The Diary of a Russian Censor

The Diary of a Russian Censor

Aleksandr Nikitenko

Abridged, edited & translated
by Helen Saltz Jacobson

The University of Massachusetts Press   Amherst

FOR GENE, PETE & JAN

I would like to express my appreciation to Ann Dunnigan, George Ivask, Phillipe Radley, Nina Berberova and Laura Fox for their helpful suggestions during the preparation of this work; to Donna Amariglio, reference librarian at the State University of New York at Stony Brook; to the administration of Pushkinskii dom in Leningrad, where the Nikitenko archives are housed; to Ada Bridge, my typist; and last, but not least, to Gene, Jan and Pete for their constant encouragement and patience.

CONTENTS

ACKNOWLEDGEMENTS ix

INTRODUCTION xi

THE DIARY OF A RUSSIAN CENSOR 1

NOTES 375

INDEX 383

INTRODUCTION

In an almost daily record kept over a span of fifty-one years, Aleksandr Vasili-evich Nikitenko, who served for over forty years in various offices of the Censorship Department and Ministry of Education of tsarist Russia, has left to literary scholars, historians, political scientists and sociologists a wealth of material on the literary, historical and social life of the Russian people during the period 1826 to 1877.

It would be misleading to ascribe the fame and interest of his diary to his censorship activities alone, for throughout his life he was engaged in a variety of pursuits: for fifty years he published literary criticism, articles on aesthetics and the history of literature; he edited newspapers and literary journals; for thirty years he was a professor of literature at St. Petersburg University and other institutions and, finally, a member of the Academy of Sciences. He played an active policy-making role on scores of governmental committees and commissions and was also active in social organizations. Thus, for most of his adult life he was to be found in the very midst of the literary, political and social scene.

Moderate in his views, always seeking a balance between the radicals and reactionaries of his time, he adds a new dimension to the vast literature that has reached the West from the representatives of extremist camps.

What gives the diary a particular poignance and significance are the lowly origins of its author and his courageous struggle against almost overwhelming obstacles to win freedom, obtain an education, and gain the dignity and respect that are the right of all human beings. By origin a serf, he never forgot that he was, as he said in his diary, "a plebian from head to toe."

Aleksandr Vasilievich Nikitenko was born in a Ukrainian hamlet in 1804, the son of an illiterate, but warm-hearted, intelligent, and affectionate mother and a brilliant, self-educated father. His parents were owned by the wealthy Count Sheremetev whose three hundred thousand serfs and vast estates were to be found in many provinces of Russia. Although a serf, his father received some formal education as a member of the count's choir in Moscow. At the age of seventeen, when his voice changed, he was discharged from the choir and returned from Moscow to the Ukraine, where he was variously employed as a clerk and school teacher. He continued to educate himself, was fluent in French, read widely (Voltaire was one of his favorite authors) and maintained a correspondence with men of high standing. He even accumulated sufficient knowledge to practice medicine of sorts, treating himself, his family, and fellow villagers who sought his help for common ailments. However, he was a restless romantic, a dreamer, an impractical fellow whose brilliance and education were, in his shackled state, a constant source of personal irritation and frustration. Consequently, he frequently ran up against the authorities, was imprisoned, was exiled with his family, and was constantly forced to seek new means of support. It was the stability, courage and, most of all, the sympathetic understanding of Nikitenko's mother that kept the family together physically and spiritually.

Nikitenko received his early education from his father, and an excellent one at that, for when he was sent off to grammar school in Voronezh, he soon won the respect of his teachers and schoolmates of all social classes as an honor pupil. Although he graduated at the top of his class, he was barred by his serf status from entering the gymnasium. So distressed were his teachers by this circumstance that they conspired to forge his graduation certificate by stating that he was the son of a collegiate assessor. His father, astute enough to realize the dangers inherent in such a conspiracy, would not permit his son to use the document. He hoped that, since his son was a star graduate, he would be considered an exception to the general rule barring serf-children from gymnasium. Accordingly, he sent him to Voronezh again at the beginning of the school year. When, however, he learned that one of his benefactors had already pleaded unsuccessfully on his behalf, Nikitenko himself lost heart completely. He spent his days and nights leafing through his old notebooks and rarely going outdoors. "I watched the boys, my former schoolmates, now gymnasium students, with longing," he recalled afterwards, "as they proudly marched off to school with their new books under their arms. They seemed to be so favored by fate, that in my eyes they assumed the proportions of higher beings, and the small yellow building on Dvoryanskaya Street which housed the school, appeared to me to be a palace with its doors shut tightly against me alone." Thus ended Nikitenko's formal education until his admission to St. Petersburg University many years later under unusual circumstances.

In 1816, when Nikitenko was twelve, his family moved to Ostrogorsk, where his intellectual horizons widened and his dreams began to take shape. He was warmly accepted by an enlightened circle of educated citizens, members of the upper classes, who had an intense interest in literature, art, science, politics and social issues. They hated slavery and wanted radical changes in the structure of the state. These people—merchants, aristocrats, clergymen, the school inspector—gave him a helping hand and started him on the road to success. At the age of fourteen, Nikitenko was invited to teach their children, and within two years he had a whole school of pupils which met at the home of the local burgomaster. He was recognized by the community as a talented teacher although, as a serf lacking academic credentials and official authorization, he was teaching illegally. Yet, the most respected and high-ranking families preferred to have their children educated by this serf-youth. Nikitenko, in his autobiography, explains their preference as a form of protest, a defiance of officialdom. They had little faith, he said, in government institutions and, therefore, avoided official teachers.

Their warmth, hospitality and companionship inspired him toward further self-education. He read voraciously from their libraries of serious works. It was here, in Ostrogorsk, that his determination to enter St. Petersburg University took root. But the thought of his frustrating attempt to gain admission to the Voronezh gymnasium only a few years earlier depressed him. So strong was his yearning for freedom and a university education, so seemingly invincible were the obstacles in his path, that he was driven to the point of seriously considering suicide. He managed to obtain a pistol, and the very idea that life or death was now his to choose armed him with the confidence, courage and will to continue his struggle toward freedom. "Though I may not be my own master," he wrote, "though I am nothing in the eyes of people and their laws, I shall have one right which no one can deprive me of: the right to die. If worst comes to worst, I shall not ignore the opportunity to take my life. Until then—boldly onward!"

In the spring of 1818 an event occurred which left a deep impression on the inhabitants of Ostrogorsk. "One fine day," wrote Nikitenko, "its dreamy streets sprang to life, brilliant with colorful flags and uniforms, vibrant with the clatter of horses and the sound of military music. Everyone, not only the townspeople, but all the local farmers and peasants from surrounding areas poured into Ostrogorsk to meet the heroes, to enjoy the kind of spectacle they had never before witnessed, and to welcome the special guests. . . ." In this manner, a regiment of the first dragoon division, returning from a victorious campaign abroad, settled in various sections of Ostrogorsk and its environs.*

Social life in the city began to hum with the appearance of these educated officers, who were not only interested in military service but also excited by political and social issues, literature and philosophy. They befriended young Nikitenko and he became a regular participant in their discussions, their evening gatherings and entertainment. "They saw in me," wrote Nikitenko, "a victim of the order of things which they hated—and under the influence of this hate they looked at me as through magnifying spectacles, exaggerating my gifts and, with them, the tragedy of my fate." The literary evenings which Nikitenko attended focused on contemporary Russian literature, and it was at such a gathering that he first became acquainted with the works of the poets Batyushkov and Zhukovsky.

At this time Nikitenko first met the Decembrist Ryleev,† whom years later he came to know well. He was serving in one of the regiments of the dragoon division. It was purely a chance meeting in a bookshop, but it left an indelible impression on the young Nikitenko.

At the beginning of the 1820s, branches of the Bible Society began to spring

---

* The army of Alexander I had entered Paris in 1814.
† Ryleev, an outstanding poet, was one of the leaders of an unsuccessful attempt by liberal noblemen in December 1825 to overthrow the regime and establish a constitutional form of government.

up all over Russia, and Ostrogorsk, in Nikitenko's words, didn't want to lag
behind. As secretary of the Ostrogorsk branch, he soon came to the attention
of the president of the society, Prince A. N. Golitsyn, a religious mystic who
was Minister of Religious Affairs and Education under Alexander I. A speech
delivered by Nikitenko at the first annual meeting of the society, on 1 April
1824, so captivated his audience that the membership voted unanimously to
present his speech to Prince Golitsyn and ask for permission to publish it.
Nikitenko felt that it was "now or never," that this was the turning point in
his life. "I was so excited that I could neither eat nor sleep and wandered
about like a restless ghost."

After receiving the speech with the petition for its publication, Prince
Golitsyn soon became interested in Nikitenko himself. He arranged for Count
Sheremetev (Nikitenko's master) to permit the young man to come to St.
Petersburg. However, while Nikitenko made the long and difficult journey to
the capital, much had changed there: Prince Golitsyn had been removed from
his ministerial post, and his influence, in the eyes of St. Petersburg's aristocracy, had faded.

It was then that Decembrist Ryleev took up the cause of Nikitenko's freedom with all his energy. He devoted a great deal of attention to the problem
of securing Nikitenko's freedom and developed a whole plan of action, a campaign. His plan consisted in first acquainting a wide circle of cavalry officers,
friends of the young Count Sheremetev, with Nikitenko's biography and with
one of his writings, and then creating the kind of social pressure and impasse
which would leave the count but one course. Ryleev's influence even reached
the palace and Sheremetev's private chancery, where one of the count's subordinates managed to execute the deal and extract a signed release for Nikitenko's freedom on 11 October 1824.

That same year, through Prince Golitsyn's efforts (he had recouped himself
after his temporary fall), Nikitenko was admitted to St. Petersburg University. Meanwhile, he had continued his friendship with Ryleev, who helped
him obtain living quarters in the home of Decembrist E. P. Obolensky (who
had also worked to obtain Nikitenko's freedom) as a tutor to Obolensky's
adolescent brother.

At that time Obolensky's apartment was the meeting place of the members
of a secret group, *The Northern Society*, but it is difficult to say with any certainty whether Nikitenko was aware of the existence of this organization.
Nikitenko's daughter wrote after his death that her father had lived in the very
midst of the progressive movement of that time, but that because of his youth
and inexperience, or, perhaps, his immaturity, they did not involve him in
their secret plans for overthrowing the regime and establishing a constitutional
form of government.

At any rate, immediately following the tragic events on Senate Square where
the conspirators were defeated, Nikitenko learned of the arrest of his closest
friends and burned his diary for 1825. The first entry in the diary which he

kept from 1826 to 1877 expresses his deep concern over his precarious position two weeks after the abortive uprising. "But why," writes I. E. Tolstoy in an essay on Nikitenko, "was the author of the *Diary* so worried? What was contained in those notes which he so quickly destroyed? One can only guess. Probably, the meticulous Nikitenko recorded all that he had seen and heard during the meetings of the Decembrists in Obolensky's and Ryleev's apartments (he had visited Ryleev on the very eve of the uprising), and it is possible that he recorded the content of their conversations and meetings, if he were permitted to attend them."[*]

According to one of his biographers, this tragic event leading to the execution of five of the Decembrists, among them his dear friend Ryleev, had a profoundly painful impact on his views and personality; it forced this so richly endowed nature to withdraw into itself; it convinced Nikitenko of the uselessness of sacrifice and taught him for many years to look upon liberation impulses with unhappy distrust. Although he admired the courage of the Decembrists, the entire event inclined him toward moderation: he now became an advocate of gradual reform in Russia. During the early years of the reign of Nicholas I, Nikitenko speaks of him in a conciliatory tone and blames his faulty deeds on his lack of real advisors, on the negative qualities of his ministers and administrators. Gradually, however, Nikitenko's attitude and tone change, and soon his diary entries are filled with bitterness and rage.

Almost from the very beginning of his university days to the end of his life, Nikitenko pursued two careers simultaneously. One was in government service, the other in literature.

Nikitenko was introduced into government service in his student days when, penniless, he was given work in the office of K. M. Borozdin, superintendent of the St. Petersburg school district. Borozdin, an archaeologist and historian in his own right, became the student's patron and protector. A warm father-son relationship developed between them and, after graduation from the university, Nikitenko was employed by Borozdin as his full-time secretary. Here Nikitenko soon applied his talents to a variety of responsible tasks, composing reports, proposals and commentaries on important documents. One such document was the new censorship code, and Nikitenko's commentary on it was very well received.

His career as an official censor began in 1833 when he was twenty-nine years old. He knew the censor's position to be a precarious one. At the time of his appointment he wrote in his diary: "I am taking a very dangerous step. Today the minister had a long talk with me about the spirit in which I must approach the duties of my new position. . . .

" 'You must perform your duties,' he said to me, 'in such a manner that you not only base your judgements on the censorship code, but also on the particular set of circumstances with which you are faced and the course of events.

[*]I. E. Tolstoy, *Ocherki literaturnoi zhizni voronezhskogo kraya* [Essays on the literary life of the Voronezh Region] (Voronezh, 1970), p. 166.

Also, you must work in such a way that the public has no cause to conclude that the government is hounding culture.'"

Nikitenko's description of his move into the Censorship Department as a "dangerous step" was an accurate one, for the censor was literally trapped in a vise. He was subject to various punishments, ranging from reprimands to confinement in the guardhouse for an indeterminate period, for approving material for publication which to all appearances complied with the censorship code but which, for some innocuous and usually asinine reason, caught the eye and provoked the wrath of some administrator or important personage. Nikitenko himself was twice imprisoned in the guardhouse for an "oversight," the first time in 1834 for passing Victor Hugo's poem, "To a Beauty." In a sense even more difficult to bear than the punitive measures were the constant tension and anxiety: one never knew when the axe might fall.

In spite of harsh censorship practices, which could be attributed more to fear on the part of the censor than to the diligent application of the censorship code, many articles and books managed to slip through the net. True, once published and distributed, "oversights" could catch someone's malicious imagination and stir up trouble for the censor, author and publisher, but frequently not before the material had seen wide distribution. If it were too late to stop the presses or recall the work from booksellers and other distributors, the stable would be locked after the horse had taken off, that is, the guilty parties would be subjected to punitive measures.

Until 1804, the powers of censorship in Russia were not defined by law and were left to the whim of ignorant administrators. The first censorship law, passed in 1804, established what came to be known as preliminary or preventative censorship: all manuscripts were to be submitted to the Ministry of Education prior to publication. However, this law offered little protection to the censor, author or publisher, who could be punished after the article was approved and published if it offended or irritated some tyrannical official. Preliminary censorship remained in effect until 1865, although revisions in the censorship code were made from time to time. The revised code of 1865 called for partial abolition of preliminary censorship, excluding books of specified lengths and permitting journals published in Moscow and St. Petersburg the option of preliminary censorship or punitive controls. Punitive controls consisted of a system of warnings and fines and subsequent suspensions, bans and judicial procedures, so that, in essence, censorship measures were not applied until after a work had been published and circulated.

No matter what system was in operation, preliminary censorship or punitive controls, the degree of vigilance and harshness exercised by the Censorship Department depended on two factors: the political views and attitudes of the administrators in office at any particular moment (and there was considerable turnover) and the calibre of the censors. Of course, foreign as well as internal politics had an impact on the policies of the administrators, particularly when revolution broke out in the West or internal enemies posed a threat to the state.

In 1848, as a direct result of the revolution in France, a period of extreme reaction began which continued until the ascent of Alexander II to the throne in 1855. On 2 April 1848 the infamous Buturlin Committee was created, a super-censorship organ which had the final word on the publication of all printed matter in Russia. During its seven year existence it officially bore the title "The Committee of April 2," but among the intelligentsia it was known as the "secret committee." With the creation of this committee the press was surrounded on all sides by vigilant authorities. Every book that came out was examined first by the regular censor, then by officials hand picked for the task by the ministry of education, and finally by the Buturlin Committee.

The terror wrought by this committee from the very beginning of its operations is described by Nikitenko in his diary: "The minister of education was not invited to the meeting of this committee; explanations were not demanded of anyone; no one was informed of the charges against him, while the charges were extremely serious. Terror gripped everyone who thought or wrote. Secret denunciations and spying complicated the situation even more. People began to fear for each day of their existence, thinking that it might be their last among their loved ones and friends."

Despite the restrictions, persecutions and oppressions which marked the reign of Nicholas I, literary productivity flourished. For thirty years until this despot's death in 1855 literature managed to sneak through the seemingly impossible barriers which at any moment threatened to extinguish it altogether. The fact that this period marked the beginning of the era known as the golden age of Russian literature makes it appear all the more remarkable and naturally raises the question: how was it possible? Was the stifling atmosphere itself responsible for such an apparently contradictory phenomenon? Suppose, one wonders, writers did not have to contend with a repressive society, would they have been so productive? Some historians and critics offer the theory that literature in Russia took the place of free institutions, and by the use of subterfuge, by the use of Aesopian language, writers were able to convey their ideas to their readers.

When Alexander II ascended the throne in 1855, all Russia drew a sigh of relief. True, the censorship apparatus remained very much a part of literary life, but it was a considerably eased censorship and one which underwent revisions culminating in the new censorship laws of 1865. In a general atmosphere of reform, the most significant part of which was the emancipation of the serfs, Russia's golden age of literature was at its zenith.

Russian journals have always played an important role in Russian literature. Today in the Soviet Union many novels appear in journals before they are published in book form. Under Nicholas I and Alexander II, they not only created and shaped a body of public opinion but brought to their readers many of the novels and short stories which we now know as classics. The works of such writers as Tolstoy, Pushkin, Gogol, Goncharov and Turgenev were often serialized in journals before they were published as books. Each journal was assigned by the censorship department to a censor, and it was not uncommon for a litterateur serving as a censor of one journal to be editing or working on the editorial board of another. Thus, while serving in the censorship department, Nikitenko was invited by Nekrasov and Panaev in 1847 to become editor of the *Contemporary*, an organ of the liberal-radical camp. The association did not last very long; shortly after the revolutionary events in Europe in 1848, Nikitenko resigned from the *Contemporary*. Nikitenko indicates in his diary that numerous disagreements over the journal's basic policies and the feeling that he was being "used" by its publishers because of his influence as a censor had prompted his decision to resign. According to Bugaenko,[*] ideological differences between Nikitenko and his publishers, along with the fears engendered by the administration's reaction to the revolutionary events in Europe, were the real reasons for Nikitenko's resignation. Nikitenko, he claims, was simply scared. On 6 April 1848 Nikitenko, writes Bugaenko, had been summoned by Count Orlov, Chief of the Third Section (Russia's political police) and compelled to acknowledge with his signature a statement reading: "His Imperial Highness . . . has noted that the journal *Contemporary* (edited by Nikitenko), has permitted ideas in its articles which are of a most extremely criminal nature and are capable of implanting in our society the principles of communism."

Among the censors, there were several distinct types. The staffs of the mass of censorship units (some twelve in all—secular, ecclesiastical, military, judiciary, foreign, textbook, and others) were drawn in part from the ranks of scholars and litterateurs, but mostly from the ranks of genuine ignoramuses. The composition of the Censorship Department shifted from time to time, depending on who happened to be in power in the Ministry of Education or the Ministry of Internal Affairs, which, after 1865, was mainly responsible for censorship. Such eminent writers as Goncharov and Tyutchev worked as censors. At the other extreme were the uncultured, stupid and frightened censors whose practices were completely unpredictable. They were utterly incapable of distinguishing so-called harmful writings from material which no intelligent individual, no matter what his political bias, could conceivably regard as inimical to the interests of the state. In this latter category fell such actions as refusing to approve a mathematics textbook because its author had inserted ellipses between a series of numbers which, according to the censor, might signify the presence of some sort of conspiracy, or censoring a physics book for such terms as "forces of nature."

"The censor, who was fully responsible for every word he passed, positively lost his head. Constantly expecting reprimands, arrest, discharge from his

* P. A. Bugaenko, "Esteticheskie vzglyady A. V. Nikitenko" [The aesthetic views of A. V. Nikitenko], *Ezhegodnik* [Annual bulletin] of the Philology Department of Saratov University (USSR, 1958), 20.

position, he groped about in the darkness, without having any clear notion of
what could be passed without dangerous consequences or what might unleash
the unexpected fury of the authorities against him. This made him suspicious
and carping to the point of totally clouding his reasoning powers. This panic
also explains why censors were able to find the spirit of revolution even in
cookbooks."[*]

Nikitenko was regarded by the writers of his day as the "wisest of censors,"
and Pushkin himself preferred Nikitenko above all others, despite moments of
friction between them. Gogol, too, spoke favorably of Nikitenko, describing
his "kindness" and "goodwill" in letters to his friends. He is credited with
saving Gogol's *Dead Souls* by suggesting certain changes in *The Tale of Captain
Kopeykin*, which Gogol then reworked. During his tenure as a censor and afterwards, when he served on high-ranking censorship committees, he helped, pro-
tected and defended writers as much as he could within established legal limits.
He viewed censorship as a necessary evil, but as a cultured, enlightened man,
as a litterateur in his own right, tried to grant literature the widest possible
latitude. Throughout his entire career in government service, he fought for
changes in the censorship code, for a well-defined, enlightened censorship, if
one can call any kind of censorship enlightened. This view of censorship as a
necessary social function in nineteenth-century Russia was held by many of its
most eminent writers. Pushkin, who was one of its worst victims, expressed the
sentiment that "what was right for London was early for Moscow."

The widely held view of censorship as a necessary evil stemmed from the
fear that the people were not mature or sophisticated enough to evaluate
printed matter objectively. Only an educated elite was capable of intelligent
judgement. When Nikitenko wrote the following words in his diary he was
calling not for the blanket elimination of censorship but for an intelligent application of a system that was necessary for the protection of a so-called ignorant
public: "What the devil is going on here? A Christian crusade against knowledge? These people are blind;[†] they don't see that by keeping learned ideas
from being advanced through the printed word, they are forcing them to be
transmitted by word of mouth. And this is far more dangerous, for bitterness
born of irritation and indignation is unconsciously added in speech, while, in
the press, it is restrained by censorship and decorum. It is time, it seems, to
change this petty policy of threats and oppression to *a policy of guidance*"
(translator's emphasis).

In another diary entry he emphasizes the government's responsibility to protect the public: ". . . the government had no right to ignore such writings
which have deep impact on morality, especially in our country where learning

---

[*] A. M. Skabichevskii, *Ocherki istorii russkoi tsenzury* [Essays on the history of Russian
censorship] (St. Petersburg, 1892; The Hague, Europe Printing, 1965), p. 369.
[†] Nikitenko is referring to the Buturlin Committee.

and public opinion are still so poorly developed that we can't stand up against false and pernicious teachings and neutralize their influence."

Nikitenko's almost hopeless struggle against bureaucracy and tyranny, against disorder and immorality in government and society, was so frustrating that he frequently became depressed to the point of morbidity. His anger and bitterness spill over into his diary with increasing frequency.

Deeply distressed by the lack of freedom of thought and expression in Russia, he wrote on 28 October 1841: "I am supposed to be teaching Russian literature—but where is it? Does literature in our land enjoy civil rights? One refuge remains—the lifeless sphere of theory. I am deceiving myself and others when I utter such words as *development, trend of ideas, basic ideas of art*. These words have meaning, a great deal of meaning, where public opinion and intellectual and aesthetic interests exist, but here they are merely words being tossed about in the air. Words, words, words! To spend one's whole life with empty words, when one's soul is thirsting for truth, when one's mind is striving for something real and vital—this is indeed a terrible fate." Often he considered resigning from his post as censor, but was persuaded by his fellow writers and scholars that he was indispensable to the cause of enlightenment. Even after he did resign, he served for many years on high-ranking censorship committees, including policy-making committees for the revision of the censorship code.

Nikitenko prided himself on his position as a moderate progressive and as an independent without ties to any bloc or camp. He lashed out at both the right and left and, toward the end of his life, was particularly vehement in his attacks on what he termed "extremist liberals." He considered them to be as dangerous and despotic as the extreme right; he deplored their violent tactics and was especially critical of what he viewed as intolerant, dogmatic attitudes and blatant opportunism. For his independent stance he was attacked by both sides and made enemies in both government and literary circles. The arch-reactionary Bulgarin described Nikitenko as "a worthy pupil of Ryleev," a dangerous man who was undermining the government. "Fourierism is being spread over the pages of *Notes of the Fatherland* under Nikitenko's censorial supervision, and, finally, the communist camp has chosen him as an editor of the *Contemporary*, a brother publication to *Notes of the Fatherland*."

Though himself of peasant origin he had little faith in the masses and repeatedly expressed the hope that "the people must be ruled, and not themselves rule. I do not accept the idea that it is wise to give the people power." He regarded the Russian *muzhik*[*] as "a perfect savage." Yet, he insisted, *"the muzhik is sincere . . . but our educated Russian is a liar from head to toe."*

Throughout the diary he blames many of Russia's ills on weaknesses inherent in the Russian character and sees those weaknesses as negative forces which have operated and will continue to operate to the detriment of any worthy

[*] Peasant (male).

undertaking. Frequently he refers to these character traits as the "curse of
the Slavs." Originality, fortitude, and a cooperative spirit are qualities Nikitenko sees in other nations, particularly in the German scientists who occupied
important positions in the Russian Academy of Sciences, but he decries the
absence of such traits in his fellow countrymen. "The Germans occupy a pre-
eminent position in many special areas," he writes in speaking of the Russian
Academy of Sciences, "because they are more industrious and, mainly, because
they strive harmoniously toward their common goals. That is the secret of
their success. But, in the first place, we try to get things done any old way, in
typical bureaucratic fashion, so that the authorities will be pleased and reward
us. Secondly, when three or four of our people assemble in behalf of some idea
or common cause, you can expect, without fail, that by the second or third day
they will have quarrelled, played dirty tricks on each other and split up. Our
only salvation lies in the intercession of authority."

Nikitenko's autobiographical notes (1804-24) and diary (1826-77) were
published for the first time in the journal *Russkaya Starina* [Russian an-
tiquity] over a period of five years, from 1888 to 1893. In 1893 and 1905
both appeared in book form, but the Soviet three volume edition (Leningrad:
Goslitizdat, 1955-56) on which this translation is based is considered the most
accurate and most complete reproduction. Five eminent Soviet scholars were
involved in its preparation: N. L. Brodsky, F. V. Gladkov, F. M. Golovenchenko,
N. K. Gudzii, and I. Aizenshtok. Working from copies (the original was believed to have been destroyed by Nikitenko's daughter, S.A. Nikitenko[*]), they
made extensive use of original materials in the Nikitenko archives,[†] including
correspondence and notes, to verify, fill in and reconstruct passages that had
been tampered with by Nikitenko's daughter, by *Russkaya Starina's* publisher
and by tsarist censorship.

The notes accompanying the Soviet edition are voluminous, occupying 219
pages in small print, and are an excellent resource for literary scholars, historians, sociologists and political scientists.

In order to make a translation accessible to a broader public, an abridgement
was deemed necessary. It was no easy task to reduce some 1500 pages of
closely packed Russian text (excluding introduction and notes) to its present
size. In deciding what to eliminate and what to retain, what to abridge and
edit, an effort was made to present an overall picture of the period from
1826 to 1877.

Some readers may be struck by the absence of entries on such an important
literary figure as Lermontov, or the relative dearth of material on other writers,
gaps which Soviet scholars also note in their introduction to the Soviet edition.
They can only speculate that Nikitenko's daughter, who had edited and prepared

---

[*] In his will Nikitenko specifically directed his daughters not to permit the original copy
of his diary to leave the family's hands.

[†] The Nikitenko archives are located in Pushinskii dom (the Institute of Russian Literature of the Academy of Sciences) in Leningrad.

the original text for publication in *Russkaya Starina,* may have been responsible for such deficiencies. Nikitenko had also exercised a form of self-censorship, indicating to his family in margin notes on the original text what should be deleted in order to avoid censorship difficulties.

The published diary contained few references to his personal life, again in keeping with his instructions to his daughters. From the rare references to his family, one gets the impression that he was a devoted husband and father. However, his autobiographical notes covering the period 1804-24 and including much material on his parents and grandparents are a fascinating personal account of a serf-boy and his family and their struggle for spiritual and physical freedom. These notes have not been included in the text following, but some high points have been included in this introduction.

The diary begins in 1826. As noted earlier, Nikitenko destroyed all his notes for 1825, the year of the Decembrist uprising.

Throughout the text, dates are given according to the Julian calendar (in force in Russia until 1918), which lagged behind the Gregorian calendar by twelve days in the nineteenth century. Personal and place names with Anglicized spelling in widely accepted usage follow that spelling. In most cases System I is used; for bibliographical citations System II is used.*

* J. Thomas Shaw, *The Transliteration of modern Russian for English Language Publications* (Madison, Milwaukee, and London: The University of Wisconsin Press, 1967), pp. 3-15.

1826

*The diary opens with twenty-one year old Nikitenko recovering from the
shock of the abortive Decembrist uprising. Although he had been living in
the apartment of one of the conspirators and had been closely associated with
several other members of the group, he had been totally unaware of the plans
of these liberal-minded young aristocrats to overthrow the regime and establish a constitutional form of government.*

1 January. I woke up in a wretched mood today. The terrible events of recent days have been oppressing me like a dark cloud. The future looked so
very bleak and hopeless. I was becoming more and more depressed. Suddenly
Rostovtsev dropped in. He had left his room for the first time since he was
wounded on that disastrous day, December 14th.[a]

After the usual exchange of greetings and good wishes for the New Year,
he cheered me up with two pieces of good news. The first was that the general is permitting me to change my apartment,[1] which means that I am no
longer under suspicion and free of the extremely unpleasant situation that has
been tormenting me for more than two weeks. The second, that Fyodor
Nikolaevich Glinka,[2] who fully deserves our love and esteem and whom I
deeply respect, has cleared himself before the emperor of every suspicion
which had been cast upon him.

Glinka's papers had been confiscated and he had been taken to the palace.
However, his innocence soon became apparent and the emperor sent him
home with these words:

"Come now, Gospodin[b] Glinka, you needn't scowl and be angry! Times
are so bad now that sometimes we can't help hurting innocent people. I have
always thought of you as a man of intelligence and nobility. Tell all your
friends that the promises I gave in the manifesto[c] established a clear distinction between suspicion and truth, between a desire for improvement and a
mad rush toward revolution. Tell them that these promises were inscribed
not only on paper, but in my heart. Go home now! You are innocent, completely innocent."

When I heard the news about the arrest of this truly fine man, I became

[a] On December 12, 1825, Rostovtsev, an officer, sent a letter to Tsar Nicholas I informing him of the planned uprising in which many of his close friends were involved. He was
beaten up by some of the soldiers supporting the rebellion.

[b] "Mister."

[c] Coronation manifesto.

very upset. But the emperor's acumen prevented him from misjudging the principles and spirit of our dear poet-Christian.

And so the new year has begun, not badly for me personally—but, how will it be for many others?

3 January. I would like to take advantage now of the general's permitting me to move. This apartment has become as depressing as a grave. But I haven't a single kopek, and without money you can neither get an apartment anywhere nor the furnishings for one. I'm in an extremely difficult position. All my former connections which could have been of use to me now, have been severed.[d] I can remain here, perhaps, a few days longer, that is, while the young prince, my charge, is here. But this is a problem, too, for the youth has always had a stubborn nature. He has given me a lot of trouble. I've tried hard to cultivate some decent values in him and to curb his wild ways. Having set these goals for myself, I patiently bore all the distress, all the rudeness, which his wilfulness inflicted upon me. From time to time I would manage to elicit some decent feelings, but even these were only momentary flashes. Since the day of his brother's misfortune he has become utterly unbearable. I've tried to admonish him gently, but he responds with rudeness and our relations are badly strained.

His brother is a fine man but, misinterpreting Schelling's philosophy, he has resolved that "nothing should restrict the freedom of a spiritual being," meaning his dear little brother. I've already mentioned the consequences. This, however, is pretty much the case with the upbringing of almost all our nobility, especially in the most prominent families. It is our custom to educate young people for "high society" rather than "society." Their minds are trained in the various niceties of manners and decorum, but their hearts are left to their natural whims. A French tutor guarantees their success in "high society," but chance alone is responsible for their morality.

Almost the same thing can be said about our educational system. Good habits are almost an alien subject. Knowledge is imparted superficially. The administrators of educational institutions are more interested in their pockets than in the hearts of their pupils. It is only in the middle class that a passion for intellectual growth and a zeal for knowledge is noticeable. Thus, as our aristocracy, drowning in ignorance, gradually falls into decay, the middle class is preparing to become the real governing class.

5 January. Rostovtsev has asked me to move in with him. Only extreme circumstances would compel me to take such a step. I am sure of his friendly

[d] Several of the young noblemen involved in the Decembrist uprising had previously taken a warm interest in Nikitenko. Ryleev, a poet and one of the principal leaders of the conspiracy, played a major role in gaining Nikitenko his freedom from serfdom. Ryleev had also helped Nikitenko to obtain living quarters in the home of Decembrist E. P. Obolensky. At the time of this diary entry he was still living in the apartment and taking care of Obolensky's younger brother.

attitude toward me, but this in itself, in view of present events, obliges me to be particularly cautious. His Majesty thanked him with great pomp for his act. His name has become a topic of heated discussion in the capital.

6 January. The very moment that I was grieving over my sad plight, our dear house steward, Egor, informed me that the wife of General Shterich, a distant relative of the prince, wished to see me. I wasn't at all surprised, thinking that she wanted to discuss my charge (the prince) with me. But that wasn't the case.

I went to her home at 5 o'clock. I was conducted to the bedroom. There, before me, lay a sick, middle-aged woman with a pleasant, intelligent face. It was Madame Shterich.

She invited me to sit down and, after the usual conversation these days about recent stormy events, said:

"I've heard many nice things about you. I know that you are in a difficult position now. If you can't find anything better, I would like to offer you room and board with us."

Her offer was very timely, but I was stunned by its unexpectedness.

"But how can I, in turn, be of use to you and pay for the kindness you are offering me? "

"That's quite unnecessary," she replied. "I simply want to help you as a deserving young man. If you wish, you can move in next Sunday."

After chatting a little longer, I took my leave and went home in confusion. I still haven't made up my mind.

8 January. After a difficult struggle with myself, having given the offer a great deal of thought, I decided to move to Madame Shterich's home. I'm sure I'll find something to do there.

10 January. Madame Shterich invited me to dinner yesterday and, after beating about the bush, indicated that she would have no objection to my devoting some of my time to tutoring her son in Russian literature and some other subjects, too (if I have free time!) which are necessary for the diplomatic corps, which the young man has recently entered.

11 January. Exam in Latin. I received three points. I am ashamed of myself because one of my friends had helped me do the translation by which our professors judge our progress. Were it not for this transgression I would not receive student rank and would not be advanced to the second year course in spite of my excellent performance in other subjects. I promise myself that I shall be more sensible, more industrious and steadfast in the future.

16 January. Exams are over. I passed them during the stormiest period of my life and can say that I passed them honorably, except for Latin, the memory of which makes me blush with shame.

23 January. Rostovtsev visited me today. He told me that Prince Evgeny

Obolensky implicated many people in his testimony, including Glinka, who
expects to be arrested again. Should this occur, he intends to call me as a
witness, as one who, having always been present at his meetings with Prince
Obolensky, would be able to corroborate his testimony that there was nothing
political in their conversations. He instructed Rostovtsev to ask me about this.
Why should he ask me to do this? If he does call me as a witness as he intends
to, I would have to tell the truth anyway, which would not be harmful to him
in the least. But, of course, I would prefer to avoid this fresh complication.

24 January. The so-called high society of the capital gathers at Madame
Shterich's soirées, which gives me the opportunity to make some useful observations. So far I have only managed to note that the "creatures" inhabit-
ing "the great world" are rank automatons. They appear to be absolutely
devoid of soul. They live, think and feel mechanically, utterly detached from
their hearts and intellects, and unmindful of their obligations as human beings.
Social decorum dictates every aspect of their behavior. Their guiding principle
is not to appear ridiculous. And not to appear ridiculous means to conform
slavishly to fashion in one's speech, opinions and conduct, just as one con-
forms to fashion in dress. In "refined" society they simply do not understand
what is truly elegant, for this society is totally dependent on certain temporarily prevailing modes which frequently run counter to what is elegant. Constraint drives out grace, and the systematic pursuit of pleasure serves to blunt
one's sense of enjoyment and to compel a constant search for new sources of
pleasure. And beneath all this are hidden the most vulgar passions. True, a
cloak of decorum is thrown over them, but it is so transparent that it cannot
entirely conceal them. I find here the very same vices that are present in the
lowest class, but without the virtues innate in the latter. I am particularly
struck by the women. They possess a self-confidence which excludes modesty.
By modesty I mean not only a sense of diffidence in relations between the
sexes, but also that inner quality which teaches them to find a happy medium
between self-confidence and feelings of inferiority. I know now that the
"adroitness" and "amiable manner" of a society woman is nothing more than
her ability to render gracefully what has been carefully memorized. And here
is the guiding rule for this "adroitness" and "amiability": "dress and position
your feet, hands and eyes as Madame French Governess has instructed you.
Don't give your tongue a moment's rest while keeping in mind that French
words should be the only sounds released by this human clavichord, a clavichord which is set in motion only by a frivolous mind." Indeed, a knowledge
of French serves as entrée into the most "refined" salons. It frequently determines your status in the eyes of an entire community and frees you, if not
forever, then at least for a while, from the necessity of displaying other very
serious claims to the public's attention and good will.

8 February. Saw Rostovtsev. I had begun to wonder if the favors being
showered upon him might change his attitude toward me. However, he hasn't

given me the slightest reason to feel this way. But I know him; I know he is
ambitious, and ambition accompanied by success finally ends up with the
ambitious individual blind to everything and everyone but himself. If this
should happen to Rostovtsev I shall have no choice but to wish him sweet
dreams in the arms of fortune, and to go my own way. But, I repeat, I still
haven't the slightest basis for such feelings. My heart tells me to consider
Rostovtsev above the crowd and to ascribe his ambition to his membership in
the ranks of the lofty and educated.

10 February. Attended Professor Butyrsky's lecture. There is a great deal of
truth in his theory of literature which is especially useful at this time when a
kind of writer has begun to appear who rejects the rules of common sense and
thinks that, instead of mastering language and all sorts of other knowledge, it
is quite sufficient to possess imagination and a dubious wit in order to win
the right to immortality. We Russians tend to be superficial, we don't care to
get to the heart of things. We can't bear to exert ourselves. We have many
people, even with talent, who are infected with the scourge of laziness and
look for the easy way to elicit praise and admiration. For such people momentary enthusiasm is all that counts: they call this "inspiration" and, after that
momentary surge, nothing else is important to them. We have a good many
such people among our fashionable writers. I know some of them personally
and am often amazed by their ignorance and their blunt judgements of things
they know little or absolutely nothing about. They call work pedantry. For
them it is enough to learn French and read a few little books in it in order to
consider their educations complete. Then, after they have written several
articles for journals or a few madrigals and tunes which are applauded in salons,
they assume the pompous air of distinguished writers and majestically rest on
their laurels, dreaming alternately of posterity and a sumptuous repast at the
home of some Maecenas.

1 March. My present situation is as follows. I have very pleasant living quarters plus dinner and a cup or two of tea every morning and evening. But I
don't have a kopek to my name nor any hope of getting money from anywhere. Thus, half my needs are taken care of, but how I shall manage to
clothe myself still depends on the future indulgence of fate. Everyone in this
house is very kind to me and the young man is especially courteous. This is
my schedule: I rise at five o'clock, sometimes at six, never later. On days when
I have classes, I go to the university, return home at noon, jot down my lecture
notes or read works related to my university studies. At two o'clock Madame
Shterich usually sends for me. I go downstairs and usually find several guests
for dinner. Dinner is served at three. This is the most unproductive time of
my day. It is spent in uninspiring conversation. They usually talk about city
news and, for lack of it, will reminisce about the old days. There is nothing
more boring than such conversation. Their sole aim consists of avoiding lapses
in conversation, which society people dread like the plague. I've assumed the

privilege of going to my room directly after dinner, where, for about an hour, I relax with a book that doesn't require any mental effort. Then I proceed to my new duties; I am giving young Shterich courses in philology and history. I go downstairs again for tea, where the dinner routine is repeated, and go to bed at eleven.

7 March. Yesterday, Prince Evgeny Obolensky's steward asked me to come and sort out his master's books, which still remain to be disposed of. He wanted to arrange them according to subject matter and send them to the prince's father in Moscow. With a feeling of bitterness and oppression I entered the apartment where I had spent so many remarkable months of my life and where the blow had struck which almost reduced me to dust. Everything was in a state of disorder and neglect. Standing by the window I grew very pensive. The sun was setting and its dying rays scarcely managed to break through the clouds which were rapidly covering the sky. A gravelike silence reigned in these sad rooms smelling of decay and despair. What happened to the life that had so recently been seething here? Where now were those courageous men who conceived the idea of opposing fate and, with one stroke, destroying century-old evils? What a terrible misfortune has befallen them! It would have been better to die at once on that bloody day when their impotence before the unfavorable tide of events became clear to them!

My thoughts were interrupted by the arrival of Prince Obolensky's aide-de-camp who had come for his own books. We talked for a few minutes and I left with a heavy heart.

12 March. I was twenty-three years old today, if one can believe an obsolete calendar in which 1803 is recorded in my father's hand as my birth date. So, my youth is fading away. There are few who could have passed through such a stormy, active youth without any kind of guidance. I attained my goal.[e] I threw off the hateful yoke under whose burden I almost broke down, and I embarked on a noble career. But every step of the way was paid for with suffering and the exertion of every ounce of my strength. My future course is outlined in the main, and the present is brightened by the attitude of my professors and the love of my comrades, among whom I even enjoy a kind of prestige. That's the positive side of my present situation, but there is a negative side, too, no less important. I have two more years at the university with no provision for my most basic needs. And now, when I am apparently settled in many respects, I must still suffer from such wants, so painful to me, to say nothing of my mother's sad plight which is a constant source of torment to me . . .[f]

6 April. I received sad news from Little Russia [Ukraine]. I was informed of

[e] Freedom from serfdom.
[f] Nikitenko's mother was still a serf.

Vladimir Ivanovich Astafiev's death.[g] He was one of my closest friends and was instrumental in bringing about the happy change in my fate.

I was terribly upset by the news of his passing. I shall always revere his memory. He was, in the full sense of the word, a second father to me. My first father gave me life, while my second made it possible for me to live it as it should be lived.

12 May. I've spent the past week at my usual duties. My situation grows worse with each passing day. Apart from my room and board, not a single one of my other needs is provided for; neither my clothing nor my textbooks. And my time, with the exception of the hours spent in class, belongs almost entirely to Madame Shterich. I am not only occupied with her son, but with all her business affairs as well. Since I have no formal agreement with her, I, of course, have no right to expect anything. What should I do? I see only one possibility, and that is to ask the emperor to give me the opportunity to complete my studies at the university. I shall have to give it some thought and ask Academician Yazykov's advice. But I think it would be better to wait until after the coronation.

14 June. I watched the funeral procession for Empress Elizaveta Alekseevna. I left the house too early, so, with three of my friends, I strolled about the Summer Garden. We watched the crowd, colorful and extremely varied, and studied their faces. Finally, I got tired of waiting and was about to start for home when shots signalled the approach of the procession. I wasn't standing in a particularly good spot, but had to be content with it, since the crush was incredible. Meanwhile, the procession approached. I adjusted my lorgnette and began to study the scene; and I must confess my insensibility, because I saw nothing that could move me strongly. However, I must admit that it was my own fault. I am generally not enthusiastic about spectacles that make such great distinctions among people. . . . The girls from the Patriotic Society, walking in pairs, the muzhiks[h] in the rich kaftans given to them by the late Empress; the figures in black cloaks; the deceased's luxurious carriage; the splendid coffin with its worthless remains of grandeur—all this was like a Chinese shadow play.

17 June. The Master of Ceremonies of yesterday's sad procession took me today to the Peter and Paul Fortress, or, rather, to its church, to see its sad adornment. The church is not spacious, but with its tombs of the late tsars, with its magnificent high bier on which new remains now reclined, ready to take their place beneath the sad vaulting, it expressed something macabre and majestic. At first this scene made a strong impression on me. But my solemn

[g] Astafiev was an Ostrogorsk landowner who played an important role in helping Nikitenko gain his freedom.

[h] Peasants (male).

mood soon came to an end. A crowd of ladies and gentlemen of the Court swarmed around the bier like a pack of drones. They whispered, shuffled, payed each other compliments, and dragged themselves about with an air of such business-like importance, evidently imagining they were performing a great service to their country. "Ah, yes, ladies and gentlemen," I thought to myself, "that's your job. You always fit in well where there is nothing to do." How they were fussing about; what concerned expressions, what smugness in those faces!

As I left the fortress I glanced at the barred windows of the prison. And these, too, were coffins! Poor martyrs![i] Oh, if only they had known, as did these other men, how to find gratification and self-satisfaction in their lives. It could even brighten up hell itself.

Reckoning with your heart, naturally you will feel fulfilled, but reckoning with reason, I dare say, you will be left, in the end, with the bitter remnants of dissatisfaction and doubt. If a righteous man wants to be effective, he must be wise, for a righteous man without wisdom is like a helpless child.

8 August. I heard about the publication of my article, "On Overcoming Misfortune," in *Son of The Fatherland.* I had submitted it for review to the censorship department last October, but due to events in the following months, publication was delayed until now. Scanning it, I noticed many faulty statements and several passages where my exposition of ideas was more pompous than precise. This, to a great extent, marred the pleasure of seeing myself in print for the first time. So far I haven't heard any reports about it.

17 August. Our vacation, which lasted more than a month and a half, ends today, and tomorrow I must return to the university. I must confess that I did far less during vacation than I should have, especially in Latin, where I've made very little progress. I anticipate problems with it. But in addition to my scholarly activities and my academic studies, I have so many other cares! Madame Shterich is returning from Moscow in a few days and my time will be at her disposal again. In the meantime my needs are growing. I've already had to sell several books in order to purchase a supply of ink, paper and pens. It was hard for me to part with these dear friends; they were my sole possessions and I had to sacrifice them to necessity. But now I've nothing left to sell.

18 August. The students assembled today at the university in the large auditorium, where the professors, too, shortly made their appearance. Suddenly, our literature professor, Butyrsky, came up to me and asked in a warm but skeptical tone of voice:

"Was it your article that I read in *Son of the Fatherland?* "

"Yes, sir, it was."

"Really? I never would have thought that you, a young student, could

[i] The imprisoned Decembrists.

have been the author of a work which would do honor to a far more experienced man of letters. Its richness and maturity of ideas is striking," he added, addressing a colleague standing nearby. "There are several errors in style and I shall explain them to you. I also noticed some vagueness in two or three places. But otherwise, everything is splendid."

I had scarcely managed to thank him for such a flattering response, when other professors came up to me. All of them had read my article and had hastened to express their pleasure. I became completely flustered by this unexpected triumph and wanted to fall through the floor to escape all those eyes that were focussed upon me. Butyrsky promised to discuss my article at his very first lecture.

22 August. I saw Bulgarin this morning. He received me very courteously, praised my article, and asked me to continue to contribute to his journal. After talking about this and that, Bulgarin asked me to visit him, promised to introduce me to prominent literary figures, and, shaking hands with me upon leaving, said "If you ever need anything, let me know. I can be helpful to you and shall consider it a pleasure to be of service to you. You are a child of knowledge and therefore one of us."

26 August. I was at Grech's printing house today. When he learned that I was waiting for copies of my article, he invited me into his office.

"I am delighted to meet you," he said warmly. "You have written a piece which does you honor."

"I would welcome your comments on it. I have just begun my literary career and need guidance and advice."

"Well in this instance, I must say there is nothing I can suggest. Fyodor Nikolaevich Glinka wrote to me about you several days ago from Petrozavodsk. He was very delighted with your article and asked me to thank you for him. Please, do us a favor, and be sure to submit your work to us in the future."

Again there was nothing I could do but express my gratitude, which I did from the bottom of my heart.

30 August. I finally went to see Academician Yazykov and did what I had planned a long time ago: that is, I told him about my hopeless situation and my plan to appeal to the emperor for aid in completing my university studies. Yazykov listened to me attentively and, after thinking a little while, said: "No, I would advise you not to trouble the emperor with this matter. Why not come to an agreement with this generous woman who is now recompensing your labor with respect instead of money? In such circumstances, there's no reason to stand on ceremony. Your work with her son alone is surely worth something."

"No, Your Excellency," I replied. "In any case, Madame Shterich is giving me room and board and feels that this is sufficient compensation. When I agreed to move into her home, I didn't even have that. I don't feel that I have the right to demand something more from her now. Besides, this would lead to nothing but a break in our relationship. She is very economical, and even her son never has spare cash at his disposal."

After giving it some thought, Yazykov said:

"Petition the minister."

I understood what this meant and had resolved to express my firm intention never to be enslaved again, although it would not be as cruel a situation as the one from which I had recently been delivered. Nevertheless, it would be most distressing to me.

"I am afraid, Your Excellency," I said, "that if I petition the minister for assistance, I shall become an indentured student.[j] Then an insuperable barrier would again appear in my path." After turning this over in his mind for some time, Yazykov replied: "Well, wait a bit—until the new superintendent takes up his duties. Then I'll consult him about your situation."

I thanked him for his interest in me and took my leave. I had expected more from my meeting with Yazykov, but now at least I know that he is opposed to my appealing to the emperor for assistance. Regarding his discussions with the superintendent, I am afraid that they will lead to that same proposal, so distasteful to me, namely, to become an indentured student. Anything would be better than that. But I shall wait a little longer, as Yazykov suggested, and I'll see if I can find some kind of work.

21 October. When I returned home from the university at four o'clock today, I found a note on my desk from Rostovtsev, informing me of his arrival from Moscow and asking me to see him. I set out immediately for Vasily Island and found him at home. We were delighted to see each other and spent about four hours in friendly, lively conversation. We reminisced about the past, particularly about that stormy period during which we had witnessed and experienced so much. He spoke frankly about his present situation. The grand duke is favorably disposed towards him, as before, but the emperor is cold. Rostovtsev thinks that this is the effect of a prudent policy: that is, the emporor is afraid of turning Rostovtsev's head by displaying excessive kindness, and since he actually has higher aims for him in mind, he is, by this policy, saving him for his own as well as the country's benefit.

I think otherwise. I expected that in time the emperor would view Rostovtsev's act differently and would feel differently about the letter he had written on the eve of the Decembrist uprising. This letter was eloquent and intelligent but, beyond its republican daring it contained a certain fancifulness and strained patriotism. When the stormy period had passed and overheated passions had died down some people noticed this and interpreted it a certain way.

[j] Students receiving financial assistance from the government were required, after graduation, to work off their obligation in the provinces for several years.

In any case, Rostovtsev's act involved a great deal of determination and courage, to which I, myself, was a witness. But it seems to me that he was too eager to appear noble. This, in the light of his dubious position, could have given the impression that his move was simply a cunning strategy by means of which he hoped, at one stroke, to extricate himself from difficulty and appear heroic. It's quite natural for the emperor to share this view.

This interpretation could be reinforced by the fact that Rostovtsev inform-ed the conspirators about his conversation with the emperor on the eve of the uprising and gave them a copy of his letter to the emperor, a fact which the conspirators themselves confirmed during the interrogations. This act could also have sprung from decent motives, from a desire to stop the con-spirators by showing them that the government was aware of their plans, and that, therefore, it was ready to act. On the other hand, this could have been simply due to weakness, an inevitable consequence of his former ties with Prince Obolensky and Ryleev—that is, he wanted to show them that he was not acting as a traitor. But to do this, he probably should not have given the names of the conspirators to the emperor, but rather have given them the option of revealing themselves or hiding.[3] But the kind of situation in which Rostovtsev found himself made it difficult for him not to make a mistake.

1 November. My Tuesday and Saturday mornings are devoted to tutoring Shterich. My main goal is to improve the young man's Russian to the point where he can use it to compose letters and official papers. His mother is grooming him for a government career and, therefore, has heroically re-solved to force her son to occasionally think and write in Russian. The young man is kind and gentle, because nature has not endowed him with any strong inclinations. He dances superbly and therefore was appointed a gentleman of the emperor's bed-chamber. He has exhausted the entire science of social amenity. No one can recall his ever having committed a blunder at the table, at a soirée, or, generally speaking, at any gathering of "refined" people. He speaks impeccable French since he's a true Russian and, besides, has studied with a Frenchman—not with a mere baker or shoemaker who thought it would be profitable to work as a teacher in Russia—but with someone who was himself a teacher in France (ah, what supreme good fortune!).

Yet with all these important and generally useful skills and talents, the young man feels an aversion for serious intellectual activity. He cannot spend half an hour at his desk working alone. At our last lesson his thinking was particularly sluggish and, evidently, he preferred to listen to me rather than work by himself. So that the lesson would not be a complete loss, I began to talk about history. While I was talking, his mother walked in. I expected her to comment on my indulgence. But this was not at all the case. When her beloved son had left the room, she thanked me effusively for having occupied his mind so well.

"But we really lost time," I objected, "since we did what was pleasant rather than what was useful."

"That's the only way you can handle young people," she said. "You can teach them only by amusing them. You can teach him more with your stories and conversations than all the professors can with their pedantic methods. He loves you and believes you; therefore, you will easily pass on to him all he needs to know without troubling him."

It's doubtful that, at the age of eighteen, one can successfully learn mechanically, using only one's ears but not one's will and attentiveness of mind.

But most of the people whose vocation it is to sparkle in high society are like that. How many of them feel entitled to ranks, decorations and power—and what's more they get them! You can't help feeling outraged when you think that a single word from such individuals can deprive thousands of mortals of their peaceful sleep and daily bread and can decide their fate.

8 November. Our present emperor knows how to rule. They say he works tirelessly, reviews everything himself, and tries to understand everything. He lives simply. His strictness with others mirrors his strictness with himself. Of course this is rare in autocratic sovereigns. But he lacks something very important, namely, people who could be genuine aides. We have courtiers, but not ministers. We have efficient people, but not people of independent mind and noble spirit. Speransky is the only one.

Oh, if only our emperor would devise some means of breaking the chains of our ten million slaves! How it would revitalize our nation! How many hands whose only function now is to serve the parasites, would turn to generally useful labor! In the home of Count Sheremetev alone, for example, live 400 people whose existence consists solely in their eating, drinking and sleeping peacefully at the expense of a producing class.

12 November. There's talk about great changes in the university and about the kind of changes that will subject the students to great restrictions both in matters of thought and dress. The students are most upset by the first of these. I am exerting all my influence on my friends to prevent angry outbursts on their part. These days, whoever is noble and imprudent perishes.

Can they really impose on us a logic of expediency, that is, can they tell us what to think and force us to call black white and white black, simply because our social order is so perverted? People can be forced not to talk in a certain way and not to discuss certain subjects—which is already a good deal—but not to think?! But, that's precisely what they want to do, forgetting, that when coercion stands in the way of fulfilment of the eternal laws of human development, it does so only temporarily, for the barbarian and slave have but their appointed time, while humanity lives on forever.

3 December. Today, Polenov, our superintendent's nephew, asked me on behalf of the superintendent to come to his uncle's house this evening around six o'clock. This unexpected invitation both delighted and surprised me, for after my last visit with the superintendent I had lost all hope of improving my situation soon.

I went to see him. The superintendent told me that he could now employ me in his office at a yearly salary of 500 rubles, since the composition of his staff had been approved as of today. My chief responsibility will be to take care of correspondence requiring special processing, so that I will be, in essence, his secretary. I am very pleased: 500 rubles in my present circumstances seems very nearly wealth to me.[k]

20 December. I was reading Byron. His poetry is like a storm playing an Aeolian harp. Harmony is absent, but you hear chords which shake you like the moaning of a dying friend or mistress.

Napoleon, Byron and Schelling are the representatives of our age. They will reveal the secrets of this age to future generations and will show them how, in our time, the human spirit wanted to triumph over fate and collapsed in unequal battle with it.

[k] Nikitenko was employed by Konstantin Matveevich Borozdin, superintendent (curator) of the St. Petersburg school district.

1827

30 January. I was under a great deal of pressure all month. Everything piled up on me: my dissertation, exams, my job at the superintendent's office, pressing needs. The superintendent becomes kinder to me from day to day. He treats me more as a friend than a subordinate. I am deeply touched by his trust in me, and my work with him is developing my skill in administrative affairs.

9 February. In reviewing the past academic year, one can't help noticing that not all young people at the university are equally inspired with a love of learning. Some of the students work only for the sake of a certificate and, therefore, do poorly. Their ultimate goal is not moral and intellectual improvement, but rank, without which, in our society, you cannot enjoy civil rights. Under such circumstances one really can't be too hard on them, or on anyone in Russia who is obsessed with a passion for rank, which Butyrsky aptly enough refers to as rank-madness.

23 March. I've entertained the following idea for a long time. I would like to spur my friends to do some serious work in literature. They could write articles and do translations, and the best would be published at the end of the year. There are many among my friends who could do this. The superintendent sympathizes with me and approves of the idea, but there are serious obstacles in the way. These days anything that is done by collective effort and even faintly suggests a social character is viewed with suspicion. In the plan I have outlined I have tried to avoid anything that would suggest this, but I couldn't ignore the need for student meetings where authors and translators could perfect themselves in their native language and literature by analyzing and criticizing each other's work. I must ask the permission of the University Council for such meetings.

5 April. The superintendent received a copy of the new regulations for educational institutions from the committee for school reform. He gave it to me for review, and asked me to prepare a commentary. The latter, together with his own remarks will comprise the opinion which he must submit to the committee.

The regulations concern parish and public schools, gymnasiums and gymnasium boarding schools.[1] I was struck by the tenor of these regulations. The idea of spreading education among the lower classes in Russia is so resolute and is expressed in such strong measures that even I feel they have gone beyond

[1] High schools.

the limits of reasonable gradualism. The establishment of Lancaster schools,[m] one or two to each parish, ought to improve our national spirit with lightning rapidity. The establishment of boarding facilities at gymnasiums is a new and effective means of educating our middle class. All this prepares the way for important radical changes.

What will happen to slavery? The superintendent flatly condemns this plan of universal education. His feelings are that of a patriot, but he labors under the misapprehensions of an aristocrat. I think the main thing is to remove the shackles from our sixteen million countrymen. The question is: should education destroy slavery or should freedom precede education? In other words, will the people themselves cast off their bonds or will they receive freedom from the government itself? God save us from the former! But this is inevitable if the government merely educates the people without slackening their bonds as national self-awareness awakens. It is important that educational measures go hand in hand with a new civil code.

14 April. Professor Senkovsky is an excellent orientalist, but I dare say, not a particularly pleasant man. He was evidently badly brought up, for at times he is extremely impolite. He is reproached for being servile to those above him and rude to those below him. His colleagues and students dislike him and he uses every opportunity to irritate the former and hurt the latter. Nature has endowed him with a nimble and sharp mind which he uses to wound anyone who becomes friendly with him.

23 May. Several days ago Madame Shterich celebrated her name-day. She had many guests, including a new face, which, I must confess, made a rather strong impression on me. When I went down to the drawing room in the evening, my attention was instantly riveted on the face of a young woman of striking beauty. I was attracted above all by the touching languor of her eyes, her smile, and the sounds of her voice.

This young woman was Anna Petrovna Kern, née Poltoratskaya, the wife of General Kern. Her father, a Little Russian [Ukrainian] landowner, had imagined that a general was necessary to his daughter's happiness. Worthy suitors had sought her hand, but all were rejected in the hope that a general would turn up. Finally, one did. He was past fifty. Thick epaulettes were his only claim to the title of human being. The beautiful, but also perceptive and sensitive, Aneta was sacrificed to these epaulettes. Her life became a web of cruel tribulations. Her husband was not only coarse and immune to the gentling influence of her beauty and intellect, but also extremely jealous. Malicious and uncontrollable, he subjected her to every possible form of humiliation. He was even jealous of her father. For eight years the young woman suffered

---

[m] The principal feature of the Lancaster system was the teaching of the less advanced pupils by the more advanced.

in his grip. When she could bear it no longer, she demanded a separation, and finally got what she wanted. Since then she has been living in seclusion in St. Petersburg. She has a daughter who is being educated at Smolny Convent. On Madame Shterich's name-day I had occasion to sit next to Madame Kern at supper. Our conversation began with some small talk but rapidly developed a personal, intimate quality. Some two hours flew by like an instant. She has an apartment in Serafima Ivanovna Shterich's house and hence the two women see each other almost daily. And since the name-day party, I've run into her several times. Each time I am more and more attracted to her, not only by her beauty and her charming manner, but also by the flattering attention she shows me.

Today, I spent the whole evening with her at Madame Shterich's. We talked about literature, our feelings, our life, about the world. We remained alone for several minutes, and she asked me to visit her.

"I cannot remain in an undefined relationship with anyone fate brings into my life," she said. "Either I am completely cold toward them, or I become attached to them with all my heart and for always."

The meaning of these words was further heightened by the tone in which she uttered them and the way she looked at me.

I returned to my room in a daze, feeling slightly intoxicated.

24 May. This was the shortest-lived and, hence, the best kind of romance. In the evening I had stopped in at Serafima Ivanovna's drawing room, knowing that I would find Madame Kern there. I entered. I was given a cold look. It were as if nothing had ever happened between us. Anna Petrovna was in utter ecstasy over the arrival of the poet, Pushkin, with whom she has long been on very close terms. She had spent the entire previous day with him at his father's home and couldn't find words to express her delight. Two or three icy compliments fell my way, and purely literary ones at that. Old friendships should take precedence over new ones. That's true. Nevertheless, I soon went to my room. I promise myself not to give this beauty another thought.

26 May. I went out onto my balcony. From her window she invited me into her apartment. About three hours passed quickly in lively conversation. At first I was restrained but she soon managed to stir me and fill me with trust for her again. How can one speak so movingly and tenderly and with such expression in one's eyes—and not feel anything? I completely forgot about Pushkin then. She said that she understood me, that she wanted to participate in my literary activity, that she loved solitude, that she was constant in her feelings, that her ideas coincided with mine in almost everything. Finally she asked me to visit her in Pavlovsk for several days when she goes there.

After the 24th I had kept my emotions under control and had resolved not to see her again, but she herself had invited me into her apartment.

29 May. I wanted to see her today, got within a few steps of her door and turned back.

8 June. Madame Kern moved to another apartment. I had resolved not to see
her until chance might bring us together again. But today I received a note
from her inviting me to accompany her to Pavlovsk. I went to see her: there
was no further mention of Pavlovsk. I stayed until ten o'clock. As I was taking leave of her, the poet Pushkin arrived. He is a man of small stature who,
at first glance, appears rather ordinary. If you study his face below the eyes
you will search it in vain for a sign of poetic talent. But the eyes are startling:
you see in them the rays of fire with which his poems are kindled—beautiful,
like a bouquet of fresh spring roses, sonorous, full of strength and feeling. I
can't comment on his manner and conversation because I left too quickly.

12 June. Anna Petrovna and I exchanged letters today. The pretext was some
books which I had promised to get for her. Her reply was clever, subtle but
elusive. I received a second note from her in the evening, in which she asked
me to bring her some excerpts from my work and read them together with her.
For lack of time I did not go.

22 June. Madame Kern sent me some of her autobiographical notes today to
use as the plot of my novel which she is urging me to continue writing. In
these notes she had produced an image of herself, which, it seems to me, was
created from everything that her fertile imagination has lifted from her reading. Dreaminess, vagueness, and inconsistency of ideas are regarded these days
as virtues, and people with noble inclinations who are carried away by the spirit
of the times model their behavior on the heroes of today's romantic poetry.
I don't know if philosophy will overcome this affliction of our age. But I, for
one, would like to write a philosophical novel, and in it I would like to prescribe some simple but effective remedy against it. We've become lost in a
mass of complicated ideas. We must return to simplicity. We must force ourselves to think, for this is the only way to eliminate dreaminess and vagueness
of ideas in which people, today, see something lofty, something very beautiful, but in which there is really nothing but the crackling and smoke of overheated imaginations.

23 June. I read excerpts from my novel to Madame Kern this evening. She
sees everything only in terms of herself, and, therefore, I doubt that she would
like anything in which she didn't see herself. She asked me to leave these
pages with her.

I don't know if my friendship with this woman will last. Her behavior is
amazingly erratic and, besides, when she encounters in others the slightest
opposition to her own feelings she is immediately alienated.

Yesterday, when we were talking about the human heart, I said: "I, for one,
shall never rely on it unless it is combined with strength of character. The
human heart in itself is in a constant state of agitation, like the blood which
drives it, and so, it is inconstant and fickle."

"Oh, how mistrustful you are," she replied. "I don't like it. It is my faith
in people which gives me all my pleasure. No! No! This is perfectly awful!"

The tone in which she said this implied that I had lost all right to her respect.

"You misunderstood me," I answered in turn with displeasure. "Whoever lives in constant fear of being deceived, deserves to be deceived. But if your heart finds its happiness only in the hearts of others, then reason demands that you do not trust earthly happiness, and greatness of character dictates that you not be seduced by it."

The evening ended on a friendly note.

24 June. I was not wrong in my expectations. Madame Kern literally criticized my novel to pieces. In her opinion, my hero is too cold in his declaration of love and philosophizes too much or simply tries to be too clever.

I would like to respect her for her frankness, especially since the main character, in view of the central idea of my novel, ought to be precisely as she pictures him. But the demanding tone of her latest letters to me, the insistently expressed desire that I must use features of her character and life in my work, and the reproaches for not doing this, indicate that she is simply angry with me because I am not working according to her prescription.

She wanted to make me her historiographer and wanted this historiographer to be a panegyrist. This is why she drew me to her and sustained my enthusiasm for her. But, then, after squeezing all the juice from the lemon, she would have tossed the peel out the window, and all would have ended. This is not merely speculation, but my direct conclusion from her very unequivocal last letters.

She is a very vain and capricious woman. She is vain from all the flattery which she herself admitted was constantly showered upon her beauty, upon that something divine and inexplicably beautiful in her. She is capricious because her vanity was combined with a careless upbringing and indiscriminate reading.

I expressed some of this in my reply to the letter she had written today, but naturally I phrased it in the most gentle terms.

26 June. In reply to my letter, I received a note from Madame Kern today which said: "Thank you for your trust. You have not erred in believing that I am capable of understanding you."

4 July. I went to Madame Kern's. Neither of us mentioned our recent disagreement, with the possible exception of a gentle hint from her, a vindictive remark. When I arrived, I found her at work.

"Sit down and wind silk with me," she said.

I obeyed. She placed the skein on my hands, showed me how to hold it and started to work.

"They say that Hercules spun at Omphale's feet," I remarked. "Although I am not Hercules, I find myself in a similar position with only one difference—

and that is, that Madame Omphale could scarcely compare with the person whom I now have the honor to serve."

"Well said! " she replied. "But, watch out, you keep tangling the silk." Again, she began to show me how to hold it.

This didn't help.

"Give it to me. I'll do it myself," I said.

I took it, untangled it, placed it on my hands my own way and everything went smoothly.

"That's fine now," she said with a pleasant smile.

"That's because I figured out the problem by myself, in my own head," I remarked.

She said nothing.

"Try to wind the thread like this," she began again after several minutes.

I obeyed, and indeed the work went even better than before. I mentioned this to her.

"Well now, you see," she said with a triumphant air, "two heads are better than one."

I, in turn, had to hold my tongue.

16 August. Since the eleventh, I've been working very hard and have been very upset. On the evening of the eleventh I had received word that His Majesty had ordered a very severe reprimand for the superintendent, which was also to be noted on his service record. He also ordered the confinement of the director of the ministry of education's office, D. I. Yazykov, to the guardhouse for his delay in submitting information on the Kronstadt School, which he had requested two months ago. This unprecedented punishment, particularly of Yazykov, left us horror-stricken and in utter despair. As acting manager of the superintendent's office I didn't sleep for several nights in order to finish some other business which could have brought us new troubles if left undone. Being so close to Borozdin and Yazykov, I shared their misfortune from the bottom of my heart, a heart grateful for the kindness they have shown me.

The chief cause of the trouble lies in the slowness and slovenliness of the university administration, upon whom the speedy delivery of the information depended. The superintendent is guilty only of not having been strict enough. This enlightened, cultured and noble man always tries to act first and foremost as an ordinary citizen and often forgets that he is an administrator.

23 August. In general, a healthy philosophical spirit prevails in our theology lectures, a spirit which puts religion on firm ground, inaccessible to fanatics. I must admit that our clerical teachers are often more successful in their subjects than our secular professors. I think one reason for it is that our clergy's public activity is confined to a certain sphere beyond whose limits it cannot go. But our other scholars, who place no limits on their ambitions, often sacrifice their subject to them.

2 September. The weather is beautiful. I felt like taking a stroll and went to the Academy of Arts which has been opened since yesterday to art lovers and the curious. The rooms were crowded, mainly with ordinary folk. People of so-called "good breeding" usually come here in the morning.

I am not an expert on painting and judge it only by the kind of impression that a work makes on me.

Here is a portrait of the poet, Pushkin. Don't look at the name plaque: if you have seen him in the flesh even once, you will immediately recognize his penetrating eyes and that mouth, which lacks only the constant quivering. This portrait was painted by O.A. Kiprensky.

20 September. Today, some brilliant young people of "good breeding" are dining with the young gentleman of the emperor's bed-chamber, E.P. Shterich. He urged me not to leave today and to dine at home with them. The descendants of the famous Dolgorukys, the Golitsyns and the like will be here. Well, we shall see!

. . . My dear Pushkin looked at the girls as a child looks at candy he is forbidden to touch. He has a good mind and a fine heart—unfortunately much too sensitive. It was as much created for love as his face and figure were created to inspire the exact opposite. He is very ugly. The rougish females sitting opposite him were slyly chattering about his appearance.

One important comment: the hair-dos of young girls today are far from elegant. Instead of curls falling gracefully onto their bosoms or being arranged with taste, knots of hair—not their own—stick out on their temples. A braid is twisted on top of the head so that it comes to a sharp point. A face like a poodle peers out of this mass of hideously-arranged hair.

The custom of tightly clinching the waist with a corset doesn't deserve any praise either. Rousseau rightly compares girls who compress their waists to wasps, bent over double. Besides, it's very unhealthy!

22 September. Pushkin has gone off to the country. He has been losing at cards. They say that he has gone through 17,000 rubles in the past two months. His behavior certainly doesn't befit a man who speaks the language of the gods and is trying to embody in living forms a loftier ideal of beauty. Such a moral contradiction combined with great natural talent is deplorable. Not a single Russian poet has mastered so deeply the secrets of our language; no one can rival him in the liveliness, the brilliance and freshness of colors re-created in pictures by his flaming imagination. No one's poetry so charms the soul with captivating harmony. Yet, they say he is a bad son and an untrustworthy friend. That's unbelievable! In any case there is a great deal of exaggeration and absurdity in the gossip about him, as is always the case with people who, having risen above the crowd and having attracted universal attention, evoke surprise in some and envy in others.

2 October. My article "On Political Economy" was cut in many places by the censor. In one place I had said: "Adam Smith, believing that free enterprise was the cornerstone of the wealth of nations" and so forth. The word *corner* was deleted because, as the censor so profoundly remarked, the cornerstone *is* Christ, and, therefore, this epithet cannot be applied to anything else.

12 October. I saw Bulgarin. He complained to the minister of education about the censorship department's deletion of many parts of my article. The minister directed him to submit a formal petition. Is such rabid persecution of ideas necessary? Without such ideas, no government can become strong and prosperous. No matter what may be said, people do need to be enlightened. You can't conclude that enlightenment is harmful on the basis of the revolutionary propaganda of dreamers who create and preach nonsense, and who preach it not because they know so much, but because they know so little and are only half-educated.

15 October. I recently read the third published chapter of Pushkin's *Onegin.* The basic theme of the work is not yet clear, but what has already been published does present a vivid picture of the contemporary scene. In my opinion this new chapter is even superior to the preceding ones in its expression of the heart's deepest and most subtle feelings. The entire chapter is permeated with the movement of a poetic spirit. There are passages so charming and fascinating that, reading them, you are completely carried away and surrender yourself totally to the emotions concealed in them; you literally merge with the poet's soul. Tatyana's letter harmonizes, in an amazing way, elements which appear discordant: the frenzy of passion and the voice of pure innocence. Her flight into the garden when Onegin arrived was full of that sweet confusion of love which, it would seem, one can only feel and not describe—but Pushkin did describe it. This part, in my opinion, together with the Russian folk song of the maidens gathering berries in the distance, is the best in the entire chapter, where each line yields new beauty.

Here the poet has totally fulfilled the function of poetry: he has steeped my soul in the pure joy of a full and free life. He has mixed this joy with a tender reverie as inseparable from a person as the stamp of his unknown destiny, as the promise of something higher which is linked with his existence. The poet has quenched the inexplicable thirst of the human heart.

There are no words to describe his artistry! If, according to the ancients, the muses expressed themselves in verse, then I know of no other verse as worthy to serve as a medium for the graces. I should point out still another quality of Pushkin's language which shows both an unusual talent and a deep understanding of the Russian language; this is an exceptional precision even among his most arbitrary turns of speech. In his powerful hands, the language is so lithe, that you are afraid it will crumble. In reality this doesn't happen. Instead you see the most versatile and charming forms where you fear that the hand of the poet, in its too rapid manipulations, will crumple his material. And you see pure Russian forms, too.

16 October. His Majesty has ordered that the twenty best students be sent abroad for further education so they can occupy professorial positions upon their return. For the study of philosophy and law they will be sent to Berlin, and for the natural sciences, to Paris. The superintendent, while consulting with me today about their selection, proposed that I go, too. There is one obstacle—my lack of knowledge of foreign languages, but Konstantin Matveevich promised to have it waived. He wants to ask Prince Golitsyn to obtain the emperor's permission. He gave me several days to think it over and urged me to feel completely free in making my final decision.

This is it, and I shall tell him frankly how I feel about it. Upon my return from abroad I would have to be a professor for fourteen years as stipulated by the government. I love learning and thirst for knowledge, but not, as a drudge, and the main thing is that I cannot reconcile myself to anything that in the slightest smacks of *enslaving* me. The wounds of my recent bondage are still too fresh for me to agree to experience it personally again, even a gentler and improved version. Naturally, the temptation to broaden one's knowledge in Germany is great, but I prefer to be *free* to arrange my own future in Russia.

1828

7 January. I haven't written anything in my diary for a long time. Preparation for exams took all my time. This is my last one, and with it my student days will come to an end—and I shall be an ordinary citizen.

26 January. My article was published a few days ago. My professors are very pleased with it and the public couldn't have been more receptive. From this I draw two conclusions: first, that our public is still very poorly versed in political economy, second, that it is beginning to develop a taste for serious reading.

29 January. I spoke with the superintendent about my work. He offered me a secretarial post in his office at 1,200 rubles per year. In any case I shall remain with him for a year since I find it particularly pleasant to work with a man who is so cultured and noble and to whom I owe so much. Besides, a secretarial position with him would not be burdensome and, therefore, would not interfere with my further pursuit of knowledge.

30 January. Rostovtsev came to see me today. We had a very pleasant talk. In general, this man's feelings have not changed, nor has he changed in his friendly attitude toward me. We chatted about the past, reminisced about the Decembrists.

"Well, what will posterity say about me? " Rostovtsev remarked. "I fear its judgment. Will it understand and recognize the motives that guided me during those disastrous December days? Will it consider me an informer or coward who thought only of himself? "

"Posterity," I replied, "will judge you not by this act alone, but by the character of all your future activity. It will clarify for posterity the real meaning of your feelings and actions at that time."

He embraced me with tears in his eyes.

11 March. The concert I had heard in rehearsal several days ago was held today at the Naryshkin Music Academy. I arrived at six o'clock sharp. Several ladies were already strolling about the richly decorated rooms. In the first of them stood footmen and blackamoors dressed in splendid livery and arranged in two rows. Gradually the rooms filled with St. Petersburg's aristocracy. Here were counts, princes, top ranking courtiers and government officials with their wives and daughters. They scattered about the rooms and buzzed like a swarm of bees. One had to move cautiously in the crowd to avoid colliding with some lady-in-waiting or beautiful woman. There were quite a few of the latter—at least many appeared to be beauties beneath the glitter of the lights and their splendid finery. And one must give these high-society ladies their due. for their training in manners is so exquisite that it conceals the vacuum inside them very successfully. If they are essentially nothing more than dolls, they are still very charming dolls who move about with poise and ease and converse according to the well-memorized rules of their art. Their attire is generally proper and pretty with the exception of the married women's caps which look like bags stretched horizontally over their heads.

16 March. The capital was informed today about the conclusion of peace with the Persians.[1] Sixty-four million rubles and the Nakhichevan and Erivan provinces—for Russia, these are the fruits of the war which has ended. A million rubles and the title of Count Erivansky were awarded to General Paskevich. Obrezkov, who conducted peace negotiations, received 300,000 rubles, the rank of Privy Councillor and a decoration. Generous rewards! They say that the emperor is overjoyed by this event. By rewarding the participants, he wants to demonstrate that he is as ready to grant favors as he is to mete out punishment.

So, Russia's broad domain has increased by still another shred of earth. The politicians claim that this is a useful acquisition because it will serve as a defense of our borders. I think, however, that it only offers Europe new proof of the fact that we can take care of ourselves. But, Europe has stopped doubting this anyway. We really aren't interested in wresting India from the English. In any case, weakening the Persians further isn't enough for that. Besides, there's still another question. Is it we who would triumph over the English with our superior physical strength, or they over us with their politics and education?

8 April. A part of the guard leaves St. Petersburg for Turkey almost every day.[2] The emperor, together with all the generals and the diplomatic corps, accompanies the soldiers to the city gates.

And so, the fateful hour has struck for Turkey. Ask anyone in St. Petersburg, from a day laborer to a high official, what he thinks of the impending war, and he will tell you. "Turkey is finished, what else! " So confident are the Russians today of their strength!

Judging from the policy England is pursuing, Turkey may not perish after all. But there is no doubt that she will suffer only defeat and disgrace in a war with Russia. Our people have a great deal of confidence in the emperor's strong will.

They say the emperor informed Europe that he would not seek conquest in the coming war, but would punish Turkey for insulting him and Russia in its first *hatti-sherif*.[n] England is visibly worried. They say that she sent our Court this question: "How does Russia plan to make use of her victories in Turkey?" We didn't reply. Why bother? England doesn't believe that Nicho-

[n] A decree signed in the sultan's own hand.

las acts unselfishly; it doesn't understand that he needs glory and not territory—
and in this day and age there is still only one kind of glory that makes an impression—the glory associated with magnanimity. England fears for India.
But if Russia really has her eye on India, she will in any case move quietly
and gradually. Try and stop her then.

26 April. The emperor has left to join his army. If war begins, its only purpose will be to increase Russia's strength and glorify Nicholas's reign. What
kind of order of things will emerge from all this? There will be a struggle, a
bloody struggle for first place among world empires—a struggle between a new
Rome and a new Carthage, that is, between Russia and England. Which way
will the scales tip? England is powerful and Russia is both powerful and
young.

9 May. I moved to a new apartment today. I had planned to do it for some
time, but Madame Shterich kept persuading me to wait a little longer.

2 June. Today, as usual, I went to see my general and sat in the waiting room
until the officials with their reports emerged from his office. Suddenly I was
informed that a police report had been made on Professor Galich.° He was
accused of holding forbidden philosophy meetings at his home. None of the
visitors were named except me. Evidently they want to ruin this noble, pure
and gentle sage, this teacher of virtue—and me along with him.

By ruining Galich, the person who made this denunciation will, of course,
win acclaim as a patriot and loyalist. And by ruining me he will satisfy his
personal hatred. For what purpose?

As far as I am concerned, he has made a slight miscalculation. I have not
made a secret of my visits to Galich's lectures. My chief, Borozdin, and Bludov,
too, know about them—the former because I consider it my duty to reciprocate his trust in me, and the latter because of his connection with the former.
But Galich will probably be forbidden to give private lectures. This will be a
great loss to me personally, for I am already greatly indebted to him and his
teachings, and the best of it was yet to come.

23 August. I have completed my commentary on the new censorship code.[3]
The new rules came as a shock to some, who have already complained that the
code permits too much freedom of thought.

The most rabid foes of enlightenment disguise their real designs against the
spirit of this new code and attack the vagueness of some of its details. They
would like to induce the government to review the rules and to strengthen
them, that is, to set limitations where, guided by political expediency, it has
intentionally said nothing.

In order to counteract the influence of these people, the superintendent in-

° Aleksandr Ivanovich Galich (1783–1848), Russian philosopher-idealist, professor at
St. Petersburg University and Nikitenko's teacher in philosophy and esthetics.

structed me to compose a defense of the code's basic tenets and to determine what additions were necessary for its administration, for indeed, in this respect, certain clarifications were necessary.

It took me three weeks to complete this difficult task. It's supposed to be presented to the minister in a day or two. I must admit that the thought of what I have accomplished gives me great pleasure, for this was my first effort in a legislative matter, and it was aimed at something closer to my heart than anything else, that is, the spreading of enlightenment in Russia and the protection of the right of Russian citizens to a free spiritual life. Some, who are well-informed and support enlightenment, wanted to meet me after reading my interpretations and additions, and they expressed their delight in most complimentary terms.

1829

1 January. It's midnight. I am welcoming the new year with pen in hand: I am preparing lectures for my law course. But it is especially difficult to work tonight. My apartment is adjacent to the quarters of some old woman who resembles the sorceress in Sir Walter Scott's novels. The wild songs of the Bacchantes, who, it seems, have drunk heavily in honor of the new year, go on endlessly. It's amazing how our lower class women are given to drunkenness. The entire building in which I live is full of these coarse creatures, who do not miss any opportunity to indulge in the most reckless orgies. Their conversations usually end in quarrels and downright brawls, and only the policeman's threat to make them sweep the streets subdues these pitiful children of ignorance.

But, here I am, welcoming the new year with a discussion of most inelegant subjects. Human nature, however, should be observed in all its aspects and, unfortunately, human vices present an abundant harvest of truths. They are bitter, of course, but their observation is necessary for a precise understanding of man.

What will the new year bring? Much that was new occurred last year in our Russia. Nicholas's resolute activity produced many changes in internal administration.

It is sufficient to mention the new censorship code, which most truly reflects the spirit and intentions of our tsar. He answers or at least tries to answer in it the question which fanatics and adherents of old prejudices raised with insidious ambiguity: is enlightenment beneficial to Russia? And it gives a positive answer. Naturally, this is all theoretical; we shall have to see how it works out in practice.

My personal situation is as follows: I am working as a secretary for the superintendent of the St. Petersburg School District, Konstantin Matveevich Borozdin. I don't know a man of more noble heart. He awaits a better order of things for Russia and, loving it more than anything else, more than himself, humbly bears society's burdens. In this respect, I can only call him a righteous citizen. But this man, so educated, so noble, lacks the will-power to manipulate circumstances and things to conform to his own ideas. Motivated by lofty feelings, he appears prepared to fight against the wrongs to which we all fall prey in the strange game of life. But, intimidated by that whirlpool of passions in which people are churning, he retreats, not because of cowardice, but because of insufficient strength and courage.

I enjoy his trust and love which I fully reciprocate.

1830

3 January. The university has offered me a teaching post in political economy as an assistant to Professor Butyrsky. Yesterday, I began to teach in the Kurnand boarding school—higher law and statistics, and Russian literature, two hours each per week.

30 January. Voeikov printed a poem, "The Censor," in the first issue of the *Slav,* in which a certain "G," a hypocrite and ignoramus, came under attack. We were ordered to ask the censor who had reviewed this poem how he had dared to pass it, and to learn from Voeikov the identity of the person who had requested him to print it. I was looking for Voeikov almost all day in order to get evidence from him, but couldn't find him. The censorship code directs that writers not be prosecuted. It would be a good thing to adhere to this fine rule not only in theory, but in practice, too.

In the end, Voeikov answered, as was to be expected, that he didn't remember who had delivered the aforementioned poem to him for publication. Censor Serbinovich answered that he couldn't have known that the poem contained a reference to a particular individual, especially since it was a translation from the French.[P]

31 January. Voeikov was put in the guardhouse. At the same time, Grech and Bulgarin were put there, too, apparently for some intemperate and biased literary reviews. In Moscow censor S.N. Glinka was also imprisoned for two weeks. The poor writing class!

We complain about a dearth of good writers. There are gifted people, but their talent remains undeveloped. Such development is generally wanting among us. And why? The reasons are obvious.

We can only be as developed and enlightened as the conditions under which we live permit us to be.

5 February. Many people in the city are glad that Voeikov, Bulgarin and Grech have been put in the guardhouse. People have grown sick and tired of their brazen egoism.

True, but at the same time, no one thinks about the damage to one of the best articles in our censorship code.

24 February. I delivered my first lecture in political economy at the univer-

[P] The poem was not a translation from the French but was written by the Russian poet Vyazemsky in 1823. Without the latter's knowledge, Voeikov introduced changes into the text and presented it as a French fable.

sity. There was a large audience, including two professors from the philosophy and law department and the superintendent. They say that I came off very well in this initial test. But I myself am unhappy about my performance. I felt very nervous speaking before a large audience.

5 September. A terrible disease, cholera, raged in Astrakhan last month, whence it moved on to Saratov, Tambov, Penza, and now has struck Vologda, according to a report by the local authorities to the minister of internal affairs. People are very worried in the capital.

While a monster grows and develops in northern Europe, ready to swallow a mass of human victims, political diseases rage in the west and south. France succeeded in pushing back the hand that was ready to bind it in chains [the July revolution]. After three days only ruins remained of the insane despotism which Charles X attempted to foist on it. France's example has awakened the southern part of the Netherlands. Bloody fighting took place in Brussels. People are uneasy in Spain, too. In Portugal, people are beginning to grow weary of Dom Miguel's cruel deeds.

What are they saying in our country about these events? People are afraid to think out loud here, but evidently they do a great deal of thinking in private.

25 September. Cholera is already in Moscow. This is official. They say it is in Tver, too.

We are making serious preparations for the reception of this terrible guest. Prayers are being offered in the churches for the salvation of our Russian land. The common people, however, more willingly visit the taverns than God's temples. They, alone, do not grieve, while grief reigns among the upper classes. A sort of quarantine has been imposed along the road to Moscow, in Izhor, because a courier who had come there died yesterday, they say, of cholera. Everyone is sprinkling himself with chlorine and hoarding tar and vinegar. There is activity everywhere. Life, scenting the enemy, is bracing itself and preparing for a struggle with it. But what can we pit against cholera? Pluck, submission to the inevitable . . .

11 October. Here is a poem that appeared in the last issue of the *Literary Gazette:*

> France, dis-moi leurs noms! Je n'en vois point paraître
> Sur ce funèbre monument:
> Ils ont vaincu si promptement,
> Que tu fus libre avant de les connaître.[q]

[q]
> France, tell me their names! I do not see them
> On this gravestone:
> They so quickly conquered,
> That you were liberated before you learned their names.

As a result, we received a note from Benkendorf[r] today. It ordered us to inform him how the censor had dared to pass this poem and to identify its contributor. The answers are already prepared. Such incidents are common in our censorship department.

2 and 3 December. I have been invited to teach Russian literature to the senior class at Catherine Institute.

The girls have another year until graduation. They know almost nothing about literature, and this year I must cover what is usually covered in three. The salary is low: 1,050 rubles per year for nine hours of instruction per week. However, the position is considered respectable and presents a great opportunity to gain teaching experience. Besides, it is pleasant to deal with such sweet, blooming creatures. And to sow even one of my ideas in the hearts of our future mothers, to further their education, and to contribute to the progress of Russian society, can prove most rewarding.

30 December. Russian writers have received a New Year's present: the Censorship Department has received a directive forbidding the publication of unsigned articles. The author's name must be printed together with his article.

In general, the outgoing year has been of little comfort to the forces of enlightenment in Russia. They felt stifled by an atmosphere of oppression. Many prose and poetic works were forbidden for the most petty reasons; one might even say, for no reason at all, because the censors have been gripped by a sense of panic. The censorship code has been completely subverted. We have been forced to acknowledge the bitter truth, that not a shadow of legality exists on our Russian soil. People are growing more and more corrupt, as they see our laws being violated by the very individuals who created them or being replaced in rapid succession by other laws, and so forth. A spirit of opposition is growing with increasing intensity in the educated circles of our society. The more covert it is, the worse it is, like a worm gnawing at a tree. The Jacobins will be delighted with this state of affairs, but intelligent men will regret these political errors whose end is not difficult to foresee. Living conditions, industry, justice, and so on, have not improved this past year, either. May the Lord protect Russia!

[r] Count Benkendorf was chief of gendarmes and chief of the Third Section of His Majesty's Chancery. The Third Section, Russia's political police, exercised a wide range of powers. It kept the censorship apparatus under constant surveillance.

1831

1 January. I was deluged with greetings on New Year's morning. I have never been visited by such a variety of people—probably a sign that I, too, am beginning to win respect as a man.

16 January. Baron Delvig died after an illness of four days.[s] Further evidence of man's insignificance. He was thirty-three. He was, it seemed, in blooming health. I made his acquaintance not so long ago, and was charmed by him. Everyone mourns his passing as the passing of a noble man.

28 January. The public blames Benkendorf for Baron Delvig's premature death. Benkendorf had accused Delvig practically to his face of Jacobin tendencies for his publication of Casimir Delavigne's quatrain in the *Literary Gazette,* and had given him to understand that he was under government surveillance.

After that he was also forbidden to publish the *Literary Gazette.* This seriously affected a noble and sensitive man and accelerated the course of an illness which, possibly, had been developing in him for a long time.

9 February. After a brilliant beginning at the institute, I am now beginning to experience difficulties in my new career. Herman admonished me at length about my lectures at the institute, saying that they should be as short as possible, that they should not go too deeply into theory or sparkle with exalted or novel ideas, that one had to avoid erudition as much as possible with the girls, and so on. Yet, he and his assistant, Timaev, had insisted at the beginning that I should feel free to teach as I saw fit. The first lecture that I had delivered in this spirit was approved by Herman and Timaev. This has led me to seriously consider the idea of resigning.

More unpleasant news. I went to see Butyrsky yesterday evening. It seems that I shall not be recommended for an assistant professorship this year.

"First, it is necessary for you to show some achievements in your field," he said.

To sum up: I have satisfied neither the political economists nor the literary scholars.

11 February. I had a talk today with Inspector Shtatnikova. She told me that not only was everyone in the institute satisfied with me, but that Gospo-

---

[s] Delvig was a poet and editor of the *Literary Gazette.* Public opinion accused Benkendorf of hastening his death by harsh treatment of him in the censorship incident which involved the publication of a poem in his journal. The poet is cited in Nikitenko's entry of 31 October 1830.

din Villamov himself, who had attended my lectures three times, had congratulated the institute on acquiring me.

"We understand what you are trying to do here," she continued. "You are not concerned merely with the girls echoing some rules of rhetoric and poetics that they have learned by heart. You want to mold their taste, to give them a feeling for literature. This is what our scholars here don't like. Like Gospodin Pletnyov and our law instructor, both of whom use a similar approach, you will often be criticized. But I beg you to ignore them! Go your own way; we understand you completely. You have aroused the enthusiasm of your pupils."

15 February. I went to see Pletnyov this morning. His manner is very unpretentious. There is more gentleness than strength in his feelings and speech. He told me details about the inner workings of the institute that were amazing. But what he told me hasn't changed my approach to my work at the institute.

We also talked about the state of Russian literature, that is, we bemoaned its paltriness. He asked me to lend support to the *Literary Gazette* by contributing articles. This publication represents for Pletnyov the legacy of the noble Baron Delvig. We parted, it seems, good friends and he asked me to visit him on Wednesday evenings.

16 February. I attended a performance of Griboedov's comedy, *Woe from Wit.* Someone made the witty and apt remark that nothing but woe was left in this play, for it was badly mutilated by the deadly knife wielded by Benkendorf's literary department. The acting was also poor. Many of the actors, including V. A. Karatygin, have absolutely no understanding of the characters and situations created by the witty and brilliant Griboedov.

The play is performed every week. They say that the director of the theatre is making a pile of money out of it.

25 February. A few days ago I enjoyed reading the novel, *Adolphe,* by the eminent writer Benjamin Constant.

Prince Vyazemsky translated it. The censorship department hesitated passing this novel because it was a work of Benjamin Constant! What a chore it was trying to convince the chairman of the censorship committee, an educated man, that an author's name alone could not be equated with an article insulting the government or threatening Russia with revolution. And to think, under the influence of such notions we are supposed to improve ourselves and the younger generation!

6 March. I am reading the lectures of Laharpe. What a slave of Aristotle he is! Aristotle, Bathier, Blaire, Laharpe. All these men speak of literature as of a trade. For them compositions are prepared—tragedies, comedies, speeches, and so on—as shoes, clothing, furniture are made. They don't look upon literary production as the manifestation of the human spirit seeking a full-bodied development of the true, the good and the beautiful.

Our century is afforded the honor of restoring to poetry its rights; that is, of showing that poetry is life, the better life of the human heart, and that its purpose is not the vain amusement of idle people, but the awakening in man of all that is divine, a positive, direct development of all that is noble in his spirit.

I read *The Last Day of the Man Condemned to Death* by Victor Hugo. One cannot read this work without a shudder, especially the chapter where the unhappy man bids farewell to his little daughter. Is it fair to reproach today's novelists for picking subjects so gloomy? I think not, when I take into consideration the idea inspiring them. These writers, on the contrary, deserve our thanks. In the gloomiest depths of the human heart, in the midst of the difficult tension of passions, they seek sparks of moral beauty and save the human soul from despair, for without this, it would be appalled with itself at the sight of certain vices and evil deeds. This is the poetic side of works in which murderers and all kinds of evildoers and criminals play a role. In these works, the reader's attention is drawn to the causes of such bloody events, in which man seems to have fallen so low. They point to a bright spot in the heart of the ill-starred man that was once the core of fine inclinations but, in the end, was covered as with slime, with the torments of poverty, with early undeserved sufferings, with a scorn with which the world burdens many at their first appearance on the scene of life. But, one asks, why do they do this? So that the oppressors will shudder and the oppressed will awaken.

22 May. The censors are being hounded again. A humorous article by Bulgarin, *The Stationmaster*, was printed in *The Northern Bee*. Bulgarin compares a man to a horse who needs only a good master and driver to be a good horse. Our minister, Prince Lieven, interpreted this as a call to revolt. He submitted a report to the emperor requesting the dismissal of censor Semyonov and punishment for the author. Semyonov came to see me today, very worried. Benkendorf, however, has promised to intercede for him. In the city, people are amazed and indignant. They say the minister became angry because he thought the article was aimed at him. What a strange way to pacify the public and still the rumbling of ideas! There's a world of difference between firm measures and coercive measures! But they are confusing the two.

28 May. Censor Semyonov's case was disposed of sensibly. It was dropped without further ado. However, poor Semyonov suffered much in the interim.

19 June. Cholera, in all its horror, has finally appeared in St. Petersburg, too. Severe, stern precautionary measures are being taken everywhere. The city is in distress. Almost all communication has been interrupted. People leave their homes only in extreme necessity or to go to work.

20 June. We are setting up an infirmary for our own officials. I spent the whole day with our superintendent making arrangements. I went to see Kaidanov to ask his advice about a doctor.

There are few doctors in the capital and it's difficult to get hold of them now.

People are very unhappy in the city with the way the government is handling the situation. The emperor has left the capital and almost all the members of the State Council have left, too. The governor-general can scarcely be relied upon. The infirmaries are organized in such a way that they are nothing more than a stopover from home to the grave. Superintendents were appointed in every section of the city, but they were chosen from among people who were weak, indecisive, and indifferent to the public welfare. The sick are carelessly tended. It is understandable that poor people consider themselves lost if the question of moving them to a hospital is merely raised. Meanwhile, the sick are being taken there indiscriminately, with and without cholera. Sometimes drunks are simply picked up in the street and thrown in together with them. People with ordinary ailments are infected by those with cholera and meet the same end. Our police, who have always been noted for their insolence and extortionary practices, have become even more shameful, instead of being helpful in these sad times. Since there is no one to rouse the people and inspire them with trust for the government, disturbances are beginning to break out in various sections of the city. People are grumbling and, as usual, believing absurd rumors: for example, the doctors are poisoning the sick, or there is no cholera, but some evil-minded people devised this whole scare for their own ends, and so forth. They are shouting against the German doctors and the Poles and are threatening to kill them all. The government appears to be asleep for it does nothing to calm the public.

21 June. There was a riot on Sennaya Square. A mob stopped a carriage transporting the sick to an infirmary, smashed it and released them. The people are clearly threatening revolt; they shout that this is not Moscow and that they'll let the German doctors and police know whom they are dealing with here. The government is deaf, dumb and blind.

The superintendent and I inspected our schools. Thanks to fate, they are still free of cholera.

We are very busy trying to get our infirmary set up as quickly as possible.

Today I visited the academic secretary of the Academy of Surgery and Medicine, Charukovsky, to ask for a doctor and two medical students for our hospital. He sent me to the chief physician, Reman. I heard plenty here, too, about the government's failure to act. The sick are being sacrificed to cholera. Everything is done only for the sake of appearance.

22 June. At one o'clock in the morning I was awakened by the news that a real rebellion had broken out on Sennaya Square. I dressed quickly, but arrived too late to find my general; he had already gone with Bludov to the scene of the disturbance. I went as far as Fontanka. It was quiet there except for small knots of people gathered everywhere. Their faces mirrored fear and despair.

The general returned and said that the army and artillery had surrounded Sennaya Square, but that the mob had already succeeded in destroying one infirmary and had killed several doctors.

23 June. The people tore three hospitals to the ground. Today, next to my apartment, a mob stopped a hospital carriage transporting the sick and ripped it to shreds.

"What are you doing there? " I asked one muzhik, who was returning triumphantly from the field of battle.

"Nothing," he replied. "The people have kicked up a bit of a row. But we didn't catch the doctor; the damn fellow managed to get away."

"And if you had caught him? "

"We'd let 'im know who he's dealing with, all right! You don't take healthy people to the infirmary instead of sick ones! Anyway, he got a coupl'uv rocks in his neck; he sure won't forget us for a long time."

Tomorrow is Ivanov Day. And the mob has some real business in mind for it.

They say that the police have seized several Poles who incited the people to riot. They were disguised in peasant dress, and were distributing money to the people.

The emperor has returned. He appeared before the people on Sennaya Square. You can't make sense out of the newsmongers' reports; each one gives a different version of the emperor's words.

All we do know is that measures have been taken to restore order.

27 June. [7 a.m.] Yesterday was a sad day. Victims were dropping all around me, struck down by an invisible but terrible enemy. The superintendent was so upset that he became ill; and these days illness is synonymous with death. At least that's the way everyone thinks. A kind of apathy toward life is beginning to take hold of me. Of the several hundred thousand people now living in St. Petersburg, all now stand at the brink of death, while hundreds are flying headlong into an abyss which yawns, so to say, under the feet of each one of us.

28 June. The disease is raging with diabolical force. One has only to step outside to run into dozens of coffins on their way to the cemetery. The people have shifted from a rebellious mood to mute, deep despair. It seems as if the end of the world has come and people, like condemned men, wander among the graves, not knowing whether their own final hour has already struck, too.

30 June. 237 people died yesterday.

30 July. I haven't recorded anything in my diary for a long time. Meanwhile, cholera has almost disappeared. Fate has spared me. Why?

3 September. The institute is open today and I began my lectures once again.

23 September. I went to Pletnyov's this evening. I thought I would find Pushkin there, but didn't. Instead he sent a stinging article against Bulgarin and Grech, and several new poems for *Northern Flowers*.

7 November. Yesterday I went to a literary dinner at the home of Vasily Nikolaevich Semyonov. Grech, Somov, Baron Rosen, and Verderevsky were there. Pogodin and Karatygin were expected, but couldn't make it. Grech sparkled with his inexhaustible wit. He is extremely amiable in public. After dinner everyone warmed up and talk flowed freely. I, by the way, was showered with exaggerated compliments by the entire literary brotherhood. Somov brought me regards from Pushkin and his regrets that he hadn't joined me last time at Pletnyov's.

Toward the end of the evening Grech was urged to sever his ties with Bulgarin, who was not referred to in the most dignified terms. Grech wouldn't agree to anything except that Bulgarin was crazy.

1832

25 January. I forgot to record in my diary that I was finally confirmed as an assistant professor of political economy. If I am worthy of it, why did they delay the matter; and if I am unworthy of it, why did they give it to me now?

10 February. I spent the evening at Pletnyov's. Pushkin was there. The *European* has been banned.[1] Ugh! So, what are we supposed to do now in Russia? Drink and brawl? It's distressing, shameful and sad!

12 March. Today at Pletnyov's, Pushkin related some very interesting tales of his travels to Georgia and Asia Minor during the last Turkish war. Very entertaining. Pushkin had been in several skirmishes with the enemy.

21 March. I heard a fascinating lecture recently on practical psychology— from a district police officer. He had come to my office on some sort of business. I struck up a conversation with him about his work. According to him, the worst corruption exists in the lowest ranks of civil servants and among the more well-to-do petty bourgeoisie and merchants. This police officer suggested two reasons for it: lack of education and a craving for luxury.

"Our system of justice and our administration are no better!" continued the police officer. "Here, for example, in my district, there are several confirmed thieves who have been acquitted two or three times by the criminal court. Other petty thieves are acting as spies. There are several manufacturers who provide pleasant entertainment for high-ranking individuals, and these manufacturers also enjoy great privileges."

"And what is the police force like?" I asked.

"Just what you'd expect. You'd be amazed at how skilful they are at manipulating police regulations. We usually begin our service on the police force as complete ignoramuses. But whoever has any brains becomes a splendid official in two or three years. He will know precisely how to protect his own interests, and for their sake will avoid his most obvious responsibilities. What can you expect us, the police, to do, when there isn't honesty anywhere?"

3 April. I read Khomyakov's tragedy, *Dimitry, The Imposter.* Khomyakov definitely lacks talent for writing drama. Not a single character is properly constructed; there's no action, but only conversations which could be reduced by half without any damage to the play's unity. The verse is good. But a drama needs action, not talk.

20 April. There exists today in Russia a group of people of what you might call mediocre mentality, who are educated and are true patriots. They constitute a kind of alliance against foreigners, chiefly against the Germans. I call them *mediocre* because they are passably noble and passably enlightened. At least they have broken out of the narrow confines of their egoism. Yet they are simply incapable of asking themselves if their total rejection of the Germans is a good thing. They are one-sided and, acting on the basis of emotions, naturally go too far. Most of these people come from the ranks of scholars.

The Germans know that such a group exists. Therefore, they try to keep together as much as possible, support all that is German, and work as methodically as they do steadily. Moreover, their activity doesn't consist as it generally does with us of loud exclamations and appeals, but of deeds. Should the occasion arise, this struggle can have harmful consequences. With us it won't be as in France, between classes and parties fighting for their ideas, but it will be tribal, which is the worst possible thing for multi-tribal Russia.

We, the Russians, are more richly endowed than all other peoples when it comes to warmth and feelings. But we rank below them when it comes to fortitude and that is why there is so wide a gulf between our passions and ideas.

22 April. I went to a soirée at Gogol's, author of the very delightful (particularly for the Little Russians) *Tales of Rudi Panko.* He is a young man, about twenty-six, of rather pleasing appearance. However, there is an air of slyness about him which tends to arouse mistrust.

14 May. We have a new deputy minister of education, Sergei Semyonovich Uvarov. He asked to see me, and I did today. He spoke with me for a long time about political economy and literature. The university wants to offer me a position in literature. I've been hoping for it for a long time.

Uvarov is a man educated in the European tradition who has long been considered enlightened. With his help, "a purification system" has been adopted which is now operating at the universities, that is, incompetent professors are being dismissed.

17 June. Intellectual life is beginning to develop rapidly in our generation. But for the moment it's still in its infancy. Everything in it is immature except for our impulses toward the noble and the beautiful. Our concepts of humanity's most important tasks are shaky and vague, because we do not yet have independence of thought and feeling.

27 June. Today we received a confidential communiqué from the minister about the reappearance of cholera in St. Petersburg. They say that several people died within a period of three hours.

It appears that the matter concerning my transfer to the Department of Russian Literature as an assistant to Pletnyov has been settled. Naturally, this is much closer to my heart than political economy.

26 August. Today I delivered my first lecture on Russian literature at the university, or, I should say, I delivered a speech, in which I attempted to express my philosophy of teaching. There was a large audience consisting not only of students, but of outsiders, too. As a result, I must say I lectured badly. I feel very dissatisfied with myself. I was advised to write out my speech and lecture from my notes, but, as usual, I wanted to improvise; and I was too nervous for this and couldn't catch my breath. My lecture was weak and colorless, and I left the platform with an extremely unpleasant feeling.

26 October. Literature is being hounded again. Some sort of frightful design against sovereign power, etc., was found in Lugansky's (Dal's) fairy tales.

I read them and they are nothing more than harmless Russian chatter. Their principal merit lies in their ethnic character. But people close to the Court see some sort of political design here. They will certainly not miss the opportunity to prosecute him. It is painful, truly painful, to an honest man to see them stir passions with these strange measures, passions which otherwise would either slumber peacefully or be turned to better purposes. If an individual is not permitted to express himself freely, to pour out his thoughts and feelings, he will be forced to withdraw within himself and secretly nourish radical ideas, and dream of a better order of things. In a political sense this is dangerous.

1833

26 January. Asia is sending Europe a new scourge—some kind of plague. They say it has already appeared in Orenburg. It's typhus.

29 January. The weather is awful. It's raining. The snow on the streets has almost completely disappeared. There are many sick people in the city. Many are dying. It's not the plague, but a certain kind of epidemic. At any rate, people are dying like flies.

Yesterday I stayed at Herman's ball until 4 A.M. The conversation among officials centered long and tediously on the awards showered on those who had compiled the Code of Laws. Stars, ranks, leases and money fell like hail on these people. The officials were very agitated about it: "and how come?" "and for what?" and "why" did he get this or that? and so on and so forth. There was no end to this kind of talk. While listening to all this I involuntarily turned down the facings of my uniform, to hide the buttons, symbol of my officialdom. Yet these people are right in wanting a cross or rank, because without it, who would recognize them as people? If you want society to indulge your heart or passions, you must show it all your shining trinkets. If you want to have a nice, educated female companion, first you must reckon with the table of ranks. Respect, the love of people, everything—everything must be purchased by the display of your titles, which more often than not you don't possess. But if you want to be free you must be at war with society. You're lucky if you can manage to save your body from cold and hunger. Don't ask for anything more.

30 January. *King Richard* was staged at the Bolshoi Theatre exactly, or almost exactly, as Shakespeare's creative mind had conceived it. We rushed as fast as the hackie's old nag could carry us and arrived at the theatre just as the first act was ending. Oh Shakespeare, Shakespeare! What barbarians you have come to! Only seven or eight people in the whole theatre (which was full) expressed enthusiasm; all the rest of this human mass, or human vacuum, were deaf, dumb and without hands, for there were neither exclamations, nor applause! But our dear Pecherin returned home with swollen hands; he didn't spare them for the great Shakespeare. No, our public has definitely not emerged from its childhood. It needs dolls, flights of fantasy, metamorphoses. It is incapable of understanding the depths of passions and the ideas of art.

16 March. I attended poor Shterich's funeral today. He died of a cruel case of consumption after suffering for six months. I have lost someone whom I loved dearly and who was sincerely interested in my welfare. It is a bitter loss. Three days before the end he summoned all his serfs to his side, gave them their freedom and rewarded some of them as well.

4 April. The day before yesterday I read the superintendent my introductory lecture, "On the Origin and Spirit of Literature," which I am sending to press. He advised me to delete several passages.

"But why?" I asked.

"Because," he replied, "they might be misinterpreted and get you and the censor into trouble."

However, I left them in, for without them the article would have neither meaning nor force.

Is it really possible that everything honest and enlightened is so incompatible with our social order? A fine social order! Why establish universities? Incomprehensible! Once again orders have been issued to send twenty of our finest students abroad for further training. And what will they do with their knowledge when they return, with their lofty desire to illume their generation with the lamp of truth?

There was a time when one could not speak of fertilizing the soil unless one could cite supporting texts from holy scripture. Then, the Magnitskys and Runichs insisted that philosophy be taught according to a program developed in the ministry of education. They insisted that teachers of logic should also try to convince their students that the laws of reason did not exist. And history teachers should say that Greece and Rome were definitely not republics, but resembled absolute monarchies in the Turkish or Mongol style. Could science produce any kind of truth when it was so distorted? And now? Ah, now it's quite a different matter. Now they demand that literature blossom forth, but that no one should write anything in either prose or poetry. They insist that we teach as well as possible, but that teachers shouldn't think, because after all, what are teachers but officers who deal with truth (sternly) and force it to twist and turn in all directions before their audience. Now, they insist that youth should study hard, and not mechanically. But, they say, it should not read books, nor should it dare to think that it might be more useful to the state if its citizens had developed minds rather than shiny buttons on their uniforms.

10 April. Nikolai Pavlovich[t] visited Gymnasium No. 1 today and was displeased for the following reasons. The children were at their lessons. He entered the fifth grade where Turchaninov was teaching history. During the lesson, one of the pupils, who happens to be the best behaved and most studious, was listening attentively to the teacher, but was leaning on his elbows. This was seen as a breach of discipline. The superintendent was ordered to discharge the teacher, Turchaninov.

Then, the emperor entered the priest's class—where the same thing happened.

[t] Nicholas I.

The class was in complete order, but, unfortunately, one boy was leaning against the desk in back of him. The priest was reprimanded, to which he responded with appropriate respect, saying:

"Your Majesty, I am more concerned with how they listen to my instruction than with the way they sit."

More grief for the superintendent. This is already the third such incident.

12 April. The emperor's visit to Gymnasium No. 1 had more serious consequences than it seemed at first. Konstantin Matveevich Borozdin, our noble, enlightened superintendent, full of love for people and his country—a man who had neither the strong will nor luck needed for one of the most important government posts, was forced to resign. He had written a letter to the minister yesterday.

But here is an example of his character which personally involved me and touched me very deeply. He had summoned me to his office and said:

"You know, to me you were never just another civil servant or subordinate, but a son. I am sorry we must part. But here is what I can do for you, as far as my sad circumstances permit: when your boat, too, begins to flounder in this sea of politics and must be saved from the shoals and rocks—come to me immediately. I've assigned twenty serfs to you and almost two hundred dessiatinas[u] of land from my estate. There, at least, you will find refuge."[v]

I couldn't say anything. Tears rolled down my cheeks and we embraced warmly.

They want to appoint Count Wielgorski in his place.

16 April. The minister has appointed me a censor, and the emperor has confirmed the appointment. I am taking a very dangerous step. Today the minister had a long talk with me about the spirit in which I must approach the duties of my new position. He impressed me as a rather statesmanlike and enlightened individual.

"You must perform your duties," he said to me, "in such a manner that you not only base your judgements on the censorship code, but also on the particular set of circumstances with which you are faced and the course of events. Also, you must work in such a way that the public has no cause to conclude that the government is hounding culture."

I wanted to ask him to release me from my present post as manager of the superintendent's office, but he expressed his firm desire that I retain that position, too.

4 May. Prince Mikhail Aleksandrovich Dondukov-Korsakov was appointed superintendent. He took up his new duties on May 1st. He appears to be a noble, well-educated man.

I've been worn out these past weeks by my work at the superintendent's

[u] One dessiatina equals 2.7 acres.

[v] Nikitenko never received this gift.

office. I am overwhelmed with office duties and don't have time for my own literary work. And so the months and years go by, taking with them the best part of my strength.

19 August. I've been married a month.[w]

[w] Nikitenko makes no previous mention of his marriage.

1834

1 January, midnight. I am resuming my diary entries which I had almost abandoned since my marriage. My time has been pilfered by the petty cares of
office life. How can one avoid this? Woe to those who are fated to live in an
age such as this, when any attempt to develop one's intellect is considered a
violation of law and order. It's no wonder that my university lectures, too,
are not what I would want them to be and what I could make them be. True,
from all sides I hear that I am creating a new school of thought, that I am
throwing off rays of light—but I don't feel as if I am generating either heat or
light.

Administrative work is crushing me in its claws and draining all my energy.
I often have to think out my lectures at the very gates of the university.

Again, I requested a release from my position in the superintendent's office.
But the minister says I am needed and asks me to remain longer. We'll work
ourselves to death here.

3 January. The minister summoned me on censorship business. Olin had
written a eulogy of our present reign in which pompous praise was lavished on
the emperor and Paskevich. This wretched little book was assigned to me for
examination. The censor is faced with a dilemma in such cases because he
can't ban books of this sort, and to approve them is awkward, too. Fortunately,
the emperor himself settled the problem on this occasion. I passed this little
book, but only after deleting several passages; for example, where the author
called Nicholas I a god. The emperor still disliked the excessive praise, and he
told the minister to inform the censors that similar works should not be approved in the future. My thanks to him!

8 January. The *Reader's Library*, a journal published by Smirdin, was assigned
to me for censorship. This was done at the special request of its editors who
flatter me, calling me the "wisest of censors."

I am having many problems with this journal. The government gives it a
thorough going-over. Informers are sharpening their claws for it, while its
editors are literally tearing ahead with their attacks on everyone and everything. Moreover, our respectable literary figures are infuriated because Smirdin
is paying Senkovsky 15,000 rubles per year. Each of them wants to wring
Senkovsky's neck and I am already hearing cries of "How is that possible?"
They are letting a Pole guide public opinion! And he's a revolutionary to
boot! He and Lelewel nearly incited a Polish rebellion. Senkovsky himself
causes me a lot of trouble with his stubbornness. We clash frequently. In
brief, I am besieged on all sides. I must reconcile three conflicting elements: I

must satisfy the government's demands, the demands of the writers, and the demands of my own inner feelings. A censor is considered the natural enemy of writers—and this certainly appears to be true.

10 January. A terrible row has been raised about Senkovsky. All the contributers to the *Reader's Library* have become very upset.

Rumor has it that he has taken it upon himself to alter, to his own taste, articles that have been submitted to him for publication.

Judging by his rashness and his rather insolent nature, this is entirely possible. Gogol came to see me yesterday, seething about Senkovsky.

16 January. A political storm has finally engulfed Senkovsky. I received an order from the minister to keep a very strict watch on the spirit and direction of the *Reader's Library.* If one were to execute this order to the letter, Senkovsky would be better off taking a clerk's job than remaining in literature. The minister spoke very sharply about his "polonism," his "gutter jokes," and so forth. When he noticed my desire to object, he quickly changed the subject and then abruptly excused me. To tell the truth, I really don't know what Senkovsky is guilty of as a litterateur. Lack of taste? That's no concern of the government. He doesn't praise anyone, but mostly rails at people; and his satire happens to be very general. Of course I can't vouch for his patriotic or ultra-monarchal sentiments. But it is certain that, out of fear or prudence, he never parades himself as a liberal. What's so surprising about that? Indeed, even Delvig, who was too lazy to be an active liberal, was accused of disloyal sentiments.

I was appointed adjunct professor of Russian literature.

21 January. I went to see the minister to thank him for my promotion. I was very well received. Again, the same talk about Senkovsky. I spoke up in favor of Smirdin, trying to save his journal from misfortune, a journal which still does mean something in our pitiful culture, or, rather, our semi-culture. The minister said he would make it difficult for Senkovsky. It appears that he wants the latter to resign from his editorial post.

26 January. Senkovsky was finally forced to resign as editor of the *Reader's Library.* But it's only for the sake of appearance. At any rate, he is still managing all journal affairs although he did publish his resignation in the *Bee.* It has caused quite a stir among the public. Those who are ill-disposed toward Uvarov strongly censure him. In this instance he really acted despotically. An absurd rumor has it that he is appointing me in Senkovsky's place. My humble thanks!

5 February. Yesterday I went with Kukolnik to a soirée at the home of Vice President of the Academy of Arts, Count Fyodor Petrovich Tolstoy. His family is cultured and pleasant. I met Lobanov there, who in an outburst of patriotic fury attacked poor Senkovsky from all sides. What kind of people are these pedant-patriots, who think that all you have to do to be considered a loyal subject is to keep shouting at the top of your lungs: "Let's be patriots, let's be *narodny!*"[x] They forget that first of all one must be a man, and an honest one at that. Patriotism is the fruit of honor, but where in our country is this honor to be found?

10 February. Father F.F. Sidonsky wrote a very intelligent philosophy book, *Introduction to Philosophy.* For this the monks removed him from his position as a teacher of philosophy at the Aleksandr Nevsky Academy. I am surprised that they still haven't pounced on me, for I was the censor of this book.[y]

16 March. There was a large gathering of literary figures at Grech's today of about seventy people. The subject of the meeting was the publication of a Russian encyclopedia. This is being undertaken by the printer, Pluchart. Any-one known as a scholar or man of letters was invited to participate. Grech opened the meeting with a brief speech about the usefulness of such a work and read the plan of the encyclopedia, which will consist of twenty-four volumes and contain, besides general scholarly topics, articles on Russia.

Then, each person signed his name on a sheet under the heading of the special field to which he would contribute his work. I signed up for "Russian literature." But when I saw that the sheet marked "Russian Language" was blank, I decided to sign my name there, too.

Pushkin and Prince Odoevsky made a minor blunder which irritated many and angered others. All those present either affixed their signatures as a sign of agreement or, if they didn't agree, simply didn't sign. But Prince Odoevsky wrote: "I agree, if this venture and its terms coincide with my aims." A. Push-kin added to this: "provided that my name not be displayed." Many took this pettiness as a personal insult.[z]

After the meeting we drank champagne. I saw many of the literary figures whom I knew: Pletnyov, Kukolnik, Masalsky, Ustryalov, Galich, Father Sidonsky, and others.

Sidonsky told me about the persecution he was subjected to by the monks (meaning Filaret) on account of his book *Introduction to Philosophy.* I also heard an amusing anecdote from him about how Filaret complained to Benk-endorf about a line in Pushkin's *Onegin.* Describing Moscow, Pushkin says: "and a flock of jackdaws on the crosses." Filaret found this insulting to things

---

[x] There is no one-word equivalent in English. *Narodny* refers to patriotism as well as the ethnic or national character of things or people. A close translation in this context is "Let's be Russians to the core."

[y] The higher clergy was indignant about Sidonsky not only because it found his book very liberal but also because the author dared to publish his work with the permission of the secular rather than the clerical censorship department.

[z] Pushkin refers to this meeting in his diary, quoting Grech's warning to him about Plu-chart. Grech had called the latter a charlatan.

holy. The censor, who was summoned for an explanation, said that jackdaws, as far as he knew, really did perch on the crosses of Moscow churches, but that in his opinion it was not the poet and the censor who were guilty here, but rather the Moscow Chief of Police, for permitting this. Benkendorf replied to Filaret politely, saying that this matter wasn't worthy of the intervention of such a respectable clerical personage.

5 April. The *Moscow Telegraph* has been banned on Uvarov's orders.[1] At first the emperor wanted to be very strict with Polevoy. "But," he said later to the minister, "we ourselves are to blame for tolerating this misconduct for so long."

There is a lot of talk everywhere about the *Telegraph.* Some complain bitterly "that our only good journal no longer exists."

"It serves him right," others say. "He even dared to attack Karamzin. He didn't spare my novel either. He's a liberal, a Jacobin—everyone knows it," and so on and so forth.

9 April. I went to see the minister today. I reported to him about some novels translated from the French.

He ordered us not to pass Victor Hugo's *Notre Dame de Paris.* However, he had praise for this work. The minister feels it is still too early for us to read such books, forgetting, moreover, that Victor Hugo is read in the original anyway by all those for whom he considers such reading dangerous. There isn't a single book forbidden by the foreign censorship department that can't be purchased here, even from secondhand book dealers. When Sir Walter Scott's *Life of Napoleon Bonaparte* first appeared, in all of St. Petersburg only some six or seven government figures were permitted to own it. But at that same time, my friend, Ochkin, bartered a copy from a book peddler in exchange for some stupid novels. The minister ordered me to prepare a memorandum for him on Balzac's stories, on Paul de Kock's novels and Nodier's stories.

I also showed him Pushkin's *Angelo.* In the past the emperor himself had examined his poems, and I did not know if I had the right to censor them now. The minister has ordered me to judge Pushkin's work according to the regular censorship rules. He himself had read *Angelo* and had demanded the exclusion of several lines. Evidently this poem or fragment was begun in a moment of inspiration which was not sustained to the very end.

The minister talked at length about Polevoy, trying to justify the ban on his journal.

"It is a vehicle for revolution," said Uvarov. "He has been systematically disseminating destructive principles for several years now. He doesn't like Russia. I've been observing him for a long time, but I didn't want to be too hasty in taking strong measures. I personally advised him in Moscow to restrain himself and showed him that our aristocrats were not as stupid as he thought they were. Later, he was officially reprimanded, but this didn't help. At first I considered bringing him to trial, but this would have ruined him. It was necessary to deprive him of the right to address the public. The government always has the power to do this, and, moreover, on completely legal grounds, for the right to address the public in print is not among the rights possessed by Russian citizens. This is a privilege which the government can give or take away at will. However," he continued, "it is well known that there is a group in our country which hungers for revolution. The Decembrists were not destroyed and Polevoy wanted to be their organ. But they are well aware that they will always encounter firm opposition from the emperor and his ministers. I would deal differently with Grech or Senkovsky; they are cowards. Merely threaten them with the guardhouse and they will quiet down. But Polevoy—I know him; this man is a fanatic. He is ready to suffer anything for an idea. With him one must take firm measures. The Moscow censor was inexcusably weak."

11 April. Something happened which caused a rift between Pushkin and myself. Pushkin asked me to examine his *Tales of Belkin*, which he wants to publish in a second edition. I told him the following: "I am always ready to fulfil your wishes with the greatest pleasure. May your genius bless you with new moments of inspiration; we are at your service. (What could I say? —clip his wings? I won't be a party to that.) Kindly send me everything mentioned in your note and let me know by what date you would like this dispute between the political apparatus and art settled, or to put it more simply, by what date do you want my censorship check completed?"

Meanwhile his *Angelo* had been returned to him with several lines deleted by the minister. He was furious because Smirdin pays him ten rubles for every line: thus Pushkin will lose several ten ruble notes. He demanded that dots be substituted for the deleted lines so that Smirdin would still have to pay him.

12 April. Ivan Andreevich Krylov has written three weak fables which suggest that his talent is waning. He made an agreement with Smirdin to pay him 300 rubles for each one. But now he is demanding 500 rubles for each fable from Smirdin, saying that he is going to buy a carriage and he needs money!

14 April. I went to Pletnyov's and saw Gogol there. He is angry with me for having deleted several passages from his story which is being published in *The Housewarming*.[2] Poor writer! Poor censor!

I spoke with Pletnyov about Pushkin. They are close friends. I said: "Aleksandr Sergeevich is wrong to be angry at me. I must do my job, but in this instance it wasn't I that caused him trouble, but the minister himself."[a]

Pletnyov began to inveigh against Senkovsky, and rather coarsely, too, for his articles in the *Reader's Library*, saying they were written for money and that Senkovsky was robbing Smirdin.

[a] Nikitenko is referring to the deletions in Pushkin's *Angelo*. Pushkin was under the impression that Nikitenko and Smirdin were responsible for them.

"As far as robbery is concerned," I rejoined, "I can assure you that one of
our most eminent literary figures is in no way inferior to Senkovsky in this
respect."

He understood and said nothing.[b]

15 April. We are living in strange times. People who lay claim to spiritual
leadership of society are totally devoid of morality themselves. All faith in a
loftier order of things, in nobler deeds, has disappeared. There is neither a
love of society nor of humanity; a shallow, repulsive egoism is being propa-
gated by those who are supposed to teach our youth, spread culture and be
the mainspring of our social order.

Immorality and cynicism have gripped us to such an extent that even in
books the noble and lofty are spoken of in mocking tones. The people most
strongly infected with this cynicism are those with the most intelligent minds—
the writers. Their works sing the praises of pure beauty, but they themselves
are guilty of shamefully immoral actions. They talk about ideals, yet they
live without any awareness of higher spiritual needs, and their lives reflect
the lowest levels of morality.

Perhaps it has always been this way, but for quite different reasons. The
reason for the present moral decline in our country, as I see it, lies in the political scheme of things. The present generation of thinking people was not
that way when, bursting with youthful energy, it entered the arena of intellectual activity for the first time. It was not permeated with such deep mistrust, it did not display such cynicism toward all that was fine and noble. But
the older generation declared itself the enemy of any kind of intellectual progress, of any kind of spiritual freedom. While destroying neither learning nor
the academic apparatus, it made things so difficult for us with its censorship,
personal persecutions, and unequivocal course toward an existence devoid of
all moral self-knowledge, that we suddenly saw ourselves hemmed in spiritually on all sides, torn from that very soil which stimulates the development
and perfection of the intellect.

At first we longed feverishly for society. But when we saw that they, the
members of the older generation, were dead serious; that they demanded only
silence and inactivity from us; that talent and intelligence were condemned to
languish and rot in the depths of one's soul which now had become a prison;
that any bright idea was a crime against the social order—when, in a word,
we were told that educated people in our society were considered pariahs,
that blind submission was the sole path to acceptance, and that soldier-like
discipline was the most important element in all behavior—then the entire
younger generation suddenly deteriorated morally. All its lofty feelings, all
the ideals which had warmed its heart, inspiring it to strive for truth and goodness, became dreams devoid of any real meaning—and for intelligent people

[b] Nikitenko's reply was probably aimed at Pushkin, who had just received 1,200 rubles
for his *Hussar.*

to do nothing but dream is ridiculous. Everything was ready for, attuned to, and set for a spiritual flowering—and suddenly this mode of life and activity appeared inopportune, unsuitable; they had to smash it and on its ruins build their bureaucratic offices and soldiers' booths.

Perhaps it will be said that during this time new universities were opened, the number of teachers and professors was increased, and young people were sent abroad for further education.

This only served to increase the mass of unfortunates who didn't know where to go with their developed intellects, with their demands for a loftier intellectual life.

This is the picture of our generation; it is an unenviable one. Is it any wonder that we, trained for a higher calling and destroyed in our very own eyes, fall like starving dogs on any crumb, if only to nourish ourselves with something?

Of course, we have people, too, who function today in a different spirit, but there are very few of them and they are too weak, too timid, too mistrusting of their own pure motives to tip the scales in the direction of good. And there are hermits, postniks [fasters], who are determined to remain true to their ideas to the end and would rather die than betray them. But these people are an exception and more unfortunate than the first group, for they do not taste the delights of even momentary oblivion. It is not surprising that some of our young people are driven to suicide, as was the case with our Popov.

Of course, this period will pass as everything on this earth does; but it can drag on for a long time, for some fifty or sixty years. By that time one will have managed to die in this remote, savage, stony Arabia, far from the holyland, from Zion, where one can live and sing heavenly songs. Alas!

> Slaves, dragging their chains,
> Do not sing heavenly songs.

29 May. Smirdin is really an honest and good man, but he is uneducated and, worst of all, lacks strength of character. Our litterateurs have a tight hold on his pocket. Thanks to them he could go broke. That would be a real disaster for our literature! It would have a hard time finding another publisher with such an unselfish, generous nature. I've cautioned him repeatedly.

30 May. I went to the country to see Aleksandr Maksimovich Knyazhevich and Del. I stopped by for a minute at Pletnyov's where I met Pushkin and Gogol. Pushkin honored me with the cold bow of a gentleman of the bed-chamber.

21 June. Kalmykov, who had returned several days ago from Berlin, visited me. He is one of the students who had been sent abroad for further training in law. Through him I received a letter from Pecherin.

Russians, said Kalmykov, are despised everywhere in Germany, Berlin included. The celebrated Kreutzer himself told Kalmykov after the capture of Warsaw that from that day on we would be firmly despised. One woman became very indignant when our poor student tried to defend his countrymen. "They are enemies of freedom," she shouted. "They are vile slaves!"

16 July. Tomorrow I am setting out on a journey with Prince Dondukov-Korsakov. The purpose of this trip is to inspect educational institutions in the Olonets, Archangel and Vologda provinces. We are chiefly concerned with the gymnasiums there.

17 July. We spent the night in Schlüsselburg. The inn was a real pigsty, full of cockroaches. But this didn't prevent me from sleeping soundly after I had wrapped myself up in my overcoat. We went to inspect the school in the morning. Both inside and outside it looked even worse than the inn. The gate-keeper was drunk.

20 July. Olenets is a very poor city. Some of the pupils spend mornings in school and then leave to beg alms. There are many Karelians among its inhabitants, and the real Karelia begins just beyond Olenets. We were warned that the Karelians were very rude and evil. But, to the very gates of Petrozavodsk, everyone we met was friendly and helpful. They are a very tidy people. The floors and benches in their homes are clean; every house has a samovar and cups from which you can safely drink. We never saw any cockroaches. The local Karelians are rather well-off and are engaged in various occupations on the waterways, which add color to this rather barren country. But, they say, the inhabitants of Pudozh and Povenets counties are very poor; they subsist on bark.

23 July. We tested the pupils at the gymnasium. Kopasov is a fine teacher. Here the system of rote memorization still flourishes. Where doesn't it in our country?

31 July. We are already in Archangel and are staying at the home of the civil governor, Ilya Ivanovich Ogarev, who received us very cordially.

ARCHANGEL NOTES

The governor told me many interesting things. The city is divided into two sections—the German and the Russian.

The German section of the city is distinguished by its neat and attractive little houses. The Russian merchants live in filth and trade like swindlers. Drunkenness is very widespread. The governor complained that he didn't have a single functionary who wasn't either a thief or a drunkard. So, he must keep a close watch on them, as one does with spoiled children. He tries to keep them close at hand so they will drink as little as possible, and often he compels them to have breakfast and dinner with him. Whoever does not respond to an invitation is sent for with a droshky and brought back, drunk or sober. After he is sobered up he is given his assignment. When a match is being arranged, the fiancée's relatives, inquiring about the fiancé, no longer ask "Is he a sober type? " but rather "What's he like when he's drunk? " for the first possibility is almost inconceivable. Most of the civil servants and other city dwellers are wallowing in ignorance.

1 August. We also visited the Solovets Monastery. Solvets Island is seventeen versts wide and twenty-five long. Its monastery is one of the oldest in Russia and it has more than one hundred monks. The section of the monastery where political criminals are confined is very interesting. They are sent here for an indeterminate period, mostly for life. There are forty of these unfortunates here now, among them two students from Moscow University who were sent here for participating in the conspiracy against the emperor. One of the prisoners, Gorozhansky, who was sent to the monastery for his complicity with the Decembrists, killed a guard during a fit of insanity. Each of the prisoners occupies a separate cell, a store room, or, I should say, a grave; from here he goes straight to the cemetery.

The prisoners are forbidden to communicate with each other. They have neither books nor writing implements. They are not even permitted to walk about the monastery yard. They can't even commit suicide, for they haven't a pen knife or nail in their possession. Escape is impossible since they are surrounded by water; and, in the winter, any poor unfortunate attempting to escape would face cruel cold and death by starvation before he could reach the opposite shore.

The archimandrate looks like the kind of canon that Voltaire loved to laugh at. He wrote *A History of Solovets Monastery*, using the records from his archives, but the Holy Synod refuses to pass it. Since there are many raskolniks,[c] particularly eunuchs, among the prisoners, the archimandrate succeeded in compiling a precise account of their heresies from their testimony. The eunuchs adhere to the following belief: the Saviour came to Earth a second time in order to teach those who had strayed. He is none other than the son of Elizaveta Petrovna, the empress; he was raised in Holstein, ruled as Peter III, and still lives somewhere today.

Archangel province has a great many raskolniks. The local bishop maintains that only one percent of the entire population here belongs to the Orthodox church. Some sects include debauchery in the practice of their faith. They go so far in their licentiousness that even the wild Samoyeds, who were recently baptized, disdain forming family ties with them. At least that's what the local bishop claims.

13 August. We arrived in Vologda at eight in the morning. We inspected the gymnasium hastily and then set out for the village of Assanova, which belonged to Dmitry Mikhailovich Maksheev and was about three versts from the city. An apartment had been prepared for us at his home.

The following day we visited the gymnasium again, and this time we made a thorough inspection. I examined the pupils, and they showed up fairly well in history and literature.

[c] Members of a dissenting group which developed in the Russian Orthodox Church during the seventeenth century.

When the examination was over, a gendarme colonel came up to me and, after greeting me, asked if I knew Konstantin Nikolaevich Batyushkov.[d]

"No, I don't know him personally at all."

"That's odd; he does mention your name often."

"My name? That's surprising! And where is he now?"

"Here. He's a relative of mine."

I decided to visit Batyushkov.

15 August. In the morning I stopped by at the gendarme colonel's and we went together to see the unfortunate poet. When they informed him of my arrival, he said: "Very good: the Virgin Mary, too, will come with him to see me."

This man's mind is completely gone. I read several lines to him from his own work, *The Dying Tasso,* but he didn't understand them. Their remarkable harmony did not strike a familiar cord in the soul of the man who had once created them.

He babbled some terrible nonsense about having concluded some sort of alliance with England, Europe, Asia and America; that somewhere he had seen someone dragging Karamzin and the Russian language through the mud. He reminisced about Ekaterina Karamzina and ended with an indecent outburst against the English. Then he jumped up quickly and ran into the garden. We followed him, but he said nothing more; he was morose and silent. He is well cared-for. His rooms are excellently furnished and he himself is dressed neatly and even smartly—in a blue silk dressing gown and a skull cap. He flung the hem of his gown over his shoulder, like a Roman toga, and kept trying to assume a serious, tragic pose.

He had a terrible effect on me and I was unable to recover from it for quite some time.

[d] Konstantin Nikolaevich Batyushkov (1787–1855), poet.

1835

1 January. The final days of last year were very stormy ones for me. I spent eight days under arrest in the guardhouse.

Here's the story:

A translation of Victor Hugo's poem was printed in the twelfth issue of the *Reader's Library,* of which I am the censor:

TO A BEAUTY

If I were king of the whole world,
Sorceress! I would lay before you
All, all that power gives to a national idol:
Power, scepter, throne, crown and purple.
For a look, for just one look from you!

And if I were God—by the village saints
I swear—I would give up the coolness
Of heavenly streams
And the assembly of angels with their lively songs,
The harmony of the worlds and my power over them
For just one kiss from you!

More than two weeks had passed since the poem had been printed and it didn't worry me. But then, about two days before my arrest, Senkovsky came to see me to tell me that this poem had upset the clergy and that the Metropolitan was preparing to submit a complaint about me to the emperor. I braced myself for the storm.

On Monday, December 16th, in the middle of one of my lectures at the university, I received a note from the superintendent requesting me to see him immediately. The note made reference to "a matter with which you are familiar." It was clear what he was referring to. I steeled myself and appeared before the prince calm and collected, prepared to face courageously the misfortune which had descended upon me.

My kind chief (Dondukov-Korsakov) sadly informed me that on Sunday the Metropolitan (Serafim) had obtained a special audience with the emperor, read to him the poem cited above, and appealed to him as tsar of the Orthodox faith to guard the church and faith from the profanation of poetry. The emperor ordered that the censor who had passed this poem be put in the guardhouse. I received the sentence rather calmly. The worst that I could be reproached for was an oversight. Perhaps the words "God" and "by the village saints" should have been deleted; then there would not have been any reason to find fault with it. But judging from the way ideas are treated here, even this would scarcely have saved me from the guardhouse.

At any rate, I had to go to the palace commandant. First I stopped to warn my family of my misfortune and then I went to the commandant. I found him at dinner. I was taken to the quarters of the officer on duty. He was pacing the room with long strides, a grim expression on his face. Rows of spurs taken from officers under arrest hung on the columns. I sat down. Within half an hour the office door opened and I was summoned to the commandant.

I must admit that I expected to be treated roughly, for rumor has it that he is an uncultured man. And I had prepared myself for this. But, I was mistaken.

The general asked me politely if it was I or censor Krylov who had passed the poem in the *Reader's Library*. He showed it to me.

"It was I," I replied.

"His Majesty has ordered your confinement in the guardhouse."

And that was all. Then I left him. I was asked my rank, which was recorded with my name, and a minute later I was already speeding away along Galernaya Street, pulled by a pair of spirited horses. An aide-de-camp, extremely polite and even kindly, accompanied me. We chatted about the weather and the theater. Finally I asked where I was being confined.

"In the New Admiralty guardhouse," he replied. "It's one of the best in the city. Besides, I think it's not too far from your apartment."

We arrived, entered the guardroom, which was full of soldiers and suffocating tobacco smoke, and then found ourselves in another small room where the duty officer was stationed. I was handed over to him. Now I was a prisoner. One other prisoner was present, an artillery officer, Fadeev, and about a minute later a third was brought in.

Fortunately, behind the guardroom there was still another tiny room, otherwise we would have been very cramped. When it was learned that I was a censor, everyone expressed surprise and questioned me about the reason for my arrest. Krusenstern, a very cultured young man and son of the famous admiral, was on duty at the time. He had made a voyage around the world with Captain F.P. Litke and our Professor A.F. Postels.

Lieutenant Fadeev also proved to be an intelligent and cultured person. Grand Duke Mikhail Pavlovich had arrested him for three days for some deficiency in the dress of the cadets who were being presented to His Highness.

The other officer under arrest, Kiselev, was very upset. He had served for fifteen years. Until today he had commanded a company, and now he was stripped of his command and under arrest for an unspecified period because of some error his men had made while marching.

I stood through all my conversations with these gentlemen because there was no other furniture in the room, save a worn out Voltaire armchair for the sentry officer, a small dirty bench, and a broken down table.

Both rooms assigned to us were light but extremely untidy. The floor was terribly dirty and the walls were covered with damp spots. I was advised to send home for a bed and bedding. I sent only for the latter and later regretted it. I had to sleep on a disgusting floor, my head against a musty cold wall. I tucked my head inside my overcoat and dropped down on the mattress. Sleep soon forced me to forget all the troubles of this stormy day.

Nikitenko kept a diary while under arrest. It begins with an entry dated 17 December 1834.

17 December. I woke up in the morning with a severe headache and my clothes reeking of bedbugs. I immediately sent home for a bed and some other things. My fellow prisoners have already started some real housekeeping.

The commandant's assistant, Boldyrev, the greatest ignoramus of all the majors in the world, came to inspect the guardhouse. He scolded Krusenstern for some blunder he had committed on guard duty, picked on the guard for something and, with the flat of his sabre, cruelly beat the old man. Having clearly established his authority by raising a row, raging, using foul language, and beating people, this venerable soldier then proceeded directly to the card table, where, they say, he spends all his free time.

My dear Del appeared a little later with messages from Prince Dondukov-Korsakov. He told me that the minister had submitted a report about me. It presented me in an excellent light and stated that I had passed the unfortunate poem purely through an oversight, which was very understandable in such complicated and difficult work as censorship.

The prince himself arrived directly after Del. He confirmed everything that my friend had told me.

18 December. Commandant Martynov himself visited me. He was kind and told me not to worry, adding that many people were making a fuss on my behalf. He, on his part, promised to report to the emperor about me that very day.

My wife wrote to me that my arrest had caused quite a stir in the city and that droves of people have been coming to our apartment to express their sympathy. Since most of them don't know where I am confined, no end of people have been asking to see me at various guardhouses.

I spent the whole day chatting with Fadeev and Muratov, the sentry officer, who is also very kind to us.

19 December. I hear that my arrest continues to arouse excitement and widespread sympathy. Pletnyov visited me this morning. Fadeev served out his sentence; Kiselev was also released. I remained alone. Little by little I've managed to make myself comfortable. I receive two letters from home every day, and dinner, too.

I've already been here three days and there's no sign that I shall be released soon. Martynov actually reported to the emperor about me and asked if it would not suit His Majesty to release me. The emperor replied: "I shall designate the day myself."

20, 21, 22 December. These were monotonous days, as one would expect in the guardhouse. Friends visit from time to time but I feel ill at ease, because prisoners are not permitted to have visitors. Some of the sentry officers have been so kind as to suggest that I go home to see my family. Of course I didn't agree to this, for they could have paid dearly for it. Among my visitors was Voeikov, and I received a very kind letter from the prince.

The guard officers assigned here for guard duty are generally people who have been educated in keeping with high society. They complain about the pettiness and futility of their service. But they do not suffer from an abundance of ideas: they want a little more freedom during drills, a little less rudeness on the part of their commanding officers, and a little more time for dancing. This is their conception of the good life.

23 December. A new cell-mate arrived this evening. It was that same Muratov who recently was on sentry duty here. He was sentenced to two weeks in the guardhouse for a mistake he had made while on duty.

24 December. I spent a fairly interesting day chatting with Muratov. There still isn't the slightest indication that I shall be released soon. For the time being I am calm, as my family's needs are taken care of for another month.

We were visited this evening by the admiralty's official-on-duty, a so-called councillor. Apparently he was sent to spy on us. He was stupid, and as underhanded as a Jew.[e] He tried, with the most repulsive grimaces and absurd circumlocutions, to goad us into a discussion of the government. Naturally, we were extremely cautious.

25 December. I finally decided to ask the commandant for permission to see my wife. I had already written a letter requesting permission and was about to hand it to the guard for delivery, when a Cossack appeared with an order for my release. After saying good-by to Muratov and wishing him a speedy release, I collected my things and left for home. I had spent exactly eight days under the hospitable roof of the New Admiralty guardhouse.

At home I was welcomed like a traveller returning from a long and hazardous journey. That very same day I went to see the prince. He welcomed me with genuine delight. From there I went to see the minister, and was received favorably by him, too. There was not a word of reproach or even advice for the future. He said: "The emperor was not angry with you at all. After he read the poem you had passed, he merely remarked 'An oversight!' But he had to appease the head of the clergy and, moreover, he had to do it publicly. During your imprisonment he asked the commandant if you weren't too upset, and he expressed pleasure upon learning that you were taking it well. In general,

[e] Nikitenko uses the word "zhid," which is a contemptuous, derogatory term equivalent to "yid."

the Metropolitan didn't gain very much by his complaint. The emperor is annoyed at having been bothered with such a trivial matter. So, don't worry, you're completely out of danger now."

1 January. The news of my release spread quickly through the city, and visitors began to appear. I was welcomed with noisy expressions of delight at the institute. I was told that my pupils had cried when they had learned of my arrest and that one of them had admitted to the priest at confession that she had cursed the Metropolitan because he had complained about me to the emperor.

I found out who was chiefly responsible for my imprisonment: it was Andrei Nikolaevich Muraviev, author of *Journeys to Holy Places* and the unsuccessful tragedy *Tiberiada.* I don't know him personally, but from everything I've heard about him, it appears that this man is a fanatic who knows how to feather his nest: that is, as the saying goes, he is building his earthly happiness on the saintliness of his spiritual convictions.

But he gained very little from his complaint about me. Muraviev's name is now openly decried in public, and the emperor, through Benkendorf, has already let the Metropolitan know that he certainly is not grateful to him for the fuss that has stirred the capital for almost two weeks. Evidently, Muraviev and his brethren hadn't wanted that to happen.

I went to see Commandant Martynov, who received me very courteously. But I am already tired of hearing about my arrest everywhere I go. It's time to consign it to oblivion.

2 January. New troubles in the censorship department. A poem in honor of the tsar appeared in the first issue of the *Reader's Library.* It is a wretched poem, by an officer, Markov, who, for a similar work, had already received a diamond ring and probably wanted another now. I submitted the poem to the minister, but both of us failed to catch a certain stupid line, or rather a word at the end of the first stanza. The author, discussing Nicholas's great deeds, called him "a champion of evil things to come." The minister learned about this yesterday and informed the prince. This good, noble man didn't want to upset me on the first day of the new year and so soon after my recent misfortune. Saying nothing to me, he went to Smirdin himself and took decisive measures. Few copies of this issue had been distributed in the capital, and it had not had time to reach the palace. All available copies were collected immediately and the first page was reprinted; the word "champion" was replaced by "destroyer." And the affair was settled.

Semyonov also made a slip. In a recent issue of *Son of the Fatherland,* an article was printed about French and English novels, in which a female saint was called "a representative of the weaker sex." The censor received a severe reprimand from the minister.

Senkovsky did a foolish thing. He had noticed the word "champion" on the eve of the journal's distribution, but he didn't want to change it himself or inform me about it. But Bulgarin is a fine one, all right! He had also noticed the ill-fated word and was about to go to Mordvinov with a complaint. But they forestalled him by collecting all the copies of the journal and replacing the word with another. Bulgarin is angry with Senkovsky because the latter makes a good deal of money from the *Reader's Library*. Such are the ways of our literary luminaries.

9 January. I visited the eminent fabulist, Ivan Andreevich Krylov. He has assumed the editorship of the *Reader's Library*.

Krylov's rooms look more like a bear's den than the living quarters of a respectable man. Everything—the floors, the walls, the staircase leading to it, the kitchen, which doubles as an entrance hall, the furniture—all this was in a most slovenly state. I found Krylov himself in a dirty dressing-gown, sitting cross-legged on a dilapidated sofa and enveloped in clouds of cigar smoke. He received me very courteously, expressed regret over my arrest and began to talk about contemporary literature. In general he is very intelligent and astute, though his thinking smacks of the past century. Yet there was a certain lifelessness about everything he said. I don't know if he was truly inspired when he wrote his wonderful fables or if they flowed from his mind like the silk threads a worm unconsciously releases and winds around itself. He complained about the mercenary trend of contemporary literature, although he himself had accepted 9,000 rubles from Smirdin for assuming the editorship of the *Reader's Library*. True, he is not selling his talent, since one can be sure he will do nothing for the journal. However, he is putting his fame to use, for Smirdin is giving him money for his name alone.

21 January. Nikolai Vasilievich Gogol. He is 28 or 29 and an assistant professor of history at our university where he lectures on medieval history. He teaches the same subject at the Patriotic Institute for Women. He is a writer. He studied at the Nezhin Gymnasium together with Kukolnik, Prokopovich, etc. With the publication of *Evenings On A Farm: Tales of The Beekeeper Rudi Panko* he gained fame. They are remarkable for the distinctive Little Russian flavor of some of their characters and their lively, often very humorous, stories. He has also written several other stories that humorously depict contemporary customs. His talent is pure Teniersian.[f] Moreover, he writes about anything and everything: he is now compiling a history of Little Russia; composes treatises on painting, music and architecture, history, and so on and so forth. But when he moves from the physical to the ideal world he becomes haughty and pedantic or gets lost in childish ecstasies. Then, even his style becomes involved, sterile and hollow. That same blend of Little Russian humor and a Teniersian concern for detail, combined with pomposity, is characteristic of his personality, too. He very comically relates various episodes dealing with common folk which he takes from the daily life of the Little Russians or

[f] The reference is to David Teniers (1610–90), Flemish artist.

borrows from the scandal chronicles. But no sooner does he begin to discuss lofty ideas, than his thinking, feeling and language lose all their originality. Yet he takes no note of this and aspires only to become a genius.

Here's an episode from his life that should have taught him a lesson if fantastic vanity can learn from experience. Taking advantage of Zhukovsky's special interest in him, he decided to become a professor. Zhukovsky spoke of him in such glowing terms that Uvarov really believed that Gogol would prove to be an excellent history professor, although Gogol had not presented a shred of evidence of his knowledge or aptitude for the position. He was offered a position as an associate professor of history at Kiev University. But Gogol imagined that his genius entitled him to higher claims, so he demanded an appointment as a full professor and 6,000 rubles outright for the payment of his debts.

This young man, although he had already made a name for himself in literature, lacked academic rank and showed neither knowledge nor aptitude for the chair. And what a chair—a university chair, no less! Yet he demanded for himself what Guerin himself would probably have hesitated to ask for. This could only happen in Russia, where influence gives one the right to do anything. The minister, however, rejected Gogol's demand. Then, having learned that the history department of our university needed a history teacher, he applied for the position, demanding, this time, at least the rank of associate professor. I must confess that even I thought that a man who was so self-confident could not fail to do well, and I tried to promote friendly relations between him and the superintendent. I even tried to have him appointed an associate professor, but they wouldn't listen to us and appointed him an assistant professor.

The result? "The titmouse came to set the sea on fire," and no more. Gogol gave such miserable lectures at the university that he became the laughing-stock of the students. The administration feared they might play some prank on him, which is usual in such cases, but has unpleasant consequences. It was necessary to take decisive action. The superintendent summoned him to his office and very gently informed him of the unpleasant rumors about his lectures. For an instant his pride surrendered to the bitter realization of his inexperience and ineffectiveness as a teacher. He came to me and admitted that university teaching required more experience.

That is how the famous demand for a professorial chair ended. But in the end this did not shake Gogol's faith in his own boundless brilliance. Although, after the superintendent's talk with him, he had to change his haughty tone with the rector, the dean, and other members of the university faculty, in his own circle of friends he has remained the very same, all-knowing, profound, brilliant Gogol he had always been. This ridiculous, inflated, childish pride is, however, not only characteristic of Gogol, but of nearly all our celebrities who have seen their names in print.

18 March. A remarkable session at the University Council. At Moscow University and other Russian universities, our academics do not deem it reprehensible to accept bribes at examinations for civil servants. But our university could not claim this distinction. For some time now, however, the mercenary spirit, a spirit which happens to be common to all Russian institutions, has begun to make its way into our university, too. Three or four of our local professors have already acquired notoriety in this respect, far greater than they had acquired in their respective disciplines. Several others considered it their responsibility to lay this problem before the prince and to spur him to act on it, for the more confidence society has in the morality of the academic class, the more influence the latter will have on education in Russia. At least let education in Russia be permeated by a spirit of honor!

The prince decided to appear at the University Council, allegedly for a consultation on various matters, but in reality, to let everyone sense how necessary it was for us to preserve the honor of academia in this respect. He handled this tactfully and very well.

19 March. Pogodin, a professor at Moscow University, visited me. He came here, by the way, with a complaint to the minister about the Moscow censorship department, which permits nothing to be printed. After my arrest it turned into a real literary inquisition. Pogodin says that in Moscow they are amazed at the freedom of the press here. So, one can well imagine what it's like there!

11 April. The state of our literature is depressing. It doesn't contain a single shining idea, not an ounce of feeling. Everything is banal, shallow and uninspired. Because of his position, only the censor has the opportunity to read everything that is being written in our country. What else can we expect under such circumstances? We don't lack talent. There are young people with noble aspirations who could perfect their talent. But how can they write when they are forbidden to think? And I'm not just talking about channeling thought or restraining still vaguely formed, dangerous impulses. The basic principle behind current policy is very simple: only an administration based on fear can be strong; only a people that does not think is a peaceful people. From this it follows that nothing remains for the mediocre but to wallow in bestiality. People with talent are forced to live only for themselves. Therefore, the characteristic feature of our time is a cold, callous egoism. Another is a passion for money: everyone is trying to grab a little more, knowing that it is the only path to relative independence. There's no ambition, no lofty enthusiasm for creative work. One bitter feeling inspires some of our most eminent writers, and with a terrible, burning intensity; and that feeling is indignation.

15 June. The students from the Institute of Advanced Studies have returned from abroad. Pecherin, Kutorga and Chivilev have already visited me. Kalmykov had returned earlier. They have grown unaccustomed to Russian ways and are disturbed at the thought of vegetating forever in this kingdom of slavery. Pecherin is particularly depressed. He lived in Rome and Naples for a long time and saw the greater part of Europe until fate cast him back in Asia again. According to them, Russians abroad encounter deep hostility everywhere. Often they had to conceal their Russian citizenship in order to gain a glance or kind word from a foreigner. We are considered Huns who are threatening Europe with a new barbarism. Their professors are proclaiming this from the rostrum, trying to arouse in their students a fear of our might.

8 August. I went to see Minister Uvarov with a report on censorship.

He was in excellent speaking form today. Here is the entire monologue which he delivered in my presence:

"We, that is, the people of the nineteenth century, are in a difficult position: we are living amidst political storms and political unrest. Nations are changing their way of life; they are experiencing rebirth, are in ferment, and advancing. No one can prescribe their own rules here. But Russia is young and virgin, and she should not taste, at least for the time being, these bitter troubles. We must extend her youth and educate her in the meantime. That is my political approach. I know what our liberals, our journalists and their minions, want: Grech, Polevoy, Senkovsky and the others. But they won't succeed in casting their seeds on to the field that I am sowing and guarding— no, they will not succeed. My task is not only to keep an eye on education, but also on the spirit of this generation. If I can succeed in delaying for fifty years the kind of future that theories are brewing for Russia, I shall have performed my duty and shall die in peace. That is my theory; I hope I shall realize it. For this I am equipped with both good will and the political means. I know that people are crying out against me, but I do not heed their cries. Let them call me an obscurantist. A statesman must stand above the crowd."

He spoke very harshly about Grech:

"I have," he said, "an order from the emperor, which could wipe him out in an instant. These gentlemen don't seem to realize the kind of vise they're in and that I have been more lenient with them than they think."

1836

10 January. Kukolnik read his *Domenichino* at my place. It is an excellent work. Kukolnik demonstrates here that he is a true artist, for he is a poet of both form and content. We had a long talk together. He is disillusioned with the Court. I don't know whether he sought its favors or simply wanted to use it as a shield. At any rate his position is not an enviable one. He must submit everything he writes to Benkendorf for examination. On the other hand, his coarse patriotic farces, *Skopin-Shuisky* in particular, have served to antagonize free-thinking people and destroy their trust in him. I am not referring to those intrigues of petty envy which usually fling mud at talent, because talent should simply ignore them.

Pushkin's opinion of Kukolnik is interesting. Once, at Pletnyov's, the conversation touched on him and I happened to be there. Pushkin, as usual, chewing his nails or an apple—I don't remember which—said:

"So you think that Kukolnik writes good poems? Well, you know, they say he even has ideas, too."

These words were uttered in the tone of a double aristocrat, an aristocrat by birth and social position. Pushkin lapses into this tone at times which makes him very obnoxious.

The reading of *Domenichino* continued at my home until 2 A.M., but my guests didn't leave until much later.

17 January. Yesterday was one of my usual Fridays. Pushkin wrote a sort of lampoon directed at the minister of education, with whom he is very angry because the latter had consigned his works to the general censorship department for review. Formerly his works were examined in the emperor's own chancery, and sometimes the emperor even read them himself. For example, his poem, *The Bronze Horseman,* was personally rejected by the emperor.

Pushkin's lampoon is called *Lucullus' Recovery,* and it was printed in the *Moscow Observer.* He once boasted he would eventually land one of the local censors in the guardhouse, especially me, whom he couldn't forgive for *Angelo.* Apparently his boast will be realized in Moscow, for his poem has caused an uproar in the city. Everyone recognizes Uvarov as the target.

20 January. The whole city is gossiping about *Lucullus' Recovery.* Uvarov's enemies are reading the piece with delight, but most of the educated public are displeased with their poet. Actually, this poem gained very little for Pushkin in terms of public opinion, which he values very highly, his pride notwithstanding. The emperor ordered Benkendorf to give him a severe reprimand.

But, about three days earlier, Pushkin had already received permission to publish a journal similar to the *Edinburgh Quarterly Review:* it will be called the *Contemporary*. Our superintendent appointed Krylov[g] censor of the new journal, the most cowardly and, therefore, the harshest censor of us all. He wanted to appoint me, but I earnestly requested to be spared this task; it is too difficult to deal with Pushkin.

14 April. Pushkin is terribly harassed by censorship. He complained about Krylov and requested the appointment of a second censor to assist Krylov in examining his works. Gaevsky was appointed. Pushkin now regrets his action, but it's too late. Gaevsky is so afraid of the guardhouse, where he once spent eight days, that now some innocuous item like the death of a king would scarcely get by him into the press.

28 April. Gogol's comedy *The Inspector General* has created quite a sensation. It is performed continuously—almost every other day. The emperor attended the first performance, applauded and laughed a great deal. I saw the third performance. The empress, the heir to the throne, and the grand duchesses were there and they enjoyed it very much. The emperor even ordered his ministers to see *The Inspector General.* In front of me, in the stalls, sat Prince Chernyshev and Count Kankrin. The former expressed his utter delight; the latter said only: "Was it worth going to see such a stupid farce?"

Many people feel that the government should not approve a play in which it is so harshly censured. I saw Gogol yesterday. He wears the expression of a great man tormented by a wounded pride. Gogol, however, has really performed a great service. The impression produced by his comedy adds substantially to what we are coming to realize about the existing order of things in our country.

29 April. A real-life tragedy followed in the wake of Gogol's stage comedy. Pavlov, a civil servant, killed Actual State Councillor Aprelev as the latter was returning from church with his young bride. This and *The Inspector General* are the talk of the town.

10 May. A fantastic business! St. Petersburg, as far as we know, is not under martial law, yet orders were given for a military tribunal to try and sentence Pavlov within twenty-four hours. The public rose in wrath against Pavlov as a "base murderer," and the minister of education imposed an embargo on all French novels and stories, particularly on the works of Dumas, considering them the real culprits in the Aprelev murder.

16 October. Censor Korsakov took over the editing of the *Encyclopedic Dictionary* in Shenin's absence. He approved and ordered the printing of Shenin's article, "The Eighteenth of Brumaire," for volume seven. Grech submitted a complaint to the Censorship Committee, stating that the article was disloyal, liberal and harmful to Russia because revolutions and constitutions

[g] Krylov the censor is not to be confused with Krylov the fabulist.

were discussed in it. The article was read at the committee meeting. Even the most cowardly of our censors, Gaevsky and Krylov, could not find anything objectionable in it. Moreover, it had been approved by the minister himself. I raised the following question at the meeting: should we consider the French revolution a revolution, and should we be permitted to print in Russia that Rome was a republic and that France and England have constitutional governments—or would it not be better to pretend in our thinking and writing that nothing of the sort exists and never had existed?

Krylov replied that history and facts could not be altered. The other censors agreed with this. But, the chairman of the committee (M.A. Dondukov-Korsakov) felt that the following statement should be censored from "The Eighteenth of Brumaire:" "*Good Frenchmen* were distressed when they saw that the government was weak and that anarchy reigned everywhere in France." He argued that there could not have been a single good Frenchman in France at that time, and that these words must be deleted. In the end it was decided that "The Eighteenth of Brumaire" was not a harmful article.

25 October. A terrible uproar in the censorship department and the literary world. An article, entitled "Philosophical Letters," appeared in the October 15 issue of the *Telescope.* It was beautifully written. The author is P.Y. Chaadaev.[h] But it paints our Russian way of life in the most dismal colors. Our politics, morals, even our religion, are portrayed as an absurd, monstrous exception to the general laws of humanity. It is incomprehensible how censor Boldyrev could have passed it.

Naturally, people raised a big row about it. The journal was banned. Boldyrev, who served as a professor and rector at Moscow University, was relieved of all his duties. Both he and Nadezhdin, publisher of the *Telescope,* are being brought here for an explanation.

I went to see the prince today, and he said that the minister was terribly upset. It is suspected that the article was purposely printed so that the journal would be banned and a fuss would be raised similar to the one precipitated by the ban on the *Telegraph.* It is also believed that this was the handiwork of some secret group. But, I think this was nothing more than a spontaneous outburst of new ideas which had remained concealed and simply awaited an opportune moment to emerge and generate excitement. This has happened many times despite the unprecedented strictness of censorship and all kinds of persecution. If one observes things more closely and objectively, one can see quite clearly what the entire present generation is striving for. And, one must admit that the behavior of our authorities only serves to push people all

[h] Pyotr Yakovlevich Chaadaev (c. 1793–1856) was a leading Russian philosopher. In his letter to the *Telescope* he strongly criticized Russian history and saw her culture as inferior to the West's. As a result of the letter's publication, the author was officially declared insane and confined to his home. The Chaadaev persecution is one of the most celebrated in Russian literature.

the more in this direction. The authorities acknowledge the existence of a policy of oppression, but consider it a policy of firmness. And they are wrong. No matter how you look at it, oppression is still oppression, particularly when it is born of anger (on the part of the government) and not of intelligently calculated measures.

28 October. The publishers of all local journals were summoned to the Censorship Committee today. Smirdin, Gintze, publisher of the Polish journal, and others were present. Grech had appeared earlier. They were called in to hear an imperial order banning the *Telescope,* and were warned to beware of a similar fate. They slunk into the room with terrified expressions, like schoolboys.

11 December. Nadezhdin's fate has been decided: exile to Ust-Sysolsk, where he must exist on 40 kopeks a day.[i] However, a concession was made in regard to the latter. When he was informed of his exile, he asked Benkendorf for incarceration in the fortress instead, because there, at least, he would not starve to death. Benkendorf then secured permission for him to write and publish articles under his own name while in exile.

They say that Nadezhdin initially became very depressed, but later recovered his spirits and is now rather calm. He spoke about Benkendorf and Dubbelt, in particular, with gratitude. Orders were given to relieve Boldyrev of all his posts, that is, as rector, professor, and censor. They say that our minister behaved very harshly toward Nadezhdin.

23 December. Pecherin went abroad on leave in July for two months and has not yet returned. Judging from the ideas he had revealed even when he was here, he has probably considered leaving Russia for good. This seems increasingly evident. Chizhov received a letter from him a few days ago begging him to send about 500 rubles, or at least 200. But he didn't say a word about his plans. We, that is, Chizhov, Gebhardt, Polenov, and myself, had a little meeting to discuss Pecherin, and we decided to send him 100 rubles each, 400 in all, for his return to Russia. He is now in Lugano, a rather small town on the Swiss-Italian border.

30 December. A new law: all young people, upon graduation from an institution of higher learning, must serve for three years at a government post in the provinces. It is forbidden to accept a ministry post immediately following graduation. There is a great deal of talk and grumbling about it.

[i] Nadezhdin was editor of the *Telescope,* which published Chaadaev's famous philosophical letter.

1837

2 January. Celebrated New Year's eve yesterday at Shenin's. The guests: Rostovtsev, Shulgin, Pletnyov, and several corps officers and teachers. It was lively.

Shenin is an intelligent man with a strong will. However, I am not very familiar with the way he thinks. There is no doubt that he loves education; it is clear from everything he says and does.

Rostovtsev has done a great deal to improve education in the corps. Shenin assisted him in this. Rostovtsev can be characterized as follows: he is a clever man and shrewd when it comes to doing good. In any case, he is certainly a gratifying phenomenon in these times. He is responsible for the change in Grand Duke Mikhail Pavlovich. He has inspired him with the noble desire to perform outstanding deeds in the realm of education. He has a great influence on him and uses it as befits an honest man and government official. He can accomplish a great deal more in the future if he is not driven from his course. Incidentally, public opinion is in his favor; he knows how to win people over. I have a great deal of respect for him.

20 January. Kleinmichel awarded me an Anna Cross, third degree, for my work with the Auditor's School. He was present during examinations and raged like a hurricane. He is a terror and scourge to his subordinates. The generals, who tremble before him, are like sheep at the mercy of a wolf. I, however, cannot complain; he was very courteous to me.

He invited me to dine with him several days ago. He was a totally different person. He was kind, polite, hospitable—simply a cordial host. His wife is the height of graciousness. It seems that he deliberately rages at his subordinates, believing that you must be a beast if you want to give orders.

21 January. I spent the evening at Pletnyov's. Pushkin was there. He's still peeved at me. He's become quite the aristocrat. What a pity that he values himself so little as a man and as a poet and insists on gaining entrance to one very closed social circle when he could reign supreme over all society. Above all he wants to be looked upon as a true nobleman, but, indeed, in our country it is the man with the greater income who is considered the true nobleman. This affectation, this conceited manner which at any moment could be irreversibly shattered by disfavor, does not suit him at all. Besides being very talented, he really is very clever. For instance, today he made many keen and astute observations about the Russian language. He also admitted that one could not write a history of Peter the Great at this time; its publication would be prohibited. It's evident that he has read a great deal about Peter.

25 January. My lectures at the university are going very well. Sometimes I even succeed in fascinating my listeners. I am fighting against all sorts of shoddy thinking and expression in literature, against tinsel glitter and unnaturalness. I am greatly hindered, of course, by my ignorance of foreign languages. Because of this I do not have sufficient material for comparison and facts, for general historical conclusions. I am trying to fill this gap by reading everything that has been translated into Russian. For the moment, my principal aim is to warm the hearts of my students with a love of pure beauty and truth, and to awaken in them a desire to strive towards a courageous, vigorous and noble use of their moral strengths. If I succeed in doing this, even to a small degree, I shall feel that I have not labored in vain.

29 January. An important and terribly sad event in our literature: Pushkin died today of a wound he received in a duel.

Last night I was at Pletnyov's: it was from him that I first heard of this tragedy. D'Anthès, a cavalry officer and Pushkin's opponent, was the first to fire; the bullet entered Pushkin's stomach. Nevertheless Pushkin managed a return shot which shattered d'Anthès's hand. Today, Pushkin is no longer in this world.

I still haven't heard a good account of all the details. This much is beyond doubt: we have borne a grievous, irreplaceable loss. Pushkin's most recent works are admittedly somewhat weaker than his earlier ones, but he might have been going through a period of transition, the result of some inner revolution, after which would have ensued a period of new grandeur.

Poor Pushkin! Here is how you have paid for the right of citizenship in those aristocratic salons where you frittered away your time and gifts! You should have gone the way of humanity, and not of caste; once a member of the latter, you could not help but obey its laws. You were meant for a higher calling.

30 January. What noise, what confusion in opinions about Pushkin! What we have is no longer a single black patch on the threadbare tatters of a singer, but thousands of patches, red, white, black, of all colors and shades. Still, here is some information about his death, culled from the most reliable source.

D'Anthès is a shallow man, but an adroit, friendly Frenchman who has sparkled in our salons as a star of the first magnitude. He would often visit the Pushkins. We all know that the poet's wife is beautiful. D'Anthès, as a Frenchman and a frequenter of salons, became too friendly with her, and she did not have enough tact to draw a line between herself and him, a line beyond which no man must pass in his relations with a woman who does not belong to him. In society there are always people who feed on the reputations of their friends: they welcomed this opportunity and spread rumors of a relationship between d'Anthès and Pushkin's wife. These reached Pushkin and, of course, troubled his already agitated soul. He forbad d'Anthès's visits.

The latter was insulted and declared that he was visiting not Pushkin's wife, but his sister-in-law, with whom he was in love. Thereupon Pushkin demanded that he marry the young girl, and the match was arranged.

In the meantime the poet received, on successive days, anonymous letters that congratulated him on being a cuckold. In one letter he was even sent a membership card in the society of cuckolds, with an imaginary signature of President Naryshkin. Moreover, Baron von Heckeren, who had adopted d'Anthès, was very dissatisfied with his marriage to Pushkin's sister-in-law, who, it was said, was older than her husband and without means. To von Heckeren are ascribed the following words: "Pushkin thinks that with this marriage, he has split up d'Anthès and his wife. On the contrary he has merely brought them closer together, thanks to a new family relationship."

Pushkin flew into a rage and wrote von Heckeren a letter, full of insults. He demanded that the latter, as a father, curb his young man. The letter was of course read by d'Anthès—he demanded satisfaction and the affair ended beyond the city limits, at ten paces. D'Anthès was the first to fire. Pushkin fell. D'Anthès ran towards him, but the poet, gathering up his strength, ordered his adversary to return to his place, aimed at his heart but hit his hand which d'Anthès, either owing to an awkward movement or out of precaution, had placed over his chest.

Pushkin was wounded in the abdomen, the bullet entering his stomach. When he was brought home, he summoned his wife and children, blessed them and requested Dr. Arendt to ask the emperor not to abandon them and to pardon Danzas, his second.

The emperor wrote him a letter in his own hand, promising to take care of his family and do all for Danzas that was possible. In addition he asked that before his death he do all that a Christian should. Pushkin demanded a priest. He died on the 29th, Friday, at 3 p.m. In his reception room, from morning till night, visitors gathered, seeking information about his condition. It became necessary to post bulletins.

31 January. I went to see the minister today. He is very busy trying to quell the loud cries over Pushkin's death. He is also very displeased with the elaborate tribute printed in "The Literary Supplement" of the *Russian Veteran.*

And so, Uvarov cannot even forgive a dead Pushkin for *Lucullus's Recovery.*

I just received an order from the chairman of the Censorship Committee not to permit anything to be printed about Pushkin without first submitting the article to him or the minister.

The funeral is tomorrow. I received a ticket.

1 February. Pushkin's funeral. It was a real "people's" funeral. Anyone and everyone in St. Petersburg who thinks or reads thronged to the church where the mass was being sung for the poet. This took place in the church on Konyushennaya Street. The square was covered with carriages and people, but not a single homespun or sheepskin coat was to be seen among them.

The church was filled with notables. The entire diplomatic corps was present. Only those in uniform or holding tickets were admitted. Every face expressed sadness—at least on the surface. Alongside me stood Baron Rosen, Karlhof, Kukolnik and Pletnyov. I said my last farewell to Pushkin. His face had changed significantly, for decay had set in. I left the church with Kukolnik.

"At least we managed to move up ahead," he said, pointing to the crowd coming to pay homage to the remains of one of its finest sons.

Platon Obodovsky fell on my breast, sobbing like a child.

But here, as usual, there were some very clumsy arrangements. The populace was fooled: they were told that the mass for Pushkin was to be sung in Saint Isaac's—so it was written on the admission tickets—while the body was in fact taken from the apartment at night, in secret, and put in the church on Konyushennaya Street. At the university a strict order was received stating that professors must not absent themselves from their courses and that students must be present at lectures. I could not restrain myself and expressed my distress about this to the superintendent. Russians cannot mourn their countryman who honored them with his existence! Foreigners came to bow at the poet's coffin, while university professors and Russian youth were forbidden to do so. In secret, like robbers, they had to steal their way to it.

The superintendent told me that it would be better if the students were not present at the funeral: they might band together and carry Pushkin's coffin—they could "go too far," as he put it.

Grech was severely reprimanded by Benkendorf for this statement which appeared in the *Northern Bee:* "Russia owes a debt of gratitude to Pushkin for his twenty-two years of service in the field of literature." (Issue no. 24.)

Kraevsky, editor of "The Literary Supplement" to the *Russian Veteran,* also ran into difficulty for several lines printed in tribute to the poet. I received an order to delete in their entirety several such lines scheduled for publication in the *Reader's Library.*

Amidst universal sympathy and deep universal mourning for the deceased, all these measures were being taken. They were afraid—but of what?

The ceremony ended at 12:30. Then I went to my lecture. But instead of my regular lecture, I delivered a lecture to the students on Pushkin's contributions to our literature. What will be, will be!

12 February. Details about Pushkin's last moments have come to me from reliable sources. He died honorably, like a man. As soon as the bullet had entered his body, he knew that this was the kiss of death. He did not groan, and when Dr. Dal advised him to do so he replied: "So, this nonsense really can't be licked? Besides, my groans would upset my wife."

He kept asking Dal: "Will it be over soon?" And very calmly, without any mincing of words, he would refute Dal when the latter tried to reassure him with the usual words of comfort. A few minutes before his death, he asked to be raised and turned to the other side.

"My life is over," he said.

"What's that? " asked Dal, not quite hearing his words.

"My life is over," repeated Pushkin. "Can't breathe."

After uttering these words, his labours ceased, for he had stopped breathing. His life was over; the light on the altar had gone out. Pushkin died well.

About three days after the requiem mass for Pushkin, he was taken in *secret* to the country. My wife was returning from Mogilev, and at one depot not far from St. Petersburg she saw a simple cart; on the cart was straw, under the straw a coffin wrapped in bast matting. Three gendarmes were scurrying about in the depot yard, pleading that the horses be reharnessed more quickly for they had to ride on further with the coffin.

"What's that? " my wife asked of one of the peasants there.

"God only knows what! You see, some fellow by the name of Pushkin was killed, and they are speeding him away on this post chaise in matting and straw—may God forgive them!—like a dog."

The measure prohibiting publication of anything about Pushkin is still in effect and the public is very disturbed by it.

14 February. I defended my doctoral dissertation, "On Creative Force in Poetry, or, on the Nature of Poetic Genius," at a public session yesterday at the university. I emerged victorious from the field of battle. My opponents were Fischer, Professor of Philosophy, and Pletnyov, Professor of Russian Literature. The defense began at 12:30 and ended at 2:30. The session was attended by so many people that the hall was packed. First, the rector read a biography of me. I stood my ground well and did not lose my presence of mind. The public was very pleased. But here's what was particularly gratifying to me. Following the disputation, the leading members of the university went up to Konstantin Matveevich Borozdin, former superintendent of the St. Petersburg school district, who was present at my defense, and thanked him on behalf of the university "for educating and preparing me so well." My kind protector and friend was moved to tears.

About thirty people gathered at my home in the evening. We had supper and, as is customary, toasts were drunk in honor of the new doctor.

22 March. I visited Zhukovsky. He showed me Pushkin's manuscript of *Boris Godunov* with the passages censored by the emperor. He had cut out a great deal. That's why the published version of *Godunov* appears incomplete and why there appear to be so many gaps, causing some critics to say that this play is only a collection of fragments.

I also saw the emperor's resolution concerning a new edition of Pushkin's works. It said:

"Approved, but on condition that everything that I have found to be improper in previously published works be excluded, and that works not yet printed be subject to strict examination."

30 March. Today I had a big battle with the chairman of the Censorship Committee, Prince Dondukov-Korsakov, over Pushkin's works, of which I was appointed censor. The emperor had ordered their publication under the minister's supervision. The latter interpreted this to mean that all previous published works of the poet should be carefully re-examined and, therefore, our red ink should not be spared.

All Russia knows Pushkin's works by heart, works which have seen several editions and were always published with His Majesty's permission. Wouldn't such a measure focus the attention of the public on passages that might be excluded? The public would be indignant and, consequently, would all the more zealously learn them by heart.

At the meeting of the committee I delivered a speech against this measure and strongly disagreed with the prince, who kept citing the imperial order as interpreted by the minister. Of course I didn't win an official victory. But I, as an honest man, had to raise my voice in defense of common sense.

Kutorga was the only one of my colleagues to support me, and then only with two or three sentences from time to time. Krylov was assigned to assist me in the censorship of Pushkin's works. His is a name frightening to literature for he knows nothing except prohibition. It was amusing when Kutorga referred to public opinion, which, of course, would criticise any distortion of Pushkin. The prince replied that the government must ignore public opinion and move firmly toward its goal.

"Yes," I remarked, "if this goal is worth the sacrifice of public opinion. But what would the government gain by distorting in Pushkin what all Russia knows by heart? Besides, it might not be a bad idea to respect public opinion sometimes. Russia does not exist only for today, and when we provoke indignation needlessly, we are paving the way for an uneasy future."

After this, however, the prince and I parted on rather good terms. Shaking my hand, he said:

"I understand you. You, as a man of letters, as a professor, naturally have reason to want Pushkin's works published without any changes."

That's hitting the nail on the head, as the saying goes.

31 March. Zhukovsky told me the good news: the emperor has ordered the printing of Pushkin's previously published work without any changes. This was a result of Zhukovsky's intercession. How furious a certain person will be!

I feel sorry for the prince, who is a good, kind person. Minister Uvarov uses him as a tool. It must be quite unpleasant for him now.

3 April. A new censorship law: henceforth, every magazine article must be examined by two censors, and either of them can exclude whatever he pleases. Moreover, a new censorship post has been created, a sort of controller, whose responsibility it will be to re-read and check everything that has been approved by the other censors. Yesterday the chairman of the Censorship Committee called me in to make a considerate suggestion—namely, that I myself should select the colleague with whom I would like to work. I told him it made no difference to me, and he assigned Gaevsky to work with me on the *Reader's Library*.

The question is: is it possible to write or publish anything in Russia today? With all my desire to remain staunchly at my post as a guardian of Russian thought and expression, sometimes I can't help feeling completely discouraged But I should neither be shocked nor deterred by this state of affairs.

13 April. I couldn't restrain myself any longer: I've resigned my position as censor. At today's meeting a memorandum on the new law was read to us. The censor is becoming a pathetic figure, so utterly meaningless, yet he is saddled with an enormous responsibility and must labor under the constant spying of a higher censor whose presence in the superintendent's office has been ordered.

As we were leaving the Censorship Committee meeting, I told the prince of my intention to resign. Naturally he was surprised at first; then he advised me not to take such a step at this time in order to avoid the terrible reproach of revolt.

14 April. After a heated discussion with the prince, an honorable peace was concluded, and for the time being I shall remain at my post as a censor. The prince and I had clashed about the new censorship statute at a meeting of the Censorship Committee. He started to defend it, and not as chairman, but as an individual. I objected strongly, and this was the reason for our disagreement. But matters took a different turn when he admitted frankly this morning that he fully shared my opinion on the new measure, but that he could not make this known in committee. He asked me not to abandon him in this difficult situation and to always be frank with him. We parted amicably, embraced, and promised to be more temperate in the future. That's no easy task for the prince! He's an honorable and noble man, but, unfortunately, too subservient to Minister Uvarov.

17 April. I am waiting for the first peal of the bells so I can set out for matins. I love Easter; it is filled with much that is grand and comforting. Meanwhile, I am at my desk, writing a tribute to Peter the Great, at the request of the University Council. It must be ready by May 1. Not much time. Oh, these works that one must produce on order! On the other hand I must admit that I work better under the pressure of a deadline. Man is weak and, without pressure, tends to succumb too easily to fatigue.

1838

Nikitenko's daughter comments here on the dearth of entries for 1838, the year her father visited his native region. He left very little material besides some statistical data about his trip, which she felt would be of no interest to his readers.

1839

30 June. [Notes from my stay in the country village of Timokhovka in Mogilev province.] I visited the huts of the local peasants; what filth and poverty! The children were in rags and dirty; almost all of them had an eye disease or boils on their faces and bodies. The faces of the adults were lifeless and dull, although some people would have you believe that both intelligence and cunning are concealed behind this mask. They evidently suffer from extreme want and oppression. Their faces, movements, clothing, or, rather, the tatters covering their bodies, and their living quarters, testify to this. Instead of windows in their huts, there are chinks covered with dirty fragments of glass. A prison cell has more light. The deepest ignorance and superstition dwell in these stuffy holes. Their religious notions are the most primitive. The peasant men and women, going off to church, say that they "are going to pray to their gods and idols."

A young man and girl appeared before me. They fell to their knees and, lying prostrate on the floor, tried to kiss my feet. Bewildered and indignant, I asked:

"What is the meaning of this? What do they want of me?"

"This is a bridegroom and his bride," I was told, "and this is the custom here."

My Little Russian footman added with his characteristic Little Russian sense of humor:

"They managed it after all. They presented themselves to the gentleman!"

"So what of it?"

"Well, you see, it's a very frightening matter for them to approach a gentleman."

"But why?"

"That's the way it is. They're scared of getting their ears boxed."

At this point I couldn't help wondering what kind of national philosophy could be deduced from one's observations of Russians and their way of life. Most likely a philosophy of utter desperation.

I gave the bridegroom and bride five rubles each and asked them to stop their bowing and scraping.

"Are you pleased that you're getting married?" I asked the bride.

"No," she replied.

"Why not?"

"It's better to live free!"

"Not bad," I thought to myself, and continued:

"Then why are you getting married if you don't want to?"

"The masters order it!"
Yes, they are brought together like cattle, for breeding!

15 July. I am getting ready to leave. What did I accomplish during my stay here? The constant activity in the fresh air and swimming were very beneficial to my health; I worked out a general plan for my university lectures for the coming academic year; I also wrote several articles; but the main thing is that I had a good rest.

25 August. There is an article in the censorship code, on the strength of which, books of moral content, although based on holy writings and supported by them, are subject to review by the secular censor. Only works dealing with dogma and church history are sent to the ecclesiastical censor. Now we have received an order from the minister based on a report from the Holy Synod, stating that all works "of ecclesiastical content to whatever degree" must be sent to the ecclesiastical censor. What does this mean? Is the law promulgated by autocratic power being abrogated by the chief procurator of the Synod? These things are not happening for the first time in our administration. In this instance the censorship department finds itself in great difficulty. The rare journal article falling into this category should not be sent to the ecclesiastical censor. I asked Prince Volkonsky to submit a recommendation to the minister about this. He already has and we are now asking: "What should we follow—the new directive or the text of the censorship code approved by imperial order?"

2 November. Smirdin is taking over the publication of *Son of the Fatherland* from Grech. He asked me to be its managing editor. I agreed, and the proposal has already been sent to the minister for approval.

8 November. I signed a contract with Smirdin today. I shall be responsible for half of the journal, that is, the following sections: science, art, Russian and foreign literature. Literary criticism, bibliography, politics, and miscellany will remain Polevoy's responsibility. Moreover, I am the managing editor, accountable to the government for the entire journal. Each of us will receive 7,500 rubles a year.

1840

11 January. I am ill.

26 February. I'm feeling better. I still wasn't up to lecturing, but went to
see Zhukovsky who is going abroad with the heir next week, and asked to see
me right away. He gave me Pushkin's works for censorship, which will supplement the seven volumes already issued. There are three volumes of these new
works. Many poems had already appeared in the *Contemporary.* Zhukovsky
asked me to go through all of it by Saturday. A difficult task! But it must
be done.

"I heard," Zhukovsky said to me in passing, "that you are preparing a work
on Russian poets. That sounds like a fine project. I can help you with material."

I thanked him, and certainly intend to take advantage of his offer. Zhukovsky asked me to send him everything I had already written about him.

28 February. I visited Vasily Andreevich Zhukovsky again and found him
ill. We talked about literature. He read my study of Batyushkov and praised
it highly.

"You have succeeded in capturing the essence of Batyushkov's poetry and
expressing it concisely," he said.

Then, Zhukovsky complained about *Notes of the Fatherland* which lauds
him to the skies, but so clumsily, that it's already having the opposite effect.

"It's odd," he added, "that many people consider me a poet of despair,
when I am very much inclined toward gaiety, humor, and even caricature."

He also spoke a great deal about the mercenary trend of our literature,
and added in conclusion:

"Thank God, I was never a man of letters by profession, but have only
written because I felt like writing!"

7 May. An evening, or, rather, a whole night at Strugovshchikov's.

After dinner Glinka sang excerpts from his new opera *Russlan and Lud-
milla.* What a charming piece! Glinka is a true poet and artist.

Kukolnik dispensed the drinks, being sure to take good care of his own
thirst. He drained glasses of champagne with amazing adroitness and speed.
But Glinka was no second to him in this. First, Glinka had to be livened up
with a few, and then sustained with a steady intake. On the other hand, they
say, he doesn't use any other kind of wine.

10 May. Polevoy finally decided to resign from *Son of the Fatherland.* This
was, indeed, necessary. We don't agree about many things. He has literary

enemies. My enemies, however, if there are any—are ideas, and not people.

25 June. I moved to the country at the beginning of the month and feel more energetic and fit here. Nature, as usual, is a source of great pleasure to me. I walk a great deal, which is most salutory when I am involved in concentrated, sedentary work. The journal absorbs much of my time and energy and, in return, pays poorly. Right now for instance, I am in very bad financial straits. Smirdin went to Moscow without paying me a kopek, although he had promised to settle accounts with me before his departure. In the meantime I am completely responsible for the journal.

8 August. Bryullov, the celebrated painter of *The Last Days of Pompeii*, dined at my home. Two or three other people were here plus several ladies from Smolny Convent. We had a pleasant time.

Bryullov not only possesses artistic talent, but a fine mind, too. He doesn't impress one as being tactful or particularly charming; however, he certainly is lively and pleasant. He lived in Europe for about fifteen years, and now it appears that he is not particularly happy about living in Russia. This, I dare say, is quite understandable. We don't know how to respect talent. Take for example, something that happened only today. We were strolling in the Bekleshov Gardens. An Actual State Councillor, whom I know, called me aside and said:

"Is that Bryullov with you? I'm glad to see him; I've never seen him before. A very, very remarkable man! Tell me, please, is he really a drunkard? They're all that way, these actors and artists!"

That's the kind of opinions we have about "remarkable people."

Bryullov left late in the evening. At dinner he admired my wife.

"A marvellous head," he said. "How it begs to be painted. I shall finish *The Siege of Pskov* and then ask your wife to sit for a portrait."

20 November. Koltsov came to see me—the once good, intelligent, good-natured Koltsov—creator of poems so beautiful in their simplicity and feeling. Unfortunately, he became friendly with the editor of *Notes of the Fatherland* and its chief contributor, and they have corrupted him. Poor Koltsov began to babble about subjects and objects and to get lost in the abstractions of Hegelian philosophy. He talked such nonsense that my heart ached for him. Unschooled and inexperienced, defenseless against the amateur philosophizing of his "patrons," Koltsov, in passing through their hands, has lost his most valuable treasure: simple, sincere feeling and common sense. Vladimir Stroev, who was also present, even suspected him of being drunk.

30 November. For about two weeks Senkovsky and I have been conducting negotiations over *Son of the Fatherland.* Smirdin is relinquishing the journal to him temporarily, and he is doing the right thing because he would not be able to continue publishing it next year. Senkovsky, however, is fully capable of handling journal affairs. He suggested that I remain in my position as editor of *Son of the Fatherland,* with the right to run it as I saw fit. I agreed, although unwillingly, and am still not sure that I shall get on with Osip Ivano-vich.[j] He sent me a draft of the announcement. But the role of the editor turns out to be completely different from what was originally promised to me. In a long letter I told him that under such conditions I must decline the editorship. Today I went to see him for a definitive discussion, but he wasn't at home.

5 December. I finally managed to come to an understanding with Senkovsky. It was decided to state in the announcement that I would be the independent editor of everything related to the journal's literary tone.

[j] Senkovsky.

1841

11 January. I didn't have a single free day during the holidays. I worked hard on the first few issues of *Son of the Fatherland,* and placed my review of Lermontov's poems in the first issue.[1]

15 January. Our contemporary society presents a sad spectacle: in it there are neither noble aspirations, justice, simplicity; nor is there honor in our ways. In brief, there is no evidence of a healthy, natural and vigorous development of our spiritual forces.

Petty souls wear themselves out in the petty gossip of our social chaos. There is not even a proper notion of what is beneficial, nor any serious striving toward it. All our energies are spent on "swindling," to use a Russian expression. Intelligence and cheating are synonyms. The words "honest man" mean simpleton. Public corruption is so great that notions of honor and justice are considered either a sign of a weak mind or a romantic imagination. And this is understandable; since they are not applied in real life, they remain empty words, book words. Our erudition is pure hypocrisy. We study without a real love of learning, unaware of the virtue of truth and the need for it. And indeed, why worry about acquiring knowledge in school, when our mode of life and our society stand in opposition to all great ideas and truths, when any attempt to realize any sort of idea related to justice, good or the public welfare, is branded and persecuted like a crime? Why cultivate noble aspirations in one's self when, indeed, sooner or later, one will have to join the crowd to avoid becoming its victim.

11 March. Smirdin is close to bankruptcy. I must say that I have no luck; again I've worked a whole year for nothing. This was a particularly bad time for this to happen because I have been getting ready to offer payment for the freedom of my mother and brother. I wrote a letter about it to Count Sheremetov. People close to him give me hope of success, but I haven't heard a single word from him yet. God almighty! What kind of order of things is this? Here I am, already a full-fledged member of society and enjoying even a certain fame and influence, and I cannot bring about—what? The freedom of my mother and brother! A half-witted noble has the right to refuse me, and this is called a right! All my blood boils within me, and I can understand how people can go to extremes! I am impatiently awaiting Zhukovsky's arrival from Moscow; perhaps his influence will bring results.

23 March. I went to see Zhukovsky today and asked for his assistance in my mother's and brother's case. He listened, with indignation, to the story of my unsuccessful attempts to buy their freedom and openly expressed his disgust with the count's policy and the order of things responsible for it. Vasily Andreevich Zhukovsky promised to exert all his influence. I, on my part, will not stop at any price to buy their freedom, if a price is demanded, no matter what I shall have to do to raise the money. My God! My God! If only I can hold out in this struggle.

3 April. No news yet from Zhukovsky!

9 April. Today, at long last, an unbearable weight has been lifted from my heart: at last, my mother, my pious, fine, noble mother and my brother can breathe freely with me. Count Sheremetov has already signed the release documents, and without payment. I received the news today. To whom am I indebted? To Zhukovsky? Or, finally, to the count's own resolution to free them? In any case, the past is forgotten and forgiven.

Meanwhile, strange rumors are circulating. It's said that a manifesto on the liberation of the peasants is being prepared for the heir's wedding day.² If this is true, this reign will be marked by an event which will exalt it in the pages of history. But many educated people consider this measure premature. They say that it will lead to disorders, that one must approach this question gradually, and so on. And just what moment, in their opinion, will be opportune? What else is there to wait for? For the landowners themselves to renounce their rights? Or for a little more education among the peasants? Both are impossible with the existing order of things. Any attempt to tread slowly along this path would be a half-measure, and half-measures are always wrong, and often disastrous, because they create a false state of affairs. As far as disorders are concerned, they are, of course, possible, but what are they in comparison with the evil contained in this loathsome system of slavery? The small landowners will inevitably suffer, but are positive changes in a nation ever achieved without victims? These words are attributed to Emperor Nicholas: "I do not want to die without having completed two tasks: the issuing of a Code of Laws and the abolition of serfdom." If this comes to pass it will contribute a glorious page to the history of his reign. But all this is only guesswork. Let's wait until Wednesday, the day designated for the heir's wedding, and then we'll have the answer. I have, however, little hope. Though why shouldn't Nicholas do it? He is omnipotent; whom and what is there for him to fear? What better use could he make of his autocratic power?

14 April. My mother's and brother's case ended so happily only because of Zhukovsky's intercession. God bless him! Today I went to see him and thanked him.

5 May. I am extremely happy today: I sent off the release documents to my mother and brother.

9 May. I dined today with Karl Bryullov in a miserable tavern on Vasily

Island. Bryullov ate his shchi[k] and beef with gusto, food which, in my opinion, looked as if it would sooner kill than whet one's appetite. Nevertheless, we had a splendid time. Bryullov was entertaining, witty and warm. He is considered immoral—I don't know whether this is just or not—but I haven't detected the slightest trace of cynicism in his conversation. For example, today, he not only spoke intelligently and astutely, but absolutely decently, too, with respect for good people and honest ideas.

12 July. All of June and the beginning of July were spent at my usual duties. When I managed to snatch a free day, I went to the country, mostly on foot, and passed the time roaming about the woods and fields. But I didn't forget about my censorship duties. There, in Kushelevka, I worked up two important matters: my memorandum on the need for instruction in Russian literature for law students and the draft of the law on periodicals.

I composed the draft on periodicals under the following circumstances. The emperor had placed a very strict ban on the publication of new journals. But the human mind is cunning and resourceful. An imperial order on this ban has been in existence for almost three years, during which period it has been reconfirmed many times. Meanwhile, during this period, the *Muscovite, Notes of the Fatherland,* and the *Russian Messenger* had appeared on the scene. The first of these was completely new, the other two were apparent revivals, but actually in name only, for their content had changed completely. Moreover, our men of letters have contrived to publish books in installments, but these so-called books are actually periodical publications. Such are the *Lighthouse,* the *Pantheon of Russian Theatres and All European Theatres,* the *Repertoire,* and the *Economist.* Quite a few others of this type have been devised. Thus, the necessity arose for a law which would define a journal. The Censorship Committee had been directed to compose such a law, and the committee passed this task on to me. It's not an easy one, for I would like to incline the government to take a milder view of the matter; I would like to save all new publications and remove obstacles from the path of future ones. I foresee a struggle with Gaevsky and Krylov. The day before yesterday I wrote all through the night; and apparently I worked it out pretty well. My proposal will be read at the next censorship meeting.

18 August. We had a splendid time in the country. Although I didn't accomplish much, I worked spiritedly. I concentrated on the series of public lectures I want to begin this winter. I must admit, however, that the thought of speaking before an audience is somewhat frightening to me, especially since I would like to lecture, as Grech does, without notes.

Meanwhile I am tirelessly gathering material: that is, I am thinking about and examining principles, basic positions, facts, and so on. I want to strengthen the basis of the literary idea and establish the direction of our literature through its chief representatives. What is meant by the literary

[k] Cabbage soup.

idea?   In the main it means to arouse in the hearts of people a respect for intellectual and educational achievements.   Let at least a few bright, noble ideas sweep through the foggy and lifeless field of our society!

7 September. I have definitely resigned as editor of *Notes of the Fatherland* and have published my resignation in the journals.   Smirdin's inconsistency and Senkovsky's self-seeking attitude compelled me to take this decisive step.

24 September. Yesterday, I dined at the home of Dmitry Maksimovich Khyazhevich, who had recently returned from abroad.   Nadezhdin, who had gone with him, had also returned.   The conversation centered on the Slavs and Austria.   My beliefs were confirmed.   I have always felt that Slavic patriotism, dreaming of the unification of the Slavic world, existed only in the minds of certain fanatics, like Shafarik, Gank, Pogodin, and others, and that in general the Slavic peoples lived very peacefully under Austrian rule, not in the least concerned with any kind of political independence.   The only exception, I thought, were the Hungarian Slavs and Ruthenians, who were very oppressed by the noblemen.   All this was confirmed by Nadezhdin, who is not one of the above mentioned slavophiles.

I am drowning in paper work and galley proofs.   My students' compositions, my lectures, censorship commentaries, and the works of writers sent to me for my opinion—my God, what a variety and, often, what an awful waste of time!   I go to bed at three in the morning, rise at seven, and still can't cope with everything.   In addition to all this I am usually occupied until four o'clock with academic work, exams, and censorship matters.   Also, Count Kleinmichel has temporarily placed me in charge of the Auditor's School.   What do I get out of all this?   The chance to live, that is, to eat and dress modestly and have a roof over my head.

8 October. Letters have come from Chizhov, who is now abroad.   He had seen Pecherin.   There is a Jesuit monastery of Saint Vitus not far from Liège, which Pecherin had entered and where he had taken monastic vows.   Thus, both a political and religious conversion at one stroke.   What a strange transformation, and what an upheaval must occur in a man's soul to bring him to this.   Chizhov speaks angrily about the moral decline in which he found our dear friend Pecherin; he had accepted not only the positive ideas of his new calling, but all its prejudices, too.   Chizhov thinks he was attracted by the poverty and charm of the Jesuits, to whom he can be very useful with his vast knowledge, especially in philosophy.   All this leads us to believe that Pecherin's act was not a result of a bold, but carefully thought out decision and firm convictions; rather was it a fortuitous escape from a difficult situation under the pressure of circumstances.   It was the fruit of an immature idea.   He reproached Chizhov and all his friends, particularly me, for indulging his vanity, for inspiring him with an exaggerated opinion of his gifts. But this, too, is not true.   When he returned from abroad I sharply criticized his egoism and immature philosophy, as a result of which our relations cooled. By the time he left for Moscow to assume a professorial post, our relationship had changed considerably. And yet, I still cannot get over the shock and cannot find an explanation for so strange a moral phenomenon. Pecherin—a Catholic monk! Simply incredible. Woe to him who is endowed with powerful emotions and a brilliant mind but lacks will-power and character of equal strength.

26 October. I am up to my ears in censorship work. I am now examining Polevoy's *History of Peter the Great,* Professor Lorentz's *World History,* and Telemachus's *History of Philosophy.* Also, an enormous work on political economy, several stories, the journals, *Notes of the Fatherland* and the *Russian Messenger.* No sooner do I finish with one, than I have another on my hands. That's the way life slips by.

28 October. The time is not yet ripe in Russia for the cultivation of spiritual needs. Our social system crushes any attempt to develop one's spiritual forces, and woe to him who finds himself in such a position. It is the most difficult position because it is a false one. It is not spiritual development that we need, we are told. To be a soldier or a man—that is our only function. To proclaim knowledge? Where's the need for that? It has no support in real life and, therefore, is only a schoolboy's weaving of ideas. So, against your will, you join the ranks of charlatans.

My field, in particular, is a downright absurdity and contradiction. I am supposed to be teaching Russian literature—but where is it? Does literature in our land enjoy civil rights? One refuge remains—the lifeless sphere of theory. I am deceiving myself and others when I utter such words as *development, trend of ideas, basic ideas of art.* These words have meaning, a great deal of meaning, where public opinion and intellectual and aesthetic interests exist, but here they are merely words being tossed about in the air. Words, words, words! To spend one's whole life with empty words, when one's soul is thirsting for truth, when one's mind is striving for something real and vital—this is indeed a terrible fate. Often, very often—for example, today, I am struck by the deep, dismal awareness of my insignificance. If I lived among savages, I would hunt and fish. I would be doing something real—but now I, like a child, like a fool, play at dreams and shadows! Oh, I could write the story of my inner life with my heart's blood. This is an accursed epoch in which a contrived, official need for moral activity exists, when there is no real need for it, an epoch in which society imposes an obligation on you for which society itself has contempt. It's already 2 A.M., and I keep thinking about the same thing. I shall fall asleep, and tomorrow I shall emerge from this mental chaos and shall again try to deceive myself and others so as not to perish from physical and spiritual hunger, until I shall really die and take with me to the grave the bitter knowledge of my fruitless, wasted efforts.

1842

11 January. I went to see Count Wielgorski. He asked me if it wasn't possible to approve Miklashevich's novel. No, it was not. It contained many ecclesiastical characters. A bishop, robber-landowner, swindler-governor and so forth appear in the novel.

The count told me that the emperor had recently spoken to him with indignation about the hostile tone of our literature and about its attacks on the upper classes. As an example he cited *Tale After Tale.* In one of them our nobility was portrayed in a bad light, and censor Ochkin was severely reprimanded for passing it.

22 January. A new scare in the censorship department. Bashutsky is publishing a book, *Ours,* in installments, each of which contains essays by different writers. One of them, "The Water Carrier," has caused a big fuss. There is no question about its democratic tone. It says that our people are oppressed and that their virtue consists in their passive acceptance of this state of affairs. The emperor was most displeased. To everyone's surprise, the affair was settled quietly. The censor was not even given an official reprimand, and Benkendorf summoned the author and merely admonished him gently. It was Korsakov who had censored the article. Our litterateurs frequently use him as their tool, particularly Grech and Bulgarin. He gets away with a lot of things which others can't. It's nice to have your brother for your chief.[1] The nobility are very irritated by these literary squabbles. Recently, a certain prince who is a member of the State Council complained to me with great indignation about the democratic tone of our literature. So, it means they are beginning to read Russian books. Woe to our books and censorship!

However, it is true that the striving of our literature for a so-called *narodnost* and its effort, in general, to arouse national consciousness is hardly favorable to the upper classes. All litterateurs writing in this nationalistic spirit, beginning with Polevoy and so on, harbor a secret desire to arouse the masses. Our upper class has no moral foundation and, naturally, must decline with the development of education in the middle and lower classes. But doesn't it have only itself to blame for this? It is totally unconcerned with the acquisition of moral superiority. Who, for example, is studying at our universities? Plebeians, while the aristocrats merely "go through" mechanically for their certificates.

24 February. I met Princess Shcherbatova, who struck up a conversation

---

[1] M. A. Dondukov-Korsakov was superintendent of the St. Petersburg school district and chairman of the St. Petersburg Censorship Committee.

with me about *Elena Glinskaya.* She recently attended a performance. Yes, our aristocrats are not only beginning to read books, but to visit the Russian theatre, too. Here is all they managed to say, for example, after seeing *Elena Glinskaya:* "Why show the Russian Court on the stage in such an indecent light?" Since I had not read or seen the play I could not reply to this. I remarked only that Russian history was generally lacking in material for good drama and therefore it was difficult for the writer to make a choice. So, when he comes across something lively, he is delighted with his find.

25 March. Convocation at the university. I delivered a speech, "On Criticism." The public received it very warmly and many came up to me to thank me. There were many in the audience who came only to hear my speech. In general, I am, at this time, in favor with the public. It's said that my lectures produce an impression. That's splendid, but will all this last?

16 April. There's a great deal of talk regarding the edict issued about the peasants.[m] I feel that it is not a final measure; it's much too strange and contrary to our politics. It means one of two things: either it is a first step to be followed by others, or there exist secret supplementary directives to local authorities to persuade the nobility to understand the emperor's will and to enter into a voluntary transaction with the peasants. This might lead people to think that all this was being done at the request of the nobility, and thus the latter would not be compromised.

26 April. I heard Liszt today for the first time. Prince von Oldenburg invited him to Smolny Convent, and the director invited me to hear the famous artist. This man is a real genius. What power, what fire in his playing! The instrument vanishes beneath his hands. He transports you into a world of sounds, where he is the absolute master. Each sound he draws from the instrument is either a thought or emotion. No, I have never heard anything like it! I don't think it's possible to go any further in music.

Liszt's appearance is very distinctive. He has fine facial features and is thin and pale. His long, light brown hair falls on his shoulders. When he plays, his face becomes animated and literally breathes fire. His entire bearing points to a man of European education. He was welcomed like a tsar. Everyone rose when he entered. Prince von Oldenburg, Minister of Education Uvarov, and the director of Smolny Convent, met him at the stage, where two aide-de-camps of the emperor awaited him. Count Wielgorski, himself a musician, accompanied Liszt and never left his side, like a tsar's gentleman-in-waiting. I am still under the spell of Liszt's marvelous performance.

[m] On April 2, 1842, an edict by Nicholas I was published, which permitted landowners to grant the peasants "obligatory status" in a voluntary agreement with them. "Obligatory peasants" received the right to personal freedom, but the right to their land was fully retained by the landowner. As a result of this edict only twenty-four thousand out of ten million serfs received "obligatory status."

16 May. We have a new superintendent, Prince Grigory Petrovich Volkonsky. Will he have sufficient will-power and endurance to sustain his desire to do good? Many people begin their careers with the best of intentions, but soon betray them. Society and life transform them so radically that they begin to act in a spirit completely contrary to their original aims. People are corrupted with amazing speed in Russia.

1 November. In the past three months four disasters have befallen Russia: the Kazan fire, the Perm fire, the shipwreck of the vessel *Ingermanland,* and finally, Kleinmichel's orders. You simply don't know what to be more amazed at in these orders: their cynical wording and tone or the blind arbitrariness which stops at nothing, unwilling to recognize causes, circumstances or the law itself. To scoff at major government wrongdoing, to vulgarize executions, to spit in society's eyes by jeering at its suffering—this is an utter outrage.

25 November. Benkendorf wrote to the minister that our men of letters have again begun to bicker with each other in a most undignified manner. As an example he cited "The Mosquitoes," by Bulgarin, which, in his words, contains inexcusably abusive language. An order was issued to the censors to deal more strictly in the future with this type of literary back-biting.

I was invited to occupy a professorial post in the reorganized Roman Catholic Holy Academy. They are planning to educate up to forty Poles, to indoctrinate them with the notion that the Pope should not be considered their master and that no other head of the church exists besides the emperor. My role is a modest one—the teaching of Russian literature.

12 December. An unexpected and absurd episode occurred which deserves a detailed account. Yesterday morning, around noon, I returned from my lecture at Catherine Institute and worked in my study, not suspecting that anything was amiss. Suddenly a gendarme officer appeared and graciously asked me to pay a visit to Leonty Vasilievich Dubbelt.[n] "Probably something to do with censorship," I thought, and immediately headed for the Third Section of His Majesty's Own Chancery.

On the way I mentally sorted through all my censorship dealings and searched in vain for a solitary blunder. In the course of ten years I had managed to acquire a certain acumen, but I was now hopelessly lost in guesswork.

The officer who had come to fetch me inquired about Kutorga's apartment, for he, too, was ordered to appear before Dubbelt. This meant that trouble was brewing for us over *Notes of the Fatherland.*

I arrived in the chancery before Kutorga; he arrived half an hour later. We were taken to Dubbelt.

"Oh, my dear gentlemen," he said, taking our hands. "How distressing it is

[n] Dubbelt was office director of the Third Section of His Majesty's Own Chancery from 1839 to 1856.

for me to see you concerning such an unpleasant case. You'll never guess why the emperor is displeased with you."

With these words, he opened the No. 8 issue of *Son of the Fatherland* and pointed to two passages marked off with a pencil. Here they are, from Efebovsky's story, *The Governess*. He describes a ball at the home of a government official in Peski: "May I ask you, what's so bad about the figure, for example, of this courier with his splendid, brand-new aiguillettes? Since he considers himself a military man and, even better, a cavalryman, Gospodin courier is fully entitled to consider himself attractive when he rattles his spurs and twirls his mustaches, which are smeared with a wax whose rosy smell pleasantly envelopes both himself and his dancing partner . . . " The other objectionable passage: "an ensign from a construction unit of the Engineer Corps, wearing enormous epaulettes, a high collar and a still higher tie . . . "

"And *that's* it? I asked Dubbelt.

"Yes," he replied. "Count Kleimmichel complained to the emperor that his officers were insulted by this."

I was so noticeably relieved, that Vladislavlev remarked:

"It appears that you are very pleased! "

"Yes, I am," I said. "I was very upset until I learned what we were being accused of. Because of the complexity and difficulty of censorship, we could easily have overlooked something and given cause for punitive measures. But now I see that this case is like a lump of snow falling down on you from some roof as you chance to be walking along the sidewalk. There are no precautions one can take against such punitive measures because they are beyond reason, beyond the sphere of human logic."

Dubbelt escorted us to Benkendorf.

Benkendorf, a venerable old man, whom I met for the first time, received us with a serious and grieved expression.

"Gentlemen," he said in a gentle, soft voice, "I deeply regret that I must give you some unpleasant news. The emperor is very upset by the passages in the journal which have already been shown to you. He considers it improper to attack members of his Court or officers. I presented the most favorable evidence about you and spoke about your fine reputation among the public. In short, I did everything I could in your favor. Despite my efforts, he ordered your arrest for one day."

After expressing regret at having incurred the emperor's wrath, I said:

"Your Excellency, speak to His Majesty for us. Explain to His Majesty the difficult position we censors find ourselves in. We never know what is expected of us and what position to take; we frequently suffer only because some outsider takes it into his head to meddle in our affairs. Thus, we are never safe; there will be no end to punitive measures, and we shall find ourselves unable to fulfill our responsibilities."

Benkendorf took our hands and assured us that he would report all this to the emperor. We left. Vladislavlev prepared a paper for the commandant and gave it to us. It was almost 4 P. M. We were permitted to go home to eat, provided we would report to the commandant by ten. At eight I went to get Kutorga who was terribly upset. He didn't know how to break the news of his arrest to his sick wife. Finally, we left to report to the commandant at the Winter Palace. He wasn't in, and we gave our dispatch to the aide-de-camp. He led us to a tiny room where a clerk was working on some papers, placed a sentry at the door, and then went to the commandant for orders. He returned in half an hour and announced that I would be confined in either the Petrovsky or Senate guardhouse, and Kutorga in the Sennaya guard-house.

I was led away first. I found myself in an enormous basement room with vaulting, in the company of the sentry officer. The town adjutant was always very courteous to us. Then, he and Kutorga left and I remained alone with the officer. He was a young man from the Obraztsov Regiment, apparently a very decent fellow. He took a kindly interest in me, saw to it that I received a bed, and gave me his overcoat to cover myself for the night. In short he surrounded me with attention and concern.

The next day the same aide-de-camp came to tell me that I was free. We went together to the Sennaya to release Kutorga. After parting with the town adjutant and thanking him for his kindness, we went to see Prince Volkonsky, our superintendent.

He not only received us kindly, but even warmly. I spoke plainly about everything that had been seething inside me. Censors are treated like little boys or smooth-faced ensigns; we are placed under arrest for trifles not worthy of attention. At the same time we are saddled with the responsibility of protecting minds and morals from anything that might lead them astray, of safeguarding the public spirit, the laws, and finally, the very government it-self. What kind of logical activity can be expected of us when everything is decided by blind whim and arbitrary desire.

After leaving the prince, we went to see the minister. The same regrets and kind words.

"Whom can you complain about or blame in this case?" said the minister. "This case was unusual. I couldn't do a thing; it was already over with before I learned about it. I would have gone to the emperor immediately, but couldn't because we have the measles at our house. All I could possibly do was write a letter and ask Benkendorf to present it to the emperor."

The prince read us this letter. It was written intelligently and forcefully. While describing us, that is, Kutorga and myself, as the finest of censors and professors, the minister stated that he was now in a great predicament with regard to censorship. Reliable people didn't want to take on this wretched responsibility, and if Kutorga and I were still at our posts, it was only because the minister had pleaded with us to stay. He is afraid that censorship duties will soon become abhorrent to everyone.

They say the emperor read this letter without saying a word.

Kutorga expressed the fear that such an incident could happen again.

"I can assure you," replied the minister, "that in the first such instance I shall resign. What just happened to you is more of a blot on my reputation—if there is any kind of blot here—than on yours."°

14 December. New troubles! The students took it into their heads to express their sympathy because of the misfortune that had befallen me. In my first course I delivered a lecture "On The Relationship of Art to Nature and the Imitation of Nature." I must say that I delivered it with great enthusiasm, for it is a rich subject. I had already finished and had started to leave the platform, when suddenly loud applause and shouts of "bravo" rang out. The stuents came at me in a solid mass. For a moment I was confused, but quickly regained my composure.

"Quiet, gentlemen, quiet, please," I said to the students. "What are you doing! Stop it!"

I finally managed to make my way out of the auditorium and hold the students back in it.

What will come of this? I don't know. A new storm, perhaps!

16 December. Rumors had reached me that the students were contemplating similar demonstrations. I wondered if I ought to go to the university. Finally, I decided to go, simply to avoid giving the impression that I attached any importance to such things. I gave lectures in two courses—in the first and second. Thank God everything went peacefully!

19 December. Prince Volkonsky was at the palace last Monday evening. He said nothing to the emperor about the incident at the university, but did relate it to Grand Duchess Olga Nikolaevna, who mentioned that she knew me.

Meanwhile, my case has been stirring up a lot of talk in the city. Public opinion is for me; everyone attacks Kleinmichel. It's said that many of the nobility attending the palace ball had rebuked him. He apologized to Uvarov.

22 December. The emperor asked Benkendorf if he knew what had happened at Professor Nikitenko's lecture at the university.

Benkendorf replied that he did, but that he considered it too trivial to bother with, especially since Professor Nikitenko himself tried to restore order instantly.

"The minister acted improperly by not informing me about it immediately," continued the emperor. "And tell him so. Meanwhile I want a list of students who attended the lecture that day."

Prince Volkonsky, who heard all this from his father-in-law, immediately wrote a back-dated report to the minister concerning the incident at the uni-

° See entry of 24 December 1842 for the effect of this incident on the publication of Gogol's work.

versity, as a consequence of which he and the minister had jointly decided that same day not to notify the emperor and bother him with so trivial a matter.

Benkendorf transmitted all this together with a list of students to the emperor.

The emperor said:

"If everyone considers this so unimportant, then why shouldn't I? Let's see the list!"

He scanned it and merely remarked: "How few well-known names!"—and that was the end of it.

Meanwhile, gossip about my arrest has not subsided. They say that Kleinmichel had grown tipsy from the tsar's favors and that nothing more was expected of him after those infamous orders he issued not so long ago which produced a painful impression on the public by their arbitrariness and coarse cynicism. And to think that our tsar has placed his trust in such people!

24 December. They say that the emperor is very displeased about the recent trouble in the censorship department. He realizes that a lot of nonsense was stirred up. Apparently, this petty incident really made a deep impression on people.

A kind of stupor has taken hold of the censorship department. No one knows what position to take. The censors are afraid of perishing for the most insignificant line going to press under their signature of approval. I had examined the new edition of Gogol's works, where several new pieces such as *The Overcoat*, a story; *The Marriage*, a play; and an *Afterpiece*[p] had been added. I had presented these works to the Censorship Committee and it was decided to publish them. They were printed. Only a certificate for their release from the printer was needed. This coincided with my arrest, so at that point the committee not only halted the new edition of Gogol, but even Dal's novel, *Vakkh Sidorovich Chaikin*, which had already been printed, too.[q]

Gogol and Dal write stories (and the former writes comedies, too), in which present-day evils are attacked. All kinds of people are portrayed: landowners, civil servants, officers, as in *Woe From Wit*, *The Inspector-General*, and many other plays which have been published, performed in the theatre, and passed by the emperor himself. Now, all of this has suddenly become criminal and is forbidden. The committee has asked me to compose a report to the minister concerning its problems; it is requesting instructions and guidance.

[p] An *Afterpiece to The Inspector General.*

[q] After Nikitenko's arrest, the Censorship Committee felt it should halt the publication of Gogol's new edition, since Nikitenko had been involved in its approval.

29 December. I've spent the past few days composing a report to the minister. The committee and the prince, too, approved it. It is now being copied. This document is very interesting. I am saving a copy of it among my papers. Perhaps it will be useful to a future historian of Russian education and literature.

1843

4 January. I made a few holiday visits, hoping as much as possible to avoid discussion of my arrest and student expression of sympathy for me.

I am sick of all this talk and tired of all these expressions of sympathy! As if it would improve matters and the deplorable state of our literature!

10 January. I am seriously considering resigning from the censorship department. It is impossible to serve; one can't conceivably do good under such conditions. I consulted some people about it, among them Vronchenko. Everyone approves of my motives, but they don't approve of my intentions, feeling that my resignation would be disastrous for literature. Vronchenko particularly stressed this point with me. I would say that all this is an exaggeration, for no man is indispensable. Nevertheless, I must think it over.

28 January. Received official confirmation of my appointment as a professor at the Roman Catholic Academy.

7 February. I went to see Prince Volkonsky today, had a heated discussion with him and asked to be released from my censorship position. What is there left for an honest man to do at such a post? Being a censor these days is worse than being a police officer. The prince was in complete agreement with me but extremely upset over my plans.

9 February. Minister of Internal Affairs Perovsky has acquired an excellent reputation by keeping a sharp eye on weights and measures, so Russian merchants cannot cheat, a practice as vital to them as the air they breathe. He is the first minister to focus attention where it is needed, and this has delighted everyone. It would seem there is nothing unusual here, for it is only a simple performance of one's duty. This is, however, a great rarity with us. All the others, as Pushkin says, dream of becoming Napoleons; they are determined to make their place in history "with their grand ideas, profound theories and endless, sweeping designs;" they set their sights above Russia, and no one cares that poor Russia is nothing; no one cares that thieving officials are robbing the people of everything they have; no one cares that there is no justice in our land.

14 February. I had a long talk with the prince today and finally had to promise to postpone my resignation. We embraced warmly on parting.

10 May. Zhukovsky sent me his new play, *Nala and Damayanti*, for censorship. It is an episode from the Indian poem, *Mahabharata*. What can I say about it? The hexameters are splendid, the language is fresh, harmonious and magnificently fragrant. But the fantastic structure of the poem won't have immediate appeal to our European taste.

21 May. Belinsky came to see me several days ago. He is a clever man. His observations are often correct, intelligent and witty, but filled with bitterness.

25 May. Government thievery and so-called abuses play an important role in Russian life, for it is our way of protesting against unlimited despotism. The authorities think that nothing is impossible for them, that their will cannot encounter resistance anywhere. In the meantime, not one of their orders is executed properly. Their subordinates sham a servile willingness to do everything demanded of them, but, in reality, do not perform as they are expected to.

14 September. Attempt on the emperor's life. People are still talking in whispers about it.

15 September. The attempted assassination is finally being discussed openly. Prayers of thanks were offered in the Court church and in the churches of some educational institutions. The son of Court physician Markus visited me this evening and told me that the empress had shown his father a letter from the emperor in which he informed her of the villainous attempt on his life.

23 October. Poor Sorokin was confined to the guardhouse on imperial orders, and here's the reason. Last Wednesday, posters advertised Garcia's first appearance in *The Barber of Seville*. Kraevsky, editor of the literary section of the *Russian Veteran,* assigned Sorokin to write a review and asked him to write it before the performance. He assumed that *The Barber of Seville* would certainly be performed on Wednesday as scheduled, that Garcia would delight her audience, and that a review of it would be ready early Thursday morning and would appear in his journal before it appeared in other journals and newspapers. Sorokin wrote a review in which he praised the singing and acting of the famous artist to the skies. The public, in his words, was absolutely wild about it; two wreathes of flowers were tossed on to the stage, and so on.

Meanwhile, on account of Rubini's illness, the performance was cancelled. One can imagine the surprise and laughter that greeted the ecstatic praise in Wednesday's *Veteran* for the brilliant performance that wasn't held.

The emperor ordered immediate imprisonment for Sorokin and forbad the *Veteran* to publish articles on the theatre.

30 October. I submitted a request to resign from Smolny Convent. I need time, time, time!

31 October. Discussions with the director of Smolny Convent. No, I've definitely decided to leave this institution. Even my dreams of doing some good here, too, are only dreams! My lectures made an impression and often aroused enthusiasm in my students. I liked them, and they liked me, but what

good is all this if the whole system is a sham. In general, our institutes for
women pay so little attention to the academic and moral aspects of education,
that an honest man becomes discouraged and feels that he is wasting his time.
Their only concern is dancing, singing and curtsying. They turn the girls' heads
with gold lace and red livery and so forth. Neither moral strength nor an
awareness of their domestic and social responsibilities is developed in them.
And they will be the mothers of our next generation. So, the result is that
our Russian nobility raises its sons to wield the whip and its daughters for
Court debauchery. Of course, not all of them will be Court maids-of-honor
not all of them will bring the immorality and hurly-burly of pompous high
society into their homes. But, much time will be needed to make good wives
and mothers out of these chiseled dolls.

9 November. Some officer decided to glorify Kleinmichel, to reproduce his
portrait, and approached him for permission.

"Do you plan to sell the portrait?" Kleinmichel asked.

"Yes, Your Excellency."

"Well, I guarantee you that no one will pay a single kopek for my portrait
and you'll lose on it."

It appears that even Kleinmichel himself shares the opinion that many hold
of him. Only a few days ago the director of Smolny Convent, Madame Leontieva, said to me: "Rest assured that Kleinmichel's power at Court will increase
in proportion to the growth of the public's hostility and contempt for him.
This hostility and contempt will assuredly endear him all the more to the
hearts of the courtiers." The more we oppress the people and insult national
feeling, the more faithfully we serve sovereign power.

They say that Kiselev has fallen into disfavor because of the liberalism un-
covered in his administration.

15 November. The director of Smolny Convent invited me to mass today at
her church, where the Metropolitan was due to perform the service. I went.
I hadn't witnessed a bishop's service for a long time. The first impression was
striking; it had a kind of dramatic grandeur. Then it became monotonous.
The endless liturgical prayers were particularly wearisome. Oh, servile Byzan-
tine! You have given us a religion of slaves! Damn you! Indeed, the best
of Christianity drowns in this gilded rubbish of ritual which despots have in-
vented to keep the prayer itself from reaching God. They are everywhere—
and nothing but them! There are no people, ideas or universal equality!
There is only an oppressive hierarchy, a dazzling splendor to divert the eyes,
to confuse people. Yes, there is everything here except simple Christian
simplicity and humanity.

16 November. A certain individual[r] saw the singer, Assandri, perform in War-

---

[r] Said to be Nicholas I.

saw. She was very beautiful and he wanted her to come to St. Petersburg. She was invited to perform here in an Italian opera for a large sum of money. Unfortunately for Assandri, her singing is in inverse proportion to her great beauty. Either sheer gall or her reliance on the patronage of a highly placed individual inspired her to accept the invitation. She decided to appear on stage following the greatest singer of our time, Garcia-Viardot, and was cruelly hissed. The public knew who was responsible for her appearance in St. Petersburg, and their treatment of her may have had a hidden motive. At any rate, this certain individual didn't like this, and when Assandri appeared on the stage a second time, she was loudly applauded by hands which could slap every cheek in Russia. In the meantime, the no. 256 issue of the *Bee* said the following about the first performance of *Norma* in which the charming and thrice fortunate Assandri appeared: "We won't say a single word about this performance, for, as they say in Latin: aut bene, aut nihil.[s] We enjoyed Gospodin Zam's menagerie far more," and so on.

This last sentence unleashed a terrible storm at the censorship department. Prince Volkonsky (Court minister) demanded an explanation for his report to the emperor. He asked: "On what basis did you dare pass such an indecent statement (the comparison of the opera with a menagerie) and who wrote it? " We remained at a meeting until 5 o'clock, composing a reply to this profound question. We replied that the censorship department had found nothing offensive to anyone in this article, and "in the simple comparison of two different things—an opera and a menagerie, it sees only poor taste on the part of the author. And, further, there are no censorship rules against poor taste, but, on the contrary, the censorship code requires that censors refrain from interfering in matters of personal taste." (The appropriate paragraphs of the code were cited.)

Will posterity believe that blind whim could quarrel so childishly with common sense, demanding for its own satisfaction that black be called white? The censors of *The Northern Bee*, Ochkin and Korsakov, are preparing to go to the guardhouse. We'll see what comes of this.[t]

7 December. Bulgarin filed a complaint against the censorship department, against Superintendent Prince Volkonsky, and against the minister himself. Here's what it's all about. Last Tuesday, at a Censorship Committee meeting, it was decided to take steps to put an end to the abusive language which the journalists were flinging at each other, particularly Bulgarin and Kraevsky. Prince Volkonsky directed the committee to inform Bulgarin, not officially, but in the form of a warning, that he had better stop writing such abomina-

---

[s] "Either (say something) good, or nothing at all."

[t] As a result of this incident, Bulgarin was severely reprimanded. Simultaneously, Nicholas I issued a general order to the censorship department to submit all articles on imperial theaters to him first for personal examination in the Third Section of His Majesty's Personal Chancery. Only then were they to go through regular censorship channels.

tions because the censorship department would censor them unmercifully.
However, this directive was aimed at all journalists using abusive language.
In response to this warning, Bulgarin wrote Prince Volkonsky an insolent and
absurd letter. He wrote that "there exists a Martinist group which has set as
its goal the overthrow of the existing order of things, and that the mouthpiece
for this group was *Notes of the Fatherland*. The censorship department
clearly encourages them." He enclosed several weak excerpts from *Notes of
the Fatherland*, which were absolutely harmless. In conclusion, he told the
prince, "but, since you have been chairman of the committee, much stronger
and clearer examples of such things have been passed."

Then he reproaches the minister for not seeing what goes on under his very
nose, thereby implying that he is either a simpleton or a champion of liberalism. He demands the creation of an investigating commission, before which
he will appear as an informer in order to expose a group which is shaking
the throne and the very foundations of religion. He will ask the emperor to
investigate this matter. He ends his letter with these strong and meaningful
words: "I will not permit censorship to muzzle me like a dog."

16 December. Superintendent Prince Grigory Petrovich (Volkonsky) reported the following to the Censorship Committee yesterday on the Bulgarin affair. Minister Uvarov had submitted a recommendation to the emperor about
the need to supplement and alter the censorship code. In its present form it
supposedly contained few provisions for controlling writers, journalists in
particular. The minister referred to the superintendent, implying that the
latter had requested his assistance, while he himself was limited in what he
could do. Evidently Minister Uvarov wanted to extend his authority. They
say he requested the right to shut down journals the instant anything of an
abusive nature was found in them.

The emperor replied that the censorship code was good enough and that
there was no need to supplement it, and even less need to alter it. "Censors
have sufficient authority," he said. "They have pencils; these are their scep-
ters." The emperor ordered a severe reprimand for Prince Volkonsky for requesting assistance because he should have found it among the powers he
already possessed.

There's something very shady here. It appears that the prince had conspired with the emperor to give the matter such a turn, and the minister was
duped. Something good did come of it: the censorship code remains intact.
Otherwise, God knows what new constraints would have come from a re-
examination of it in times like these.

What Bulgarin gained or lost by his denunciation is unknown. The prince
said there were details here he could not reveal.

I requested to be replaced as censor of *Notes of the Fatherland*, because
Bulgarin voices the suspicion that Kutorga and I are taking particular pains to
protect its liberalism or, as he expresses it, its Martinist spirit. The prince re-

plied that the journal ought not to change hands at this particular time. So, for next year I am again saddled with this thick monthly. The *Reader's Library* has also been added to this load.

20 December. I went to see the prince to discuss censorship matters. What chaos and confusion. Apparently they want to smother the last spark of thought. A request to resign is always with me, tucked away in my pocket.

21 December. An unexpected, absurd order was issued by the minister of education. The Censorship Committee received a memorandum from him saying: "I have actually found journal articles which disseminate harmful ideas under the guise of philosophical and literary studies." Therefore, he directed the censors "to be as strict as possible." The order to exercise greater vigilance over translations of French stories and novels was also repeated.

I went to see the prince about it. He was very angry with the minister for issuing these directives. The minister had told him that he "wanted" to see an end to Russian literature. Then, at least we would know where things stand. And the main result would be "that I shall sleep peacefully."

The minister had also declared he would punish censors unmercifully. A pleasant prospect!

The most interesting thing about the minister's new orders is that they would seem to justify completely Bulgarin's charges against the minister himself, Prince Volkonsky, and the rest of us.

They say the emperor, after reading Bulgarin's letter, returned it to Benkendorf with these words: "Act as if I knew and know nothing about this."

1844

12 January. Kiev Governor-General Bibikov sent a complaint to the minister of internal affairs about censorship, or, more specifically, about the *Reader's Library*, for its articles on Markevich's history of Little Russia, which had appeared last year. The *Reader's Library* is accused of clearly favoring Poland, of making disparaging remarks about Russia and Little Russia, of insulting Little Russian nationality by saying that "its people came from runaway Polish serfs," of a generally abusive tone and, finally, of the most pernicious anti-national tendencies. Perovsky forwarded this complaint to our minister, and the latter issued a mild reprimand to Korsakov and Freigang.

14 January. At the Censorship Committee meeting we read censors Korsakov's and Freigang's reply to Bibikov's complaint. It was rather well written. I proposed minor changes which were also accepted. The censors based their arguments on the fact that the *Reader's Library* expressed only its learned opinion regarding the Little Russians—an opinion with which anyone was free to disagree. As far as the journal's general tone is concerned, the notion that they pander to Polish ideas is absolutely unjustified. On the contrary, one can point to passages where Poland is strongly criticized. But the censors based their main defense on the following idea which ran through the articles in the *Reader's Library* : Little Russia was never a separate political community; it committed many foolish and evil acts against its neighbors, and all this ceased only after it became part of Russia.

Saw Count Kleinmichel, who invited me to teach literature at the Communications Institute.

20 January. Bibikov's complaint finally reached the emperor. He settled the case splendidly. He said: "If the articles in the *Reader's Library* contain lies, then they must be refuted by literary means, but without name-calling."

4 March. Saw Count Kleinmichel and was received most warmly. He invited me into his study and asked me to concentrate on reorganizing Russian language instruction at the Communications Institute, where it was deteriorating very rapidly.

"In general," he added, "this institution has been a hotbed of debauchery, brigandage and liberalism: I shall eradicate this spirit! "

19 March. A decree raising the tax on foreign travel has been issued. Anyone leaving the country for six months must pay 100 rubles in silver. Travel abroad is absolutely prohibited for those under twenty-five. And if illness should require a trip to Carlsbad, Marienbad or other watering places? In such cases the government will mercifully permit the patient to die in his own home. Moreover, governor-generals will no longer be permitted to issue passports for foreign travel. In short, all possible measures are being taken to transform Russia into a China. They say this move was prompted by the last debate in the English parliament, where our government was strongly attacked. People are grumbling a great deal about this measure. Indeed, it is terribly clumsy, to say nothing of its coercive character. As a result of the ban imposed on European travel, Europe is becoming some kind of promised land. But can ideas from Europe really be prevented from reaching us? And where's the justification for such coercion, for not permitting me to breathe the air I want to breathe. Everywhere we have coercion and more coercion, oppression and restrictions. Nowhere is there freedom for the poor Russian spirit. Oh, when and where will there be an end to this?

28 March. If you want to rule the people through bureaucracy alone without their participation, you will simultaneously oppress them, corrupt them, and give the bureaucrats a pretext to commit countless abuses. There are areas of administration that should certainly involve the public or society. For example, the judiciary. And this can be achieved without usurping the rights of sovereign power. What we need is less egoism on the part of the latter.

22 June. There was an uproar recently in the censorship department. Someone wrote a book, *Deception in the Caucasus*, under a fictitious name. The chaos in the administration of the Caucasus and the abominations committed by the authorities were rather bluntly described in it. The book was passed by Moscow censor Krylov. The minister of war read it and was horrified. He showed it to Dubbelt, saying, "This book is particularly dangerous because there's truth in every single line of it."

On the 25th the book was recalled from all local book dealers, but it had already received wide distribution in Moscow. I knew nothing about this recall measure or about the book itself. In the meantime I had received a review of it for examination for the June issue of *Notes of the Fatherland.* The review quoted several passages from it. I felt that these passages, to use censorship terminology, were "suspicious and indicated malicious intent." But there was nothing I could do but pass what had already been passed by the censor of the book itself.

On June 2nd Vladislavlev's office informed me that the article in *Notes of the Fatherland* was causing a furor and he was afraid that it would lead to a lot of trouble. I hurried to him and learned then for the first time that *Deception in the Caucasus* had been banned and that, therefore, it could not be discussed at all, while an even stricter ban had been imposed on the reproduction of any passages from it. But it was too late; the deed had already been done. Still, I advised Kraevsky to remove the article from the undistributed copies of the journal.

Is it possible that I shall have to pay for someone else's mistakes again? And why expect otherwise?

30 June. Moscow censor Krylov was summoned here for an explanation. Everything indicates that both he and the Moscow Censorship Committee had committed a blunder. He was, however, permitted to return to Moscow. We still don't know how it will end.

20 September. Some people make a big fuss about the church, but are absolutely unconcerned about religion, for it is not in their hearts. They have no sincere interest in God or people but are interested only in their own reputations and ideologies. Their slogan, "to be the leaders of society at any price," hides behind a cloak of nationalism and patriotism.

1 October. I went to see our minister this morning. It appears that the Muscovites' technique of flattery certainly was effective. He recently returned from Moscow. The delicate nerves of this lively, but weak-willed man cannot stand up against this sort of thing. He's terribly set against *Notes of the Fatherland,* claiming that it harbors pernicious tendencies—socialism, communism and so forth. Evidently this attitude was inspired by those Moscow patriots who are determined to be the leaders of our time at any price. The minister will show no mercy toward *Notes of the Fatherland.* Yet, was it so very long ago that he, in word and deed, had criticized Bulgarin's denunciation, which had been composed in the very same spirit?

22 October. I had a talk with Volkonsky about the clergy's complaint against the censorship department or, rather, the complaint lodged by the rector of the local holy academy, Bishop Afanasy. He charged the department with passing articles about the Reformation for *Notes of the Fatherland,* which were drawn from Ranke's work. I learned that the matter had already gone to the synod. Afanasy is considered a fanatic, a champion of the kind of orthodoxy that sticks not to the spirit of religion, but to the letter of religion, and which has more respect for tradition than for the Gospel. I spoke with his henchman, Raikovsky, our religion instructor at the university, and I asked him what he found objectionable in the articles about the Reformation. His reply was completely irrelevant, and he said in conclusion that "many among our own clergy are imbued with protestant ideas; therefore we must attack the Reformation."

"But, after all, the Reformation is a fact," I objected. "Can you really dismiss it from history? Besides, what does it have in common with our church? The Reformation was a result of abuse of clerical power in the West. Have we had such abuse here or was it even likely to occur here? If our priests do lean toward protestantism, what business is it of the secular censor? The clerical authorities are at fault: why do they tolerate this?"

The prince wanted to have a talk with Voitsekhovich about this and asked me to discuss it also with Odoevsky, who is very friendly with Voitsekhovich. But I would prefer to have an official explanation demanded of me: then I could teach that monk, Afanasy, a lesson. This isn't the first time he has shown a predilection for meddling in someone else's affairs. To give the

monks free reign would be disastrous: it would mean another Magnitsky era.[u]
As it is, they talk too much talk nowadays about Orthodoxy; they attack
Peter the Great and want to revive the blissful times of pre-Petrine Russia, and
so on.

I had dinner at Savva Mikhailovich Martynov's. He is friendly with the fabulist Krylov and told me the following story about him. This summer Krylov
had suddenly decided to buy a house somewhere near the Tuchkov Bridge on
the St. Petersburg side. But when he inspected it carefully, he noticed that
the house was not in good condition, and required extensive alterations and
consequently, more money than he could afford. Krylov abandoned his plan.
Several days later a rich merchant, whose name I don't know, came to see
him and said:

"I heard, my dear Ivan Andreevich, that you want to buy a certain house."

"No," replied Krylov, "I've already changed my mind."

"But why?"

"Why should I bother with it? It needs a lot of repairs, and besides I don't
have enough money for it."

"But the house is an exceptionally good buy. Permit me, my dear Ivan
Andreevich, to arrange this matter for you. We'll work out the costs."

"Why do you want to do this for me? I don't even know you."

"The fact that you don't know me is not at all surprising. But it would be
surprising if a Russian didn't know Krylov. Permit me to render you a small
service."

Krylov had to agree, and now the house is being fixed up. The merchant
looks after everything painstakingly and furnishes the finest materials. The
work is going well under his supervision and he's putting up half the cost of
everything. In short, Ivan Andreevich will have a well-constructed house without any fuss for a sum which is insignificant compared to the return on his
investment.

Such respect for talent in a simple Russian man was a pleasant surprise for
me. That is what being a people's writer means! This was not, however, the
first time that Krylov had had such an experience. Once, two merchants from
Kazan came to see him.

"My dear Ivan Andreevich, we are tea merchants. Like all Kazanians, we
love and respect you. Do allow us to supply you with the finest tea every
year."

And indeed, every year Krylov receives enough superb tea to keep the brilliant fabulist's capacious belly well filled.

Marvellous! Would to God that the ordinary people of our land rather than
literary cliques might judge our intellectual exploits.

[u] In 1819 Magnitsky directed a purge of free-thinking professors from the University
of Kazan. Other universities followed suit.

1845

6 January. I am drowning in work. Another new task has been assigned to me—the drafting of a proposal for amendments to the censorship code. For some reason they are suddenly in a big rush about it.

24 February. I went to see our former superintendent, Prince Grigory Petrovich Volkonsky. I say former, because several days ago he was unexpectedly transferred to a superintendent's post in Odessa.

This is a great loss for us. The prince was not a zealous administrator. But he is a very noble person, educated, with a European outlook; and his position at Court was such that he will prove irreplaceable in dealing with those complex situations that arise in university and censorship affairs. How many times has his influence saved us from disaster! Take, for example, the last incident involving secret student meetings, which was settled without a fuss only because of his intervention. Now we fearfully await the new superintendent. At the last meeting of the Censorship Committee, Pletnyov, our temporary chairman, had already raised the question of the need for a stricter and more vigilant censorship because now the censorship department had been deprived of its protector and defender. Yet this unfortunate censorship department, even during the prince's tenure, had hung by a thread. He told me himself, today, that he had planned to make every effort to have censorship removed from his responsibilities as superintendent. On the whole, the prince performed his censorship duties very unwillingly and, at times, even expressed contempt for anything called "Russian" literature. Perhaps he was right, too, particularly at its present stage of development, or, to be more precise, at its present stage of stagnation.

26 February. An imperial order was received by the Censorship Committee directing it to ban the publication of any article relating to construction activities in the communications department, unless permission was given by the chief administrator. Every section chief among us avoids publicity and tries to surround all his activities with an impenetrable curtain of darkness. It's so much easier that way: anything goes in the dark. Russian administration is certainly a remarkable phenomenon!

8 March. Pletnyov is now chairman of the Censorship Committee. The first benefit he has bestowed on literature with his newly acquired authority is the oppression of journals hostile to him! Almost all of them are, for they ignore his poor journal, the *Contemporary*. He is most harsh with *Notes of the Fatherland;* it had once scoffed at *The Family,* a novel which he had recommended. Now

Pletnyov has suddenly decided to check, point for point, whether the journals are complying with the programs approved by the government: that is, whether the journals are printing articles which were not specified in their original programs. It turned out that all of them had strayed from them more or less and had done so in the very first year of their existence. Particularly guilty in this respect is *Notes of the Fatherland,* which had agreed initially not to publish foreign stories, but now does. This was never considered a serious problem in the censorship department; it knew that all our journals were trying to be comprehensive, and that this was very understandable because highly specialized journals still cannot support themselves here. Every editor tries to outdo his competitors in volume and variety. The censorship department concerned itself only with violations of its rules and did not bother with subject matter of concern to other censors, such as clerical and military writings. By raising this question, Pletnyov stirred up a terrible storm and caused a lot of trouble for the minister who, at the beginning of each year, approves each journal in the identical form that it had previously appeared. I argued with Pletnyov and succeeded in forcing him to withdraw his proposal. But my colleagues are fine fellows! Some of them yessed Pletnyov, while others said nothing, leaving me to fight it out and win by myself. I was particularly surprised by Kutorga, who is always talking about humane principles. On this occasion he insisted on the execution of the chairman's proposal. There was, however, no malicious intention on his part—he is an honest man—he took this stand out of thoughtlessness and because he is weak-willed, which often causes him to be in conflict with himself. At any rate it was a heated battle, and, although I won a victory, I am not sure it will be a lasting one.

15 March. My doubts about Pletnyov were not without good reason. At the last committee meeting he had agreed not to take action on his proposal regarding the journals. In a friendly conversation on Wednesday he confirmed this, but today we received a directive from the minister which stated: "I have noticed that some journals have arbitrarily strayed from their programs; they must stay within these limits." This time, however, the entire committee rebelled. I was charged with the task of composing a reply to the minister. There was a sharp debate. Pletnyov, who, in addition, had attempted to impose other repressive censorship measures, was defeated on all points. I cited the law more than anyone else in our efforts to defeat him. The article of the censorship code which sharply limits a chairman's rights in censorship matters was read to him. This time everyone was unanimous and firm, and Pletnyov was routed. He tried to find fault with the *Reader's Library.* Its original program stated that it would publish translated stories, but it is publishing *novels* like *The Wandering Jew.*

"Now what real difference do you think there is between a story and a novel?" I asked. "We are both professors of literature, and I, for one, can only define 'a story as a novel' and 'a novel as a story.'"

Our poor, poor literature!

8 May. I went to see the minister on Sunday. He spoke at length about the indecent and mercenary trend of our literature. He reminisced about the old days when the literary profession was considered respectable.

"Take, for example," he continued, "our literary circle, which consisted of Dashkov, Bludov, Karamzin, Zhukovsky, Batyushkov, and myself. Karamzin read his history to us. We were still very young, but so well educated, that he listened to our comments and made use of them. Once the late tsar struck up a conversation with Karamzin about academies. Here's what our historian said to him: 'Do you know, Your Majesty, which is the most useful of all our academies? The one made up of those scamps and young people who, with their good-natured banter, manage to convey many useful truths and valid observations.' He meant our circle. But now things are different. The literary profession doesn't command anyone's respect."

Uvarov wanted to show me a letter he had received from Gogol, but he couldn't find it among his papers. He conveyed its contents to me orally, vouching for its authenticity. Gogol expressed his thanks for receiving financial assistance from the emperor, and said in his letter: "I am grieved when I see how little I have written that deserves this kindness. Everything that I have written until now is so weak and insignificant, that I do not know how to make amends to the emperor for having failed to fulfill his expectations. Perhaps God will help me to do something that will please him."

What pathetic self-abasement on Gogol's part! This was written by a man who had assumed the task of exposing our social ills and not only exposed them pointedly and authentically, but also with the tact and talent of a brilliant artist. What a terrible pity! This will suit Uvarov as well as some others very well.

10 May. I stopped in at Komovsky's office at the minister's request to read Gogol's letter. It is essentially what Uvarov had told me earlier.

24 July. The new superintendent, Musin-Pushkin, has arrived.

18 October. Minister Uvarov is taking terribly repressive measures against journals. The *Literary Gazette* was ordered several days ago to stop publishing three issues a week (although it did not stray from its original program in any respect whatsoever) and to stop shifting articles around: for example, stories should not be printed in the feuilleton section, etc., although such changes had previously been permitted or, rather, had not been noticed because they didn't deserve to be noticed.

Of course one can cite important official reasons for all this. We are unusually rich in official reasons. If you were forbidden to brush a fly off your nose, it would be for official reasons. Indeed, three years ago our local governor-general issued a proclamation stating that children were not to deviate in their dress from the prescribed uniform, but no one knew what it was. There probably was an official reason for this too. People who not only tolerate all this, but cite the term "official reasons" as justification, probably deserve to be ruled in such a way—and that in itself, to be sure, is official reason enough.

21 October. I am beginning to think that 1812 never even happened, that all this was only a dream or a figment of the imagination. It left not a single trace on our national spirit, nor did it stir an iota of pride, self-awareness, or respect for ourselves. Neither did it yield social benefits, the fruits of peace and tranquility. A terrible oppression, a silent servility—that is what Russia harvested on this bloody field, a field on which other nations have acquired a wealth of rights and self-awareness. What is one to make of all this? Did the people really act in 1812? Do we really know what happened? Isn't everything they say about a people's uprising and patriotism a distortion of the truth? Isn't it a lie, something which is ingrained in our servile nature? We are whipped as in Biron's day;[v] we are treated like stupid cattle. Or maybe our people never actually did anything at all, and it was always the authorities and the important figures who acted in their behalf? Do the people owe everything to their eternal obedience, to this abominable talent of slaves? What a terrifying thought!

[v] E. Biron (1690–1772), a favorite of Anna Ivanovna (Empress Anne), who wielded enormous influence in all government affairs in the 1730s during the latter's rule (1730–40).

1846

2 January. At the end of December, I completed a large project assigned to me by the minister of education, which I had worked on uninterruptedly during the last two months of the year. It is "The Draft of Amendments to the Censorship Code." It appears that the minister wants to issue a new code—and we all know very well in what spirit. I was determined to do all I could to prevent this, and I assembled all the arguments I could use to prove the need for preserving the present code, which in these times is still the least of a mass of evils hanging over us. I also had to persuade the Censorship Committee. Finally, a meeting was held to discuss my draft and everything was accepted with very minor changes. Kutorga tried to voice objections, but all the others supported me.

5 January. What sort of person is the new superintendent, Musin-Pushkin? Doesn't he occasionally have bouts of insanity? How he treats his subordinates! Recently, he summoned several gymnasium teachers to his office and called them "blockheads," "fools," "numbskulls," "buffoons," and the like. He behaves this way toward all his subordinates who are dependent upon him, except the university professors. A few days ago he drove one of his employees from his office, threatening him with his fists. To the ladies who come to him with petitions, he shouts: "Off with you!" In short, this man is a beast! He tried to treat the students the same way, but they threatened him, saying that first they would hiss him, and if that had no effect, they would beat him up. He calmed down. And this is the kind of man that has been chosen to be superintendent of the university of our capital! Again, however, I must repeat, any society is ruled as it deserves to be ruled; not one of the people insulted by the new superintendent has complained to the minister. Two, however, did resign.

6 January. The new superintendent doesn't understand anything about censorship and keeps ranting about too much liberalism in Russian literature, particularly in the journals. Most of his attacks are reserved for *Notes of the Fatherland.* Fortunately, he doesn't carry any weight here because it's not he who does the censoring.

22 February. Polevoy is dead. This is a great loss. He was an unusual man. Everyone is saddened by his passing.

7 March. Our superintendent has changed a great deal. It seems he has decided to curb his haughty, insolent behavior toward his subordinates.

12 October. Notes of the Fatherland was hounded again. Bulgarin, Grech, and Boris Fyodorov filed a complaint against it with the Third Section. As soon as I learned about this, I informed Kraevsky and advised him to go to the minister and then to Dubbelt. The latter, as the expression goes, raked him over the coals for his liberalism, but finally declared that nothing would come of it.

Several Moscow litterateurs, represented by Panaev, invited me to serve as an editor of a journal which they want to purchase from its present owner: it is the *Contemporary*.[1] I accepted. The preliminary contract has been drafted. They are only waiting for Uvarov who is now in Moscow.

The day before yesterday I met Herzen.[2] He came to see me. A remarkable man. Yesterday we dined together at Legrand's. Other litterateurs were there, including Count Sollogub. There was plenty of intelligent talk, but champagne finally managed to drown it.

14 October. The minister agreed to my appointment as an editor of the *Contemporary*.

1847

4 January. The first issue of the *Contemporary* under new editorship appeared on January 1st. It made a fine impression. I have been receiving favorable reports from all sides on its tone and direction.

5 January. The city is in an uproar and buzzing with gossip. Several poems by Countess Rostopchina were printed in the December 17th issue of the *Northern Bee,* and among them appeared her ballad, "The Forced Marriage." A knight-baron complains that his wife doesn't love him and is unfaithful to him, and she replies that she cannot love him because he had taken her by force. What could appear more innocent in respect to censorship? At first, both the censorship department and the public thought that Countess Rostopchina was talking about her own relations with her husband, which everyone knows are most unfriendly. I am simply amazed by the boldness with which she aired her family affairs before the public and also by the fact that she became involved with the *Northern Bee.*

But now it turns out that the baron represents Russia, and the wife taken by force, Poland. It is really amazing how the poem fits either possibility, and since it is well-written, everyone is memorizing it. For example, the baron says:

> I sheltered her as an orphan
> Brought her here impoverished,
> And gave her my protection
> With a sovereign hand;
> I clothed her in brocade and gold,
> Surrounded her with countless guards;
> And I myself stand over her with a sword
> So the enemy will not entice her . . .
> But sad and unhappy
> Is my unappreciative wife.
> I know—with complaint, with slander
> She brands me everywhere.
> I know—before the whole world
> She curses my shelter and shield,
> And looks at me askance, scowling,
> And repeating the lie of our vow,
> She prepares a plot . . . sharpens her knife . . .
> Fans the fires of internecine wars;
> She is whispering with a monk,
> My treacherous wife! ! ! . . .

To this the wife replies:

> Whether I am a slave or a spouse
> God alone knows! . . . Was it I that
> Chose for myself a cruel mate?
> Did I myself take the vow? . . .
> I lived freely and happily,
> I loved my freedom . . .
> But evil neighbors swooped down,
> Conquered me, captured me . . .
> I was betrayed . . . I was sold . . .
> I am a captive, and not a wife.
>
> .   .   .   .
>
> He forbids me to speak
> In my native tongue.
> He forbids me to wear
> My coat of arms . . .
> I daren't show pride in my
> Ancient name before him,
> Nor pray to the age-old temples
> Of my forebears as did my glorious forebears . . .
> This unhappy wife must
> Accept another's ways.
> He sent into exile, into prison
> All my loyal, true servants;
> And surrendered me to the oppression
> Of his slaves, of his spies. . . .

There can be no doubt about the real meaning and significance of this poem. Bulgarin has already been summoned to Count Orlov. The censorship department awaits the storm.

11 January. Gossip about Countess Rostopchina's poem does not cease. St. Petersburg, in its apathetic existence, is delighted that it has picked up some kind of news, a lively morsel that can engage it for several days. The emperor was very displeased and was about to prohibit Bulgarin from publishing the *Bee.* But Count Orlov came to his defense, explaining that Bulgarin had not grasped the real meaning of the poem. They say that the count's remark was followed by this reply:

"If he [Bulgarin] is not guilty as a *Polyák,* he is guilty as a *durák.*"[w]

However, the matter ended with that. But Rostopchina was summoned to St. Petersburg. The censorship department breathed a sigh of relief.

31 January. Differences have arisen between the publishers and myself since the publication of the second issue of the *Contemporary.* I had to exclude

[w] "Fool."

several articles for literary and censorship reasons. For example, they wanted
to publish a nasty lampoon of Kukolnik and I opposed it. My publishers were
indignant with me, having forgotten that according to our original agreement,
they themselves had granted me complete freedom in the selection of
articles and in the setting of the journal's tone. It was only under these
specific conditions that I could have consented to sign my name to the agreement.

5 February. I am beginning to think about resigning my editorial position
on the *Contemporary.* It's rather soon, but what can I do. It's too burdensome for me to be in constant conflict with the publishers, who, in turn, may
also be disturbed by my impact on the journal. They probably counted on
my being a convenient tool, and wanted to operate independently under the
protection of my name. I cannot agree to this.

7 February. I informed Gebhardt and Rebinder of my intentions regarding
the *Contemporary.* Panaev and Nekrasov became alarmed and decided to discuss the situation with me. In the presence of Gebhardt and Rebinder, a meeting was arranged at my home. I had considered inviting Dal, too, but didn't,
not wanting to embarrass my adversaries. Everyone gathered at my home in
the evening. I expressed my ideas concerning the spirit and direction of the
journal and also my opinion regarding my rights as an editor. Then I explained
the reasons for some of the things I had done which had irritated the publishers. We gradually came to an agreement but I strongly doubt that this is
a durable peace.

2 May. Last year a brief history of Little Russia appeared in several issues of
the children's magazine *Little Star,* published by Ishimova. Its author was
Kulish. Now an awful fuss has been raised about it. Kulish was a lecturer in
Russian at our university; Pletnyov had written to him to come here and had
found this position for him. As a result of Pletnyov's efforts, the Academy of
Sciences deemed him worthy of further study abroad at government expense.
He was sent to study Slavic dialects.

He left and took with him a stack of offprints of his "History of Little Russia"
and distributed them on the way, wherever possible. Now, both the history
and Kulish himself have been seized. He had already been in Warsaw with his
young bride. Censor Ivanovsky was asked how he came to pass Kulish's work.
He replied that it was a mistake and that he was guilty. Kutorga's name appeared on the offprints, so he, too, was summoned for questioning.

I finally obtained a copy of *Little Star* and read Kulish's history. Now I can
see why Ivanovsky could give no other reply than "guilty." When the emperor
saw censor Kutorga's name on the offprints, he ordered his confinement in
the *fortress.* But Count Orlov proposed that it was necessary, first of all, to
get all the facts. It is difficult to predict the outcome.

They say Kulish's *History* is implicated in something far more serious. In the South, in Kiev, an organization was discovered which has as its goal a federated union of all Slavs in Europe, based on democratic principles, similar to the United States.[x] Some professors from Kiev University belong to this organization: Kostomarov, Kulish, Shevchenko, Gulak, and others. It is not known if these southern Slavs have any connection with the Moscow slavophiles, but it appears that the government intends to do something about them.

7 May. I received a *secret* order today from the minister (via the superintendent): "Upon examining articles on our country's history, which have been appearing in periodical publications, I have noticed that discussions of national and political problems often creep in, discussions which should be permitted only with great caution and within very well-defined, moderate limits. Special note should be made of the efforts of some authors to incite rash displays of general or provincial patriotism among the reading public, displays which are, at times, if not dangerous, then at least unwise, because of their possible consequences."

1 June. During these fatal days I had lost track of events.[y] My eyes, full of tears, look dimly at external objects: they wander about only in the terrible abyss of my own misfortune, trying, in vain, to catch at least one ray of comfort. Meanwhile much of interest had transpired. Chizhov was seized, on government orders, at the border, near the customs house and, as a dangerous bearded slavophile, was taken to the Third Section. After nine days of imprisonment and several interrogations, he was released the day before yesterday.

He came to see me and told me many interesting things about the questions which were put to him and his replies. He divided his confession into two parts. In the first part he apparently confessed to some mistakes, particularly in regard to uniting all Slavs into a single monarchy under the Russian scepter. It goes without saying, that this mistake was readily forgiven, as a mistake which flowed from an excess of love. In the second part of his confession he emerged a passionate patriot, wholly in the spirit of autocracy, Orthodoxy and nationalism, alien to everything European, and even hostile to Europe. In an outburst of fanaticism, he even exclaimed that "Peter I was the greatest and most dangerous revolutionary" (this is not my invention, for Chizhov had actually said this, as he himself admitted to me). In the end, his respectable confessors, Leonty Vasilevich Dubbelt and Count Orlov, were fully satisfied with him. Of course, in his confession he did not touch upon the democratic principles of slavophile teachings and emerged from the inquiry completely pure and innocent. They even thanked him, but remarked to him as he was leaving that he was too hot-tempered and, therefore, still would not be permitted to publish his journal in Moscow. How he will now combine his slavo-

---

[x] The organization, known as the Ukrainian-Slavic Society or the Cyril and Methodius Society, was founded by Kostomarov and Gulak in 1846.

[y] Nikitenko had lost his favorite son.

phile ideas with what he must write and do—I don't know. It is all the more difficult because he must submit all his articles to the Third Section for censorship from now on.

Yesterday an emergency meeting of the University Council was called and chaired by Superintendent Musin-Pushkin. The director of the Pedagogical Institute, Davydov, was also invited. A directive from the minister, composed on imperial orders, was read to us. It explained how we should view our *narodnost,* and what slavism meant in relation to Russia. Our *narodnost,* it says, consists of a boundless devotion and obedience to autocracy, and western slavism should not arouse any sympathy in us. It has its own way, and we have ours. We hereby solemnly renounce it. It does not even deserve our attention, because we have built our state without it; without it we have suffered and become exalted, while it has always been dependent on others, could not create anything, and now has lived out its historical existence.

Based on this, the minister wants professors to promote our *narodnost* from their rostrums precisely as outlined in this program and ordered by the government. This particularly concerns professors of slavic dialects, Russian history, and history of Russian law.

After reading this document, the superintendent declared that he had no doubts about our loyalty or our readiness to respond to this appeal; that he saw how moved we were and that he would certainly inform the minister about it. The rector considered it fitting to thank the superintendent in the name of the Council for the government's trust in us and assured him of our common zeal in this endeavor, and so on and so forth. Upon emerging from the Council the censors held an emergency session of the Censorship Committee. After a brief discussion, it hastily banned the witty and completely innocent article by Senkovsky against the slavophiles, an article wholly in the spirit of those ideas which we had just listened to for half an hour at the Council meeting. And only three days ago, Kraevsky was thanked by the Third Section in the name of the emperor for exactly the same kind of article which appeared in *Notes of the Fatherland.*

My God, what chaos, what confusion in their thinking!

20 June. An order from the minister: "Although French novels and stories printed in some journals are altered to such a degree in Russian translation that nothing harmful remains, it would be better not to allow them at all—and censors are directed to be strict in this respect. In general, the printing of any kind of translation must not be permitted unless presented in advance to the superintendent, at whose discretion the work will or will not be approved." In other words, the censorship department will no longer examine these works, the Censorship Committee will be abolished, and the imperial law will no longer be in force. I went to have a talk with Komovsky and had planned to go from his office to the minister, but after my conversation with Komovsky, I saw the futility of this. However, I did go to the superintendent, told him about the violation of the code and about the impossibility of executing the minister's order. He agreed. Then I asked him to inform the Censorship Committee, which he did. And so it was decided not to carry out the minister's order and to leave everything as before.

5 August. I returned from a meeting of the Censorship Committee. I argued with the superintendent who declared that "it is necessary to eliminate all novels in Russia, so that no one will read novels." In my entire career I have never met such a blockhead. He usually doesn't have a reason for anything. He talks a lot, shouts, waves his arms and leaps across all logical bounds in expressing his opinions, until finally he bumps his head against something so fantastically absurd, that he stops on his own.

2 November. St. Petersburg has come to life: something to think, talk and gossip about has appeared on the scene. Indeed, there really is something to think and talk about here. Cholera, engulfing all of Russia in its sweeping embrace, is approaching St. Petersburg at a slow but steady pace. Yet the public appears to be more curious than fearful. Perhaps it's because it still threatens from afar. Or perhaps it's because our society's vitality is so badly sapped that we are now spiritually closer to death than we should be, and, therefore, the prospect of physical death evokes less natural horror in us.

Nothing has changed in our literature. Bulgarin continues to submit complaints against journals. His lustful passion for them usually increases in intensity toward the end of the year because it's subscription time. Every new subscriber to a journal not published by him gets his bile up. What a villainous heart this man has! If one were to believe what he prints about his competitors, all of them should be locked up in the fortress and their publications suspended. Then, in all of Russia only his journal, the *Northern Bee*, would remain, and, of course, it would be the only one left to subscribe to. The public has expressed its contempt for Bulgarin, but it hasn't moved him at all. He has a sort of delusion of grandeur, for he fears no one or nothing except the knout, and since the knout is not used these days, he considers himself completely safe.

Censor Krylov is in trouble. He generally doesn't know how to handle his job: one day he will ban the most innocent piece, while the next he will pass things which are considered dangerous under the present system. Therefore, he gets into difficulty more often than other censors. At the moment he is the target of two complaints from Kleinmichel for passing articles contrary to the interests of the communications department, and a third complaint from the ministry of government property for not passing an article on trade in its journal. Krylov had forwarded the latter article to Kleinmichel for examination only because it said in it that grain is transported by water in Russia. Incredible—but true. Nonetheless, Krylov is in the good graces of the chairman of the Censorship Committee.

1848

17 January. *Notes of the Fatherland* is in danger. About three months ago liberal ideas were discovered among some students of the Mining Institute. One of them admitted he had picked them up from *Notes of the Fatherland.*

22 January. They say there have been unfavorable reports about the *Contemporary*, too. Meanwhile, Bulgarin, Kalashnikov, and Boris Fyodorov do not tire of spreading the blackest slander about the *Contemporary*. Every week Bulgarin suggests through various innuendos in the *Northern Bee* that the *Contemporary* is a vicious journal like *Notes of the Fatherland.* The time has come to discredit these spies! I am now preparing an article which I would like to publish in the Academy newspaper (the *St. Petersburg Bulletin*) in order to avoid involving the *Contemporary* in a polemic. Kalashnikov is playing an active role in the machinations against both journals. At one time this man was an incompetent author and incompetent teacher who finally entered the civil service. Now he is the director of the horsebreeding department. Hoping to make some easy money, he wrote a special little book for the peasants working for his department. He wheedled 2,000 silver rubles from the administration for its printing. The book was published, but proved to be very bad. The *Contemporary*, showing all due restraint, could not avoid giving it a negative review. *Notes of the Fatherland* was more critical of it, and the Academy newspaper's review even harsher. Kalashnikov became enraged and, at a meeting with Bulgarin, who is a member of his chancery, plotted to persuade the administration that the journals which had criticized him were excessively liberal and, therefore, dangerous. After all, hadn't they dared to find fault with his book, a book which was published with the administration's approval?

25 April. I haven't worked on my diary for more than three months, and, meanwhile, very important historical events have been taking place. The peoples of Europe have matured to the point where they have decided to assert their desire for independence. France, as usual, set the example. Germany and Italy followed suit. The sovereign authority of individuals has been destroyed, and in its place has come an authority which rests on the principles of humanity, legality and rights. Our spiritual and political bondsmen are filled with indignation. They call this anarchy, the willful overthrow of an order bright with tradition. But indeed, this is an order in which, in their opinion, the masses should remain in bestial immobility and suffer for the sake of the grandeur and prosperity of a few. Perhaps this is right for some societies —for the Asians. But the peoples of Europe have acquired the right—and at no little cost—the right to be what they want to be. And so the time has come to crown their bloody labors, to fulfil their fervent vows. May God be with them as they stride toward their great future. Undoubtedly they will not realize all the ideals of human reason. They will have their share of troubles, suffering and victims.

While issues of world-wide significance are being decided in Europe, a drama is also unfolding in our country. It is an absurd and savage one, pathetic for human dignity and comical to the outside observer, but unspeakably sad for those involved in it. Several wretched litterateurs, together with Bulgarin and Kalashnikov, with Boris Fyodorov as their leader, attempted to ruin the reputations of our journals in the eyes of the government (*Notes of the Fatherland* and the *Contemporary* in particular), even prior to the events in Europe. But the thunder of European revolutions had scarcely rung out when far more powerful and dangerous individuals emerged as informers. Count Stroganov, former superintendent of Moscow University, furious with Minister of Education Uvarov, who was responsible for his removal from office, presented a note to the emperor about the frightening ideas allegedly prevailing in our literature, particularly in the journals. This, he charged, was due to the incompetency of the minister and his censorship department. Baron Korf, hoping to overturn Count Uvarov so that he could take over his post, presented another such note. And so the public suddenly learned that, as a result of these notes, a committee was organized under the chairmanship of Minister of the Navy Prince Menshikov, and was composed of the following members: Buturlin, Korf, Count A.G. Stroganov (brother of the former superintendent), Degai, and Dubbelt.[z] The purpose and significance of this committee was shrouded in mystery, and, therefore, it seemed even more frightening. It gradually became clear that the committee was created to investigate current trends in Russian literature, particularly in journals, and to develop means to control it in the future. People were gripped by a panicky fear. Rumors spread that the committee was particularly busy ferreting out and interpreting the pernicious ideas of communism, socialism, and all kinds of liberalism and that it was devising cruel punishments for people who espoused such ideas in print or with whose knowledge they had reached the public. As usual, *Notes of the Fatherland* and the *Contemporary* were regarded as the chief culprits in the dissemination of these ideas. The minister of education was not invited to the meeting of this committee; explanations were not demanded of anyone; no one was informed of the charges against them, while the charges were extremely serious. Terror gripped everyone who thought or wrote. Secret denunciations and spying complicated the situation even more. People began to fear for each day of their existence, thinking that it might be their last among their loved ones and friends.[1]

[z] Nikitenko henceforth refers to this committee as the Buturlin Committee, the Committee of April 2nd, or the secret committee. (See endnote 1 for 1848 for details of this committee.)

22 August. I have written nothing in my diary for four months, but, during this period, I, too, could very easily have reached the end of my days. From the very beginning of June, cholera began to rage in St. Petersburg, and, by the middle of July, some 15,000 people had died. During this time everyone stood, so to say, face to face with death. It spared no one, the lower classes in particular. The slightest carelessness with food, the slightest cold, was enough to kill a person in a matter of four or five hours.

Terror reigned everywhere during the entire summer. There were almost no deaths in the dachas near Lesnoy Korpus, but, nevertheless, everyone was distraught and tense. The news coming from the city each day was sad, especially from mid-June to the end of July.

27 October. Cholera continues to reap victims which it overlooked during its great harvest. Recently, it has spread among the upper and middle classes. People continue to be as cautious as they had been during the summer. Fruits, smoked and pickled foods, and kvass[a] are avoided.

1 December. What a fantastic place is our Russian land! For 150 years we feigned a yearning for education. It seems this was all sham and pretense, for we are bolting backwards faster than we have ever gone forward. An amazing, fantastic land! When Buturlin proposed closing the universities, many considered this impossible. Simpletons! They had forgotten that one couldn't close what never was really opened. Now, for example, that very same Buturlin is serving as chairman of some higher censorship organ (not the Chief Censorship Committee), and he operates in such a way that it is becoming utterly impossible to write or publish anything at all. Here's a recent example. Dal was forbidden to write. What? Yes, Dal, that intelligent, good, noble Dal! Could he, too, have become a communist or socialist? Two of his stories were published in the *Muscovite.* One is the story of a gypsy-thief in hiding who cannot be found even with the help of local authorities. Buturlin asked the minister of internal affairs if its author wasn't the same Dal who was serving in his ministry? Perovsky summoned Dal to his office and reprimanded him for spending his time composing literature rather than office documents, and, in conclusion, told him to choose between writing or serving.

But that wasn't the end of it. Buturlin presented this matter to the emperor in the following form: Although Dal's story does inspire the public with distrust of the authorities, this was evidently not his intent, and since his work is generally harmless, then he, Buturlin, would suggest a reproof for the author and a reprimand for the censor. A resolution followed: "to reprimand the author as well, in view of the fact that he, too, is a civil servant."

Count Uvarov had removed Count Stroganov as superintendent of Moscow University. Stroganov took his revenge on him in March by presenting a note to the emperor about the liberalism (communism and socialism) prevailing in the censorship department and in the entire ministry of education, so that

---

[a] A drink made from rye bread and malt.

Count Uvarov barely managed to hold on to his own post. In September he went to Moscow. The Moscow Society of History and Antiquities, chaired by S.G. Stroganov, was working at the time on the publication of a translation of Fletcher's memoirs.[b] Publication was undertaken on the basis of an article in the censorship code which permits the uncensored publication of anything written about pre-Romanov Russia.

Count Stroganov personally passed Fletcher's notes in which Ivan IV, Fyodor, and various church rituals were described disparagingly. However, a similar description had been published a long time ago in Behr's notes.[c] Shevyrev, who once courted Stroganov, told the minister that this was the wrong time to publish Fletcher and that Stroganov was acting improperly by allowing it. He supported his recommendation with assurances of his own devotion and loyalty to God and the tsar, as we always do in holy Russia.

Uvarov ordered the printing to be halted and brought it to the attention of the emperor. An order followed: Count Stroganov was to be given a most severe reprimand via the Moscow governor-general.

The point I want to make here is that it's all a matter of "tit for tat." Stroganov, to use an expression of Gogol's, "played a dirty trick" on Uvarov, and Uvarov on Stroganov. This is in the very nature of things in holy Russia, where such incidents involving government officials only demonstrate the deep, pervasive immorality to which everyone is accustomed here. But why did Fletcher's book, so useful for our study of history, have to perish? Why did the secretary of the Society, Bodyansky, who was expelled to Kazan, have to suffer for it? Why was the Society, which has contributed so much to science, paralyzed?

In our circle, that is, in the scientific and academic world, here's how people are judged. If you lack talent and do your job badly, you are fired for incompetence. If you are talented and do your job well, you are fired because you are an able person and therefore dangerous. What is one to do? Be a little of each: slightly stupid and slightly intelligent. In the middle ages people were burned at the stake for their ideas and opinions, but at least everyone knew what he could and couldn't do. But now we are confronted with the kind of idiocy the world has never witnessed. There's your Russian erudition for you.

The minister ordered the deans to keep a watchful eye on instruction at the university, especially in political and jurisprudence courses. The university community is frightened and depressed.

2 December. Events in the West have caused a terrible panic in the Sandwich Islands.[d] Barbarism is celebrating its savage victory over the human mind,

---

[b] Giles-Fletcher—English poet, ambassador to Russia in 1588.

[c] Behr, a German merchant, left notes on his journey to Moscow at the turn of the sixteenth century.

[d] Nikitenko's reference to the Sandwich Islands is a camouflage for his personal thoughts on Russia's internal situation.

which was just beginning to think, and over education, which was just beginning to come into its own.

But the bastions of education and thought were still so weak that they were unable to stand up against the very first puff from the winds of barbarism. And those who were inclined to consider thought a human virtue and a necessity reverted once again to nonsense and to the belief that only what is ordered from above can be good. The arbitrariness displayed by the authorities is at its zenith; it has never been considered so thoroughly legitimate as it is today.

Events in the West and Western ideas about a better order of things are used as a pretext to avoid all thought about improving things here. Therefore, any inclination to think, any noble impulse, modest as it may be, is maligned, destined to be persecuted, and doomed to perish. And the ease with which these ideas and impulses perish clearly indicates they are not original, are always borrowed, and that nothing original of this sort ever did exist here.

The emancipation issue nearly came up. The gentlemen became frightened and are now using the present state of affairs in the West to label any movement in this direction as disastrous for the nation.

Science is growing feeble and is in hiding. Ignorance is achieving status in the system. A little more of this sort of thing and everything accomplished by Peter and Catherine in the course of 150 years will be cast down and trampled upon . . . And now simple-hearted folk are sighing: "Well, you can see that science is really a German affair and none of our business."

5 December. German affairs are deteriorating in the West, too. The rebellion has come to naught. Physical force came to the rescue of the jolted authorities and gained the upper hand in Paris, Vienna, Frankfurt and Berlin.

15 December. The newly invested Catholic Bishop Borovsky told me about his audience with the emperor. Golovinsky and other bishops were presented together with him. The emperor said to Golovinsky:

"Wasn't I right when I told you a year and a half ago that there would be rebellion in Europe?"

Golovinsky replied: "As soon as I heard about these disturbances I recalled the exalted words of Your Majesty and was amazed at their prophetic significance."

"But it will get even worse," remarked the emperor. "All this is due to godlessness, and, therefore, I hope that you, gentlemen, as pastors, will make every effort to strengthen religion in the hearts of our people. As far as I am concerned," he added, making a sweeping gesture, "I will not permit godlessness to be disseminated in Russia, for it will surely reach us from the West."

20 December. What is fashionable now is the patriotism that rejects everything European, including science and art, and assures us that Russia is so blessed by God that it can thrive on Orthodoxy alone, without science and art. Patriots of this type have no understanding of history and think that the presence of physics, chemistry, astronomy, poetry, painting, etc., in the world is responsible for France having proclaimed herself a republic and for Germany's revolt. They really don't know what Orthodox Byzantium reeked of, although its science and art were in a dreadful state of decay. Everything indicates that the work of Peter the Great has no fewer enemies today than it did during the raskolniki and streltsi[e] rebellions. However, in those days they did not dare crawl out of their dark holes where the government, by encouraging the Enlightenment, had driven them. But now, having heard that the Enlightenment was freezing up, growing torpid and decaying, all these secret, underground swamp reptiles have crawled out again.

27 December. Some scoundrel by the name of Aristov, a Ryazan landowner, having run through his fortune, came to St. Petersburg to wind up his affairs. After he had taken care of everything, he devised an amazing scheme to replenish his depleted purse. He appeared at the Third Section and announced that he knew of the existence of a conspiracy against the government, all of whose participants he would expose and hand over, if they would provide him with the means to do it, that is, with money. Dubbelt, they say, didn't believe this, but the others not only believed it, but were frightened. The informer was paid. He began to give banquets in taverns and, immediately after wining and dining his guests, would turn them over, as conspirators, to gendarmes in disguise. About seventy people were seized in this manner. A certain Lavrov, nephew of a department director who knew Dubbelt very well, turned out to be one of them. He appeared before Dubbelt and explained that his nephew was the most innocent of creatures, who had never read anything liberal, was not a person given to serious thinking, was not only completely incapable of conspiracy, but of carrying on an ordinary conversation. But this still didn't untangle the affair, which could have continued and, perhaps, have ended badly for many. Fortunately, this very same director received a letter from some friend in Ryazan, asking him to make arrangements for the extradition from St. Petersburg of one Aristov, a known swindler, petty thief, and card sharp, who had filled the whole province with his adventures and debts. This letter was presented to the Third Section, and thus the comedy which this scoundrel had staged in order to have a spree on fraudulently obtained money was finally exposed. In the end, he himself confessed to everything. Of course, all the innocent people who were arrested were released and this fine fellow was sent off to a convict labor gang.

[e] Russian sharpshooters, the bodyguards of the Russian tsars until the reign of Peter the Great. In 1698, following desertions, revolts and petitions, they were executed wholesale by Peter the Great.

1849

30 January. I have been offered a new post. It's in the ministry of finance, with the department of foreign trade, where they appear to need someone to edit the emperor's most important notes, etc.

Of course I certainly welcome this offer as I have suffered enormous financial losses by resigning my position as censor and my editorial post on the *Contemporary.*[1]

12 February. An unusually interesting article by Professor Soloviev of Moscow University appeared in the *Contemporary.* Not a single one of our historians has yet presented such a thorough and deep analysis as has this scholar. He has shown great promise as a student of our history, which until now has lacked this sort of critical approach. But here is what happened. The "Secret" censorship committee, or rather, the Buturlin committee, felt that Soloviev's articles, though well-meaning and harmless, ought not to have discussed Bolotnikov!![f]—especially in a journal. A reprimand was ordered for the censor.

I dropped in at a meeting of the Censorship Committee. Fantastic things are going on there. For example, censor Mekhelin is expurgating from ancient history the names of all great people who fought for the freedom of their country or were of a republican turn of mind in the republics of Greece and Rome. The discussions aren't being expurgated, but simply the names and facts in them. This intimidation of the censors was inspired by Buturlin and his crew, that is, by Korf and Degai.

What the devil is going on here? A Christian crusade against knowledge? These people are blind; they don't see that by keeping learned ideas from being advanced through the printed word, they are forcing them to be transmitted by word of mouth. And this is far more dangerous, for bitterness born of irritation and indignation is unconsciously added in speech, while, in the press, it is restrained by censorship and decorum. It is time, it seems, to change this petty policy of threats and oppression to a policy of guidance. But for this, something other than a Buturlin mentality is needed. Indeed, in this instance, discontent is not being provoked in some scribbling youngsters or magazine pen-pushers, but in established writers who have talent and reputations, people of a serious turn of mind who have already had some influence on the public and have made important contributions to our education and language. At least we ought to distinguish one kind of writer from another, and if we are going to curb some when they lie, then at least let's encourage the others. But here, everyone is lumped together indiscriminately: you are all dangerous people simply because you think and publish your thoughts.

No wonder we can't think straight. The younger generation, unable to find a noble outlet for its aspirations, moves away from science and the arts, con-

[f] Leader of a peasant uprising at the beginning of the seventeenth century.

fuses all the basic concepts of life and the purpose of man and society. There is nothing to hold on to in our society; we stagger about like madmen or drunkards. Only thieves and swindlers are vigorous and sober. They alone maintain presence of mind and clearly see the purpose of their lives—in money grubbing. Abuses are committed openly and brazenly everywhere, and those committing them are unafraid of punishment which some powerful hand, rather than the law itself, might chance to mete out to them. Immorality is spreading rapidly and, like cholera, infects even people who are simple and not without a sense of honor, but who cannot find security in honest convictions and deeds. Our superintendent, Musin-Pushkin, was appointed to the Senate. Several days ago he told me that when he reads the Senate records, he is appalled at the chaos and abuses rampant in civil and criminal cases. He is still a novice in this sphere and therefore is shocked by this corrupt atmosphere.

8 March. There is a fellow by the name of Samarin, a young and wealthy aristocrat, a well-educated man with remarkable talents. This Samarin is now imprisoned in the fortress. He served in Riga with the local governor-general, Prince Suvorov. Samarin took it into his head to describe the Ostsee Germans and their administration in the form of letters to friends. Both Suvorov and the Germans were strongly taken to task by the author. He has a Slavophile point of view. These letters, assembled in a notebook, were passed from hand to hand here and in Moscow. Initially, Suvorov complained to Perovsky, and when the latter received his complaint indifferently, he complained to the emperor himself. As a result the author was imprisoned in the fortress.

21 March. Samarin was not only released from the fortress, but under conditions rather complimentary to him. The emperor summoned him directly from the fortress to the palace. Thus he appeared in the palace just as he was—unshaven, and certainly not in Court dress. The emperor greeted him as follows:

"Have you considered your position, young man, and the meaning of your action? You've certainly had enough time for that."

"If, by my action, I had the misfortune to offend Your Majesty unintentionally," replied Samarin, "then I beg you mercifully to forgive me."

"Well, our accounts are settled now," said the emperor, who embraced him, kissed him and then added: "Don't worry about your father; he's all right. Sit down."

At a second invitation, Samarin sat down.

"Now we'll have a chat. Do you realize what the fifth chapter of your work could have caused? Another December 14th."

Samarin recoiled in horror.

"Hold your tongue! I know this was not your intention. But you exposed the people to a dangerous idea by saying that Russian tsars since the time of Peter the Great acted only on the counsel of the Germans and under their influence. If such an idea were to spread among our people, it could have terrible consequences."

In Moscow there was a lot of talk about Samarin's arrest because he belongs to one of the most well-known Russian families and is related to many noble houses. Now, I.S. Aksakov, instead of Samarin, is imprisoned in the fortress. He is the brother of the famous Slavophile who strolls about Moscow sporting a beard and wearing an old-fashioned Russian okhaben and murmolka.[g]

26 March. Aksakov has been released, too. However, he wasn't in the fortress. He was only held for three days at the Third Section. They wanted to ascertain his way of thinking and interrogated him with this in mind, and he gave written answers. They say the emperor reacted to his replies very favorably. Aksakov belongs to a circle of those Slavophiles who stir up national spirit from its very depths and cling to patterns of olden days. Their dislike for the Germans is nothing more than an expression of the idea that it is high time we made something of ourselves. This idea goes much deeper than it would appear to a lot of people. Such a bloc of Slavophiles must be strong, for it actually leans on the people. In open opposition to them is a Western-oriented bloc, post-Petrine champions who base themselves on ideas common to all mankind, on the ideas of science and art. But, within both camps are shades which reflect extremes. The main thing is that both camps are beginning to have a definite and distinct impact on the scene.

29 March. I attended an examination at the Mariinsky Institute. Grand Duchess Elena Pavlovna was present. She was very gracious and warm to everyone. She asked me if I were satisfied with the girls' responses to the examiner's questions, and she expressed the hope that they would not merely repeat what they had memorized from their textbooks, but would give some thought to what they were saying. "And I," she remarked afterwards, "well, you can hear how badly I speak Russian. But he's the one to blame for it." Smiling, she pointed to Pletnyov.

Here, by the way, is something interesting she said during the examination. One girl had to talk on conditions in Russia before Peter the Great, and, of course, she had to discuss ignorance and barbaric ways, and so on. At a sign from the teacher the pupil began to hesitate and became more selective in her language. The grand duchess noticed this and said: "Come now, speak freely. You should express yourself with Russian feeling, but you must speak the truth about Russia."

The questions which she herself asked, as well as her comments on the girls' replies, were very intelligent. She is obviously a well-educated woman. Upon leaving she came up to me and said with a warm smile: "Thank you for the patience you have shown today in staying with us for so many hours."

Indeed, the exam lasted from one till six. But because of the grand duchess's relaxed attitude and warmth no one felt especially fatigued when it was over.

[g] Peasant cloak and fur or velvet cap.

1 April. Cholera is on the rise again. Every day about fifty people fall ill, and about thirty die. Almost all of March was cold, but the days were clear. Suddenly a thaw began; the streets are now clogged with mud and piles of broken ice. People are breathing foul vapors, and mortality from infection has increased proportionately.

3 April. An article in defense of the university appeared in the last issue of the *Contemporary.* It made a strong impression on sensible people and on those who value learning. Davydov wrote it. The minister revised and expanded it, and finally gave permission for its publication. Displeasure was expressed over the article and an order was issued stating that, henceforth, nothing was to be printed about academic institutions without special permission from higher authorities.

4 April. I presented myself to the new minister; saw a lot of people, including Dondukov and Davydov. The Buturlin committee posed the following question to the minister: "On what grounds did you permit the publication of the article about the universities?" The minister replied that the article was written on his order, in his office, and printed on his order also. He considered and still considers the article necessary in order to reassure teachers and students in the universities and gymnasiums, as well as all those seriously disturbed by rumors concerning the closing of the universities. These rumors upset everyone connected with educational affairs.

The article achieved its purpose. With its appearance in the press, everyone calmed down.

It is forbidden to print anything not only about academic institutions, but also about any kind of government institution, measure or order. This means that national statistical data will not be available.

16 April. Ivan III unified in a mechanical way what had merely been separated mechanically. The Tver, Ryazan, and Novgorod principalities were populated by Russians who were linked by an inner unity of spirit, their way of life, and religious beliefs. It was only necessary to push aside the princes for the separate parts to grow together by themselves. Would that work today? Can the Germans, Poles, Moslems and others be united with Russia in a mechanical way? They can be kept side by side, but it isn't possible to blend them into one indivisible, spiritual whole. They should feel content in their cohabitation with Russia, for they do have one thing in common under these conditions: their unity of interests.

But such notions are mere baseless dreams. If one takes a closer look at things, one can't help noticing that Providence does a better job of managing things, after all, than we often think it does. The main thing is that we must honestly believe in something better, which is being created by Providence, and not by us. It is this thought that buoys me amidst troubled opinions and doubts and gives me the quiet strength to fulfill my obligations to society.

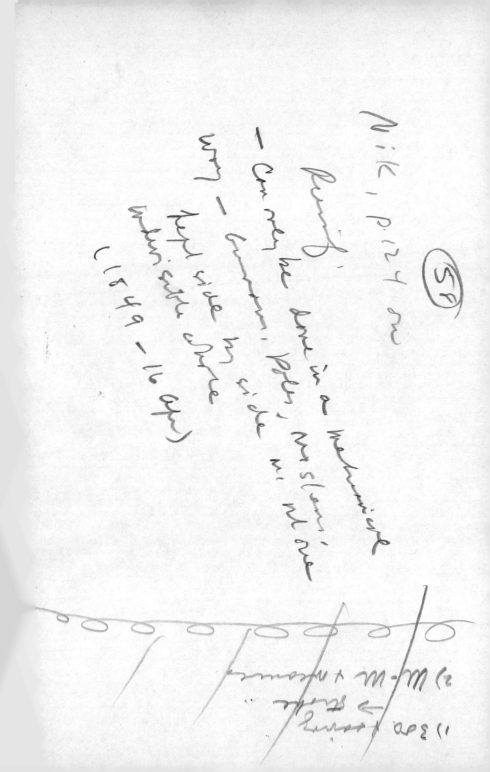

Nik, p.124 on

Rivolog'

— Can only be done in a mechanistic
way — Contain, polar, non-slavic
fiptd side by side in at one
within ciable whole

((1849 — 16 Ap))

(5 F)

1850

6 February. Minister of Education Shirinsky-Shikhmatov confirmed my appointment today as a full professor of Russian literature on the recommendation of the University Council.

12 February. Avraam Sergeevich Norov was appointed deputy minister of education. I went to see him today and he was very pleased to see me. I was welcomed with open arms, assurances of enduring friendship and trust, and entreaties to be his assistant.

16 March. Philosophy is being hounded again. There is a proposal to limit the instruction of philosophy in the university to logic and psychology by putting clergymen in charge of both of them. The proponents of this change cite the Scottish school. Bludov, we hear, insists that the history of philosophy should also be included in the curriculum. The minister doesn't agree. Fischer (currently professor of philosophy) came to see me and repeated his conversation with the minister. The minister bases his argument mainly on the reasoning that "the usefulness of philosophy has not been proven, but the possibility of its being harmful is a fact."

18 March. I visited the Censorship Committee to inquire about new literary works. There were no books, nor were there even manuscripts which promised books. Meanwhile we received a confidential memorandum from the minister regarding an inquiry by the Supreme Censorship Committee, or, as it is called, the "secret" committee, which contained the following: "A book on fortune-telling has been published. The Censorship Committee is requested to submit a report identifying the author of this book and stating why the author thinks stars have an influence on people's fortunes." The Committee replied that "some bookseller had published it in a new edition (probably the hundredth) and that the Committee had no idea why the author thought stars had an influence on people's fortunes."

Adjutant-General Nikolai Nikolaevich Annenkov now chairs the "secret" censorship committee instead of Buturlin.

It appears that our literary output certainly has been very modest of late, so modest that educated people, who had barely begun to read literature in Russian, are compelled to turn to foreign books again, to French in particular. Annenkov, however, found sixteen incriminatory points in certain books and journal articles in his case against French literature. Naturally, all of these were out of context, and he prepared a report on it. Korf managed to prove the absurdity of these petty objections, but was forced to concede two points. Korf told his brother that the activities of the "secret" committee were sickening and that he would have left it long ago but for the hope of occasionally being of some use to those being persecuted by it. I went to see the superintendent today, and he told me many strange and utterly fantastic things about the committee's activities.

22 March. A new censorship section was created for textbooks and all books related to learning and educational matters. It is a committee consisting of the directors of local gymnasiums and the inspector of government schools, and it is chaired by the director of the Pedagogical Institute. Here are the censorship sections we now have: a general one in the ministry of education, a Chief Censorship Administration, a supreme "secret" committee, an ecclesiastical section, a military section, a censorship section in the ministry of foreign affairs, a theatrical one in the ministry of the imperial court, a newspaper section in the Post Office Department, a censorship unit in the Third Section of His Majesty's Private Chancery, and now a new one—the pedagogical. In all there are ten censorship departments. If you add up all the people in charge of censorship, the total will exceed the number of books published in a single year.

I'm mistaken: there are still others. There is also a section for works on jurisprudence in the Second Section of His Majesty's Private Chancery, and there's the foreign book section—which makes twelve in all.

24 April. The Easter holidays are here; lots of noise, crowds, hustle and bustle. I went to matins at the Theatrical School's church. The singing was awful, and they whisked through the service so fast that I was home by two o'clock. The minister was on hand today to receive holiday greetings. Many people came, or rather, creatures whom we call people. It was amusing to see them embracing and kissing each other like brothers. It was evident that the minister still hadn't adjusted to his new position. He also joined in the Easter kissing ritual in true Christian fashion.

17 December. A new decree on civil servants. A superior has the right to fire a subordinate for being untrustworthy or "for offenses which cannot be proven" without giving him an explanation for his removal. And if the employee should want to clear himself, "there is nowhere he can submit his case."

Thus a significant number of government employees have been deprived of the protection of the law by a single stroke of the pen. Meanwhile, the civil servant who has committed a real, clear-cut crime and is tried in a criminal court, has the right to clear himself before such a court. I read the entire decree and didn't know what surprised me more, its lack of simple justice or its lack of common sense. It is interesting, incidentally, that the possibility of administrators abusing their authority was foreseen in this decree; and yet nothing was done to limit their right of arbitrary decision over a person's fate!

There are no entries for 1851. Apparently the notebooks for that year were lost.

1852

6 January. Count D.A. Tolstoy and I spent the evening at the home of the charming Madame Opochinina, neé Skobeleva. Her late brother's wife was also there, the former Poltavtseva, not as charming as our hostess, but evidently a very clever woman. In general, both women do read (even in Russian),[h] are interested in ideas, poetry and art; and they conversed about subjects which are rarely discussed in our salons. They talked about the pettiness and emptiness of high society life and the stereotyped behavior of the present generation of aristocrats; about the deplorable necessity, however, to conform; about the charm of life abroad; and about nature . . . Opochinina was particularly delighted with Naples. During the evening, Maikov's *Choice of Death* and my article about Countess Rostopchina were read. The reading was accompanied by lively discussion and often by astute comments from both ladies. Thus, the evening flew by and I returned home after 2 A.M.

11 January. Count Uvarov told me several days ago about his battle with the censorship department during the printing of his book, *On Greek Antiquities Discovered in Southern Russia,* which was recently published. He had to translate several Greek inscriptions into Russian. The censor came across the word *demos,* meaning people; he would simply not permit this translation and replaced it with *citizens.* The author had a hard time convincing him that this would not be a translation but a distortion of the original. Nor would the censor permit mention of the fact that Roman emperors had been assassinated and ordered the word *perished* substituted, and so on.

24 February. Today I received the news of Gogol's death. I was in the hall of the Dvoryanskoe Sobranie,[i] at the drawing of the lottery to aid the Society for the Visitation of the Poor. There I met Panaev, and he was the first to tell me this most distressing news. Then Turgenev, who had received letters from Moscow, told me several details. They are quite strange. Gogol was very disturbed by the death of Khomyakov's wife. About three weeks before his own demise, he awoke one night, ordered his servant to light the stove, and burnt all his papers. The following day he told his friends that the devil had given him the idea of burning some papers, and then egged him on so, that he burned them all. Several days later he fell ill. A doctor prescribed medicines for him, but he refused all manner of medicines, saying that he had unquestionably to submit himself to the Lord's will, which obviously was content to have Gogol end his life. He wouldn't even listen to Filaret, who called his refusal to take

[h] The nobility generally read French.
[i] Nobles' Assembly.

medicine a sin, suicide. Obviously, Gogol was under the influence of a mystical mental disturbance which had inspired those "Letters" several years ago, that had caused such a furor.

In any case, this is another sad loss for our intellectual life—and a very great loss! Gogol awakened in our society many ideas about itself. He doubtless provided some of the strongest props for the party of action, light and thought, for the party of post-Petrine Russia. The destruction of his papers only adds further to our grief.

The minds of our age are in some kind of unnatural, feverish state. The man who possesses exceptional mental abilities inevitably rushes into some kind of extremism. He does not pursue his idea with the persistence of a stubborn will which is rationally conscious of itself, but feverishly seizes this idea as if afraid to let it, along with the blessings it promises, slip from his grasp. There is a certain lack of intellectual maturity, of a clear, chaste outlook on life and man. There is a certain lack of simplicity and spontaneous courage in these impulsive strivings for intellectual distinction. Others see in this a restlessness of powerful spiritual forces which toss and turn so, because they feel hemmed in. It seems to me that this represents a defect in a spiritual force that cannot control itself. Life is always crowded for the spirit, everywhere, but the latter must rise above life. Only a man of great character can accommodate himself to any sphere.

Society must renew itself with fresh and clear beliefs, or vice will devour it. The support of these beliefs must be found in man himself.

25 February. At the Dvoryanskoe Sobranie I met Annenkov, publisher of Pushkin's works. The emperor has permitted their publication without any changes. But any new works which may be discovered among the poet's papers must undergo regular censorship examination. Annenkov says there are many new works. Of course it will be difficult to include them in the forthcoming edition. Annenkov paid Pushkin's widow 5,000 silver rubles for everything, including the right to publish 5,000 copies. A profitable deal!

26 February. No! It was not religious feeling that inspired Gogol's behavior. Religious feeling revives and saves, but doesn't tear the soul apart and destroy it. For Gogol it was either mental illness or simply the distraught state of a weak soul unable to cope with the grandeur of the ideas coming to it and collapsing beneath the burden of its half-formed beliefs and half-formed convictions . . .

17 April. Turgenev, author of *The Hunting Sketches,* was *jailed* yesterday on imperial orders for his article about Gogol in the *Moscow Bulletin,* in which he called Gogol *great.* The order called for Turgenev to be held in the local police station for a month and then to be exiled from the capital to the country under police surveillance.

I just met Yazykov who told me that he had visited Turgenev. He is imprisoned in a real jail, but is well and calm. "I am calm," he told Yazykov, "because I am not tortured by suspense. I was told exactly what to expect, so I no longer fear that I shall be tortured."

They wanted to use the example of Turgenev, of course, to give the literary profession a bad name, but besides being a man of letters he is also a pureblooded Russian nobleman, and the humiliating punishment to which he was subjected will scarcely produce the kind of impression on the public that they counted on. Both the nobility and all educated people were insulted in the person of Turgenev.

Such measures never prevent the spread of ideas. Moreover, one such measure is more dangerous than ten published liberal articles. It is wrongly assumed that only what is printed can be evil; what people think can be evil, too.

18 April. The misfortune that has befallen Turgenev has had a terrible, depressing effect on me. I can scarcely recall anything that has moved and upset me so much. I do realize that there is still nothing extraordinary about his case, that Turgenev is still not a martyr for the truth, and that by calling Gogol "great" he is essentially suffering not for an idea, but for a rhetorical figure of speech. But this only makes me feel all the more keenly the defenseless position of thought these days.

20 April. An order was issued to place Pogodin under police surveillance for his article in the *Muscovite* on Kukolnik's play *The Orderly,* and also for having printed the no. 5 issue of his journal with a black mourning border on the occasion of Gogol's death. Meanwhile, Bulgarin, in his *Bee,* strikes them when they're down—Gogol, Turgenev and Pogodin. Bulgarin's last article in a Sunday feuilleton aroused universal disgust. There wasn't a line in it without a police denunciation.

Turgenev wasn't even told why he was jailed. He learned about it only from friends visiting him. Incidentally, A.N. Karamzin visited him on Saturday. Turgenev is well, in good spirits, and even cheerful. He has great praise for the courteous, even deferential treatment accorded him by the police. The district police officer simply amazed him with his humanity. He transferred him from the thieves' jail to a clean, bright, spacious chamber.

The arrest of Turgenev has produced the most painful impression on everyone. Even if he were considered guilty, his guilt would be completely drowned in the disproportionate treatment meted out to him. The police order to arrest Turgenev did not cite his article as the reason, but rather the circumstances under which it was published. This article had been written for the *St. Petersburg Bulletin* and was submitted by its editor to the censor. The chairman of the Censorship Committee had stated earlier that he would not pass articles praising Gogol, "a lackey writer." He did ban the article submitted to him by the editor of the *St. Petersburg Bulletin,* but without issuing any formal statement; therefore, this ban certainly could not have been considered official. Turgenev, feeling this was merely caprice on the part of the chairman, sent his article on to Moscow, where it was published. The arrest order stated that "despite the ban on his article issued to the landowner Turgenev, he dared to . . . " etc. But a formal statement of this kind was never issued to him. No explanation was demanded of Turgenev; no one interrogated him; yet he was immediately subjected to punishment. They say that Bulgarin, with his influence on the chairman of the Censorship Committee and his suggestions to him, was more to blame than anyone else in this shameful affair.

22 April. It is now known that the cause of all this trouble was Musin-Pushkin's denunciation, which was inspired by Bulgarin. It is indeed a sad state of affairs when, innocent of any criminal intent and equipped with a clear conscience, you feel yourself in constant danger of perishing for no reason at all as a result of some secret denunciation, slander, some misunderstanding and haste, someone's miserable frame of mind, or because of a false interpretation of your words and deeds. And you are subjected to this only because nature has endowed you with some intellectual powers and society has acknowledged their presence in you. What principles can you call upon for help? Where can you turn for support? There is but one alternative—to completely scorn this stupid nonsense, this contemporary life, while consoling yourself (if you can) with faith in a brighter future, which, alas! even our own grandchildren will scarcely live to see. It would be better for you, crippled and tormented, to renounce at once all rights to life and work—in the name of . . . In the name of what, I ask, O Lord?

26 April. So many friends visited Turgenev in jail that a ban was finally imposed on visitors.

28 April. A commotion in Moscow again. An anthology was published there by Khomyakov, Kireevsky and Aksakov which is said to contain some very powerful words. I managed to read only the article about Gogol, in whose behalf they evidently want to raise a banner. They call Gogol "the great satirist-Christian." His path through life was a sad one because he was doomed to tread it through the kind of society portrayed in his *Dead Souls,* and so forth. Khomyakov's poetry is even more powerful. People are already talking a great deal about the collection. Dark clouds are gathering for the storm. And who is to blame?

10 May. Pogodin visited me this morning. I hadn't seen him for about twelve years, if not more. He hasn't changed in the least, has the same simple face, the same heavy, bearish ways, and coarse manner. But he is a very intelligent man and deserves our full respect for his many labors in behalf of the advancement of knowledge. I was delighted by his visit. We chatted about these bitter times, about the turmoil in people's minds, about Gogol, Turgenev, and the *Moscow Anthology,* now in danger. Pogodin asked the minister for permission to place a black mourning border in the *Muscovite* around the news of Zhukovsky's death. The minister granted it.

12 May. The Third Section and the secret censorship committee have already sounded the alarm on account of the *Moscow Anthology.* The deputy minister told me about it today. He said that the minister had already severely reprimanded the censor, Prince Lvov. I advised him to inform the secret committee of this reprimand: hopefully, it would consider it sufficient.

27 November. I went to see censor Freigang yesterday with my article about Zhukovsky. He noticed one sentence, or rather, two words, that he felt should be changed: "intellectual ferment." I heard fantastic things from Freigang about censorship; about how Elagin will not pass the expression used in physics, "forces of nature;" about the spying of various lackeys; about the thousands of restrictions to which everyone who has dealings with censorship is subjected. In my time, Freigang was considered one of the most suspicious censors, and now he is known as the most indulgent.

22 December. I completed my business with Freigang. He passed my entire article except for several passages which I had to change. I had no choice in the matter. I hardly protested, realizing that the system followed by the most reasonable censors, like Freigang, allowed no alternative. The others aren't worth discussing. They don't follow any system, and their decisions are guided only by fear. The system of the first type of censor, like Freigang, consists of guessing how the enemies of literature and education will interpret a given article. Freigang frankly admitted this to me. So one can imagine what the conclusions of such censors must be like, censors who are guided by this kind of guesswork rather than by the real sense of an article, by directives, or their own personal convictions. It means that everything depends on the interpretation of ignoramuses and malevolent individuals who are ready to see a crime in every idea.

1853

8 January. The holidays are over. Lectures again at the university. Pletnyov greeted me with effusive thanks for my article about Zhukovsky, which he had already read in the first issue of *Notes of the Fatherland.*

"You got right to the heart of it," he said to me, "and analyzed Zhukovsky superbly from every angle."

14 January. I went to see two ministers today: Minister of Internal Affairs Bibikov and Minister of Education Prince Shirinsky-Shikhmatov. I introduced myself to Bibikov for the first time. The conversation naturally focussed on the Roman Catholic Academy. I had to explain to him in brief outline the rules I followed there: "Stay clear of politics and religion, and try, as far as possible, to inspire the students with love for our common Mother-Russia and with trust in her."

"So, you don't discuss geographical questions with them or the question of uniting the churches?" asked Bibikov.

"That has nothing to do with my subject," I replied. "I am only concerned with their national and spiritual sentiments."

"Are you satisfied with them?"

"Completely. I've been teaching there for ten years and can only speak well of them."

"Excellent. And how is their Russian?" the minister continued to probe.

"Very satisfactory. Of course they do make some grammatical errors, but I would rather they made slips of the tongue than slips of the heart. I concentrate mainly on getting them to like our language, our traditions, our way of life. They are very attentive at my lectures."

"Well, that's very good. Exactly as it should be and what the emperor wants."

9 February. I attended convocation at the university and then dined at Karamzin's. Unpublished chapters from Gogol's *Dead Souls* were read to us after dinner. The reading lasted exactly five hours, from seven to midnight. Those five hours were a real pleasure. Obolensky read, and very well, too.

10 February. In studying the life and works of the representatives of our intellectual activity from Karamzin to Gogol inclusive, one clearly sees two large layers. What reigns in one, so to speak, is the first spring breath of the spirit of truth and beauty. Receptive, noble, gently inclined souls felt the power of the great faiths of mankind over themselves and, happily, selflessly, surrendered to the initial impressions of this joyful encounter. Karamzin and Zhukovsky were like this. But in this *roseate* state there is still a narrow outlook on things. This is a state of adolescent inexperience which does not know evil. It is, if one can put it this way, a voluptuous attitude toward truth and beauty, and not an activity for men for whom life is not a game of beautiful feelings, but rather of action and conquest. But the better minds are gradually sobering up and ceasing to look at the world through the nearsighted spectacles of their own hearts, which see only what they want to see, that is, what will delight and pacify them. They begin to look more deeply into things and find that there is no room here for the Sybaritic luxury of feelings. The soul ails from mankind's abominations and sufferings. What is one to do? To sink into a poetic euphoria, fruitlessly to languish in tender sympathy for one's brothers, to console oneself with fruitless expectations of better things to come, but to leave unsolved the serious earthshaking problems of the urgent, material sufferings of man—in a word, to let the world go its own way, if only not to disturb the harmony of our inner life? No, a thousand times no! . . . And so, under the influence of a new Weltanschaung, a new layer formed in our literature. The connecting link here was Pushkin: he was dissatisfied, troubled, caustic, though still in a personal sense. In his wake came Lermontov, and then, suddenly, Gogol emerged . . .

20 February. Prince Dimitry Aleksandrovich Obolensky paid a visit and read Gogol's *Confession* to me. It is an extremely curious piece.

Prince Obolensky told me the following details about Gogol, whom he knew very well. He was in Moscow when Gogol died.

Gogol finished his *Dead Souls* abroad and burned it. Then he re-wrote it, and this time was satisfied. But in Moscow he was gripped by fits of religious frenzy, and while in this state, he became obsessed with the idea of burning this manuscript, too. One day, Count A.P. Tolstoy, with whom he was always close friends, visited him. Gogol said to him:

"Please, take these notebooks and hide them. I have moments when I feel like burning all of them. But I myself would regret it if I did. I think there is possibly something worthwhile here."

Count Tolstoy tactfully refused. He knew that Gogol was succumbing to gloomy thoughts about death, and he didn't want to give seeming confirmation to Gogol's hypochondriacal fears by fulfilling his request. About three days later the count visited Gogol again and found him in a depressed state.

"Well, you see," Gogol told him, "the Devil confused me after all: I burned *Dead Souls.*"

He said many times that some sort of vision would appear before him. About three days before his demise, he was convinced of his impending death.

Gogol's *Confession* is permeated by a religious mood that does not exclude, however, other feelings. This mood is both noble and humble. But toward the end, in Moscow, he had indulged in strange, religious excesses which were baffling. It was as if church formalism had crushed all genuine religious feeling in him. Could this be the usual psychological course of religious enthusiasm?

25 February. The actions of the censorship department are beyond belief. What do they want to achieve by this? Stop the process of thinking? It's like ordering a river to reverse its course. Here are the most recent examples of thousands of such instances. Censor Akhmatov halted the printing of an arithmetic textbook because a series of dots had been placed between the figures in some problem. He suspected the author of some sort of hidden design.

Censor Elagin would not approve a passage in an article on geography which stated that dogs were used for transportation in Siberia. He justified his action by saying that this information had to receive preliminary confirmation from the ministry of internal affairs.

Censor Peiker would not approve a meteorological table where the dates of the month were indicated by both the old and new systems according to the usually accepted formula:

$$\frac{\text{old style}}{\text{new style}}.$$

He demanded that the formula be reversed, with the words "new style" appearing above the line, and "old style" below.

The censors shift the blame for their absurd behavior on to the secret censorship committee, and they speak of it as an ogre who threatens to punish them for every printed word.

15 April. This evening I visited our deputy minister Norov, who is now in charge of the ministry. He talked about his difficult position and complained of his lack of friends. The department functionaries are mere chancery hacks. He touchingly recalled our old friendship and begged me to help him. We agreed that he would acquaint me with the most important matters for preliminary discussion and review. First on the agenda is an important matter: the Bludov proposal for university reforms. Abram Sergeevich asked me to prepare a memorandum on it.

5 May. Prince Platon Aleksandrovich Shirinsky-Shikhmatov died today. He was a good man who was just, simple and approachable. He was not noted for a brilliant mind or a gift for words as was his predecessor, Uvarov. His mind revolved around practical administrative matters, in which he acquired much knowledge and skill. He was not really a statesman (where are our statesmen anyway?)—and the ministerial post took him, so to say, unawares, unexpectedly. He himself realized his weakness in this respect. But it must be said that the job of running the ministry fell on his shoulders at a difficult time when, on the one hand, champions of pre-Petrine darkness rebelled against enlightenment and, on the other hand, a confused administration became flustered and didn't know which way to turn. The ministry was being undermined from all sides; it became a kind of dubious arm of state administration, and its representative, the minister, was more of a respondent in interrogations than a government official. Prince Shikhmatov wanted to execute his difficult mission honorably and conscientiously. In the documents I used to receive from his deputy (Norov) on various important matters, his noble efforts to defend enlightenment and to reject radical reform measures which might lead to its constraint, were always in evidence. But he lacked both the moral and civic courage to turn the wheel of his ship boldly into the wind, a ship buffeted on all sides by the stormy battle of the elements. He grew weak in this struggle, and one can say with certainty that it shortened his life. His illness and death were a result of overwork and grief. He didn't carry any weight in the eyes of his own subordinates. They regarded him with a certain contempt which was the natural consequence of his political impotence, but which neither his feelings nor his aims deserved. How much mud was slung at him! And the way it was done, both in public and in scholarly circles! Meanwhile, no one even suspected how painful this was for him.

Now, two ministers of education, he and Uvarov, have become victims of a storm which has swooped down on our educational system, weak and shaky as it is. Uvarov also endured much in his last days in office. When his position became precarious, much became clear to him, and many times I had occasion to be a witness to his grief. Then I, too, understood this man better and could appreciate his good qualities—his unmistakable intelligence, which, at the height of his power, was often obscured by vanity and petty pride. Unfortunately, he, too, like Shikhmatov, was not endowed with the strength needed for stormy and dangerous times. Rostovtsev was right in what he told me several days ago: "Not a single individual of depth and insight will agree to take on the job of minister of education at this time. It requires a tremendous amount of strength which no one in our country has."

Will Norov hold his ground? Or will he, too, become a victim? He has a noble heart and is well meaning, but will barely have sufficient strength. Although he insists he is prepared to sacrifice himself, that is, his official status, for the cause of education, will he have the courage to do this? Besides, he lacks that practical turn of mind and administrative skill which Shikhmatov certainly had, and he doesn't have any real assistants either. As long as he trusts me, I am ready, at his bidding, to assist him most conscientiously in any noble undertaking, in so far as my skill permits—and I gave him my word on that. But there are problems: in the first place, my position with him is not an official one; therefore many things can bypass me. Secondly, I cannot give up my other commitments for the sake of this work: I must also work to feed my family . . . Well, we won't cross our bridges until we come to them; rather, let us follow the dictates of our conscience.

8 May. In the evening Avraam Sergeevich Norov summoned me again. He complained even more strongly about his problems and said he was pinning all his hopes on me. Oh, Lord! How can staying power be expected of a man who doesn't rely primarily on himself and the strength of his own convictions? No matter how educated and humane he may be, he will be incapable of resisting the onslaught of hostile circumstances for long. . . .

2 June. I'm back in the city. It's sweltering. I spent yesterday evening work-ing on ministry business with Avraam Sergeevich. The memorandum on the Bludov committee's proposal was finally finished. The minister was pleased. He wanted only to tone down some strongly-worded passages. My basic idea, with which he also agreed, was that nothing should be changed, but only im-proved. There are times when the spirit of reform can only do harm when it touches deeply-rooted institutions whose usefulness has been proven by ex-perience. The idea of reforming the ministry of education grew out of the panicky fear aroused by events in Europe in 1848. At that time it became customary to blame everything on the ministry of education. The emperor received several proposals for its reform which were completely amateurish. Some of them were even remarkable for their amazing illiteracy.

When you delve into all these state and administrative matters you reach a sad conclusion: how badly we lack qualified administrators! Some ignoramus can set an utterly absurd idea going and rock the very foundations of many institutions with it, all the while shielded by his feigned devotion and zeal. You are struck everywhere by the instability of basic principles, by super-ficiality, impulsiveness, and inconsistency, by the inability to see salient and subtle relationships between things, which is necessary if you want to create a harmonious system which yields abundant results.

16 June. Niebuhr[j] takes the following position: "Great epidemics or scourges coincide with the epochs of decline of civilizations." I was taken by this thought. Our times appear to confirm it. Cholera and moral decay are going hand in hand before our very eyes, undermining our finest and greatest beliefs. We can even see that people with stronger moral fibre appear to have a greater resistance to disease and a greater capacity to conquer it.

27 September. I went to Pavlovsk to see Norov. Much discussion of ministry affairs. He asked me to prepare two memorandums: one about censorship in general, the other about the Davydov committee.[k] Perchance we shall succeed in curbing both of them.

16 October. Avraam Sergeevich sent the draft I had composed on our educa-tional system (our university in particular) to Yakov Ivanovich Rostovtsev, with a request for his opinion. The draft also serves as the ministry's reply to the Bludov Committee's proposals. Rostovtsev didn't suggest any changes.

20 October. War.[l] They say the Turks have crossed the Danube or occupied one of the islets that command the crossing. Rumor has it that our fleet suf-fered losses on the Danube.

[j] Barthold Georg Niebuhr, a German historian.

[k] Since 1850, I. I. Davydov had been chairman of the committee for the review of text-books in the ministry of education.

[l] The Crimean War.

21 October. I saw Gaevsky. Negotiations are in progress to transfer the editorship of the *Journal of the Ministry of Education* to me.

17 December. From 9 A.M. to 3:30, scarcely rising from my seat, I worked on an important memorandum to the emperor. It concerns the merging of the committee of April 2nd with the Chief Censorship Administration. This is a bold step. The committee is doing a great deal of harm. Avraam Sergeevich wants to show the memorandum first to Count Bludov, who is also very critical of the committee's activities.

30 December. Yesterday, at the grand annual meeting of the Academy of Sciences I was elected a corresponding member of the Russian language section. I was not present.

1854

14 February. There was a terrible snowstorm on Thursday. I walked to the university, because walking is so much healthier, cheaper, and pleasanter. I say pleasanter, because of all the wintertime delights Russian nature has to offer. I love a snow storm more than anything else, and in the summertime— a thunderstorm. As I crossed the Neva, the wind swept me off my feet, covering the path and my galoshes with snow. I paid for it with a cold. This is the third day I've been resting at home and taking medicine. I feel better today.

18 February. The director of the ministry chancery went to see the emperor on commencement day with a personal report. The emperor received him graciously and approved all our reports, including one proposing the establishment of a department of oriental languages at St. Petersburg University. The other report was very important for our literature. The emperor's permission was requested for the presentation of thrice-yearly reports to him on our best Russian works and translations. A brief outline of their contents and a notation on their merits would be included. Thus, the emperor would see that trash isn't the only commodity produced by our intelligentsia as the infamous April 2nd committee would have him believe with its constant complaints to him. The emperor received this proposal favorably, too.

12 March. I worked until 2 A.M. yesterday with the director of the ministry chancery. I think we've managed to eliminate one evil. I've been hammering away for a long time at the vile Davydov textbook review committee. Avraam Sergeevich fully agreed with me. With the idea in mind of eliminating this miserable creation of the late minister, it was decided to submit a report to the emperor calling for the revival of the Chief School Board, with which this committee would merge and vanish. I prepared the report yesterday. The director of the ministry chancery had also drawn up a proposal, but contrary to mine in spirit, and inclined toward continuing the committee. We clashed, but I managed to win. Amazing people—these chancery directors! No one expects them to be intelligent, shrewd or politically astute, but they can't even compose an intelligible document. Take, for example, the director of the ministry chancery, Actual State Councillor Berte. Anything of importance passing through his hands must be completely re-worked by either me or the minister himself. And with all that—the conceit, the arrogance! What contempt for knowledge and its representatives!

13 March. The emperor approved our proposal to merge the Davydov committee with the Chief School Board.

11 April. Easter. Avraam Sergeevich was confirmed as minister of education. I went to matins at the ministry church. Today is a holiday and it was not without pleasant surprises for me, too. It was finally acknowledged that it was not too soon to promote me to the rank of Actual State Councillor.[m] But the most pleasant news of all was that Avraam Sergeevich managed to get me a grant of 1,000 silver rubles. It came just in the nick of time, for two serious illnesses in the family left me utterly unable to make ends meet.

14 April. The minister received holiday greetings today in the department hall. My appearance there had a surprising effect. When I entered, a sea of faces turned my way so that I automatically turned around to see what important personage was following me. The *personage* turned out to be me. I was showered with congratulations, compliments, smiles, and handshakes. Evidently I had risen in everyone's eyes but my own. Tomorrow the wheel of fortune will turn again, and once more I shall be flattened and dwarfed to insignificance. But each day has its cares, so let us put aside worrying about tomorrow and go forth boldly today. The influence which is attributed to me now in regard to ministry affairs imposes a new responsibility on me, and no matter how fleeting this influence may be, I must extract every possible benefit from it for our educational system and for those struggling for its good.

9 May. I fully realize the precariousness of my position with the minister and, consequently, the shakiness of my dealings with him. I am afraid that most of our hopes will go up in smoke. I know his character. He is well-meaning, enlightened, humane, but weak. Woe to him and to our labors for the common good if he should fall into the unscrupulous hands of those who seek personal gain. They are already secretly planning to drive him into their arms! Then many mistakes will be made. That is why I have been trying and am still trying to protect him from harmful influences, to shield him, as it were, with my own body. It is a difficult and thankless role. One must be constantly on one's guard.

11 May. My family moved to the dacha, but I am remaining in the city a little longer. I am involved with exams, committees, and the like.

15 May. I'm now in the country, too. I've grown awfully sick of Lesnoy Korpus. Everything has changed—the woods have been destroyed, the fields taken up with kitchen gardens, the population has grown, taverns have multiplied—in a word, it has turned into a wretched little town.

17 June. I scarcely live in the country, but spend most of my time going to the city or Pavlovsk for meetings with the minister. Yesterday I went to Tsarskoye Selo to have a talk with the superintendent about the establishment of a department of oriental languages at our university. From there I

---

[m] Equivalent in rank to major-general.

went to Pavlovsk again, and in the evening I returned to the city with Avraam Sergeevich, where we continued to work far beyond midnight. I can scarcely find the time to even think about my own literary work. Meanwhile I want very much to do a biography of Galich, a task that has been begging my pen for ever so long.[n]

8 September. We moved from the country today. For me the most interesting event of the summer was my trip to Moscow. I went there July 19th and returned August 4th. There, my learned colleagues welcomed me with open arms: Katkov, Soloviev, Leontiev, Kudryavtsev and Drashusov. I spent several days at Katkov's in Petrovsky Park.

19 September. The struggle is on. Hopes for improvement in censorship are fading. I started to tell the minister today about its abuses and senselessness. But he displayed such indifference that I became annoyed and abruptly changed the subject. We'll postpone the attack until a more favorable moment.

During a discussion of current events the statement was made that we had no competent people on the highest levels of government and public activity. I remarked that this was true of our whole administrative system. They agreed with me. Indeed, our present epoch is represented by moral and intellectual nonentities. It's amusing that everyone is aware of this and yet the attitude is, "Very well, so be it." On our return trip from Moscow, Rostovtsev had strongly emphasized the fact that we had excellent resources but that we didn't have the administrators who could use them intelligently in their work. "Yes," he added, "this is our problem everywhere, in both civilian and military life."

25 September. Several folk songs of dubious moral content were published in the *Saratov Provincial Bulletin* as material, of course, for study of our national culture. The secret censorship committee, now headed by Korf, submitted a complaint to the emperor. Orders were issued to reprimand the governor; to hold the director of the gymnasium, who was responsible for censoring the newspaper, in the guardhouse for a month; and to ask the minister "if the director was deemed sufficiently trustworthy to be permitted to continue in his position." The minister himself wrote a very intelligent report in defense of the poor director, who was one of the best of our provincial directors. The report was sent out today.

A lady living in Moscow wanted to publish an anthology of fine articles, each of which had been contributed by various Moscow intellectuals whom she knew. Ex-minister Shirinsky-Shikhmatov had obtained an order classifying the anthology as a journal; therefore imperial permission had to be requested for the publication of this new collection. This decision followed: "There's enough being published as it is." Indeed, there are absolutely no books being published here and, with anthologies being banned, too, our literature is at a

[n] See footnote, p. 25.

complete standstill. There are only the journals, *Notes of the Fatherland,* the *Contemporary, Reader's Library,* the *Muscovite,* and the *Pantheon.* But even they, for the most part, publish rather miserable, dull material.

26 September. Thank God! The Saratov director who had passed the afore-mentioned folk songs was pardoned through the intercession of the minister. He was told to announce the one-month sentence and a pardon simultan-eously.

But, right on its heels followed new grief for our literature. A story, "The Dreamer," by Likhachev, was published in the Muscovite (in the June issue, I believe). There were three or four passages that it would have been better to omit in order to avoid trouble, but censors Pokhvistnev and Rzhevsky passed them. The minister ordered their dismissal. Despite my efforts to persuade him not to treat them so harshly, the minister stuck to his decision this time. Unfortunately this will provide a pretext for our local censors to exercise even less restraint in their imposition of bans.

30 September. As far back as the beginning of August, I had written and sub-mitted to the minister a proposal for the reform and improvement of the *Ministry of Education Journal,* of which I was to become the new editor. Avraam Sergeevich had pressured me, as usual, to draw up preliminary plans for the journal; and when I did, he completely ignored them. The journal is in a terrible state.

1 October. What is the matter with Avraam Sergeevich? I don't understand him! He handles censorship matters in a manner almost as bad as his timid predecessor's. Some sort of panicky fear has gripped him. He latches on to the most innocent sentences. All anyone like Komarovsky or Volkov has to do to upset him, is to show him some totally innocuous passage in some book or journal, and there he is on the spot with a harsh order or reprimand.

8 October. I submitted to the office for re-copying my report to the emperor together with a list of the sixteen best works in science and literature from January to October.

16 October. Several important questions concerning the university were turned over to me by the minister for my examination and opinion. A stack of files was sent to me for reference and study. I'm up to my neck in them now.

24 October. Much gossip about the discharged censors. Pogodin came from Moscow to appeal on behalf of himself and the others. I saw him when I was at the minister's office.

25 October. I am dissatisfied with myself. I feel a terrible weariness, which is why I probably didn't display the necessary fortitude in several instances. I was utterly unable to defend one of the measures I had proposed during this time, and two others were subjected to chancery alterations and changes which seriously distorted them. My views are honest and I must support them most energetically both in word and deed.

28 October. Disorganization—this is the motto of our society, and falsehood is its idol. It lies incessantly in thought and deed, consciously and unconsciously. Under the influence of recent extraordinary events,° it seems that an idea has begun to stir in it: it is longing to go somewhere, it wants to understand and is searching for an answer. But it has not succeeded in developing logically! It lacks a scientific base; it is circling in space and struggling like a wounded bird . . . We need another full century for some kind of rational force to develop.

29 October. Had a long talk today with Avraam Sergeevich. I told him, by the way, what an unpleasant impression the discharge of the two censors (Pokhvistnev and Rzhevsky) was making on the public under the present circumstances; and that the public was ascribing it to Count Panin's influence. He had focussed attention, as it were, on some stupid sentences which no one else had noticed.

30 October. I spoke to the minister about the need to compose an instruction manual for censors so they would know what policy to follow. Thus, their arbitrariness, often born of ignorance and egoism, could be curbed. This time the minister heard me out, appeared convinced, and asked me to work on it.

Karolina Karlovna Pavlova is a very pompous woman. She is not without talent, but bores everyone to death with her chatter and obtrusiveness. Besides, the sole topic of her conversation is herself, her writing, and her poems. She recites them to everyone she meets, or rather, shouts and sings them. Last summer she lived near me in the country and never gave me or Pletnyov any peace. We literally ran away from her.

Incidentally, about poets. Patriotic poems are now in vogue. Of course, there's nothing reprehensible in this. But the trouble is that all these recognized and unrecognized poets—particularly the latter—are not so much inspired by patriotism, as by a craving for rings, snuff-boxes, and the like.

15 December. At last, all our reports have been re-read, re-copied, re-read again, and are completely ready. The minister thanked me as a friend. It was a lot of work, but worthwhile, serious work, and I did not tire, worked with enthusiasm—and I might even say—with love. If the minister's good intentions are realized, I shall have the right to say: "I had a hand in this, too." The most important of all current business concerns censorship, that is *the abolition of the secret censorship committee* and, with it, the elimination of most of censorship's troubles and absurd conduct. Our task is to put censorship into a framework that leaves no room for the arbitrariness of unscrupulous

---

° Nikitenko is probably referring to the severe reverses suffered by Russian forces in the Crimean War.

and ignorant people who now use it to harm enlightenment. I can relax a little with a clear conscience now.

17 December. I picked the wrong moment to think of relaxing. No sooner had I shed my armour than I had to don it once again. I had returned from Smolny and found a note from the minister asking me to see him. I went. He gave me to re-work another memorandum to the emperor which had been composed by a department staff member. I re-wrote it; he approved it and sent it back to the department, where it was re-written a second time. And, of course, they were annoyed at me for this. This was a very clumsy move on the part of Avraam Sergeevich, which puts me on a bad footing with his staff. It is a minor thing, but it does serve to make matters worse. Upon returning home around midnight I found a member of my family dangerously ill: my poor boy had the croup.

18 December. The danger has passed. I can breathe freely again.

19 December. The emperor has granted the minister an audience for 11:30 A.M. tomorrow. Avraam Sergeevich is leaving today for Gatchina where he will spend the night. He asked me to see him tomorrow evening to learn the results of his report. "Pray for success," he said to me on leaving.

And how I'll pray! These reports are for the benefit of our educational system; and, truly, Russia needs education more than anything else.

Here's an example of how the truth is regarded in our country by those who have been called upon to be its heralds and champions in educational matters. Several days ago the committee for the review of textbooks examined Smaragdov's *History* (new edition). Ivan Ivanovich Davydov, chairman of the committee, demanded the deletion from the book of all references to Mohammed, since he was "a scoundrel and founder of a false religion." The committee members were astounded. Professor Fischer addressed the chairman and said: "What do you want, Your Excellency? Do you want students of history to remain ignorant of what has happened in the world? Then why teach them history? What do you propose we tell students about the Mohammedans and the religion they preach? Does education really consist of knowingly spreading lies?" Fischer said much more in this vein without sparing Davydov, who finally had to withdraw his proposal.

1855

18 February. Sometime after two o'clock, Zvegintsev, my wife's sister's husband, who works as a purser for the heir to the throne, entered my study. His face was completely changed, and his eyes were bloodshot.

"Did you hear the news?" he asked.

I hadn't, but for some reason my thoughts immediately turned to the palace; I thought that the empress had died; she had long been ill and had lately taken a turn for the worse. But my visitor suddenly blurted out:

"The emperor is dead!"

The news shocked me first of all by its unexpectedness. I had always thought, like everyone else, that Emperor Nicholas would outlive us all, even our children, and almost our grandchildren. This wretched war was responsible for his death. When he began it, he did not foresee that it would become such a burden, that he would have neither the mental or physical strength to endure it. Under the present circumstances his death is a particularly significant event which can have unforeseen consequences. A new era will begin for Russia. The emperor is dead; long live the emperor! A long and, I must say, joyless page in the history of the Russian empire has come to an end. A new page is being turned by the hand of time. What new events will the new ruling hand inscribe in it; what hopes will it fulfill?

23 February. The minister visited me several times during my illness. Though he claims he needs me very much, he advised me not to rush with my work and not to go out too soon. Besides, I still don't feel up to working.

I have been having many visitors. Of course, everyone thinks and talks about only one thing—Nicholas's death. You hear rumors galore about the past and even more about the future, one more absurd than the other.

My illness can damage my relationship with the minister. However, I have long ceased to entertain any confidence in the notion that my activity is necessary and beneficial to society.

27 February. My strength is returning slowly.

Funeral services are being held today; the body is being transferred to Peter and Paul Cathedral. It is silent outside; almost no one can be seen. Everyone has converged on the route which the procession is expected to follow. The funeral bells have begun to toll in the churches. It is now 11:30 A.M.

What a lesson for human arrogance!

13 March. I did not err in my assumptions regarding my relationship with the minister. There is something that has inclined this eternally vacillating and easily swayed man against me. Of course it's still a vague feeling, but I can definitely sense it. Evidently, the chancery plays havoc with one's reason. I must have a talk with him.

16 March. The dominant vice of people today is that *they pretend to be what they are not.* Everthing is deceptive and there is deception in everything: there is deception in the boot which pinches the foot instead of serving it as footwear; deception in the hat which doesn't protect the head from cold; deception in the too-tight and too-short tail-coat which covers the backside and remains open in front; deception in a smile of greeting and in the mind that deceives and is deceived; deception in the language which is used, as Talleyrand says, to conceal one's thoughts; deception in shallow, superficial education which lacks depth, strength and truth. Lies, lies, and more lies; an endless chain of lies. What is most amazing about this order of things is that it is a lie and, at the same time, constitutes a system. How can you talk about the need for truth when without it one can manage so well and derive such benefits for one's self?

20 March. I went to see the minister this morning. We discussed ministry business. He told me that several important matters awaited my attention. I suggested, first of all, that we work on the censorship issue, so if the emperor[p] himself should chance to think of it, we would have everything ready. Avraam Sergeevich jumped at this idea with enthusiasm and asked me to devote myself exclusively to the task of composing instructions for the censors. So I must immerse myself completely in this work. It is a very important matter. It's time to put an end to this terrible hounding of ideas, to these arbitrary actions of ignoramuses who have transformed the censorship department into a jailhouse and treat ideas like thieves and drunkards. Composing these instructions is no easy task.

3 April. Avraam Sergeevich is suddenly in a big hurry with the censorship instructions, but it's the kind of task that you can't finish in even a month of steady work. And I began it only recently. However, today I read him what I had done—almost half the job. He was delighted and embraced me.

"I had expected a lot from you," he said, "but this has exceeded my expectations."

"That's fine," I thought, "but for how long will he feel this way?"

We decided, as a preliminary step, to present the emperor with a kind of brief introductory memorandum about censorship and the need to give it more intelligent guidance; then we would submit the instructions.

"The only trouble is," remarked Avraam Sergeevich, "that our present censors will be unable to follow the rules which you are proposing for them."

"Are you really thinking of retaining them?" I replied. "Nothing will work with them, of course. If you are going to improve censorship, it will be necessary to discharge our present censors for their utter incompetency and replace

[p] Alexander II.

them with better people. It is more important to place intelligent people in these positions than in any other. We ought to definitely make it a rule that those who do not have at least a candidate's degree cannot be censors."

It was decided that as soon as the emperor approved the instructions, the present censors would be discharged and new ones appointed. In this instance I am allowing myself to work for the common good to the detriment of a few. Besides, who told these gentlemen to assume a burden that was beyond their capabilities? They certainly received fine salaries. But, indeed, how many abominations and stupidities have been committeed and, worst of all, the foul deeds! Sometimes it reached the point where you didn't have the slightest bit of sympathy for all these gentlemen, these Elagins, Akhmatovs, Peikers, and Shidlovskys. It was Shirinsky-Shikhmatov and Musin-Pushkin who collected this crowd. Elagin ran Shikhmatov's stable. Akhmatov, a Kazan landowner, was appointed a censor because his chief was in debt to him and B. was related to him. Only Freigang remained from the old staff. He had served back in my day; at that time he was considered the most carping and petty censor, and now he is considered the best of the lot, although he hasn't changed a whit for the better.

6 April. I submitted the memorandum on censorship which will be presented to His Majesty with the minister's personal report. It was approved.

7 April. A general meeting at the Academy of Sciences. I attended for the first time. An imperial order confirming me as an ordinarius[q] academician was read.

The main business of the meeting was the election of a new permanent secretary to take the place of the late Fuss. Two factions struggled for the post: the so-called Russian and German factions. One tried to advance its own candidate, Bunyakovsky, the other—Middendorf. The German group has a voting majority; consequently, its will had to prevail.

Hostility toward the Germans has become a sickness with many of our people. Of course it's fine to stand up for one's own—but how? By deeds, talent, industry, and conscientiousness, and not by shouting that "We are Russians." The Germans occupy a preeminent position in many special areas because they are more industrious and, mainly, because they strive harmoniously toward their common goals. That is the secret of their success. But, in the first place, we try to get things done any old way, in "typical bureaucratic fashion," so that the authorities will be pleased and reward us. Secondly, when three or four of our people assemble on behalf of some idea or common cause, you can expect, without fail, that by the second or third day they will have quarrelled, played dirty tricks on each other and split up. Our only salvation lies in the intercession of authority. Take the Russian faction in the Academy: Davydov and Pletnyov can't stand each other; Davydov can't stand Pletnyov because he is highly regarded in the imperial Court, and Plet-

[q] Extraordinary rank of professor, equivalent to the rank of full professor.

nyov can't tolerate Davydov because he chairs the department and received the Vladimir Star before he did. Sreznevsky will do the bidding of whoever happens to be the strongest. Ustryalov—if he has dined well and slept well— doesn't give a hang about anything. Ostrogradsky has been playing the role of the terrible Slavophile for some time, but basically, this man is a cunning *Khokol*[r] who, on the sly, makes fun of both the Germans and the Russians. He loves money, the lazy life and comfort. In brief, everyone goes his own way. Naturally, there are many capable people among us, but they were not endowed with the ability to make good use of their gifts.

Middendorf was elected. However, Bunyakovsky received only two votes less, which means that even the Germans voted for him. There are grounds for preferring Middendorf to Bunyakovsky, since the latter doesn't know German, and all the Academy's correspondence with European scholars is conducted in German and French.

9 April. I was presented to Grand Duke Konstantin Nikolaevich together with other members of the Commission appointed to inspect naval academies. Here is what he said to us.

"Gentlemen, may I ask you to feel completely free and to be frank with us about the shortcomings of our schools. My sole purpose is to learn the truth about them. People are usually wrong when they think they have achieved perfection. We must know what our weaknesses are, for only then can we improve ourselves. Our naval academies have many weaknesses, but we want to know what they are and how we can correct them. That is what I expect of you. Take your time. Work on this when you find it most convenient and when time and other responsibilities permit."

I mentioned the curricula. "Yes," he said, "the curricula must be carefully reviewed and put into order. They are very well set up in military schools, but how they work out in practice—I don't know. They look good on the surface."

I gathered from what he said and the way he said it that the grand duke didn't have much faith in the curricula and external evidence of flourishing courses at the military schools. He was very friendly and displayed a great deal of intelligence as well as a fine attitude in some of the things he said. He understands how much falsehood, how much lust for power there is in Russia. He wants the truth and is proving this by his actions. We left, completely satisfied with him. The grand duke not only talks well, but eloquently, too. A desire for truth and clarity prevails in everything he does.

13 April. I just came from the minister. He had presented a personal report to the emperor. I don't understand why Avraam Sergeevich did not handle the censorship matter as we had agreed he would. Instead of reading our prepared memorandum to the emperor, he explained it to him in his own words. Consequently, the results were not what they could and should have been.

---

[r] A colloquial and facetious term for a Ukrainian.

The minister attacked the committee of April 2nd, but did not explain why he considered it harmful. The reasons had been set forth in the memorandum. The emperor replied that since the minister himself was now a member of the committee, it could no longer be so harmful. Avraam Sergeevich mentioned nothing at all about the instructions for censors, and this was a very important matter. I'm afraid that the whole business was ruined.

Everything indicates that although the present emperor is kindly disposed toward us, he has some reservations about us, too. This was also the attitude of the late emperor toward the end of his reign.

19 April. There's a great deal of talk in the city about censorship. Like most rumors and gossip, it contains both truth and falsehood. Unfortunately, Avraam Sergeevich's actions are responsible for much of this kind of talk. Censorship is the most delicate and sensitive nerve in the life of our society and, therefore, it must be touched with care.

23 May. I finished my instructions for censors. The rough draft came to 52 pages. I gave it a final review this morning and read it to the minister in the evening. There were the usual embraces and expressions of delight.

I myself am very well aware of the significance of this piece of work. The ministry had started work on such a project many times, but never got anywhere with it. What has emerged now is a real censorship code, as precise as only a code of this kind can be. Censorial arbitrariness is curbed, literature is given scope, and measures against abuses are specified. This is a solution to a difficult problem. I read the proposal to Mark Lyuboshchinsky, whose opinion means a great deal to me, for he is chief prosecutor of the senate, one of our finest lawyers, and a man who is not only clever in theory, but in practice as well. He was enthusiastic about it. The minister and I decided that it would be presented first to the Chief Censorship Administration and then to the emperor with a brief abstract. Fine, if it works out that way. However, the draft still remains to be read to Rostovtsev.

I requested, and in very strong terms, that no changes be made without consulting me. Avraam Sergeevich solemnly gave his word.

19 June. I worked with Avraam Sergeevich on ministry business from noon until three. He is preparing a personal report to the emperor. We discussed many important subjects, but I don't know whether it will bear any fruit. Our affairs are making less progress with the present emperor than they had with the late emperor toward the end. Our minister bore greater weight with Nicholas, who liked Avraam Sergeevich's frankness and directness. The late emperor made his decisions himself, and quickly too, and we could submit many things to him without fearing rejection, particularly if the presentation were well edited. It's different now. The emperor is evidently depressed by the war and doesn't give his full attention to matters unrelated to it. He is always in a hurry and hesitates to undertake many things because he's afraid of making mistakes.

25 June. I talked to Avraam Sergeevich about Yershov's *The Hunchback Horse,* which the publishers want to issue in a new edition, but stupid censorship won't pass. Censor Elagin had stated in his report that "impossible events" were depicted in this fairy tale.

The censorship project is being held up in the chancery. On the minister's instructions I had submitted my memorandum for recopying: a month has almost gone by and it's still being recopied. It's incredible! I told the minister about it. He replied that his chancery staff was stupid, and the director, a fool. He promised to push it but keeps forgetting about it. That's how serious business is conducted here!

5 August. P.A. Vyazemsky was appointed deputy minister of education.

27 August. The department of oriental studies opened at the university today. There were public prayers, speeches by Professors Popov and Kazembek, and a luncheon. I was invited as a member and secretary of the committee responsible for establishing the department, and, principally, as the individual responsible for the original idea of establishing a department instead of the separate institute which had been proposed.

Avraam Sergeevich introduced me to Prince Vyazemsky. During the minister's absence we were instructed to concentrate on the censorship project.

30 August. Today is my nameday. My wife went to the city and returned with sad news: *Sevastopol has been taken!* Here's the bulletin of August 27th, word-for-word: "*Midnight.* The enemy is receiving new reinforcements almost daily. Terrific bombardments are continuing. Our losses exceed 2,500 per day.

"10 A.M. The armies of our Imperial Majesty are defending Sevastopol to the end, but it is impossible to hold out any longer under the terrific fire to which the city is being subjected. The armies are shifting to the northern front after having finally repulsed, on August 27th, six out of seven attacks led by the enemy on the western and naval fronts; only at the Kornilov Bastion was it impossible to repulse them. The enemy will find only bloody ruins in Sevastopol."

My God, how many victims! What a disaster for Russia! Poor humanity! A single nod from a madman, drunk with despotic power and arrogance, was enough to wipe off the face of the earth so many souls in the bloom of life, to spill so much blood and tears, to cause so much suffering.

We have been conducting a war not for two years, but for thirty, by maintaining a million men under arms and constantly threatening Europe. Why? What benefits, what glory, has Russia reaped from this?

19 September. There is a great deal of discussion of the Pogodin article which was written in connection with the emperor's arrival in Moscow. In my opinion it is too full of self-praise: "We are the leading nation in the world; we are better than anyone else," and so forth. But it does contain one passage which is noteworthy because it expresses a general sentiment; it is where the author speaks about "those names so dear to us—Peter, Catherine, and Alexander"— and doesn't say a single word about Nicholas. They say the emperor personally approved the article for release to the press. But Musin-Pushkin would not permit it to be reprinted in our local newspapers.

25 September. I went to Tsarskoe Selo to see the deputy minister, Prince Vyazemsky. I read him the draft of instructions to censors. He approved it enthusiastically. After I have corrected the clerk's errors, I must deliver it to the prince for dispatch to Count Bludov. I spoke with the prince about many things concerning our ministry. He is still unfamiliar with ministry affairs and agreed with me about everything. However, I doubt that it will do any good. Nearly all our high officials agree to everything and yet nothing is accomplished. At any rate, the prince is what we would call a cultured, educated man.

6 October. Only now is the truth beginning to emerge about how dreadful the past twenty-nine years have been for Russia. The administration was in chaos; moral inclinations were suppressed; intellectual development was halted; abuses and embezzlement grew to monstrous proportions. All this was the fruit of contempt for truth and a blind barbarian faith in physical force.

9 October. Still another death, but only a political one, and, moreover, one that is being greeted with joy rather than sadness. Kleinmichel, finally, like Bibikov, has fallen and been destroyed. They say he received a note yesterday from the emperor in Nikolaev suggesting that he resign.[s]

12 October. The universal joy over Kleinmichel's downfall continues. Everyone is exchanging congratulations on a victory, which, for lack of real victories, constitutes a genuine triumph for the public.

Is he really to blame? He is a limited person. He has a prison keeper's mentality, but is not naturally evil. The evil lay not within him, but within his position, a position in which fate had placed him by transforming him from an all-powerful noble into a man who jeered at the Russian public.

16 October. A yearning for a better order of things is beginning to make itself felt in our society. But one's hopes ought not to be raised too high. Everything that has been good or bad until now has not been produced by society's free and independent activity, but by the orders and will of a higher authority which controlled everything and also led us wherever it wished. Outstanding personalities and individual phenomena are of minor significance in a totality of stagnation: they are like bubbles popping out on the surface of sluggish water which is suddenly agitated by some weight that has fallen into it.

Many people are now beginning to talk about the need for legality and an

[s] The public's intense hostility toward Kleinmichel, whom it saw as a symbol of Nicholas' regime, finally compelled Alexander II to request his resignation.

end to secrecy; they are talking about replacing bureaucratic administration with more efficient management. If only all these fine ideas didn't dissolve in words! The Russian mind is amazingly inclined to content itself with words rather than deeds—to begin and end with some very fine intentions which the road to hell is paved with, as the saying goes.

There's no end to the gossip about Kleinmichel! What is he guilty of? His head had been cruelly turned by honors and power. It was too much for him.

18 October. I received an imperial order appointing me a member of Count Bludov's committee for the examination of Zhukovsky's posthumous works, which they want to publish now. The other members are Pletnyov, Prince Vyazemsky, Korf (Modest Andreevich), and Tyutchev.

19 November. Soirée at the home of Countess Rostopchina. She read her new drama. Rather a bore. Several princesses, countesses, Prince Vyazemsky, Tyutchev, Pletnyov, and Prince Odoevsky were present. I returned home at 2 A.M.

The countess was very haughty, attacked the lower classes, and praised the higher nobility. Tyutchev came back at her very cleverly. All I, a plebian, could do, was to hold my tongue, and so I did. Besides, what good would it have done to say anything to a chatterbox who listens only to what she herself has to say?

24 November. In the evening I went from Avraam Sergeevich's to Turgenev's. There I found many literary figures: Maikov, Druzhinin, Pisemsky, Goncharov, L.N. Tolstoy, who had come from Sevastopol, and others.

Incidentally, about Maikov. He read his new poem, "Dreams," at my home the other day. This poem is written in a quite different spirit than his recent ones. I have been advising Maikov not to get involved in any futile doctrines or groups, but to stay with his art because he has a genuine aptitude for it. He has great talent and, therefore, should treat it all the more carefully.

I finally succeeded in getting Goncharov an appointment as a censor. Three censors, the most stupid ones, will be replaced by January 1st. Goncharov will replace one of them, with the idea, of course, of doing a better job than his predecessor. He is intelligent, very tactful, and will be an honest and fine censor. On the other hand, this post will serve to rescue him from the chancery drudgery which is now destroying him.

30 November. Count Bludov was appointed president of the Academy of Sciences. I believe this is a good appointment.

3 December. A copy of a remarkable order which Grand Duke Konstantin Nikolaevich distributed to his department is circulating from hand to hand. The order says that administrators should not lie in their reports by assuring us that everything is in wonderful shape, as they usually do. There is reference in the order to a memorandum which sharply attacked various real and official lies. It is stirring up a lot of excitement in the city. The ministers and other administrators who must submit reports are very unhappy about the order. Actually this order was a marvelous thing. Many people are generally displeased that we are beginning to give some thought to eliminating secrecy and respecting public opinion.

10 December. My ambiguous position with the minister has finally compelled me to take definite measures. Avraam Sergeevich calls me "his friend" and entrusts me with important matters. I work with him, I can say, completely unselfishly, for I do not receive any pay at all for it. But I can never be certain of the one reward which I basically need—that is, the sure knowledge of the usefulness and durability of my work. For "my friend" has other friends in his chancery to whom he is often more receptive and at whose prodding he occasionally polishes up what we, it seems, had just worked out so well together. In the meantime my energy is being sapped in this exhausting work, since I must still worry about earning my daily bread for myself and my family. I wrote a letter to Avraam Sergeevich in which I outlined the present state of affairs to him, of which he is well aware, however. I asked if he couldn't find it possible for the protection of our common efforts to make my position in the ministry official so that I could devote more time to it and enjoy equal rights in defending myself against chancery intrigues.

1856

3 January. I spent New Year's Eve at Avraam Sergeevich's. It was dull. There are rumors of peace.

16 January. The public is extremely dissatisfied with the peace treaty and our acceptance of its four points.[1] "We must fight," say the super-patriots, "we must fight to the last drop of blood, to the last man." The government is very wise—it hears this gossip, but ignores it. I feel that the emperor by his compliance, and by his acceptance of the four points, has demonstrated not only nobility of character and his desire to avoid useless bloodshed, but intelligent and keen judgment, too. He feels we should begin by coming to terms with European public opinion. Seeing that our overtures have been well received there, one must agree that he has achieved his goal. He ought not, as his father had done, set a force against himself and Russia which, as Talleyrand expressed it, was more clever and more powerful than even he or Napoleon—and that force was public opinion. Nicholas himself didn't understand what he was doing. He did not weigh all the consequences of his hostile views toward Europe and paid for it with his life when, finally, these consequences revealed themselves to him in all their horror. It is impossible to tread further along this path and to stand up against a coalition of all Europe. Peace would come anyway, but an inglorious and disastrous one. No, a thousand times, no! Our praise and gratitude to Alexander II, who had the noble courage to reject the voice of pride in favor of real benefits and real glory.

31 January. Confirmation of my appointment as editor of the *Ministry of Education Journal* appeared today in the *St. Petersburg Bulletin* (order issued January 24).

26 February. I made a report to the minister about the program of future activities of the Chief School Board, which he must personally present to the emperor. Avraam Sergeevich was especially pleasant and thanked me warmly. "What would I do without you?" he added.

29 February. Pletnyov told me something encouraging today. Last week the emperor attended a private performance at the home of Grand Duchess Mariya Nikolaevna. Sollogub's *The Official* was staged. It contains many bold statements about immorality, that is, about the thievery prevalent among our administrators.

At the end of the performance, the emperor, upon meeting Pletnyov, remarked:

"It was a very fine play, wasn' it?"

"It's not only a fine work, Your Majesty," replied Pletnyov, "but a mile-stone in our literature. It says things about the state of our public morals and manners that one didn't even dare think about before, no less say publicly."

"It's long overdue," said the emperor.

Several days ago I attended two literary readings: the first, at Prince Vyazemsky's home, where Count Lev Tolstoy read his work;[t] the second, at Turgenev's, where Ostrovsky read his short play, *A Family Portrait,* and then a drama, also based on Russian customs and daily life.

Ostrovsky is undoubtedly one of the most gifted of our contemporary writers who base their works on the folk element, or rather, the common-folk element in our society. It's a shame he's so onesided—always dealing with the merchant class. As a result, he tends to repeat himself, often reproduces the very same types, and harps on the same theme. But he knows the life of the merchant class inside out and he doesn't create mere cardboard images. His works have comical elements and humor, and characters who emerge inde-pendently from a mass of skillfully arranged material. Ostrovsky himself is absolutely not what a certain literary circle has proclaimed him to be. He behaves modestly and respectably; he certainly does not resemble the alcoholic they claim him to be; and his manner is very pleasant, too. He reads his plays beautifully.

10 March. Troubles again, thanks to the pathetic spinelessness of our minister. It's impossible to follow a smooth, direct and open course with him, and yet he is basically a good man. But that's what it means not to have a strong will or a mind capable of making its own decisions without outside assistance. Moreover, there's the ever-present fear that his dependency on someone will be exposed.

12 March. Still another spiritual affliction of our so-called thinking genera-tion is its *superficial thinking.* We do not tread the path of thought with a firm, logical step, but rush madly along it and, moreover, without any definite aim, often attracted only by a desire to stand out and draw attention to our-selves. In this race we seize upon any idea, any knowledge, any conviction, injudiciously, superficially, without a solid base of stalwart and sober labor. And we, a great people, geniuses in our own eyes, dare to offer incontrovert-ible judgments on the West, North, South, and East, on science and litera-ture, etc.

13 March. It looks as if I shall eventually have to disengage myself from my work in the ministry.

Since my honest way of doing things is not understood here, I have no choice but to resign.

22 March. The Academy of Sciences' department of Russian letters elected

[t] Tolstoy read his tale "The Snowstorm."

me to represent them on the commission for review of academy regulations. I was very anxious to avoid this. In this situation one will unquestionably find oneself clashing with certain members who, in the name of the so-called Russian element, want to fight with the Germans. I, of course, shall support neither the Russians nor the Germans, but only what I shall consider to be just. And what is the Russian element? Davydov with his personal schemes and Sreznevsky with his Yusy.[u] Surely, no one is preventing the Russians from distinguishing themselves in the academy by displaying moral virtues and scholarly achievements. But the fact is that it is far more difficult to distinguish oneself in such ways than to shout: "It's the Germans; it's always the Germans."

4 April. I have been feeling extremely fatigued from the dizzying pace of my government work and other commitments. Committees, commissions, lectures, supervision of instruction in various departments, reading journal galley-proofs, ministry assignments, taking defensive measures against department drudges—all this and much else creates such a constant turbulence that I am choking in it and can scarcely catch my breath. My health is broken. It's time to relax for a few months. But how? I need money, money, and more money. I haven't saved any; I couldn't. So, I'm not even entitled to rest! Alas! I have done so much in my lifetime that life has not required, and I have not done what it did require.

12 April. Those suspicions and fears that haunted me as far back as a year ago have been realized. The ministry of education is being placed under a trusteeship. However, I hadn't foreseen who the chief trustee would be. The fact is that the Chief School Board, by will of the emperor, is acquiring a structure that will permit it to function as a kind of independent board with the right to contest the minister's decisions, decisions related to the most important issues in education, training, and administration. And, as Rostovtsev was appointed a member of the board, it is clear who will play the leading role. It must be conceded that the notoriety of our ministerial bureaucracy, with its eminent representative, Kislovsky, was greatly responsible for this shake-up. Many rumors flew about the city concerning the minister's dependence on this bureaucracy. Besides, the very behavior of Avraam Sergeevich, who is a good man and, as we say, well-meaning, but who is absolutely lacking in tact and self-reliance, contributed much to the imposition of this restriction. At any rate, we are now on the eve of serious upheavals in the ministry. Several days ago Rostovtsev's aide-de-camp, Kossikovsky, came to see me and told me many interesting things. Yakov Ivanovich Rostovtsev, by the way, wants to see me.

13 April. Pletnyov was confirmed as a member of the Chief School Board. Since both of us were nominated for this post, it means that I have been re-

[u] Old Russian nasal vowels.

jected. So, this whole routine about my appointment to the Chief School Board was a farce. But what was the purpose? Why did Avraam Sergeevich resort to this? Besides, what did I do to deserve this humiliation?

The ministry just informed me that the emperor does not wish to confirm my appointment to the School Board on the grounds that I am not yet a senior Actual State Councillor. Yet only recently, Avraam Sergeevich assured me that the emperor had already expressed his consent to my appointment. Something strange is going on here—but, mainly, something nasty.

21 April. I went to see Rostovtsev yesterday. He detained me for a long time. He told me all the facts; how the present Chief School Board was organized and how a trusteeship was imposed on the ministry. Moreover, he also gave me some examples of Avraam Sergeevich's amazing spinelessness. He was even more familiar than I with Kislovsky's bureaucratic machinations and his power over this weak man. I heard many new details from him. Yakov Ivanovich says it is inconceivable that the emperor would not confirm me as a member of the Chief School Board. Avraam Sergeevich had fabricated this explanation in order to extricate himself from his promises to me. It is more likely that, terrified of his chancery staff, he never even presented a recommendation to the emperor for my appointment. Frequently his rashness has put him in such a position that he didn't know how to extricate himself and resorted to schoolboy subterfuges. In any case, I am no longer in his cast of players, because Avraam Sergeevich's hands are now tied, and he himself has already definitely rejected me.

28 April. Fet read his fantastic tale in verse, "The Dream," at my home yesterday. The verse is good. It is full of pictures and images, but lacks a theme. These poets think that they can write without presenting any definite idea and that it is the reader's responsibility and not the author's to discover it or impart it to a work. I told him what I thought and also hazarded a guess about what the author was trying to say. He was amazed that anyone would look for meaning here. Panaev felt as I did.

I haven't mentioned an event of great importance for our university. Superintendent Musin-Pushkin was relieved of his post on the first day of the holiday and simultaneously promoted to the rank of Actual State Councillor. This honorable retirement was forced upon him. Everyone is overjoyed at the news. Yet it happens that he was not one of the worst administrators of our time. He had three points in his favor. First: in the most troubled times he did not consciously try to undermine education; he didn't advance in the service by fawning or looking for something subversive; he did not interfere with academic freedom. On the contrary, he showed respect for education in his own way and recognized its rights. His second quality: he could appreciate scholarly contributions and threw all his support behind his colleagues, protecting them from all sorts of traps. I myself witnessed this. In those troubled times, in 1849, when legions of informers spied on the university and followed our every move, when they confiscated our notes, mine included—Musin-Pushkin, like a true knight, rushed to defend our honor and safety and wrote a strong, firm, bold, and courageous statement in our defense. It would often happen that he would refuse requests from people like Count Orlov who were seeking a post for someone, a post which justice demanded should be awarded to a deserving scholar or civil servant. Whatever he did, he did out of conviction. His third strong point was his fidelity to his word. But all these good points were, unfortunately, hidden under such thick bark that few were able to get to know them well enough to appreciate them. With all his fine qualities, he nevertheless rode a mad steed which, taking the bit into its teeth, often tossed him headlong into the mud, an abyss, or swamp, anywhere at all, where he risked knocking down someone or breaking his own neck. This mad steed was his own turbulent nature. With his subordinates, and even with his equals, he would stage the most absurd scenes, raging and cursing away. This is what gave him the nasty reputation which finally led to his downfall. Our present emperor, with his fine, humane inclinations, could not bear him. Ofttimes he and the minister would express their displeasure at Musin-Pushkin's behavior. His greatest weakness was his handling of censorship. He would often do absurd things. To tell the truth, it was impossible, anyway, to make any headway with the kind of censors we have had lately. However, the system wasn't of his making; it had been organized higher up. Yet he himself had no respect for literature; he lacked that something called sympathy.

24 May. I went to the city yesterday. I spent the evening at Kavelin's. Dmitry Alekseevich Milyutin, whom I always enjoy seeing, was also there. Also present were two young professors: one, Eshevsky, from Kazan; the other, Kapustin, from Moscow. Kavelin's supplement to his very intelligent article about the emancipation of the serfs was read, an article which is being circulated in manuscript form and which he recently gave me to read. The two main points are: 1) to bring about emancipation by compensating the owners, 2) the peasants must be redeemed together with their land allotments.

27 May. Here are the main things that I strove for and supported with all my strength during my three years with the minister:

1. not to act impulsively on ideas of the moment, but to determine the ministry's views clearly and distinctly, and then systematically and unswervingly to act in the spirit of these views.

2. to establish gymnasiums.

3. to establish a Chief School Board (this was primary).

4. our universities were on the brink of disaster because of a lack of competent, qualified professors. Therefore, I quickly undertook the preparation of qualified personnel by: a) charging the universities to prepare talented young people to fill professorial posts; b) providing retirement security for professors, so that such capable individuals could give their undivided attention to their work at the university during their tenure.

5. to give censorship intelligent direction in keeping with the requirements of enlightenment. To accomplish this, it was necessary to, a) replace incompetent censors with more able ones, and b) to give them instructions to supplement the censorship code, which would curb their arbitrariness and give literature more latitude by providing them as far as possible with precise guidelines.

Of course, almost all my efforts were as futile as a voice crying out in the wilderness.

3 June. Some literary figures recently reproached me for not being associated with any particular literary faction and for not fighting exclusively for any one of them.

"My creed," I replied, "is independence in my personal opinions and a respect for the opinions of others. Everyone knows that this is the way I have always thought and acted and I see no reason for me to change this policy in the future."

11 June. The attempt to give the educated class an understanding of the lowest class through the medium of literature and, thereby, open the way to education among the latter is a splendid idea. However, we ought not to portray the ignorance, coarseness and prejudices of this class as something romantic and capable of evoking only tender emotions. In this class, no less than in others, there are shortcomings and vulgarity. Never mind that they are natural and not adopted—vulgarity is vulgarity no matter what its origin. And daguerreotype images of them neither speak well of what does exist nor pave the way for something better. Literature, by focussing exclusively on these subjects, demonstrates a lack of creative ability and a reluctance to perfect itself. For indeed, it is far simpler to copy coarse reality with all its ugly details, than to think and create.

18 September. I was chosen a member of the Theatre Committee for the examination of plays written for the one hundredth anniversary of the theatre.

9 October. Pletnyov writes from Paris that the most striking feature of the French is their unity of national feeling. He attributes this to their belief in their national superiority. "Why," he asks, "doesn't Russian national feeling yield such splendid results?" And he answers: "Because of a lack of faith in our moral qualities!" But I think it's because we have failed to develop our moral qualities. We have many talents, but alas!—we have plenty of immorality, too.

20 November. I dined today with Count Bludov. After dinner we remained alone. The main topic of our conversation was the ministry of education. The count was very indignant about what was going on there.

He also told me many interesting things from his recollections of the past. Somehow, the conversation lighted on Bulgarin and Grech. The count positively knew for a fact that Bulgarin had been in the service of the secret police during Benkendorf's tenure. Amongst other things he related the following episode from the history of secret operations.

"I don't recall the exact year the late emperor was absent from St. Petersburg for a long period," said the count. "Count Benkendorf and Dashkov former minister of justice, had accompanied him. These two were very friendly.

"One day Benkendorf said to Dashkov:

" 'How would you like to read a report delivered to me from the Third Section? Naturally, a secret report. It concerns the trend of thought at St. Petersburg University. I haven't read it yet, but it will probably be of interest to you.'

"Dashkov took the report and, to his amazement, here is what he found. Charges of extreme liberalism against Prince Vyazemsky, Count Bludov, and many other such figures—and, finally, against himself. He immediately jotted down his comments in the margins, and the next day, upon returning the report to Benkendorf, said: 'I read this interesting document, Count, and I must insist that you promise to include my comments on it, should you decide to present it to the emperor.'

" 'I'll do better than that,' replied the Count. 'I won't present anything to him at all.'

"And he didn't."

26 November. I read a memorandum, at a departmental meeting, on the need to teach philosophy at the university. It met with strong approval, and the department decided to send it up through administrative channels.

The academy's department of Russian letters and the university charged me to write reports for convocations on December 29th and February 8th. It will take a lot of my time.

6 December. I saw Voitsekhovich this morning and had a long talk with him. He told me the strangest things about the *raskolniki*, whose affairs the administration had entrusted to him about three years ago. According to Voitsekhovich, they constitute an enormous force in our country. There are almost ten million of them. They have contact with Austria, where one of their central offices is located. Some of their beliefs are very crude, others, to a great degree, are rational. Some sects are remarkable for their immorality. For example, there are sects that consider wives common property, and it is their practice to kill off their young. Voitsekhovich assured me that in one *raskolnik* settlement, the district police officer, on his orders, had fished more than forty infant corpses from a pond! !

22 December. Went to Posen's. Had a most interesting chat. He repeated word for word the conversation he had had with the emperor several days ago. Posen had come to St. Petersburg with his proposal for the emancipation of the peasants and for this reason had been invited to an audience with the emperor. His Majesty had lent a willing ear to Posen's explanatory comments and promised to read the proposal very carefully. Posen, meanwhile, had warned the emperor that he, Posen, had many enemies.

"Oh, and how!" the emperor agreed with him.

"Therefore it shouldn't be surprising if my ideas are rejected by many."

"Have you signed your proposal?" asked the emperor.

"No, Your Majesty," replied Posen.

"Fine, just fine," remarked the emperor.

In the meantime, some three days after this conversation, Prince Dolgoruky, on the emperor's orders, visited Posen for further discussion of his proposal.

30 December. I've just returned from a soirée with a feeling of intense disgust for everything I saw and heard there. The so-called cream of society was present, really many intelligent people, but they all swim along with the tide, thinking only of their own personal gain, their petty ambition, vanity, and so forth. Such is the spirit of our times, and there are few who consider it necessary to resist and oppose it.

1857

1 January. Went to Posen's and stayed about an hour. A committee has been organized to study his emancipation proposal. The emperor himself will head it. The members are: Count Orlov, Rostovtsev, Brok, Gagarin, Prince Dolgoruky and Adlerberg.

10 January. Had dinner at Posen's. He let me read the letters he had written to the emperor. They had accompanied his proposals for changes in various branches of government administration. Posen had prepared these proposals at the request of His Majesty. Posen accepts four basic principles: orthodoxy, autocracy, humanity and *narodnost,* but he assigns three of them a different meaning than did Uvarov. His letters are more remarkable than anything else. They are bold, clever, and even eloquent. There is an interesting passage in one of them where he says that the people expected their lot to be improved after the war and that if their expectations were not met, we must anticipate widespread discontent. He calls the living conditions of our people intolerable.

The emancipation committee hasn't decided anything yet. Posen is leaving on Tuesday.

12 February. Prince Vyazemsky, now in charge of censorship, asked me to work out a proposal for its reorganization because it was in a terribly chaotic state. I repeated to him what I had repeated a hundred times to both him and the minister, namely, that, first of all, it was necessary to do three things: a) give precise instructions to the censors; b) free the censors from the restrictions of various directives, especially those that had been accumulating since 1848. Because of their extreme irrationality and harshness they cannot be carried out, and, meanwhile, they hang over censors' heads like the sword of Damocles; c) abolish the rule which obliges censors to consult every department on which a literary work, by its nature or content, may have bearing. The prince asked me to invite one of the censors to explore and discuss all these problems with me, and then to present our findings to him. However, I explained to the prince that I could not assume the role of legislator and advised him to appoint a committee. For preliminary discussions I selected Freigang as my assistant, for lack of a better choice.

26 February. My request for leave was read at the University Council yesterday. My health is very poor. I am so worn out, that if I don't take immediate measures to restore my health, I am afraid it will be completely destroyed.

27 March. At Count Bludov's. Conversation about our administration and

Brok, who insists that nothing concerning finances should be published without his permission and openly states that our writers are leading us to revolution. I remarked that he was mistaken, that it wasn't writers that made revolutions, but incompetent ministers. Also present was Tyutchev, who coined a very biting witticism about one of our administrators.

28 April. I spent the entire month suffering fierce bouts of illness and arranging a trip abroad, where the doctors insist on sending me. After running into various difficulties, the matter was finally settled.

27 October. I received a document from Count Adlerberg informing me of my appointment as chairman of the Theatre Committee.

I glanced through various journals which had come out in my absence.[v] Many articles, particularly in the *Contemporary,* surprise me with their extreme boldness and the paradoxical nature of their aspirations.

After all that our society has experienced in the recent past, protest and opposition are inevitable phenomena. Moreover, they are necessary elements in the life of our society and in our political life, both of which would lose their equilibrium, stagnate and decay, without them. So, therefore, gentlemen, protest!—it is your right and even your duty—but let your protests rest on firm principles of reason and be offered in the name of broad humanitarian ideals of truth and goodness common to all mankind, and not in the name of your personal, narrow philosophy of life and your passions. But our modern protestants don't think and act this way. Blinded by a hatred for the maladies of the past, they condemn and curse indiscriminately; they are up in arms against everything, often contrary to reason and history. They don't notice that they still lack a solid base for their ideas and that, in their intolerance, they are becoming representatives of a new and almost greater despotism than the previous one. No, gentlemen, the truth isn't come by so easily.

8 December. Krasovsky is dead. He was chairman of the Foreign Censorship Committee. He was a man with wild ideas, a fanatic and hypocrite who spent his whole life trying as hard as he could to extinguish enlightenment. Davydov proposed writing a panegyric on him (Krasovsky was a member of the Russian Academy). I opposed this, saying, "What can we say of true merit and worth after praising someone like Krasovsky? Besides, who would believe such praise? The saying that 'one must not speak badly of the dead,' applies only to personal friends and enemies, and not to public figures."

9 December. I dined with Count Bludov several days ago. He talked a great deal about Speransky and told me the following story. Speransky was an unusual man. He was a great admirer of Napoleon and the French administrative system, which he introduced later on in our country. He subsequently took a dislike to Emperor Alexander I, who returned like sentiments and, once, in a frank conversation, said to one of his intimates about Speransky: "You

---

[v] Nikitenko was back in St. Petersburg after a trip abroad.

can't imagine what a coward and scoundrel he is." However, Speransky was neither. He was accused of treason in 1812, but this was unjust, although Emperor Alexander I believed it. At any rate, the emperor cited as proof of Speransky's guilt his frequent contacts with the French ambassador. Karamzin defended him on this charge before the emperor.

Also, said Count Bludov, Speransky displayed unusual respect for his mother. When he was in power and she (a simple village priest's wife) would come to see him, he, upon meeting her, would fall before her onto his knees, according to the old Russian custom, and offer her every possible token of a son's love and respect.

16 December. Prince Shcherbatov is beginning to act very strangely. He wants to eliminate boarding arrangements at gymnasiums and stipends for indigent university students. Things are going badly at the university. The students are without any moral guidance. Evidently the prince is trying to win them over. For example, the students put out two handwritten journals which they fill with all sorts of abusive language. One is called the *Herald of Free Opinion,* and the other, in imitation of Herzen, is called the *Bell.* The superintendent is aware of it and permits it. But in order to avoid trouble he told the students that he would assume the responsibility of censoring these journals and wanted all articles shown to him in advance. So, they show him five or six innocuous articles and then, afterwards, add on a few others, which they also release under the aegis of the superintendent's approval. Instead of urging young people to study, he encourages them to be journalists and to waste their time on nonsense which, in the end, might harm them and also have serious consequences for the entire student body and the institution.

19 December. Talk everywhere about the so-called emancipation. Everyone read the initial steps toward it in the rescript to Nazimov and the memorandum from the minister of internal affairs.[1] Both had appeared in the newspapers on the 17th. The main thing is that a beginning has been made and there is no turning back.

22 December. People are very concerned about the possible consequences of the emancipation rescript; they fear disturbances among the peasants. Many are hesitant about going to their dachas next summer.

No one thinks that the emancipation of the peasants will yield any positive benefits for the nobility itself. It seems to me this is precisely what one ought to expect it will do because it will enhance the nobility's political significance. By ruling slaves, they too were enslaved. As soon as the idea of rights is established between the nobility and their subjects, the concept of such rights will most certainly penetrate other social relationships and will receive universal application. By taking this step we have started on the path of many reforms whose significance cannot be fully ascertained at this time. The force of the torrent into which we have hurled ourselves will carry us whither we cannot yet foresee.

23 December. In the No. 270 issue of the *St. Petersburg Bulletin,* I published my objections to Dal's notion about the dangers of literacy for our common folk. My objections were received very well by the public. Many people have expressed their pleasure and appreciation.

24 December. Our journals today are filled almost exclusively with descriptions of all kinds of vile deeds and scandals. I am far from rejecting the significance and usefulness of a literature which bares the truth, particularly at this time. But I am distressed by the extreme exclusiveness of such a trend and its excessively narrow concern with momentary interests. It not only excludes everything that smacks of universality and nobility, any sort of striving toward the ideal, but even hounds it with a vengeance. Such an exclusive trend in literature must inevitably prove harmful to society, as does everything narrow and personal which is infected by intolerance.

1858

3 *January*. Panaev told us about his meeting with Chevkin, Chief of the Communications Bureau.[W] This government man tried to show him that the current trend in literature, which consisted of the exposé of all sorts of thievery, was harmful. Recently, in some article, officials of the Communications Bureau were offended on this score. Many of our present department heads don't like this literary castigation of irregularities occurring in their departments. They feel it will encourage disrespect for the government. These people, especially Count Panin, feel it is dangerous to air and strengthen public opinion where social issues are involved. But they are wrong: this has nothing to do with respect or disrespect for the government. The government itself is annoyed by the existence of various administrative abuses, and it should see publicity and public opinion as its strongest ally in its struggle against this evil.

The minister gave Beketov a real tongue-lashing the other day because, when the rescript on emancipation was published, he permitted *Son of the Fatherland*, in the same edition, to print an excerpt from the decrees on the Baltic peasants. This occurred in Prince G. A. Shcherbatov's absence. When the prince returned he insisted that Beketov not be fired as the minister had threatened. This was the handiwork of Kislovsky, who thought he could irritate the prince with Beketov's dismissal. But the prince acted very forcefully, put pressure on the minister, and did not let the scheming mentality of a petty official triumph over justice this time.

5 *January*. Soirée at Prince Shcherbatov's. I was informed on his behalf that he was very sorry he hadn't seen me for so long. We talked it over.

"I think," said the prince, "that you are angry with me." I did not hide the fact that I had been puzzled by certain words and deeds ascribed to him. The prince denied many things, and explained others as the exaggerations of his enemies. We promised each other that we would be completely frank with each other in the future.

Then the prince complained bitterly about the chaos in our ministry. Kislovsky is everywhere.

6 *January*. Visited Count Bludov. The superintendent of Moscow University, Kovalevsky, was also there.

The superintendent complained about the struggle between the Slavophiles and *zapadniki* at Moscow University. It has reached the point where the protagonists even resort to foul play. This particularly affects those seeking degrees and chairs. The *zapadniki* are even rejecting gifted candidates who don't happen to belong to their camp. The Slavophiles take their revenge in the same way.

11 January. Meeting of the Theatre Committee. There wasn't one decent play, although we examined five of them this time.

Revolt of worker-peasants on the Luga-Ostrov road. They say several land-owners were killed in Smolensk province.

13 January. Endless talk about the emancipation of the peasants, and there certainly is plenty to talk about. But, my God, how much nonsense in all this talk. Through all the various, more or less biased, opinions, however, the spirit of two hostile camps clearly emerges—those who favor emancipation and those who oppose it. All the so-called thinking people, or, those who pretend to think, belong to the first group: litterateurs, scholars and so on. To the second group belong all those whose material interests are involved in this gigantic game: that is, most of the serf-holding landowners. Two shades of opinion are discernible in the latter group: the one feels that the emancipation measure is unjust under the terms proposed by the government; the other feels that it is unquestionably harmful or at least premature. Naturally, they have reason to be fearful. The issue directly concerns their welfare. It involves their landholdings, which they certainly do not wish to give up. Others simply dislike the idea of seeing their *gentry* destroyed—and these are the people who seem to be raising the biggest fuss.

Kavelin, whom, incidentally, one can't help liking and respecting, often goes to extremes in his passionate enthusiasm. Now, for example, he is lashing out against the nobility as the worst evil in the world, as if evil were inherent in the nobility itself rather than in the nature of its position in our society.

15 January. Korkunov, a member of the Academy of Science's department of Russian letters, died. He was ill with typhus for two weeks.

16 January. I was elected secretary of the department of Russian letters in Korkunov's place.

I dined with Count Bludov. Other guests were I. V. Annenkov, publisher of Pushkin's works, and Kovalevsky, director of the Asiatic department. We talked about the literary world and censorship. The former is very eager to discuss the most important issue of the day—freedom, or the so-called emancipation, while the latter is strongly opposed to permitting such discussions. The countess read K. S. Aksakov's poem dedicated to the emancipation. This poem was not passed by censorship despite Grand Duke's Konstantin Nikolaevich's efforts.

18 January. We heard that the minister of education had suffered a terrible defeat at a session of the Council of Ministers last Thursday, where he had delivered a report. The beginning of the report, apparently, went well. The minister read a statement about the need to approach censorship in a conciliatory spirit. It was prepared by Prince Vyazemsky with Goncharov's help. Count Panin, an enemy of thought and of any kind of civic, intellectual and moral improvement, opposed Norov. Although Panin doesn't lack intelligence, his strong point is his way with words. Poor Norov attempted to defend education and literature, but his defense, they say, came out worse than the opposition's attacks. Panin, of course, won, and stricter censorship was ordered.

21 January. Panin, Brok and Chevkin, it seems, are all obsessed with the idea that literature is the cause of all the revolutions in the world. They don't want to understand that literature merely echoes ideas and convictions nurtured in society; that, if it focusses the government's attention on some administrative irregularities, it is doing it a service; that one must distinguish attacks on the law from attacks on failure to enforce it, and that attacks of this sort only raise the dignity of the law and legislative power.

26 January. There is *lightning* progress and *gradual* progress. If I had to label myself according to one of these categories, into which it is customary to subdivide political opinions in Europe, I would call myself a moderate progressive. I have little faith in those doctrines which promise society infinite happiness and perfection, but I do believe in mankind's need to develop. At every stage of this development there emerges for mankind certain blessings along with an unavoidable admixture of certain evils. For mankind not to follow the path of this development means to oppose the law of nature and to subject itself arbitrarily to the dangers and misfortunes which it is the duty of rational beings to avoid. As nature experiences the changes of the seasons, and with each change produces new creatures and new phenomena without breaking out of the sphere which defines its activity, so mankind cannot remain motionless and must uncover in historical sequence those forces which constitute its makeup.

29 January. A good deal was said at Count Bludov's today about Count Panin, who burns with such hatred for education and literature, that he is forever proposing new, oppressive censorship measures. For example, in order to force censors to be even stricter, he proposed immediate punishment for any oversight; and only afterwards would an investigation determine whether the punishment fit the crime. Isn't this reverse logic? So fitting for a minister of justice! My God!—when you look around, you see what strange things are produced by blind hatred of truth and reason.

6 February. First session of the committee organized to review the old censorship code and compile a new one. First there was a reading of Prince Vyazemsky's memorandum on the trend of present-day literature, which the minister of education had submitted to the emperor. It clears literature of the accusations made against it. It was cleverly composed and beautifully worded. It does honor to Prince Vyazemsky for the fine ideas in favor of thought and education he managed to put into it. It serves to refute the view of many people that he had become a mere aristocrat-courtier; and he especially refutes Herzen, who has been castigating him unmercifully in every issue of the *Bell*. The tsar's comments on this memorandum are interesting, too. He approves of some parts, while he appears suspicious of others; and a seeming dislike of literature and mistrust of its good intentions show through his remarks. Generally speaking, he considers vigilant censorial supervision of literature necessary.

16 February. I worked terribly hard all week. I drafted two charters: for the Theatre Committee and the Writer's and Scholar's Fund. The first has already been examined and approved by the committee; the second will be examined this week. Moreover, the committee for review of the censorship code is now having meetings. There's a lot of talk and a lot of changes. All this has produced a jumble of ideas which must be given order and clarity. Prince Vyazemsky is taking a noble and intelligent view of things, but isn't involving himself directly in this task. The prince proposed at the last meeting of the committee on censorship that I should compose and edit the draft-proposal for changes in the censorship code.

24 February. Session of the committee for review of the censorship code. I read the entire first section which I had reworked, where the basic principles of censorship are laid out. I added a few new paragraphs with the aim of giving literature more latitude in its views on social issues. Everything but one paragraph was accepted this time.

This is only the beginning of my labors. Much more work lies ahead of me. What it will lead to—I know not. I feel bitter when I think how many times my work in this area has gone for nought! But one never wants to lag behind, and each time one places one's hopes in that *maybe*, so portentous in our Russian life.

The draft of the Theatre Committee's charter was copied and then signed by its members.

7 March. Saw Count Adlerberg. Discussed the Theatre Committee's charter. The count said he was pleased with it and thanked me for it. He asked my opinion about the advantage of such a committee. I replied that its advantage was primarily a negative one: it would keep the stage from being cluttered with bad plays. But there was also a positive benefit: namely, that writers, especially young ones, would find encouragement in the thought that the fate of their work, from now on, would not be decided arbitrarily, often ignorantly, but by a literary court, and, as far as possible, a just one.

The count remarked that we had few gifted dramatists today. Then he talked about censorship and how difficult it was to control it. He remarked that our literature was pursuing quite undesirable goals. I replied that there was nothing absolutely malicious or harmful in it, and that if some of our young writers were sometimes carried away by fiery ideas, this could not have

a generally decisive influence on people, since they would always find a coun-
terbalance in the works of people who were more mature and had a more settled way of thinking.

16 March. Visited Count Bludov. Important news. Norov submitted his
resignation and it was accepted.

17 March. University Council meeting at which the superintendent presented
his draft of new university regulations for review. Everyone here already
knew about Norov's resignation. They say that Kovalevsky, the Moscow
superintendent, is being appointed in his place. The general consensus is that
nothing could be worse than what we had. Poor Avraam Sergeevich, this is
what all your shilly-shallying has led to.

18 March. Prince Vyazemsky told me today that he had also submitted his
resignation and that it had been accepted. What a pity. He didn't accomplish
very much and couldn't; but he is a noble, enlightened, intelligent man.

19 March. Kovalevsky has taken Norov's place.

24 March. I read Herzen's analysis of Korf's history of the Decembrist uprising. Herzen judges Rostovtsev too harshly. There was much that was childish
in Rostovtsev's letter, and his act was due more to weakness than the baseness
which Herzen ascribes to him. I knew Rostovtsev well then, and I well remember all the circumstances of the affair and the moral frame of mind of Rostovtsev himself. He was very young and hardly capable of being motivated by
selfishness and baseness, those subtle calculations which are the province of a
man wizened by experience and life. The role of historical personage might
have appealed to him, but one can say with assurance that he did not foresee
all the consequences of his act. He warned the conspirators that he intended
to inform on them, and, having informed, told them about it. This was a matter of self-preservation, but he had hardly counted on any future rewards. It
was another matter later, when his eyes were dazzled by the braid of a tsar's
aide-de-camp (immediately after December 14th). It was at this moment that
he might have conceived an entire plan for a brilliant future, although he had
then assured me that the rank of aide-de-camp would bring him much grief.

I went to see Posen this morning. He was visited by an endless stream of
dignitaries. There was a great deal of talk about the emancipation issue.

7 April. Visited the new minister. Talked about censorship. The emperor is
very concerned about it. His faith in literature has been shaken and he has
been turned against it. Now he demands stricter censorship, although he
doesn't want to stifle thought. How could the two be reconciled? The minister said he was counting on me to work this out.

"This responsibility," he said, "falls on two people: you and me. Of course,
neither you nor I could act in a spirit of constraint."

I remarked that the mistakes and inclinations of individual writers should
not be held against all literature nor taken as an indication of its general tenor.

The minister agreed with me. At any rate, the emperor is demanding a solution to the censorship problem from the minister, and the minister expects that solution from me. Yet the fact of the matter is that whatever may be the expectations of some and the concerns of others, everything will end only as it suits the good Lord. One thing is clear: you cannot, by imposing restrictions, direct and control minds that have awakened from centuries of slumber. These are discordant forces, not sobered either by tradition or religion, that are trying to act without firm convictions or conscious aim—and are therefore unbridled. They could only encounter suitable opposition in a literature which, left to its own devices, would not be long in producing from its own ranks the necessary fighters and bridlers.

10 April. Reported to the minister this evening on the committee for review of the censorship code. We worked for about two hours, and both of us got thoroughly tired. Yes, it is hard, very hard, to guarantee freedom of thought. We seek improvements and think we can attain them through that same bureaucracy which has so wallowed in thievery, rather than with the help of public opinion. For the government, meanwhile, it is obviously better and safer to join with the press than to war with it. If it tells the press which way it must go, it will begin to move in secretive ways and will become impossible to control. No force can keep track of an idea labored over in secret, an idea that has been frustrated and forced to resort to cunning. Indeed, we still do not know how that terrifying system of police persecution of thought and speech in France will end. But, at least there, the system is well defined, while we vacillate between permitting and not permitting, between constraining and not constraining.

The minister raised the issue today of the responsibility of journal editors. He feels that this is the only way to save something so vital to our literature.

18 April. I saw the minister. He was rushing off to a meeting of the Chief School Board, but did not let me go without some discussion of censorship. What could I say that was new? I could merely repeat the same thing: namely, that literature needs more latitude; that one should not even think of writing a code today in any other spirit; that justice and political wisdom demanded this spirit; that if this were not done, a handwritten literature would come into being that would be impossible to control.

Finally, the minister asked me again to intensify my efforts on the censorship code and added that he had even informed the emperor that the matter rested with me. The emperor then remarked that he knew me and ordered the work on the code to be rushed.

"Can't it be finished in a month?" His Majesty asked. The minister replied that this task was too difficult and important to rush, but that every effort would be made to bring it to a most speedy and satisfactory conclusion.

20 April. Spent the evening with Count Bludov, who had invited Davydov, Veselovsky and me for a conference on the inscription for the medal being stamped in the late emperor's honor. Conversation on the peasant question. A statute had been composed in 1830 which contained a first and an important step toward emancipation: it was forbidden to take peasants as house serfs, thus granting a measure of personal freedom. But Mordvinov dissuaded Emperor Nicholas from promulgating this directive before returning from his journey: he was going to Vilnius. After this the matter dragged on. In the meantime, revolution had broken out in France, also in Poland, and, until 1847, there was no longer any discussion of the emancipation of the peasants.

Really, one can't help liking Count Bludov. How alert and spirited he is although he is past seventy! And so kind! What if he does show off his mind and rhetoric a bit? Thank goodness there is something to show off!

Prince Shcherbatov was reprimanded for passing Kavelin's article "New Conditions in Rural Life," printed in the April issue of the *Contemporary*. The article disputed the emancipation measures contained in the rescript, which is why the ministry of internal affairs censor would not pass it. Despite the ban, Prince Shcherbatov permitted it to be printed and, as a result, was reprimanded.

A clique of the heir's military mentors are labeling Kavelin and Babst reds, hoping thereby to smear Titov and get the youth into their own hands.

The new minister of finance, Knyazhevich, obtained the emperor's permission to allow material about financial operations to be written and published freely, except where administrative measures or directives already in force were attacked by the writer.

26 April. The publication of Kavelin's article in the *Contemporary* had the following sad consequences: Prince Shcherbatov received an imperial reprimand which was entered on his service record; Titov resigned as the heir's tutor; Kavelin was discharged as preceptor. They say Titov resigned because he was told of imperial displeasure with his choice of such preceptors as Kavelin. But this was not the main reason. Some three months ago, Pogodin's letter to Titov, containing advice on how to bring up the heir, was published in Leipzig in Russian. The letter was very caustic. At that point Titov began to feel unsure of himself. The faction that sought to raise the heir in the spirit of times past, made use of this incident and delivered the final blow to Titov. But, generally speaking, another faction is playing a role in this whole affair, a broader and stronger faction which is opposed to so-called progress, to emancipation of the peasants, to the advancement of learning, to *glasnost*[x] —in brief, to all the improvements which public opinion began to demand after Nicholas's death. Prince Orlov, Prince Dolgoruky and Count Panin are considered the leaders of this faction. As one might expect.

I was summoned by the minister this evening. Again, talk about censorship and the censorship code. After returning home I went with Rebinder to visit Yazykov. There I met Redkin and Panaev. Yazykov gave me Pogodin's letter

[x] A policy of nonsecrecy, openness, of releasing information to the public.

to read. It contained several passages about education in general and several bold, but wild, ideas about the education of the heir. The main thing that struck me was the tone of the letter and several extremely caustic remarks, the kind that Pogodin likes to scatter about recklessly on paper. But what was most imprudent (if not something worse) was his circulation of the letter and its release to the press. Could Pogodin have assumed it would have a positive influence on those entrusted with the heir's education? It was invective and not advice, and we all know that invective irritates and doesn't educate. How amazing these gentlemen are! They wail about the public good, but don't want to do what is necessary to attain it.

8 May. I stayed until 10 P.M. at a meeting of the committee organized to examine the draft of university regulations. This is toil, like a lot of other such toil, all to no avail. The improvements we are proposing for the university are sheer utopian thinking. There is still not the firm realization in our country that learning needs latitude, financial support, and respect. Some people rejoice in vain, claiming that now we have a real triumph of learning. We are still far from it. It will come when it is honored not only in words, but in our hearts, too; when it will be deemed not merely a need of the state, but of human nature.

At 10 P.M. I went to see Count Bludov. This unfortunate, noble, old man has changed visibly in the past month. His health is declining rapidly. He is going to Vichy on his doctor's orders and at the insistence of the emperor. May God grant him a few more years. This is a man with a warm heart and a cultivated mind, a man with a sincere, passionate love for everything beautiful and good. I consider myself extremely lucky to have been so close to him for some three years now. Never has a week gone by without my dining with him at least once or twice and spending the evening with him. He loves to discuss literature with me and various current social issues. His mind retains the brilliance of its finest hour, and his heart, its warmth. His memory is amazing: he remembers not only the major and outstanding things he has read, seen, studied, or heard, but even the most minute details, names and dates. After every chat with him, I always carried away with me some new piece of knowledge, my mind refreshed and my heart at peace with man. And to think that we shall soon lose him! He is visibly fading away. Who can replace him? Alas! I must repeat: in our time this was one of the few highly placed people whose heart had room for all sorts of fine ideas and lofty social interests; this was a man who could grasp with his mind and heart the most delicate and subtle strands of the best in life, human knowledge, and the human heart.

9 May. Three things are foremost in the minds of thinking Russians today: emancipation of the peasants, or, the so-called peasant question, freedom of the press, and public judicial procedures. One must admit that these are the three most burning needs of a society which neither wants to return, nor can

return, to the time of Nicholas. When the government vacillates, the ultraconservatives push everything back. The government vacillates in vain. The
worst of all systems is not to adhere to any system at all, to think that, perchance, everything will work out all by itself. The ultraconservatives are behaving foolishly in seeking the impossible, for there is no turning back. If all
they want to do is to slow things up, they have no case. What would they or
society gain by it? But they are not even thinking of society. They are egotists, who would like, if they could, to stop the sun itself in its course, only
because it does not shine on them alone.

At the present time this bloc is strong. It overthrew Titov and is trying to
surround the heir with moral and intellectual nonentities. It takes repressive
measures against the press. It is delaying the solution to the peasant question.

Grand Duke Konstantin Nikolaevich enjoys a reputation as the defender
and leader of a faction composed of all thinking people, as the leader of so-
called progress.

17 May. I'm feeling better. I saw Prince Shcherbatov this morning and we
had a disquieting discussion of current affairs. He told me that Governor-
General Ignatiev, at a meeting of the Chief School Board, had attacked the
wretched leaflets that were now in mass circulation and were being sold on the
street for five kopeks. This frightens him. Yet these leaflets contain nothing
that is either clever or dangerous. The printing of anything related to social
issues is strictly forbidden. They contain nothing more than meaningless
chatter for the amusement of arcade shopkeepers, literate janitors, and the
like. One litterateur even remarked to me that they should be banned.
"Why?" I replied. "Of course it's nonsense, but it does get literate people
into the habit of reading, which is better than having them waste their time in
bars and taverns. In the meantime they will gradually shift from nonsensical
to sensible reading material. Grain you know, does grow from manure. Besides, what kind of system is it that bans everything? If a Russian merely
reaches for something in the most innocent way, he immediately receives a
slap on the wrist. Even in olden days, crude picture books with stories and
fairy tales were printed for the people! But our great administrators see danger lurking in everything."

20 May. I've been in the country since Saturday and am working on the censorship code.

22 May. I received a number of messages from the city today, summoning me
to various committee meetings, including one from the minister asking me to
see him, also letters and so forth. In brief, during the time I've been in Pavlovsk a lot of business has piled up which demands my presence in the city. In
the meantime I've been struggling with a stubborn and insidious enemy—my
illness.

Lyuboshchinsky came to dinner and brought various pieces of unpleasant news: at Panin's suggestion Russia was being divided into military districts to be administered by military governors-general; military administrations were now being set up in the districts; the press was being terribly oppressed, and so on. In other words, by pursuing imaginary evils everywhere, those who are pushing us backward are bringing down a mass of real evils upon us and themselves.

24 May. Mark Nikolaevich Lyuboshchinsky wrote me that he had seen the minister and had told him about my illness. The minister said the emperor was pressing him for the censorship code.

25 May. S. Baranovsky came to see me. He was on his way to Paris to have a railroad car built to his specifications for his project, a car which will be propelled by air rather than steam. Some company granted him 10,000 silver rubles for this project.

31 May. The word "progress" is banned from print. It is, indeed, a meaningless word when applied to the nineteenth century, which the utopians extol to the skies as the century that would give birth to the miracles of progress. A great thing—this progress, when a Europe, amidst terrible political upheavals, after passing through a bloodbath, has finally acquired a Napoleon III, a man who has put an educated, progressive, and great nation of 37 million under police surveillance. This sort of progress is a great thing in our country too, when we are even forbidden to use this word.

Certain measures indicate very clearly that we are moving backwards: for example, the military control to which Russia is being subjected following France's example, repressive censorship measures, and so on.

5 June. In the city. I gave the minister the freshly copied notebooks with the censorship code. It was decided that the explanatory memorandum and everything else would be ready for the emperor's return from Archangel, where he is going on the 12th for 18 or 19 days.

I talked at great length with the minister about censorship and suggested to him that, before sending our code to the State Council, we should submit it to the emperor with the explanatory memorandum. The heart of it lies in that memorandum. The minister approved all my suggestions.

7 June. Dined at Donon's restaurant with several litterateurs—Turgenev, Goncharov, Nekrasov, Panaev, Chernyshevsky and others. The artist, Ivanov, who had recently returned from abroad, was also there. Lots of talk; nothing especially clever or stupid. We didn't drink much. Yazykov was as witty as ever.

2 July. I went to see the minister today. He thanked me for my work on the censorship code and granted me a two-week leave. It was decided to launch the project with my explanatory memorandum upon my return, and, meanwhile, I would finish the memorandum at my brother's in Korcheva. And so, I am going.

8 July. This miserable Korcheva is as dull as a graveyard. It is poor, dirty and disorderly. Neither groves nor fields nearby. The Volga lies in a bed of mud, and, gazing at her, you wonder how such a venerable river, dear mother and wet nurse to many a province, could have decided to wend its way through such a hideous swamp and, what's more, to bear on its shoulder this Korcheva, with its taverns and drunkards.

10 July. I went to the village of Ustya, whose lady of the manor is so typical of her class. She had travelled abroad and returned with an enormous quantity of crinolines, a passion for extravagance, harsh opinions of Napoleon III, Paris, Switzerland, the emancipation and contempt for anything Russian. Moreover, her wine cellar was well stocked with champagne and she didn't spare it.

In general one sees or hears little that is comforting in this province. Swindles, abuses in judicial and administrative affairs are rampant here. Widespread drunkenness among the common folk produces a particularly unpleasant impression.

16 July. I'm home. I read a book yesterday which left me with some distressing thoughts. How depressing it is to think that people have absorbed so little of true Christianity and have hardly applied it in their daily lives. The book I am referring to is *The Rural Clergy in Russia*. It was written by a real expert on the subject, evidently a priest, and was printed abroad. What a dreadful picture of the state of our clergy! They say this book was presented to the Metropolitan and other clerical authorities. They became furious and called it slander. Only Bazhanov did not agree with them.[y]

4 August. Entrance examinations at the university. I stayed overnight in the city.

5 August. A huge tide of applicants are seeking admission to the university. Most are badly prepared—backward, with little knowledge. There are many Poles, Germans and foreigners. They are better prepared, as are our own gymnasium graduates. The youths educated at home are like drab cloth woven by the fingers of mamas under the supervision of wise papas. Yet I would not close the university's doors to anyone, save the most unsuited: what little knowledge we give them will be worthwhile.

Most of them have chosen to specialize in administration and economics. Of 250 applicants, only one wants to study in the Department of History and Philology.

7 August. I was notified by Minister of the Imperial Court Count Adlerberg that His Imperial Majesty was pleased to appoint me a member of the commission for reorganization of the Theatre Board.

19 August. We have had many catastrophes this summer. There have been

[y] V. B. Bazhanov, professor of religion at St. Petersburg University and Court priest.

forest fires everywhere and worst of all, peat fires, which have destroyed many villages. A station on the Moscow railroad burned down and several miles of wooden crossties on the roadbed burned out, forcing trains to come to a halt. It's almost a month now that we residents of Pavlovsk have been literally drowning in dense clouds of smoke coming from burning peat.

30 August. As for the peasant question, only the dull-witted or hopelessly malicious can question the need for emancipation.

I've just come from a fire again. Barely had they managed to extinguish the first one, when a second broke out. It flared up next to the first, only a little higher, and engulfed a whole block. Sixteen buildings were in flames.

Several friends had dined with me in honor of my name-day. Now they're gone and we are alone, watching a majestic glow in the sky. It's 9 P.M. There is talk of arson. A whole pile of inflammable materials was found somewhere on another block, but the arsonists failed to ignite them. There's no doubt that, during the confusion of the fire, the soldiers of the local Obraztsov Regiment, summoned to help, engaged in terrible looting.

10 September. At Goncharov's this evening I heard a reading of his new novel *Oblomov.* It contains much sensitive analysis of the heart. The language is beautiful. The character of the woman and her love are superbly understood and portrayed. But there is much more of this sort of thing that can only be explained as a whole. Besides unquestionable talent and poetic inspiration in this work, there is much that is clever, and much careful, intelligent workmanship. It has an entirely different tone from all our current novels and stories. Also present at the reading were Kraevsky, who bought the novel for *Notes of the Fatherland,* Dudyshkin, and V. N. Maikov, publisher of the children's magazine *Snowdrop.* It was decided to continue the reading on Saturday.

16 September. Present day extremist liberals, with their negative attitude and despotism, are simply dreadful. They are like despots, but stand at the opposite pole. They are as egotistical and intolerant as the ultraconservatives.

The most terrible and unbearable tyranny is one that encroaches on our cherished thoughts, on the sanctity of our beliefs. According to the liberal code of present-day extremist liberals, you must stand at one with them until, finally, there is nothing left of your own—neither a thought, nor a feeling to your name! No!—freedom itself is created by the power of things alone, and not by someone's arbitrary will. If it is based on passion, it is unstable and unreliable. Only a freedom which history has produced, which no one has imposed upon a people, which has not emerged as an abstract doctrine but as the fruit of genuine toil and genuine inspiration, will endure and yield blessings abundant.

The students are seething with anger and bringing down disaster upon the university.[1] There was a clash of sorts with the police. The chief of police complained to the superintendent about the students' behavior. A sharp exchange of words followed. Alas, dear students, you are helping neither the university nor the cause of learning with your foolish antics!

21 September. I spoke today with the student Bogolyubov, who has influence over his fellow students. I urged him to calm the students, to persuade them to behave more humbly, to think more about learning, and not to give the university's enemies any excuse to harm it in the eyes of both the emperor and the public.

25 September. The student disturbances are causing quite an uproar. What a shame! It is forcing young people to exaggerate their importance and is taking them further and further away from their studies, which alone should reign supreme within a university's walls.

28 September. We apparently gained little from a change in ministers. Evgraf Petrovich Kovalevsky is also a very fine man, but, as before, nothing is getting done in the ministry. The fates of learning and education, as before, remain in the hands of Gaevsky, Kislovsky, and Berte. A few days ago I was visited by the chairman of the Committee for Foreign Censorship, Fyodor Ivanovich Tyutchev, who complained that the new minister would decide one thing in words and another on paper. Ah, yes, this is *norovism* all over again.

I am going to see the minister today. Will he have something to tell me? He seems to have forgotten completely about censorship and the censorship code. Yet how many times has he kept telling me about the crying need for a code and even urged me on in the name of the emperor. Now July, August, and September have passed; my project is ready, but everyone appears to have forgotten about the censorship issue.

I just came from the minister. Evgraf Petrovich has surpassed my expectations. I found him in the very same study where I had so often seen Norov, sitting in the very same armchair. A sinister omen! We began to talk and—oh, horrors! It was Norov himself, whole, with all his instability, his lack of character, his inability to cope with anything beyond ordinary office routine, and, finally, with his repudiation of what he had pompously and enthusiastically approved so recently. Instead of going to the emperor and explaining, with this same enthusiasm, the state of censorship and the need for the solutions worked out by the censorship committee, he is now turning over the project to the tortures of the Chief Censorship Administration; and in his own words, he hasn't any faith at all in most of its members. Such is the end to my labors and hopes! I left him, distressed and annoyed, weary of hearing how difficult it was to cope with censorship matters, and similar complaints, that people who are weak and unsuited for demanding work are prone to air.

5 October. I went to see Tyutchev this morning to discuss ways of getting the censorship project moving. Fydor Ivanovich told me, by the way, about a proposal sent here from Berlin by our ambassador, Baron Budberg, suggesting we create a system of *warnings and fines,* following France's example.

"Fine! But what about our present system of preliminary censorship? Would we keep that too?" I asked.

"That's exactly the problem!" replied Tyutchev.

On imperial orders a committee composed of Prince Gorchakov, Prince Dolgoruky, Timashev, our minister, and Tyutchev, had been organized to review the proposal. Tyutchev protested strongly against this double censorship—preliminary censorship plus a system of warnings and fines. Our minister agreed with him.

"But," remarked Prince Dolgoruky, "something must be done to appease the emperor; he's very disturbed by the state of censorship."

I went to see Knyazhevich this evening. Aleksandr Maksimovich is very friendly with our minister, and I wanted to persuade him to influence his friend and get him to speak directly to the emperor about the censorship matter; otherwise there is no hope of success. He promised to read my memorandum.

6 October. Sent Knyazhevich my explanatory memorandum. Visited Count Bludov. I was delighted to find him in a cheerful mood despite the fact that the day before yesterday he had been badly shaken by a fire in an adjacent building. We had a very pleasant chat after dinner. Talked about everything; discussed censorship, too. He wanted to read my memorandum. The minister, he said, wanted to present it directly to the emperor. However, I, on my part, had done all I could, and considered my obligation finished, which I told the minister in a letter enclosed with the memorandum.

Trouble at the local religious academy. The students, dissatisfied with their inspector, the monk Victorin, complained to the Metropolitan and threatened to turn to secular authorities for help if they weren't given satisfaction. They sharply condemned the general state of our academic and seminary training. This criticism, people say, stems from a book published in Leipzig, *The Russian Rural Clergy.*

But the ecclesiastical authorities are hardly concerned about improving their affairs and prefer to promote such pamphlets as the following: *A Warning Against Being Carried Away By the Spirit of Our Times* and *Are Modern Ideas in Keeping With the Orthodox Faith?* In the first pamphlet they try to show that progress consists of the preservation of church traditions and that all knowledge is contained in theology. There is nothing to discuss, and one must stick to the letter of church doctrine. In other brochures, extremely ascetic rules for public morals, manners and behavior are given; concerts, tableaux vivants, charity balls, etc. are anathematized.

8 October. I sent my explanatory memorandum to Count Bludov. We now have a veritable reign of chaos. There is chaos in everything: in administration, in moral principles, in convictions, and in the minds of those who hope to control public opinion.

11 October. I spent the evening with Prince Shcherbatov, who had come from the country to St. Petersburg on his way abroad. He told me about some incidents of rebellion among the peasants. In some places the peasants refused to work; in others, they wouldn't pay the steward the *obrok*,[z] and elsewhere nearly thrashed the district police inspector and the district police officer. But most of these incidents were directed at landowners whose peasants were on *barshchina*.[a]

12 October. Saw the minister. He fully endorses my explanatory memorandum and agrees with all my ideas. But it will have to be shortened somewhat for the State Council. There was much discussion of censorship and the proposal to establish a special bureau which would deal with literature by employing moral suasion rather than administrative measures. I remarked that this was wishful thinking. The minister agreed, but said some people wanted this.

Kovalevsky thanked me again for the memorandum and for my work on the censorship code, but my hopes for success along the lines I wished to give it have been blasted.

21 October. My work on the censorship code is getting completely snarled up in bureaucracy. Some clerk is now cutting it up into excerpts, notes and Lord knows what else! In brief, a labor of so many months— is lost. . . .

30 October. They say that Herzen, in no. 25 of the *Bell*, has let loose a stream of invective at various people, not excluding some very high placed ones. This was not very clever. Herzen did not conduct himself like a man who wanted to promote a good cause and thus chose the best means for this purpose, but like a hell-bent fanatic who takes pleasure in shouting his lungs out. It's a pity, for he could be very useful. Now, however, as a result of his excesses, those who feared him are beginning to become indifferent toward him, and those who considered him to be one of our most useful social activists are losing respect for him, so that little by little he might lose all his influence in Russia.

Meanwhile, some official documents were reprinted in the *Bell*, and an investigation is now under way to determine how they were obtained.

9 November. I dined with Count Bludov this week. Among other things, we discussed Herzen and his *Bell*. The emperor is very distressed and displeased over his latest escapades. The government wanted to lithograph some memo on the Peasant Committee so its members might have easier access to it. The emperor would not permit it, saying that "no sooner is something lithographed, than it appears in the *Bell*."

The government wants to have its own organ in literature which would be run by several litterateurs. We discussed this at Count Bludov's. The count said he discerned among us three kinds of writers: the first are malicious and

---

[z] An annual payment to the state or landowner, exacted from the serfs.

[a] Compulsory service due the landowners from their serfs.

stubborn in their extreme ambitions; the second have no ambitions at all save those of filling their pockets; and the third are noble and gifted people who can act only out of conviction. The government cannot win over members of the third group unless it gives them a role in its fine plans. The count questions the success of the proposal, but is not against trying it out as an experiment.

10 November. Went to the theatre, to a performance of *Othello*. The mulatto, or as the poster called him, the African, Aldridge, who had come here for several days, played the role of Othello in English with German actors. I can't speak or understand English, but since I know the play well, I went to the theatre—which I don't regret. Aldridge is a great artist. One can hardly go further than this actor in expressing strong and deep passions. In the third act, in the scene with Iago, he is so terrifying that it is difficult for people with weak nerves to bear, and you are choked with tears in the heartbreaking scene in the last act.

22 November. Our university youth is in a state of ferment everywhere for, I believe, the following reasons. Our society has been caught, as it were, unawares, by the privileges it has so recently acquired. Many are giddy with the new freedom, particularly our young people, who are not, in any case, too inclined towards moderation. A man who is suddenly led out of the darkness into the light, from a suffocating atmosphere into pure air, is always stunned at first and giddy. On the other hand, the majority of our leaders cling to the old regime and are classic examples of an inability to adapt to new conditions. The third cause of university disorders lies, finally, in the very organization of the universities, which deprived professors of their moral influence on youth the moment supervision passed into the hands of the inspector and his aides. Young people see him as a police officer, and he, by the very nature of his position, cannot carry any moral weight with them.

In general, dissonance and disorder abound in our country. Russian society now resembles a large lake, in whose depths burn subterranean fires, while bubbles keep popping up, bursting and popping out again on its surface. This effervescence in itself does not represent anything unusual; it is not yet a great problem. But the real problem lies in the total absence of any organizational principle, in the absence of strong wills and higher moral convictions. And here's still another problem: there is not a single idea of yesterday, however solidly founded, which would not today seem obsolete. The enthusiasm that greeted some measure yesterday, has already cooled today. Every day something new is begun, and the next day—what was just begun is discarded unfinished, and not because something better has been found but because of some blind, uncontrollable, drive. Whither are we going? Some kind of invisible force, like a demon, drives us, whirls us about and throws us off our course. Everyone goes his own way and struggles not to make things easier and better for all, but to make them conform to his own desires. We have as many factions as we have ambitions. Someone will make a fuss not because he is interested in defending some principle, but so that he can say: "This is *I*, gentlemen: this is *mine*."

28 November. Dined with Count Bludov. No one was there except the well-known singer, Isabella Greenberg. Talked about contemporary literature. The count felt that the literary protest printed in the *St. Petersburg Bulletin* in defense of the Jews, who were reviled by *Illustration,* was preposterous.[2] Then the count expressed surprise at the great number of new journals appearing among us and could not understand who would fill them and who would read them. He also complained about some journals taking such excessive liberties that it became difficult to defend them.

Our minister has gone to Moscow. They say something has happened at the university again.

6 December. They say the emperor expressed his displeasure at the Council of Ministers over the opposition he was encountering in the Committee on the Emancipation of the Peasants. He referred directly to Muraviev and Butkov, who, during their summer travels around Russia, spread rumors everywhere that the emancipation proposal existed only for show: there would be a lot of talk, they said, and with that, the whole matter would end. What a strange state of affairs! The emperor sees in some people direct opposition to his generous intentions, yet these same people remain firmly entrenched in their positions.

17 December. Drama at the university. A student delegation approached me today with a petition to the superintendent requesting protection from the police and soldiers. (They had had an encounter with them two days ago at the fire.) The petition described the episode as follows: the students rushed in to save property of fellow students in the burning building; the soldiers, who had formed a chain around the fire, not only would not allow them through, but, when they pushed them back, beat them with their gun butts, egged on by the officer in command of the chain. "Beat the rascals!" he kept repeating.

I could not, of course, sign the petition, but promised to speak to the rector. The students were terribly agitated. Ah, yes, the rector is a fine chap, all right. Instead of calming the students and controlling them, he sent them off to their professors and kept himself well out of sight.

18 December. An inquiry was ordered on the student affair.

22 December. I saw the superintendent. He was in a turmoil over the student affair. I proposed the following to him: form a small council consisting of the rector and three or four faculty members to establish closer contact with the students. By being in direct and constant contact with them, such a council, backed by university authority, could anticipate any dangerous plans far more effectively than an inspector, who hasn't the slightest moral influence on the student body. The superintendent promised to discuss this with the minister.

A proposal has been made to replace the student uniform with ordinary dress, so students would be indistinguishable from anyone else subject to the authority of the regular police. Of course this would ease things for the university. But, on the other hand, it would put these poor youths completely at the mercy of our barbarous police.

24 December. Dined with Count Bludov. Pletnyov and Tyutchev were there. Talk about the celebrated apparatus recently organized to curb writers who, in the opinion of Chevkin, Panin and others, are preparing a revolution for Russia. They conceived the idea of creating a committee which would *lovingly, paternally* and *wisely* guide our literature, particularly our journalists, on to the right path. It would have direct contact with them and employ friendly persuasion without assuming any censorship powers.

"And what if our litterateurs ignore them?" I asked the count.

"Well, so they'll ignore them."

"If it doesn't matter one way or another," I remarked, "the committee won't matter, either."

"Fine! You see, this would be something like the French Bureau de la Presse, remodeled on the Russian style. An amazing thing! There is nothing too absurd or too irrational that couldn't be proposed as a government measure in our country."

Count Bludov, was, of course, opposed to this absurd apparatus, which, most certainly, would either turn into a secret Buturlin Committee (which had thrived under Nicholas) or into the most ridiculous nothing.

Who, then, are the members of this "triumvirate" as Tyutchev calls it? This is the most curious thing of all. They are Mukhanov (our minister's deputy), Count A. V. Adlerberg (son of V. G. Adlerberg), and Timashev. If one had deliberately tried to seek out the people least suited for this role, better ones could not have been found. They are going to guide our litterateurs, advise them, reason with them about questions of the greatest importance, moral, political and literary—they—who never reasoned about anything, never read and still don't read anything. How comic and tragic!

The minister had strongly opposed the organization of such an apparatus, and, before his departure for Moscow, it was decided to drop the idea. When he returned, he found the committee an accomplished fact. This was the handiwork of Minister of Foreign Affairs Prince Gorchakov.

It's interesting how Timashev managed to get on the committee. Initially he was rejected because of his reputation as chief of the secret police. He desperately wanted, however, to be included among the three great guardians of purity of Russian thought, and so he devised the following ingenious argument. "Since," he said, "I don't enjoy popularity, permit me to be a member of the committee, so I can have the opportunity to acquire it."

28 December. I visited I. S. Turgenev. He has written a new novel of completely artistic bent. How marvelous! It is high time literature became more than a collection of memorandums on extraordinary events and we stopped thinking of it as only a disciplinary whip.

Turgenev told me about his dinner with Prince Orlov. The prince also considered the recent establishment of a literary "triumvirate" a foolish move. But he thought that those who sought to create this apparatus had something else in mind. They wanted to arrogate unto themselves controlling power over all the ministries, and literature served as a convenient pretext. This was what Adlerberg, in particular, had in mind. Fine plans, fine people, fine everything! Alas, poor Russian land, who has not abused you, and how you have been abused!

This "triumvirate" business is very obvious: it will turn into a secret committee. I had a visit today from a student who had graduated this year and whom Mukhanov had invited to work as a staff member, that is, as a spy, for this committee. Mukhanov wanted him to read the journals and report anything improper to the committee. The young man was very perplexed by this offer and had come to me for advice. I pointed out the shady side of this proposal, and by the time he left, he appeared firmly convinced of the importance of honor and integrity.

A proclamation was posted at the university forbidding students to applaud professors at lectures or to express their approval or disapproval.

30 December. The minister told me today that he felt ashamed to face me. He had recommended me for a decoration for my work on censorship legislation but the emperor had rejected his request. The minister went so far as to ask the emperor to regard it as a personal favor to him and he still refused. Evgraf Petrovich expressed his profound displeasure and regrets to me, and I, in turn, thanked him as warmly for his kind interest in me and hastened to assuage his feelings. What happened was very understandable. Why should there be any rewards for one's efforts to advance knowledge and literature? I worked hard and conscientiously but only for the sake of an idea. There should never be any thought of reward. Now, if only this idea were to become a reality and bear fruit. But all such hopes are mere dreams, dreams, dreams, and completely joyless ones at that!

1859

1 January. Yesterday I dined at Goncharov's with several other litterateurs—Turgenev, Botkin, Annenkov, Panaev, Nekrasov, Polonsky, Druzhinin. It was a sumptuous and rather lively dinner. A toast was drunk "to our finest citizen," in my honor.

After dinner, Nekrasov read his remarkable poem "Cemetery," and then Botkin and I left for the theatre where my family was waiting for me.

11 January. We are diseased with committees. I just received an invitation from General Levshin to join a committee created to draw up detailed science curricula and to select textbooks for schools under military jurisdiction. In the meantime I've been thinking of quitting all these committees as soon as I go on pension. They are a complete waste of time. Mine included.

16 January. The case of the students who were beaten at the fire on the commandant's order, was investigated by a special commission set up on imperial orders. It turned out that the students were completely innocent.

Shchebalsky was asked to prepare a monthly survey for the emperor of the most outstanding articles in our journals and to include excerpts from them, as was done with books during Norov's tenure, in order to acquaint the emperor with our best literary and scientific works.

17 January. I finished my twenty-fifth year as a professor today. So, I'm now an emeritus! At their next meeting the University Council will decide whether I can stay on for another five years. How quickly those twenty-five years flew by!

The students are circulating a sheet containing the names of professors whom they want to drive out of the university.

23 January. We are being inundated by periodicals these days. It's becoming simply impossible to go through them all, and, to tell the truth, there's no point to it either. There's nothing different about any of the new ones. Our best sources of intellectual nourishment among the journals still are the *Russian Messenger, Notes of the Fatherland,* the *Contemporary,* the *Reader's Library;* and among the newspapers—the *St. Petersburg Bulletin.* The *Russian Diary* hasn't found its niche yet. If it continues on its present course, that is, of publishing dry statistics and data, reports of fires and murders in the provinces, I suppose it will become a kind of useful specialized newspaper, but dry, boring and intellectually unstimulating.

They say Timashev is trying his best to get the *Sail's* publisher, I. S. Aksakov, packed off to Vyatka. An excellent idea; one that is most up to date, patriotic and useful for the government; an idea that reminds every trusting person, every utopian and optimist, that we are not as far removed from the times of Nicholas I as they may think. But I don't think the emperor will agree to this. It would be a big mistake.

26 January. Aksakov wasn't sent to Vyatka, but his journal was banned. Kraevsky repeated an interesting conversation to me that took place between Aksakov and Timashev. Aksakov, in the course of the conversation, said:

"Your Eminence, you fear revolution. You are right—we are really threatened by revolution, for there are conspirators."

"What did you say?" asked Timashev, horrified. "Where are they?"

"In the Third Section. The Third Section with its persecution of ideas and its oppressive measures is brewing revolution by pitting those who think against our most kind emperor."

29 January. Gorlov was forbidden to give lectures on political economy. Ah, yes! A great advance for *glasnost!* We seem, in all seriousness, to be calling up the ghost of Nicholas I. This could be very dangerous now. The government is wrong to reject the consequences after accepting the principle of *glasnost.*

30 January. I have based everything I have ever done on a set of moral principles built around ideas of a lofty image of human dignity and perfection. I wanted to influence people with these ideas. I tried to make these ideas attractive by giving them beauty and grace, elements which I had taken from my store of moral principles. My actions were not dictated by the demands of people and circumstances, but by my personal inspiration. It happened that I frequently drew attention to myself, but since I had little in common with what was most vital to people of my milieu or with their passions and aspirations, I was soon forgotten. When it was convenient, they used me, but when the need passed, they abandoned me. I did not want concessions or was unable to grant them, but this wasn't out of pride or lack of understanding, but stemmed from principles and inclinations that had developed in me since childhood. In a word, I always was, am, and, I suppose, will always be, a so-called doctrinaire person . . .

1 February. My relations with Pletnyov have been strained for a long time. In the course of our twenty-five-year-long protestations of friendship, he has stepped on my toes more than once, and, upon my arrival from abroad had tried surreptitiously to make things difficult for me again. I noticed this and took a defensive stance, switching from friendly relations to a mere observance of decorum. And so it has continued until now. But it is repugnant to me to meet a person so often in this way, a man with whom I once broke daily spiritual bread, although to tell the truth, I rarely received a piece of pure, fresh bread from him. The thought occurred to me a long time ago to have a frank talk with him, to give him an opportunity to clear himself completely, so that I, on my part, could completely forget his sneaky behavior toward me. Yesterday morning I finally made up my mind to do this and went to his home. He wasn't in—he had gone to mass. Too bad. On the way home I stopped by at Zvegintsev's, where I accidentally learned something that completely thwarted my sentimental impulse and showed me again that I was dealing with an ungracious, cold egotist, spoiled by his long contact with all sorts of earthly abominations and hypocrisy, who would inwardly scoff at your fine impulses and, at the first opportunity, would deceive you again with sweet talk while actually trying to harm you. I didn't make a second trip to Pletnyov's.

4 February. Yesterday, the University Council elected me distinguished professor for another five years.

6 February. Dined with our minister, Kovalevsky. After dinner he called me aside and told me that the new Committee for Supervision of the Press (Adlerberg, Mukhanov and Timashev)[b] wanted to consult me about its organization and operations. Evgraf Petrovich wouldn't let me get a word in edgewise, and, taking my hand, added: "Please, please, don't refuse."

I told him that it was difficult to give advice where the aims of an organization were either vague or unlimited.

"Please, don't say no!" said the minister. "Come to their meeting and give them a lecture. You will find among them one member who understands—Count Adlerberg."

Tyutchev, too, confirmed this later.

I finally told the minister to have them set a date and I would come.

Deputy Minister Mukhanov also spoke to me, hinting at something that I would hear later from the minister.

Mukhanov enjoys the Court's favor, but outside he is known as a shallow man. I spoke to him today for the first time, and, after some fifteen minutes with him, concluded that public opinion had scarcely misjudged him. He spewed forth hackneyed platitudes, but with an air of enormous respect for himself and his utterances.

In the meantime, the committee, as I had feared, threatens to turn into another "secret" committee and, judging from the people on it, will undoubtedly produce some appalling nonsense. A fine way to go about the business of guiding thought.

7 February. The "secret" committee finally came into its own by asking the minister to announce to all concerned, that censors and writers must appear before it for explanations and guidance when summoned. Mukhanov was given the power to withhold certificates for the release of books or journals from the printer's until he personally granted permission. This is far worse than the Buturlin secret committee. Even Emperor Nicholas I didn't resort to

[b] This committee is referred to earlier as "the triumvirate" and later as the Press or Publishing Committee.

this. How low they've sunk! What can I possibly say to them when they invite me? Any attempt to reason with them is completely out of the question.

What a shame that events have taken such a turn. They are destroying any possibility of a rapprochement between the thinking Russian and his government; and, as accustomed as we are to bad administration, and as scant as are our means to oppose it, now we are faced with an evil, and a terrible one at that. On the one hand, we are rapidly drowning in all kinds of administrative disorders, confusion, and chaos; on the other hand, we have an outpouring of opinions which are completely opposed to any kind of reactionary course—and these opinions are dangerous when they become a normal state of mind. Yes, they are always dangerous, even for us. And at the top there is a deplorable inability to provide any sort of orderly and rational direction. It is really bad, very, very bad!

The government is frightened by the unrest that has been growing among us for some time now. The government doesn't want to sit idly by, and it knows only one approach to the problem—that is—restraint, oppression and intimidation. It doesn't understand that its function is to *govern* and *guide*; and it is difficult for it to understand this because it won't allow any kind of talent to penetrate administration and has surrounded itself with an impenetrable wall of weak minds and faint hearts. The situation is even more deplorable when you think of how and by whom the heir is being educated.

8 February. Student dinner. About sixty people gathered at the home of Timofeev, one of our former students. It was a noisy, gay, but decent affair. Sakharov delivered a speech. Then a toast was offered to the university, followed by one in my honor. I proposed a toast to Turgenev and said: "Gentlemen! Fate has cast us into various fields of endeavor, but each of us, wherever he may be, whatever path he may have taken, always carries in his heart a deep love of Russian thought and the Russian language, and, therefore, of Russian literature. Let us drink to one of the finest builders of our literature —to Ivan Sergeevich Turgenev, who in his works has been so true to both artistic beauty and our national spirit, that one doesn't know which he loves more —art or Russia. I think he loves both equally." Afterwards, another toast was drunk to my health and even to my wife's. Then we sang, and left at 10 o'clock.

17 February. I received an official communication stating that the emperor, in deference to the reasons outlined in my letter to Zhikharev, has granted his imperial consent to my resignation from the Committee for Theatre Reform. And so I am gradually cutting off the branches of my official tree, branches which have never offered either shade, flowers or fruit and which only drain the sap from the very roots of my life. Under other circumstances my conscience would not permit me to renounce a social obligation, but in this situation, I must say that no one is concerned about art. All we'll get is a torrent of words, proposals and statistics, and the matter itself will be put aside and will die in the chancery. Besides, I now need to consolidate my efforts. I've wasted a lot of time and energy on incidental issues.

18 February. I am working on a project I conceived a long time ago on the study of philosophy and the need to teach it in higher educational institutions.

20 February. The minister of education summoned me for a talk. I arrived at 1 o'clock.

"The matter of your appointment to the Press Committee," the minister said to me, "has taken a rather serious and delicate turn. The emperor has expressed his desire for your appointment, and now I am conveying his wish to you. Count Adlerberg has informed me about it."

"Yes," I replied, "this really puts me in an awkward position. I am prepared to undertake any kind of work which would offer at least some hope for a cause which means so much to me as learning and literature. But if this committee was created for the moral supervision of literature, as its members claim it was, there are no grounds for its existence and it doesn't have a leg to stand on. If it is going to turn into a secret committee, it is standing on muddy ground and I don't want to soil myself on it."

We talked about it for a long time and finally I promised Evgraf Petrovich that I would try my best to change this whole situation for the better.

While we were discussing this, Mukhanov arrived, and I immediately got involved in a conversation with him on this issue.

Mukhanov tried to prove to me that the committee had no reactionary intentions; that it did not have anything in common with the Committee of April 2; that the emperor was certainly not interested in creating a similar apparatus.

"Personally, Your Excellency," I replied, "I am not worried about it becoming another Committee of April 2, because I think that's impossible. I consider the very thought of it repugnant to the spirit of our times as well as an insult to our enlightened emperor. But I can't hide the fact from you that the public is very prejudiced against this new committee."

26 February. All week I've been busy thinking about the proposal to join the committee and have been involved in discussions with them about it. I was invited to a meeting on Monday, the 23rd, where I came face to face with Count Adlerberg, Timashev and Mukhanov.

I was received very courteously, particularly by Count Adlerberg. I had made up my mind to express frankly both my convictions and my views on the committee, so they could decide for themselves whether I could participate in their affairs. They listened to me very attentively.

I told them of the public's negative attitude toward the committee; that it considered it another April 2nd committee; that I personally considered it an impossibility today and thought their committee could not be either repressive or reactionary; that its sole function was to serve as an intermediary between literature and the emperor and to influence public opinion by getting the government's views and aims across via the press in much the same way as literature did by bringing its ideas to the public.

They took all this very well. Then I added that if I were to sit on the committee, it would have to be with the right to vote. It was decided that I would give them a memorandum containing the gist of my remarks and that I would bring it with me on Thursday.

Today, Thursday, I read my memorandum to them in which I outlined my ideas in greater detail. Enlarging upon the thesis that literature did not nurture any revolutionary schemes, I took the position that there wasn't the slightest reason to take repressive measures against it; that ordinary censorship measures were completely adequate; that literature couldn't and shouldn't be restrained by administrative measures; and that, perhaps, the committee should limit itself, according to the emperor's wishes, to keeping a watchful eye on the mood of the public and to guiding public opinion, rather than literature, on to the right path.

I forgot to mention that, on Monday, after my discussion with the committee, I went to see the minister and told him that I was demanding voting rights. He completely supported my demand and tried to persuade me to accept the position of administrative director of the committee on that condition, since the voting right would put me in a position where I could undoubtedly be a force for good.

He also told me that, on Sunday, at the ball, he had spoken to the emperor about me and referred to me as one, who, in his opinion, could be more useful on the committee than anyone else. The emperor turned to Adlerberg and said: "Hear that, Aleksandr?" Earlier, too, while the committee was being formed, the minister had proposed my name for membership along with the names of Vyazemsky, Tyutchev, Pletnyov, and E. P. Kovalevsky (his brother).

After all this my memorandum was accepted, and tomorrow a report goes to the emperor. The die is cast. I am now embarking on a new career in public service. I shall certainly encounter difficulties—and enormous ones, too. But it would be wrong and dishonest of me to evade them, to refuse to do my part. There will be a great deal of gossip. Perhaps many will reproach me because I, with my spotless reputation, have decided to sit on a tribunal which is considered repressive. But that's exactly the point, gentlemen. I want to stifle its appetite for repression. If I can work effectively—fine. If I can't, I'll leave.

In any case, I am absolutely determined to fight to the bitter end against repressive measures. But, at the same time, I am convinced that literature ought not to sever all its ties with the government and assume a hostile stance. If I am right, then it is incumbent on one of us to hold on to this tie and to assume the role, so to say, of a connecting link. I shall try to be that link.

Perhaps I shall succeed in convincing the committee that it must approach this sort of business in broad statesmanlike fashion; that it should not war with ideas, with literature, or with anything at all, because it is not a clique, but a public figure; that it should not irritate people; that it has an enormous responsibility toward Russia, the emperor and posterity, and that because of this responsibility, it must not get involved in petty literary squabbles, but should look beyond all that and view literature as a social force which can do a great deal of good for society. Yes, I shall assume this new responsibility, *if I am given the right to vote.* Tyutchev, Goncharov, and Lyuboshchinsky warmly endorse my decision.

I think even the committee understood the purity of my intentions. Not a word was mentioned there about any kind of benefits or rewards. As far as salary is concerned, I shall be satisfied with the first figure to be named. As far as my other activities are concerned, it goes without saying that I shall have to curtail them.

27 February. Can this be true? I am told that the editor of the Polish newspaper, Ogryzko, has been imprisoned in the fortress. It's true that the newspaper was banned, but that the editor himself was arrested, I learned only today from one of my Friday visitors. The culprit in this case is said to be Prince Gorchakov, viceroy of Poland, who is here now. He attacked the editor for a letter by Lelewel which appeared in his newspaper, a letter which, in itself, perhaps, is innocent, but is incriminating because it links the editor to a political criminal. Is there anything that cannot be made to appear sinister? In any case this is a very deplorable event. It is the first harsh measure directed at the press by the present regime.

The main trouble with Nicholas I's reign was that the whole thing was a mistake. His twenty-nine-year-long fight against freedom of thought not only failed to extinguish it, but created a force in opposition to the government.

Everything that I heard about Ogryzko and his Polish newspaper, the *Word,* is true.

1 March. I received a document with imperial confirmation of my appointment as administrative director of the Publishing Committee. Bless me, Oh Lord, that I may work for the good of thought and literature in a spirit of harmony and conciliation.

I saw the minister this morning and conveyed the contents of my memorandum, which had been read at the committee meeting on Thursday. He was very pleased and said he now felt reassured, knowing that the cause of literature was in good hands. We talked for a long time in this spirit. What an upright, noble man!

2 March. Went to see Delyanov this morning. He told me the story of the banning of the *Word* and Ogryzov's imprisonment in the fortress. This punishment befell him for his dealings with a political criminal. Delyanov made strong pleas on his behalf to Dolgoruky, considering himself basically responsible for the appearance of the letter in the paper.

At 3 o'clock I went to Mukhanov's office for a committee meeting, where I was now greeted as a colleague. The emperor had read my entire memorandum and, they say, was extremely pleased with it. This was fine news, for it contained a great deal in defense of literature. Count Adlerberg told me, incidentally, that I must be presented to the emperor.

4 March. I have heard that my appointment to the committee was generally received with joy in the literary community. Some of the *extremists* feel, however, that by affiliating myself with the committee, I have firmly established its existence; that if I had refused the appointment, it would have realized its inability to attract anyone worthwhile connected with literature, and would have been forced to close down as a wholly unsuccessful and impossible venture. But suppose they didn't close down? Then wouldn't the committee become repressive? It is unlikely that it would so kindly take to suicide. On the contrary, wouldn't literature's deliberate move to alienate itself from the government provide the committee with a new pretext to frighten the government; and wouldn't the committee then feel committed to attack literature in every possible way? The government very likely would again resort to *harsh measures,* and suspensions would be slapped on journals left and right. What then? Isn't it better to get what you want by peaceful means? If I had the courage to assume the arduous role of an intermediary between literature and the government, it was only because I wanted to be in a position to defend the interests of literature should they be threatened.

Literature can be menaced by still another powerful enemy, the kind of enemy that would make its alliance with the government a necessity—and that enemy is the reactionary, ultraconservative and obscurantist encroachments of our ecclesiastical authorities.

5 March. Meeting at Count Adlerberg's. The committee wants to employ special readers who would comb all the journals and note down harmful passages. I explained to them that such a step would serve only to reinforce the negative impression the public already had; it would remember that the April 2nd Committee also had special readers for this purpose. Instead, I proposed that we place the responsibility on the collaborators of the journal we are planning to publish. In the course of their work they would have to follow all the journals; thus the committee, without resorting to artificial means, would be in a position to know what was going on in literature. I hoped, through this proposal, to eliminate the idea of professional readers. They cast a shadow on the committee which, as it is, doesn't enjoy the public's confidence. Mukhanov replied that professional readers were necessary as the journal's collaborators would be unable to cope with the huge mass of journals. The other members also agreed with him.

7 March. I read my memorandum to Delyanov. He warmly endorsed it. Ogryzko has become the main topic of conversation. His imprisonment in the fortress and the banning of his paper have made an extremely bad impression on the public. They say the emperor agreed to this measure only because Gorchakov had stated that he would not return to Warsaw unless Ogryzko were put in the fortress.

At the Council of Ministers, Kovalevsky, Rostovtsev and Prince Dolgoruky took a strong stand in favor of Ogryzko.

9 March. The Committee on Publishing discussed the problem of temperance societies, which have sprung up rapidly throughout the empire and have placed the government in a difficult predicament. On the one hand, it threatens to undermine *otkup*,[c] which would result in significant losses for the state treasury, and, on the other hand, the government can't block such a noble impulse on the part of the people to reduce alcoholism. Mukhanov called for the publication of an article, not as a criticism of temperance, but as a criticism of the illegal action of those peasants who decree the flogging and fining of drunkards. It was decided to discuss this further at the next session.

Discussion of the proposed journal. I told them again how difficult it was to set it up, but that I was working on a plan. The main problem was finding assistants: the literary world is suspicious of the committee's activities.

Count Adlerberg told me that the emperor would like to grant me an audience on Wednesday at 1 P.M.

I'm extremely disturbed by all the gossip. But I must learn to cope with all these problems: the advice of well-intentioned people, the machinations of my enemies, and the difficulties of the job before me. Ah, yes, many people can talk eloquently about doing this and that for literature. I don't want to talk, I want to act. It's easy to sermonize, but difficult to act. It was not I who created the committee. But when I became aware of the yoke it would impose on literature, I tried to direct its shafts toward public opinion and to put the committee face to face with it, on an open, non-secretive basis.

I may not be successful in my efforts to be peacemaker between free thought and the government. But to do nothing at all would be cowardly; more than that—it would represent betrayal of society's most cherished hopes.

I am not motivated by greed or vanity. I am relying on my humane ideas and will power.

My hopes have been given quite a lift. While literature is being showered with accusations of harboring revolutionary designs, and while the Panins, Chevkins, and the like are firing away at it, I have already succeeded in persuading the committee to recognize the falsity of these charges and to convey this to the emperor.

I am to be presented to the emperor. But, after what? After he has read my plea for literature, *glasnost,* and freedom of thought; after I had expressed the opinion that the committee could only be effective if it operated openly and concentrated on influencing public opinion rather than literature?

[c] The granting of exclusive rights to an individual in certain business enterprises.

10 March. Dinner at Dusseau's, given by writers in honor of the actor, Martynov. About forty people came. Martynov was given a letter, signed by everyone present, and a beautifully bound album with their pictures. Druzhinin read the letter during a toast. Then Nekrasov read a poem in honor of Martynov. The dinner was gay and lively, but without the yelling, shouting and other excesses which usually accompany our dinner celebrations. Everything was sincere, simple and, therefore, good. Oh, yes, I also forgot to mention that Ostrovsky delivered a rather long speech on behalf of our playwrights. At dinner I sat between Shevchenko and Yazykov.

I was greeted with warmth and affection by all the writers. Many expressed their pleasure over my new position. I was delighted with this as proof that they understood my intentions and were doing them justice.

11 March. A remarkable day: I was presented to the emperor. I arrived at the palace at 12:30. In the reception room facing the admiralty there were several generals and aides-de-camp.

As I waited with nothing to do, I walked about the room, glancing out the windows, at the walls, at the standards hanging in the corner.

Finally, around 2 o'clock, Count Adlerberg summoned me into the emperor's study.

"I am delighted to meet you," the emperor said with a kindness beyond description. "I read your memorandum very carefully and with pleasure. I hope you can influence literature to work in harmony with the government for the common good, rather than in a hostile spirit."

"This, Your Majesty," I replied, "is the only path one can follow to lead Russia to greatness and prosperity. I shall do all I can to serve this cause."

"There are ambitions," continued the emperor, "which are at odds with the government's views. They must be restrained. But I don't want any repressive measures. I would like to see important issues studied and evaluated scientifically, although our scientific approach is still poorly developed. Popular articles should be moderate in tone, especially those dealing with politics."

The emperor laid particular stress on the word "politics."

"Your Majesty," I replied, "may I take the liberty to state that, based on my lengthy observations and experience, I find that the best minds and therefore, the most influential in literature, do not entertain any notions inimical to the government. If mistakes or delusions of this sort are encountered, it is only in some still unstable and inexperienced people who do not merit special attention."

"Don't think," remarked the emperor, "that your task is an easy one. I know that the committee does not enjoy the public's favor and confidence."

"My role, as I understand it, Your Majesty, is to be a peacemaker between both sides."

"Again, I repeat," added the emperor, "that I do not want any repressive

measures, and if the committee understands my views, then, despite the difficulties it will encounter, it can still manage to accomplish something."

With the words "if the committee understands my views," the emperor
glanced meaningfully at Adlerberg.

A few more words were spoken about the proposed government journal.
Then, the emperor shook my hand warmly and said in an extremely kind
voice: "Do try!" and bowed and left me.

I cannot describe the gentleness, nobility, and kindness with which the emperor spoke. What struck me particularly about his whole manner was a certain openness and simplicity. He didn't affect the slightest show of regal
grandeur. It is clear that this is a man filled with love and benevolence who
can't help but capture your heart.

"Ah," I thought as I left him, "how much good one could achieve together
with you and how much good you could do if you were surrounded by people
more worthy of you and more dedicated to you and Russia's welfare!"

As I left the palace, I met Adlerberg again and told him how enchanted I
was by the emperor.

"The emperor is counting on you," he said to me.

It was also comforting to find that the emperor understood the difficulties
involved in this task. He mentioned this several times. I had feared that he
would take a very imperious attitude, as much as to say that the task must be
done at any cost and that whatever was ordered could be accomplished. Instead, he merely expressed his desires and views, and gave advice, rather than
dictatorial orders. He also understood, it seems, that there was no room in
our current undertaking for cold, administrative formality.

12 March. I saw the minister this morning and gave him a detailed account
of my audience with the emperor.

"You see what sort of person he is," said Kovalevsky. "You can't help being
wholeheartedly devoted to him. There have been times when I have felt so
overwhelmed that I was ready to give up everything. But after talking with
him, I would feel better about it. It's hard to resist him. Oh, if only he could
show a firmer hand and had better advisors."

At our committee meeting Timashev presented a poem from the *Spark* (No.
9) with his comments on its harmful tone. Unfortunately, the poem does
warrant censure. But Mukhanov attacked it as if it were a political crime. He
demanded the guardhouse for the editor. Timashev was far more moderate.
He declared that, as director of the Third Section's chancery, he would summon the editor and reprimand him. He completely agreed with my view that
it wasn't worth making a fuss over this case.

We discussed my audience with the emperor. I deliberately turned the committee's attention to the magnanimous and noble thought expressed by the
emperor against any repressive measures.

My main concern now is the proposed journal. I must persuade the committee that this is the only way it can hope to influence public opinion, that is, by public airing of information.

Mukhanov will probably give me the most trouble, for he is incapable of responding to appeals to his mind or heart. He is only interested in one thing—wielding influence. The other two members should be clever enough to realize that it is in their own interest not to scorn public opinion.

Also, they should be shown that their sense of honor demands opposition to people like Chevkin and Panin.

13 March. Spent the evening with Count Bludov. I met Egor Petrovich Kovalevsky there. He felt it was wrong for me to have accepted the appointment.

"No one doubts your good intentions," he said, "but you won't be able to accomplish anything."

"If I find that I can't get anywhere, I'll resign. Certainly no harm can come from trying, and maybe some good will come of it."

"No," he objected, "it could lead to harm."

"What kind?"

"It's hard to say at the moment."

"But it would be cowardly on my part to do nothing."

Egor Petrovich is an intelligent, noble man, but he's a hypocondriac and has a very irritable temperament.

26 March. I delivered a long speech today about the difficult position of censorship. It was in a quandary because of the absence of an orderly system and guidelines, and because of the meddling of outside authorities. I tried to show them how important it was for censorship to be centralized and independent. My aim was to place censorship beyond the influence and reach of our committee and to allow the minister of education himself to work without the constant interference of outsiders. "What kind of detectives are we," I said, "that we must pursue every article and hinder censorship from functioning properly by terrifying it and totally confusing it! We are not policemen—we should act like government officials and rise above all that. Our task is to keep track of the way people are thinking, and not of some petty blunders or deviations committed by censorship which should be left to the appropriate authorities." This was, it seems, well received by the committee members, especially Timashev, who is more receptive than the others to reasonable suggestions. Even Mukhanov did not object. "The committee's task," I added, "is not to war with public opinion or literature, but to defend the latter against the Chevkins and their ilk."

There was also discussion of the new censorship code. I tried to make two changes in it: to enlarge the 1828 code to conform to current needs; to introduce *regulations* for censors and establish a censorship administration with power concentrated in a single authority, the Chief Censorship Administration. The spirit of the code is liberal-conservative. No one objected to this either. Today's session was interesting; I changed, it seems to me, many of the committee's earlier notions.

28 March. So far I haven't noticed anything particularly hostile in the Publishing Committee's actions. Originally, it sought to *guide* literature and to control censorship through *reprimands* and *fear*. But it is clear to me now that this earlier approach was more likely due to lack of understanding than any purposeful design. As far as guiding literature is concerned, I have succeeded in completely eliminating that idea and greatly diminished the committee's encroachments on literature.

29 March. Saw the minister. He had received word from Moscow that the benefits of my participation on the committee were beginning to be felt there and that, in Evgraf Petrovich's words, they were very apparent both here and in Moscow. Whether this is true or not, at least we know no harm has come of it yet.

Had a lengthy conversation with Strugovshchikov, whom I had called on after leaving the minister.

I am being criticized for one thing—that I am delaying a crisis by eliminating those reactionary measures which, more than anything else would serve to expose the absurdity of reactionary activities. There is something to this. But is the reactionary bloc really so weak that it would completely surrender after one or two failures? On the other hand, is the liberal bloc so strong that it can truly count on the success of its opposition to the reactionaries? Indeed, power still rests in the hands of the reactionaries, and what if they should suddenly decide to use it and should begin clamping down on one organ of thought after another?

Has the time really come for a complete rupture between the camp of thought and progress and the government? Is our choice limited to two extremes? I don't believe it. And if, as they claim, I am wrong? Perhaps I am. But I must be convinced of this. Blind hatred would be criminal. One ought not to give way to anger lightly and decide such important issues in the heat of passion or enthusiasm.

I am convinced that the time is not ripe for such a crisis. I would say the time is ripe only when a crisis can lead to a well-defined state of affairs and can guarantee a well-structured future. Where are the elements that would make this possible? "But a crisis would certainly produce them," they say. No! A crisis would most likely produce chaos and nothing more. I know there are people who are counting on chaos. But chaos will most certainly lead either to anarchy or to a worse despotism.

I must say the following to the committee: true patriotism and a real government policy consist of the preservation of the basic principles of our social order, and not in fussing over trifles. A dozen trifles which have somehow slipped into print will never do as much harm as a single attempt to persecute them. These trifles stir up a momentary fuss and then disappear, while every attempt to persecute arouses indignation and keeps people in a constant state of agitation.

30 March. The committee made an important admission as a result of my powerful arguments: namely, that it had committed a very serious error by announcing via its circular that it planned to call in writers and censors for explanations and reprimands. This mistake, as I told them, had completely set them at loggerheads with literature and public opinion and had given rise to endless unfavorable rumors which were also encouraged in no small measure by the committee's decision to publish its own articles in journals. I tried my best to get the committee to adopt a policy of noninterference in the affairs of literature and censorship and I think I succeeded. This is an important victory for justice and sensible liberalism.

Mukhanov told me that the emperor was very anxious for me to present the plans for our newspaper.

After the usual discussion of irrelevant matters, the meeting ended rather early.

5 April. Visited Timashev in the evening. Assuming he wasn't putting on an act with me, I must say he stands far above the reputation he now enjoys in literary circles, and I am compelled to modify my original opinion of him considerably. He appears to be more liberal than a good many of the dignitaries with whom I've had discussions and dealings. For example, he told the emperor openly that his government didn't enjoy the public's trust and that such trust could only be acquired by making concessions to public opinion and not by coercion. He read me his memo containing this view. In addition, he claimed to be opposed to harsh measures and completely agreed with the idea that we must follow a course of moderate and sensible liberalism. Thus, he is apparently not a reactionary at all, but he doesn't hide the fact that, in his opinion, the overzealous drives of the ultraliberals must be stopped. In brief, one can see that this is an intelligent man who understands the needs of the times and recognizes the need for reforms. He says that he is absolutely not opposed to *glasnost*, but only against its abuse.

25 April. What am I going to do with those petty minds that screen out mosquitoes and swallow camels whole? I want to save something great and vital, the political principle on which our society rests, making whatever concessions are necessary, and thereby ensuring the peaceful, even development of our society. But our petty minds rage over trifles and think they are saving society from disaster when they tear apart some insignificant article or sentence.

30 April. Dined at Dusseau's with Goncharov, Nekrasov, Panaev, Rebinder and others. It was a farewell party for Turgenev, who was going abroad.

10 May. I appeared before the emperor in Tsarskoe Selo to express my official thanks for the decoration awarded to me.[d] After mass the emperor received us in a small room upstairs. It was quite crowded. He entered at 12:30 wearing a white uniform with yellow side stripes on his trousers. He

---

[d] Nikitenko nowhere identifies this decoration.

greeted some with a smile, some with only a bow, and exchanged a few words with others. Finally, my turn came.

"Thank you," he said to me with a warm smile. "Are you working on your project?"[e]

"I am, Your Majesty," I replied.

"How soon do you think you'll finish it?"

"I hope to finish the plans during the summer, and we can start publishing at the beginning of next year."

He smiled again, bowed, and then turned to the others.

In about five minutes he had covered the entire circle and had exchanged greetings with everyone.

10 June. St. Petersburg seems to be experiencing an unprecedented summer. Delicious southern warmth, tempered, but not spoiled, by frequent rains with those rather fierce thunderstorms that we know here. Lush vegetation. Everything is delightful! However, I am so busy working on my project that I scarcely have time to enjoy these delights. I work in my study until dinner time, and in the evening I am physically too exhausted to enjoy a stroll. My work on the project is making headway. But there is still much work and so many problems ahead! The main difficulty is finding people who have some talent, nobility, and sense; people who would understand that one can and must, while remaining neutral, firmly uphold one's own unselfish convictions in the face of outside pressures; people who would understand that it is still too early to think of radical changes, that it is still possible to accomplish many good things through gradualism, and that our disorderly state and political immaturity are not yet able to withstand a complete break with a powerful, centralized authority. And if such people can't be found, will it be possible to carry out my plan?

19 June. Meeting of the committee in Tsarskoe Selo. Only three of us were present: Count Adlerberg, Mukhanov and I. Timashev was on leave. It was decided to begin the reading of my nearly finished proposal. The reading had, in fact, only begun, when again, I ran up against the kind of remarks I no longer had expected. For example: there was no such thing among us as public opinion, and it was hardly possible to have one; the kind of talk we heard every day or what we read in journals did not constitute public opinion, and so on. This came from Count Adlerberg. Mukhanov objected to it and, I must say, rather cleverly and successfully. Where the count picked up these ideas—I don't know. That he thinks so little of our public opinion is not the point I want to make here, but, rather, that this time he generally displayed a kind of resistance, a hostility to everything intellectual, which I hadn't noticed in him before. Apparently, some recent development brought this on. What is most

---

[e] The emperor was referring to the plans for the government publication which Nikitenko was working out.

important here is the implication that his thinking reflects views coming from higher up.

We read a while, but constant discussion and debate kept us from getting anywhere. However, for me it was a very important session. I realize now that I must change my tactics. I thought I could be direct, that the truth would stand up for itself. Since we think along different lines, I'll have to do some maneuvering. I wanted to explain things to them so they would arrive at certain convictions themselves; now they'll have to accept them against their will. They will accept them, too, unless they are ready to throw up their hands and let fate take over. What a pity! They aren't bad people, particularly Count Adlerberg, but their world of ideas is so limited to the narrow ideas of the Court, that they are almost wholly incapable of understanding what is going on in the world outside, in this age, and in history. I said: "Suppose all this is so and you are absolutely correct in your mistrust of public opinion. But what you are attacking now exists as a fact of life. And since this fact is a force in society, and a significant one, too, then it's no longer a question of whether it's a good or bad one, but a question of how to relate to it, what steps to take, not only to render it as harmless as possible, but to make it a useful tool as well."

We decided to continue the reading tomorrow.

12 July. In Peterhof. I read the committee the plan for the newspaper. It was approved. Same argument that took place at the last meeting, about a revolutionary current in society. I tried my best to show them that such a current did not exist either in our literature or our society; that we lacked the necessary elements for revolution—history had not produced them; that if we had anything to fear, it was complete chaos in our society and administration; and yet even this would not produce a political revolution, but rather only disorder and aimless slaughter. But we must not and should not allow matters to reach that stage.

18, 19, 20, 21, 22 July. The ultraliberals don't even suspect what despots and tyrants they are. Just as our despots and tyrants don't want anyone to make a move without their knowledge or against their will, so our ultraliberals will not tolerate anyone whose thinking doesn't agree with theirs. The worst of all these tyrannies is the tyranny of the mind. Why does this or that gentleman feel that he has the right to proclaim his way as the best way to serve humanity, and to damn those who differ with him?

"In my Father's house are many mansions."

I believe, if our ideas and literature are fated to come into open conflict with the government, that time has not yet come.

A great gulf divides the activists or leaders of our society from each other, a gulf which will always prevent them from uniting for the common good. This gulf is ambition. Our pettiness and immaturity are further evidenced by the fact that no one even tries to judge the next fellow objectively. No one wants to acknowledge another's deeds if they were not accomplished by a method or means that he considered best.

In my personal discussion with the emperor, he expressed such fine intentions that it decidedly raised my hopes. But if, surrounded by limited and self-seeking people, he betrays my expectations, I, at least, shall have a clear conscience: it cannot reproach me for either cowardice or neglect of duty. I shall pursue a course that I consider correct until the bitter end.

The main problem is that I can not find decent co-workers. The so-called progressives are so hostile to the government that they look coldly upon me— not because, they say, they doubt the purity of my motives, but because they seem to think I am only delaying the coming crisis. In the final analysis, gentlemen, exactly what do you want to achieve? What immediate results? Revolution? And without the participation of the people?

But such revolutions are senseless and immoral!

27 September. Moved from our dacha on Friday the 12th. I spent the month of August working on the Publishing Committee's affairs. Since I first expressed and continued to uphold the belief that the committee was a mistake, it has accomplished nothing. It heard only a part of my newspaper proposal. Mukhanov kept trying to get the committee to assert its power over the censorship department, which he felt was permitting literature to take terrible liberties. But since Count Adlerberg and Timashev responded to his zealous attempts with silence, and I kept repeating that this was not our business, Mukhanov's words fell upon deaf ears and he turned, instead, to telling anecdotes and the like. Finally he grew weary of doing nothing and, at one of our meetings, he enthusiastically suggested there was nothing for us to do but to merge with the ministry of education. This is exactly what I was waiting for. My entire strategy was leading up to this moment. But I didn't want this idea to come from me. I wanted it to come from one of the members, once he saw its obvious necessity. This is exactly what happened. Then I proceeded to use all my dialectical skills to support this fine idea, and, at the following meeting, I read the proposal I had already prepared on the merging of the committee with the Chief Censorship Administration under the chairmanship of the minister of education. It was approved, read to the minister, approved again, and, today, the 27th, I am taking it to Timashev for presentation to the emperor by Count Adlerberg.

Censors and litterateurs will be admitted to meetings of the Chief Censorship Administration. I was very fearful that this would meet with resistance, particularly the admission of writers. But it didn't because of the kind of arguments I had presented earlier.

All through August I was plagued by headaches which would come on every day after work. At times I had to leave my desk and walk about, and this would give me some relief.

28 September. Visited Posen. The Kiev provincial marshal of the nobility[f] was there. Both he and Posen were furious at the Emancipation Committee for rejecting their proposals. From their conversation, I gathered that they wanted to impose large monetary payments on the peasants for their land allotments, which the committee did not want. They complained that the committee was dominated by a bureaucratic element; that the committee had summoned them not to hear their opinion and to consult with them, but to get their unconditional agreement to a plan which had been worked out in advance.

They say the deputies had made allusions to something resembling a constitution. But the emperor replied very calmly that they had assembled to discuss the emancipation issue and must work on that alone, rather than on irrelevant issues.

I heard also that, at the first meeting of the Main Committee on Emancipation which the emperor attended, Prince Orlov expressed his fear that the emancipation of the peasants might lead to the idea of a constitution. To this the emperor replied:

"Why not, if Russia will want this; and if it is ready for it, I am ready!"

29 September. Perhaps some other responsibilities might be imposed on our Publishing Committee—but not in matters of censorship, because its exclusive role in that area, according to the sense of our proposal, has ended. The whole idea of the proposal was to centralize censorship and free it from any kind of outside interference.

The idea of the proposal, that is, the centralization and establishment of closer relations between censorship authorities, their agents and writers has been accepted.

8 October. Mukhanov and Timashev are up in arms against literature, particularly so-called accusatory literature and its latest escapades. They seem inclined toward very harsh measures. Mukhanov, in response to my objections, remarked jokingly that the writer in me was showing. I told him I believed that literature was created for Russia and not Russia for literature, and since literature was a force called upon to serve her, it must be permitted to function. You don't throw out the wheat with the chaff.

17 October. I'm sick!

23 October. Feeling a little better. Meeting with the minister of education on the merging of the Publishing Committee with the Chief Censorship Administration. Present were the minister, Timashev, Count Adlerberg and myself. The merging of the committee with the Chief Censorship Administration is a

---

[f] Provincial marshals of the nobility served as chairmen of committees set up in every province between January 1858 and April 1859 to work on emancipation reforms.

very important matter. We decided to present a report on it to the emperor in a day or two. The committee itself, in a note I had prepared for this purpose, described in precise and sharp terms not only its uselessness, but its harmfulness, too.

There was discussion at the minister's of Pisemsky's new drama, which Palauzov was about to pass. It is a drama of peasant life. In it a landowner seduces a peasant's wife, and the peasant, in a fit of anger, kills him. It was felt it would be unwise to publish the play at this time when work on the emancipation issue is in full swing. However, since the play is supposed to be a very fine one, it should not be permanently banned, but only temporarily shelved.

They say there is disagreement on the emancipation issue between the commission and the deputies. The deputies seem to be pressing for a constitution.

26 October. The minister called in Pisemsky, praised his play highly, and promised to pass it, but not right away.

Much gossip about the emancipation issue. Five deputies signed a petition to the emperor for public trials, juries, greater freedom of the press, and the right of the nobility to present its needs to the emperor. It is said that this document was favorably received by the emperor and that he promised to transmit it to the State Council for examination.[g] But why did only 5 out of 20 deputies sign it?

1 November. Went to see Dr. Zdekauer this morning about my health, which is playing tricks on me.

5 November. Went to Tsarskoe Selo to see Count Adlerberg. The emperor is in complete agreement with our proposal to merge the committee with the Chief Censorship Administration. There was only one thing he didn't support —the proposal that the president of the Academy of Sciences should be a member of the Chief Censorship Administration.

8 November. The minister told me what had happened on Thursday at the Council of Minister's meeting on the censorship proposal. There was a sharp debate. However, the proposal to merge "the Bureau de la Presse" with the Chief Censorship Administration did not encounter resistance. Apparently the matter is settled.

15 November. There are many rumors about separating censorship from the ministry of education. I gave Count Adlerberg my views on the political inexpediency of such a move. "However," I added, "the main thing is to adhere consistently to some set of principles and not to get frightened by every article that doesn't happen to agree with accepted and established ideas. Censorship

---

[g] In reality, Alexander II was extremely irritated by this petition and the delegates were reprimanded for their action.

should safeguard the basic principles of our state structure. Everything else will be taken care of by the normal processes of a growing and developing society."

21 November. I went to Tsarskoe Selo to see Count Adlerberg. My role on the Publishing Committee is ended, and Baron Korf is now selecting his members for the new chief committee.

22 November. My head feels terrible these days. I even felt faint today. I went to Dr. Zdekauer again for advice. From there I went to see Timashev. Timashev confidently predicts that Korf's new censorship administration will not last more than a year. Korf made a serious mistake when he let it be known among writers that he would follow a liberal course. In so doing he raised hopes and expectations which he won't be able to fulfill. He'll have to reverse himself. Korf was in too much of a hurry to gain popularity, and his chief mistake was in making his desire known.

A coalition is beginning to form against the new censorship administration.

Rumor has it that the minister himself is responsible for the proposal to separate censorship from the ministry of education. And yet a month before, here's what he had said to me:

"As Minister Kovalevsky, I would like to see censorship removed from my jurisdiction because it is a terrific burden. But, as a citizen, as a Russian, I shall oppose with all my strength any attempt to separate it from the ministry of education because this could have disastrous consequences for literature."

Yet they say that he was the very first to propose this measure at the Council of Ministers.

The fact is that a censorship torn from the ministry of education would become prey to anyone seeking power and influence. Even now, many have an eye on it and are spinning intrigues against Korf, and it's not impossible that Timashev's prophecy will be fulfilled. Then, for all we know, censorship may even find itself in the Third Section. In general, it has become more than ever a plaything of chance. The more I think of it, the more I feel that our proposal was the most sensible and the most in keeping with the interests of literature and the government itself.

24 November. Korf wrote me yesterday, asking me to see him on official business. I replied that illness had kept me in for the past five days, but as soon as I felt better, I would have the honor of appearing before him.

The minister wants me to see him tomorrow. The doctor will allow me to go out tomorrow.

27 November. My health is still poor. I am waiting for the doctor now; afterwards I'll go to see the minister and Korf.

Why did Korf call me in? I don't understand! Did he think that I was going to ask him to put me on the new censorship committee? If so, he's mistaken. What he finally asked me to do was to meet with Troinitsky for discussions. What kind? About what? It's a mystery to me.

From Korf's I went to see Adlerberg, who spent the whole time talking about Korf and his activities. The count wanted to see him.

The minister explained to me how the idea of separating censorship from the ministry of education had originated. The emperor himself had initiated this move, and it was not inspired by Count Stroganov.

1860

3 February. I hadn't made any entries in my diary since November 27 of last year. This has been one of the most trying periods of my life. I was stricken with a grave, painful illness.

I experienced such physical suffering that I often believed the end was near, that one more jolting sensation in my head would transport me to the place from which there is no return and to which every living being fears to go. It apparently began with a cold, but when it passed, I couldn't seem to get rid of the endless remnants which hung on and still plague me.

A weakness of my whole body, combined with a miserable depression, nagged me during the daytime, and, at night, my head was beseiged by jolting sensations, by some strange repetitive movement, by twitching, surging and falling sensations . . . One minute my spirits would sink so low, the next— they would rise to do courageous battle with nature. Thoughts of death never left me. Added to this were some superstitious signs which upset me terribly. Apparently my entire nervous system was shaken up. Both doctors, Waltz, and Zdekauer, who was called in for consultation, agreed that it was. Yet they did not feel that this condition was potentially dangerous. However, they felt that my strength would be fully restored only in the summer in the complete absence of any serious work. I must either go abroad or to the country.

6 February. My health is scarcely improving. I do feel better than I did a month ago. But these seizures of weakness, particularly of depression, and this disorder in my head, are still the same. However, I am gradually returning to normal activity.

7 February. In general, a very unfavorable period has dawned for literature. The main problem is that the emperor is so firmly set against it.

The minister had a frank talk with me and expressed the view that literature had virtually no defenders in the Chief Censorship Administration save Delyanov, himself, and me.

The minister's report to the emperor on censorship reforms, from beginning to end, was nothing less than an intelligent and noble defense of literature. The emperor approved this report and it was read at the first session as a statement of principles which our censorship apparatus should follow. There is no doubt, however, that it will not be followed.

9 February. And so I have a ticket for the funeral of Rostovtsev, who died Saturday at 7 A.M. He is being buried today. The emperor himself closed Rostovtsev's eyes. They say he sobbed heavily in his grief. Everyone, save the enemies of emancipation, is deeply saddened by this death. Of course, this is Rostovtsev's finest funeral oration.

15 February. There was no business of any importance today at the Chief Censorship Administration. I was given O. A. Przhetslavsky's opinion to read on *glasnost,* which, in Delyanov's words, if accepted, would completely gag literature on social issues.

By and large, this gentleman makes it very clear that he is an inveterate advocate of darkness and silence.

Mark Lyuboshchinsky visited this evening and told me the news. Count Panin had been appointed to take Rostovtsev's place on the Emancipation Committee. Friends of freedom and reform were thunderstruck by this appointment. Panin's way of thinking is well known. He has constantly blocked any kind of intellectual, material or judicial progress, in fact, any progress at all. People are used to regarding him as the chief spokesman of ignorance, silence, immorality and other such fine things. How will he behave now in a situation which demands the very opposite of everything he has ever stood for and done?

Clearly we have lost much that is good with Rostovtsev's death. This feeling is universal. Apparently, the enemies of thought and all that is decent are rearing their heads. My poor country! All your fine projects are so unstable! One man makes his exit, and, suddenly, everything reverses its course.

11 March. My doctors insist that I go abroad. The idea scarcely appeals to me. I would prefer to go to the country, but the doctors will not even hear of it.

13 March. I submitted a request to the minister for a four-month leave from May 15 to September 15 to go abroad.

27 March. The minister informed me yesterday that the emperor agreed to give me leave. Also, the minister is trying to get me a grant.

29 March. About five or six years ago Goncharov read Turgenev an outline of his novel *The Artist.* When Turgenev published his book *A Nest of Gentlefolk,* Goncharov noticed that several places in Turgenev's novel resembled parts of his outline for his own novel. He suspected Turgenev of having lifted these parts from his work, and he informed the author of *A Nest of Gentlefolk* of this belief. Turgenev replied with a letter, stating that, naturally, it had never occurred to him to borrow anything from Goncharov deliberately, but since some of the details of Goncharov's outline had made such a deep impression on him, it was not surprising that they could have been unconsciously repeated in his story. This simple-hearted confession triggered a big scandal. In Goncharov's suspicious, cruel, egotistical, and cunning mind, the idea took hold that Turgenev had intentionally taken almost everything from him, or, at any rate, that he had been robbed. He spoke bitterly about this to some writers and also to me. I tried to point out to him that even if Turgenev had actually taken anything from him, it ought not to distress him so much; their talents were so different, that it would never occur to anyone to accuse either one of imitating the other, and when Goncharov's novel came out, certainly no one would reproach him with this.

Turgenev's novel *On the Eve* came out this year. Looking at it with an already jaundiced eye, Goncharov found in it, too, similarities to his own plan, and became enraged. He wrote Turgenev a strange, ironical letter which the latter ignored. A few days ago, when Goncharov met Dudyshkin and learned that he was going to Turgenev's to dine, he said to him rudely and nastily: "Tell Turgenev that he's giving dinners at my expense." (Turgenev had received 4,000 rubles from the *Russian Messenger* for his novel.) Dudyshkin, seeing that he was dealing with a person who had positively lost control of himself, should have been more discreet; but he told Turgenev what Goncharov had said, word for word. Naturally, this must have been the last straw for Turgenev. He wrote Goncharov a very serious letter, accused him of slander, and demanded an explanation in the presence of a group of trusted people selected by both of them; otherwise he would challenge him to a duel. However, this was not the threat of some dandy, but the last resort of an intelligent, gentle, but cruelly insulted person. Mediators and witnesses were selected for the meeting by mutual agreement: Annenkov, Druzhinin, Dudyshkin and myself. This famous encounter took place today at 1:00 P.M. Turgenev was visibly disturbed; however he recounted the whole course of events very clearly, simply and without the slightest show of anger. Goncharov replied to this in a vague and unsatisfactory manner. The similarities he cited between *On the Eve* and his projected work were scarcely convincing so it was clear that victory favored Turgenev, and it turned out that Goncharov had been carried away by his suspicious nature and had exaggerated things, as he himself expressed it. Then Turgenev announced the immediate end of their friendship and departed. What we had been most afraid of were the things that Goncharov had said to Dudyshkin, which the latter had transmitted to Turgenev; but since Goncharov himself admitted that what he had said was stupid and unintentional, and not meant to be taken at face value, and by his own admission was tactless and crude, and since Dudyshkin stated he had no right to repeat these words to Turgenev, we solemnly proclaimed that these words had never really been spoken, thereby removing the most important casus belli for the quarrel. All in all, one must admit that my friend, Ivan Aleksandrovich, did not play a very enviable role in this affair; that he showed himself to be a kind of irritable, terribly superficial and crude person, while Turgenev, overall, and especially during this meeting, which was undoubtedly very distressing for him, conducted himself with dignity, tact, refinement, and the kind of special graciousness that is reserved for respectable people of good breeding.

30 March. I received an official notice from the minister giving me a four-month leave to go abroad for my health and awarding me a grant in place of the salary I would normally receive from the Chief Censorship Administration and the university.

3 April. Easter Sunday. In all my life, except for maybe five occasions due to circumstances beyond my control, I have never missed matins or mass on this holiday. I love this majestic drama—mystery, whose theme is the comforting and profound idea of resurrection. The very solemnity and splendor which our church imparts to this drama is wholly in keeping with its meaning. There's only one thing that has often irritated me—the carelessness with which it is generally performed in our churches. The priests simply rush through matins and mass and distort them by conducting them hurriedly and disinterestedly. The worshipers, as well as the priests, seem just as impatient for the service to end. No one is inspired, no one experiences the real, great poetry of this sacred act in which the human spirit, swathed in elegant symbols, seeks and welcomes its future, a future that has been lost in the stormy troubles and vicissitudes of life under the existing order of things.

10 April. My father used to say when some unexpected misfortune would strike: "This has befallen me so I would not be a stranger to any kind of trouble." And, indeed, this was a privilege of sorts reserved for him alone. Since last November, the same thing has applied to me. All this time my family has been besieged by a series of illnesses, one worse than the other. The burden of suffering shifted constantly among us. Of course it would be foolish to ascribe it to fate or the like. It's all a game of chance, stemming from our poor natural environment and living conditions.

23 April. I come from the ranks of the people. I am a plebian from head to toe, but I do not accept the idea that it is wise to give the people power. Not everybody in this world can be content, educated, or virtuous. There will always be some who stand out above the rest, possessing a superabundance of the qualities others lack. The masses will never acquire the qualities needed for a just, wise and enlightened use of power—and, out of necessity, they will either abuse it or put it into the hands of one man, which will inevitably lead to despotism. The people must be ruled, and not themselves rule. But they must have the right to express their needs, to point out to the government the vices and abuses of those who have been appointed to preserve and enforce the law.

30 April. Received my passports yesterday for my trip abroad.

Meeting of the Chief Censorship Administration. Heated debate over Arseniev's article on the need for public court trials. Przhetslavsky, of course, opposed publication of the article as did Berte. The rest favored it, including Timashev and Mukhanov.

7 May. We said goodbye on the English Embankment to our friends who were seeing us off. We set out for Kronstadt, where, at the anchorage, we transferred to the steamer *Prussian Eagle* that was to take us to Stettin.

16 May. We left Berlin at 7 A.M. and arrived in Dresden at noon. We went to the Hotel Frankfurt, recommended by Goncharov, who was already waiting there for us. It's not luxurious, but the owner is very eager to please. We'll have to stay here until we find an apartment for the children.

22 May. We spend our days looking for an apartment and strolling around the city with Goncharov, who is obsessed with a mad passion for wandering about the city and making all sorts of unnecessary purchases. We sampled the cigars in almost every one of the finest tobacconist shops.

6 July. We are preparing to leave Kissingen. In the morning we stopped by at the casino. A mass of new faces. A new generation seeking the cure has replaced the old one. As before, the doctors, standing beneath the trees, question each of their patients as they come up to them in turn. As before, hundreds of people converge on the Rakoczy and Pandur springs with hands outstretched for glasses of the healing waters. As before, music fills the air, giving an impression of gaiety which is utterly false, because no one here is in the mood for fun. I met several friends here, and, as before, heard the same old talk: how they had slept last night, how many mineral baths they had taken and how many more they still had to take, and so on. As before, on the tree-lined avenues, the ladies flash by in their voluminous crinolines. You search their faces for a glimpse of real grace or charm, but, for the most part, you find faces worn with suffering or made up to look young and beautiful. It's all so false.

12 July. Generally speaking, I must say that tourists are often treated very dishonestly in large European cities. Hotels frequently charge three times the standard rate, covering it up with polite words and smiles. Cold egotism and greed for profit are in evidence everywhere.

In general, honesty is strictly observed among one's countrymen, but it's another matter when it comes to foreigners. This can be explained very simply. Every citizen fears the law and public opinion here—those two great forces in Western civilization. Woe to him who, in his own city or village, is caught in an unscrupulous act; the people will rise up against him. But neither public opinion nor the law will stand up for a foreigner. They can deceive and, I dare say, persecute him with impunity. This means that respect for the rights of others, and honesty, which is so highly extolled in Europe, especially in Germany, do not stem at all from that lofty humanity which our ultra-Westerners see in it, but spring solely from firmly established mutual relationships. Of course this is a fine thing too, because the members of such a society have security. But Europe has not yet attained the kind of civilization in which a man and everything belonging to him is respected purely out of a feeling for humanity. . . .

5 August. We are leaving Interlaken today. Farewell, oh charming, peaceful, hospitable valley! Here I have spent the most pleasurable days of all my wanderings abroad.

13 August. We arrived in Boulogne at 5 o'clock. We were warmly welcomed at the station by Goncharov and Grot. They took us to their hotel where we also took up lodging in two small rooms.

14 August. Goncharov, already well acquainted with Boulogne, became my host and guide. He helped me arrange ocean baths and recommended his own swimming attendant.

29 August. Every morning we walk to the railroad station and pick up the latest newspaper at the book stand, either *Constitutionel* or *Patrie.* Today we bought the latest edition of *Constitutionel.* I am very interested in Italian affairs. The people here seem ready for a new system, for unity. There is popular agitation everywhere in favor of this unity, and with each day the status of the pitiful remains of the Neapolitan king's Bourbon dynasty diminishes. He couldn't understand an important and simple political truth, that you can't rule people only as you wish, but you must give some consideration to their wishes, too. Whatever the needs of the times may be, they must be met within certain limits. Therefore, nothing is more foolish than the kind of conservatism that wants not only to restrain and temper excesses in an outburst of new ideas, but to destroy them and turn things back or maintain the status quo. Isn't it foolish to think it possible to establish this or that system for eternity when there is nothing eternal in this world except death?

Garibaldi is a wonderful man. He's not a genius, but something even greater and more noble—a good man, one of humanity's heroes, in the most judicious and highest sense of the word.

My stay in Boulogne is coming to an end. What has it done for my health? I shall review the results, which are scarcely comforting. During my entire stay here I felt better than at Interlaken. They say that the beneficial effects of ocean bathing are felt later on. Let's hope so, and meanwhile, the only thing I can do, as before, is keep up my courage.

30 August. My nameday. This is the first time I've spent it without my children. Poor things! They are miserable without me on this day; and here I am, feeling low, sending them my greetings.

Tomorrow we are going to Paris. And then to the children. It's high time! I want so much to embrace them. I feel badly that my return will scarcely bring them joy for I am bringing them a sick body and a troubled mind. Farewell, Boulogne by-the-sea!

1 September. There is something attractive about the French. They have neither the awkwardness nor coarseness one encounters in the Germans, nor that democratic crudeness noticeable in the Swiss. Their liveliness has a certain grace of its own, which points to the aesthetic superiority of this race.

I spent almost three weeks in Boulogne. A great many people, who cannot boast of having much education, are crowded into this small city; they are tradesmen, workers, sailors and fishermen. Perhaps this was coincidence, but during my entire stay, I never witnessed any commotion in the most bustling places; no quarrels, incidents, or the like. Everything is done briskly and rapidly, without any shoving or confusion. I frequently stopped in at Marten's Tavern or, as Goncharov and I called it, Martynich's. Lower class people gathered there, too. They would drink, eat, smoke, read newspapers, but with the utmost decorum. Only once did I see drunks—two workmen. The soldiers were young, gallant, free and easy, but also, it seemed to me, humble for their calling. Taking a detached look at them then, in a period of calm, it was difficult to imagine that the French were a people who have made so many revolutions.

The French have acquired a universal reputation for their kindness and courtesy. But they can also be terribly impolite and crude as soon as they no longer feel the need to be kind and courteous. When they utter certain polite phrases and present such smiling faces, it is not dictated by a noble human desire to avoid hurting someone, but rather is it dictated by habit. By nature, the French are cold and false. They are sincere only when they try to show their superiority or occupy the center of the stage.

One must give the French people their due: they are amazingly attractive. Frenchmen are very lovely at a certain distance—from afar. But their claim disappears as soon as you come close to them and begin to examine their faces. Amazed and somewhat horrified, you suddenly behold a mask, a wretched imitation of life, instead of the striking, pleasing features which captivated you from a distance.

10 September. Dresden. My dear children and Goncharov met us at the station. We were overjoyed to see each other—it was indescribable. We hadn't seen each other for 3 months and 10 days. My children and I had never experienced such a long separation. Thank God that I found them healthy and happy.

14 September. While in Dresden I am trying to live in as carefree a way as possible and, at least for the next few days, trying not to think of all the work and problems awaiting me in St. Petersburg. The weather is certainly helpful in this respect, too. The days have been clear and warm, the kind we've seen so little of during this trip. We love to stroll through Grossgarten and Bryulov terrace; or I wander aimlessly about the city with Goncharov, who continues to be frantically preoccupied with shopping. At the moment it's cigars and stereoscopic pictures of various sights. . . .

16 September. Goncharov read me this evening the new chapter of his novel which he had written in Dresden.[1] He had read me something from it earlier. The parts he had read to me up to now were very good. His strong point is his skillful shading, his ability to color faithfully each detail, to give it a meaning in keeping with the picture as a whole. Moreover, his brush is especially light, and his language lithe and graceful. In the new chapter he read to me today the character of Vera is starting to develop. I was not completely satisfied this time. I felt that this character was created in mid-air in another atmosphere, whence it was brought to our world, and was not a natural outgrowth of the world in which we live and move. Yet he poured so much beauty into it. It is dazzling and vivid. I shared my opinion and doubts with the author.

28 September. It's raining and cold. There's a biting wind today which sweeps down the streets and cuts right through you. The rooms are terribly cold but we're afraid to heat them because of the fumes. German stoves are not made like ours. They can't give off or hold heat. The devil only knows what it is. These muddleheaded Germans, who have written thousands of brilliant and stupid books, have not yet learned the secret of heating their dwellings in the wintertime. They don't have dampers in their stoves, and the stoves themselves seem to be constructed merely to scare away the cold rather than battle with it seriously and drive it out. Oh, you muddleheaded Germans!

I am reading a translation of the Bible which is being published in London. Only the Pentateuch has come out so far. Vadim[h] is listed as the translator and it is being printed by Herzen's press. The translation is being made from the Hebrew original with the help of an English translation by the Jew, Doctor Benish. Therefore the translation is free of pompous and obscure Slavic phraseology. It reads like Homer's *Iliad*. I don't know what impression it would produce in Russia with its patriarchal simplicity and colloquial style. But I do think that our notion of the Bible's divinity and classical grandeur would be severely shaken. Essentially it is made up of the history and laws of a people ruled by theocracy, and in this sense the Bible is understandable and natural. But its concept of divinity is incompatible with our Christian ideas; its God is too human and terrifying. Moses, of course, had reason to present him to the Jews in such a light. They needed a strict ruler who was always ready to mete out punishment without sparing anyone or anything in His outbursts of anger, and God actually was, according to Moses, such a ruler for them. But we Christians cannot understand such a God and have no need of such a ruler.

29 September. Literary critics and historians err in looking at literature in a one-sided way. They see in it a force which either rises above society and pulls it upward or a force which is exclusively dedicated to society's interests and dependent on them. As a result, some fall into abstract and dreary idealism, others into extreme realism. Literature, however, has a dual function. It simultaneously serves ideals and reality.

Only those works in which the ideal is not opposed to the real and the real does not destroy the ideal, completely fulfill the true mission of literature.

Every writer who has had a strong influence on his society either awakens or reaffirms in it certain moral and social principles; he opens new vistas for intellectual activity and inclines the mind and heart toward certain ideas and convictions. This is what distinguishes the writer-activist from the writer-

[h] The pseudonym for V. I. Kelsiev.

artist, who nourishes only the aesthetic sense with his elegant images and
pictures.

We recognize Pushkin's dual significance: 1) his significance as an artist, cul-
tivating an aesthetic sense in his society, and 2) his significance as a public figure, developing certain moral principles in society; persuading it to face certain
tasks and issues; giving direction to the ideas and feelings of his generation.
Before this, life's high ideals were a plaything; they flashed before us, we never
bothered to analyze them or relate them to life. Both in literature and reality,
they remained abstractions in the realm of fantasy. Pushkin was the first to
consider them seriously, the first to teach us to combine the finest strivings of
the spirit, the finest ideals, with a reality based on the life and history of our
society.

Pushkin's works have been criticized lately as lacking social significance. I
have a deep respect for this social orientation which strongly concerns today's
literature. I fully recognize its role in this sense and am far from imposing on
it a so-called artistic character to the exclusion of all else. But I give a much
broader meaning to the concept "social," than is customarily given to it of
late. I include in it not only current social problems, no matter how important
they may be, not only the exposure of current needs, various ailments and
abuses, but everything contained in the basic beliefs and aspirations of our
national spirit, everything related to the means and ends of its development,
in brief—the entire moral order of things, the entire realm of ideas of this era.
Thus, social writers are not only those who point out the disparity that exists
between our social mores and what the ideals of humanity and *narodnost* call
for, but also those who elevate these ideals by purifying them of all temporary
distortions and perversions. It is essential that these latter writers should not
offer us abstract ideals or those that are alien to our national character or
society. Their ideals should be supremely humane, but at the same time they
should be realistic in terms of our national and social concepts. These ideals
and these concepts should be linked together in people's minds, even if only
on the basis of vague intuition or vague feelings, or on the basis of their striving toward the ideal, or not necessarily toward the ideal, but at least toward
a certain definite Weltanschauung.

We find all this in Pushkin, and, therefore, fully regard him as a social
writer.

Such a writer must, of course, clothe society's vague feelings, intuitions, and
aspirations in faithful, lively images which are powerful enough to influence
it. Whether he can do this depends, of course, on the extent of his aesthetic
or artistic talent. And Pushkin was tremendously gifted in this respect.

30 September. Today we are leaving for Russia via Breslau and Warsaw at
11 P.M., on the night train.

The image of the French, as I saw them under Napoleon III, sticks in my
memory. They seem to have been born with a love of theatre and a bent to
create it—they were created for showmanship. Emotions, principles, honor,

revolution are all treated as play, as games. Yet they must be given their due; they are superb at everything related to performance: their understanding of their roles, facial expressions, recitation, the entire setting. Their calling is not simply "to be," if one can phrase it that way; instead, nature has provided them abundantly with the means of "seeming to be" and to produce effects: to assume the role of warrior, conspirator, lover, fanatic, liberal, slave—all this appears on their stage, all these roles executed brilliantly and skillfully. They possess the kind of skill that permits them to slip into any role, at least to master it outwardly, which often fools the inexperienced eye. Initially, I dare say, you don't take them for actors, but for real people; but when you go behind the scenes, and take a closer look, you can see the rouge, tinsel and make-up in everything.

2 October. Every city, village and region, like a person, has its own personality, that special elusive quality which makes a certain kind of impression on the observer. Warsaw does not leave me with a pleasant impression. In general, it seems somewhat dirty and coarse. The square opposite Saxon Gardens could have been beautiful if it hadn't been spoiled by some unsightly and gloomy-looking structures—the guardhouse on one side, and the stables and barracks on the other. But the most ugly thing of all is the monument in the center of it . . . Yet the strictly Polish face of the city is not without some interest. Here you can see traces of history which give evidence of a distinctive national culture. The population as a whole displays traits of originality and even has a kind of grace about it. There is a great deal of life in their movements and faces, which are expressive and beautiful.

4 October. A letter from Goncharov, now in St. Petersburg, where he had arrived on September 26th. He describes the trials and tribulations he experienced on his homeward journey as a result of all kinds of difficulties stemming from our typical Russian barbarism and chaotic ways. Goncharov cautions me about what he encountered.

I paid a visit to Starynkevich and, in the course of our conversation, learned of the changing moods of our censorship apparatus. An article had appeared in the *Russian Word* about Gogol, which said that Gogol enjoyed the public's respect until he began "to burn incense for the King of Heaven and Earth." They say the emperor called in the minister on account of this article and said to him:

"I pay no attention to what is said about me. You can't expect everyone to love you; some do and some don't. Earthly kings have their weaknesses. But one must not talk like that about the King of Heaven."

Well said! It is indeed a pity that our literature says such tactless things. It has no understanding of its position or mission today. It is to guide people and enlighten them, not to irritate or upset them. This is a fine role and it can't be carried out in a frenzy of invective, as Herzen, for example, is doing now. Herzen has his undeniable merit, but he, too, would do far better if he

refrained from invective. However, he is in a different position from all our
other writers. He has openly assumed the role of an agitator rather than a
leader. In this respect he doesn't have the same responsibilities as do others.
Herzen doesn't participate directly in our affairs. In general, he doesn't have
to observe various conventions which no writer can ignore if he hopes to make
a favorable impression on society.

My conscience and my understanding dictate the need for restraining those
blind drives which stir up storms from the dark reaches of our minds and are
more difficult to stop than to arouse once they have begun their destructive
course. I was born, grew up, matured, and am now aging, with a feeling of
revulsion and hostility for any yoke, for any kind of oppression. My personal
feelings, my entire being are on the side of freedom and rights. But I have
never toyed frivolously with people's lives for the sake of any utopia which
guarantees freedom and rights. I have never felt and still do not feel that
these things are possible without the support of the law. I well know, like
everyone, that these blessings are purchased with victims, and that without
crises society cannot make the transition from one system to another. But it
is not my business to accelerate or force these crises. On the contrary, I feel
it is the duty of an honorable man to cushion these crises and promote whatever will bring about a minimum of sacrifice. If history gives nothing away
free, then we must at least purchase the good it promises or gives us as cheaply
as possible. It is a terrible crime to bandy about ideas at the expense of human
blood, and it is the responsibility of those who are fated to participate in this
transaction to act wisely, and not to rush blindly into the abyss along with
the crowd, which doesn't think of the consequences.

13 October. Arrived in St. Petersburg on Monday the 10th at 5 P.M. The
following day, Tuesday, various people had already begun to call on me.

5 November. I found, upon my return, that the Chief Censorship Administration was even more irritated with literature than before. It seems they
want to pursue a repressive policy. All this was precipitated by one article in
the *Russian Word,* or rather, by one sentence, that "Gogol was respected by
the Russian public until he began slavishly to burn incense for the King of
Heaven and Earth." Censor Yaroslavtsev was discharged for this sentence,
and Count Kushelev Bezborodko, the publisher, was reprimanded.

26 November. Meeting of the Chief Censorship Administration. Debate over
Nekrasov's verse, which the author wants to publish in a new edition. This
edition had once been banned by Norov. I now submitted my written opinion
favoring publication of this book with the possible exception of several lines.
The other members opposed it because they felt the tone of Nekrasov's poetry
was too democratic. It is difficult to reason with such gentlemen as Przhetslavsky and Berte. However, it was decided to send the poetry to the Censorship Committee for re-examination.[2]

1 December. Faculty meeting at the university. Talk about the competition for appointment to the chair of philosophy. Some people are priming Lavrov for the post. I am opposed to it. Lavrov has a talent for clouding minds rather than enlightening them.

3 December. Meeting of the Chief Censorship Administration. Berte delivered a report stating that an article on the North American States[i] which appeared in the *Northern Bee* dwelt excessively on the right of people to check abuses in government administration and to change their form of government. I defended the newspaper on the ground that these were not their arguments, but, rather, extracts from North American articles.

"These are plain facts," I added, "and facts that occur every now and then in Europe and America. So there is nothing left for us to do but forbid the press to mention any facts of this sort; that is, we must close our eyes and ears to what is going on in the world."

The minister agreed with me. Delyanov and Troinitsky supported me. It was decided to drop the matter.

8 December. At the beginning of the present reign our writers were not sufficiently tactful to benefit from the increased freedom bestowed on the press. They could have done a great deal to strengthen certain principles of society and incline the government toward various liberal measures, but instead they went to extremes and spoiled everything. Dazzled by their initial successes, they lost all sense of proportion and became much too demanding, forgetting that only a year or so ago they would scarcely have been allowed to hold a pen in their hands. They wanted everything at once and began to attack everything in sight like zealots incapable of guiding public opinion. Instead of using the printed word, they abused it. I tried in vain to be the mediator between literature and the government, but literature had gone so far that it suddenly found itself in open and bitter opposition to the government, while the government shuddered and began in earnest to tighten the reins. People like Chernyshevsky, Bov, and others, imagined they could usurp rights to which they were not yet entitled. They embarked on an ill-timed mission beyond their strength, and instead of advancing their cause, they hindered it.

While thinking of themselves as progressives, as leaders of public opinion, they acted like instigators and demagogues, thereby demonstrating their immaturity and inability to lead a social movement. A really fine role lay before them, a leadership role, in a realm where everything was so unstable, immature, and backward. But they didn't understand this and, carried away by romantic impulses, themselves became part of the crowd which needed guidance. It were as if they wanted to challenge the government to a duel, to summon it to battle, instead of joining their progressive aims with the government's best ideas (whose existence cannot be completely denied), thereby acquiring, so to say, a helper, while helping the government in its good works without trying, at one stroke, to wipe out all its mistakes and traditions.

[i] United States.

Moreover, they lumped people who stood close to center with those in the center, and whatever had been bad in previous rulers they ascribed to our very system of government. In short, these were people who craved distinction and wanted to acquire popularity at any price and, following the example of those Western luminaries of journalism, to gain renown as political figures, rather than remain mere public figures who let time and gradual progress do their work.

11 December. Went to see Rebinder and Delyanov this morning. Discussed the projected appointment to the university's chair of philosophy. I stressed the importance of proceeding as carefully as possible in this matter. The best thing would be to use the requirements for the post as a means of removing some of those gentlemen whose candidacy is being pushed by a group of ultra-progressives who are unconcerned with the havoc these philosophers are causing in the minds of our young people. Lavrov and Bulich are, for example, such philosophers. The latter is a man of very few talents who has great pretensions toward popularity, which he counts on acquiring by disseminating the latest philosophic ideas of the German materialists, but, of course, in undigested form. Lavrov does not lack intelligence or talent, but is a materialist through and through who lashes out unrelentingly against anything and everything. The reds are very anxious for his appointment to the chair of philosophy, but this should not be permitted.

17 December. Meeting of the Chief Censorship Administration. This evening I had to stay for a long time, and this, plus the strain of speaking, gave me a miserable headache. There was fierce debate. I was terribly distressed to hear Count Adlerberg's opinion concerning an article about which Troinitsky had delivered a report. The count exhibited an incredible lack of knowledge and understanding of the simplest facts of intellectual and political life. Indeed, this man is supposed to be the emperor's representative, and his utterances are supposed to echo him. Can this really be the way they think up there, and is this the extent of their knowledge? It is utterly incredible and impossible! The following idea was expressed at the meeting: no one should be allowed to write on subjects relating to finance, politics and economics, the courts or administrative matters, because it would infringe on the rights of sovereign power even if such subjects were discussed very generally and, moreover, did not contain the slightest suggestion of a desire for any kind of change. If an individual should come up with an idea for improvements in various public or government matters, he should write a personal letter to the department directly concerned. In short, not a single social issue should be discussed in the press. Troinitsky justly remarked that this meant a return to the past. Delyanov, he and I tried, in vain, to demonstrate the inexpediency of such a system and point out that the government itself, for its own good, ought to welcome public discussion of various public, social and administrative matters, and that there was a vast difference between the expression of one's ideas in print and the delivery of a police denunciation. I tried, in vain, to explain the difference between the inviolability of the political principle on which our state rests and the inviolability of some local authority or the like. Adlerberg stubbornly insisted on his point of view.

There is a strong tendency in today's youth toward disobedience and insolence. One constantly hears of incidents in some university or other educational institution. These sad events are undoubtedly a direct result of the suppression of all thought under the previous regime, of its subjection to a discipline which amounted to complete contempt for the highest principles of morality. In short, they are the result of a cruel despotism which stifled everything. Now, everyone, especially our youth, are filled with wrath not only toward oppression of any kind, but even toward legitimate restraints.

23 December. Campaign against Sunday schools.[3] Prince Dolgoruky gave the emperor a note, which was inspired by Count Stroganov, criticizing them. Three or four days ago our minister advised the emperor that their popular activity was harmless and that it should not be suppressed. The emperor agreed with him. Now, again, they want to begin a campaign against teaching the people to read and write, which, of course, is not yet education, but does give people the key to it. Do they want to condemn our people to eternal obduracy at a time like this—when they are giving them their freedom? Does this make sense?

Of course the real issue is not the Sunday schools as such, but the popular movement they represent. Would it not be wiser to control this movement than to destroy it, only for a more harmful and dangerous movement to rise in its place? How nearsighted are our government officials!

30 December. Maikov read his new work, *The Spanish Inquisition,* at my home this evening. It is undoubtedly one of his best poems. The spirit of the times (Isabella), of Catholicism, and of Jesuitism, are superbly conveyed. The conversation between Isabella and the confessor is masterly; Maikov's portrayal of her as a woman, a queen and a Catholic is a brilliant display of lyrical beauty. Moreover, the whole work, in its complexity, is such that you can't add or subtract a single word, for everything is so precisely, completely and carefully thought out.

Rebinder, Goncharov and Chivilev were also here this evening. Incidentally —about Chivilev. He was appointed tutor of the grand dukes in place of Grimm. He found the young princes' intellectual development terribly neglected. Absolutely no thought had been given until now to their general development or intellectual training. Yet Chivilev found the tsarina to be a fine woman with a kind, warm heart and lofty ideas. How could it have happened that the education of the princes was managed so carelessly? The fault is not Grimm's, but of those who chose him and tolerated him for so long. Chivilev consulted me about certain tutors for Russian. I advised him to take on Orest Miller.

1861

5 January. Rumors about Sunday schools. Prince Dolgoruky gave the emperor
a note about their danger, saying they threatened revolution and the devil
only knows what else. They say Count Stroganov initiated the whole affair.
Both the prince and the count frightened the emperor. They want to take
repressive measures. Indeed, only his enemies could suggest such measures to
the emperor. There will be a debate about it today in the Council of Mininsters.
The minister of education will defend the schools.

Of course, this is only one side of the story; the Sunday schools are not
above reproach and do give the government some grounds for attack. But
in this case, the government should assume a guiding role, and not close them
down.

6 January. A victory for the Sunday schools. There was a debate about them
yesterday at the Council of Ministers. They say our minister delivered a passionate and superb defense of the schools. The party chiefly responsible for
their persecution was not Count Stroganov, as rumor had it, but Ignatiev.

Yes, the Sunday schools won a victory. The minister defended them this
time, but will they be able to defend themselves and uphold their lofty aims
for long? Or, will they go the way of most fine intentions and undertakings
these days; will bad seeds be sown along with the good?

22 January. Visited Prince Odoevsky this morning. We hadn't seen each other
for a long time. The princess was most gracious. They have soirées on Wednesday evenings, and I promised to come.

29 January. An important day for all Russia. The emancipation proposal was
introduced at the State Council. The emperor himself was present. It lasted
from 10 o'clock until 6:30 or 6:45. They say the emperor delivered a very
fine speech in which he said: "Autocracy established serfdom firmly in Russia,
and it is autocracy that must end it." He staunchly expressed his unbending
royal will on this issue. Some members protested against the basic tenets of
the new freedom, and one in particular, they say, cut a pathetic figure as he
expressed his distress over the termination of the tender patriarchal relationship between landowners and peasants. Kleinmichel, addressing the emperor, said: "Your Majesty has deigned to promise to grant the gentry patri-
monial police power over the peasants."

The government's proposal was strongly supported by Grand Duke Konstantin Nikolaevich, Count Panin and Chevkin. Among the opposition, incidentally,
stood the enlightened, liberal-minded Count Stroganov. It's clear that his liberalism and enlightened views are rather limited.

It seems that the faction opposing freedom is ready, in its impotence, to resort to all kinds of foul measures. It is spreading absurd rumors about the city, designed to frighten the government.

5 February. Several days ago I read Lavrov's article, "Three Talks on Philosophy," in the No. 1 issue of *Notes of the Fatherland.* My God! This is philosophy? To say nothing of the fact that it's all solid materialism. What a chaotic mess of ideas! Nowhere else, save on the Sandwich Islands, would all this rubbish be recognized as philosophy. And they want to force this Lavrov on the university as a professor! I am particularly disturbed by the fact that Kavelin supports his candidacy.

8 February. Commencement exercises at the university, which ended unexpectedly in a huge student demonstration. Kostomarov was supposed to give a speech.[1] He had composed a kind of biography of Aksakov. The minister cancelled it. Then, at the end of the exercises, shouts suddenly rang out: "Speech, speech, give us Kostomarov!" The shouting was accompanied by stamping and banging and soon became a wild roar. The authorities hid. Only the inspector, like a ghost, wandered along the corridor. Several sensible students asked me if I could persuade Rector Pletnyov to come out and reason with the unruly crowd. I went to the rector and found him alarmed, but he immediately agreed to go. I followed him and saw him enter the crowd, but because of the noise I couldn't hear anything. In the meantime I saw his wife, pale and frightened, accompanied by two students. I offered her my arm and led her away. A little later the rector returned, and I went home. A very nasty business! Our young people are losing their senses.

11 February. Conversation with Count Adlerberg about the commencement incident. I could not, in all good conscience, defend the students' actions, but I said that what was needed here, in any case, was a firm but friendly hand. The main reason for all this trouble was the immaturity of our youth, who needed, therefore, to apply themselves all the more seriously to their studies.

15 February. Some of the professors are even ready to defend the students' actions. I had a big argument today with one of them. Come now, gentlemen! It's not your love of young people or of learning that motivates you, but merely your desire to be popular with your students. Instead of giving them knowledge, you are enticing them into politics. This appeals to our unreasonable youth, which is now seriously beginning to consider itself a force that can make demands on the government and control its actions.

18 February. People are very tense over the emancipation issue. Everyone expected the manifesto on the 19th. Then rumors began to circulate about a delay. The public began to think it was being duped.

The governor-general released a statement to the press yesterday which said that "the government will not issue any orders in regard to the emancipation issue" despite rumors to the contrary.[2] This strange announcement, without any explanation of the fact that the matter was being postponed for only a short time, is irritating many people. Disturbances and demonstrations are feared.

An article appeared in today's (St. Petersburg) newspaper about an attempted uprising in Warsaw.

There's something ominous in the air. I hope to God everything turns out all right.

20 February. Baron Medem has composed instructions for the censors. They were sent to me today for review. I spent the day working on a plan counter to these instructions for they must be countered in every possible way. Above all I shall demonstrate that such rules for the censors are unworkable.

22 February. I stopped by at Delyanov's to discuss Baron Medem's instructions for censors. He also felt they were unworkable. Well, I now have one ally for the coming debate.

23 February. With the emancipation of the serfs our nobility's relationship with the government must change. It will have to acquire new moral and political authority. Political authority is emerging by itself from the changed circumstances in which the reform has involved the nobility. In freeing the serfs, the government could not avoid discussing the issue with the nobility, could not avoid inviting them to participate in their plans. This is an embryo which can grow into even broader rights for the nobility, if, of course, it knows how to use this first opportunity to participate in the government's affairs which has come its way; but only if it knows how to use it by relying on moral authority. Then it will acquire political significance, though not, in fact, as a nobility (it doesn't have sufficient legal or historical grounds for that), but as the cream of our nation, a sector which is more educated, developed, and more capable of understanding all manner of rights and of upholding them in the face of sovereign power.

24 February. I worked on the proposal for the elimination of outside censors. This task was entrusted to a commission consisting of Troinitsky, Berte and myself.

25 February. Meeting of the Chief Censorship Administration from noon until 4:45. Much current business. Several requests for permission to publish new journals, which are now springing up in countless numbers in Russia. Vernadsky, according to one member, is raging in his *Economic Index* against censorship rules, and has gone so far as to discuss the need for a constitution in Russia. We decided to call him in to the next meeting of the Chief Censorship Administration and inform him that since he has repeatedly shown he doesn't deserve the government's trust, he will be forbidden to publish his journal at his first new escapade. Some of the members demanded immediate suspension, but I persuaded Timashev, who was sitting next to me, to be satisfied this time with a reprimand. The others, too, agreed with us.

5 March. A great day: the emancipation manifesto! I received a copy around noon. I cannot express my joy at reading this precious act which scarcely has its equal in the thousand-year history of the Russian people. I read it aloud to my wife, my children and a friend of ours in my study, under Alexander II's portrait, as we gazed at it with deep reverence and gratitude. I tried to explain to my ten-year-old son as simply as possible the essence of the manifesto and bid him to keep inscribed in his heart forever the date of March 5 and the name of Alexander II, the Liberator.

I couldn't stay at home. I had to wander about the streets and mingle, so to say, with my regenerated fellow citizens. Announcements from the governor-general were posted at all crossways, and knots of people were gathered around them. One would read while the others listened. I encountered happy, but calm faces everywhere. Here and there people were reading the proclamation aloud, and, as I walked, I continually caught phrases like "decree on liberty," "freedom." One fellow who was reading the announcement and reached the place where it said that manor serfs were obligated to their masters for another two years, exclaimed indignantly "The hell with this paper! Two years? I'll do nothing of the sort." The others remained silent.

I ran into my friend, Galakhov. "Christ has risen!" I said to him. "He has indeed!" he answered, and we expressed our great joy to each other.

Then I went to see Rebinder. He ordered champagne and we drank a toast to Alexander II.

11 March. Meeting of the Chief Censorship Administration. Vernadsky, publisher of the *Economic Index,* received a reprimand together with a warning that his journal would be shut down if he weren't more careful. Vernadsky was embarrassed and defended himself rather clumsily.

16 March. The fate of our universities should catch the attention of our thinking people and our society if they are capable of bothering with such trifles. Our universities are obviously heading for a decline. Their students are demoralized; the professors lack prestige. Many positions are vacant, others will soon become vacant, with no one to occupy them. There are no replacements, because young, gifted people prefer other careers to university service. In a word—utter depletion. Indeed, it seems that our universities, even under Nicholas I in 1848, were never in such a critical state as they are now.

18 March. Meeting of the Chief Censorship Administration. I was asked to compose a set of guidelines for censors on certain current, rather ticklish, issues.

This task was in danger of falling into the hands of that great master composer of instructions, Baron Medem, or that bureaucrat, Berte, who is a master at raising issues which the government itself would much prefer to forget. Berte isn't worth talking about, while Medem thinks that censorship rules can be composed which cover every conceivable exercise of the human brain, thus instantly freeing humanity from all undesirable ideas. So, I had to take on the task.

A warning was issued at a meeting of the Chief Censorship Administration to the *Contemporary*, stating that it would be banned unless it changed its tone. This was a result of Berte's report.

31 March. Dinner with Count Bludov. Other guests were Tyutchev, Egor Kovalevsky, and Annenkov and his young wife. The countess was delighted with Khomyakov's poem, while Annenkov didn't care for it at all. The count attacked present-day writers for not knowing how to write, and repeated his favorite line for the hundredth time: "our current crop of writers doesn't understand that there is such a thing on earth called the art of writing." Kovalevsky and I remained silent. The count's point of view was disputed by Annenkov, though rather feebly, and by Tyutchev.

1 April. Meeting of the Chief Censorship Administration. It seems that the minister wanted to impress Count Adlerberg today with his strict and vigilant attitude toward literature. For example, he intensified his efforts to ban Nekrasov's work, although everyone except Przhetslavsky was ready to approve it with the exception of a few passages. In the end even Count Adlerberg stood up for Nekrasov.

8 April. A very significant session for me of the Chief Censorship Administration. I won a victory. It involved the refutation of Baron Medem's instructions, and to this end I had written a circular to the censors contrary in spirit to Medem's instructions. It cost me a great deal of time and thought. I feared I would encounter resistance from some of the members. However, my victory was complete. They listened attentively to my circular and everyone approved it in the end, even Przhetslavsky—which I never expected.

10 April. In various districts of some provinces demonstrations have already taken place among the peasants who refuse to fulfill their obligations to the landowners. The landowners, in turn, are very upset. Clashes are feared when the land is reallocated. In the meantime, the so-called educated class and progressives, as they call themselves, are ranting about a constitution, socialism and and so forth. Our youth is in a state of complete demoralization. Poland is seething—and not only the Polish Kingdom, but Lithuania, too. All this portends something ominous.

12 April. Spent the evening at Rebinder's. The emperor had summoned the minister and told him that the disorders now rocking the universities could no longer be tolerated and that he intended to close down some universities. The minister replied to this, saying that such a measure would provoke general displeasure, and he asked him not to resort to it. "Then you think of something," the emperor said, "but I warn you that such disorders can no longer be tolerated and I am determined to take stern measures."

The minister was at a complete loss: he hadn't, up to now, thought of any measures; he had gone about his business as if everything had been going well. Our kind, good emperor has had no luck in his choice of administrators. For the past three years the most flagrant misdeeds have been committed under Kovalevsky's very own nose—and he didn't realize that something had to be done.

15 April. There was a debate on the universities at the Council of Ministers on Thursday. Our minister was strongly attacked for the student disorders. In vain he referred to the spirit of the times. The emperor assigned Count Stroganov, Panin and Prince Dolgoruky to review the minister's memorandum on measures he is now proposing. Strictly speaking, this means subjecting the ministry to control and giving custody of its affairs to outside powers. So that's how Evgraf Petrovich has ended up! Incidentally, Count Stroganov asked him this: "What would you do if some professor, in your presence, began to deliver a lecture on a constitution for Russia?"

25 April. Reception at the minister's. Endless talk about the crisis in the ministry of education. Everyone sees a victory here for the reactionary bloc, while Kovalevsky, little by little, grows in the public's esteem. He is not only insulted, but embittered, too. However, I feel that he isn't entirely in the right. He should have given some serious thought long ago to the university disorders. Now that a triumverate has been appointed to examine his proposals, he has no alternative but to resign. Kovalevsky lacks firmness and the breadth and boldness of intellect demanded by the times.

They say Stroganov was offered the ministry, but declined it. They also say he is very powerful in the Court and that his machinations produced the current crisis. The Moscow superintendent, Isakov, has arrived here. The emperor asked him to look over Kovalevsky's proposals and give his opinion. Isakov replied that he was in complete agreement with them. "Go and tell that to Count Stroganov," said the emperor.

What do these proposals consist of? Their main point is that neither repressive measures nor harshness can lead to any good, but that it is necessary to improve the financial status of the universities and to give them the opportunity to do scientific work in keeping with the needs of the times and the advances science has made in Europe. But these are only general principles. Where are the measures which should and could make them a reality?

3 May. The once good-natured Russian people, who, in Pogodin's words, welcomed the emancipation humbly and gratefully, are now beginning here and there to display their eternal ignorance and coarse understanding of law

and rights. A Tambov landowner told me yesterday again that there were
incidents on his estate of disobedience to the authorities: "We don't want to
work; and give us land—as much as we want." Again they were compelled to
summon soldiers to explain to them that they must work and that all of the
land was not theirs. On another estate the peasants descended on their
master's woods with axes and felled all of it before it could be divided up.

5 May. Goncharov, Kraevsky, Lkhovsky and a few others visited this evening.
Kraevsky arrived from Moscow yesterday. There, he said, the students were
behaving worse than in St. Petersburg. They are openly demanding the replacement of certain individuals and freedom from the university administration's interference in their affairs. Mainly, they don't want to study anything
at all. The Moscow nobility, in Kraevsky's words, keeps fuming about the
present state of affairs. In short, dissension and disgraceful incidents are becoming the order of the day.

6 May. Meeting of the Chief Censorship Administration. Lots of business to
cover—we stayed until 4 o'clock. Debate on Zotov—which I stirred up again,
by trying to show that one cannot so lightly strip a writer of the right to edit
a journal. Berte, the one chiefly responsible for this discussion, asserted that
Zotov deserved it for violating censorship rules. I replied that such a harsh
decision should not have been made without first exhausting other more temperate measures. It ended, without abandoning the original decision, with
an agreement to let Zotov remain as editor of *Illustration* for an indeterminate period during which he could mend his ways.

More discussion on the ban on using names in accusatory articles. In addition, Przhetslavsky protested strongly against the importation of foreign
books via Poland.

16 May. It is definitely confirmed that Count Putyatin has been named minister of education and Taneev his deputy minister.

19 May. Goncharov, Shchebalsky, Strugovshchikov, Timkovsky and others
visited this evening. Talk of the new minister, Count Putyatin. It is impossible
from all the talk one hears to form any sort of clear picture of this man, for
opinions of him are so diverse. It is rare in our society for anyone to emerge
with a clearly defined image; for the most part reputations are based on false
facts—they rise and fall without sufficient cause or at least without well
founded or just cause. It seems that no one is concerned with the truth, and
everyone is determined to put his own thoughts into circulation. This is our
accursed habit of seeing an excuse in everything to display ourselves, to show
off.

Everyone is lauding Kovalevsky for leaving the ministry in such a blaze of
glory after standing up for the principle of progress and the like at the Council
of Ministers. I don't quite share this view. Rather do I have the impression
that he sacrificed the emperor for the sake of acquiring a good reputation,
for a flattering response from a certain camp.

Should he, at such a critical moment, have abandoned our kind, honest, well-meaning emperor, who is guilty only of being surrounded by unworthy people? But, comes the objection, what else could Kovalevsky have done, seeing that the emperor had not invited him to stay on and was, apparently, inclined to favor the opposite camp? True enough, but Kovalevsky himself had alienated the emperor, even before this, after the Aksakov affair. Indeed, even on the university issue he acted remiss at the very least. For some three years the universities had apparently been going downhill financially, academically and morally. Did Kovalevsky do anything to improve this situation? Kovalesvsky seemed afraid of being accused of opposing the liberal movement, were he to resort to any restrictive measures against the students. He, if it can be put this way, assumed a neutral position, concerned only with avoiding a charge of inertia by the public.

I don't know, but in my opinion, in this instance he did not conduct himself like a government official who must face problems squarely, but like a man awaiting favorable circumstances in order to perform some good deed. Now he has become a martyr for a just cause. But how will the future judge him?

22 May. I submitted a request for a two-month leave. Through the entire winter my poor health did not change one iota and my nightly distress continued. My doctors prescribe another sojourn by the sea.

23 May. Professor Soloviev visited me this evening and we had a long talk about current affairs, about the new minister, etc. He brought me volumes X and XI of his history.

8 June. I spent the whole day packing. My papers went into my briefcase— and now all mental labor must cease. At least that's what I promised the doctor, my family, and myself.

Farewell, my dear study, for the next three months.

1 August. I took my last swim yesterday. I am leaving Libava tomorrow. Thus, my summer health cure comes to an end. What it will do for me in the days to come—I do not know. Meanwhile, the paroxysms have become even more severe.

10 August. Upon his arrival from abroad, Nikitenko goes directly to his dacha.
Finally, at noon, I arrived at my so-called estate. The rest of my family met me at the edge of the birch grove. There was general rejoicing, embraces, noisy exclamations, and questions left and right. Together, we walked to the house, which I now can call all ours. It is small but very pretty, cozy and comfortable. My study was clean and bright—a charm to behold. My dear wife's careful hand was in evidence everywhere; she had done everything to make my home pleasant, and at very little cost, too.

11 August. Yesterday ended noisily and uniquely. Toward evening, on the little square in front of our house, the peasants gathered in their holiday apparel, which is very unpretentious. They wore long white caftans. A young girl brought me an enormous wreath of corn ears and, as her girlfriends sang lustily, presented it to me. This is their way of celebrating the end of harvest. Then came refreshments—wine and apples. A violin appeared and dancing followed, which continued late into the night. I spoke with some of the peasants who had come up to me and thanked me for my kind treatment of them. Well, this is something that I really can't take the credit for and must ascribe wholly to my tenant's intelligent and kind management. Two huge bonfires were lit at the end and the peasants dispersed to their homes while the flames still danced brightly.

13 August. Went to matins. Our church is made of stone but is very dilapidated and in need of extensive repairs. However, it is certainly adequately equipped. Some articles—namely the vestments, standards, two or three icons, chandeliers and holy vessels, would do credit even to a fair-sized village. But the service and singing are somehow lifeless and senseless. The priest himself seems completely disinterested in what he is doing and reading. He reads the Gospel particularly badly, although his diction and voice are not unpleasant. The main fault lies in the deacon's utter disinterest and the parishioners obtuse indifference. But external decorum was observed. They even tried to make a show of it for us. The sermon to the people was not forgotten either; it was taken from some book, but delivered without the slightest attempt to adapt it to its listeners, and so lifelessly, that the only thing it could possibly arouse was boredom. What a pity and how annoying! You can't blame the priest for it: that's the kind of training, direction and guidance he received . . . At least, thank God, he's not an alcoholic. The pitiful state of our rural clergy is truly a serious problem.

I invited the priest to my house for tea. In due time he appeared. At first he was very flustered, but later regained his composure and conversed very intelligently. He complained that the peasants came to church most reluctantly and were generally extremely backward.

Also here was my wife's niece, Madame Bykovskaya, a neighboring landowner who owned 350 peasants and a great deal of land. Like most of the local gentry she was very unhappy about the present state of affairs. She and many other landowners felt that the peasants should be given their freedom without land. I tried, in vain, to show her that this was wrong from a moral and political point of view. I tried to console her by saying that in time everything would work out and all sides would benefit—but this, too, fell on deaf ears. Of course this is a very difficult time for the gentry, but there is no other way to carry out such an enormous reform, and they don't want to understand this and are furious at the government.

17 August. I went to the country with my pockets full of gingerbread for the kiddies and to visit the sick peasant, Terekha. This fellow is amazing. Yesterday, in the course of several hours, he drank up all the medicine the doctor had prescribed for him to take over three days, thinking that this would hasten his recovery. We were horrified when we heard about it. Poor Terekha has grown very weak. We don't know if he will live. We sent for the doctor again. As for the kiddies who ran up to me for the gingercakes, you can't, by any stretch of the imagination, conceive of anything filthier. The pretty little faces of some of them were almost completely hidden by layers of dirt. But they were all outdone by one Tit, who presented the classic image of a filthy urchin. I distributed the cakes, sat down on a log and talked with them. Only a few of them knew one or two prayers, most of them had scarcely even heard of God. They were all perfect little savages. An unpenetrable darkness will long reign in our rural areas unless the government opens schools and compels parents to send their children to them, and unless the priests come better prepared to their rural parishes and establish a different kind of relationship with their parishioners.

18 August. I had a talk with the *starosta*[j] today about the important benefits conferred on the peasants with their freedom. I couldn't convince him. He listened to me with head bowed and kept saying that everything had been fine for them until now, and that now only God knew what would become of them. I singled out to him one of the most important advantages of the new system—that they would have their own courts, that they could choose their own administrators and would not be at the mercy of someone's whim. To this my *starosta* replied that all this would only overburden them, that until now they had thanked God for their way of life and prayed for their mistress. Finally, he cited the state peasants, and then I understood the reason for his fear. The local peasants think that henceforth they will be in a similar position to the state peasants; thus, from a tolerable dependence, in this case, on the landowner, they would shift to a more oppressive dependence on government officials. This is at the base of their panic.

The Russian official is a wretched individual. What he will be like in the future is something we don't know, but until now he has been the worst natural enemy of the people.

30 August. Tables were set up in our courtyard after matins today with pies, wine and various sweets, and all this was offered to the peasants. After dinner the violin began to sing, and the dancing began, lasting until 5 P.M. The weather was conducive to gaiety. It was rather cool, but clear and windless. When dinner began, I went up to one of the tables, poured a glass of wine and offered a toast to the emperor, father of us all, and liberator of the peasants. "May God grant him a long life and a long reign," I said. But, alas, even my attempt to elicit sympathy in these good people for the new system was useless. They were constantly at my side and addressed their wishes and gratitude to *me* alone. The *muzhiks* were very pleased with the treat, conducted

---

[j] The village elder.

themselves properly and kept repeating one thing: only God knew what would happen to them under the new system, that they could not want a better life in the future than they had known in the past ten years, that is, when the estate passed into the actual possession of my wife. Evidently their desires did not and do not go beyond some material comforts and decent treatment on the part of the authorities. Their understanding of freedom, political, or whatever, is very hazy. The women were given presents: caps, aprons and ribbons. I took the children under my wing and treated them to apples and gingerbread, and, when my supply of these goodies was exhausted, gave them lumps of sugar which they accepted with no less pleasure.

8 September. I introduced myself to the new minister, Putyatin. He did not make a favorable impression on me.

13 September. For the third time some sort of leaflets are circulating, calling upon the people to rebel. The first batch bore the heading, "Great Russia," and the latest ones are simply a kind of proclamation. Could this be the work of Herzen and his cohorts? The leaflets are, of course, coming from abroad. It's all really very stupid and vicious.[3]

18 September. I finally read that famous appeal "To the Younger Generation." Its falseness, absurdity and insolence could amaze any thinking person, if anything can amaze anyone these days. For example, their idea of slaughtering 100,000 nobles is a fine one, indeed! "Why, wars kill more than that; even the Crimean War did," and so forth. Superb logic! Even better: "Let them all die." What we have here is nothing more than vulgar, revolutionary invective which could once be heard in every tavern in France. It contains not a single intelligent word which would indicate that its author or authors know anything about the problems of government, about the political life of nations, or about the science of administration. Their poor, raving minds can't figure out any alternative to slaughter. Their amazing ignorance about everything concerning Russia, its national spirit, its moral, intellectual and material resources, are evident in every sentence. They demand that it shed blood like water for the realization of those utopian ideas coming from London's printing houses. Whether Russia wants this or not doesn't concern them at all. Our wise reformers have learned nothing from the French carnage. They didn't learn that anarchy's horrors and pillaging lead to dictatorship of the most horrible kind imaginable, to a reactionary dictatorship armed with a sword and executioner's axe to replace the knife it has wrested from the hands of anarchy. Can this be what Herzen is preaching? A fine thing it is to stir up popular passions, to preach carnage, to summon rebels to the square, in a word, to push thousands of people, like sheep, into a whirlpool of boundless misfortunes, while you sit in your comfortable armchair in a peaceful study and, from there, 3,000 versts away from all these horrors, dispose of the blood and lives of millions without risking a drop of your own blood or a hair of your own head. Cheap patriotism; that's all it is! Yes, gentlemen! It is an ignoble, cowardly greed for popularity and a leading role in society, for the worship of gullible and nearsighted people (if only there could be more of them for you); it is a vain and criminal desire to pass as a second Mazzini or the like at the expense of others. Poor Russia!

20 September. It is generally clear that Count Putyatin has very little understanding of ministry affairs and administration. Many of his ideas are rather strange, if not absurd. I feel he is very limited. It's difficult to hammer any fine, useful, idea into his head, for he is stubborn, too, as are all limited people. He is very rigid in all his views. So it seemed to me this evening. Perhaps he will reveal more of himself to us and make a more favorable impression.

22 September. Student meetings are forbidden, but they held one today and raised an awful row. Will the authorities do anything about it? It's amazing how some people are coming to the defense of disorderly students and are not only ready to defend them but to encourage similar escapades.

There were several arrests. They say the great apostle of socialism and materialism, Chernyshevsky, was arrested too.[k] My God—what are these people ruining themselves and others for! Let them sacrifice themselves for their own teachings, but why drag in others, especially these poor, irrational young people.

23 September. Meeting of the Chief Censorship Administration. The new minister finds himself in a quandary about censorship. He has no fixed viewpoint on it. The main topic of today's meeting was the matter of the *Contemporary*, which Berte raised. According to him it preached revolutionary ideas. It was decided that all the members would read the pages and articles singled out by Berte and give their opinions.

Meanwhile, disorders are continuing at the university. Meetings are forbidden, but they are held anyway. The students are raising a row and demanding the elimination of all restraints. Like the peasants in some provinces, they shout: "Liberty, liberty!" without giving the slightest thought to the kind of liberty they're howling for. And what does the government do? —It exclaims: "Oh, what terrible, terrible times these are!" and posts appeals and rules on the walls of the university calling for the preservation of order, rules which are often ripped down by the students and replaced by appeals and announcements of another sort. In brief, complete chaos reigns. No one thinks about learning.

What can be done about this distressing situation? Various ideas come to mind. I thought of suggesting the following measure at the first opportunity. A commission should be created consisting of several professors, to which each young person desiring to study at the university would have to give his word of honor that he was entering for the sole purpose of attending lectures. If, after this, he was seen at demonstrations or found violating the rules of university decorum he would be subject to expulsion.

[k] The rumor of Chernyshevsky's arrest turned out to be false.

24 September. A sad day. A meeting with the minister. He delivered a brief speech to us, asking us to help him restore order. Then he talked about the need and justification for a fee system, whereby students would pay to attend lectures. But this was incidental. The main thing we learned was that the university was closing for some time as a result of yesterday's student disorders. And so, it has come to pass! My worst fears have been realized. The university is closing, and not as a result of obscurantist persecutions, but of internal breakdown, which demands temporary use of the surgeon's scalpel to preserve its future existence. All the professors were stunned by this. Yet no one expressed the view that this measure was not called for under the present circumstances. Everyone, so to say, hung their heads, including those who had, perhaps, much abetted this by encouraging the hollow aspirations of the students.

Yesterday, besides shouting and wild speeches against the authorities, the students forced their way into the large auditorium which had been intentionally locked against them, smashed chairs, broke in the door and smashed windows.

Just came from Philipson's (7 P.M.). We exchanged ideas on measures which should be taken at the university. He's a wonderful person; he has a noble and sensible outlook; he loves young people, and is unhappy about what is happening, but is unruffled. He can't act independently; he's bound hand and foot.

"Do you know," he said, "how difficult it is for me merely to get information about the real state of affairs at the university? Reliable information about everything comes to me from the minister, while the minister gets it from the Third Section; and the Third Section learns everything through its spies. You can imagine how pleasant this is!"

So, I thought to myself, the local university administration is either so blind that they can't see what's happening under their very noses, or, are so ignoble, that they cover it up out of cowardice, fearing student reaction. Meanwhile, the evil continues to grow and has grown to the point of closing the university. I keep thinking that timely and unanimous pressure on the students by the professors and superintendent could still put out the fire without outside assistance. It's really disgusting to think how spineless we are.

25 September. At 12:45, on the street where I live (Vladimirskaya), a huge crowd of young people wearing blue collars and blue bands on their caps appeared. A gendarme detachment and a crowd followed close on their heels. The crowd turned into Kolokolnaya Street and swarmed around the university superintendent's flat. These were our students, but here and there one could see the outfits and uniforms of officers and medical students. I dressed quickly and set out for the scene of action. A detachment of firemen was hurrying there, too. An absurd and sad drama of student disorder was being enacted here. The crowd had come to the superintendent's quarters to demand the abolition of various university decrees.

As I neared Philipson's flat, the crowd was in a turmoil and shouting wildly in the middle of the street. The gendarmes cordoned it off. Amidst all the chaos and shouting, it was impossible to make out what was being said, but the gestures, waving of shawls, canes and hats, were testimony to the frenzied state of these young people. I made my way with difficulty to the sidewalk which was also overrun by crowds of students. Some, evidently the more moderate ones, were exclaiming: "Gentlemen, let's not make a scene! " A small group was observing its fuming comrades. I turned to them and expressed my regret about what was happening. I don't know whether the regrets they expressed in return were sincere or not. But when I said that they were harming the university by such escapades, my words were seized upon by one of the shouting students, who answered: "Who cares about learning, Aleksandr Vasilievich! We're deciding vital issues here!"

The crush got so bad that I was forced to climb onto the parapet of the enclosure surrounding the church on Vladimirskaya Street and somehow made it to Philipson's flat. Of course he wasn't there: he was outside with the students. But I had wanted to reassure his wife, whom, however, I found unruffled by the disturbance.

Finally, after shouting and demonstrating for a long time—about a half hour—the crowd moved on toward the university with the superintendent at its head. I took a cab and headed there, too.

The superintendent was already there. When he saw me, he was delighted and asked me to stay and participate in the commission which was to hear the statements of student representatives.

Meanwhile, the young people had poured into the university courtyard and gatekeeper's lodge; there was also a huge crowd outside; people jammed all the nearest vantage points; carriages and droshkys blocked the roadway. Everything was in a state of confusion and an air of tense expectancy prevailed.

Chief of Police Patkul appeared, followed by Governor-General Ignatiev. The student delegation, consisting of Mikhaelis, Gen and Stefanovich, entered. The governor-general delivered a speech to them in which he expressed his sympathy for youth, but, at the same time, his determination to prevent student disorders outside university walls. His speech would have been satisfactory, if it weren't, I felt, so vague. Then he asked the students to disperse, but the superintendent announced that the commission he had hastily assembled planned to hear the student representatives. Then the governor-general agreed to wait and went into the other room.

We took our places before the mirror of justice in the council hall, and the delegate, Mikhaelis, began to put forth the students' demands. They were: a) that students be permitted to use the university library while the university was closed, b) elimination of the rules imposed by the matriculation oath.

The chairman, that is, the superintendent, told them that the rules could not be abolished; that the students, on the contrary, had to promise to adhere to matriculation rules, and only under those conditions would they be permitted

to enter the university. If they didn't want to take such an oath, they could
leave the university: it was completely up to them. This was a kind of contract which the university was concluding with its students. To this Mikhaelis
replied that they would take the oath but wouldn't uphold it. I expressed my
surprise at hearing such words from the young man, and remarked that one
should not take oaths lightly. "Well, why not," he replied, "when we are
forced to take them?" It was explained to him that acceptance or rejection
was a matter for each individual to decide freely, and that there was no coercion involved.

At the end of the meeting the governor-general asked the students to disperse. However, they continued to mass at the gatekeeper's lodge in the
courtyard and at the university gates for a long time afterwards. A variety of
spectators jammed the nearest street and the embankment. I returned home
late in the evening, terribly distressed and exhausted.

27 September. Student demonstrations again. Some had been arrested during
the night. As a result, a crowd of young people—about 600—gathered in the
university courtyard. There were many inflammatory speeches. Some woman
also burst into the crowd and shouted something. The noise got louder and
the turmoil grew, too. The governor-general was informed of this, and, on his
orders, a battalion of a Finnish regiment moved in and formed a square on
the street opposite the university gates. Ignatiev himself appeared. Six students pushed their way through the crowd. They went up to Ignatiev and
informed him of their desire to go to the minister, as delegates, to appeal for
the release of their arrested comrades. They were told that the minister would
not receive any student delegation. Then, upon the governor-general's insistence, the students dispersed.

I heard all this from the superintendent.

28 September. Meeting at the Academy. From there I went to the university
where I was confronted with a very sad spectacle. Students were milling
around the Neva entrance—not many—some fifty. The doors of the university
would not open for them. The youths wore sullen, dejected expressions, but
they were peaceful and not raising a fuss.

Philipson sent for me. Despite my fatigue, I immediately went to see him.
He told me that, on the minister's orders, I was being appointed to represent
the university on the commission investigating the recent disorders.

I don't feel like taking it on! It will involve many difficulties and many unpleasant situations, and my health is poor. But, as a citizen and true friend of
youth, I do not have the right to refuse simply because it is a difficult and unpleasant task.

I was at the governor-general's at 6 o'clock. He greeted me with expressions
of regret over what had happened. I expressed the hope that the young people
would not be looked upon as political criminals. These are merely children,
and the authorities must take a paternal view of them. "God is merciful, and

everything will end well," replied the governor-general. Then he added that many people were criticizing his orders, although they were indebted to these very orders for averting bloodshed.

From the governor-general I went to see the minister and told him that I had to be at the fortress at 8 o'clock, where the commission was to meet.

At the fortress, at 8 o'clock. Not all the members were present. We could not proceed because we had no facts on which to base an interrogation of the detained youths; that is, we didn't have precise data on the reason for their arrest and the charges. We drew up an official report, stating our decision to secure information from the appropriate parties and then adjourned. We accomplished little at the first session. General confusion and inconsistency were very much in evidence.

The members who were present seemed to me to be decent people. They are not anxious to treat as political criminals young people who have gone astray; at least that was the general sentiment they expressed. God, I hope so! It would make our task a lot easier, a task which not only involves justice, but mercy too.

The commandant also impressed me as an unpretentious, kindly person. Thirty-seven students had been arrested. One had fallen ill and was taken to the hospital.

29 September. Several members of the university faculty came to see me this evening to ask me to step down from the commission because they said that this affair required a lawyer, a member of the Department of Law. Naturally, I did not argue, especially since their words, if not their intentions, did have some validity. People are upset, and, should things turn out badly, the ministry could be reproached for choosing a delegate who was not a lawyer. I shall ask the minister tomorrow to release me from the commission for health reasons.

30 September. I submitted a request to the minister for my release from the commission. He appointed Gorlov in my place. He was very angered by the faculty appeal submitted to him today requesting his intercession on behalf of the students imprisoned in the fortress. I couldn't sign it because I was still a member of the commission and in that capacity could not participate in any kind of action.

Some people would like to transform the university into a political club, and have almost done so.

Incidentally, not only university students are involved in the current unrest. All the local higher educational institutions are in sympathy with them; and not only the local ones, but the provincial ones, too. All the theoreticians of liberalism and the journalists are on their side, too. There is no doubt that the events of the last two days are connected with the leaflets "Great Russia," and "To The Younger Generation," which openly called for revolution. In a word, this is a symptom of the revolutionary fever which has gripped a lot of

frivolous writers and pompous minds. I suppose it is a very natural development, but it must be intelligently and firmly resisted or it will lead us to anarchy; and anarchy, as everyone knows, ends in that most terrible of all des-
potisms—reactionary despotism. It appears that we must accept the incontro-
vertible truth—that historical events are beginning, and not only wisdom and
virtue, but madness and violence, too, are involved in the making of these
events.

It is unfortunate that, in such trying times, power usually rests in the hands
of unreliable people.

1 October. In one respect the current agitation for change could be turned to
advantage if the government would make proper use of it. In the first place,
it should understand that it should not ignore certain demands of the educated
sector of society. Secondly, it should not shelve projected reforms and should
act more judiciously and with greater deference to the law. Thus, it could
avert much evil and do much good. It should stand at the head of this movement and not let itself be drawn into a position of surrendering to the inevitable demands of the times in the form of concessions. This would be a terrible
failure, on its part, to act. No one knows where to call a halt to these concessions, or whether we can call a halt. Such failure could lead directly to revolution, probably the most disorderly the world has ever known.

But firmness on the part of the government must not, in any case, turn into
anger or cruelty. God forbid! And it must not, in fact, look upon unruly
children as real enemies. Young people should be forgiven their enthusiasm;
especially if it turns out, as it most likely will, that they were stirred up by
outsiders. If not, they should still be absolved of their sin, for they know not
what they do.

2 October. I visited Glebov, vice-president of the Academy of Medicine and
Surgery, yesterday. He told me that their students were not necessarily involved in overt acts as were ours, but that their sympathies certainly did lie
with ours. The students had organized a joint meeting for Thursday in the
Academy courtyard. But, measures were taken to block it: the Academy
courtyard was locked, and outsiders were not allowed to enter. Several
coaches, carriages, and droshkys drove up to the gates, young people jumped
out and went up to the gates, which refused to budge. The uninvited visitors
were forced to leave.

There is one thing that is producing awful confusion among the public; it is
the terrible lies being spread in the city by unscrupulous progressives about
any incident or any new move of the government. The government should
really do something to silence this slander. There's only one way to do it—and
that is by letting the public know what is going on. The government should
issue short factual bulletins about any unusual occurrence, but the facts as
well as the refutation of false rumors should be accurate. The Academy's
Bulletin (the *St. Petersburg Bulletin*) could be used for this purpose.

Students are again massing near the university; also crowds of onlookers are gathering. Troops have been brought in. No one is allowed to enter the university.

There would appear to be no doubt that the students are lambs being led by outside forces—not by real shepherds, but by wolves in sheep's clothing.

3 October. Mikhailov has confessed that he wanted to start a revolution.[4]

4 October. Ran into a friend [I.A. Goncharov], who advised me to be careful. He had dined at the club yesterday and heard some people attacking me for not approving of the students' actions. "And do you?" I asked him. "No," he replied. "So, you were attacked, too?" I added. He stopped short.

University Council meeting. Held an election to the university court. I received two votes. The majority is obviously displeased with me. This doesn't surprise me and no longer distresses me. I expressed myself openly against this majority during the student disorders; so, it's very natural that they are against me.

5 October. All the *ultraprogressives* at the university have turned against me because I don't approve of the students' actions and, in general, oppose the principle which gives the students the right *to demand* the cancellation of any order they please. These gentlemen are employing the usual demagogic tactics: they lie, slander, and ascribe thoughts to me which I never had, as well as words which I never uttered. My friend[1] came to see me again, today, and we had a long talk. He, out of his own boundless laziness and apathy, out of his own political and moral indifference, advised me to straddle the fence. But such tactics, which smack of hypocrisy and baseness, are not for me, and, moreover, these days it is easier to give advice than to follow it. Of course, it is safer to go whichever way the wind is blowing, but these days there are all kinds of winds blowing, and they're blowing against each other, too. In such times, every honest man active in the life of our society must take a definite stand; he must be *something;* he cannot be *everything,* which is the same as being nothing.

7 October. What is being done now—arresting students and holding them in the fortress for more than ten days—is something I certainly disapprove of. But, on the other hand, we must understand the nature of the Mikhailov case, the leaflets that were issued, and whether our students were not involved here, too. That would be simply awful.

Philipson told me that the minister wants me to draw up a memorandum on university reform. I gave Philipson my views on this issue and promised to set them down in a special memorandum.

11 October. The university was opened today. The sentry was removed from the gatekeeper's lodge. But the barracks odor had so permeated the air that it was difficult to breathe. Meanwhile small bands of students wandered back

[1] Nikitenko is probably referring to Goncharov.

and forth between the main entrance and the Neva entrance like sinners at the threshhold of paradise who are forbidden to enter. Apparently these were the ones who had applied for and not taken the matriculation oath. There was talk that they were here with the idea of starting some kind of demonstration again. And so, the first day of the university's reopening, which our administration had feared, went well.[m] Will this calm continue?

12 October. Around 11 o'clock, as I rode across the Dvortsovy Bridge toward the Academy of Sciences for a meeting, I noticed a crowd on the Ostrovsky Bank and a gendarme detachment. Just as I thought; student disorders again. I did not go to the Academy, but headed for the university. Near the Neva entrance stood a small crowd of students. However, the real action was not here, but at the main entrance. A detachment of gendarmes was deployed there. Spectators strolled about the square and several carriages stood there. However, there was no great commotion. I entered the university and found everything quiet. Several students who had matriculated and attended lectures were wandering along the corridor. The lecture halls were empty.

Students were still hanging around the Neva entrance, and nearby stood several members of the municipal guard. I went upstairs to my lecture hall. About fifty students were gathered in the corridor near the rector, and he was lecturing them about something. Meanwhile, the gendarmes had pushed a crowd of about 150 students away from the main entrance and chased them into the university courtyard where about 100 of them were taken under convoy to the fortress.

Here is what happened. About 700 students had taken the matriculation oath and declared that they wished to attend lectures according to the rules set forth in the oath. Those who had not applied for matriculation—and there were some 300 of them scattered about the city—decided to descend on the university en masse, somehow entice from it those who had matriculated, attack them, seize their ill-starred matriculation certificates and there, on the spot on the university's doorstep, destroy them. This is what the police wished to prevent, and the incident ended with most of these anti-matriculates being led away to the fortress.

Very few students attended lectures. Most of them, expecting trouble, did not go, fearing ill treatment at the hands of fellow students who belonged to the opposition.

17 October. Here is what I would like to say and will say to a red at the first opportunity: We should not be enemies. We are both striving toward the same goal. You and I both favor progress; but you stand for *lightning* progress, whereas we stand for *gradual* progress. The whole point is to keep each other from going to extremes. Unrestrained speed and dawdling are equally bad.

---

[m] Notes in the Soviet edition of Nikitenko's diary claim that he was mistaken, that clashes did occur between the students, police and soldiers, and that, as a result, about three hundred students were arrested.

You will not permit society to stagnate, to go along in just any old way; and we don't want to let you race along at breakneck speed, for this could lead to great harm, anarchy, for example. In a word, we serve as a counterweight which keeps the scale evenly balanced. In essence, neither you nor your opponents will achieve what you want, rather will something quite different emerge from the mutual resistance of forces, something which neither of you expect—something which has to be. This is the crux of the matter. You want blood, while we allow for the possibility that blood may flow, but we don't want it. You say that nothing can be attained unless blood flows. In the first place, where did you get that idea? It doesn't necessarily follow that what was true in the past must always hold true in the future. In the second place, blood is a marvelous substance when it stays where it belongs—in one's veins, but not quite so marvelous when it gushes out of them.

You say the old must be *completely destroyed* so the new can then be created. But is this really possible? Mankind is steeped in the old: in science, art, and all the experiences and discoveries of centuries past. The old is the totality from which emerges the new. To destroy everything old is to destroy history and culture.

There is such a thing in our social order as reconstruction, where we don't start from scratch, as if nothing had ever existed before. And when we rebuild, some things are discarded, other things are improved, and some things are left untouched to keep everything from being destroyed.

18 October. They say that during the student demonstrations in Moscow many students were beaten by a mob who thought it was a rebellion against the authorities.[n] If this is true, it is a very significant fact. How will our reds, who are summoning the people to rebellion in the name of progress and all kinds of social improvements, react to this?

Six students attended my lecture today. Some professors are not giving any lectures because there's no one to give them for.

19 October. The emperor has returned.[o] Some five students attended my lecture today; other professors had even less. Sreznevsky, for example, had three. A total of 75 students have been attending the university, although almost 700 had originally submitted requests to attend. Why don't they come? It is mostly law students who are staying away, the most restive section of the student body. They seem almost determined to follow the Hungarian example of *passive resistance*. We are great imitators. The students took the matriculation

[n] According to a note in the Soviet edition of Nikitenko's diary, the beating of the students was organized and executed by the police and gendarmes. The Moscow administration circulated various rumors that the students were rebellious Poles who wanted serfdom restored.

[o] The emperor had returned from a vacation in the Crimea because of the student demonstrations.

oath, submitted requests to attend lectures, but still want to display a form of silent protest. How long will this continue, and how will it end?

20 October. Some students wanted to involve the soldiers, too, in their demonstration. They moved through the barracks and urged the soldiers to rebel, circulating the kind of ideas preached by the *Great Russia* leaflet about reducing the term of military service, etc. According to these students, the soldiers must win this through armed struggle, and they will be assisted in their struggle by students and all good people. My Lord, what it's come to! And there are mature adults who sympathize with such demonstrations. I would like to believe that they are unaware of all such schemes. They ought to foresee the consequences of this absurd movement among our youth, of their contempt for law and order, of the audacity with which it pressed at its meetings for a voice in political matters and government reforms.

22 October. Students who had taken the matriculation oath, but were not attending lectures, planted four notes in the university, cursing their fellow students who were attending lectures. Savelich, the gatekeeper, told me sadly that some of the students (troublemakers, as he calls them) were wandering about the corridors trying to persuade their fellow students to skip lectures.

No wonder the university is empty. A great many students are in the law department and the professors in this department agreed not to hold lectures. Spasovich and Kavelin go along with them. This particularly encourages the students' spirit of rebellion.

Another installment of the *Great Russia* leaflets appeared and was distributed, it seems, to the editorial offices of all the journals, or at least the major ones. Some secret committee is again appealing to patriots, and this time, primarily, to the patriots of the moderate-liberal camp. It concerns the demand for a constitution. The committee, as a kind of concession to the moderate-liberal camp, decided for the time being to shelve the idea of forcing the emperor to grant a constitution, or the idea of overthrowing the dynasty. Instead, it proposed a petition to the emperor and appended a draft of this petition.

Both the appeal and the petition are moderate in tone and, therefore, they can make a deep impression on the public if they are widely circulated. It seems they will be because, under the very nose of the police, they are quietly finding their way about the city in badly printed—but, nevertheless, printed copies. You don't need many copies circulating for everyone to get a chance to read them, as they are passing from hand to hand.

It is remarkable that the leaflet scarcely deals with the student disorders. They are mentioned only as an object lesson in connection with the propaganda that youthful minds should be stimulated, but, at the same time, inappropriate, immoderate impulses should be curbed.

23 October. Meeting at the minister's this evening. We deliberated the university reforms suggested in Baron Korf's proposal. He proposes opening university admission to the general public, thereby eliminating the classification of "student" and their role as a corporate body. Promotion exams and courses would be abolished—in a word, universities would no longer function as schools.[p] I voted in favor of this proposal, feeling that it was almost the only way at this time to break up the corporate spirit of university youth. This spirit, in its present form, is such a profound evil, that I do not consider any sacrifice to weaken it too great. Pletnyov also voiced the same feeling, but Savich was the most vocal and forceful of us all. The minister questioned the effectiveness of such steps, and defended examinations. But the rest firmly supported Baron Korf's proposal. Delyanov also supported us strongly. Apparently, the minister did not want to agree with Korf.

There will be a debate on this proposal at the Council of Ministers on Thursday.

25 October. I am a monarchist on principle (of course not an absolutist), and have been sincerely devoted to Alexander II since the emancipation. But I am really afraid of losing my respect for him. How can people like Count Putyatin be appointed to ministerial posts? A half hour's conversation with him is sufficient to convince you of his limited mentality. Is it possible that the one who chose him has so little understanding of people and the tasks that his appointees must undertake? This is incomprehensible.

28 October. I went to see the minister of internal affairs after dinner. He asked me to assume the editorship of the newspaper the ministry has decided to publish next year. I gave him my views: that the newspaper should, above all, have its own well-defined character, as well as a definite orientation. And this, I felt, could only be a moderately liberal one. If I assumed the post, I asked, would I be able to maintain such an orientation in the interest of the government? The minister replied that one would have to tread cautiously here. "You know," he added, "that the government itself is not even clear about its own views."

After a rather lengthy conversation, the minister gave me forty-eight hours to think it over. I must give him a definite answer on Monday.

30 October. Saw the minister of internal affairs. I submitted a memo to him outlining the conditions under which I would accept the newspaper post. He read it in my presence and agreed to everything. And so, the die is cast. I shall be editor of this paper, and, at long last, shall try to realize my cherished hope of laying a foundation for conciliation in our society. The minister will make a report to the emperor about me on Friday.

The minister and I also talked about the minister of education. Valuev also feels that he is simply a limited person, incapable of dealing with certain ideas or coping with his position.

[p] Korf's view was that formal education belonged in the home and lower schools, that the only function of a university was to impart knowledge to the student, and that universities should be breeding grounds of pure science.

1 November. Not a single student appeared for my lecture. Since philology students, from the day the university reopened, had been attending my lectures fairly regularly, I am wondering if their complete absence now is not a demonstration against me personally.

This would be the first time such a thing had occurred during my entire university career. But this should neither surprise nor distress me. The demoralization in our university is so great, that one can expect anything. However, it appears that no one attended the lectures of the other professors in our department today.

2 November. No students again today at my lectures or my departmental colleagues'.

I stopped in to see Delyanov. Talked about the minister. He makes mistakes every step of the way. He is already reneging on his word to invite professors from all our universities to work on university reforms and is retreating on the issue of open admissions at the universities.

Delyanov told me to what wild extremes the Moscow students have gone. They cursed the superintendent to his face, calling him a [?].

3 November. Saw Valuev this evening. He told me that he had reported to the emperor about my appointment as editor-in-chief of the newspaper, and the emperor agreed to it "with great pleasure."

Saw Pletnyov this morning. He told me how Putyatin had been appointed minister of education. Metropolitan Filaret had recommended him as a highly religious man. The empress, enchanted by the stories of the count's piety and devoutness, had forgotten that a minister needed other qualities, too, and began to press the emperor to appoint him in Kovalevsky's place. Of course, other members of the palace clique joined in. Unfortunately, the emperor surrendered to this intrigue—and so Putyatin was appointed minister, to the government's shame, the detriment of Russia, and his own disgrace. They say Grand Duke Konstantin strongly opposed the appointment. As commander of the fleet, he knew Putyatin well. But this was of no use.

5 November. Received official notice from Minister Valuev of my appointment as editor of the *Northern Post.*

11 November. Meeting of the Chief Censorship Administration at 8 P.M. Report on the *Russian Word.* The minister insisted that the journal be banned. The other members and I suggested a warning instead. We decided on the latter course.[5]

16 November. The minister sent for me this evening. He asked me to outline for him in writing the main problems facing the universities and those which demanded immediate attention. He is obviously incapable of coping with the problems of the universities, their needs, or the means of reforming and improving them. I promised to write the report.

19 November. Spent the whole morning with Delyanov. Count Dimitry

Andreevich Tolstoy,[q] who was appointed to succeed Delyanov as director of the education department, and whom I know intimately, was also there. Talked about Putyatin. Delyanov didn't spare him. Count Tolstoy defended him for his honesty. The conversation then turned to the present state of affairs in Russia, which presented a most disturbing picture. The count had spent the summer in the countryside and had traveled around various provinces, observing conditions and the way people were thinking. He was convinced that in about two years—1863—a slaughter would begin. The nobility was preparing petitions to the emperor, asking him to grant some constitutional privileges or something on that order, without insisting however, on a constitution itself. The *Bell* was delighted with the student disorders and was openly inviting the students to ignore their studies and to spread propaganda for rebellion. Let's face it; Herzen has been behaving dishonestly and foully: he is operating underhandedly, without any understanding whatsoever of Russia's problems or giving any thought to the consequences of his actions.

Aren't all these problems nothing more than the pangs of Russia's rebirth—this general floundering, the rapid, alarming disintegration of social relations, the demoralization, the senseless infatuations of the young, the obtuse inertia of mature, adult minds—this general ferment, this fever of worthless ambitions, this raving about theories with which one is scarcely familiar and which have withstood neither analysis nor testing? Is it not a painful and disturbing process, this regeneration of a people which until now had not experienced a natural and sound development, a people which history has tormented and not educated?

There is no room here for either fear or anger; one must discard one's usual prejudices. One must show courage in one's thoughts, desires, and actions.

Yet, I find my faith in our national ability to control our own fate crumbling. I find myself thinking that the Russian people are inherently incapable of self-control and of moral and political originality. Isn't this the common curse of all Slavs? God save us!

21 November. This morning I went to see Troinitsky, whom I often consult on matters related to the newspaper. We always got on well together at meetings of the Chief Censorship Administration, and now we agree on almost everything. As deputy minister, he will help us get materials from the ministry for the paper, and will serve as a middleman between the ministry and the newspaper staff. This is very important.

I met a colonel at Troinitsky's who had been present on the square during the student disorders in Moscow. Assuming that he, as a witness, could give me an exact account of the affair, I asked if it were true that the populace had played a role in this sad event, and exactly what they had done. The colonel replied that the people had actually rushed at the students in a frenzy and beaten some of them half to death. He managed to rescue three of them, getting roughed up himself in the scuffle and losing his cap. Someone in the

[q] Not to be confused with the writer, Count Lev (Leo) Tolstoy.

crowd had shouted: "These fellows want serfdom!" and then the crowd went wild.

22 November. Went to see Kraevsky this morning about some details relating to the publication of the newspaper. He has a lot of experience. He gave me many useful suggestions.

I left my article about universities with him for publication in the *St. Petersburg Bulletin*, no. 265.

Bankruptcy threatens many journals and newspapers next year. Subscriptions are going badly. No one has any money. I was told that, two days ago, at the funeral of Dobrolyubov, who wrote for the *Contemporary*, Chernyshevsky delivered an amazing speech at the Volkov Cemetery. The essence of it was that Dobrolyubov died a victim of censorship. It had cut his articles, thereby bringing on the kidney ailment that led to his death. He repeatedly cried out to the crowd assembled there: "But what do we do? Nothing, simply nothing. All we do is talk."

1 December. The minister of education sent for me. I went to see him. He asked me to give him the report on university problems which he had requested earlier. Among other things, he spoke at length about the sad state of our universities. He said that one of the main causes of the disorders was the joint action taken by several professors to embarrass the government.[r]

2 December. The students started more trouble at the university. A large crowd of them had assembled and they were discussing or reading something. Deputy Inspector Schmidt, suspecting that they were holding a meeting, asked them to disperse, to which they responded rudely. Spotting a nonmatriculated student among them who, as a nonmatriculate, did not have the right to attend the university, he grabbed his arm and asked: "What are you doing here?" Poor Schmidt was then showered with blows and knocked off his feet, that is, thoroughly beaten. A faculty court was assigned to the case with myself as a member, but I asked to be released because I was terribly busy with the newspaper and preparation of an Academy report. Steinman and Sukhomlinov were chosen from our department.

4 December. I gave the minister my memorandum about universities. I am glad to be rid of this fruitless task. In the meantime I had wanted to do a good turn for Goncharov. I suggested to the minister that he appoint him a member of the Chief Censorship Administration in place of Troinitsky, who was appointed deputy minister of internal affairs and, therefore, had left the Censorship Administration. Naturally, one couldn't make a better choice. Yet, what did the minister, who knew Goncharov well, reply?

"I've already appointed someone," he said.

"Whom?" I asked.

[r] A group of liberal professors had resigned from the university in protest against government policy toward the universities and the students.

"Kislovsky"!!

Kislovsky capable of judging literary matters?! That ignoramus, whose knowledge is limited to chancery routine?! The minister is ousting Delyanov and Voronov and making way for Kislovsky!

5 December. I received a note between 7 and 8 A.M. from Philipson, asking me to see him at 9 o'clock. They want me to be a member of the commission for review of the university charter. This is so important that I cannot refuse, despite my very busy schedule. May God give me the strength!

7 December. First meeting of the commission. Bradke began with a very intelligent and clear exposition of its task. Philipson, somewhat awkwardly and too emotionally, aired the advantages of open university admissions over other systems in the same sense that I had in my article in the *St. Petersburg Bulletin.* What I had in mind was to break up the corporate spirit of the students as it now exists. Meanwhile there are other, no less important conditions, which must be taken into consideration in reorganizing our universities. The delegates from Moscow University, Soloviev and Babst, showed up rather late, having just arrived from Moscow. At this session, after a rather lengthy debate between the chairman and Philipson, we decided to start with a review of the 1825 charter and the proposals offered by our university, Kiev and Moscow universities to amend and change the charter in keeping with current needs.

9 December. Third meeting of the commission. Babst also raised the question of whether student writings should be subject to regular censorship or simply printed with the permission of their respective departments? The Moscow delegates strongly insisted on the latter. A vote was taken. The majority agreed with the Muscovites. I was against it, the chairman, too. It was decided to insert this difference of opinion into the official record. Prince Vyazemsky agreed with the chairman.

11 December. Meeting of the Commission. We accomplished much today. Bradke informed us of the plans relating to student discipline. Where there are governor-generals, that is, in large cities like St. Petersburg, Moscow and Kiev, university students will be subject to the authority of the governor-generals, who will have special officials to keep an eye on them. The Kharkov and Kazan delegates announced that they would deal with the students themselves and would be responsible for order in their universities. This is remarkable!

15 December. Sharp debate at the commission on two issues: 1) whether to allow women to attend lectures, and 2) on tuition fees. The majority was against the first. Debate on the second is still continuing. However, there is little sympathy for a fee reduction. I supported a decrease, particularly for poor gifted students.

21 December. An imperial decree to close St. Petersburg University. In reality it has already been closed by the students themselves, who have refused to attend lectures.

27 December. Golovnin was appointed minister of education.

1862

13 January. Meeting of the Chief Censorship Administration at 8 P.M.—the first with the new minister of education (Golovnin) presiding.

The minister announced that the emperor wants the censorship department *to be stricter and more vigilant with respect to periodical literature.* So, my dear red gentlemen, what would you say now? On whose conscience does the guilt lie?

21 January. I welcome Sunday like a schoolboy. I don't have to go to the newspaper office or the printers and I can spend the evening at home.

Life has its difficult and trying moments. I am experiencing one of them now. Everything is raging and seething around me, and I am like a helmsman who must steer his ship amid shoals and rocks. There is the confusion surrounding the publication of the newspaper, which I must struggle with daily; the lack of honest colleagues; the poverty of material which could enliven the paper and give it a literary tone; the endless constraints I am subjected to by the ministry; the finnicky public, demanding instantly what normally takes months and years to accomplish; the hostile cries of the extremist groups; my broken health—and amidst all this chaos, I must struggle alone, without anyone or anything to rely on except the purity of my own intentions. These are only a few of the charming aspects of my current position.

28 January. State presentation to the new minister. Here is my estimation of Golovnin: he is aloof, cold, intelligent, resourceful. That's all I can say for the time being.

5 February. Oh, what a dreadful business! The minister of internal affairs issued a circular to the governors, directing them to compel everyone, through the police, to subscribe to the *Northern Post*, because it was a government newspaper and was supposed to counteract the influence of the Russian press! The circular's very words! I am terribly upset and must do something to counter it.

6 February. Today I read to two of my chief colleagues, Rzhevsky and Arseniev, a draft of my letter to the minister of internal affairs, outlining our protest against compulsory subscription to the newspaper and especially against the reasoning in his circulars for this absurd measure. Without the slightest hesitation they agreed to sign my letter. It will be sent out tomorrow.

7 February. I sent the letter to Valuev. I think it was convincing and strongly worded. At any rate, I held nothing back.

It was sent out around 4 o'clock, and I received an answer at 6 o'clock. The answer indicates that the minister realizes his mistake, but since it is difficult to correct, he is trying to find a way to extricate himself. However, he promises to furnish a satisfactory explanation.

16 February. They say a disturbance took place in Tver among the gentry. Annenkov, several gendarme officers, and the chief prosecutor of the Senate were sent there to restore order. Tver is a liberal city. Since the very beginning of peasant reform it has often made demands, and rather bold ones too.[1]

18 February. I met Panaev, who has grown very thin. He complains about his fellow litterateurs and journalists, those progressives who are doing such great harm to the cause of genuine freedom. Now, Panaev, too, is beginning to be convinced of this. Incidentally, the new minister, Golovnin, asked for their opinion of censorship affairs, and this gave them such swelled heads, they began to spread reports that both censorship and the minister himself were now under their thumb.

20 February. I sent the minister an explanation of the Tver affair for publication in the newspaper. A rather nasty business. Thirteen nobles had decided to protest the "Emancipation Act of February 19th." They were arrested, taken to the fortress and their case turned over to the Senate for trial.

5 March. Professor Pavlov has been expelled under police surveillance to a remote *uyezdny gorod*[s] as a result of his speech last Friday at a public benefit reading for writers.[2]

7 March. I feel it was a big mistake for Golovnin to reopen the university in the Duma Hall. In so doing, he has apparently encouraged in our youth the idea that one can study with abandon, on the run, at public gatherings, rather than at a school or university. This is a dangerous step leading toward superficial knowledge rather than serious learning, for which we feel an urgent need.

10 March. Gossip about the incident which occurred in the Duma auditorium at Kostomarov's lecture. Here are the details. After Pavlov was banished to Vetluga, the professors lecturing at the Duma and (Pavlov's) former students agreed to the suspension of lectures. But Blagoveshchensky and Kostomarov did not. Kostomarov appeared at his lecture at the scheduled time. He was received badly. He delivered a speech to the assembled crowd, in which he declared that he had no intention of being a gladiator for the amusement of those who had gathered for a spectacle rather than the pursuit of knowledge; that he didn't intend to indulge their empty liberalism. This was followed by shouting, whistling and cursing. But Kostomarov left, not very moved by the flood of uncouth anger unleashed at him.

There is talk now among the public, too, that the young are not as much to blame for these escapades as their teachers and leaders who have been prematurely arousing liberal sentiments in them instead of providing them with sound and practical knowledge. It's long overdue.

11 March. The Chief Censorship Administration has been abolished. Censor-

[s] Chief town of an uyezd, which is the lowest administrative division.

ship is now being transferred definitively to the ministry of internal affairs and is being organized along special lines.[3]

12 March. 11 P.M. Just came from Golovnin's. Talk about censorship. He asked me to help him get the Geographical Society exempt from censorship.

18 March. Just came from an informal party at Valuev's. (It's midnight.) It was an enormous gathering. Heard all sorts of news. Nothing comforting. The confusion in ideas is growing. Valuev, it seems, won't be holding on to his post much longer.

Grand Duke Konstantin had indeed been appointed chairman of the State Council in place of Bludov, who has been granted sick leave for six weeks.

19 March. The future looks gloomier and gloomier. If a certain group is victorious, it will mean the end of all rational, liberal, moderate principles, and the representatives of these principles will be trampled by that crowd which bounds ahead at breakneck speed and smashes everything in its path. Then, what will we have: a new brand of oppression and despotism? . . .

It seems that Golovnin, too, is concerned more with his popularity than proper administration. Isn't this why he dumped censorship on the minister of internal affairs and reopened the university in the Duma?

22 March. Meeting yesterday with the deputy minister of internal affairs. Present were members of the former Chief Censorship Administration and its staff. Censorship is in a strange position now. It has split in two somehow: it has one foot in the ministry of education, and the other in the ministry of internal affairs. The ministry of education retains the preliminary censorship apparatus, while the ministry of internal affairs has the power to supervise, to check and, we hear, will have punitive powers in the future.[4]

2 April. The deputy minister visited our editorial office and told me that the *Northern Post* would not have a special censor.

8 April. Easter Sunday. Went to matins. The speed with which they ran through the service was fantastic. It was all over in no more than half an hour. The church was full of ladies, decked out in all their finery, and their dashing admirers, who kept a lively conversation going through the entire service. Goncharov and I went home together and chatted over an Easter loaf and ham until 3 A.M.

13 April. The minister of internal affairs called a meeting today at 2 o'clock of the entire staff of the department responsible for the supervision of publishing matters. Indeed, this entire supervisory council, the very idea of supervision, and the entire state of censorship today is perfectly ridiculous. So this is what Valuev's proposals for changes in the censorship apparatus have come to! He wanted to create a punitive censorship apparatus, started the task, couldn't handle it, and procrastinated until Golovnin appeared on the scene. Now Golovnin, too, has bypassed him. Golovnin took over the heart of the censorship apparatus, and left its murky, unattractive side to Valuev. It's turned out to be something like the fable, "The Crow and the Fox."

29 April. Here's the kind of cunning our minister used. He wants to please the students and the defenders of their wild pranks, and open the university. But he doesn't want to take the initiative himself in this risky matter. He uses every possible strategy, trying to induce the university itself to raise its voice in favor of reopening. In the meantime, here is what is being ascribed to him: he induced first the German, and then, they say, the Russian edition of the *St. Petersburg Bulletin* to say that the public was very anxious for the university to reopen, and that the university had nothing more to fear from the students since they were taking their meetings outside the university's walls to the Society for Aid to Needy Writers. Indeed, if this is true, it surpasses even the lowest kind of pandering to the crowd . . . At least the blood spilled in France was in the name of impracticable, but great theories; with us it would be spilled because of the stupidity or baseness of some individuals and the completely chaotic approach we Russians have in everything we do.

Yesterday, Andreevsky demanded that the university itself compose its own new rules, and that this be done in such a way that the ministry would have no influence in the matter; not even its approval would be sought. To this, someone objected. "So you want to give the university dictatorial powers?" "Yes," he replied. "Well," I remarked to Kutorga who was sitting opposite me, "this fellow is going pretty far, but whether he'll be successful or not, I don't know." And when I said that any rules we devised would be considered arbitrary and that it would be better to await the new charter, which would, nevertheless, be an organic law, and, so to say, a legitimate law, Blagoveshchensky replied: "Do you think anyone really respects the law these days?" "Well, in that case there's no use even reopening the universities," I answered.

Indeed, if, in the past, people didn't respect the law, they respected the government or at least recognized its power and feared it, but now there's no restraint whatsoever, no self-control, and everyone goes his own way. At least the minister should understand the importance of all this and not act like a scoundrel or coward.

If the suggested temporary rules are composed in a spirit which limits the students' arbitrary behavior, they will not like it, and will carry on again. If these rules are weak and indulgent, the students will like them, and again they will do whatever they please, except study.

1 May. Discussion with Minister Valuev. He has begun to cut funds for the government newspaper. As a result, editors Rzhevsky and Varadinov were fired. This saves 7,500 rubles. I suppose I can manage without Rzhevsky, but where will these cuts end? The minister might not stop at that and could extend his cuts to the fees paid to our contributors, and this would inevitably destroy the literary tone of the paper. Consequently, I decided to exert every effort to oppose any new cuts, and if I am unsuccessful, I shall resign. The minister criticized the expansion of the paper's political section and I defended it.

7 May. Things are going very badly between Valuev and myself. If, dating from the incident involving the famous circular (to the governors, about compulsory subscriptions), I had been standing with one foot in my editorial post, now I am hanging by a thread, which I myself am ready to cut at any moment.

He doesn't like the idea of my wanting a certain degree of independence for the editorial staff, without which it is impossible to give the paper an image worthy of the public's attention and trust. We've had several clashes. He keeps complaining that he is being ignored. Yes, it's becoming quite clear that the minister, after all his fine intentions and twaddle about our broad perspectives and tasks, wants, in the end, to shrink the original plan of the newspaper. If he is really such a flighty person, I am no longer interested in working with him.

15 May. Meeting of the University Council (or rather of the faculty, because, properly speaking, there is no Council) with Superintendent Delyanov presiding. It was decided to reopen the Council in August, and the university about the first of October.

24 May. There were four simultaneous fires in various parts of St. Petersburg yesterday. One of them, the worst of all, was not far from my home, near Ligovka. There's talk of arson. Some people think it is connected with certain proclamations in the name of young Russia which were scattered about in various places.[5]

28 May. A day full of anxiety and fear for all St. Petersburg. For the past four or five days there have been fires in the city and, sometimes, several going at once. On Friday, for instance, there were six simultaneous fires in various regions. Rumors are circulating about arson. The government is amazingly careless. The city is in obvious danger, especially after the latest leaflets that have been scattered everywhere—on streets, squares, in houses, in barracks. Thank God, we have enough troops. Shouldn't we have reinforced our patrols and cordoned off the more dangerous and suspicious areas? But none of this was done. I didn't even run into ordinary Cossack patrols. With the authorities being so lax, fear of even worse disasters was quite natural. And they have come.

30 May. Fire at Peski. I went to the city at 11 A.M. The troops and the emperor were on Tsaritsyn Meadow. Lots of excitement in the city. No one doubts that it's arson.

There's no end to stories, rumor and gossip.

31 May. It appears certain that the fires are related to the recent leaflets. If the fires were laid by ordinary thieves, there would have been attempts at robbery but there weren't any anywhere. The police announced that a commission for aid to fire victims has been created by imperial order. Many people have lost absolutely everything. The government announced that anyone caught with incendiary equipment and materials or held as a suspected arsonist, as well as anyone picked up for inciting disorders, would be tried by a military court within twenty-four hours.

Also, punishment was meted out on Mytnaya Square today to Obruchev for distributing seditious literature against the emperor and sovereign power. A sword was broken over his head and he was sentenced to hard labor for three years, to be followed by permanent exile in Siberia.

Measures were taken. All courtyards are now locked; caretakers have been stationed at their gates to bar entrance to suspicious parties. Patrols have been reinforced.

2 June. Terribly cold in our rooms; 45° outside. The fires have died down.

I received an article from the deputy minister at 8 o'clock this evening for tomorrow's edition, which describes the discovery of seditious teaching in the Sampson and Vvedensk Schools. The students were being told that St. Petersburg must be burned, etc. This was being taught in the Sunday schools which had been established within these schools for the working class. A commission was organized to investigate this. I immediately went to the printer's and the article was set up in my presence!

3 June. Saw the deputy minister this morning. Discussed some editorial business. Asked him, too, to get me some facts about the fire; otherwise we couldn't print anything. He promised to get them.

Two arsonists were caught and confessed: a *muzhik* and *baba*.[t] Someone had given twenty-five rubles to each of them for this horrible deed. But the person or persons responsible cannot be found, and they are the key to the whole affair.

The emperor won't agree to capital punishment. The public still thinks that students are setting the fires. Golovnin wrote Valuev, asking him to make an announcement to the effect that the students were being falsely accused. Valuev refused.

12 June. Here it is—the logical reaction to the senseless and vile deeds committed by our reds. The Sunday schools have been ordered to close. Also, the women's boarding school in Vilnius. The schools will be reorganized and placed under strict government control. The *Contemporary* and the *Russian Word* were suspended for eight months. The real problem involved in any reaction, and particularly in our reactions, is that the innocent must suffer together with the guilty. Stagnation and oppression threaten again, while thinking people, writers and scholars—are threatened by the hostile attacks of ignoramuses and reactionaries.

Visited the deputy minister this evening. The commission set up to find the arsonists is not making any progress. It has turned up very little so far.

16 June. It is customary now to label any intelligent article or opinion in literature insipid if it is not sufficiently cutting or radical in tone. Thus, do we teach our people how to drink: we try to keep them from acquiring a taste for anything which doesn't intoxicate at once.

[t] Peasant woman.

27 June. I had a talk with Troinitsky this morning. He confirmed my feeling that the minister was displeased with the newspaper, picked on everything, and inflated such trifles as misprints while glossing over important matters. I told Troinitsky of my decision to resign. He didn't try to dissuade me, agreeing that it was impossible to continue in this way.

When I arrived home I wrote a letter of resignation and a rather brief letter to the minister explaining the reasons which were compelling me to give up my position as editor-in-chief.

30 June. I received a letter from Minister Valuev about my release as editor-in-chief of the *Northern Post.* The letter is full of the most flattering comments. We are parting "on the most friendly terms." And yet, we were unable to work together!

The doctors are chasing me to the sea again. Now, I suppose, I can go.

1 July. Went to see Valuev. Was received very well. I requested leave. He agreed.

7 July. Arseniev came over late this evening, and together we composed a telegram to Goncharov in Moscow, asking him to hurry back to St. Petersburg. Valuev plans to appoint him editor-in-chief of the *Northern Post.*

10 July. They say Serno-Solovievich, Chernyshevsky, and Pisarev have been arrested.

13 July. Preparations for departure. Another journey to the sea. I can't say that I like the idea of making this trip for the third time in pursuit of health. But my doctors insist, and my own family is pressuring me and imploring me to go—and so, we're going.

14 July. I am leaving today.

19 July. (Abroad.) Strakhov and I ran into each other back in Berlin and since then we've been exploring Dresden together, too. Good to the point of naïveté, gentle and intelligent, he is a very pleasant companion.

4 August. I ran into Prince Yusupov in Dresden. Our conversation touched on Herzen and the revolutionary leaflets with which he is flooding Russia. Here's what he told me apropos of this: "I was buying some German books in a bookshop in Berlin. 'Would you care for some Russian books?' a helpful salesman asked me. 'What kind?' 'Well, for example, Herzen's: I have every one of his works, the older ones and the very latest.' 'No,' I replied. 'They watch such things very carefully these days, and I am afraid that I would never get them to St. Petersburg: they'd be confiscated at the border.' 'That's a lot of nonsense! I'll deliver as many as you want to St. Petersburg, directly to your home, in fact right to your study.' 'Amazing! But what if I suddenly decided to detain the person who delivered them?' 'Don't worry about that! You wouldn't be able to do that; you wouldn't even see the person delivering them to you.'"

15 August. Here is an important point about the countries I've been visiting: each individual recognizes his own worth. The lowliest day laborer, sweeping refuse on the street, would no sooner permit himself to be insulted or treated unfairly and illegally as would some deputy attending a legislative session.

17 August. Everything appears to be going rather uneventfully in St. Petersburg. I assume this is so because there hasn't been a single word in the local press about Russia (except for some telegraph dispatches about trouble in Warsaw). One would think Russia wasn't even on the map of Europe. Since the press feeds on such sensational news as fires, slaughters, and hangings, we Russians should refrain from supplying it with material. Italy alone is giving it enough of that now. It seems that poor Garibaldi has blundered. I hope Italy doesn't fall into Napoleon III's hands. They are saying here that the Zouaves [French colonial troops] are advancing from the Shalon camp toward Nice.

19 August. I read in the *Constitutionnel* today that Garibaldi was captured by Victor Emmanuel's armies. According to all the rules, Garibaldi ought to be sentenced to death. But, it goes without saying, his prior services and the entire character of his activity place him outside the law, that is—above the law. He undoubtedly will be pardoned.

27 September. (Berlin.) I read Koshelev's pamphlet *Constitution, Autocracy and the Zemstvos,* which I bought in a local shop. It contains a great deal of truth. I think the idea of *zemstvos* is both proper and workable, should the emperor want them, and no one hinders him.[u] But this raises a ticklish question: wouldn't the introduction of *zemstvos* violate the principle of autocracy? Koshelev doesn't see it as a legislative body, but only as a *deliberative one.* But will he want to stop at that? We have the historical elements for the creation of a deliberative duma. It would be a thoroughly national institution for us.

I also read the latest issue of the *Bell.* Herzen calls Mazzini and Garibaldi "Saint Don Quixotes." Bakunin lies about Poland.

30 August. We arrived in St. Petersburg at exactly 11 P.M., where we were met by the rest of my family. I was home in half an hour—and happy to be there.

Something dreadful occurred in my absence: we were badly robbed. All our clothes disappeared, and anything of any value was taken from my study.

5 October. I've spent the past few days putting my study in order and making some calls. I went to see the chief of police today to complain about the improper conduct of the police assigned to investigate the robbery, especially Inspector Kupriyanov. Instead of giving my wife legal aid and assistance, he made things as difficult as possible for her and demanded her presence at police headquarters for depositions.

[u] *Zemstvos,* institutions of local government, were established by law in 1864.

10 October. I read the proposal approved by the emperor for reforms in legal proceedings and the court system.[6] What unbelievable progress Russia has made under the present tsar. If anyone had dared to think of dreaming such things during Nicholas's reign, and his dreams had, somehow, become known— he would have been considered a madman or political criminal. Now we shall have public trials, public airing of information, juries, a legal profession, a court free of the administration's despotism. And all this is the work of an emperor who is reproached for being weak, unintelligent, and the like. No, you red gentlemen, you followers of Herzen! You have not understood this man, and all you want to do is perform before a crowd for the sake of ap- plause. No, you are not the moving force behind Russia in its drive toward progress, but its brakes! If only the emperor can stand his ground against the turbulent waves surging at the foot of his throne. He is obviously fully de- voted to Russia, but the trouble is with those surrounding him.

21 October. I hate all forms of despotism equally—the despotism of the rabble as much as the despotism of a single individual; the despotism of opinion as much as the despotism of crude, physical force; the despotism which turns me into a robot in some shop for the good of the commune as much as the des- potism of a wealthy man who thinks he owns me, my labor, and knowledge, because he has a lot of money.

I, you, he—are individual personalities. Society is an abstract concept, but the socialists and communists want society to be made up of individuals who would be enslaved to it and live for it alone. Shouldn't it be the other way around? Shouldn't society be structured in such a way that each individual could live freely, free to arrange his own life, while society's function would be to protect that freedom?

11 December. I am beset, once again, by an inner restlessness and discontent with myself. This has been going on for the past few days. I feel disgusted with myself; my life is like an incoherent, empty dream, a cloud of noble, lofty intentions which the winds of circumstance and my own impotence are carry- ing off into endless space.

13 December. In our entire administration, there is only one man whose hon- esty and patriotism can be trusted—and that man is Tsar Aleksandr Nikolaevich.

26 December. In keeping with custom, I had to read my report to the presi- dent before delivering it on Public Speech Day at the Academy on December 29th. He told me to come this evening at eight. I had barely opened my note- book and read the first few lines when the venerable old man dozed off. What was I to do? To stop reading would have been awkward. So, I continued as if I hadn't noticed, rushed through it somehow, and finished in 10 minutes. "Good," he said, as he awoke, "very good." After chatting with him for a few minutes, I left.

28 December. The commission set up by Golovnin, under Obolensky's chairmanship, for the reorganization of the censorship department and the censorship code, has finished its work and presented its proposal to the minister.[7] Baron Nikolai literally criticized it to pieces. Golovnin, deducing from this that the proposal would never pass in the State Council, pounced on it himself and declared it unworkable because it was *much too harsh*. Yet, Prince Obolensky has in his possession a pile of memos from him which endorse the commission's ideas, so it is obvious that the proposal had developed under his guidance and influence. What exactly does his new stance mean? It means that if the proposal should be approved, Golovnin can wash his hands of it before the ultraliberals, claiming that "despite my opposition, a reactionary law was passed." And if it isn't approved he will take the credit himself for blocking such a vicious proposal. That's how Golovnin spends his time—in tricky maneuvering and fancy intrigue. Poor Russia! Obolensky, Golovnin's former friend and, in part, his creation, now curses his name outright everywhere.

1863

1 January. New Year's Day. With all this frenzied activity, one might think that everyone had suddenly gone mad! What is the meaning of all this? Is it nature that has suddenly changed so radically, or is it people? There isn't the slightest indication that anything new has occurred to distinguish 1862 from 1863. Yet the air rings with New Year's greetings; and everyone is succumbing to hopes which are probably as unfounded this year as they were last year. But I suppose there's something to say for such a custom. Lacking true blessings, a man must at least have lofty illusions. All this frantic running about is a kind of pastime which brightens our prosaic lives.

3 January. At the palace ball. The guests began arriving around nine. I arrived at the Jordan entrance. The entrance to the hall was magnificent. The illumination was dazzling. The Pompei Gallery was decorated with foliage and transformed into a lush garden path which, in fact, led into a garden illuminated from above by lights sparkling like diamonds. First, the guests thronged into two large rooms to await the entrance of the emperor and his family. It was quite stuffy. Around 10 o'clock the door of the inner chambers opened, the band began to play, and the polonaise began to drift through the room with the emperor leading the empress, members of the royal family and various ladies and their partners. Then, everyone began to mingle and wander off to various rooms. They say that some 2,200 guests were present, but only the dance floor was crowded. In one room, cards were being played, and there too, many ladies, newly appointed gentlemen-of-the-bed chamber, and chamberlains, were presented to the empress. She exchanged a few words with each of them. The emperor strolled about all the rooms, stopping now and then to chat. Decorum prevailed until supper was announced. At the entrance to the hall where tables had been set, a terrific commotion arose, complete with pushing and crowding. The way they rushed in with such unrestrained greed, pushing each other for seats at the elaborately set tables, one would have thought that all these bemedalled and beribboned people had just come through a strict fast . . . The emperor walked around the tables asking people to remain seated in his presence; and when they did not heed him, he would raise his voice and, annoyed, almost shouting, would say: "Now, stay seated!" I arrived home around 2 A.M.

15 January. A telegram was received on Sunday about an insurrection in Poland.[1] What treachery! Killing soldiers, at night, who are unarmed and asleep!

22 January. It is evident from the telegrams coming in that Polish priests are among the most active forces behind the Polish insurrection. I feel that we are behaving very stupidly in this situation. We have spread our troops too thin over an enormous area and settled down with small units, forgetting that we are in greater danger on the soil of domestic foes than of foreign ones. That is why our soldiers were slaughtered like sheep, even as they slept.

23 January. Dinner at Dusseau's, given by Klevanov for some of his friends and the staff of the *Northern Post.* The paper's entire staff complains that it has become a police sheet and censures Valuev for bringing it down to such a low level after he had originally planned to make it a government organ which would influence public opinion.

25 January. Of what use is the *Northern Post* in its present form? None! None, whatsoever,—either to the government or society. Does it serve as a government organ? Definitely not! It contains neither explanations of government's plans nor simple facts—although that was part of the original plan.

A decree was published yesterday transferring censorship to the ministry of internal affairs (decree issued January 14th, No. 20, the *Northern Post*).

26 January. Visited Chivilev this evening. He told me some details about the emperor's family life. It seems that this entire family is very kind and wonderful. But they all lack one quality—firmness. This same weakness is noticeable in the heir. He is intelligent, able to think and shows an interest in higher intellectual matters, but is too softhearted. Perhaps he'll grow a little firmer with time and experience. He must, for a stormy future lies ahead of him.

28 January. The censorship administration's main problem will be how to define those deviations of the press which would be subject to review by the courts. These deviations are frequently very difficult to pin down.

Saw Valuev. New tasks await me on the Censorship Commission, and also some kind of work which he'll tell me about later. I found him in his study, amidst a pile of papers, unshaven, tired, but, as usual, genial and engaging.

29 January. I was notified by the minister of internal affairs of my appointment to the commission created by imperial order for the review of press laws, under the chairmanship of Prince Obolensky.

30 January. There is something very adolescent about our literature: extreme arrogance, a know-it-all attitude and a spirit of intolerance.

Saw Prince Obolensky. Preliminary talks on press laws. His views seem to give promise of being sound and fair. In any case, it's evident that he has thoroughly investigated this subject in its theoretical as well as its practical, legislative aspects. He showed me a pile of books, kept for reference, which he had read in part while presiding over the earlier commission. Here was almost everything that had been written on the subject of censorship in Germany, France, England, and Belgium, as well as legislation pertaining to censorship. He also has a lot of documents on censorship affairs issued by the ministry of education. It included much of my previous work, too.

I feel we shall get on very well with Prince Obolensky. He is evidently a sober, intelligent, educated man, and free of extreme prejudices. Rzhevsky and Tyutchev were appointed together with me from the ministry of internal affairs.

10 February. The current state of public opinion is extremely unsatisfactory. The government is losing its prestige with each passing day. Of course our head of state is liked and in favor with the masses. But some among the thinking public, because of their ultraliberal principles, hate him; others, anxious to go along with him, are irritated by many measures which expose either governmental ineptness or weakness; and the cream of this thinking sector of society is deeply distressed.

Almost everyone ascribes the Polish uprising to the Warsaw governor's ineptness. Nothing was done even when many ominous signs pointed unquestionably to an uprising. Not a single precaution was taken, and the butchering of our soldiers as they slept should be blamed not only on the cruelty of the rebels, but also on the incredible negligence of our administrators.

11 February. Saw Prince Obolensky. He described in detail what was involved in censorship legislation and how it had been handled under Golovnin. He showed me his entire correspondence with him. It appears that the unprecedented ineptness and unscrupulousness of this gentleman was far greater than the public had imagined. It would be hard to believe this without the evidence of his very own letters. My God! how the ruler of our country is being deceived!

14 February. They say Victor Hugo has composed a leaflet for the Poles.[v] What else can this bombastic chatterbox do but stir up the public, this chatterbox who, while preaching equality, knows very well how to manage his own affairs. For example, he has just presented Europe with a brilliant new product of his monstrous imagination for the sum of 400,000 francs.[w]

The hostility of the European press toward Russia and the delight it takes at the sight of confusion in our affairs is, on the whole, strange. Does it really fear the ghost of Nicholas I? Is it fair or rational to link Nicholas's regime to the present one and to take vengeance on an entire people for the mistakes or guilt of one man? This is Europe's celebrated humanity; this is what our ultraliberals are learning there!

15 February. The superintendent called a meeting of the history and philology department for discussion of appointments to the university. It is scheduled to open next August, as the charter has already been reviewed and revised by the Stroganov Commission. My status was also discussed. I stated that my five years had already come to an end, and asked to be released. The department (and I don't know if it was sincere or not) asked me to remain. They asked me to stay on for a while, at least until the university had begun to

[v] The leaflet was, in fact, an appeal to the Russian troops to stop their fratricidal slaughter.

[w] Nikitenko is referring to Victor Hugo's novel *Les Misérables*.

function again, and not to abandon it so suddenly. I agreed rather halfheart-
edly, not certain even in my own mind of my decision.

I want to talk to Delyanov and get his opinion, but in the end I suppose I'll
ask to retire anyway.

We have a wealth of great publicists and great thinkers writing for our newspapers and feuilletons; but when it came to finding professors, we had to
wrack our brains over almost every chair.

16 February. I had a talk with Delyanov about yesterday's meeting and the
appointment of professors to the university. The faculty asked me to remain.
I consented, but only for a short time, until the university manages to get on
its feet again, and only because everyone agreed to our need to retain reliable
people during that interim period, that is, people known for their long and
dedicated service to the university. However, Golovnin may have other ideas
on the subject.

19 February. Gilyarov-Platonov, who was called here to sit on the Censorship
Commission, came to see me. You hear the very same remarks from any intelligent and honest person you chance to talk to: Russia, they say, is going
through a terrible period. Europe threatens to intervene in our Polish affairs,
and, hating us with a terrible intensity, appears ready to tear Russia to pieces.
.What has Russia done to them? They have forgotten 1812. Evidently, man
is more ready to do evil than good. What kind of civilization is this that fails
to make people more generous or more just? Worst of all are our domestic
enemies. Those petty journal liberals who don't give a damn about their country and who, for the sake of gaining twenty-five or fifty subscribers, are ready
to preach any villainy or do anything to increase our confusion and grief. Oh,
what deep, loathsome depravity in this generation, led by sages like Herzen,
Bakunin and others.

The Polish rebellion is undoubtedly nothing more than a symptom of the
general revolutionary socialist movement. According to the leaders of this
movement, Europe must be rebuilt and revived; but storm and general destruction must precede this revival. A new world, a golden age will rise from the
dust and ruins. What is the meaning of all this? Are these people madmen or
are they apostles of a new religion without faith, of a new revelation without
miracles, a new morality without virtue, a society without laws and authority,
a complete dominion of reason without passions, without science, art and
poetry, a new Christianity without God, Christ and the Church; and, finally,
a life without suffering and death?

Let us assume that there is a grain of truth in these doctrines; but how many
lies and how much madness they contain!

28 February. The socialists want people to live without government. Perhaps humanity will put it to the test some day. But what does it imply?
One must lack an understanding of people or have blind faith in the most
fantastic utopia to believe that man is capable of managing without an external
force to curb and control him. If such a force, which would by cunning or

coercion take him in hand, fails to appear, he must create it himself. If it abuses its power, it will either fall or he will overthrow it, but it will be created anew. This force can assume various forms, but it cannot be eliminated as long as passions and unequal abilities exist on this earth, as long as one man is capable of ruling and it is more to another's benefit to obey and relax than to maintain eternal vigilance.

18 March. Derzhavin used three kinds of tools in his work: a golden pen, a goose quill with a dull point, and something resembling a hearth broom.

I sleep badly: I am besiged by disturbing and alarming thoughts about Russia. These are truly grave times—almost a question of "to be or not to be"— and more critical than 1812.

1 April. I read the manifesto about amnesty for the Poles. It could have been worded better.

Rumor has it that Europe is assuming an increasingly threatening attitude toward us. Power in world affairs belongs to the most crafty and most shameless. Now, Louis Napoleon has that power. It seems he intends to use it, having assured everyone that Russia must be destroyed for the safety of Europe, which is, in fact, being threatened by him.

The kind of policy we are pursuing is shrouded in mystery. It seems we have almost deliberately chosen this wretched system of concessions and peace *at any price*. Nothing can be more deplorable. Not only will it fail to avert war, but it will lead directly to it. The only way of avoiding war is to *show* Europe that we don't fear it. But we must *show* this without fail and impress this upon them.

7 April. They say that Russia has received notes from the three powers. Will our government make a decisive move? Woe to us, if it displays weakness. This would be the first step toward Russia's political degradation. The government would lose its last shred of prestige, and it would be hard to imagine the kind of internal chaos it would lead to. Of course, this is exactly what our enemies want.[2]

8 April. God save the government from granting concessions inimical to Russia's honor and safety. Patriotism is beginning to stir vigorously everywhere, both here and in the provinces. Should Napoleon declare that public opinion might force him to break his friendship treaty with Russia, Alexander could tell him that he could not predict what his people, seething with anger and hostility toward foreign meddling, might do. Europe cannot want the kind of war which Napoleon's meddling threatens to trigger, and, therefore, it is highly possible that the public opinion on which Napoleon is relying, will not support him.

9 April. A huge demonstration took place on Sunday on the square outside the Winter Palace. A tremendous crowd assembled beneath the balcony facing the Admiralty, and it thundered a "hurrah" that finally brought the emperor to the balcony. The crowd greeted him with indescribable enthusiasm. The people asked for the tsarina, too. She appeared on the balcony to the same enthusiastic shouting and rejoicing.

The emperor received the same unusually warm welcome at the benefit concert for veterans. The musicians, incidentally, had to repeat the hymn, "God Save the Tsar," four times.

The liberal St. Petersburg press has maintained complete silence.

10 April. If a choice must be made, Russia is more necessary to humanity than Poland.

Only a nation that has not exhausted its moral reserves can serve humanity, and Poland, it seems, has already exhausted hers. Russia, however, has a future.

12 April. The intemperate reading of shallow books, such as novels, has a debilitating effect on the mind like drinking, lying about lazily on the sofa, or wandering aimlessly about the streets.

13 April. Threatening and ominous signs are growing stronger and stronger. Everyone is almost certain that war is inevitable. Meanwhile, calm apparently prevails in government circles where there is no sign of movement. What the devil is this—inertia or confidence in their strength? The latter would hardly be fitting. We are unquestionably in great danger. We are insufficiently armed. We have neither able generals nor able government officials.

14 April. Things look gloomier and gloomier. Many people feel we are in a very dangerous position. Although strong patriotic sentiment is stirring among the people, we are poorly armed in comparison with our enemies. Our troops are brave, but are they as well armed and trained as, say, the French? Kronstadt is inadequately fortified. We don't have armored vessels. Naval authorities have given little attention to the fleet since the Crimean war. Our finances are in dreadful shape.

17 April. 8 P.M. Just received the decree on the abolition of corporal punishment. This will be a landmark in the history of the Russian people.

The festive lights[x] were on this evening and Nevsky Prospekt was literally overflowing with people and carriages. Somehow, I reached or, rather, was carried along by the crowd to the Duma. It was impossible to go further: a solid wall of people, scarcely moving, and the awful crush, finally forced me to retreat. I kept wondering if the emperor would come—I wanted to wait for him. But by 10 o'clock he still hadn't appeared.

The festive lights were dazzling. The Benardak and Kokorev houses, Gostiny Dvor, and the Duma were particularly beautifully illuminated. Bands played in three places. The people were surprisingly orderly and conducted themselves with decorum. There wasn't the slightest interference from the police. I didn't see a single drunkard.

[x] April 17 was Alexander II's birthday.

19 April. There was an overwhelming demonstration of popular support for the emperor in Moscow on the 17th. The people demanded a service on the square opposite the palace windows of the room where the emperor was born. They fell to their knees and prayed for Russia and the emperor with deep emotion. Witnesses say it was a wonderful and touching sight. Another demonstration of popular support occurred at the theatre on the same evening. "One's Life for the Tsar" was being performed. There was no end to the ecstatic cries and applause.

23 April. Hope for peace is reviving. Today's telegram, informing us that the Swedish Parliament has firmly rejected any idea of aiding Poland, is splendid news.

25 April. General indignation over the weakness of our administration in Warsaw. The city is, in fact, under martial law, and there, as in all of Poland, administrative power is in the hands of a revolutionary committee. How absurd! The police force is made up of Poles. The Russian element is completely suppressed. Russians are suffering unheard of insults under the very nose of [Grand Duke Konstantin Nikolaevich]. But the main problem is that the rebellion, owing to the administration's utter impotency, is dragging on and on, thus giving Europe a pretext for intervention.

The peasants in the Dinaburg district decided to deal with rebellious landowners themselves. They stirred up countless disorders on the Plater estate. The same thing is happening in the western provinces, too. What else can one expect the peasants to do? The revolutionary committee is stifling them, and the government isn't coming to their defense.

The Samara nobility passed this decree: "Call home from abroad, especially from Paris, our traveling countrymen, who, as Russians, are the target of all kinds of insults and continue to reside there."

28 April. It was an enormous mistake on Konstantin Nikolaevich's part to let the Poles go unpunished for their insulting treatment of the Russians—for slinging mud at them and even spitting at soldiers and officers. This, of course, has forced public opinion in Europe to have strong doubts about our right to Poland. . . .

3 May. Meeting at the Academy of Sciences. Session of the Commission for the award of the Uvarov drama prize. I read my report on two comedies and nominated Ostrovsky's *Sin and Sorrow Are the Common Lot* for the prize. The rest of the Commission—I don't know why—didn't seem interested in awarding it to him.[y]

This evening Maikov read his play, *Lucius's Death,* at my home.[z] A truly fine work.

[y] Ostrovsky eventually received the prize.
[z] *Lucius's Death* is the second part of Maikov's lyrical drama *Three Deaths.*

10 May. Nikolai Nikolaevich Kologrivov arrived from Paris unexpectedly. He said that Russians living there were not being insulted at all; the journals were cursing us, but Russians living in Paris were not experiencing anything like the insults ascribed to the French. The French sympathized with the Poles, whom they understood about as poorly as they did Russia.

13 May. I went to look at a dacha. The house isn't bad, and the area is clean and green, although deserted. I wouldn't care about that, except that it is expensive—300 rubles. Somehow, the whole area has lost its appeal for me but my family shouldn't be deprived of some comfort and pleasure while I have the strength to give it to them.

14 May. Disorder, confusion and tension are increasing from day to day. Moscow, we hear, is very agitated over public demonstrations led by the Warsaw Revolutionary Committee. Outrageous leaflets are flying all over Russia and, sometimes, they produce the desired effect, as in Penzen Province, for example. Prince Obolensky received a letter from there several days ago which said that the peasants, after reading a leaflet promising them some sort of new, unheard of, freedom, and all their land, etc., had refused to pay the *obrok*, to work for their master or even for themselves. In Kazan, some student who had deserted his studies stirred up a real rebellion among students and other foolhardy liberals, and so on and so forth. No one can count on being safe during the summer in St. Petersburg, either. What is the government doing? Not a thing. No energy, no foresight, no measures beyond normal police routine to cope with this urgent situation. Everyone sees this and is indignant.

17 May. Everything that exists is in danger of being destroyed. But no living being should surrender his rights without a struggle. His rights consist in the very fact that he exists. This was the point I wanted to make in my article, "The Younger Generation."

21 May. Ran into Tyutchev.
  "Will it be war or peace?"
  "War, no question about it," he replied.

22 May. We have a very important advantage over those who attack us. The advantage of defense. We don't have to win a victory; we must merely put up a stubborn and successful defense. Repulsing the enemy, pushing him back, and maintaining our own position—that alone would be a great victory for us.

26 May. The Poles are treating their Russian captives with unheard of barbarism. A soldier, who had been captured by them and then managed to escape, was brought here several days ago. His nose, ears, tongue and lips had been cut off. What the devil is this? Can you call them people? What can one say for people? What animal can compare to man in his invention of evil and villainy? The case I just described is not an isolated one; there are hundreds like it. Some have had their skin torn and turned out on their chests like facings on a uniform; others have been buried alive, and so on. They also torture and hang their own if they hesitate to join the rebellion. What's more—in Europe everyone ascribes atrocities to the Russians, while the Poles are called heroes and saints.

28 May. An article of most illicit content, "Fateful Question," and signed, "A Russian," appeared in the April issue of the journal *Time.* It lauded the Poles, called them a civilized people, while it attacked the Russians and called them barbarians. This article was not only repugnant to our national feeling, but consisted of lies. The public was amazed by its appearance in the press. Tsee[a] was dismissed from his post.

29 May. The journal *Time* has been banned. The government, that is, the ministry of internal affairs, has made a big mistake. This ban will give our enemies a plausible excuse to say that the government is using coercive methods to suppress the truth.

Here's another, even more absurd, order issued by Valuev. To replace Tsee as chairman of the Censorship Committee, one Turunov has been appointed, a ministry official without any reputation, without any contact with literature, who doesn't have the slightest understanding of such a ticklish business as censorship.

Both the ban on *Time* and this appointment have made a very negative impression on the public.

6 June. Visited Goncharov this evening. He is resigning as editor of the *Northern Post* and joining the Council on Press Affairs.

7 June. Had a long talk with Pogodin when I saw him this morning. He wrote an article, at the emperor's request, in reply to the brazen and coarse slander of Russia which had appeared in a French journal. He will show it to Prince Gorchakov tomorrow. He also wrote a letter to Garibaldi which he read to me. It is an intelligent and noble letter. He exhorts Garibaldi not to allow his pure and splendid name to get mixed up in such a dirty business as the Polish rebellion, and he explains to him briefly the utter falsity of rumors about himself and Russia which the Poles have circulated in Europe.

A real gang of the most villainous revolutionaries has been discovered in Kazan University. They say that all the leaflets, etc., were composed there. Timashev and Zhdanov were sent to investigate.

8 June. I sent a letter to Katkov. It's incredible! He still hasn't printed my article, and it must be published at the right time to have any meaning. I wrote him a polite, though far from friendly, letter, asking him to return my article. Pogodin, to whom I expressed my dissatisfaction with Katkov on this matter, says that Katkov's editorial office is a madhouse and responsible for all sorts of delays.

[a] Chairman of the St. Petersburg Censorship Committee.

9 June. The minister evidently realizes that he erred in banning *Time*. Someone, probably one of his officials, had told him that *Time* had evil tendencies.
Yet it was a thousand times less evil than the *Contemporary* and *Russian
Word*, which had been suspended for eight months. The minister didn't bother
asking for the opinion of people whose official job it is to keep a watchful eye
on periodical literature.

10 June. Strakhov, author of the ill-starred article, "Fateful Question," which
appeared in *Time,* came to see me yesterday. He was terribly upset. He asked
for my advice and for me to use my influence as far as possible. I told him
that I was sorry that he had written the article, that I could not defend it and
that it was in very bad taste. He didn't defend himself or reject my criticism.
He merely claimed that he, who considered himself a son of Russia, had no
desire to insult it. Further, he claimed that what he had hoped to do in his
article was to convince the Poles to stop gloating about "their assets and their
superior civilization," etc., but that he had failed to develop this idea fully. I
replied that all this might very well have been true, but that it was wrong to
publish such an undeveloped idea; that the impression it made was the only
one possible; that such things could not be tolerated in times like these when
our thinking people were upset, the common people extremely irritated, and
the administration troubled and confused. How could one be so careless at a
time like this? Poor Strakhov would tow the line *now*. What upset him most
of all, he said, was that people considered him a non-Russian. "True," I replied. "Do you know from whom I first learned about your article? From a
Pole, who told me about it with such relish." Then Strakhov asked me what
he should do. I said that since the authorities were not bothering him, it was
better to let this impression fade with time and later on he could find the
proper moment to explain to others and to himself that he had made a big
mistake, etc.

I saw M.M. Dostoevsky,[b] editor of *Time.* Here, indeed, is an unfortunate
man—almost completely ruined. He realizes that he is guilty, but he feels that
he was treated too harshly, which is not without foundation when you recall
that the *Contemporary* and *Russian Word* were merely *suspended* and not completely banned, and these journals constantly expressed—and frequently without beating about the bush—the most hostile ideas, not only toward the government, but toward any kind of social and moral order. *Time* never permitted itself such outrages, and its tone was more liberal-conservative. I tried to
console Dostoevsky with the thought that there was reason to believe that the
ban on his journal was only temporary.

16 June. On my way home I ran into Troinitsky who was on his way to see
me. We went to my place and talked for a rather long time. He told me that
the Council on Press Affairs would convene this week. Its members are: myself, Goncharov, Varadinov, Przhetslavsky and Turunov. Troinitsky is the

---

[b] Brother of the novelist and co-editor with Strakhov of *Time.*

chairman. Goncharov was promoted to the rank of Actual State Councillor. Well, I suppose he must be very pleased. He has wanted to be *His Excellency* for a long time.

19 June. Redkin visited this evening and stayed a rather long time. Later, Vessel, editor of the *Teacher*, came. He had arrived here about three days ago from Astrakhan by Volga steamer and had stopped at several cities on the way. He told us that the people in the villages were giving rough treatment to anyone suspected of polonism. Recently, near Simbersk, peasants beat up and disfigured five officials who, for some reason, had been sent from St. Petersburg. They had been taken for Poles.

21 June. Goncharov had tea with me. The order about his promotion in rank and his appointment to the Council on Press Affairs has already been received.

22 June. Not a peep out of Katkov. I want to write Gilyarov to see what he can do to get my manuscript back. Rumors have circulated for a long time about Katkov's insufferable egotism, his arrogance and unspeakable haughtiness. I must admit that, based on my earlier relations with him, I would never have expected such rudeness and discourtesy from him—and this is a lesson to me for being so gullible and trusting. It is clear that Katkov, like all our great people, has collapsed beneath the burden of fame. I was stupid enough to get upset about his behavior—too upset, so that I dwelt on it for several days. His behavior has done me irreparable damage. My article must remain unpublished because it would be untimely to release it now. How kindly Katkov was, how friendly and attentive, when he needed me! Of course, it's my fault for believing in his nobility.

First meeting of the Council on Press Affairs. Present were Chairman Troinitsky, Przhetslavsky, Goncharov, Vardinov, Tikhomandritsky, myself, Police Director Pokhvisnev, and Turunov. Newspapers and journals were distributed for surveillance purposes. I received *Notes of the Fatherland* and *Russian Messenger,* and several newspapers, but I haven't decided yet which ones to take on. Probably the *St. Petersburg Bulletin*, the *Voice* and the *Moscow Bulletin.*

Some observations about my Council colleagues: *Prezhetslavsky*—an old swindler, a Pole and Catholic at heart, but he very skillfully conceals his Polish and Catholic sentiments. It's difficult to tell at this point what line he'll follow on censorship. He has always adapted himself to circumstances and gone along with the strongest faction.

Varadinov scarcely believes in anything at all, except in the notion that one should obey the will of the authorities. There is much of the civil servant in him; he is most accommodating to his superiors, but stubborn with everyone else. On censorship matters he won't dare to oppose the majority and, especially, the actual or presumed desires of those above him.

My friend, *Goncharov*, makes a special effort to collect his salary of 4,000 rubles punctually and to tread cautiously so that he will please both the authorities and litterateurs.

Tikhomandritsky—nothing much to say about him.

Turunov. I think he's a bit on the stupid side, exactly as a blind tool of the ministers ought to be. However, we'll have to take a closer look at him.

Pokhvisnev—having seen him only once, it's too early to draw any conclusions.

8 July. Strakhov came to see me with an article which he wants to publish in the *Day*. It contains a defense of his "Russian Question" which had caused such an uproar and served as a pretext for banning *Time*. Moscow censorship did not pass the article and submitted it to the minister. I must say his defense is a very poor one: it consists of the kind of abstract phrases which could never change the public's mind. I expressed my opinion openly and advised the author to admit his mistake frankly. The editor of the *Day* said that he was satisfied with Strakhov's defense. Good luck! These Muscovites are strange and ridiculous in their boundless arrogance and haughtiness. They think that the public should take their every word as Holy Gospel, and woe to those impious wretches who would question their claim to intellectual dictatorship!

11 July. I witnessed a spectacle today that thrilled me. As I set out for a Council meeting, I noticed a large crowd of people on Tsaritsyn Meadow, tables loaded with bread and vodka, and regimental carts and caissons standing directly opposite the Pavlovsk barracks. "What's going on here?" I asked a cabbie. "We're welcoming the Pavlovsk soldiers returning from a campaign." I wanted very much to stay and look at our brave soldiers who had been fighting the Poles. But, I had a meeting and I wanted to take care of some of my own business before that. As I approached Bolshaya Morskaya I came upon battalions from the Pavlovsk regiment. A band played and you could hear stirring songs coming from the front of the second battalion where a little soldier was dancing with gusto. I was particularly taken by the soldiers' appearance; by their simple, generous, modest, tanned and healthy faces. "Well, boys, coming back from a campaign?" I asked one fellow with a bushy mustache and kindly face. "Yes, Your Excellency, from a campaign."

The music, songs, fluttering banners, the faces of our brave soldiers, tanned and stained by gunpowder—all made a deep impression on me. I decided to forget about the business I had planned to take care of before the meeting and to stay on the square as long as time would permit. I took the first cab I saw and asked to be taken to Tsaritsyn Meadow. I arrived just as the battalions entered the square. An altar was erected. The troops arranged themselves in a semi-square. The banners cast shadows over the lectern holding the gospel; and the recently decorated recipients of the order of Saint George stood in a semicircle, forming a wall of bayonets. The priest, a gray-haired old man, arrived and began the public service under the open sky before a vast assemblage. It was a gray day, but warm and still. I stayed until the end of the service. I wanted so much to stay while the soldiers partook of refreshments so I could listen to their talk and chat with them, too, but duty called. Less than half an hour remained until my meeting. I had no choice but to leave and left deeply moved.

12 July. Our replies to the notes sent by England, France and Austria were published yesterday. They made an extremely favorable impression on the public. Indeed they were restrained, truthful and firm. Now, the only alternative is war. Everyone is sure of it and awaits it calmly, although we know it will be difficult for us.

At a meeting, yesterday, I read my opinions on two articles scheduled for publication in *Notes of the Fatherland.* The censor wanted to pass half of one and completely reject the other. I suggested that the first one be rejected outright because it contained an idea about changing the form of government in Russia, but that the second be passed, although it did contain criticism of our administration. The Council gave its unconditional approval to both my opinions.

16 July. Pisemsky's new novel, *The Troubled Sea* (two parts have already appeared in the *Russian Messenger*), consists of pieces of rags in which Russian *narodnost* is clothed, rags which have already been used to sew a lot of goods on our literary market.

17 July. Europe is cursing us again with reckless abandon. It was very displeased with our notes. There are fewer intelligent people in Europe than one would think. It apparently thought, in all seriousness, that Russia would agree to the six points, and that it was worth while threatening us.[3] Could such hopes be born only of deep ignorance and extreme stupidity? Europe wants to deprive Russia of its right to develop, of its right to civilization, of rights a great power has acquired through enormous sacrifices and blood—and Russia is supposed to yield and submit to the abuse of the whole world and of history. This proves but one thing, that Europe is accustomed to yield only when threatened by the crudest and most brazen force. But we aren't . . .

25 July. Meeting of the Council on Press Affairs. I read my opinion on Lebedev's report. He didn't want to pass the story, "The Spanish Card-Sharper," for *Notes of the Fatherland.* I suggested that it could be passed by merely toning down a very few passages. It's not a bad piece, and I'm glad we managed to save it.

Generally speaking, the Council has been operating in a liberal spirit so far, which is considerably encouraged by Chairman Troinitsky's attitude. Of course, the literary world won't give us credit for it, and will continue to rail at us no matter what. But in doing our job it would be foolish and base to be guided by what others may think or say about us. I, for one, would not seek popularity by trying to please some clique or by satisfying some irrelevant demands, no matter what the source.

Kraevsky was reprimanded for his article against Katkov, published in the *Voice*. The minister called him in. So, Katkov is chief Court journalist after all, and there is something to the rumor that he receives a subsidy. If this is true, why does he try to give the impression of being an *independent* organ of public opinion?

1 August. Meeting of the Council on Press Affairs. Sometimes, the *Moscow Bulletin*, with its advice to the public and the administration, goes too far, and since its editors are in the habit of discussing everything in a dictatorial tone, this situation becomes intolerable, despite the fact that the government, for certain reasons, gives it more freedom than other papers. We decided to contact the Moscow Censorship Committee to ask them to try to curb the violent and unpardonable outbursts of the *Moscow Bulletin*.

Meeting of the Commission for the award of the Uvarov drama prizes. I had an altercation with Sreznevsky. I had nominated Ostrovsky to receive the award for his drama, *Sin and Sorrow Are the Common Lot*. Sreznevsky vehemently opposed this. He didn't like the play and didn't feel it deserved an award. I certainly wouldn't call it a first-class work; but, if we are going to wait for a Shakespeare or Molière, our awards can rest easy. Besides, such plays wouldn't need prizes anyway. Ostrovsky, alone, is keeping Russian drama alive, and although his *Sin and Sorrow* doesn't shine as a first-class beauty, it is not only the best we have now, but it does have some remarkable dramatic qualities. Grot supported me strongly. There were six votes in favor of my recommendation and two against, including Sreznevsky's.

14 August. We shouldn't impose masculine qualities on women. A woman is so lovely only because she doesn't possess many of the qualities that a man does, but has her own feminine traits instead. By emancipating them, you run the risk of giving them many of the defects that men possess. I'd rather her weaknesses and shortcomings remained strictly feminine.

22 August. University Council meeting—the first since the university reopened. However, the actual reopening has not yet been fully implemented. We had preliminary discussions on the reorganization of the university and the introduction of its new rules. Elections of a rector, inspector, and others are scheduled for September 2. Also, an announcement was made about a vote to be taken on the retention of those professors who had served twenty-five years or five years in addition to the twenty-five-year period. I fall in the latter category.

Since I was sure that I would receive more negative than positive votes, I announced that I did not wish to have a vote taken and would submit my statement in writing. There is a strong bloc against me which would be delighted to subject me to the unpleasantness of a negative vote. What sort of people are they? Ultraliberals, of course, the remnants of the Spasoviches, Kavelins, Kostomarovs, and others. But there are so many of them that the majority of votes would be on their side.

I regret having to leave the university.

5 September. What a rotten, wasted day—spent in very demanding, but stupid and fruitless, activity. At 10 A.M. I went to a meeting of the Academy—a total waste, then to the university for a most unfruitful examination of some blockheads who are seeking degrees and will undoubtedly get them. This went on until 1:30, and I scarcely made it to the Council of the Ministry of Internal Affairs. A meeting convened a few minutes later which didn't last long this time—until 4 P.M. Then I stopped in at Dominico's, which I left half-starved after putting out a ruble and a half. What miserable dinners are served in our hotels! They usually serve five courses, vilely prepared, and only God and the cook know what goes into them. Why not serve only three courses, but decent ones?

When I finished my cigar I went to the University Council meeting, and there I literally sat from about 6 until 10 P.M., discussing a lot of nonsense. A rotten day, wasn't it?

17 September. I was appointed to the Superintendent's Council yesterday.

25 September. I would like to abandon reason with its unmerciful logic, with its harsh Spinoza-like truths, and think with my feelings, so that life would not seem so mechanical with its terrible fulfilment of the laws of necessity. But feelings, which promise so much, vacillate and seek refuge in that same mode of thought which doesn't want to hear about anybody's rights, except one's very own. I resort to fantasy, but fantasy, after tempting me for a moment with its brilliant mirages, itself bows down before all-powerful reality, which either insists on going with its fantastic daydreams to the madhouse or resigns itself to the vicissitudes of life. How can one reconcile reason, feelings and fantasy?

6 October. Services at the university to mark the beginning of classes.

My poor Katya is sick again. This poor creature's whole life has been nothing but a series of illnesses and convalescenses.

9 October. My first lecture at the university. The large auditorium was literally jammed. The audience was very attentive.

24 October. Meeting of the Council on Press Affairs. I had been assigned to review Pavlov's petition for permission to publish his three stories banned in 1835. I proposed that two of them, *Auction* and *Nameday,* could be passed without any difficulty, but that I couldn't see passing *The Dagger.*

Then I read a note about the rapidly growing literature on the *Schism,* especially about its current movement. I advanced the argument that the administration should give more attention to the *raskolniks,* who, after the patriotic appeals made by *raskolnik* communes, have been operating openly and trying to establish their own church hierarchy. I suggested a solution: if the church can't recognize this hierarchy, then both the government and the church should show it the same *tolerance* it shows to other religious beliefs.

Moreover, I suggested a ban on articles about the *raskolniks'* current activities. The Council endorsed all my suggestions. What will the minister have to say? Troinitsky thinks the minister intends to take a liberal position on the *raskolniks,* too.

We then discussed the incredible impudence of the articles in the *Moscow Bulletin* and the *Contemporary Annals,* in which Katkov flew into a fury in his attack, for example, on the ministry of education. He throws curses around like a drunken *muzhik.* The chairman felt he would have to call upon me to compose a memorandum about this problem.

7 November. At the Superintendent's Council the question was raised whether the *raskolniks* should be granted permission to open their own schools. It was decided to grant it, allowing them at the same time to enroll their children in regular schools without compelling them to take religious instruction from Orthodox clergymen. They can get it from their own priests or teachers in their own schools.

14 November. So far it's quiet at the university; evidently our young people want to study. At least they are attending lectures conscientiously and are not starting any trouble. They merely grumbled at the ban on smoking and, since they know very well that none of our laws are rigidly enforced, they began to smoke, without raising a fuss. Of course the authorities are looking the other way. In that case, why did they bother banning it? However, the Council did want to allow it, but the minister wouldn't agree, so we ended up with the law being broken, anyway.

The new rules were generally criticized in many newspapers, but it seems that it was done simply to show opposition to anything undertaken by the government. Meanwhile, this apparently has made no impression on our youth.

24 November. Went to see Delyanov and Tyutchev this morning. At Tyutchev's I met Gendre, who had come from Kiev several days ago. He said that Annenkov, at first, also wanted to take a merciful and conciliatory approach (like Nazimov, no doubt?), but was finally convinced of the utter impossibility of dealing gently with the Poles. Gendre, who knows the region well, having served there for many years, felt that the only way to appease the country was to wipe out the Polish element completely. Their hostility toward us is irreconcilable and they are unwavering in their belief that the Polish kingdom can and must exist as it did before partition. They regard most of the Russians and Little Russians in these provinces as trash, and Poles as the nobility. Meanwhile, the Russian people hate them intensely, and, if not for the government, it would tear every Pole to pieces at the first sign of rebellion. It follows, therefore, that the only possible relationship between the nationalities is one in which both groups completely exterminate each other. Naturally, Russia cannot agree to its own extinction, and since it is stronger, the whole thing must end with the extermination of Poland as a nation. It seems that the government, too, is finally aware of this sad necessity and is beginning to initiate appropriate measures. It plans to resettle the petty landless or petty landed Polish nobility in Orenburg, Samara and other provinces, while the wealthy landowners will be forced to sell their estates to the Russians.

28 November. At a meeting of the Council on Press Affairs, Przhetslavsky called for a ban on such popular works as dream books[c] and fortunetelling books. "Why?" I asked. "So we don't reinforce popular superstitions," he replied. "These superstitions will exist regardless of books, as long as the people remain steeped in ignorance. You won't accomplish anything by banning them, but will only irritate people," I said. The Council rejected Przhetslavsky's proposal.

30 November. My poor Katya has been suffering since the day we returned from the country. It is one of those cruel misfortunes of life against which we are defenseless. Her whole life has been one of endless suffering.

2 December. Soirée at Akhmatova's, publisher of the journal of translated literature. Both Stasovs were there, V.V. with his enormous beard, and a smug and haughty expression on his face; D.V. rather more modest and with a smaller beard. Also there was Victor Gaevsky, who informed me that he was under senate investigation for his involvement with Herzen. Therefore, he wasn't working now, hoping to be cleared—which I strongly doubt, for he has, in fact, almost compromised himself by his relations with Herzen.[d] There was a time when our liberals considered it a privilege to have any kind of contact with that scoundrel, to correspond with him, to shake his hand. For this they made special trips to London, where they servilely tried to wheedle a smile or a few kind words from him.

6 December. If women want to acquire equal rights with men, they will be worse off; they will be deprived of the services and protection they receive from men in exchange for certain rights they lack. Thus, I feel that those who strive for women's so-called emancipation and for equal rights are doing them a real disservice.

Where there is inequality of strength, there is inequality of rights, too.

12 December. The president of the Academy of Sciences is pressuring us to elect Katkov and Aksakov corresponding members of our department. The department and the entire Academy are extremely annoyed by this. Moreover, Count Bludov wants us to elect Reitern and Butkov honorary academicians. All of this was discussed at today's meeting. Sreznevsky alone was not opposed to the president's solicitation. Veselovsky and Grot went to see Bludov to persuade him to change his mind about Katkov. The feeling against Aksakov isn't quite as strong. Of course, I cannot be in favor of Katkov. What a strange and ridiculous position for the Academy to be in, that it must

[c] Books of dream interpretations.
[d] Gaevsky was acquitted on 10 December 1864.

demean itself on orders from above. Is this sort of thing so unique in our country?

14 December. At Count Bludov's suggestion, Butkov and Reitern were elected honorary members at an Academy meeting yesterday, and Dal was elected a full academician. Shame on the president that he forced such a gentleman on us as Butkov. It's a disgrace for the entire Academy. How opportune it would have been to elect Prince Gorchakov.

Somehow we managed to bypass Katkov by claiming that the complement of corresponding members was already full and there were no vacancies, although, this wasn't the real reason. Ostrovsky, Tikhonravov, and Danichich in Belgrade, were elected.

19 December. Meeting of the Council on Press Affairs. I read my note on the articles appearing in various newspapers which attacked the new student rules. Golovnin's conduct doesn't make sense. The rules were composed almost literally in line with his circular. In the meantime he has been ordering written refutations of them, has been revising them himself and has sternly reprimanded the Kazan superintendent for complaining to him about the harmful effects which these critical articles have been having on the students. What the devil is this: stupidity, baseness, or something else? Meanwhile, he presents everything to the emperor in a favorable light. Is there another government in the world where such nonsense would be tolerated?

20 December. It seems that my lectures at the university are coming to an end. During the holidays I must submit a request for my release, since I do not plan to have a vote taken on my behalf. I don't feel generous enough to give my ill-wishers the pleasure of casting negative votes.

21 December. That damned Academy report that I must write!

Our academicians rummage in the very dung and bowels of science, and such probing is good for it. What is bad is that, they, in the first place, consider all the excrement discharged by the human mind to be of the greatest importance, and, in the second place, consider themselves to be such important instruments of science that, in comparison, everyone else is dwarfed to insignificance.

But there's nothing I can do about it! Here I am writing an Academy speech and, holding my nose, I must proclaim for all to hear: "Slavic garbage! You smell sweeter than honey!"

25 December. The pain in my chest grew worse this morning, but I coughed less. A slight cold. Sent for Dr. Waltz. Had to know if I could go out.

Waltz came; ordered me to stay at home and to take two drops of some bromide every two hours. I think it's a lot of nonsense. He also prescribed a diet.

26 December. This stupid bromide, like all homeopathic medicines, is a pure hoax. I'm no better today.

The hell with all these bromides! Give me something more substantial.

I gave up those stupid homeopathic drops this evening and ordered a compress for my chest of pork grease on blue sugar-paper, and also smeared my nose with it. I was also advised to drink a lot of tea made from apple and rose leaves.

27 December. Waltz, as usual, fooled me yesterday; didn't show up. The hell with him! He's probably spending more time now with his business deals than his patients. About three weeks ago he asked me to lend him some three thousand rubles. Where would I have gotten such a sum! My entire capital consists of two thousand rubles in the Commercial Bank. I'd be a fool to give it up recklessly. That's why he's probably angry with me. This is the second time he has tried to get money out of me. I pay him promptly for every visit, and more than he asks for. But man always makes a pig of himself.

1864

6 January. I don't think there have ever been as many vile things going on in St. Petersburg as there are today **under** that tenderhearted blockhead, Governor-General Suvorov. Thievery, day and night; countless instances of banditry and drunkenness every day and every night; and the drunkenness is unprecedented, even in Russia, so that drunken crowds roam the streets; they collapse and die like cattle wherever they happen to be. Among the drunks are boys of fifteen, and a cabbie told me today that he had seen a fourteen-year-old. Complete anarchy reigns in the streets: carriages racing along at headlong speed are constantly causing accidents; packs of stray dogs roam about as in Constantinople, and so on. The police are so undisciplined and powerless that everyone ignores them completely; and I have often seen a cabbie or *muzhik* struggle or fight with a policeman who wants to bring him to the stationhouse for some disorderly act. Thieves who have been imprisoned several times for stealing are released immediately on the governor-general's orders, although burglar's tools have been found on their persons. Domontovich himself was told recently by policemen and other police personnel that it wasn't worth apprehending arsonists and thieves because the authorities released them immediately. The very same people are caught several times committing criminal acts. Police Chief Banash, a friend of mine, said that he had given up trying to improve matters because the governor-general gives firm and open support to thieves and swindlers, naturally out of humane motives. Thus are lofty European ideas tailored to fit our ways in this semibarbaric land of ours.

7 January. I delivered my letter to Sreznevsky asking to be released from the university, since my five years will expire on the 17th.

9 January. I had a long talk with the deputy minister today, and he told me that the Milyutin camp was beginning to grow very rapidly. Well, that's a bad sign. Milyutin is a follower of the reds and an advocate of democratic principles. I thought that once he became minister he would abandon his red ideas, but it seems that he has strayed too far in his enthusiasm for democracy to turn back. Woe to us with our homebred doctrinaires. Russia could do very well without all these doctrines which were a natural historical development in the West. We don't need to be dominated by either aristocrats or democrats; we need but one thing—*we must broaden and strengthen our educated sector without regard to class principles.* But we stir up class antagonism by artificial and violent means, and when we pat the coarse, semibarbaric masses on the head and elevate them, we fail to see the kind of dangerous and barbarous power we are grooming them to wield. Shouldn't we concern ourselves first of all with the education of the masses? It would tame their savage instincts and equip them to cope with the power now being thrust upon them without safeguards against its abuse. Rule by the masses would be a great disaster for Russia.

10 January. Katkov returned my article completely unexpectedly.

12 January. A rumor circulated several days ago that Herzen had died, but now they say it's not true. It doesn't matter if he lives or dies: he is politically dead for Russia. He can do us neither good nor harm. Since the Polish uprising his reputation with the public has fallen so low that he has almost been forgotten.

16 January. Life is full of troubles; and mine is extra full. I am not complaining, but in talking to myself, am merely stating a fact. Meanwhile my domestic situation is as follows: both daughters are dear, good girls (and Sofia is terribly gifted), but have weak, sickly constitutions. Katya's life is an endless round of illness and convalescence. She has a disorder of the spine and there is no medicine that can help. Sasha is a good boy but without any talents. He can't concentrate, and, besides, our gymnasiums today do a poor job of teaching, which is typical of the way we do things. They are more interested in quantity than quality in instruction. In the lower grades, for example, they try to pump five subjects into the heads of ten- and twelve-year-old children, and since each teacher is more concerned with covering as much material as possible rather than treating it in depth, the children stagger about like drunkards, intoxicated by words and not ideas, and they are unable to understand anything properly. So, my poor girls are doomed to a life of poverty and work, and for work they lack what they need most—good health. The boy's future is also bleak. I worry about it day and night. But what can I do?

17 January. A few days ago I ran into Turgenev, who had recently returned from Paris. The government had called him here for a confrontation with certain prisoners in the fortress. Turgenev delayed his return for a long time, one time saying that he was ill, another that his daughter was ill (he has an illegitimate daughter in Paris). The real reason, however, was his fear that the authorities might link him with the rebels. Senator Pinsky wrote him, finally, that his presence was necessary here to settle the case and that he had absolutely nothing to fear: he would only have to give two or three depositions—and that would be the end of it. That's precisely how it worked out. Turgenev told me that, after reporting twice to the Senate, he was told he was free to go wherever he pleased.[1]

22 January. At the request of the department I am continuing my lectures at the university.

24 January. Kostomarov wrote an article defending himself against charges of separatism. It was given to me for examination. It is cleverly written, but, nevertheless, supports the favorite idea of Little Russian writers which calls for using their native tongue in Little Russian schools. For that reason I proposed banning the article. Goncharov objected weakly. It's obvious he has absolutely no understanding of the aims of these gentlemen. I insisted that we must oppose their schemes with all our strength because the idea of separation based on a ridiculous Slavic confederation is the real motive behind all of them.

My article "The Younger Generation" appeared in the *Northern Post*, No. 20.

30 January. Meeting of the council on Press Affairs. Przhetslavsky's call for a ban on the Russian edition of Mill's celebrated book, *On Liberty*, was defeated. Goncharov, the chairman, and I were the most outspoken against the ban. The rest quietly went along with us. There was also discussion of an article "On Food," scheduled for publication in the *Contemporary*. Goncharov's report on it was very vague, so it was decided that I should read the article and present my opinion.[e]

2 February. Annual meeting of the Society for Aid to Needy Writers. Turgenev's brief article in memory of Druzhinin was read. Baron Korf was elected president. I talked with Prince Shcherbatov, Turgenev and others. Nekrasov very humbly asked for my support of his petition in the Council on Press Affairs for an article which he wants to publish in the *Contemporary*. Goncharov, as usual, passed it off on me, although it's his affair since the *Contemporary* is under his jurisdiction. I am not used to dodging responsibility and told him, therefore, that I would do what I could and should do.

5 February. My great sorrow is my poor Katya. This winter she is suffering more than ever before. My heart bleeds to look at her! What can we do? Medicine can't perform miracles. She can scarcely do anything, and what little she can do, she does fumblingly.

6 February. Meeting of the Council on Press Affairs. Przhetslavsky read his report about the wide circulation of materialistic ideas and assumed that all we had to do to stem this pernicious tide was to choose good censors. I asked for the floor. First of all, I praised Gospodin Przhetslavsky's report, calling it a treatise, which apparently displeased its author, who preferred to regard it as an official document. Then I posed these questions: exactly what measures does the author of the report suggest we take to fight this evil? Could one seriously believe that the selection of a few good censors would have any effect? Moreover, finding good censors was not a simple task. Materialism is the spirit of the times. It not only is invading our reading matter, but is also occupying university chairs. Natural science has captured the spirit of the times and, together with a utilitarian trend, constitutes the character of our

[e] See Nikitenko's entry for 5 March 1864.

times. If this is evil, then we must be equally well armed against it. We must not only call upon the police, that is—censorship—for help, but upon the finest in human convictions, in reason, and in education. How can we do this? In conclusion, I pointed out that Gospodin Przhetslavsky's report was a very respectable treatise, but that it did not lead to anything workable in an administrative sense. The president, Goncharov, and Turunov, argued with Przhetslavsky in the same vein, but he defended himself with his usual ineptness. However, to assuage his feelings and not completely disregard such a serious issue as the spread of materialism, the president suggested sending the report to the St. Petersburg Censorship Committee *to be read there.* This ended a lengthy debate.

I was given the article, "On Food," to examine, which is scheduled for publication in the *Contemporary,* and for which Nekrasov had asked my support.

7 February. Dinner at Grigory Vasilievich Druzhinin's, brother of the recently deceased Aleksandr Vasilievich. A Balthasarian dinner—with especially fine wines. I stayed until about 10 P.M., chatting with several writers: Turgenev, Goncharov, Grigorovich, Annenkov, and others. Turgenev was particularly interesting. He told us many interesting things about his relations with foreign writers, Dickens in particular.

The difference between Turgenev and Goncharov is that Turgenev is a real gentleman. He is pleasant in a relaxed way, simple and noble. It is pleasant to be with him and talk with him. Goncharov is a stoutish, rather haughty gentleman, something like a provincial nobleman. He always tries to make you feel that you are dealing with someone important. His entire character can be described in terms of these traits: egotism, cowardice, and envy.

In general, the conversation at this dinner and afterwards was more entertaining and decent than the last one. Perhaps, because the ladies were constantly with us. And the children, too.

11 February. Medical men assure us that every age has, besides the usual common ailments, its own specific ailments which are strictly a product of the times. Such are the nervous disorders and softening of the brain so prevalent today. It would be interesting to investigate the psychological causes of the latter disease, which has become so common today. I think it is a result of the growth of education and the intense drives toward success that education generates; it pressures us to undertake tasks which are beyond our strength and capacity. Indeed, who is not ambitious these days? Who doesn't want to stand out, to be the center of attention, to become popular? Popularity itself is a disease of our time. The desire to acquire it puts too much strain on the brain, thus laying the groundwork for softening of the brain itself.

20 February. This morning, while I was preparing reports for the Ministry Council, I was suddenly notified by the vice-president of the Academy that I was to stand watch at Count Bludov's bier. And so, Bludov has passed away.

21 February. I stood watch at Bludov's bier this morning. The Metropolitan conducted the funeral service. My God! What a clumsy, bearlike creature! What a coarse, unpleasant, vulgar-looking face! The service, as usual, consisted of endless repetitions of one and the same thing, which (I don't know why) our church considered necessary, but could bore God himself to death. The usual singing followed. "Simplified," they call it, but I would call it "vulgarized." In their effort to avoid catholic theatricality and an operatic atmosphere, they fell into the kind of unbearable monotonous droning and wailing which neither one's ears nor heart can understand. The depressing character of our funeral sermons is overwhelming. In those appeals about eternal life, eternal peace and the like, the idea of *eternal nothingness* tears at one's very soul. Assuming this idea to be valid, why tease a man who is suffering enough as it is. It is a particularly unfitting approach for Christianity, which has provided humanity with so many fine illusions.

22 February. Sukhomlinov was here yesterday and told me what had happened on Thursday at the emergency session of the University Council, which I could not attend. The rector had read a secret report which he had received from the superintendent. It stated that three Poles had come to the university with the idea of inciting student disorders and bringing about the closing of the university again. It is true that the students have been agitated for the past few days, and it seems that they are definitely making plans again for meetings.

24 February. Student disorders are erupting at the university again. That's your younger generation for you! Really disgusting! Like a drunkard, it intrudes where it shouldn't, yells, and threatens law and order. It says to hell with learning, and turns, instead, to the press and superficial reading. How ridiculous! And this bunch is Russia's future? A fine future!

I heard from Delyanov yesterday that Litke was appointed president of the Academy. Obviously, he is Golovnin's choice. Imagine appointing a German to an academy already half-German! It all goes to show what a great patriot he is. And this Litke? He has a reputation as a fine seaman and very easy going person, but mainly as a great protector of his fellow Germans. A much more intelligent choice could have been made, more in keeping with present circumstances. Why not, for example, Korf? Or Stroganov?

25 February. That the Poles cannot bear the sight of a Russian *muzhik*, that they are filled with hostility and contempt for him, is understandable, because they are really more educated, while the Russian *muzhik* or Russian masses still languish in ancient, barbaric cimmerian gloom. What I don't understand is their attitude toward so-called educated Russians, for indeed, the Poles are in no way superior. In them you find the same intellectual and moral depravity, the same shallowness, the same lack of character, etc. Their intelligentsia is as rotten as ours, and, with their Catholicism, they are even worse.

5 March. I presented two reports to the Council on Press Affairs: one, on a most absurd drama written by the well-known literary eccentric, Velikopolsky. *Yaneterskaya* had been printed in 1839 with the approval of censor Oldekop, who had not read it. It was immediately taken from the author and burned in my and the late Stefan Kutorga's presence. Now he has decided to publish it again and had presented it for censorship review. The author has assembled in this play all the abominations, all the moral afflictions with which the human race has disgraced itself—thievery in various forms, adultery, a mother acting as a procuress for her daughter, murder, suicide, attempts at incest and the like; and all this was painted in the filthiest colors. He says in the introduction that he has purposely used such striking language in order to deter people from these vices; but it turns out that the vices he describes are not as revolting as his writing. I, of course, wanted to keep our literature from being sullied by this vile work and proposed a ban on its publication, basing my recommendation on the earlier ban. The Council agreed with me completely.

My other report was more interesting. I presented a rather strange memorandum. It concerned the publication of an article, "Food and Its Significance," written, it seems, by Antonovich, for publication in the *Contemporary*. This article openly preaches materialism, basing its arguments on man's primary need to eat. Later, when it discusses labor and its exploitation, it delivers its communistic and socialistic messages. If this were a popularization of scientific ideas or a statement of principles, I would not say a word against it, no matter how ticklish the issues discussed might be. But this article is nothing more than a proclamation to people of limited intelligence and knowledge, which tells them that man's belly determines how he lives, thinks and functions in this world; that the social system must be revised in terms of this belly and its desires. Goncharov initially examined this article and, in keeping with his policy of straddling the fence—of appeasing a certain literary faction for fear of its attacks in the journals and, at the same time trying to retain his 4,000 rubles-a-year post—presented a review that was vague, but yet substantial enough to keep him in the good graces of this literary clique. However, he used a device, not very cunning or ingenious, although adopted, apparently, with the cunning idea of avoiding responsibility for the final verdict: he asked the Council to appoint a second member to read this article. The Council assigned it to me. Since I neither favor nor fear any literary faction and, to boot, have no intention of appeasing the authorities should they make absurd or harmful demands on science, thought and education, I decided in this case, too, to act as I always have, i.e., according to the best of my knowledge and convictions. After reading the article carefully, I was convinced that this was one of many such wretched little pieces appearing in the *Contemporary* and the *Russian Word* which counted on the immaturity and ignorance of its readers, particularly of the younger generation, and tried to acquire popularity among young people by preaching eccentric and red ideas. What are these gentlemen after? Money and popularity. They haven't the slightest desire or need to earn them through serious work. One can find everything one wants in foreign literature and books; one can easily get from them all sorts of charming ideas of radical-progressive color. To us these ideas will look new, and, by passing them off as one's own it is easy to acquire the fame of a great thinker and publicist. Our ink flows rather freely. It goes without saying that we must not pander to this in our press, to this intellectual depravity and egotism which is unconcerned about consequences as long as money and popularity are forthcoming. Unfortunately, this is the sad and irrefutable truth. I expressed all this in my memorandum and pointed out that the government had no right to ignore such writings which have a deep impact on morality, especially in our country, where learning and public opinion are still so poorly developed that we can't stand up against false and pernicious teachings and neutralize their influence. The Council not only agreed with my conclusion, but decreed that my memorandum be forwarded to both the St. Petersburg and Moscow Censorship Committees as a *guideline*.

Ivan Aleksandrovich [Goncharov] was amusing: he argued with me, trying to prove, in the most ridiculous way, that it was time to expose the public to seamy ideas, too. He had forgotten that it was already quite familiar with such ideas. I argued that this was no reason for the press, which our public believed like the gospel, to be used to compound the evil. By exposing people to all these abominations without equipping them to cope with them, you are making them totally defenseless and protecting evil. Later, Ivan Aleksandrovich agreed with me and even gave his enthusiastic approval to the proposal to adopt my memo as a guideline. Now, he can rightfully inform a certain literary clique that he had staunchly defended the article, but Nikitenko had attacked it so harshly that his defense was in vain. This was the main thing he wanted to make clear, while also making the point that he hadn't opposed the Council's decision. So the goats were sated and the hay remained intact.

16 March. World revolution—the radical reform of all civilization and culture —this is where the so-called spirit of our times is taking us, this is what people are striving toward today. It is a universal movement. There are similar examples in history. We can't and shouldn't resist this movement, but we must resist the possibility of disastrous consequences. Therefore we must struggle against the shameless radical strivings of this generation, while keeping the path toward progress open. Without such restraints humanity will indeed topple into an abyss instead of reaching the promised land.

22 March. The emancipators of women are demanding equality for her. Doesn't this imply that a woman must behave like a man? Would a woman still be expected to observe a certain bashfulness, restraint and modesty in her drives to satisfy sexual needs and impulses? Or could she throw herself at a man, shamelessly, and take the initiative when her blood begins to seethe? Objection: but, men ought not to behave shamelessly, either. And this will change, too, when men are well-bred and moral. However, nature herself has made man the aggressive party and woman the submissive one. We see this in animals, too. And there's a good reason for it. Otherwise, universal debauchery would prevail, and people, dogs, horses and so on would do nothing but copulate. Animals and the human race would die out for the very reason that should serve to perpetuate them.

Women are supposed to ride only side saddle. And there is a sound physiological reason for it.

It is an irrefutable fact that a woman is weaker than a man. Doesn't she, therefore, need his protection? If she does, then the question of equality is out. The need for protection means dependence.

27 March. Tyutchev visited me. He was appointed to the Council on Press Affairs and wanted to consult me about the Council. He told me, incidentally, that Gorchakov had dissuaded the emperor from celebrating the anniversary of the capitulation of Paris.[f] Tyutchev thinks as I do—that war is inevitable.

2 April. Meetings of the Academy, Ministry of Internal Affairs Council, and the Superintendent's Council. Przhetslavsky was defeated again in the Ministry Council—this time by Goncharov, on the issue of increasing our surveillance over personal attacks in the press, caricatures, etc. Przhetslavsky wanted specific instructions given to the censors for this purpose.

4 April. Russian women have a great future ahead of them if they can learn to curb their passion for those immense crinolines whose size is commensurate to the ruin wrought their fathers, husbands, and themselves, as well.

21 April. The minister of war has ordered that women should no longer be admitted to classes at the Medical Academy. The first three or four who had been admitted applied themselves most conscientiously to their anatomy studies. Soon there were sixteen or more. The lot of them were sweet nihilists with short bobs, wearing little round caps with a feather. They began to stroll about the corridors, smoking cigarettes, arm in arm with male students, and were getting involved in various scandalous affairs with the latter. Evidently it was not a question of their anatomical studies on corpses but of experimentation on living bodies, as a result of which several of them began to gain weight and bulge. Oh, Russian society and Russian intelligentsia, how amazing are thy ways!

30 April. I had a conversation several days ago with Tyutchev about that rotter, Golovnin, and his vile administration. "What are you going to do?" Tyutchev said to me. "Everyone knows what he is; everyone has nothing but deep contempt for him. The emperor shares the general feeling of disrespect for him; and, meanwhile, there isn't a soul who would dare tell the emperor how dangerous it is to tolerate such a scoundrel and blockhead in such an important post."

5 May. Celebration of the one hundredth anniversary of Smolny Convent. I

[f] On March 31, 1814, Alexander I made a triumphal entry into Paris.

had received an invitation several days ago. I called for Polinka Sukman at
9 A.M. She had been educated at Smolny Convent and had also been invited
to the celebration; and since she is such a nice young lady, I thought it would
be pleasant to take her with me. We were at Smolny Convent church by 9:40.
A lot of old women, probably from the almshouse, stood by the fence. The
convent's pupils and several busy officials were behind the balustrade. Prince
von Oldenburg had already arrived. He came up to me in his usual unpretentious, kindly way and asked how long I had taught at the convent and
whether my students were attending university lectures conscientiously. The
church began to fill with dignitaries and alumni. I met many friends among
both. The Metropolitan conducted the mass. The court choir boys sang.
How lovely the church is! I haven't seen anything comparable to the grandeur, simplicity and gracefulness of its architecture anywhere, except, perhaps,
in the Pantheon in Paris. The emperor, empress, and entire imperial family
came for the service. The church and the convent building were temporarily
joined by a covered canvas gallery. All the invited guests passed through it into
the convent's endless corridors, which led them to the main hall. Along both
sides of the upper corridor pupils stood in two rows, producing a very interesting effect. In the main hall, opposite the entrance, shaded by beautiful green-
ery, stood a statue of Catherine II, and the entire hall was filled with tables
set for breakfast. All the tables were occupied by women except one which
had been set aside for dignitaries, among whom I, too, a little and obscure
man, took my place, between a very high ranking figure, Yazykov, director of
the Law Institute, and Minister of Justice Zamyatin.

Since this was mainly a woman's holiday and since I generally have a greater
appreciation for educated women than for our so-called educated men, I
devoted all my attention to the waves of women's heads which filled almost
the entire hall. What a variety of faces and ages! Side by side with blooming
youth of recent graduations sat the ruins of the beginning of the century,
which had once known the bloom of youth, too. They say a 104-year-old
woman was the last survivor of the convent's first graduating class. But she
didn't come. Many familiar little faces, that some 15 or 20 years ago had
radiated the charm and excitement of youth in bloom, flashed by me; but
now, alas!—they were fading, partly faded or totally faded, which eloquently
spoke of how I, too, had faded. And how many of them had faded and are
fading in want and under the stress of daily misfortunes and storms! Many,
when they noticed me, sent me their warm greetings and smiles, somberly
marked by the sad imprint of time. The men sat down immediately at the
table and were about to attack the pies, cutlets and so forth, when a gentleman-in-waiting appeared and announced that we had to wait for the emperor.
After some 20 minutes the emperor appeared, leading the empress and followed
by the grand dukes and members of the court. The band began to play. The
emperor bowed with his usual warmth and sat down at the table, which everyone else then proceeded to do. And the gluttony commenced. The feast

didn't interest me at all; I was too absorbed in contemplating the meaning of this celebration. My thoughts turned to Catherine, to whom Russia owes its understanding of the great importance of women, to whom it is indebted for their transformation from a piece of sweet meat or pie filled with physical delights, into thinking, noble beings, into great instruments for the regeneration and humanization of our people. But suddenly, foolish Yazykov interrupts my thoughts by taking my plate and piling it with cutlets. So, I had to eat. Glasses of champagne appeared; a first toast to the emperor; and charming female voices began to sing "God Save the Tsar."

My fellow guests were glad that the singing had ended and they could return to the business of feeding their stomachs. The breakfast was sumptuous, with plenty of wine, and good wine, too. All from the palace. Court servants attended us.

When the breakfast ended the emperor left quietly with his family. We all scattered about the hall. I kept running into my former pupils.

I started for home at 2:30, and, on the way, stopped at the Sukman's to deliver my companion to her parents. The Smolny Convent celebration left me with most pleasant memories.

7 May. Meeting of the Ministry Council on Press Affairs. I delivered two reports—one on the second edition of Zotov's novel *Secret Forces,* which discusses, among other things, Cagliostro's prophesy regarding Paul I. I proposed that the novel could be passed if we deleted the words: "you have a crown prince." The second report was on Strakhov's article on Polish affairs, which the St. Petersburg Censorship Committee had unjustly banned. I proposed that we pass it. Tyutchev and Goncharov agreed with me. It was decided that the other members of the Council should read it, too. Nekrasov's poems "Lullaby" and "The Railroad" were not passed.

17 May. It was announced today in the police newspaper, the *St. Petersburg Police Bulletin,* that on Tuesday, May 19th at 8 A.M. on Mytninskaya Square, Chernyshevsky would be publicly sentenced. He was given seven years hard labor, to be followed by lifelong exile in Siberia. The court had given him fourteen years hard labor, but the emperor had cut it in half.

20 May. I didn't go to the university today. Kostomarov came to see me. The censor had mutilated his article, "The Veche,"[g] written for the magazine, *Work and Play,* and, in addition, had substituted his own words. I read the article and found nothing in it which called for censorship.

Some woman by the name of Mikhaelis tossed a bouquet of flowers at Chernyshevsky as he was being led to the scaffold. Of course she was seized immediately and taken away by the gendarmes.

[g] The Veche was a popular assembly in medieval Russia. These town assemblies acquired absolute power in Novgorod, Pskov and Vyatka. Elsewhere they shared authority with the local prince.

21 May. Meeting of the Council on Press Affairs. Tyutchev and I tried, in vain, to defend Strakhov's article for the *Epoch,* but the ignorance and stupidity of the majority triumphed. Even Przhetslavsky was on our side.

I asked Turunov why the censor had not passed Kostomarov's "Veche." He said the censor had found something against autocracy in it. I read it and found absolutely nothing of the kind. One must admit that censorship is now in the hands of real ignoramuses. Especially damaging to it are such committee chairmen as Turunov, who doesn't know what science and literature are all about and views them no differently than the most commonplace civil servants. Valuev has chosen a fine chairman! It is not informed and able people that Valuev needs, but the kind who would constantly hang about his antechamber, people who are nothings and would not dwarf him with their intelligence. A most fitting point of view for a minister! Oh, this terrible fear of intelligence!

I asked Lyuboshchinsky to tell me, in his capacity as a senator, whether there was sufficient legal evidence of Chernyshevsky's guilt. He replied that legal evidence was lacking but there was, of course, a tight moral case against him. How, then, had he been judged? Some members of the State Council couldn't find sufficient evidence and proof of the charges for which he had been convicted. Then, Prince Dolgoruky showed them some papers from the Third Section—and these members suddenly dropped their opposition. But what kind of papers are these? It's a secret. Why keep them secret if they contain real proof of Chernyshevsky's guilt? What a pity! Even some people who are completely unsympathetic to Chernyshevsky are wondering if he wasn't treated too harsly, if not cruelly. These days in particular, such impressions don't do the government any good. They say that during the public sentencing on Tuesday a series of articles published in the *Contemporary* was cited. In that case, the censorship department is at fault. Why did it pass articles so obviously aimed at the overthrow of the existing order? In short, it would seem that the case was handled imprudently.[h]

23 May. Granted that the Supreme Being is all-wise and good, that he is everything you wish Him to be, except omnipotent, because, if He were, how could He permit such terrible chaos and suffering? Indeed, one must say in all honesty, that the idea of the human race was well conceived, but it could not have been more miserably executed. Could this really have been part of the Supreme Being's plan? It is truly a comedy, full of irony and tears; a joke, and not even a funny one at that.

24 May. Many people are very indignant at the government over the Chernyshevsky affair. Could they have convicted him without any legal evidence?

[h] The Soviet editors of Nikitenko's diary indicate doubt as to the complete validity of Lyuboshchinsky's statements. They feel that there would hardly have been any serious disagreement in the State Council over the Senate's decision.

Almost everyone is saying this, even those who aren't reds. The government has acquired a substantial number of new enemies.

How can one reconcile such irrationality in the affairs of mankind with the rationality of His plan and purpose—if such things do exist? It is from such contradictions that materialists derive their claims. Their chief weapon is despair. And to tell the truth there is plenty to drive one to despair. We are but one step away either from plunging into reckless nihilism or grasping the kind of heroic faith of which so few people are capable.

26 May. We moved to our dacha in Pavlovsk. The weather is beautiful here, but in the city it is getting oppressive, dusty and smelly.

28 May. Yesterday and today were beautiful. I am growing fond of our dacha. I took a long walk in the park with Sasha today. The railroad station has been greatly improved; everything else is the same.

An awful crowd of strollers came pouring in from St. Petersburg this evening. The lavishness in women's clothes is positively insane! It's really a disgrace, especially when you think of how we suffer from low incomes and high prices. For this our Russian women deserve to be censured. They carry this passion for all kinds of finery, rather than for true elegance, to a ridiculous extreme.

30 May. Meeting of the University Council this evening. It was my last. I parted with the university for good after giving it thirty of my best years. Weighing all I have done with great care, I cannot reproach myself for anything. But I shall have much more to say about that in my memoirs.

The ministry, that is, Delyanov, treated me very badly. The university was willing to let me stay on until September, but the minister and Delyanov arranged for my retirement on June 1st in order to deprive me of 600 rubles.

I wanted to deliver a brief farewell speech at the Council meeting, but figured there was no one or nothing worth giving it for. I simply rose and left without ceremony.

3 July. Meeting of the Council on Press Affairs. The minister's order calling for an end to the polemic between the Ostsee[i] and Moscow newspapers was announced. The Ostsee press had openly preached separatist ideas. It called for the separation of the Ostsee region and encouraged German Russians to hate Russia. The Moscow press opposed this. I raised my voice—I say, raised, because I literally became very vehement, and expressed the following thought: "Let us assume that the elimination of such polemics is a good thing. The minister has made such a decision, and the matter is ended. But will the German press be allowed to continue to express its bias against Russia in non-polemic articles and to demonstrate that the Ostsee provinces constitute a completely separate entity, tied more closely to Germany than to Russia by its common interests? If this is permitted, either because of weak censorship

---

[i] Baltic provinces.

measures or the connivance of Ostsee authorities, on what grounds can the
Russian press be forbidden to speak out against this campaign of the Ostsee
press? Higher censorship authorities must not allow such a situation and firm
measures to prevent it must be taken. Not only will the polemic then disappear by itself, but the pretext for it too, which is the most important
thing."

The others agreed with me.

13 July. Went to Mikhail Dostoevsky's funeral. He died of jaundice at the
age of 44. He was not so much a remarkable writer as an honest and good man.
His brother Fyodor is a better writer: he had suffered a great deal and was involved in the Petrashevsky affair. He had spent five years at hard labor in exile. I accompanied the unfortunate deceased to the cemetery. From the balcony of my dacha I have often admired the beautiful little wood on the slope,
on the other side of Slavyanka. It seems that this little wood is the peaceful
eternal resting place of Pavlovsk's inhabitants. The entire ceremony lasted
some two hours after the mass. It was terribly hot, a storm was gathering, and
majestic storm clouds were rolling in from the west. But the storm passed
over. I didn't get the least bit tired.

16 July. I went to the city just to pass the time. The Siberian plague has
made considerable inroads in St. Petersburg. Police measures have been taken,
especially in regard to butcher shops. But none of the tradesmen observe them,
while the authorities are satisfied that they have performed their duty by merely distributing the necessary circulars.

25 July. What an amazing people are the Russians! They are beyond me!
Their stealing, drinking and swindling, for example, have now reached the
point where, seriously speaking, they are almost impossible to live with. Yet
you feel drawn to them by something unique, something so good, clever and
charming, that no German, Frenchman, or, even, Englishman, can compare
with them. You struggle with them in vain. One minute their vile antics in
the taverns, on the streets, in the marketplace and workshops drive you wild;
and the next, when you are feeling low, their unsophisticated, goodnatured
and carefree disregard of all their daily misfortunes and troubles draws a cheerful smile from you; or they move you to tears with some truly generous, heroic
deed, without flaunting it or even understanding its significance. The devil
only knows what they are! It is said that our people lack education. I can
only hope that they, with the help, of course, of a few simple solid, honest
and seriously enlightened souls, will educate themselves. It would be unfortunate if they were to accept the kind of education that our liberals, our publicists and our government officials want to impose on them. (From my letter
to Goncharov.)

Sent out letters to Goncharov in Frankfurt-on-the-Main and to Rudnitsky
in Weimar.

1 August. According to our laws, a criminal cannot be punished unless he *confesses* his crime. This law is obviously a vestige of barbarian law which terminated all criminal cases very easily by confession, since authorities had at their disposal such charming, convenient instruments as knouts, racks, and the like, to elicit these confessions.

20 August. I presented my opinion to the Council on Press Affairs about an article for the *Russian Messenger* which describes scenes from the first cholera epidemic of 1830–31. The Moscow Censorship Committee didn't want to pass it because it contained many descriptions of terrible scenes and gave an account of a peasant rebellion. The Committee felt that the latter suggested class antagonism. I replied that history was obliged to tell the truth and not to varnish it. The Council agreed with my opinion.

29 August. Celebration of Academician Karl Maksimovich Baer's[j] anniversary. We Russians can't conduct anything with complete decorum and respect for one and all. In the first place, the dinner was held at Demuth's restaurant, which was so crowded that we practically had to sit on each other's knees. There wasn't the slightest semblance of order; not the slightest attention to the kind of decorum and solemnity demanded by such an occasion. Noise, hubbub, banging, frenzied shrieking during speeches, people jumping up from their places and returning to them with a lot of banging and rattling. The first speech was made by Middendorf, in German, and he managed to make himself heard. After that it was totally impossible to say or hear anything. I decided not to give my speech and to leave immediately after the cake was served, especially since I was afraid of missing the Tsarskoe Selo train and not making it home to Pavlovsk for the night. Academy Secretary Veselovsky, Betling and other organizers of the celebration stopped me, saying that this would prove awkward since I was listed on the program. "But how can I speak in this bedlam?" I asked. "Wait for a quiet moment and then begin," I was told. But it was pointless to wait. I extracted a few sentences from my speech and tossed them off somehow. The whole thing was senseless and absurd. I dashed out, sorry about the time I had lost and for Baer, who had been feted so disrespectfully. Here's still another indignity that occurred. Normally, when a toast to the emperor is offered, the band immediately strikes up "God Save the Tsar." The toast was offered, the usual "Hurrah" was repeated three times, but—no music. Litke gestured in vain to the band—and still no music. Only after he had shouted several times: "God Save the Tsar" did the band strike up the national anthem. That was the way the affair appeared to the observer, while the inside story was another matter and went like this. Apparently, the Germans wanted to crow over their defeat of the Russian faction, so Russia was completely ignored in every German speech. Then, there was a group of natural scientists present who preach materialism. They wanted to proclaim Baer as their man. But the worst thing was the presence of several

---

[j] An eminent zoologist. The celebration marked his fifty years as a doctor of philosophy.

bearded nihilists and young people—followers of the latest doctrines, who for ten rubles came to eat, drink and demonstrate in favor of their ideas. The Germans, honoring their star, wanted as many people present as possible, and admitted everyone.

I am sorry we celebrated the anniversary of one of science's most worthy representatives so wretchedly, and am even more sorry that everything combined to eclipse the Russian name and Russian thought. Serves us right! He who does not respect himself compels others to lose respect for him, too.

14 September. The blame for the fires is being placed on the Poles who had been moved en masse from the Polish Kingdom and western provinces to the inner cities of the Russian empire. I feel this was a mistake on the part of the administration. Of course they aren't burning cities, but they are encouraging the spread of inflammatory ideas among our gullible youth.

19 September. We hear that the arsonists in Simbirsk were caught, and their leader is not a Pole, but a Russian. If it's true, it hurts.

22 September. A fire broke out yesterday, but it was quickly extinguished.
Fires are becoming a chronic affliction with us.
Scarcely a day goes by that we don't read about serious fires in various cities and villages.

23 September. For several years now both the public and the Duma have been aware of the need to curb dogs who run about the city and attack horses and pedestrians. Sometimes there are sad cases of hydrophobia. The police are forever "taking measures." They keep talking in the Duma about positive steps: one time it's muzzles, another time they propose fining dog owners, and so on. They've been talking this way for several years, while dogs still roam the streets.

4 October. Discussion of Russian nationality and its predominant role in relation to other nationalities in the empire is a healthy thing and we should encourage it. But if all we are going to do is talk or shout about it as the Muscovites do, we are not going to accomplish very much. Our right to prevail over other nationalities can be demonstrated only by growth, by intellectual, moral and social progress, rather than by a display of mere numerical strength and brute force. It seems too early to shout about it, because our achievements have not been particularly brilliant. Meanwhile, our Russian nationality is only strong in numbers, in its vague awareness of its strength, and in its vague strivings toward independence. We must be more modest and temperate and not follow the example of those Moscow journalists who boast that they alone have discovered and understand what Russian patriotism is all about.

15 October. Arson is becoming something of a mania with us, a kind of pastime. Recently an arsonist was caught. He was asked what had motivated him to commit arson. Was it revenge or a desire to steal? He replied that it was neither, that he had simply set the fire and didn't understand why. Another turned himself in and gave identical replies to similar questions. Aksakov would explain these acts as the misguided expression of a great nationality's great strength which takes this destructive form. I think there is a simpler explanation. Our ordinary Russian does not grasp the meaning of rights or law. His entire moral code springs from a casual kindheartedness which, being neither developed nor firmly based on some conscious principles, will sometimes assert itself, and at other times be stifled by more savage instincts. Untill now, fear was the only means of curbing him. It no longer troubles him. The protection which the government still offers him is so weak that he hasn't the slightest respect for it. Impunity and the complete absence of moral principles encourage him to commit deeds which he considers simple acts of daring, and, frequently, he is motivated by profit, too. Impunity and cheap vodka —these are the causes of the demoralization raging among our people and turning them into a beast, despite their fine talents and many fine traits.

1 November. Had a long talk with Kostomarov. His article, "The Veche in Russia," was held back in the censorship department for God only knows what reason. The censors felt we ought not to be reminded of that time, long ago, when our people would come together to discuss their affairs. I want to help Kostomarov and, since the Council, acting on his complaint, gave the article to me to examine, I hope that I shall succeed in preventing censorship from taking ridiculous measures.

5 November. Meeting of the Council on Press Affairs. After several objections were raised, the Council approved my recommendation to permit publication of Kostomarov's article.

5 December. I read the new laws on our judicial system, which were publicized several days ago.[2] What a splendid monument to our time! It will stand side by side with the emancipation of the serfs. Meanwhile, the public scarcely discusses it or thinks about it, except for a small circle of people directly concerned with such matters. Magazine gossip seems to make more of an impression on the public than this immortal step. I tried to discuss it with several of my Academy colleagues, but got little response.

The new laws will cause a lot of confusion at first. People won't know how to interpret, evaluate or apply them. But that ought not to dismay us, just as we ought not to be dismayed by a summer rain which wets our clothes but prepares the way for an abundant harvest.

10 December. Special session of the Academy of Sciences on the draft of the new rules. My proposal for the deletion of the following words from the draft didn't encounter the opposition I had expected: "When there are two equally qualified candidates for an Academy vacancy—a foreigner and a Russian—preference should be given to the Russian." I feel that the only decisive factor should be scholarship and merit and not the candidate's nationality. However, Sreznevsky's amendment was added to the draft. It stated that a foreigner would be elected only when we didn't have a worthy candidate of our own. I did not change my stand.

21 December. I was busy all morning putting my papers in order. I scarcely managed to sort out half of my correspondence, which is only a small part of my papers. After all, I have corresponded with practically every writer, many scholars, and a vast number of people from every walk of life. I have accumulated such a vast correspondence over the course of many years that it is difficult to organize it. I didn't want to destroy it because it contained a great deal of interesting material. Nonetheless, I did destroy much of it, especially my private correspondence. I can't understand how I managed to answer all those letters. If I didn't answer all of them, I did, at least, answer most of them. There are also some brief, but interesting little notes here, which reflect the psychology of the times and history, as well.

1865

1 January. The most difficult battle I fought last year and which I shall certainly continue to fight, is the battle with my feeling of my own *worthlessness,* and, moreover, with my feeling of the worthlessness of all sorts of things: social, moral, material and physical.

Why am I writing all this in my diary? Here's why. I was overwhelmed by a fit of depression, but the instant I began to jot down these lines, I felt much better and almost cheerful, although there's little to be cheerful about. This often happens to me. My diary, playing the role of confidante, almost always restores my mental equilibrium. Psychologists, interpret this as you will, but it's an indisputable fact.

7 January. Spent the morning at Troinitsky's and at Norov's. Norov asked me to prepare a commentary on the press proposal introduced at the State Council. He gave me all the material for it. Korf evidently favors greater freedom for the press, although he recognizes the need for certain limits, such as preliminary censorship as a preventive measure. But, he feels that journal editors should have the option of subjecting their publications to preliminary censorship. He is completely opposed to the posting of bonds. He favors punitive rules. He demands limits on the minister's power and greater independence for the Council. He thinks and writes like a statesman. Panin also agrees with the idea of limiting the minister's power.

It's hard to get at the truth or make sense out of all the rumors one hears. Katkov was called to St. Petersburg. He was told that if he didn't simmer down, his newspaper would be taken from him and placed in other hands. Moscow University declared that it didn't want to change the paper's editors and was itself assuming responsibility for its censorship. This comes as a complete surprise. Moscow generally is very disturbed about the *Moscow Bulletin.*

14 January. The Moscow nobility drew up a petition calling for the convocation of a *zemskaya duma.*[k] Mark Lyuboshchinsky read a copy of it which is passing from hand to hand. The petition hasn't been signed and presented yet, but the decision to present it has been made in Moscow. 302 members agreed to it, and some 30 rejected it.[1]

15 January. Distressing news about the heir. They say he is ill, and with an illness that gives us reason to fear for his life.

[k] Nikitenko is probably referring to a *zemskii sobor* (Assembly of the Land), an institution of the sixteenth and seventeenth centuries, made up of representatives of various groups.

The idea of convening a *zemskaya duma* is not a bad one. But it's unfortunate that the initiative didn't come from the government itself rather than
from the local nobility. I remain firmly convinced that we must keep the
principle of national government inviolable in order to avoid a chaos worse
than what we have now. I think it would be wisest in this situation for the
government to tell the Moscow nobility that it is the government's responsibility, as governing body for the entire nation, to determine the needs of the
state and that it is not the task of local nobility alone; that the government
has absolutely no intention, in view of the extraordinary circumstances in
which it now finds itself, of denying the need for a *zemskaya duma* or its
usefulness. And, further, that it will come to its own decisions regarding the
time and type of discussions it will have with the delegates, whose moral support in the solution of extremely important problems it does not consider
superfluous.

16 January. Meeting of the commission appointed by the Academy to organize the one hundredth anniversary celebration of Lomonosov's death. All
those present were Russians, except Kunik. I proposed opening the celebration with a mass, since it would coincide with holy week, to be followed by
a mass for the dead, and ending with ceremonies at the Academy. The idea
was received very coldly. Veselovsky was particularly opposed to it. I said:
"If I am proposing the introduction of a religious element into our academic
celebration, I feel I have a good reason for it. We are celebrating the memory
of Lomonosov not merely as a member of the Academy, but as a famous figure to whom all Russia is indebted and whose name is repeated in every corner of our land. This is not only an Academy celebration, but a national one,
too. Therefore, I feel it would not be superfluous to give it a national character, which my proposal would do. Or, are we afraid of being accused of
having a religious tone? This appears to be an unwarranted fear. Lomonosov
was a true Russian, and his memory should be honored in true Russian fashion."

Sreznevsky, who had supported this proposal at a department meeting, now
kept as silent as a fish. Then the question of speeches was raised. I was assigned the task of preparing a speech about Lomonosov and belles-lettres.

19 January. The no. 4 edition of the newspaper, the *News*, published by
Skaryatin printed the Moscow nobility's petition together with a bombastic
editorial commentary, an account of the April 9th meeting, and Count Orlov-
Davydov's speech.

Both the petition and speech would seem to indicate the desire of the Moscow nobility to establish an oligarchy. Skaryatin's remarks are even insolent.
I ran into him today on Nevsky Prospekt and remarked: "Why did you print
that? It was a big mistake." He replied that he had foreseen all the consequences, that it was done deliberately. I congratulated him for still being at
liberty, since there were rumors that he had been arrested. "I have a better

opinion of the government than that," he said with irony. "It treated me legally. Only an inquiry is being conducted now."

Meanwhile it's rumored that 5,000 copies of the no. 4 edition of the *News* have been printed and, although they are being confiscated, a certain group is said to be preparing to circulate them in Russia and abroad.

Everything appears to indicate that the Moscow nobility's petition was not a casual demonstration, but a calculated move. Skaryatin was probably bribed. His newspaper was having financial problems. He was promised and given money. It didn't matter to him whether he was wiped out by poverty or a ban on his paper. In the latter case, he would still stand to gain, for he would acquire a certain popularity.

There is no doubt that the Moscow nobility's proposal will be greeted sympathetically by some nobles in other provinces, too. A certain sector of the nobility grew bitter toward the government after the abolition of serfdom.

The *News* has been suspended for eight months.

Some are saying openly that none of this would have happened if Grand Duke Konstantin hadn't been appointed chairman of the State Council. But I think that the nobility would have expressed its displeasure with the government anyway, particularly against the *zemstvos*, in which the common people are given the same rights as the nobility.

21 January. I went to see Norov about the draft of new press laws. He is preparing to fight for two things: a penalty system, exclusively, and a collective board. Valuev is anxious to acquire unlimited power. Norov is making a tremendous effort to win my friendship again. Let him! I have no objection. He gave me his memo for corrections and additions.

23 January. I returned the memo to Norov. He was very grateful.

When I praised Korf to Mark for his memo on press affairs, Mark said to me: "The memo may be fine, but do you really think that Korf will support his own ideas at a meeting of the Council? Believe me, he won't, if the slightest opportunity to please someone presents itself."

That's exactly what happened. When Norov, who is, at least, unquestionably honest, began to reproach Korf for retreating from his own position, Korf replied: "Now, what are you getting so upset about, Avraam Sergeevich? This doesn't mean anything."

27 January. Now, as I write about Lomonosov—about the artistic nature of his works, I am suddenly reminded of the kind of respect he enjoyed among ordinary folk during my childhood.

The name of Lomonosov as a poet was well known to us, even to those Little Russians who were barely literate. I was ten or eleven when two blind wandering minstrels came to our cottage and asked for my father's permission to sing a hymn. My father agreed, of course. I can see them now: one of them —a tall, thickset man wearing a short blue overcoat and a brave, rather severe expression; the other, somewhat shorter, with a pock-marked, expressive face.

Each held a long staff, by which a small boy led them. I sat in a corner of the room and was very taken by the play of expressions on their faces, especially on the tall blind fellow's when he sang out in his powerful, rich bass, trying to put feeling into his singing which clearly came from the bottom of his heart. Since that time this poem by Lomonosov, which the blind wandering minstrels sang to the delight of my father and all our household, still remains very much alive in my memory:

> Let my breath send praise
> To the Most High Sovereign;
> Until the end of my days
> I shall sing of him in thunderous choir.
>
> Do not place thy trust in vain
> In the power of earthly princes:
> They are born as you and I,
> And from them comes no salvation!

At first, as I mentioned, I was completely captivated by the changing expressions on their faces. But later, a sort of special, indescribable feeling gripped my little heart, and now I recall that moment with tenderness. My father told me then, that this poem was written by Lomonosov, and since that time I have come to know his name well.

28 January. Meeting of the Council on Press Affairs. The draft of the new press code was finally reviewed at the State Council and in the legal department. The Council began and continued its efforts to curb the unlimited power of the minister of internal affairs and to correct the many weaknesses in his draft. The meeting ended with full agreement on the draft.[1]

4 February. To understand life, one must suffer. It is this alone which gives it a serious character. Would it matter if I did or didn't exist, or some Little Russian animal had been born instead of me? Life isn't miserable because of suffering, which every living creature is fated to experience,—on the contrary, it's the one thing that gives it meaning.

Life is ugly because of the worthlessness of everything in it, of everything that drives it and everything toward which it drives. It is the epitome of worthlessness. What is far more terrifying and strange is the knowledge that all this is necessary and must be. Every living thing is drawn to its destiny by fate, and the only justice in it is that death comes to everything.

5 February. Typhus is raging in St. Petersburg, especially among the poor. All the hospitals are jammed. The Izmailov barracks have been turned over to the sick.

14 March. Saw Knyazhevich this morning. He introduced me to A.M. Raevs-

---

[1] See Nikitenko's entry for 14 April 1865.

kaya who is related to Lomonosov. She asked me how to go about donating money to commemorate this anniversary. She is offering 2,000 rubles to be used for university scholarships for four young people of peasant origin who come from Archangel, mainly from the Kuroostrovsk district.

Maikov came to see me and read the poem he had composed for the dinner in Lomonosov's honor. It is well written, but has strong anti-German overtones. Lamansky's influence is evident here. I remarked to Maikov. "You're throwing down the gauntlet to the Germans."

1 April. I received a very courteous note from Litke today in which he expressed the fear that my voice wouldn't be powerful enough to deliver my "splendid" speech at the Lomonosov celebration. What the devil is this? Probably he or someone else doesn't like my speech. I decided to have a talk with Litke and went to see him this evening. He greeted me very warmly and said that he had no intention of criticizing my "splendid" speech, and that he had sent the letter only for the reason stated in it. I must admit that all this was quite confusing to me. I reassured Litke that I would deliver my speech in a very strong voice.

But, did it reassure him?

7 April. The wispy clouds that had been slowly dimming my expectations for the Lomonosov celebration for some time grew so dense on the very day of festivities that it was badly spoiled for me. I had worked so hard over my speech. In any case, I felt that this speech was no worse than any other I had ever given. Yet, it was received coldly. There was scattered applause, but some hissing, too. I clearly had ill-wishers in the audience, and among my very own colleagues, too, which the president's recent note (about my voice not being strong enough) had hinted at.

We received the most distressing news yesterday about the heir: he is dying. The emperor planned to go to him yesterday. There is little sympathy among the so-called intelligent sector of our public for the enormous grief this father and tsar-liberator must bear, but the common people will be deeply grieved.

12 April. When I stopped by Bazunov's book shop, I learned the sad news of the heir's death. How very sad, especially when you think that the life of this noble youth, so promising for Russia, might have been saved if his mentors, Gogel, Zinoviev and Count Stroganov, had shown a little more concern for his physical condition and hadn't been so inexcusably careless about it. The public is seething with anger at Count Stroganov. What, indeed, did he do during the three years he spent with the heir? Why did he conceal his illness if he was aware of it; and, if he wasn't aware of it, why wasn't he?

14 April. I started work on a biography of Galich.

The new press laws have been released. One can rightfully call them Valuev's laws. Everything is subject to the minister's whims. The Council is fated to play a pitiful role.[2]

17 April. President Lincoln of the North American States has been assassinated. This was probably the separatists' way of taking revenge on him for their defeat. When a murderer strikes at a man who has a great gift for ruling a nation and with whose fate the fate of millions is linked, the effect is the same as burning and sacking a whole country and slaughtering masses of people.

Visited Tyutchev. Talked about the heir. According to him the heir was worn out by the ridiculous education he had received, especially by the kind that Stroganov had imposed on him in recent years. His physical condition was completely ignored; they exhausted him dreadfully by forcing him to study and perform beyond his capacity and by ignoring the salutary warnings of certain levelheaded doctors, like Zdekauer and others. The emperor was kept in complete ignorance of his condition. So not until several days before the heir's death did the emperor learn accidentally from a state messenger about the imminent tragedy.

It is said the heir's death sparked a demonstration in Moscow. Crowds of people gathered and cries could be heard blaming Konstantin for this tragedy. The masses, as we know, are unusually receptive to fantastic ideas and rumors.

27 April. A letter written by Boothe, Lincoln's assassin, has appeared in our press. It contains the assassin's political confession and his reasons for the crime. What incredible insolence and arrogance on the part of these self-appointed benefactors of humanity and nations! They would have you believe they are great people who have undertaken a great mission in the name of freedom and progress. This is the deep-seated and fatal disease of our age! Every dreamer, fanatic, or man of great ambition, thirsting for universal popularity, feels he has the right to undertake tasks which no one has authorized him to undertake.

28 April. Spiritualism is becoming extremely popular in St. Petersburg. Fine! This is clearly a reaction against materialism. Let one kind of madness be destroyed by another, just as one nail drives out another.

3 May. The *National Chronicle* has been banned until September. When news of the heir's death was received, all newspapers except the *National Chronicle* came out with a black mourning border. Yet, when a dispatch reporting Lincoln's death was received, the newspaper was clothed in mourning. This precipitated the ban. But the main reason for it was that Chernyshevsky's followers—Antonovich, Eliseev, and Lavrov and others, had allied themselves with this paper. The Third Section had alerted the minister of internal affairs about the paper immediately after its founding. When the time came it showed its true colors.

16 May. It appears that a cruel fate awaits our literature: Valuev has achieved his goal. He has taken it into his hands and has become its complete master. It could not have been given a worse one. As far as I can judge from certain convincing facts, it appears that he has conceived an enormous plan—a plan to destroy any tendencies in literature which he considers harmful and to mold literature into a loyal and trustworthy instrument. He is trying to accomplish what Nicholas I could not and scarcely wanted to either. Nicholas despised literature, but hardly thought it feasible to reshape it to his taste. Valuev, evidently, does. He probably has as much contempt for any intellectual movement today as did others during Nicholas's reign, and he thinks that administrative measures are far more effective and powerful than any idea can be. The press code which must be put into operation in September gives him complete authority over every idea appearing in print. Now that preliminary censorship has been eliminated, the publication of journals is becoming an extremely difficult affair. Previously the journals were at the mercy of the censor, who, despite his position, could not completely ignore the public's reaction to him. Therefore, he was forced to a certain extent to be moderate and lenient. Under his aegis publishers were, to a certain degree, free of responsibility. Now it's different. There is no preliminary censorship. Instead, the sword of Damocles now hangs over the heads of writers and editors in the form of two warnings, followed by a third, which means suspension of publication. This sword is in the minister's hands; he lets it fall at his own discretion and is not even obliged to justify his action. So, we have tyranny in its purest form; no longer the kind that petty civil servants wielded, and, therefore, less bold, but a tyranny backed by strong authority, the authority of the minister. The writing fraternity's panic is understandable. Journalists, at least those from St. Petersburg, have agreed among themselves to submit to preliminary censorship, as before, and, perhaps, in their situation, this would be the wisest thing for them to do. But here's what Fuchs, Valuev's confidante and echo, told me yesterday. "The minister knows about the journalists' plans, but they are making a big mistake. If they want to remain under censorship, they will get it, but a censorship incomparably harsher than they experienced under Nicholas I. By fair means or foul, they will have to be emancipated." What an amazing emancipation!

20 May. More stories about the late heir. You keep hearing the same thing: Stroganov is to blame for this noble youth's premature end. Tyutchev says the empress blames herself for lacking maternal insight and for not being aware of the heir's condition. However, everything had been concealed from her; and the heir himself had concealed it, not wanting to grieve her with the sad truth, of which he, however, was aware, as is evident from a letter to his fiancée, found unfinished among his papers.

25 May. A sad and solemn day! The body of the heir was brought to St. Petersburg and accompanied by a ceremonial procession to its eternal resting place in the fortress. The weather was in keeping with the mood: the sky was covered with storm clouds which constantly threatened rain. But it didn't rain and it was warm. I left my home at noon. Nevsky Prospekt was overflowing with people hurrying to Saint Isaac's Square. The procession was supposed to proceed from Nikolaevsky Bridge, past Saint Isaac's, along the square and bank to Troitsky Bridge. Soon a volley rang out. The streets were now completely empty. All St. Petersburg had converged on the square. An accommodating speculator offered me a seat in the stands for fifty kopeks. I clambered up with difficulty and had a very fine view of the ceremonial procession. A gloomy and majestic picture. Soldiers lined both sides of the square. Various courtiers with their decorations displayed on cushions marched at the head of the procession; then came an endless line of clergy in black vestments, a detachment of soldiers, and then the hearse with the remains of the youth whose death has brought all Russia to tears. Behind it rode the emperor on horseback. The people stood in complete silence, heads bared, and crossed themselves as the chariot appeared. There wasn't the slightest fuss, no pushing, no disorder. Complete silence reigned, broken only by church bells and ominous volleys from the fortress. All stores, shops, and taverns were closed. All St. Petersburg was blanketed by sadness and grief, and a gloomy sky hung over the city like a dark coverlet.

26 May. I went to Peter and Paul Cathedral at 2 o'clock to pay my last respects to the heir's remains. We had to wait a good half hour at the gates of the fortress while carriages returning from the funeral services exited. There was an enormous crowd of people: again it seemed as if all St. Petersburg were here. Suddenly they flocked into the fortress and created such a jam at the entrance that it was pointless to think of getting in without a long wait. Only a few people at a time were admitted. Many grumbled about this procedure, but I felt it to be necessary and wise.

Finally my turn came. Visitors passed through a door and, each in turn, stepped up to the bier, paid his respects and passed through another exit. Gentlemen-in-waiting and generals standing watch flanked the bier on both sides. With profound grief I stepped up to the bier and kissed the cold hand that was meant to hold the scepter of one of the greatest kingdoms in the world and now was doomed to rot. I glanced at the pale face and tears came to my eyes.

28 May. My speech on Lomonosov, despite its cold reception at the Academy ceremony, is now meeting its share of success. Pleasant rumors have been reaching me from various places. I received flattering comments and letters of thanks from Archangel, Kiev, Moscow and Kharkov. The journals maintain a deep silence, except for the *Northern Post,* which commented on my "exhibitionism," and the *Russian Veteran* which summarized my speech. I am profoundly indifferent, and have always been indifferent, to all reviews, good and bad alike. It stems neither from pride nor from a desire to appear invulnerable: on the contrary, I certainly do enjoy hearing praise. But, the point I want to make here is that we Russians do not base our praise or abuse on sound literary grounds, but rather are we motivated by a desire to spite someone or gain someone's favor.

It's now 12:30 P.M. The sad chimes have just announced the burial of the heir. I live directly opposite the church on Vladimirskaya Street and clearly hear its menacing, sad tune.

He was a man, and his father—the liberator of millions. Russia must weep if it has a grain of national feeling—if it is a nation, and not a random aggregate of heterogeneous elements that would turn its back on everything.

13 June. Are we eternally doomed to commit acts of stupidity or is this merely a transitional phase of our development? Whenever we borrow from others we never fail to select the worst of what they have, and then we hasten to make it our very own as if nothing superior to it existed in the world. When we come upon various improvements and material blessings, we always extract the superfluous, the glitter, the inordinate splendor, and we begin with incredible haste to squander our own as well as our fathers' fortunes. When we master a foreign language, we hasten to read the most shallow or racy articles; we chatter about all sorts of nonsense in the new tongue, while forgetting our own. When we go abroad, instead of becoming personally acquainted with the advances of a foreign culture, we make a point of visiting all the dens of iniquity, lose our shirts gambling in places like Baden and Weisbaden, or smuggle in forbidden books or objects, only so we can boast to our friends at home: "Well, brother, I certainly lost heavily in Paris" or someplace or other. Or take our young people who go abroad with the admirable goal of studying. They start out by criticizing and attacking their foreign professors, and end up, upon returning home, by repeating, with the air of world renowned geniuses and experts, what they had picked up from these very same professors in the most superficial fashion and hadn't digested at all; and there they stagnate, never to advance beyond that stage. When we engage in pamphleteering or politics, we hasten to embrace socialism and communism and, with a lot of fuss and fanfare, demand every conceivable kind of reform without worrying if our demands are truly an expression of popular need, or merely a play of our idle fantasy. When we take up philosophy, we hastily plunge head first into atheism and materialism and become blind and deaf to all else. I would like to think that such behavior is only a passing phase of our development and not a permanent fate.

16 June. Norov visited me again. I try to forget that he was once minister of education, and when I do succeed, I am most willing to respond to his friendly overtures. He told me the following anecdote yesterday about Pushkin. Norov ran into him a year or so before his (Pushkin's) marriage. Pushkin greeted him very warmly and embraced him. Tumansky, a friend of Pushkin's, was present. He turned to the poet and said to him: "Aleksandr Sergeevich, do you know whom you are embracing? This fellow is your enemy. When he was in Odessa, he burned the manuscript of your poem in my presence."

The fact of the matter was that Tumansky had given Norov the manuscript of Pushkin's notorious, indecent poem to read.[m] A fire was burning on the hearth, and Norov, after reading the piece, tossed it right into the fire.

"No," replied Pushkin, "I wasn't aware of it. Now that I am, I can see that Avraam Sergeevich is not my enemy, but my friend, while you, who were delighted with such a piece of filth as my unpublished poem, are my real enemy."

17 June. There is talk of postponing court reforms. In the meantime it has stimulated an unbearable thirst for change: everyone feels there can be no security without it, and everyone awaits it like manna from heaven. But administrative or bureaucratic forces do not want to relinquish their power.

What will happen if, on top of all our other problems, the threatened general famine materializes! Won't this incomprehensible inertia on the part of the authorities lead to widespread disorders and thievery, and won't this, in fact, become the starting point for a violent revolution, which the Poles, our foreign enemies, and domestic revolutionaries are hoping for?

13 July. It's rumored that cholera has appeared in St. Petersburg. Cases have already occurred in France and Italy, and in Constantinople too. There's certainly nothing to keep it from spreading here. Then what an epidemic we'll have! And no wonder. People will drink cold water with ice during hot spells and will come down with stomach colds. And the common people are always inflaming their stomachs with their cheap vodka.

14 July. A broad conspiracy to burn Russia has been unmasked in the western provinces. It's interesting that this discovery was made by private parties and not by our police, who apparently don't give a hang about anything.

31 July. Valuev recently announced at the Committee of Ministers that more than 400 fires had broken out in Russia during the two summer months. Evidently, this does not particularly worry our highest administrators.

4 August. I read an article about smoking a few days ago in one of our journals, which said that excessive smoking weakened one's vision. Since my vision has been poor for some time now, I've decided to cut down on cigars, which I had been smoking heavily. It's been several days since I reduced my usual quota by exactly half and I intend to stay with it, particularly since it is good for my purse, too.

6 August. A very interesting article about the arson episodes appeared in today's *Russian Veteran* (no. 171). The existence of a broad arson network, organized by a Polish group here and abroad, has been revealed and is now an indisputable fact. There also exists a group of Russian foreign renegades, who are working in concert with them.

28 August. When I arrived in the city yesterday, I found a letter from Turunov

[m] "Gavriliada."

with this notation on the envelope: "*urgent,* August 26th, summons from the minister." He received me with unusual warmth and began by apologizing for sending the letter to my dacha in Pavlovsk. As a result I did not receive it in time and, therefore, he did not have the opportunity to consult with me regarding a matter he must now inform me about. As of the beginning of September the Office of Press Affairs is being reorganized, thus necessitating a change in staff. Therefore, he, the minister, wanted to know if I wouldn't care to resign from the Council on Press Affairs. Moreover, His Majesty would be pleased to promote me to the rank of Privy Councillor, and he, Valuev, would try to get my pension increased. The minister added that members of the censorship administration might very likely find it uncomfortable under the new system, especially at the beginning: they might be subject to penalties and so on. "With your reputation and record of meritorious service we couldn't have you subjected to that sort of thing."

After these and many other such remarks I "was pleased" to accept Valuev's kind suggestion to resign. It's clear that he wants to get rid of me. I had spoken up openly against his censorship proposal, stressed the need to broaden the Council's rights and to limit the minister's arbitrary powers. Now that his proposal has won out and he is absolute master of the Council, my presence there could be an eyesore to him. Moreover, what could I accomplish there now? The press issue is a lost cause and I would be unable to serve honestly and independently, as I have done until now.

1 September. Received notice of my promotion to Privy Councillor.

10 September. Our ultrarussophiles are violently opposed to the West. The Western nations have suffered much, but only because they have worked so hard to accomplish something. We have suffered passively, and thus have accomplished nothing. Our common folk are steeped in barbarism; our intelligentsia is corrupt and rotten; and the government is powerless to do any kind of good.

14 September. Valuev actually tried to make my departure as rewarding as possible for me. He wanted to raise my 1,700 ruble pension by 2,500, which, of course, would have been a great comfort. But K.K. Grot opposed it and granted a total pension of 3,000.

28 September. Goncharov told me yesterday that the Council was in an utter state of chaos. The chairman, Shcherbinin, is an absolute nonentity, and Fuchs tries to take over everything. I was remembered there as the only one who could stand up and fight.

When I was at Prince Vyazemsky's, I told him frankly what a big mistake Valuev had made by assuming personal responsibility for press affairs, thus depriving the Council of this responsibility. He has paid dearly for it. The public is very angry with Valuev.

3 October. Madame Ladyzhenskaya, with whom I recently became acquainted, invited me to her home. She wanted my advice about the education of

her children—two boys and a girl. Like all parents these days, myself included, she doesn't know what to do with them—how, where, and with whose
help, to educate them. Our schools are in such a chaotic state, thanks to the
wise and solicitous management of the past few ministers of education. In
the gymnasiums, for example, the childrens' heads are stuffed with too many
subjects, names and dates, without any meaning or awareness of purpose.
And, to boot, the celebrated debate continues: should we have *classical* or
real gymnasiums? Meanwhile pedagogics, with its new theories, views and so
forth, has finally reached the point where everyone is completely confused
about how and what to teach.

5 October. The *Bell* is rattling like a cracked chunk of iron. Failure has made
Herzen lose his head. He thought he could inspire all Russia to follow him
along his path to a new Russia, or, I should say, to its own destruction—but
he didn't succeed. Now, "dipping his poisoned pen in the spittal of a mad
dog," he flings invective around in the most indecent fashion. His letter to
the emperor on the occasion of the heir's death—was the height of indecency.
It wasn't even clever. Even Herzen's wit as a pamphleteer, a talent with which
he is unquestionably endowed, was of no help here. Whom is he trying to
convince with his coarse invective? Meanwhile, how much good he could do,
even now, by talking sensibly and calmly; by criticizing boldly and energetically without resorting to invective; without giving vent to his personal anti-
pathies and allowing the bitterness of deceived or injured pride to weaken the
effectiveness of his words. One only sees his rage now, but rage isn't evidence
and doesn't convince anyone. We have so much material available for constructive criticism, and we are not only failing to deplete our stock of it, but,
on the contrary, are adding to it daily. Does he need character-types? We've
no shortage of them either. My God, Valuev alone would make a marvelous
profile of a conceited bureaucrat; or Golovnin could serve as a model for the
scheming type.

23 October. Conversation with Tyutchev. He told me that his daughter (a
maid of honor at the Court) was marrying Aksakov. Also, that the *Day* was
suspending publication because Aksakov was losing money on it at the rate of
some three thousand a year.

24 October. Dreadful rumors are circulating about the Simbirsk fires, which
a commission had just finished investigating. They say it was not Poles who
had burned Simbirsk, but a battalion of Russian soldiers, whose leader, some
colonel, was the leading culprit and instigator of this unprecedented villany.
Apparently, robbery was the motive. They say the government doesn't dare
make this information public because of the shame it would bring on the
entire nation, especially after everything that was said and written about the
Poles' role in setting the fires. Can this be true?

1 November. Received a letter and photograph from Pecherin in Dublin. How
many memories are associated with this dear face, which, judging from his

picture, has hardly changed! It's all there: the very same gentleness in his features, the same good nature, the same intelligent, distinctive expression in the whole cast of his face. His letter brims with evidence of a keen, observant, intelligent mind, of knowledge acquired through study and experience. He speaks of Russia with affection although it is not evident that he wants to return.

8 November. It is clear that Valuev is hoping with Fuchs's help to stifle anything in our press that he considers harmful. Good luck! It seems to me that Valuev has taken on a task beyond his strength and ability, and, in general, beyond the strength and ability of any civil servant.

We should do two things under these circumstances. In the first place, since the government has acknowledged our press to be so mature that it could free it from preliminary censorship, it necessarily and inescapably follows that it must, *in fact,* grant it greater freedom. Secondly, a council should be created within the ministry which would enjoy the public's respect (not the kind of council we now have)—and it should be given a certain measure of independence as well as responsibility, as suggested, for instance, in Korf's memo. Such a force would lean heavily on public opinion and would not be accused of bureaucratic tyranny. But, in Russia they want to follow the pattern of French press laws. It's quite a different matter there. In general, their system is well defined and consistently followed. It doesn't constantly vacillate like ours, and its administrators are far more intelligent and tactful than ours. Moreover, however much the French press may complain of the despotism of its administration, it still has greater freedom than ours. The French administration is mostly concerned with protecting and strengthening dynastic principles (which we don't have to worry about); unrelated matters or those that do not threaten the imperial government are not pursued. In our country, everything arouses apprehension. Therefore, it would really be better to retain preliminary censorship for a while longer. But, having already considered it obsolete—which it is—they should have made every effort to put press affairs into more dependable hands than the hands of those civil servants who see everything through the eyes of bureaucrats. The main thing is to create a *real Council!*

12 November. A first warning to the *Contemporary* was printed in the *Northern Post* for "indirectly condemning the principles of private property" (in the August issue, pages 308-321) and for directly condemning the same principles (in the September issue, pages 93-96); for inciting people against the upper and propertied classes; and for insulting the institution of marriage. Although I openly condemn the present state of our press laws, nonetheless, I can't help thinking in this case that the "thief got what he deserved!" If such journals as the *Contemporary* and the *Russian Word* deliberately run up against a third warning and its known consequences, one can scarcely have any sympathy for them. I looked through the pages cited in the *Northern*

Post: unless we allow unconditional freedom of the press, I would say that these pages contain unprintable material.

13 November. Whoever is a keen observer of the course of human events knows that there are periods in the life of human societies when affairs become so complicated and hopelessly tangled that it is totally impossible to untangle them by the usual means and the knot must be severed by the sword. It seems this is exactly our situation now. Griboedov, in his comedy, voiced this sentiment very cleverly through one of his characters, a shallow-minded individual: "radical medication is needed now, because the stomach won't digest any more."[n]

One feels the inevitability of revolution in the air, and the conviction that it is coming grows ever stronger and more widespread. We stand at the brink of anarchy; in fact, it has already begun. I don't mean the kind that has been concealed for so long in the tyranny of our authorities and officialdom under the guise of external order. Rather does this anarchy lie in the patent scorn for law, order, and the government itself, which is neither feared nor respected; it lies in the general dissoluteness; in the lack of safety for people or property; in short, in all the intellectual, moral, and administrative ferment, in this obvious chaos which pervades every area of our civil society.

The most terrifying kind of rule is rule by the rabble. Personal despotism is stifling and doesn't give people freedom to breathe. Rule by aristocracy plunges people into deep apathy. But rule by the rabble means wanton robbing and killing.

It would be disastrous if the democratizing ideas which our quill-driving lads are so fervently preaching succeed in unleashing upon us a still half-civilized, drunken people that lacks moral and religious training. What terrible deeds this rabble could commit in the name of the tsar, who couldn't possibly be everywhere at once to restrain them! Yet, it will obey no one but him.

22 November. We Russians are an awfully wordy people. We either spew forth a lot of nonsense or come out with something witty; but we never go deeply into anything. This is our passion and our curse. For that reason, whatever we undertake begins and evaporates in words. It remains where it started, and most of the time never moves beyond the proposal stage. We don't have factual information about anything and, moreover, aren't very concerned about getting the facts. Yet, we make the most final and irrevocable judgements about every conceivable subject.

3 December. A reading at my home this evening. Goncharov read Count Tolstoy's drama *The Death of Ivan the Terrible,* which has been much discussed in public. It is remarkable for its faithful portraits of Ivan the Terrible and Boris Godunov and its masterful construction. Quite a few guests came for the reading, especially ladies. A.S. Starynkevich, whom I dubbed Queen Anna

---

[n] From Griboedov's *Woe from Wit,* act 4, scene 5.

for her stately figure and outstanding beauty, was the most radiant of them all. I had also invited my Academy colleagues, including Pekarsky. I was quite certain he wouldn't come. He scoffs at poetry, considering it much beneath his academic mind.

19 December. Tyutchev described the conversation he had had with Valuev about press affairs. He told the minister frankly that the repressive system he had adopted would lead to no good. Tyutchev was furious about the Council; he definitely refused to participate in its affairs. Goncharov feels the same way. None of this is in the least surprising. The minister himself approaches problems more like a petty official than an administrator; and he doesn't appear to have any understanding of the importance of ideas. He tries to stifle them with bureaucratic office procedures and measures.

23 December. Goncharov spent the evening with me. He was very distressed about his intolerable situation at the Council on Press Affairs. It appears that censorship affairs had never been in such wretched hands, that is, in the hands of individuals who are ignorant and hostile to thought.

31 December. Pletnyov died in Paris. I just received the news from Grot, whom I met on Nevsky Prospekt. I had known Pletnyov for some thirty-five years. We frequently were very close, especially at the beginning of our friendship. Later it cooled and again revived, but in recent years it had cooled once and for all. The reason for our unstable relationship was the feeling of suspicion his behavior would arouse in me, behavior which was completely contrary to my direct and open ways. I felt there was something insincere about him, and on two occasions he actually did me great harm. On the first occasion, he succeeded in smoothing things over, and I began to believe in him again; but after the second occasion I became more cautious. In general, he didn't possess any striking positive or negative qualities. He had, on the whole, a good disposition, but wasn't capable of concentrated work or of engaging in any activity that would disturb his tranquility or interfere with his interests. He always wore the most relaxed expression and had a clean-cut look about him.

Pletnyov was always restrained, yet this restraint did not flow from strength of character, but from fear, as if he were afraid to do anything that might invite reproach. And this was a result of his inability to feel things deeply and to display his feelings sincerely and boldly.

1866

3 January. The most shocking brigandage, robberies, and savage villainy are being committed openly not only in St. Petersburg, but all over Russia. The administration consoles itself and others by saying that this is nothing new, but that it was never publicized. However, the position adopted by the government under these circumstances is a complete enigma. Why does the administration view this with complete indifference and refrain from taking any action, as if the interests of the public are completely foreign to it? In any kind of organized government, the administration, even the weakest, always makes at least a pretense of acting. But in our case one would even doubt the existence of a government if, from time to time abominations, like embezzlement of public funds, a flagrant violation of justice, or some strange measure beneficial to thieves rather than peaceful citizens, didn't bring it to the public's attention.

9 January. A polemic has developed between the *zemstvos* and the administration: that is, the ministry of internal affairs. The ministry's articles appeared in the *Northern Post.* Some *zemstvos,* particularly St. Petersburg's, have expressed their dissatisfaction with the restrictions imposed by directives coming from administrative authorities. They have decided to ask for an expansion of their rights, and, most important of all, have requested that the authorities desist from interfering in the exercise of their powers. Perhaps these pressures on the part of the *zemstvos* are not completely warranted, perhaps they are also premature, as the *Northern Post* commented. But the fact remains that our administration doesn't enjoy our trust, that everyone is fed up with their arbitrariness and abuses, and, therefore, it is not surprising that people will do their utmost to weaken it and will have as little as possible to do with it in respect to their own affairs and interests.

10 January. A second warning has been issued to the *Russian Word,* mainly for Pisarev's article on Conte's teachings.° (see *Northern Post,* no. 6). Chicanery! We are reverting to the archcensorship of the past. I far from sympathize with what the *Russian Word* preaches. But we must do one of two things: either, with the expansion of freedom of the press we must permit the expression of various opinions and discussion of subjects which were previously discussed only from an official viewpoint, and we must allow debate, or we must remain on our old course of a censored literature and a stifled press.

° Goncharov was responsible for both the first and second warnings, having submitted complaints to the Chief Censorship Administration.

It would have been better not to issue the new regulations, thereby not deluding the public and the press into thinking that we were granting the press greater freedom, when, in reality, we were only drawing the noose tighter.

15 January. A first warning was issued to the *News* for its editorial in the no. 3 issue, which proposed the creation of a central *zemstvo.* Yet this idea had actually been expressed and written about many times during the *zemstvo* meetings in St. Petersburg. In general, the ministry has been very generous with its warnings. It appears to be utterly obsessed with the idea of destroying what gains the press has made in the past ten years, many of which had been approved and guaranteed by imperial order. Of course, these tactics give the impression that it is putting a stop to abuses in the press. But the whole point is that, what the minister of internal affairs considers an abuse is only a natural consequence of an accomplished fact and is an urgent social need, a need permitted by the government itself. Such a policy can only serve to irritate the public and stifle our meagre thought and culture even more.

Kraevsky's trial took place on the 14th, according to an announcement in no. 15 of the *St. Petersburg Bulletin.*[P] He has not been sentenced yet.

16 January. The task of keeping a watchful eye on the press is one of the government's most difficult tasks. The difficulty is compounded when the government does not establish a firm policy which it intends to follow and fails to publicize its policy; when it vacillates between allowing greater liberty and the fear that it has allowed too much. Then, even the most sensible and well-meaning writers do not know what policy to follow. One minute they feel free to range beyond the commonplace; the next, sensing above them the sword of Damocles, they become confused, and the pen, dipped in ink, dies in their hand as they envision harsh and undeserved punishments. Such is now the situation with our press. The government should either have postponed the new liberalizing press law for some time, or it should have retained the system of preliminary censorship, making it as sensible as possible; or, having issued the new law, it should have accepted its inevitable consequences. A law that is not applied, a law created only for show, is deceitful and a trap, ill befitting a decent government. It is said that the government certainly cannot allow various abuses. But what exactly are these abuses? Herein lies the problem. Indeed, every citizen understands very well that it is wrong to speak out against God and Christianity, against the emperor and the existing form of government, to violate the honor and safety of other citizens; but when it comes to the press and ideas, what exactly is to be considered encroachment in these sacred areas, if it is not clearly expressed and publicized? Here is a broad area for all sorts of confusion, misunderstandings, arbitrary interpreta-

[P] As publisher of the *Voice*, Kraevsky was tried for an article written by I. A. Ostrikov on religious intolerance in the Ostsee region. The censorship department saw "an insurrection against the government" in the article and therefore demanded exile with penal servitude for Kraevsky.

tions and personal differences. And from this could stem terrible punishments
and oppression that could stifle all development of thought. For example,
Kraevsky was brought to trial and threatened with nothing less than penal
servitude. Yet, when he spoke of the administration's oppression of the
raskolniks, he based his statements on the imperial will, as expressed by the
emperor during the Polish uprising. It left no doubt that the *raskolniks* would
no longer be persecuted for their beliefs from that moment on. All that the
editors could be reproached for was two or three harsh words which it would
have been better to tone down. But penal servitude for this is a terrible thing!
And yet, the minister of internal affairs, in justifying his decision to bring the
editor to court, specifically cited the new press law. In Kraevsky's article the
strongest statements were the following: "A long time ago freedom of religion
for old believers was proclaimed among us," and thus, that is, by the tsar's
will, a "privilege" was granted. The minister interpreted the author's statements as rebellious and daring to express the royal will. But wasn't this what
the emperor himself expressed to the dissenters? Can one be accused of daring to proclaim the royal will when ministers, adjutant generals and the like
are authorized to quote these words? In the second warning to the *Russian
Word* a reason is cited: "It is an indirect attempt to give practical aid to communism." This one word, "indirect," can drive anyone who writes to despair, for what cannot be interpreted as an indirect attack on God, the tsar and
so on?

I attended a soirée at Troinitsky's. I had a lengthy conversation with Senator Tsee, who had once been chairman of the Censorship Committee. He completely agreed with my opinion on the situation regarding the press. He also
thought that it would have been better to retain preliminary censorship for
some time rather than handle the matter so clumsily. As far as the haste and
clumsiness with which this new censorship reform was introduced, I had
spoken about this as far back as a month and a half ago with Count Adlerberg
in Tsarskoe Selo.

There were many guests at Troinitsky's. Everyone expressed strong disapproval of penal servitude for Kraevsky. They felt that this [new press] law
had no relationship to the case at hand. The warning to the *News* was also
generally criticized. Everyone says that the Office of Press Affairs is in very
bad hands. People are impatiently awaiting the court's decision on Kraevsky.
The deputy minister himself sees in this affair a big blunder on the part of the
ministry. He expressed this heatedly to Goncharov who was present and who
replied that he was quite helpless in this matter. He didn't have the voice or
lung-power to shout down the council's decision, and, besides, what could
one do when the pressure came from above, that is, from the minister. Troinitsky strongly attacked this last statement. I even began to feel sorry for poor
Goncharov.

22 January. They say that the opinion of the court is divided in Kraevsky's
case. Some of the judges can find absolutely no justification for the charges,

while others are suggesting a twenty-five ruble fine. In any case, Valuev has suffered a crushing defeat. The general feeling among the public and in court ran against him and his bureaucrats. They can't fathom how it was possible to raise such a storm and compose such an absurd accusation based on laws which don't have the slightest relationship to the case.

8 February. Student banquet. One hundred people dined at Demuth's. Plenty of food and drink, drunkenness, smoke and noise, and it was jammed!

I returned home from the affair around 7 P.M. and found a note from Prince Vyazemsky, inviting me to a soirée to hear a reading of *The Death of Ivan the Terrible*. I went. Several princesses, countesses and others were there. Of my friends—Prince Obolensky, Prince Urusov, and Vladimir Karamzin. Markevich read, and very well, too. He has a particular gift for reading.

12 February. Meeting at the Academy yesterday about the Uvarov drama prize. Sreznevsky spewed forth the strangest opinions about poetry and drama. The others remained silent. A powerful coalition appears to be forming against Tolstoy's drama, *The Death of Ivan the Terrible*. Serves him right, they say! Why doesn't he belong to any literary circle; and he's an aristocrat to boot—both in name and by virtue of his position in Court. Imagine, they say, a man with such great talent, who has written such a fine piece, bringing in the likes of grave-diggers or self-styled leaders of the younger generation!

13 February. How coarsely these naturalist fellows treat the human soul, considering it part and parcel of the human flesh. They stare at it coldly through their microscopes, plunge their scalpels into it, and are disinterested in anything the microscope or the scalpel cannot divulge. Naturally, they believe only their own feelings. But is everything that is knowable available to them alone? Isn't there, my dear Horatio, something else in nature that even our wise men do not dream of, something that is concealed so deeply or contains elements that neither our feelings nor our instruments can reach? In that case, how can I, in good conscience, become a materialist? Why does materialism have a greater right to our trust in what concerns the most vital part of man than does idealism? Both of them are ignorant in this sphere. But at least our spiritual interests are harmonious with idealism, without which man would be no more than a beast, a scoundrel, and the most pathetic creature.

10 March. I read my review of Pisemsky's drama, *The Eagles of Catherine II* at the Academy. In it I generally criticize blind adherence to facts in science and art, an affliction of our realist-writers and our academicians.

11 March. I was elected to membership in the Society for Assistance to Needy Women. Time will tell me what sort of organization it is. In general I have little faith in our organizations. Many women are active in it; perhaps this will be for the better.

17 March. I visited Prince Odoevsky, who had come here for a few days. I hadn't seen him for about eight years. He has scarcely changed physically and otherwise is the same as ever. He is still the same intelligent person, inclined toward speculation; the same noble, honest man, active and involved, as before; and with that same youthful face. Only his legs, he says, are serving him poorly.

1 April. A first warning has been issued to the *Moscow Bulletin.*[q] No matter what government is in power, it cannot, until it is overthrown, tolerate the existence of any force that attempts to share the reins of power. The *Moscow Bulletin*, encouraged by success, has recently tried to assume such a role. Its followers even spread rumors that the government would not dare to treat the *Moscow Bulletin* as it did other newspapers, and they were sure that if it did happen, Moscow would be the scene of a rebellion of sorts. On the other hand, their opponents feel that it is time to pour a bucket of cold water over the heads of publishers who are drunk with success.

The warning was issued because of an article which appeared in no. 61. But it appears that this article only served as a pretext to crack down on the paper.

4 April. I just this instant heard the horrifying news of the attempt made on the emperor's life as he strolled in the Summer Garden around 3 o'clock. The details, of course, are not yet known. We'll learn them tomorrow.

So this is what Russia has finally come to. Who is responsible? Poles? Or our nihilists?

The *Moscow Bulletin* did not accept the warning and decided to pay a fine for three months. Their reply to the warning was a lengthy article, the essence of which was as follows: "I have attacked you far more harshly in the past and you have never said anything." I wonder what Valuev is up to. However, it's said that the warning was issued on imperial orders, which Katkov must have known about. It seems to me that Katkov is behaving very badly. He is trying in every possible way to harass the government, although he knows very well how harmful such tactics are these days. Success has blinded him completely and has made him arrogant to the point where he has lost all sense of decency.

5 April. I still haven't heard the details of yesterday's despicable incident. The newspapers say only that an attempt was made on the emperor's life as he was entering his carriage after a stroll in the Summer Garden. He was saved from certain death by factory-hand Komissarov, who struck the villain under the elbow just as he was aiming his pistol at the emperor. We still have not learned the villain's identity or the motive for this vile act. I went to the Roman Catholic Academy today via the Nikolaevsky Bridge and found Palace Square jammed with people. I announced at the Academy that I was not up to lecturing today. Evidently the young people shared my grief at the attempt

---

[q] The warning was dictated by the desire of the minister of internal affairs to curb this influential newspaper and subordinate it to his policies.

on the emperor's life as well as my joy that no harm had come to him. Some say the villain is a nihilist who had abandoned his gymnasium studies. Others say he is a student at the Academy of Medicine and Surgery.

No results yet: the villain is inconsistent in his testimony.

The emperor, thanking those who had gathered to congratulate him on his escape, said: "It is true, Russia still needs me." And then he added to his son and heir who, sobbing, had flung his arms about his neck: "Well, my boy, your turn has not yet come."

I went to Tyutchev's where I met Delyanov. Naturally, the assassination attempt was the main topic of conversation. Later, we discussed the *Moscow Bulletin*, for which a second warning is being prepared. Even Tyutchev, who until now had always defended it, was displeased with it.

9 April. The ovations and demonstrations in connection with the emperor's escape from death surpass anything that Russian imagination and patriotic fervor have ever conceived before. The same ecstatic mood prevails in both St. Petersburg and Moscow.

The public is literally carrying Komissarov on its shoulders. They say an aide-de-camp has been assigned to him to coach him in Court manners. Everyone is asking about the identity of the criminal. Is he Polish or Russian? It is generally hoped that he is not Russian. It's impossible to glean anything from the mass of rumors and speculation. It seems the Russian people have never been as aroused as they are now.

I keep thinking that the criminal is a tool of Russian nihilism which is tied to the revolutionary movement abroad. Their obvious intent is to produce a state of turmoil in Russia.

10 April. A second warning was not issued to the *Moscow Bulletin*, although the Council had already prepared it. The minister wouldn't agree to it. The *Moscow Bulletin*'s supporters are celebrating their victory.

13 April. The emperor's erstwhile assassin is a native of Saratov province, Serdob district and the son of a landowner. He is Dimitry Vladimirov Karakozov. It is a Tatar name meaning "dark eye." He was an auditor at Moscow University. An article about it appeared in the *Russian Veteran*, no. 93.

15 April. Komissarov doesn't drink even the weakest wine. His glass is usually filled with honey when toasts are offered at the dinners to which he is invited. His fellow villagers visited him and tried to convince him to try a jigger full. "No boys," he replied to them, "I won't drink. I must burn purely, like a candle before an icon."

Golovnin was relieved of his post as minister of education. Count Dimitry Andreevich Tolstoy was appointed in his place, at the same time retaining his post as chief procurator of the Holy Synod.

16 April. Apparently Golovnin certainly didn't expect to be overthrown so quickly.

Everyone attributes Golovnin's dismissal to Muraviev's influence. The affair of the Moscow students was also very damaging to him. It was discovered that an organization existed among the students, which had as its aim the dissemination of democratic and socialistic ideas among the masses. Several of the students were brought here before an investigating commission.

It is rumored that Pyotr Lavrovich Lavrov was arrested, too, and also Blagosvetlov, editor of the *Russian Word*. As far as Lavrov's arrest is concerned, I had expected it. He is the rabid ringleader of the nihilists and a propagandist for all sorts of freedoms.

26 April. Here is what I heard from an authoritative source. Muraviev asked the minister of internal affairs to put an end to the scandalous business with the *Moscow Bulletin*. He also added that he considered it impossible to shut down the paper.

How will Valuev manage to squirm out of this really scandalous affair? The *Moscow Bulletin* has gone so far in its resistance to the ministry, that a retreat on the part of the ministry would strongly compromise it.

Observation, experiment, the gathering of materials and facts are, it stands to reason, necessary to science and constitute its present-day orientation as well as its merit. But this approach has also generated a fad among petty scientists who apply it indiscriminately, collecting all sorts of rubbish and meaningless detail for study.

However, I am ready to accept the need for all this trivia in the total scheme of science, but I cannot tolerate it when this trivia is placed on a pedestal and is used to mute the meaning and essence of more important phenomena.

30 April. Lavrov has definitely been arrested. They say that another group of nihilists was brought here yesterday from Moscow for interrogation.

6 May. They say that the investigation of the attempt on the emperor's life is unearthing some amazing facts. An additional three or four accomplices have been discovered in this terrible affair. They said in their testimony that they had acted in the government's interest. The latter, they claimed, had clearly indicated a liking for democracy and a desire to crush, weaken, or even destroy the nobility. But a stupid and uneducated people did not understand what they were trying to do for them and, at that point, it was decided to kill the one person who was capable of restraining the people. Then it would be easy to rouse the people against the nobility, or rather, against the entire educated class.

As a result of this testimony Muraviev called an emergency session of the Council of Ministers, which was held several days ago. Supposedly a check was made of officials suspected of harboring or disseminating democratic ideas. As a result, some people's stock, Nikolai Milyutin's, for example, is said to have fallen sharply. A committee, similar to the Committee for Public Safety was organized for an investigation of Russia's internal affairs. Of course nothing sensible will come of it because the people on the committee are not equipped intellectually or morally to handle such serious, patriotic matters without giving primary consideration to their own personal ambitions. Professionally and morally they are complete vacuums.

8 May. Two warnings to the press in no. 98 of the *Northern Post:* one to the *Moscow Bulletin,* the other to the *Voice.*

The *Moscow Bulletin* encourages hostile and distrustful attitudes toward government officials. Of course our government figures are not noted for outstanding ability or character, but, to practically accuse them of treason, as does the *Moscow Bulletin,* is going a bit too far and amounts to an appeal for anarchy. Whom should we put in their place? A *zemskoe sobranie?* With the chaos we now have everywhere, it, too, would scarcely be equal to the task. Replace them with other people? But where can we get them, and where is the guarantee that they will do any better? As enormously inept and incapable as our present administration may be, the more serious problems at the moment are the widespread dissension and upheavals—the crisis which our nation is now experiencing.

The wife of our Dr. Waltz went abroad several days ago. She took with her 100 rubles in bank notes and 200 railroad bonds guaranteed by the government. Yesterday, Waltz received a letter from her asking for some other kind of money, because her money is not being accepted. She visited seven bankers and not one of them would agree to exchange her securities for hard currency. One of them said: "How can we give you money for them when nobody knows what will happen in your country in a few months?" They are sure a revolution is about to begin here.

11 May. I can't understand why the *Voice* was given a warning. I read the two feuilletons (no. 109, no. 114) cited in the warning, but simply cannot understand the legal basis for it. Perhaps the ministry wanted to demonstrate to the public that it was not singling out the *Moscow Bulletin,* but that its blows fell equally on all. With such warnings hanging over one's head, it becomes impossible to publish a newspaper. How can one possibly foresee what one might have to answer for?

The *Moscow Bulletin* is on the verge of suspension. What a shame that it has driven itself to suicide.

12 May. The *Northern Post* (no. 99) published the following announcements: publication of the *Moscow Bulletin* has been suspended for two months. The *St. Petersburg Bulletin* and the *Contemporary* are being brought to trial.

23 June. Cholera in St. Petersburg!

I can scarcely recall an administrative measure that has provoked such unanimous and widespread indignation as the . . . banning of the *Contemporary* and the *Russian Word.*

28 June. Cholera is spreading in St. Petersburg. There are distressing rumors about its savage course. They say death comes very rapidly, even when medical aid is given.

1 July. I went to the city. Cholera is spreading rapidly although this epidemic is not as severe as the epidemics of 1830 and 1848. However, the dying suffer cruelly, and few of those stricken recover.

A month and a half has passed since we've been in the country. I haven't felt up to par either physically or mentally. Physically, I feel a sort of listlessness and fatigue, and mentally—a lack of energy. I'm frequently torn by internal conflicts, am disinclined to work, and even feel despondent.

I've started work again on my autobiographical notes, which I had dropped in 1854. It's going well, thanks to my good memory and my diary. But I haven't resumed my major work—the completion of Galich's biography.

15 July. Our gymnasiums ought to meet three requirements. They should:
1. prepare young people for universities
2. prepare them for further technical education and
3. give a terminal general education to those who do not have a vocation.

It appears that the basic difference between proponents of classical schools and *Realschulen* is that the former seek to establish a foundation, an abstract base, so to say, for education, while the latter want to satisfy society's current needs. Some say we should concern ourselves with creating the kind of principles and base for intellectual development which would equip us to face the future with confidence. In brief, what they have in mind is the development of mental discipline. Others maintain that we need the most relevant kind of knowledge, the kind whose application is required at every step in our daily lives. Without it, they say, we certainly cannot follow the advances of civilization, advances which flow only from practical knowledge—from knowledge which encompasses people's basic, or, rather, real interests. Who is right and who is wrong? Both sides are right. We ought to reconcile both demands. Give both of them the necessary latitude. That is the task of an intelligent administrator.

But *real* education is senseless without technical schools.

The gymnasiums, they say, should offer general education. But this still does not answer the question: should this general education have a classical or *real* foundation? [1]

31 July. A delegation from the North American States arrived in St. Petersburg several days ago. It was given a splendid reception and ovation. [2]

The American ambassador was in Pavlovsk Monday evening. Huge crowds assembled and there was a magnificent display of festive lights. The public behaved respectably, and it seems that the Americans were very pleased.

1 September. Yesterday the Supreme Criminal Court sentenced Karakozov to death by hanging.

2 September. A third warning has been issued to the *St. Petersburg Bulletin,* and it has been suspended for three months. So, Valuev, having failed to over-power the bear in the woods (Katkov), has pounced upon a poor, defenseless hare and, together with Shcherbinin and Fuchs, is mercilessly destroying it.

3 September. Karakozov was hung on Smolensk Field. An enormous crowd watched the execution. Ought death sentences to be carried out publicly?

9 September. Meeting at the Academy of Sciences of the commission for the award of the Uvarov drama prizes. I read my review of Count Tolstoy's trag-edy *The Death of Ivan the Terrible.* I nominated the author for first prize. There were seven of us on the commission: Veselovsky—chairman, Ustryalov, Grot, Sreznevsky, Pekarsky, Kunik, and myself. Four were in favor, that is, Veselovsky, Ustryalov, Grot and myself. The rest were opposed. So, this drama remains uncrowned. It was a disgraceful and comic affair. The worst ignoramuses in belle-lettres were able to block the award since the bylaws re-quire a two-thirds majority.

4 October. It seems that the Valuev administration sees the press as its per-sonal enemy and grows increasingly hostile toward it with each passing day.

8 October. Soirèe at Goncharov's, where I made the acquaintance of Count Tolstoy, author of *The Death of Ivan the Terrible.* He is a very pleasant person with gentle aristocratic manners and is very intelligent. He thanked me for voting for his tragedy in the competition for the Uvarov prize. Yurkevich, chairman of the theatre committee, was also present, and we talked about staging *Ivan the Terrible.* Count Tolstoy read some of the ideas he had jotted down on how the actors should conceive the leading roles of Ivan and Godunov. These ideas show how much and how deeply the author has thought about his work. In many respects they coincided with those I had expressed in my re-view. The discussion continued until 2 A.M.

14 October. Count Tolstoy came to see me. He thanked me warmly for my article about him. The first half had appeared in yesterday's *St. Petersburg Bulletin.* He is now writing a second drama on the Fyodor period, in which Godunov is the central character. Judging from the plan which he briefly sketched out for me, this, too, will be a very fine work. Now he is trying to arrange for the staging of *Ivan the Terrible.* The empress is very interested, but doubts that actors can be found who could do it justice.

18 October. An article appeared in the *Voice* (no. 286) in connection with my review of *Ivan the Terrible.* The article criticized the Academy for deny-ing it the Uvarov prize and cited my review.

The public has the right to demand respect for Russian literature from the Academy's Department of Russian Language and Literature.

26 October. Valuev and Count Shuvalov are moving rapidly toward joint police rule of Russia: Valuev through the general police, Shuvalov through the secret police. Their chief goal at the moment is to undermine the courts, that is, to put them under the control of administrative authority. Valuev has already undermined the courts in press matters. He is attempting to deprive the prosecutor of the right to make his own judgements concerning charges involving press violations, which are presented to the court by the ministry of internal affairs. Norov asked me to compose a memorandum for him on this issue for the State Council, which I did and returned to him today. All it will do is make old Norov and me feel a little better, deluding ourselves into thinking that his voice carries any weight around here! In the meantime the emperor has already agreed with Valuev's opinion, and the review of his proposal in the State Council will merely be a formality. And so, bureaucracy has already won its first victory over the authority of our courts. Poor Russian justice!

2 November. They are reacting unfavorably in Moscow, too, to the Academy's failure to award the Uvarov prize to Count Tolstoy's play. An article disapproving of the Academy's action appeared in *Contemporary Annals* (no. 36). Bezobrazov, who had recently returned from Moscow, told me yesterday that the Muscovites were speaking very disparagingly about those who had voted against the play.

3 November. Storm in the Academy's Department of Russian Language and Literature on account of Count Tolstoy's play. Bychkov brought the *Annals* article to the meeting, where it was read aloud by Sreznevsky, for all to hear. There was nothing objectionable in it. Grot remarked that we had made a big mistake by denying the award to a work which fully deserved it.

4 November. Valuev put through his measure, after all, which strengthens the authority of the governors. It had been rejected by the State Council in July or August. (See the *Voice*, no. 303, for the imperial order of October 28th.)

5 November. What most thinking people have feared has come to pass: a period of reaction is setting in, a turning back.

The emancipation of the peasants was unquestionably a great event. Yet its greatness also consists of the fact that it laid the foundation for other inevitable and equally great reforms. Without this to look forward to, it would have been an incomplete measure. To abandon the liberated masses without the guidance of experienced, educated and intelligent people—is to abandon some to childish ignorance and to plant distrust in others. This would be a big mistake on the part of the government.

Here are the fruits of the famous measure to strengthen the authority of the governors. The Nizhegorod governor issued an order (the *Voice*, no. 307) which labels as nihilists all women wearing round hats, dark glasses, hoods, short hairdos, and not in crinolines. They are to be escorted to the police station where they are to be ordered to shed their garments and don crinolines. If they refuse to obey, they are to be shipped out of the province. In their zeal, the administration is going to such extremes that its strange orders are beginning to border on the comical. The order I described above was issued by Ogarev. However, this was only the beginning; the best is yet to come. Naturally, governors will be found, who, intoxicated with their unlimited power, in a burst of zeal, will compose orders outdoing this one. And not only governors, but other administrators, too.

4 December. The Office of Press Affairs is following a totally erroneous course. It has taken to applying only one kind of force—police force, having completely forgotten that there exists yet another, very important kind of force which is available to them—a moral one. It appears to have made up its mind not to recognize the importance of psychological or moral force under any circumstances.

The crassest form of blindness, not only unbefitting a statesman, but even an ordinary official, is to think that one can govern these days merely by employing police measures, by the issuance of circulars, bans and the like.

The Office of Press Affairs has decided to operate in utter defiance of the most supreme of all earthly sovereigns—the spirit of the times, a spirit which irresistibly demands freedom of thought and speech. This is a concession which it will have to make if it wants to prevent a resurgence of the most disastrous licentiousness and abuse of thought and speech in the future, when it is forced to slacken the reins. Valuev is not a stupid man, but he is a bureaucrat from head to toe, whose grasp of national affairs doesn't go beyond office memorandums and reports, although he occasionally expresses himself grandiloquently. Valuev will do what the public itself, perhaps, would not do: he will lead it to believe implicitly that nothing is believable.

8 December. Once a certain measure of free thought and speech has been permitted, there is no turning back. This freedom must be permitted and acknowledged as a new element in the life of our society in much the same way as the need for various social and administrative changes is acknowledged. Certain abuses of the printed word must then be regarded as a necessary evil. The authorities don't want to ignore them and let them go unpunished—fine! But what should be considered an abuse? The greatest degree of restraint must be exercised here. In general they ought not to show that they see a personal enemy in the printed word as our present Office of Press Affairs tends to do. Such matters should not be approached with a police mentality.

9 December. At a general meeting of the Academy, the president nominated Minister of Education Count D.A. Tolstoy, Dimitry Alekseevich Milyutin, Valuev, and Minister Zeleny for honorary membership. The first two were elected. Count Tolstoy received only three negative votes, Milyutin—two. But when it came to Valuev, four negative votes were cast and he was not elected. To what could Valuev's defeat be attributed, considering the Academy's generosity with honorary memberships? I think that Valuev's treatment of the press was responsible for it. The Academy is a natural protector of the press in its highest sense, and this was probably its way of expressing its disapproval of someone whose role in press matters until now had been limited to persecution. In general, Valuev is very unpopular with the public. His famous circular to the governors also won him few friends.

14 December. The sword of Damocles hangs over the *Moscow Bulletin.* Several days ago, Valuev, on imperial orders, introduced a memorandum to the Committee of Ministers relative to all anti-government articles published by the *Moscow Bulletin* in the past. When the committee members heard the memorandum, they asked why it had been presented to them. Was it for the purpose of passing some sort of measure? Valuev replied that it had been introduced to the committee in keeping with His Majesty's will, and as far as a measure or measures were concerned they would be taken by the administration. The blindness of the *Moscow Bulletin* is beyond comprehension.

Kraevsky has been shown leniency. Instead of being confined to the guardhouse or jail, he was placed under house arrest for two months.

29 December. Annual exercises at the Academy. I read badly, having difficulty making out my handwriting in places. That certainly was stupid of me.

Secretary [K.S. Veselovsky] chided me for having stated that we didn't have first-class talent today either in science or in literature. What about Baer, he wanted to know! I certainly had not forgotten about our Baers, but they belonged to the past.

1867

10 January. Dr. Waltz prescribed a half drop of belladonna for the night. Of course this is nonsense, but I took it anyway, for a drowning man will clutch at a straw. I began the night in an armchair and then shifted to my bed. I slept splendidly, as I haven't slept in a long time. A believer in homeopathy would naturally attribute this to the belladonna, but I attribute it to chance.

13 January. Grech died yesterday. I visited his wife today and, incidentally, asked her to give me some biographical information about him. Despite certain character traits and deeds which provoked the public's wrath time and time again, Grech was an outstanding figure in literature and a man of unquestionable talent and merit. Lately he had almost been forgotten, but such is the fate of many of our eminent people. They must die in order to be remembered and appreciated. Grech was eighty.

16 January. The St. Petersburg *zemstvo* assembly was dissolved by government authorities.[r]

21 January. We have been ruled by fear for the past twenty-five years. And what has it brought us? The disastrous Crimean War, which ended in a disgraceful peace, the Polish insurrection, dreadful disorder in our finances and, in general, all sorts of disorders, demoralization among all classes and nihilism with its villainous attempt at regicide.

23 January. What a strange comparison—nihilism and the *zemstvos!* And this was precisely the comparison that was made, because the St. Petersburg *zemstvo* assembly was dissolved like some secret nihilist society.

27 January. Complaints and grumbling about the dissolution of the St. Petersburg *zemstvo* continue. There isn't a soul who would hesitate to censure Valuev and Shuvalov, who are considered the real culprits in this affair.

Meanwhile, we hear that foreign public opinion, too, is growing increasingly negative toward Russia. Our securities have declined sharply everywhere; our credit is completely shattered; railroad negotiations have taken an unfavorable turn. An editorial in the *Times* says quite bluntly apropos our *zemstvos,* that everything in Russia is so unreliable and uncertain that one ought not to enter into any transactions with it. Bismarck, even before the catastrophe with the

---

[r] Protracted quarrels with Valuev over the budget resulted in their dissolution. The St. Petersburg *zemstvo* had insufficient funds for its operation and therefore levied an additional tax on plants, factories and other industrial institutions. Valuev rebelled against this and ordered the dissolution of the assembly.

zemstvos, delivered a speech about us in the Prussian parliament in an extremely offensive, mocking tone. And this from a power that has close and friendly relations with us! Russia's position grows gloomier and more difficult from day to day.

7 February. Count Shuvalov introduced two proposals to the State Council. The first proposal called for the saturation of the entire area with gendarme agents, because a pernicious spirit pervades the Volga provinces. The count requested 80,000 rubles for this purpose. His other proposal concerned the strengthening of punitive measures against secret societies and against harmful activities in the *zemstvo* assemblies. One member of the State Council remarked that it was highly improper to talk of secret societies and *zemstvos* in the same breath.

11 February. We look upon our government as some sort of god. We think that, like heaven itself, it must tower above society in its intellectual qualities, virtues and knowledge, and therefore we demand near perfection from it. But, is it not a product of the very people it governs? Their intelligence, virtues and vices operate unconsciously and are responsible for everything it does, whether these things are done well or badly. If the government is unstable, inconsistent and impulsive, it is only because all of us, all we Russians, are unstable, inconsistent and impulsive.

14 April. If it heeds the never-ending grandiloquent praise and splendid ovations for Komissarov,[s] folk history will most certainly portray him in an ideal light and, perhaps, make a hero out of him. Basically, he is a very shallow person. I heard some very curious details today about Komissarov from Voronov. Totleben had handed him over to Voronov, so to say, for some education. Voronov spent a whole year with him and couldn't knock anything into his head. He barely managed to upgrade his literacy a bit, or, rather, his illiteracy, and to teach him some rudimentary arithmetic. He still remains the peasant that he was, despite his noble rank and his desire to be accepted in so-called proper society. He understands very well that he has become an important personage and enjoys accepting all kinds of expressions of devotion and respect. He had almost begun to drink some, too, but has stopped for the time being due to Totleben's firm supervision. In general, he is looked after and supervised like an adolescent. Some clever sayings have been ascribed to him, like the one about his "burning purely, like a white candle," but this is pure invention. He never said anything clever, and besides, he couldn't, because he has been an utter dim-wit since the day he was born. On the other hand, here's an example of the sort of thing he is capable of producing. Several days ago, for April 4th [first anniversary of the attempted assassination], some sixty congratulatory telegrams were sent to him from various parts of Russia, including several from governors. Voronov remarked to him that this must

---

[s] Komissarov had foiled the attempt on the life of Alexander II.

give him great pleasure. Komissarov replied: "This you call a pleasure!? It would have been a greater pleasure if they had sent me the money it cost to send these telegrams." It's a good thing that he's being shipped off into the service—or joining up himself, as a hussar in the Pavlograd regiment. Otherwise, idleness would certainly turn him into an alcoholic. His wife is also a simple Russian peasant, but brighter and better looking than he. She even shows a desire to learn and has managed to learn to read and write. But her husband treats her very roughly; and her mother, who lives with them, also is inclined toward excessive drinking and swearing.

19 April. I dropped in to see Tyutchev this morning. He has had foot trouble these past two weeks. We talked for a rather long time. Always about the same thing: how depressing and dismal the picture is everywhere!

3 May. I read Turgenev's new novel, *Smoke.* It has caused quite a sensation. Many people are displeased by Turgenev's apparent criticism of Russia. Of course, he doesn't show a particularly positive attitude toward Russia. A spirit of dissatisfaction with everything that's been done and is being done in Russia runs through the novel. But the gossip and criticism of the novel are generally exaggerated. The novel scarcely deals with our *narodnost.* It is all satire, almost a lampoon of our foreign vagabonds of both sexes. Aristocrats and politicians come under particularly heavy attack, and it serves them right. As far as the novel's literary merits are concerned, I feel it is weaker than many of Turgenev's other works. The story is very lively; the sketches of manners and customs are drawn boldly and with ease. But his characters are shallow, for, in general, they are poorly developed. However, one character stands out sharply as a complete and finished portrait—Irina. All the rest, as I've already said, consist of rather lightly drawn sketches.

24 and 25 May. I have spent the past two days at "Pustynka" [little hermitage], the home of Count Tolstoy, author of *Ivan the Terrible.* Other guests were Markevich, Blagoveshchensky, and Kostomarov. "Pustynka" is a kind of luxurious castle on the banks of the Tosna, about an hour and a quarter from St. Petersburg on the Moscow railroad and about four or five versts from Sablino station. The count's wife, the former Bakhmetieva, turned out to be one of my former pupils. We were received and treated most cordially. Here, by the way, I met Miss Breze, a delightful Scottish lady who speaks poor but understandable Russian. The countess is a very intelligent woman, genial, and well educated. Everything in the house is refined, comfortable and simple. The very location of the estate is interesting. You ride along the vile Ingermanland marshland and suddenly come upon the River Tosna, flanked by high, picturesque banks. On its opposite bank stands the house which, in this setting, presents a beautiful and poetic refuge. On both days the weather was miserable—cold and rainy. Snow lay on the heights near the river. The trees were bare: not a sign of spring.

26 May. A telegram arrived from Paris about a new attempt on the emperor's life. This time it actually was a Pole, one A. Berezovsky, a native of Volynsk province.

28 May. For the past two days there has been intense excitement in the city over the villainous attempt on the emperor's life, and everyone is rejoicing over his latest escape.

Some people console themselves with the fact that it was an individual attempt, and not part of a general Polish conspiracy. But the Poles have displayed such solidarity in their plotting against Russia that one automatically blames every individual episode of this sort on all of them.

2 June. Meeting of the Academy and the commission for the award of the Uvarov prizes. I remembered last year's events, when some members did not want to award the prize to Count Tolstoy on the pretext that an outside opinion had not been submitted. At today's meeting, however, I said that if the Academy did not consider itself competent enough to judge aesthetic and moral issues, it would be better to openly decline this responsibility. This would be far more praiseworthy than acting as a mere messenger who transfers works from an author's hands to the hands of outside reviewers. This was met with deep silence. No one dared acknowledge the Academy as incapable of judging the aforementioned issues. It was decided that I should review all dramas currently being submitted for the Uvarov prize.

6 June. I served in court continuously from 11 A.M. until 8:15 P.M. Two cases involving burglary were tried. In the first case, lots were drawn and I didn't make the jury. But we were told to remain, since another case was coming up. I made the jury this time and, was selected as jury foreman. Two thieves, who had stolen money from a tavern, were being tried. The lawyers represented their clients very well, but the public prosecutor, a very young man, was somewhat tedious and inept. On the whole, I came away from the court with an extremely favorable impression. Everything was conducted with great dignity, painstakingly, and with strict regard for all legal requirements. It was clear to the defendants that nothing had been overlooked to ease their fate and that, if they were subjected to punishment, it was lawfully, and not arbitrarily, imposed.

12 June. Our most dangerous internal enemies are not the Poles, not the nihilists, but those government figures who create nihilists by irritating the public and arousing genuine disgust for the government. These are the same people who are dissolving the *zemstvos* and undermining the courts.

Anything is possible if our *zemstvos* and courts are undermined by these enemies. It is said that several days ago Minister of Justice Palen had a talk with the chairman of the local district court and remarked in passing that the jurymen didn't live up to the government's expectations; it had hoped to find a conservative element in them, but had found the reverse.

15 June. Today was my last day of jury duty. Before leaving, I had a long talk with the public prosecutor. He complained most regretfully that the administration was doing everything in its power to subvert the courts. And if the courts should have the misfortune to make a mistake, the administration almost goes wild with joy.

The public prosecutor remarked in passing that when he was going through the districts with the assessors, he was surprised at the common sense and objectivity of the peasants who served as jurors.

19 June. I do not despair of Russia's political future because the people are still a force, but I do despair of there ever being good government in Russia.

22 June. There is an enormous difference between the native intelligence of a government official and his administrative ability. You will hear it said about such-and-such minister that "he's an intelligent man," when he is very mediocre as an administrator. He is capable of coping with routine bureaucratic matters, but he lacks the insight and perspective required on the highest administrative levels. Here, his mind proves to be shallow and narrow. And never have we lacked, as we do today, high ranking administrators of high calibre. And meanwhile, the character of the times so insistently demands them.

There are two things in which it is impossible to have any confidence—Russian administration and the St. Petersburg climate.

6 July. *Moscow* has begun to publish again, and its first editorial was an attack, of course, on its recent suspension.

8 July. A warning to *Moscow* for its first editorial appeared in the *Northern Post* (no. 148). The ministry has decided for once and for all not to stand on ceremony with the press and to reduce it, if it can, to total silence. There is no indication in the warning of the exact nature of the offense, but it speaks obscurely about a violation of the law—the law! ! and about the government's intention to firmly uphold the law, that is, to prosecute the press.

New rules on the *zemstvos* were published. They are being placed under the authority of provincial administrators and chiefs.

Isn't this the first step toward their dissolution? A period of reaction is rapidly setting in.

Why must we label everything *revolution,* including *zemstvos* and court reforms? Are they not a necessity?

23 August. I met Tyutchev at the station a few days ago. He told me that the Office of Press Affairs is raging like a north-easter at *Moscow* for its article in no. 103. The article criticizes the order which states that nothing can be printed about *zemstvo* meetings without permission of the governors. Actually, the article is so clever, truthful and valid that it should provoke the wrath of the entire Valuev administration. They want to issue a second warning to Aksakov, but don't quite know how to go about it.

16 September. Ostrovsky's play, *Vasily Shumsky and Dimitry the Imposter,* was denied the Uvarov prize. Four votes in favor, four against. Exactly what I had expected. Some members openly stated that, after denying the award to Count Tolstoy, it was impossible now to give it to anyone else.

2 November. A second warning has been issued to the *Voice* (see the *Northern Post*, no. 240) for its editorial against the Ostsee Germans in its no. 299 issue. It's a strange state of affairs. The government itself was responsible for raising this storm—this polemic with the Germans—perhaps by its inopportune measure calling for Russian as the official language of the Ostsee region. The Germans raised a cry for all Europe to hear, began to threaten us with secession, Prussian intervention, and so forth. Our newspapers, naturally, replied to this. A press war broke out, and now Minister Valuev has issued a warning to one of the papers for repulsing the German attack and has accused it of having a "reprehensible tone."

11 November. Arseniev, chairman of the Moscow district court, during the trial of someone accused of passing counterfeit currency, removed the defendant's counsel, Prince Urusov, one of Moscow's best-known lawyers. They say this was a result of a secret order given to all court chairmen to remove lawyers who, for any reason, were disliked by the administration. I must say that if this is true, it is a successful, if not a brilliant, episode in a comedy called *Russian Culture and Civilization.*

14 November. The administration is pursuing the wrong policy in press matters by focussing its attention on individual, isolated phenomena rather than concentrating exclusively on the safeguarding of *principles.* Its current approach imparts a downright police character to its work. Certain principles must be safeguarded; those which flow from the spirit of society and are concerned with public safety. This is the main point and the only point. And, as long as a writer doesn't violate these principles, why set up other obstacles for him? This petty faultfinding and hounding of individuals leads nowhere. The following policy should be adopted and strictly adhered to: when the press is given greater latitude and the right to review and criticize government measures and current events, the inevitable consequences of increased freedom must be accepted, that is, the expectation that the press will make use of this right.

Perhaps it would be inappropriate at this time to eliminate the system of warnings. The system itself isn't as much to blame as is its stupid and senseless application. Of all the warnings issued lately by the Valuev administration, a single example of a fully reasonable and fair one could scarcely be found. It couldn't even formulate them properly.

The government has come into conflict with itself on the press issue. When it has been in difficult straits, it has repeatedly turned to the press for assistance and leaned on it for support, but when the need for it would pass, it would begin to look down on the press again and treat it in police fashion. The ministers themselves—Valuev, Golovnin, Count Tolstoy—have ingratiated themselves at times with the press, thereby raising its status and increasing its power. How could one expect it not to sense its importance and power after that?

22 November. I always turn to my diary as to the only friend in whom I can confide all my thoughts and feelings. A chat with it takes the place for me of both society and my so-called friends. This notebook, with its white pages, is a mere trifle; yet I see it as some sort of animated object in which my "I" is reflected and divided into several rays, like light in a prism. What would otherwise appear for an instant and then vanish without a trace, is retained in my consciousness as a small piece of my inner life.

3 December. Poyarkov, Pecherin's nephew, visited me. He corresponds with Pecherin and brought me his warmest regards. He repeated, by the way, Pecherin's explanation of the source of the psychological disturbance that had driven him to abandon Russia and convert to Catholicism. As a child he had had a Swiss tutor, a zealous radical, who had saturated him with liberalism's most burning ideas. At the same time he had a tyrannical father, an old colonel, who was determined to turn his son into a soldier. Poyarkov told me that he had a copy of Pecherin's memoirs which were kept right up to the moment of his departure from Russia. He promised to let me read them.

11 December. All our circles—both literary and social—suffer from the disease of failing to understand the limits to which they can stretch their demands.

The system of classical education which is being introduced here will most certainly fail, not only because of the excessive burden it imposes on the pupils, but also because—and this is the main thing—(the reason why any new system we try fails) because of our inability to implement properly any new system we introduce.

17 December. I visited Troinitsky this morning. He told me, in passing, a very interesting story that he had heard in Odessa from a very intelligent woman of noble family, who was very familiar with various secrets of her time. The story concerns the reason for Speransky's fall. At the beginning of 1812, or at the end of 1811, when Napoleon's intentions toward Russia were becoming more and more obvious, we began to think about our defense. It appears that a plan was presented by Barclay de Tolly, a plan of our future operations which, of course, had to be guarded with the utmost secrecy. Speransky was then at the zenith of his power. The emperor undertook nothing without his advice and this plan was given to him for review. Speransky took it home, put it on a table in his study, and left the house again. In his absence, Magnitsky arrived. He was told that Speransky would return shortly and he decided to wait for him in the study, to which he had always had free access. He noticed the notebook on the table, and since a conscience was not one of Magnitsky's virtues, he read the notebook and discovered the important government secret. About two days later the emperor learned that the French envoy was discussing the government's plan as if he were familiar with it down to the last detail. You can imagine the emperor's reaction. No one had known about the plan except himself, its author, and Speransky. The emperor could, understandably, consider Speransky a traitor, a double traitor, both to his country and their friendship, and he became furious with him. This explains Alexander I's statement in a letter to Parrot that Speransky deserved capital punishment. One thing is not clear—why the emperor said nothing to Speransky about the discovery of the government's secret, but instead, on parting with him on the very eve of his fall, was as warm and gracious to him as he had always been. If he had said something, the matter would undoubtedly have been clarified. Magnitsky's deed would have been exposed, and Speransky would only have been guilty of carelessness.

29 December. Convocation at the Academy of Sciences. Afterwards, all the academicians gathered for dinner at Donon's. The banquet was a rather noisy affair and couldn't end without some debate between the Russian and German elements.

Maikov delivered the following impromptu verse over hot punch:

> The Academy is boozing,
> Not sparing its muscle;
> It's clear who's losing,
> Rus is winning the tussle.

1868

14 February. We don't know what to believe: is or isn't there a famine in Russia? Horrifying news has been coming in from everywhere. An excellent article (by Rosenheim) on this situation appeared in the *Voice*. Finally, on imperial orders, a committee was organized with the heir as chairman. It issued an official announcement about the famine, along with a general appeal for contributions. Meanwhile, the minister of internal affairs has been assuring us in the press that there is no famine and that the people "merely suffer from want."[t] He throws all the blame on the *zemstvos*. But everyone knows that the *zemstvos* are bound hand and foot by the new statute, as a result of which, council chairmen and governors have been granted almost unlimited power over the *zemstvos*.

16 February. The *Moskvich* was banned. There is so much gossip about it that it's impossible to sort out the facts. In this instance, as usual, Valuev is the main target of criticism.

22 February. I spent the evening at Troinitsky's. No one else was there and we chatted for about two and a half hours. He told me, by the way, the real reason for the banning of the *Moskvich*. It was the editorial on the Dankov peasants.[u] After Valuev read the editorial he sent it to the emperor together with his own report on the need to halt insolent attacks on the administration, and he asked for permission to ban the paper. The emperor agreed that this matter should be introduced at the Committee of Ministers. The results are well known. However, in the published decision, this reason was not cited, but, instead, the reason given was that the *Moskvich* was nothing but *Moscow* in disguise. This was Korf's doing. It would have been better to have stated the real reason outright.

1 March. Literary soirée at Vasily Petrovich Botkin's. Count A.K. Tolstoy read his new drama, *Tsar Fyodor Ivanovich*. Present were Goncharov, Kostomarov, Maikov, Stasyulevich, and Fyodor Ivanovich Tyutchev. It is difficult to judge a play from a rapid reading, particularly if you are not doing the reading. However, the characters of Fyodor and Godunov seemed to be very skilfully constructed. The author was able to create a remarkable psychological portrait out of the complete moral and political nonentity that Fyodor was.

[t] The poor harvest of 1867 did cause severe famine in many places, although vehemently denied by the government, particularly by Valuev.

[u] The Dankov peasants were tried for not fulfilling their obligations to their former landowners. The editorial was devoted to this issue and contained a series of attacks against the local administrators and the minister of internal affairs.

4 March. Valuev has retired from the ministry, or the ministry has retired him. His place was taken by Timashev. It appears that the decisive blow was delivered by the famine, which, for incomprehensible reasons, he concealed and did nothing to alleviate. Will his successor be any better?

14 March. Timashev was director of the secret police, chief of the Third Section. Which will finally triumph in him—his police instincts or his new calling as a government official?

3 April. I spent more than two hours talking with my former teacher Vasily Vasilievich Schneider. Paralysis has deprived him of the use of his legs, but it has not affected his mind, which is crystal clear. His memory is still sharp. He told me some interesting stories from his past. He had been intimately acquainted with various important figures of his time, particularly with Speransky, and knew much about the secret course of events. Here is what he told me about the circumstances surrounding Speransky's fall. It is well known that Prince A.I. Chernyshev, who later became minister of war, was sent by Emperor Alexander I on a secret mission to Paris in 1811. Chernyshev was then in the prime of life, at his most handsome, and was noted for his charm and cunning. In Paris he became very intimate with the chief director of Napoleon's war ministry, and even more so with his wife. One night the director was summoned to Napoleon at St. Cloud, where he stayed the whole night. Chernyshev took the director's place by his wife's side and used this opportunity to fill his briefcase with papers from the director's study. He had probably planned this in advance. The following day, early in the morning, he was galloping toward France's borders, and before the disappearance of the papers was noticed, he was out of the country. The stolen papers proved to be very important, for here were the plans for Napoleon's Russian campaign, the sketches, the location of the armies, and so forth; and coded documents were also included. Everything contained in these documents was, of course, a government secret known only to the emperor, Speransky, and Bek. It happened one day that Magnitsky, who was a friend of Speransky's, came to see him when the latter was at work in his study. He managed to spot the contents of the secret documents and then, in his need to boast, broadcast it to the members of the diplomatic corps. This reached the emperor, who had to conclude that Speransky had given away a government secret. That was the reason for his downfall and the explanation of the emperor's words to Parrot: "Speransky did something for which he ought to be shot."[v]

7 April. I spent the evening at Norov's, who, incidentally, told me the following anecdote which he had heard directly from Golitsyn. Empress Catherine II had suddenly decided to visit Revel.[w] A masked ball had been organized in

[v] *Nikitenko's own footnote:* I've already recorded another version of this in my diary, but Schneider vouches for the authenticity of this version which he had heard from people close to Speransky.

[w] Now Tallin, Estonia.

her honor. She sat at her dressing table in the dressing room preparing for it. Suddenly a courier arrived from St. Petersburg with a secret report about Mirovich's conspiracy and the catastrophe that had befallen Ivan Antonovich in Schlüsselburg.[x] She was very upset by this news. She had to act quickly and could no longer bother with the ball. But her failure to appear in the ballroom would have been extremely awkward, especially under these circumstances. The resourceful empress quickly found a way to remedy the situation. She summoned Count Stroganov.

"My dear Count," she said to him, "I must ask a favor of you. Will you do it for me?"

Naturally, Stroganov expressed his complete willingness to help her.

"Here is what I must ask of you. Sit right here in this chair in front of the mirror in my place."

The count was a little surprised; however, he obeyed. Instantly one of the ladies-in-waiting in the dressing room threw a negligée over him, another began to powder him, a third stood in readiness, preparing to clothe him in a gown. Stroganov, no longer surprised, but enraged, jumped from the chair and said:

"Your Majesty, I am ready to sacrifice anything for you: my blood, my life; but to be a laughingstock and play the buffoon is something I cannot do."

The empress sent everyone out of the room, told the count about the news she had received, and added with her usual charm:

"You understand how important this is. I must work all night at my desk; I have no time for the ball, but I cannot abandon it. Otherwise it will stir rumors and cause displeasure. Here is my plan. You will dress up in my evening gown—it's just your size, conceal your face beneath the mask, and go to the ball instead of me. You will remain there for about twenty minutes; then you will plead fatigue and, feigning weakness, drop into an armchair prepared for me. Then, summon Prince Orlov; tell him that you don't feel well, and ask him to inform the guests and apologize for the fact that you cannot remain at the ball. Then, come back here."

All this was executed with precision. The count played the role of the empress, and the Revelians were delighted that the empress, though indisposed, had not refused to honor their ball with her presence. Stroganov was presumably an expert at this sort of thing, and Catherine knew to whom she was entrusting such a delicate matter.

15 April. There are many young and not so young middle-class women who are very eager to attend university lectures or would like to have a special women's university created for them. The position of poor women who, outside of needlework, have no other means of earning an honest living, really

---

[x] In 1764 a disgruntled army officer, Vasily Mirovich, attempted a palace revolution. He tried to free Ivan VI from the Schlüsselburg fortress where he had been confined since 1756. Ivan was murdered in the attempt.

deserves special attention, and it is worth thinking about opening new areas of employment for them.

A first warning has been issued to *Moscow* for its article in the first issue. Thus, the new minister has served notice that he intends to continue his predecessor's policy in press matters. Unfortunately, Aksakov provokes him with his intemperate behavior and hostility, thus compelling the government to conclude that it has an enemy in him. And one doesn't stand on ceremony with an enemy. In general, Muscovites are terribly vain. They will not only go to great lengths to tell the truth, but also to demonstrate to the whole world that they alone are its harbingers, and, therefore, there is no salvation for anyone or anything that does not hasten to bow before their victorious pen.

14 May. Apropos of the Slavic world. That the German and, particularly, the Turkish Slavs are striving for independence is understandable and natural. But the extravagant claims of the Slavophiles to a pre-eminent role among European peoples do not make sense. How can they justify such claims? What have they done for civilization, science and art? They keep talking about the future of the great Slavs, about the future of their brilliant role; but where, meanwhile, is the evidence of that great future? What services have they rendered humanity that entitles them to such conceit? Of all the Slavs, only the Czechs, Serbs, and we Russians have distinguished ourselves. In reality, only we have, because we alone have succeeded in founding a strong state. But we, too, still flatter ourselves only with hopes. Wouldn't it be wiser to await their realization before boasting about them? Meanwhile, let's have a little less arrogance and a little more real work.

5 June. According to Norov, the State Council has finally begun serious discussions of the alcoholism problem in Russia, and has already come to the conclusion that the number of taverns should be limited. It's about time! Why hadn't this occurred to them before? Many tragedies and disorders could have been averted, and maybe even last winter's famine. But as the old saying goes, *a muzhik won't cross himself until the thunder starts to roll.*

11 July. June and July have been so hot that I can't remember anything like it in St. Petersburg. In all this time it has only rained twice—once in June and again the day before yesterday. You don't feel like working in this scorching heat. The evenings would be delightful if not for the smoke coming from burning peat and woods on the outskirts. There are days when one has to shut the windows to keep out the smoke. Fires are literally a daily occurrence in St. Petersburg, and sometimes there are several burning at once. The provinces are threatened by famine—in some places because of drought—elsewhere, because of unusually heavy rains. Drunkenness and thievery are going on as usual.

18 July. Smoke, smoke, and more smoke; not Turgenev's kind, but real smoke, thick and acrid, from the peat and woods burning around St. Petersburg.

12 August. The terrible smoke continues. My room is so full of it that my eyes are burning.

7 September. I visited Prince Vyazemsky. He read me his article on Count Tolstoy's novel *War and Peace.* A very astute article.[y] Afterwards we went for a stroll.

7 October. I spent the evening at Prince Vyazemsky's in Tsarskoe Selo. He asked me to look over his work, *In Memoriam,* which contains his poem to Bibikov and recollections of the Battle of Borodino. The prince's ideas on the meaning of history and the role of the historical novel are exceptionally profound and valid, and his recollections are real jewels. I expressed the hope that he would continue to think, feel and write in the same spirit for a long time to come.

13 October. Avraam Sergeevich Norov asked me to look over and correct his article on the war of 1812 and the Battle of Borodino, written apropos of the novel *War and Peace.* The article is most interesting, particularly the details of the Battle of Borodino, where Avraam Sergeevich lost a leg. Thus, Tolstoy has encountered attacks from two sides: one from Count Vyazemsky, the other from Norov—the latter as an eye-witness. Indeed, no matter how great an artist you are, no matter how great a philosopher you may consider yourself to be, still, you cannot, with impunity, show disdain for your country and the finest pages of its glory.

22 December. Three women, representing a St. Petersburg women's organization, visited the minister of education with a petition requesting permission to establish higher education courses for women. There were four hundred signatures on the petition. They say that the minister treated them rudely and said: "These four hundred ladies of yours are nothing more than a herd of sheep, and half of them have dossiers in the Third Section."

27 December. I attended a grand soirée at Vyazemsky's. Markevich, an excellent reader, read us Prince Pyotr Andreevich's poem to Bibikov and his commentary on Count Tolstoy's *War and Peace.* Both pieces were very fine indeed, and although the prince had already read them to me in manuscript I enjoyed hearing them again.

[y] Vyazemsky attacked Tolstoy's novel, accusing him of "historical freethinking."

1869

6 January. The students are beginning to carry on again. They issued their demands for permission to hold meetings, etc.

23 January. Avraam Sergeevich Norov passed away today at 3:30 P.M. Except for the time he served as head of the ministry or, at least, except for the latter half of his tenure, I was very close to Avraam Sergeevich. I am terribly saddened. I do not want to remember him as a weak, cowardly minister and can only speak well of his human qualities and his warm feeling for me personally.

15 February. A grand soirée at Prince Vyazemsky's at which the heir was also present. Meshchersky's drama was read, a weak and dull work which bored everyone with its length. It accuses our periodicals of all sorts of dirty tricks and evil deeds. The St. Petersburg fires of 1862 are even ascribed to them.

18 February. The masses are endowed with an ability to produce, but are totally unequipped to organize or plan.

There is freedom and equality for all in North America, but it is only their *finest minds* that create laws, govern and guide the nation. Their leaders are those endowed with the finest talents, those who can develop and use them for the noblest purposes. Lincoln—the woodcutter, Johnson—the tailor, and Franklin—the printer, rose from the common people and only in this respect belonged to the masses; but in their talent and development, they stood immeasureably above them. The fact is that, there, in America, everyone has the opportunity to be and do what he is capable of.

16 March. The Academy of Medicine and Surgery has been shut down. Naturally, there are endless rumors, but no one is certain about the facts surrounding this sad event.[1]

18 March. The Duke of Leuchtenberg, Nikolai Maksimovich, gave a dinner today for the members of the Academy to mark his election to honorary membership with voting rights. The duke treated us handsomely: the food, wine, and service were fit for a tsar. But the nicest thing of all was the warmth, good nature and simplicity of the host himself. It was completely informal.

19 March. Nothing has been verified about the events at the Academy of Medicine. They say that politics had nothing to do with it. If only this were so! However, Naranovich was fired and Kozlov was appointed in his place.

Two gendarme units rushed past my windows this morning to quell disturbances, they say, at the Technological Institute.

20 March. Yes, it's true that disorders occurred at the Technological Institute yesterday and that the assistance of the gendarmes was required to suppress them. The *Voice* announced that classes had also been suspended at the Moscow Petrovsky Academy.

21 March. Even at the university our well-bred youth have rebelled. Professor Blagoveshchensky came to see me and told me some sad things. The students had rudely accosted the rector and other professors, including Blagoveshchensky, with the demand that meetings be permitted inside the university. Exhortation and explanations were of no avail. Noise, shouting, even swearing, rang out in the halls of this peaceful refuge of knowledge. Finally, it was necessary to summon the police. By the time Trepov arrived, the noise had abated somewhat. "What are you trying to start here, gentlemen?" the senior lieutenant asked the crowd. "Nothing! We're just picking up our coats and leaving."

Such scenes as the following occurred:

A professor was delivering a lecture when several students suddenly rose from their seats and demanded that the lecture be halted because they had no time to listen to it now: they had to go to a meeting. When the professor ignored them and continued with his lecture, the rowdies left and, once outside, began to bang on the doors of the lecture hall. After they had succeeded in opening them, they swore at the students who had remained to hear the lecture. "Scoundrels, villains!" they shouted.

22 March. The most stupid thing of all is the leaflets the students have been scattering around the city and distributing to the editorial offices of some newspapers. The *News* published one such leaflet, accompanied, naturally, by appropriate editorial commentary uncomplimentary to the leaflet's authors. The students are asking the public to support their demands, i.e., that they be permitted to hold meetings for deliberation of their so-called "affairs" and that they be freed from police surveillance, which they consider disgraceful.

23 March. Man, spurred on by science, particularly chemistry, in his mad pursuit of pleasure, of so-called comfort, fails to notice that he is encountering a multitude of afflictions and suffering, the likes of which people never imagined existed. I am certain that many of the new illnesses of the nervous system and the brain, etc., or the complication of older ones, have come about as a result of various improvements in our material existence.

13 April. The Aksakov case has ended in the State Council with the decision to forbid him to publish *Moscow*. Two members voted against the decision—Titov and Knyazhevich. They consider the newspaper guilty only of clumsiness and bluntness, and not of having a dangerous tone, the only legal reason for imposing a ban on a newspaper.

3 May. Soirée at Kelsiev's. His wife organized a musicale at their home. She played the piano, and beautifully, too. Kelsiev is going off to America to seek employment. He plans to give lectures on Russia. His situation here is becoming impossible. Although he was granted permission to live in Russia, he was denied the opportunity to work and earn a living.[z] This is rather absurd. Either they should not have allowed him to re-enter Russia, or they should have afforded him a legitimate means of supporting himself. He wanted to publish a paper and was not permitted to do this. There were openings in government service which he could have filled to the benefit of all concerned, but he was denied employment everywhere.

15 May. We've moved to our dacha in Pavlovsk. This is the sixth summer we have leased the same house from General Miller. Despite increased prices for dachas in Pavlovsk, I am paying the same rent as I have in the past. Prices have risen because of our stupid passion for everything foreign—because the great Johann Strauss will conduct here.[a] The director of the railroad says that Strauss was paid a fantastic sum for this season and he was practically begged on bended knee to give us the pleasure of his presence.

19 May. People should be ruled not only by *laws*, but by *fear*, which serves to preserve the law. Everyone ought to fear at least something: tsars—revolution; nobles—disfavor; civil servants—their chiefs; the rich—thieves; the poor—the rich; evil-doers—the courts; and so forth. Many people still fear the devil and, lastly, every man fears God and death. Only under the pressure and cloak of fear are the greatest number of human virtues preserved and are people prevented from sinking completely into a morass of immorality.

The main thing we lack in implementing our so-called reforms is sincerity and good faith. With one hand we make or try to make improvements, while we undermine them with the other; one hand gives, while the other takes away. We establish new procedures and immediately hasten to invalidate them as soon as they begin to produce the expected results. We would like to see changes only in minor details, provided our major structures remain intact.

10 June. People in the West still believe in something; they believe in money or capital, in labor, in comfort; some believe strongly in science. We don't believe seriously in anything. With us everything is somehow conceived and executed lightly, with a certain humor and irony. Perhaps we shall have to be cleansed in fire and revolution. However, let us not go too fast. Premature births are dangerous.

18 June. A university is being opened in Warsaw. Many people are unhappy about it, fearing that a university in Poland will become a hotbed for the most diabolical schemes against Russia. I think this is an exaggeration.

They say all the teachers will be Russians. And where in the world will they

---

[z] Vasily Ivanovich Kelsiev (1835–72), publicist, had gone abroad in 1859 and worked for some time with Herzen. In 1867 he returned to Russia and was "pardoned."

[a] Johann Strauss performed in Pavlovsk with his orchestra for fifteen seasons, from 1859 to 1874.

get them when, for lack of qualified professors, there are so many vacant posts in our own universities. To appoint anyone that happens to come along will result in its becoming a general laughingstock. As far as I am concerned, let them open the university, but first they ought to concentrate on ways and means of establishing a good university. But we've always been rich in hindsight.

8 October. The minister of internal affairs had prepared a proposal for presentation to the State Council which called for changes of a repressive nature in the press laws. Some time ago editorials about this began to appear in the press (the *Moscow Bulletin,* the *Voice,* the *St. Petersburg Bulletin*). They strongly attacked this proposal which was known to the public at that time only through rumors. Now the minister has decided to drop it, and they say Grand Duke Konstantin Nikolaevich was responsible for the decision. He had even expressed the sentiment that the public and the government owed a great deal to the press and that, therefore, it would be extremely unjust and unwise to limit it by imposing new restrictions.

25 October. They say that Timashev's proposal for imposing certain restrictions on the press is under consideration again. It is stirring up many rumors and dissatisfaction in certain sectors, that is, in intellectual and patriotic circles.

2 November. The storm threatening the press is moving ever closer. Prince Urusov was asked to form a commission to draft new press laws. But, because this commission has been assigned the task of composing laws of a repressive nature, few are willing to join it. So, its members must be drafted, which is precisely what Urusov is doing.

5 November. Prince Urusov has been commissioned to find the philosopher's stone, to produce the kind of press laws that will prove equally satisfactory to the government and the public and, while limiting freedom of thought, will not interfere with the development of science and education.

  The following question must be raised with honesty and clarity: does the government wish to share its concern for the nation's security and welfare with the public, that is, with the educated sector, or does it think it can attain its goals solely through its own agents—its administrative apparatus? It would be inadvisable to wait until the public itself, brought to its senses by bitter experience, seized the opportunity to manage its own affairs from the hands of the government. Someone once phrased it very well: *we must begin from the top, so they don't begin from the bottom.*

22 November. The usual soirée at Kornilov's. Many guests. One thing is on everybody's mind—the fate of the press. The most ominous rumors are circulating. People are repeating the statement made by Shuvalov, whom they call the new Arakcheev: "The press must be gagged." In brief, we have widespread panic. Measures worse than any adopted during Nicholas's reign are anticipated.

23 November. The Council met last Thursday to discuss the *Moscow Bulletin* and the press in general. Each member had to pledge to keep the proceedings confidential. Therefore, the public fears that something unpleasant is in the offing for the press. It is even rumoured that the *Moscow Bulletin* has already been banned.

13 December. The *Moscow Bulletin* withstood the attack on it this time. They say that Shuvalov and Timashev had raised a terrible row about the paper. The emperor organized a deliberative council, over which he presided, consisting of various trusted individuals. He ordered it to review Shuvalov's and Timashev's charges. After the charges were read, Gorchakov spoke up in defense of the press and the *Moscow Bulletin,* in particular. He said that in view of the present state of affairs in Europe, it was very important for Russia to have an independent press. With that the matter ended.

15 December. Some vile leaflets have been widely circulated again. Cherkesov, the bookseller, was arrested. We hear that several others were also arrested. A student was murdered at the Moscow Petrovsky Academy, and, it is rumored, by his very own friends. This crime apparently has something political behind it.[b]

[b] The chain of events (leaflets, arrests, murder of a student) mentioned by Nikitenko were links in the revolutionary-conspiratorial activity of S. G. Nechaev, a follower of the anarchist Bakunin. The murder of the student I. I. Ivanov, a member of Nechaev's organization, was ordered by Nechaev. The "Nechaev" affair was portrayed in Dostoevsky's novel *The Possessed.* See Nikitenko's entries for 5, 14, 22, 30 July and 28 August 1871.

1870

9 January. No. 5 issue of the *Court Messenger* has been confiscated for an editorial in which it argued that the Third Section should be abolished.

The *Moscow Bulletin* has received a warning, as a result of which it will probably be shut down.

10 January. I read the *Court Messenger*'s editorial. It is intelligent, truthful, and well written. The editor was summoned to Shuvalov. He was reprimanded and told that if another such incident occurred, the full weight of the Third Section would be brought to bear against him. Frank and comforting!

A warning was issued to the *Moscow Bulletin.* Yet only a month ago it was judged innocent and useful. The editors will presumably refuse to publish, and we shall be deprived of one of the finest of our press organs, and the government—of one of its sources of strength. The reactionary set is making fine progress.

13 January. Herzen is dead. Some rather nice statements were made about him in today's *St. Petersburg Bulletin.*

25 January. Spencer's *Principles of Biology* was translated into Russian and published here. The Office of Press Affairs initiated legal proceedings because there were passages in the book ostensibly subject to ecclesiastical censorship, as for example, theories about creation which geology has recently accepted. The ecclesiastical authorities were asked if such passages were subject to censorship. They replied they were. The publisher was brought to trial because he had not submitted those passages to the ecclesiastical censorship department. The court acquitted him.

The Office of Press Affairs isn't capable (in 1870!) of distinguishing scientific issues and ideas from the idle chatter of ignorant scribblers.

26 January. A bureaucratic administration allied with sovereign despotism has always paralyzed the spirit of our people and its ability to act. Its grip had almost begun to weaken with the introduction of the *zemstvos.* But now it appears to have revived for good.

Nothing is so harmful to the cause of freedom as the absurd demands of the radical reformers of society. They not only force the government to turn against freedom but antagonize freedom's sensible, sober champions, too, many of whom prefer to remain where they are rather than follow the dangerous path of these self-appointed benefactors of mankind.

The principle these gentlemen follow is all wrong: "Demand more if you want to get anything at all." The terror which they arouse with their *more,* serves to stifle any enthusiasm for the *less.*

27 January. The proposal to increase the power of the governors has stirred up a great deal of talk and widespread discontent. (An article about it appeared in the *Moscow Bulletin,* no 19.) This proposal arouses fears that all Russia will be placed under police surveillance. The culprits responsible for this remarkable monument to administrative wisdom are none other than Count Shuvalov and ⟨Timashev⟩. Nothing more monstrous, it seems, has been devised in these senseless times, where the pettiest personal interests—vanity, ambition and cowardice, have long ceased to feign the least concern for national interests. Are not the courts being undermined openly; are they not trying to topple the *zemstvos* and revive secrecy? All this is due to the incompetence of two or three people who have taken power into their own hands.

16 February. Why not permit our graduates of *Realschulen* to specialize in the physical and natural sciences at the universities? This would not keep those who lack the ability to master classical philology from receiving a higher education, and it would satisfy public opinion. To permit only graduates of classical gymnasiums to enter the university is truly unrealistic. Then, we would have to transform all gymnasiums into classical ones, and where would people with technical and practical goals obtain a general education? I am certainly not an enemy of classical education, but it should have its limits and not prevail exclusively.

3 March. An announcement in the *St. Petersburg Bulletin* today about the appearance of cholera in St. Petersburg.

22 March. The weather has been splendid for some two weeks. However, the winter was a sad one. Scarcely a family in St. Petersburg escaped illness. And the number of deaths! The papers were full of notices with black borders.

26 March. Soirée at Tyutchev's. Many guests. I met a refined, intelligent lady there by the name of Novikova. Among the guests was Yuzefovich, who told some clever and lively stories from his past experiences. He reminisced about the war in Asia Minor in which he had fought, and about Pushkin, whom he had met in the Caucasus. He was with him at the Battle of Erzerum. He said that Pushkin was very eager to experience the enemy's artillery fire and to hear the whistling of the shells. His wish was granted. However, the shells did not frighten him although one had fallen very close by.

Slavophile poems were read at the soirée: Tyutchev's "Huss," and Maikov's and Polonsky's "Simeon Bolgarsky," which was composed for the Easter staging of living portraits. They were all fairly good, particularly Tyutchev's.

24 May. What strange and absurd times. It's like living in a whirlpool with nothing solid to hold on to, with deception and cheating encountered every step of the way. Such are our ways. For some two years now I have refused to have a male servant in my home. Drunkenness and stealing are rife almost everywhere among male servants. Among the women, at least, drunkenness is not as widespread. How all this complicates and mars one's domestic tranquility!

4 July. Today's telegrams announce that France has declared war on Prussia.

10 July. War, war, war—that's all people are talking about. But, so far, I have not heard anyone express a desire for our involvement in this conflict.

12 July. Everyone was delighted by our government's declaration of strict neutrality. However, we hear that sympathy for the Prussians is coming through in higher circles, while the public's reaction is quite the opposite. All our leading newspapers clearly favor the French.

28 July. Prussia's victories over the French (two already)—and the war has scarcely begun—can lead to Napoleon's fall. Then, France, of course, will proclaim itself a republic. Will the proximity of such a republic prove desirable for a quasi-constitutional, but basically despotic, power like Prussia? Hardly. Socialism and democracy have sunk deep roots into Germany's masses. And who knows how soon the Hapsburgs and Hohenzollerns, too, will share the same fate which now threatens Napoleon and his dynasty.

3 August. France is on the brink of disaster. We, too, are partly to blame for this. We permitted Prussia to strengthen itself and, of course, shall continue to permit this until, finally, we, too, experience its yoke. And, in our so-called higher circles, they continue to delight in Prussian victories. On the other hand, there is, among the public, clear-cut, widespread hostility toward the Prussians and sympathy for France.

However, the reasons for our sympathy for the French go far deeper than our hate for the Prussians. We make a distinction between the French government and the French people, and it is important that we do so. We are instinctively drawn to the French people because it was they who tried to develop a new political and social system for the first time.

16 August. Germans are dead serious from head to toe, while we are frivolous and more witty than profound. Germans are stable and steady, while we are unstable and incapable of self-control. Germans are slaves to work, like oxen, while we are gay and carefree, but capable of doing more work in a day than anyone else in a month. That is why, they say, our work isn't durable. True, but we don't grieve over it, and rather than weep over the ruins of our buildings, we would sooner laugh about the fact that we tormented ourselves so long with the job of building them. Germans are egotists to the core, while Russians are goodnatured and softhearted. Don't expect generosity or self-sacrifice from a German, or that he will forget an insult, while a Russian, having fought it out with his enemy, will fraternize with him and give him his bread and money. In brief—he will forget that his face was drenched in blood by blows from his opponent's fist.

22 August. News has come that Napoleon has been captured and that MacMahon's army has surrendered.

25 August. A republic has been proclaimed in France.

15 September. Bismarck's war with France was certainly not fought for the sake of borders and the unity of Germany. France is justifiably considered the center and heart of all liberal movements in Europe. Despite Napoleon III's efforts to crush this spirit within France, he could not control her. Then Bismarck came to his aid. The war which he began with France was certainly not for German unity; it could have been achieved, and was on the verge of being achieved, without it. To humiliate France and reduce her prestige—this was the real meaning of the war and the Prussian victories. Bismarck knew very well that France with her Napoleon could not fight against a splendidly organized German army of one and a half million men. However, even he did not foresee such a turn of events; fate had served him too well. France has proclaimed herself a republic and this, of course, was something he didn't count on. But Bismarck hasn't given up. He is bearing down on France all the more harshly in order to drain her life's blood and crush her soul, and if he succeeds, Prussia's dictatorship in Europe will be firmly established—and woe to freedom. So will it be unless the Germans themselves come to their senses and understand that it certainly is not very flattering to be hauling stones, according to Bismarck's plan, for the construction of their own prison.

18 September. The following words were uttered when the new chairman of the Council on Press Affairs, Shidlovsky (a former governor of some province), was appointed to replace Pokhvisnev, who is being discharged from his post for his liberalism: "You must take the press in hand."

26 September. They say Shidlovsky tried very hard to refuse the appointment, submitting that he was totally unfamiliar with literary and press affairs. Moreover, he added that he was hot-tempered and accustomed to acting *forcefully,* which was appropriate in police work but might prove awkward in the world of science and thought. He was told that this was precisely the approach required, for they wanted the press "taken in hand."

Dissatisfaction among the public is growing by leaps and bounds. Patriotic sentiment feels insulted by Russia's humiliation in foreign politics and by the servile position we are adopting in our relations with Prussia.

27 September. The idea of "taking the press in hand" was originally conceived by Minister of Education Tolstoy. He doesn't get on well with Timashev, minister of internal affairs, and had submitted a memorandum to the emperor about the extreme laxity of our press, which he attributed to weak supervision on the part of the authorities. In Timashev's absence, his deputy, Lobanov-

Rostovsky replied to Tolstoy's charge, stating that there was no laxity or maliciousness on the part of the press, and if it existed anywhere at all, it was in the minds of those professors and teachers whom Count Tolstoy failed to watch properly. Evidently, Count Tolstoy's memorandum made no impression at first.

But, after the meeting [of Alexander II] with Wilhelm and Bismarck, Count Tolstoy's memorandum did find support in the notion that the press was acting very badly by attacking the Germans and inciting mutual hatred between the two nations. This led to Albedinsky's discharge from his post as governor-general of the Ostsee region, the resignation of Revel's Governor Galkin, and an order for restrictions on the press.

3 October. Count D.A. Tolstoy, who had provoked the current measures against the press with his memorandum, is being very harshly criticized everywhere.

During my lifetime I have seen many repressive measures taken against the press, but not a single one ever achieved its aim; it could not halt the flow of ideas. It simply distorted them and drove them underground, only for them to gush out again from beneath the earth like a raging stream.

16 October. Metz was taken. One hundred and fifty thousand Frenchmen surrendered to the Prussians.

17 October. Contemporary events have a profound, fatal significance: they fully explain the meaning of civilization and progress in the nineteenth century. Of the advanced nations of the world, one of them has become so decadent that, within two months, it finds itself on the brink of disaster. Another displays the kind of coarse passions in waging war that are strongly reminiscent of the good days of yore. And so, humanity has made little headway along the path of so-called progress! For example, what has become of the Germans' celebrated, profound, philosophical, humane aspirations in science? What has science done to improve man's condition? He still remains a slave to his animal instincts. What is the rest of Europe doing? Amidst terrible bloodshed and misfortune it engages in diplomatic babble instead of doing something positive to end this disgrace. England wants to fish in troubled waters, while Russia blissfully relaxes and venerates Prussia! It's all a matter of politics, diplomacy, political interests, etc. "Our present civilization," "our progress," "our science"—are all empty phrases. Humanity is still at a very low level of development despite its railroads, machines, its factories and political economy.

27 November. Convocation at the Artillery Academy. I was awarded a gold tobacco box decorated with diamonds and the emperor's monogram.

1 December. I was presented, together with others, to the emperor to express my gratitude for the award I had received. The presentation took place at 1 P.M. in the Winter Palace. When my turn came, the emperor said very graciously with his warm smile: "Thank you for your fine service. I am sure you will continue to serve as well in the future."

4 December. Englehardt, his wife, and a girl, Volkova, who was living with them, were arrested.[1] Five or six students from the Agricultural Institute were also arrested. I still don't know the charges. And at today's session of the Academy of Sciences, we had awarded Englehardt the Lomonosov prize for his work in chemistry!

25 December. Shuvalov works tirelessly: he is continually banishing people to distant provinces. He arrests people and puts them in the lockup—all in secret. Everyone lives in fear; there is no counting the number of spies. In brief, Pietri and his system have triumphed. All the principles of police art are being employed to trump up conspiracies; or, insignificant incidents are blown up to look like conspiracies. Is it any wonder that such tactics inspire real conspiracies, which are more difficult to cope with than the products of their own inventions?

1871

26 January. I wonder how our historians and thinkers will interpret the fall of France. German philosophers will probably say that humanity has much to gain from it and, of course, will rejoice in the shift in France's political and social status which was engineered by brute, Prussian-German force. They will say France was corrupted by ideas, and she, in turn, had corrupted the world. Prussia's mission was to restore her to reason and common sense, and of course, this could only be accomplished by spilling blood and applying an iron hand. The world will be pacified beneath a canopy of Prussian bayonets, and all society's troubles will be settled in the headquarters of the Prussian high command.

"I cannot see Europe," declared Beist, and a very accurate statement it was. It is indeed difficult to see what isn't there. The Europe of today is a country of dead and dying and of peoples just beginning to live, but beginning under the iron hand of dictators.

Religion teaches us to submit to divine will, and philosophy—to the law of necessity. What choice do we have, but to submit to such a miserable creature as man? Yet, can we remain indifferent to disasters which befall mankind? Can we look on calmly at the dead and dying on the assumption that their destruction is necessary if we want to attain a better order of things, if we want to reach a worthy goal? Indeed, may we not ask, in our deep compassion for them, why some must suffer so cruelly so that others might live a little better? Yes, one would need a great deal of faith, almost more than the human heart could sustain—in order to reconcile all this suffering with the idea of boundless mercy and omnipotence.

29 January. And so, France is perishing, and not because she is being destroyed by an external force, but because, thanks to Napoleon, she lacks the kind of spirit so necessary for the defense of her honor and independence. She must bow her head before the shameful peace terms which Bismarck has imposed on her; she must, because she lacks that unity and moral strength which, in a moment of danger, could rally her sons behind her.

31 January. It is vainly believed that real democracy will follow from the nobility's diminished role, and with it will come freedom, too. One thing is forgotten—that we cannot have complete democracy, that our people have always been and always will be divided, at least for a long time to come, into the *people proper* and *officialdom,* or *bureaucracy.* And this bureaucracy will rule us because it is directly linked to autocracy.

4 February. In the early years of the present regime I was enthralled by its splendid and noble beginnings, which promised Russia a better order of things without upheavals and victims. At that time it was considered a disgrace and crime for capable people to refuse to help the government work toward its fine goals. Since I was also counted among the capable and was called upon to assume an active role, I tackled such tasks with enthusiasm while continuing to pursue my academic and literary careers.

It wasn't very long before I became bitterly disillusioned and convinced that it was our fate to begin fine deeds but not to carry them through to their conclusion. Perhaps I did not work with the kind of subtle wisdom which, in the struggle between conflicting opinions, interests and passions, manages to achieve something constructive. It is very natural that they found me, in the general course of affairs, unable to go along with them.

And yet everything is so simple and clear. Autocracy is clinging to its divine power with both hands; government functionaries cling to autocracy and support it because they, like insects who appear and disappear with the sunshine, are wholly dependent on it for their existence; the people, not yet roused from a thousand-year sleep, stir and toss from side to side without knowing whether and whither they should bestir themselves; the intelligentsia struggles with officialdom, trying to conceal the fact that it is encroaching upon autocracy, although by daring to struggle with autocracy's instruments and slaves, it is, in reality, already making headway. How will it all end?

8 March. Two hostile forces are attacking St. Petersburg, epidemic smallpox and epidemic cholera. The latter appeared very suddenly and spread rapidly. And what a ferocious course—it's all over within a matter of hours, like the Prussians' lightning conquest of France. Although smallpox is not as deadly as cholera, everyone is having inoculations. Great times these are, with people and nature competing with each other for the destruction of human beings!

And now there is a new revolution in France.[c]

27 March. I fear for France. I feel she has ceased to be a motherland, a nation to her people, and is becoming merely a place, a territory. She has socialists, communists, constitutionalists, legitimists, Orleanists, imperialists, but no Frenchmen. These factions are tearing France apart, and each one takes a little piece for itself, unconcerned about the rest of the country.

8 April. Everyone is talking about the Odessa incident.[d] The local administration's action, or, rather, lack of it, is incomprehensible. It not only made no effort to prevent public disturbances against the Jews, which could have been anticipated on the basis of previous episodes, but permitted a real attack to break out which raged for three whole days and was accompanied by widespread plunder. They say Governor-General Kotsebu played a wretched role

[c] Nikitenko is referring to the formation of the Paris Commune.

[d] A three-day pogrom against the Jews.

in this affair. It is suspected that the administration deliberately refrained from acting. Since it was having a feud with the courts, it made it appear as if the latter had paralyzed its authority. It then cited this as the reason why police officials did not dare take strong measures. However, the administration finally did act: after three days it flogged both the innocent and guilty unmercifully, punishing whomever chanced to come its way. The newspapers say that several people were taken to the cemetery after the flogging, including a boy of fourteen. In brief, there is no end to the rumors one hears.

15 April. The public is very much aroused by the battle between classicism and so-called realism in our educational system. The issue is under discussion in the State Council. The minister of education, on the advice of Katkov and Leontiev, is defending the proposal in favor of classicism, which states, in essence, that a university should admit only those who have completed a course in a classical gymnasium: that is, only those who have studied Greek and Latin. For other students *Realschulen* are being established, and a commission of experts in various fields was organized to draft curricula. They outlined a rather lengthy proposal which would provide for general and *real* education without classical languages. Since Katkov and Leontiev had felt that such schools would lure many young people away from classical gymnasiums, they structured their proposal in such a way that *Realschulen* would resemble *technical-vocational institutes*. The minister doesn't use his own eyes or think for himself, but relies on Katkov and Leontiev. So, it was their proposal that he introduced at the State Council. There was an awful storm several days ago at the Council when Milyutin, Count Panin, Greig, Golovnin, Grot, and Chevkin rose up in opposition against the minister of education. They pointed out to him that his proposal, which denied university admission to young people who didn't know Greek, would definitely lead to the destruction of education in Russia by making it the exclusive property of those few who had the ability and opportunity to study Greek. The aforementioned members demanded for graduates of *Realschulen* the right to enter a university, and they also felt that Latin should also be permitted in the *Realschulen*. The public is awaiting the outcome with feverish impatience and the newspapers are debating the issue vigorously. This exclusive and one-sided classicism is vigorously opposed by the *Voice* and by the *St. Petersburg Bulletin,* in particular, which cleverly and convincingly defends the right of those with a general education to enter a university. Count Tolstoy, one must agree, is playing a pathetic role in this whole affair. At the State Council meeting he was unable to say anything with authority, but only became irritated and threatened to resign from the ministry. Meanwhile, Katkov practically never leaves his side, cramming him with arguments in favor of his proposal, while Markevich writes provocative articles in the *Stock Exchange Bulletin,* which, for some reason, has rallied to the support of classicism.

29 April. Analyzing it objectively, here's what I think Katkov's and Leontiev's

plan will lead to. Their intentions, perhaps, are very fine: they want to lay
the foundation for a solid and serious education, and they think that they can
achieve this through classicism. So far, so good. But their major error is this:
by insisting upon an exclusive curriculum of classical languages in gymnasiums
and by opening university doors only to their graduates and closing them
to students of so-called *Realschulen,* they will reduce *real* education almost to
the level of vocational education. But, of course, they are doing this because
the classical gymnasiums might lose students to the *Realschulen* if their level
were raised, and this would play havoc with their proposal for classical education. Now, this very neglect of the practical sciences, which threatens to kill
their proposal, is also rallying the entire public, as well as all natural scientists,
against the minister, Katkov and Leontiev.[e]

1 May. Soirée at Kornilov's. I met Katkov there. As usual, he embraced me
like an old friend but avoided any frank discussion. Evidently he was afraid
to hear my opinions, which clash with his extreme convictions in support of
classical education.

7 May. May a highly gifted writer forgive me for saying this, but his character
portrayal (of the grandmother in *The Precipice*) is psychologically false and
slanders Russian women.[f]

16 May. Many people are convinced, by the way, that Count D. Tolstoy's
proposal, if finally adopted, will encounter insurmountable difficulties, and
everyone hopes that the reform will be short-lived. The force of events and
widespread hostility toward it will kill it.

11 June. The emperor agreed with the minority opinion of the State Council.
From now on universities will be open only to those who study both Latin
and Greek. That's precisely what we ought to have expected.

5 July. The Nechaev trial has generated a tremendous amount of public interest. The newspapers talk about nothing else.[1]

14 July. The Nechaev trial continues to stir the public.

22 July. The most contradictory opinions exist among the public concerning
the Nechaev trial. Some consider it a triumph for our new judicial procedures;
others censure it for its weakness and indulgence. The latter group is particularly critical of Chairman Lyubimov's conduct. They claim that he did not
silence the defendants at those points in their testimony where they expound-
ed their extremely radical ideas and introduced irrelevant issues. The latter
criticism was aimed particularly at a speech made by Spasovich. He had turned
it into a lecture on how the government was to blame for the appearance of

---

[e] Count D. Tolstoy, Katkov and Leontiev felt that nihilism could be checked by subjecting youth to a classical education.

[f] Nikitenko is referring to Goncharov.

revolutionary movements, and that such movements were the result of conditions which forced young people to take the same path as had the defendants. Moreover, the chairman is also being criticized for the statement he made to the four acquitted defendants—that henceforth their place was among them, the judges, implying, of course, that they now could take their place in society.

30 July. Katkov's article in no. 161 of the *Moscow Bulletin* makes many sensible and valid points about the Nechaev affair and expresses them with a clever and talented pen, yet he doesn't really tell the whole truth. One simply can't do that publicly. There is no doubt that all these youthful rebellions and disturbances are nothing more than the ravings of half-educated minds. But one ought not to forget how wretchedly they have been schooled by society since childhood. What do they constantly hear and see around them in society and in our administration? In the former they see a total absence of honesty, of respect for the law, of sense of duty; they witness all sorts of drinking bouts and depravity and so on. And in the administration? Merely talking about it is most unpleasant, yet one must put up with it every step of the way. Is it possible to destroy all this at once, and by employing the nihilists' methods? Of course, it is impossible. But, speaking of the causes of our sad disturbances, one must admit that hate and contempt for such an order of things do not arise spontaneously in young people. Moral laxity alone is not the only force operating here, for there are noble motives, too. One would only wish they would not rush headlong into something which, on the one hand, is beyond their capacity, and, on the other, leads them toward criminal and immoral goals.

28 August. There is a great deal of talk about His Imperial Majesty's displeasure with the courts. Firstly, he felt that the chairman had behaved too humanely and warmly toward the defendants in the Nechaev case and that he had failed to silence the lawyers when they dwelt excessively on the nature of conspiracy and secret societies and the differences between them. Secondly, he was critical of the court's acquittal of some of the defendants; he felt that all of them should have been subjected to the same punishment. They say that Count Palen begged forgiveness for choosing a poor court chairman, and when Essen wanted to explain why the court hadn't charged all of them as a group, they didn't want to listen to him. In any case our courts have fallen into disfavor.

15 September. All St. Petersburg is grumbling about the exhorbitant prices of apartments and firewood. Landlords are raising rents on apartments to fantastic levels. For example, what once cost 700 rubles, now costs 1,000 or more. Firewood has gone from 4 or 4 ½ rubles to seven rubles per *sazhen*,[g] and threatens to reach ten. Prices in St. Petersburg are unprecedented. In general, the prices of all basic necessities have gone up terribly.

2 October. My first soirée, after a summer's respite, at Kornilov's, on neutral

[g] One *sazhen* is equal to seven feet.

soil, as Blagoveshchensky so aptly put it. Who wasn't there, and what a crowd! And each with his own political, literary and social prejudices. It stands to reason: "many men, many minds." But that's not the problem. Diversity in God's world is inexhaustible, and difference of opinion and disagreement in the Russian world is infinite. The trouble is that the vanity involved in such disagreement is insatiable. At the start of a conversation, each individual conveys the impression of his readiness to compromise. He politely invites you to express your opinion, with the apparent purpose of coming to an understanding with you or at least acknowledging your right to your own opinion. But if you should try to express it freely, if it is in any way your own independent opinion, you will be rebuffed as if you had inflicted a personal and bloody insult on your fellow conversationalist. And what a mishmash of opinions! How easily the most absurd rumors spread! How prejudices and personal bias prevail in everything. One wanders about in such a crowd dazed and groggy.

24 October. Dinner with Minister of Education Count Tolstoy. After dinner we gathered around him. He talked a great deal about the splendid state in which he had found the instruction of classical languages in Germany during his summer journey. I remarked to Delyanov, who was sitting next to me, that it was impossible to expect such success in our own country. In Germany these successes were several centuries in the making, and besides, such an approach to education was in keeping with the spirit of the German people. "Are you sure," I asked, "that your system can endure for long here: What system does last for any length of time in Russia?"

20 November. Shidlovsky was appointed deputy minister of internal affairs, replacing Obukhov who, after four trial years in office, was finally judged incompetent. Longinov took Shidlovsky's place. Longinov was the governor of Orlov and was known to the public as an inveterate opponent of emancipation, the new court system, the *zemstvos*, and, generally, of all improvements initiated during the present regime. Naturally, we expect him to take extremely hostile measures against the press.

1872

3 January. Our generation wants to make a show of its beards. They sport these masculine symbols for lack of manliness in their own souls.

17 January. Suvorov (governor-general of St. Petersburg) was dining with the emperor one day, and among the guests was some envoy. Suvorov, uninhibited as usual, cursed Chevkin, who had done something nasty to him. He swore in French. Finally, the emperor said to him: "Hold your tongue! " His Majesty took Suvorov aside after dinner and said to him: "You are a fool. If you must swear, do it in Russian so foreigners won't understand." Suvorov told this story to Knyazhevich, who passed it on to me.

6 February. A third warning and a four-month suspension has been given to the *Voice*.[1] And so the last independent newspaper in Russia has stopped publishing. The *Moscow Bulletin* doesn't count because it has turned into a mouthpiece for the administration.

9 February. The reactionary swing in Russia appears to be crystallizing into a definite trend. Its major manifestations are: the reform of secondary schools for the purpose of denying higher education to the middle and indigent classes, while granting them the right to prepare their youth for the lowest technical skills; the undermining of the independence of the new court system; and, finally, the repressive measures against the press. That is the picture in governmental spheres. And in society? The intellectual sector is alarmed and agitated; but it is helpless and, moreover, torn by conflicting ideas and disharmony. As far as the other classes are concerned, they remain steeped in ignorance, without the slightest understanding of political and social issues. They are willing to accept anything that comes down from above and serves as assurance that Russia will not democratize. We are following a reactionary course. What is left for a thinking, honest man, standing completely alone, to do?

Katkov has come to St. Petersburg to rouse and arm the ministry of education for the coming battle in the State Council on the issue of *Realschulen*. According to the Moscow ringleader these schools ought to provide professional training in the lowest technical sense, and not offer a general education. There isn't the slightest doubt that the proposal will go through.

11 February. The struggle between classical and *real* education involves something more than the issue of training and education. Concealed here is a political motive. Advocates of classical education feel that restless minds must be countered by an intelligently directed force, and this force is being sought in the solid intellectual foundation which classical subjects are supposed to create. But that isn't the whole story. By denying university admission to young people who are unschooled or weak in classical subjects, they hope to create a special force consisting of those who have classical training. This force would restrain rash impulses to democratize. It would guide people toward more serious and stable goals. It would be a kind of aristocracy which would control both public opinion and the reins of government. The masses would be engaged in technical production and would work to develop the country's physical strength. Young people who do not wish to engage in classical studies or who do not have the ability, would study technical specialties and would not be concerned with the loftier problems of society and the state. One must admit that there is something to this plan in theory. What would happen in practice is entirely another matter.

I had many visitors this evening. Goncharov was also here. He appears to be emerging from his shell and the deep depression which had kept him in complete solitude for several months.

17 February. There is a good deal of grumbling about the suspension of the *Voice.* It is said that Grand Duke Konstantin Nikolaevich expressed his anger over this measure to Timashev, who apologized by saying that the editor, Kraevsky, was a wicked man. "I hope, however," replied the Grand Duke, "that you don't consider me a wicked man, because I have always enjoyed reading the *Voice.* There are probably many people like myself. Why are you depriving the public of such a fine paper?"

18 February. The debate on *Realschulen* ended yesterday in the State Council's Commission. Six members favored the minister of education's proposal, and nine opposed it. The nine were: the heir, Count Litke, Chevkin, Milyutin, Golovnin, Grot, Greig, Titov, and Obolensky. The six in favor were: Count Tolstoy, Count Stroganov, Count Panin, Urusov, Valuev, and Putyatin.

26 March. The public is strongly opposed to the emphasis on classicism. This opposition is more than an expression of the public's distaste for the government's proposal; it also reflects a general spirit of opposition.

27 March. The administration is taking such repressive measures that one would think Russia was inhabited only by nihilists. It doesn't want to know that people have a lot of other ideas totally unrelated to nihilism and that these people belong to classes which in no way share the destructive and radical ideas of half-educated, ignorant youth.

7 April. The proposal on *Realschulen* was approved at a general session of the State Council.

8 April. The Western brand of socialist morality isn't suitable for us. Moreover, even in the West, it can only work in very small communes.

And, generally speaking, can any kind of lasting moral order be established on this earth without the help of religion?

But religion itself is on the decline. Who or what will reverse this course?

Education? But education is more concerned with Greek and Latin declensions and conjugations than the strengthening of religious feeling. This above all should be the primary function of the church, but our church is *completely divorced* from people and society. It is much like any other institution in Russia, such as the police, provincial administrations, and the like. It is totally unconcerned with the task of guiding minds and hearts and thinks only about preserving its own mode of existence.

14 April. Society should not be satisfied with merely making its needs and interests known to the administration; it must find a way to fight for them and should not be disconcerted by refusals, delays, or even prohibitive measures. For society to wait for the administration graciously to yield to its desires, is knowingly to make a fool of itself. We all know that society's most precious and complex needs can never be satisfied without some sacrifices on the part of the administration.

23 April. A deplorable incident took place in Kharkov (see no. 110 of the *St. Petersburg Bulletin*). The people rose against the police and vented their terrible anger at them. It was all caused by the stupidity of a police inspector who had decided to disperse a merrymaking crowd with firehoses, and several people were crushed by them. The people reacted to this with the fury of a hurricane, against which the administration, led by the governor, was helpless. This was a real people's revolt against police methods. It is interesting to note that there were shouts from the crowd demanding a court trial. One should not look for the cause of this lamentable incident in the isolated or momentary error of some police agent. Rather was this an expression of the public's long-smoldering hostility against the administration's arbitrary and illegal actions. Will the higher authorities understand this?

29 April. Most of April has been flaunting marvelous weather. Will it last? Doubts begin to creep in and one wonders if May won't take its revenge on us for April with snow and frost? That's the way it goes in this world. Neither fate, nor nature, nor the administration, pamper us with lasting good. Grief is humanity's normal state, joy an exception.

4 July. A new censorship law. *Finis* press! The minister of internal affairs can do as he pleases. Regardless of the specialized content of a book, he can confiscate it. If this law is applied, science and literature will be totally paralyzed in Russia.

7 July. The natural sciences and mathematics are in disfavor now. Several days ago two directors of local gymnasiums were discharged for the sole reason that they were not classicists, but scientists in the physics and mathematics department. Both had been outstanding directors for many years. Everyone feels particularly distressed about Belyaev. Acting Superintendent Yanovsky told Delyanov frankly that he would not take it upon himself personally to

discharge this noble and splendid educator: "I couldn't bring myself to tell
him that he's considered worthless."

20 July. What a wretched state of affairs! We are trapped between two evils
sent to us by nature: cholera and smallpox. Cholera is raging furiously in St.
Petersburg, and smallpox is also going about its repulsive business with zeal.
It has already appeared here, too. You are constantly threatened by disaster:
you walk, sleep, eat, and work, so to say, in the face of death. If your stomach
rumbles, or you feel slightly different from usual, or you sense the slightest
change in the normal pattern of your day, you imagine that disaster is about
to strike. What is one to do? Common sense tells us to be careful, especially with our food and, without losing heart, to leave the rest to fate.

12 September. Meeting of the Academy of Sciences' Commission for the
award of the Uvarov drama prizes. I read my reviews of the seven plays that
were submitted. This included two by Ostrovsky: *From Poverty to Riches*
and *Even a Cat Has Lean Times.* Both are weak and I could not give them
favorable reviews. So, at the moment, there are no plays worthy of drama
prizes. The Commission agreed with me.

5 October. Pisemsky read his new comedy, *Intrigues,* at Kraevsky's. This is
his finest work. But I don't know how he will make out with censorship. He
wants to have it published in Meshchersky's *Citizen.* Pisemsky reads beautifully, and I feel that anyone who has heard him give a reading of his comedy
should not go to see it performed in the theatre. It will probably be vastly
inferior to the author's recitation.

8 October. I was introduced to I.S. Aksakov at Tyutchev's. What a burly
fellow! However, he has a very gentle, modest manner so that the raging
journalist in him isn't visible. We talked about current censorship practices
which are almost more savage today than under Nicholas I.

20 October. Voronov and Blagoveshchensky came to see me today. Voronov
described many of the extremely distressing things going on at the ministry
of education. Count Tolstoy and his deputy, Delyanov, are doing a remarkable job of wreaking havoc there. The latter, incidentally, vehemently demanded at a meeting of the Committee of Ministers that the issue of *Dialogue,*
which contained a discussion of our monasteries, not only be confiscated, but
burned, too. And it was.

The minister of education ordered all gymnasium students to carry their
books and notebooks in knapsacks on their backs, like soldiers.

3 November. The *Stranger,* in his feuilleton in last Sunday's *St. Petersburg
Bulletin* announced his own death, as a joke, of course. Now, we hear that he
did, in fact, die a literary death. Censorship had hounded him so fiercely that
he had to cease all literary activity on behalf of the feuilleton. Thus, one of
the few lively streams in the paper has been frozen by an icy blast from cen-

sorship. The fact of the matter is that the *Stranger*'s feuilleton was noted for its intelligence and wit and was widely read. Therefore, it was considered harmful.

Count Tolstoy is playing detective. He searches painstakingly for any idea in the press which differs in any way with his own notions on education and then presents it to the appropriate authorities as a criminal act. This was what he did with *Dialog*. As a result, two issues were halted and one, they say, was burned in Moscow.

His chief assistant in this splendid occupation is Georgievsky, who has become an important figure these days. It is reported that Katkov is indeed ill and will hardly be able to continue publishing his newspaper, which is going downhill. The number of subscribers has fallen off considerably.

Repressive measures against the press have reached a high point and, together with the ministry of education's measures, comprise the most remarkable phenomenon of our time. The government probably feels that all these measures are useful and necessary for the restoration of good morals and respect for the administration in Russia, both of which have suffered keenly of late. That the public remains silent in the face of repressive measures, that our intellectual horizon grows ever darker, that men of science and thought are becoming discouraged, that people are growing apathetic, that trust in something loftier than material things is vanishing (and consequently corruption is increasing), is still not as serious as the paralysis that has gripped our intellectual and moral forces. We are heading straight back to that wretched era preceding the Crimean War.

5 November. The *Stranger*'s feuilletons are in print again. This means the censor is permitting him to write again provided, no doubt, that he tosses about the pearls of his wit merely for amusement, to no serious end, without aiming at or attacking anyone.

8 November. On orders from the minister of education, universities may not admit anyone coming from Saratov Seminary, only because Chernyshevsky had once studied there.

Suvorin, who writes as the *Stranger,* published a calendar for 1873 as he had done the previous year. The Office of Press Affairs ordered it to be confiscated and burned because of some biographical sketch not to their liking.

This is the second auto-da-fe in the past two or three months. It is amazing that these book-burners can not understand that their stupidity only makes them and the government look ridiculous. Book-burning in this day and age! Look here, gentlemen, if you don't like a book, confiscate it. You are consigning books to the flames not on the basis of their entire content, but on the basis of a single article. So burn the article, but why destroy a whole book and ruin the publisher as you have just done with Suvorin, the most impoverished of our impoverished litterateurs?

12 November. Why was Suvorin's calendar victimized and consigned to the

flames? Firstly, because he included an obituary of a man like Mazzini; secondly—and this appears to be the main reason—because he mentioned the salaries of high placed government officials in an article on government expendi-
tures.

18 November. A reading at Miller's. Maikov read his poem, *Two Worlds,*
which he wrote for the *Citizen.* It is a highly artistic work in which Maikov
rises to heights never achieved in his previous works. Everything is magnificent: the idea, its development, the images, the language. The author won
everyone's enthusiastic approval. When he was showered with compliments
and praise he solemnly announced that he was indebted to me and my university lectures for everything praiseworthy in his poem. I had awakened in him
as in others, a pure and lofty desire for the noble and beautiful and had given
his literary efforts direction. Naturally, it wasn't unpleasant for me to hear
these words from such a talented person as Maikov. Maikov is following a
course which is viewed unfavorably by those who champion social themes
and naturalism, but even Orest Miller had to acknowledge the first rate, non-
tendentious quality of this work.

Suvorin has been shown mercy. His calendar will not be burned, after all,
and he was told to recast only those pages that were considered harmful.

6 December. Pisemsky came to see me. The censor refuses to pass his comedy.
He had a talk with Timashev, who told him that it could be passed if he would
assign his characters a somewhat lower social rank, that is, if he would leave
directors and deputy ministers alone. He also had a talk with Longinov, but it
was fruitless. When Pisemsky asked: "How the devil is one to write, and what
can one write about?" Longinov replied: "It would be better not to write at
all." The author promised, however, to alter his play, that is, not to cast his
characters as high ranking officials.

A first warning was issued to the *Voice* on November 30 for two articles:
one from Revel on the disgraceful episode with the Ostsee Germans, and the
other from Odessa on the shameful treatment of the Jews [h] It charges the
Voice with stirring up friction among the Empire's various nationalities.

Nicholas I wanted to run the country like an army barracks. Concerned
only with disciplining his people, he systematically destroyed Russia's intellectual forces until he was left without generals or administrators, and had only
toadies who knew only how to "yes" him. The climax was Sevastapol. He
saw himself as Europe's chief policeman; he arrogantly tried to stifle any freedom movements there, too, just as he did in his own country among his own
frightened slaves. But, disgraced at Sevastapol, he died of shame and despair.

Many honest, thinking people, driven to despair by Nicholas's regime, actually hoped for our defeat at Sevastapol, seeing it as the only means of curbing
the sovereign's harsh will. Unfortunately, their hopes for a defeat were fulfilled. Did Russia learn much from this lesson? They say this shock restored

[h] The Odessa pogrom was described in Nikitenko's entry of 8 April 1871.

our sight. True, it did, momentarily, only to have us sink back to sleep once more after yawning and stretching our limbs a bit.

15 December. Neverov, superintendent of the Trans-Caucasia region, came to see me. He had come to St. Petersburg to plead for a waiver of the Greek language requirement. The problem is that the Trans-Caucasia region has almost no doctors or veterinarians, so that both people and cattle have a hard time. There is no one to treat them. Some localities have appealed directly to the viceroy (the grand duke) for doctors. But where can they get them when they don't even have them in the inner provinces? Doctors will have to be trained at the universities. But they will not accept applicants without Greek, and no one wants to study Greek. Both the grand duke and the superintendent would like to take steps to remedy this situation but Georgievsky refuses to. He states that he would not make an exception for those who want to study medicine: he doesn't give a damn about cholera, smallpox or cattle-plagues raging in Russia, as long as the Greek language lives on. So it seems that Neverov will leave, unsuccessful in his attempt to have the Greek requirement waived.

29 December. Our community spirit reveals itself only when we must struggle against a foreign enemy, although even at such times we can't seem to do without disorder, without unpleasant escapades like embezzlement of public funds, without boasting, quarrels, wrangling and the like. No sooner does a threat subside, than we return once again to our normal system of doing things, or, I should say, our lack of system. So, we are a nation; of this there is no doubt. But what kind of nation? Do we have an historical mission? That is another question.

In science, in literature, and in our administration, one finds individuals who are gifted and are apparently motivated by an awareness of society's needs. But they work in disorganized fashion and alone; each one wants to act independently, to stand out, to pamper his own aspirations. We don't have something called *principles.*

Public opinion feeds on rumor, heaving from side to side like a wave. Perhaps the government is to blame because it blocks the free flow of information.

31 December. 1872 is coming to an end. How was it for me? I existed—and nothing more. My inner world was full of anxiety and the usual discontent with myself, which has become a chronic affair with me. I would frequently analyze and review my past life and would always come to the same conclusion—that it would be difficult to conceive of anyone doing more foolish things and making more mistakes than I have.

1873

1 January. Nothing could surpass the banality that exists among us today.
A passion for gain, for the acquisition of money, is the most glaring and outstanding feature of contemporary society. In everything else either complete
apathy reigns or there are momentary outbursts of noble desires and inclinations which all go up in smoke. Although I criticized Turgenev's novel *Smoke*,
in my article on "Realism," I am inclined to think he is entirely correct. However, I spoke unfavorably of Turgenev's *Smoke* only because such a view of
his novel was in keeping with my desire to uphold the *ideal* in our literature.

7 January. Tyutchev suffered a stroke several days ago. His left side and
tongue are paralyzed. Dr. Besser said he would pull through, although not
without loss of strength. I believe he is seventy-two.

10 January. Grand Duchess Elena Pavlovna died yesterday. The Court has
been deprived of its last intellectual force. She was a highly educated woman
and played an active role in all the sensible freedom movements of our time.
Several philanthropic institutions owe their existence to her. The achievements
of the Conservatory of Music were also due to her efforts.

11 January. Provincial *zemstvos* are shutting down with increasing frequency
for lack of legal quorums. The reason? Discontent among the landowners, a
kind of passive opposition. Why the discontent? We have two kinds of landowners; those who favored serfdom, and one can see why they are now dissatisfied; and those who were not opposed to the emancipation (even with re-
distribution of their land), but had expected to receive some new rights in
return for their sacrifices. Their expectations were not fulfilled, and so now
they are dissatisfied. Although our landowners are no pillars of enlightenment,
they are far better educated than their *zemstvo* colleagues who come from the
peasantry, the petty bourgeoisie and merchant class, and they could accomplish
something if they weren't so apathetic.

13 January. The Nechaev trial, according to today's papers, is over. During
the entire trial he would not acknowledge the jurisdiction of Russian courts
over him and insisted that he was not a common murderer, but a political
criminal. It is very clear that this man is a political fanatic. He was sentenced
to twenty years of hard labor for murder. As he was being taken from court
he shouted: "I am no longer a slave of your tyrant. Long live the *zemstvos!*"
The spectators shouted, too: "Out with him!" for which they were sternly
and properly reprimanded by the chairman.

23 January. Soirée at Countess Bludova's. I spent most of the evening chatting with Princess Trubetskaya, whose husband had been governor of Voronezh. I found her to be a very intelligent and pleasant woman. She and her husband had been very friendly with Dal. Clever, talented Dal had developed a strong passion for spiritualism not long before his death.

15 March. Soirée at Bezobrazov's, where I read my review of Maikov's epic poem, *Two Worlds.* It was a brilliant, well-attended gathering. Adjutant-generals, senators, and members of the State Council were present; also several of our academicians, professors, and the minister of education. My reading was, so to say, middling. As usual, I stumbled over several words in the manuscript that I had recopied myself in my wretched, indistinct hand. However, it seems I made a fair impression. At least I didn't bore them with a lengthy reading; it took only fifty-five minutes.

16 March. At a meeting of the Academy the other day, several of my friends decided to propose a celebration to mark my fifty years in literature. Naturally, I opposed this nonsense.

25 March. Vast preparations are under way for the reception of the German emperor. Incidentally, our generals were ordered to change their red trousers, which had been modeled after the French army's.

29 March. Our officials are trying to make St. Petersburg look like a real German city for the German emperor's visit. The change in our generals' trousers, the replacement of our soldiers' headgear with Prussian helmets, the Prussian flags planted on buildings, and so forth, will all serve to enhance this impression.

A kind of epidemic of suicides has been raging here for some time. A day rarely passes without a press report of a suicide by hanging or shooting, most often by shooting. Revolvers are very popular. Even women have learned how to handle them.

4 April. If real life is so full of evil and human filth, then art and literature ought to preserve those ideals that represent the finest, most rational and most noble efforts of humanity. But they are not. Art and literature today are descending as deeply into vulgarity as they possibly can, under the pretext of being faithful to truth and reality. What do they mean by truth? The duplication of nature? The classification of daily phenomena and everything that troubles people and society? Of course all this is truth. But there is another kind of truth, too—one's *consciousness,* where the eternal ideas of reason, goodness, truth and beauty reside. When depicting the first kind, one ought not to forget about the second.

12 April. I visited several friends; saw Nebolsin, Bogdanova, Blumenfeld, and Tyutchev. Tyutchev is still half-paralyzed, but his mind is perfectly sound. He speaks quite clearly, too, except for a slight impediment. But there is no hope for his complete recovery.

20 April. Classical education, it seems, was not neglected in France, yet it did not save it from its first bloody revolution. On the contrary, it contributed to the development of republican ideas. Inciting people against their tsars was entirely in keeping with Greek republican ideas.

The new resolution on censorship, we hear, has already been passed by the State Council. It consists of two parts: 1) when articles in newspapers and journals are based on rumors, the administration has the right to compel editors to identify the source. 2) the administration has the right to forbid newspapers and journals to write about certain subjects. The first part of the resolution is especially serious. It strikes a terrible blow at so-called correspondence from the provinces: who would dare send reports with the sword of Damocles, the threat of exile, hanging over his head? This is a great pity. The free flow of information, which has been so beneficial to our society, is now becoming completely impossible. Without it we shall sink up to our ears, once again, in an abyss filled with disorders and abuses, an abyss from which we had barely begun to emerge.

20 May. Retail sales of the *Voice* have been banned.

Dyachenko, a graduate of St. Petersburg University who had been in government service for several years, had been appointed to a teaching post at Krasnoyarsk gymnasium. Now he writes me that Governor-General Sinelnikov of Siberia had him committed to an insane asylum and had taken away all his belongings. Why? For what reason? No one knows. The letter, which Dyachenko had written to Voronov and me because we had helped him get the Krasnoyarsk position, doesn't give one the slightest reason to think that he is mentally deranged. What the devil is this? No matter what he may have done, if this unfortunate fellow did not commit a major crime, is it possible to punish him this way and, to boot, threaten to flog him if he complains about what was done to him and demands to hear the reasons for this punishment? The facts clearly indicate that it is entirely possible. Dyachenko writes that the local bishop, gendarme colonel and other respected citizens had taken a lively interest in his case, but their efforts were in vain, and he is still confined to the insane asylum.

30 May. I went to Tsarskoe Selo to see poor, sick Tyutchev. His condition is most deplorable. He has no control over half his body, but his mind is alert and his mental functions are intact. A slight speech impediment is barely noticeable. He is completely alone: all his relations and friends have gone off for the summer. I didn't see any of the servants except the nurses and footman who were looking after him, and, it seems, most conscientiously, too. He was overjoyed to see me. We chatted about literature, France and Thier. Of course, like all noble and thinking people, he was indignant at the rightist faction in the National Assembly which had overthrown Thier. Everything seems to point to the restoration of the Napoleonic dynasty.

9 June. Visited ailing Tyutchev. Poor man; his mental anguish is greater than his physical suffering.

16 June. Went to Tsarskoe Selo to visit Tyutchev. But I couldn't see him: he was unconscious and doing very poorly. I had visited him on Monday; we talked for a long time and he was fine then.

21 June. Went to Tyutchev's but didn't see him. His son-in-law, Ivan Sergeevich Aksakov, told me that he had been fighting for life for days. Sometimes he would regain consciousness briefly but would lapse back into unconsciousness. Somehow, he remembered about the priest, but he could not confess because his tongue would not obey him. After he had mumbled a confession, however, he received communion and understood when the priest asked him to open his mouth. Now it is clear that his brain has been affected.

2 July. Visited Tyutchev. He regained consciousness, but he is very weak and can barely speak as his tongue is affected. His wife, Ernestina Fydorovna, a venerable old lady whom I met for the first time, seemed to be very happy about my arrival. Tyutchev had asked about me yesterday. I was taken to him. His face had changed greatly. He held out his emaciated hand to me and formed several sentences with great difficulty. I stayed with him about three minutes, afraid of upsetting him. He and his wife asked me to visit again. Aksakov and his wife had gone off to Moscow.

7 July. Went to Tsarskoe Selo to visit Tyutchev, but didn't see him. He has lost consciousness again. I learned, incidentally, his exact age. He is seventy-eight.

11 July. A second warning was issued to *Messenger of Europe.*

14 July. Two articles were responsible for the warning to *Messenger of Europe*: one, by Pypin, on repressive censorship measures; the other, "Revision of the Judicial Code." It describes the orders issued by the minister of justice which have so undermined the new courts, that nothing but a shadow of their new structure will soon remain. There go our fine reforms! The courts have already been undermined; Valuev is bending every effort to roll back emancipation reforms as far as possible, to subordinate the peasantry to the landowners. The *zemstvos* have been paralyzed for a long time, and the press is almost worse off now than it was under Nicholas.

However, we ought not to complain or grumble about this state of affairs. Every nation is ruled as it deserves to be ruled.

The very people who created the reforms are frightened by them. They expected that the most orderly existence, in harmony with their wishes, would logically follow; that our ways would immediately change for the better; that industry and agriculture would flourish; that wealth would flow through the entire country like a river. The press, they felt, would be given over to praising those who held the reins of government, and so on and so forth. All these golden dreams did not come true. You can't change overnight what has taken centuries to ruin and distort. The main object of the reforms was certainly not the immediate enjoyment of the blessings they promised, but, rather, the laying of a solid foundation for the future realization of these blessings. In short, reforms don't have the *present* in mind, but look to the *future*. Therefore we ought not to undermine them, but to ensure them and await the fine fruits they will yield.

Naturally, these reforms have produced much that is distasteful to the government. But I find it very strange that all this wasn't foreseen. Should we conclude from this that it would be better to return to the past?

17 July. When I returned from the city I read the news of Tyutchev's passing. He died Sunday, and the funeral is to be held tomorrow. The funeral train will leave for Novodevichy Monastery at 9 A.M.

18 July. I was cheated out of attending Tyutchev's funeral, in a most stupid way. I had appeared at the deceased's apartment at exactly 9 A.M. today and was told that he had been taken to the train a long time ago for the trip to Novodevichy Monastery. I dashed to the station only to see the smoke of the departing train. What could I do? After silently cursing those who had organized the funeral, I had no choice but to return home. And so, I failed to pay my last respects to the man whom I had loved so much and who had shared with me alone the last wretched fragments of his life.

21 July. Semevsky begged me to write something about Tyutchev for *Russkaya Starina* by Tuesday, in time for the August 1st issue.

23 July. I wrote the article about Tyutchev which Semevsky will pick up tomorrow on his way to Moscow.

2 August. I read the report of the Valuev Commission about the condition of the peasantry. It is an unusually fascinating report. The data in it seems to be factual as well as carefully and intelligently compiled.

The report states that the condition of the peasants has generally been improving since their emancipation. However, their mode of life is still very unsatisfactory almost everywhere in the empire. The main reasons for this are their extreme ignorance and demoralization with its resulting widespread drunkenness; the meagre land allotments in many provinces and the excessive, disproportionate compensation demanded for them; very high taxes; cattle plagues almost everywhere, against which no serious measures have been taken thus far; communal ownership of land; excessive division of peasant holdings; and finally, inept peasant administrations and courts.

To correct these evils, the report states, the causes must be eliminated, and schools can play an important role. Other important aids: the moral influence of the church and clergy; the introduction of technical knowledge in agriculture; the reduction of alcoholism by persuading the peasants of its harmfulness, and by replacing taverns with inns, where food as well as vodka would be sold; and, finally, a careful, continuous check on peasant self-rule. The latter suggestion is mentioned rather cautiously.

Meanwhile, the minister of internal affairs reposes unperturbed in his comfortable armchair as reports of calamities occurring among the people drift through his dreams. And he thinks: "What has all this to do with me? . . ." Oh Timashev, Timashev! Wasn't it you who remarked to me several years ago, before becoming minister, that our tragedy was the lack of public confidence in the government or respect for it, a fact which, in your own words, you even brought to the emperor's attention?

12 August. My family and I and two guests walked to a farm where we had tea and coffee. On our return trip through the park we met the empress riding in her carriage with her betrothed daughter. They stepped out of the carriage not far from us, and it looked as if they were going to hunt for mushrooms. Mushroom hunting in the park has become the latest craze for summer people.

16 October. There was a flood in St. Petersburg about two weeks ago reminiscent of the flood of November 7, 1824. The water rose almost ten feet (it had risen to nineteen feet in 1824). The low-lying sections of the city suffered quite badly this time, too. The water filled basements and overflowed into the streets. The storm sank many barges and tore up many trees.

21 October. I read Maikov my article on his poem, *Two Worlds.* He was very pleased with it. He brought me the latest edition of his poetry, issued in three volumes.

Maikov wants to submit his translation of *The Tale of Igor's Campaign* and a commentary on it to the Academy for the Uvarov prize. He asked for my advice and assistance. Naturally, I gave him the former, and I have promised him my full support for the prize, too.

29 November. I dined with Minister Tolstoy today. He talked at length about licentiousness in the provinces; about the Samara gymnasium for women where he had fired several teachers for nihilism, and the *zemstvo*'s subsequent complaint to the Senate; about university autonomy which he wants to replace with his own arbitrary authority, and so on and so forth. His motto can be summed up in these few words: "Everyone is a fool, except me." This man, who is an intelligent and even good person under ordinary circumstances, doesn't know the real meaning of administration and guidance, but knows only one thing—how powerful he is at Court, how to lash out at everyone and smash whatever he gets a notion to destroy, and to demand absolute obedience from everyone.

13 December. Meeting of the Academy's Department of Russian Letters. Count Lev Tolstoy and Count Aleksei Tolstoy were elected corresponding members of the Academy.

Terrible famine in Samara. The administration did nothing to prevent it, but only insisted on the collection of tax arrears. They sold the peasants' cattle and all their other property for back taxes.

17 December. It wasn't until a few days ago that we learned that the famine in Samara province had actually been raging since the very beginning of autumn, while Governor Klimov had reported that all was well. The ministry staff, too busy with the important task of furnishing its minister's apartment, naturally was not inclined, with its well-filled stomachs, to think about famines in Samara or elsewhere.

So many deaths have occurred recently that one is haunted by the thought of it. So many people of my age are dying off that the thought has begun to visit me frequently. People are rarely prepared for it. They have not managed to finish something, repent, or straighten out some business, or make provisions for their families, and so forth. I find myself in the latter position. My body is visibly wearing out: rents keep appearing which require medical repairs.

19 December. Meeting of litterateurs at Gaevsky's apartment to arrange for the publication of a literary anthology for the benefit of Samara's famine victims. A publications committee was elected: Kraevsky, Goncharov, Nekrasov and myself. Our anthology is called *Skladchina.*[i]

[i] Literally, "the pooling of resources."

1874

1 January. I received a little card from Delyanov with the following inscription some three hours before the New Year began: "I.D. Delyanov hastens to offer his congratulations to you, a recipient of the order of the *White Eagle.*" I was absolutely stunned. True, about two months ago Bunyakovsky informed me that I had been proposed for the *White Eagle.* I figured it was merely a presumption or wish on the part of dear Victor Yakovlevich and promptly forgot about it. If it is a reward for special services I have performed, I certainly do not deserve it; if it is a reward for simply serving, a mere formality, what value can it have? And here I am, receiving congratulations, as if it were already an accomplished fact.

4 January. The manifesto on military conscription was printed in today's papers, and the *Voice* published a laudatory, but intelligent and sensible editorial on the new law.[1]

8 February. A storm has developed over *Skladchina*'s publications committee. The *Moscow Bulletin*, as usual, saw something dangerous here, and its followers, or rather zealots, are raising a fuss about the appointment of Nekrasov and Kraevsky. Why, they want to know, were reds appointed? One of these chaps attacked Goncharov, and, today, I was the target. Goncharov countered the attack with a sharp rebuff, while I declared that I was not interested in Kraevsky or Nekrasov but only in helping the victims of the famine; and Kraevsky, I felt, with his knowledge of the mechanics of publishing, was indispensable to our purpose. It seems that anything good we undertake in our country can't escape the smearing tactics of the very people who should be throwing all their support behind such projects.

19 February. Present-day psychologists, particularly of the English school, resemble those dry-as-dust archaeologists who, digging in graves, uncover bones and complete human skeletons. They sort them out, can even put them together and arrange them according to age, sex and so forth, but they cannot reconstruct a human image from them.

3 March. Spent the evening at Goncharov's, who had dropped in to see me earlier to invite me to a soirée at his home. Maikov's translation of *Cassandra* from Aeschylus was read. It goes without saying that the translation was excellent; and the reading was very enjoyable—especially since it wasn't long. I was introduced to Leskov, author of the popular and, they say, very fine novel, *Soboryane.*[j]

[j] "Cathedral folk."

10 March. I had an audience with the emperor at the Winter Palace. Five of us were presented. The emperor came up to me. It is difficult to describe his pleasant smile and the warm tone in which he said: "Thank you, thank you for your zealous and faithful service. I am certain that you will continue to serve us so well. Thank you, again."

26 March. Doesn't it seem absurd that I enter every trifle in my diary with such precision? Ever since I can remember, almost since childhood, my guiding principle was to keep a watchful eye on myself. For many years I limited this careful review of myself to my moral and intellectual state exclusively, without the slightest regard for my physical condition and health. I kept driving toward my moral ideal, to the realization of my human responsibilities and, of course, have made many mistakes. But for some time now, since my health began to undergo various stresses, I have been keeping track of my physical as well as my moral and intellectual well-being and, perhaps, I owe what little health I have managed to preserve to this care.

My corporeal sheath is visibly deteriorating: my vision is growing weak, but those damned jolting sensations in my head have worn me down more than anything else.

10 September. Award of the Uvarov prizes at the Academy of Sciences. I had examined six plays and found two of them, Pisemsky's *Vaal* and Minaev's *Ruined Nest*, worthy of special attention. I wrote detailed reviews, praising both of them, but left the final decision to the commission. However, I tended to favor Minaev's play, although I did want to see Pisemsky get a prize, too. He had submitted a second play, *Intrigues*, but it was weaker. The commission expressed negative feelings about Pisemsky's play and preferred Minaev's. There was a debate and the prize was unanimously awarded today to Minaev's *Ruined Nest*.

7 October. Many people are being arrested: more than five hundred, they say, in the provinces, including many women.

Everyone's attention is focussed on the trial of Mother-Superior Mitrofaniya, who tried to acquire huge sums of money for the benefit of her convent's philanthropic enterprises with forged promissory notes.

Trying a high ranking member of the clergy for a capital crime and, to boot, publicly and completely openly, is unprecedented in Russia.

20 October. Mother Superior Mitrofaniya's trial has ended. The jury's verdict was: "guilty, but with a recommendation for leniency." This trial stirred no less excitement here than did Arnim's in Europe. Our trial was very significant for two reasons: one, the rank of the accused, who was tried in a public court and sentenced to criminal punishment; two, the conduct of the trial, which did honor to our judges. Influence played no role in their decision.

24 October. There was an uproar at the Academy of Medicine and Surgery several days ago. The students announced that they would not attend lectures given by Professor Tsion of the Department of Physiology, and they split up into two groups: some whistled, while others clapped.[k] One hears a variety of explanations for the incident. In general, it's impossible in St. Petersburg to learn the facts about anything that happens. Everyone offers his own version, often embellishing it, while solemnly assuring you that he obtained his information from a most reliable source.

3 November. The disturbance at the Academy of Medicine was repeated at the Mining Institute, the Technological Institute, and the university, but on a smaller scale at the latter. The students demanded the dismissal of Tsion, who was finally relieved of his post. The official excuse given to the public was that he was taking a year's leave abroad. Gendarmes were dispatched to the Mining Institute and the Technological Institute. Since our press has been reduced to silence, not a word about these events appears in them, and, therefore, the most fantastic rumors are circulating around the city.

What is behind this epidemic of revolts in the schools? Young people don't like this or that school administrator or instructor, so they demand his immediate discharge. This should not be permitted. But the point is that such demands are being made and are reaching epidemic proportions. Alas! These are merely symptoms of the disorder reigning everywhere in our country, our administration and our society.

Morality is sinking lower and lower. Our young people have noble impulses, but these noble impulses are constantly directed against the existing order of things.

Everyone is dissatisfied, everyone is suffering, and suffering unbearably, because there is no confidence in what tomorrow will bring. I truly fear for Russia's future.

It seems that no human effort can save us from our fate. We are in the hands of history, which is drawing us irresistibly toward a fateful, inevitable crisis.

[k] According to a note by the Soviet editors of the *Diary,* "I. F. Tsion . . . , from the very first, set himself in opposition to the progressive camp of professors and students. . . ."

1875

1 January. Everything in my beloved country is a pack of lies, lies and more lies. We have a fine Eastern Orthodox religion. But crude, superstitious beliefs predominate among the masses; and the upper classes camouflage their total indifference and skepticism toward religion with new ideas or scientific arrogance. We have laws; but what administrator, in whose interest it is to ignore them, carries them out; what kind of people have been chosen to check on their execution? We have science, but who is so dedicated to it and morally uplifted by it that he will not sacrifice it for so-called material goals?

There is one thing we don't lie about: the fact that we are building a powerful state capable of repulsing any foreign enemy who dares to attack us. And another thing we don't lie about is the state of our morals and manners. We promise nothing, but frankly state that we don't have an iota of community spirit; we steal, get drunk, and try to outswindle each other, openly and without hypocrisy.

12 January. The Valuev Commission has decided that graduation examinations at the universities should henceforth be prepared by appointees of the minister in order to check on the kind of instruction professors are giving. It was also decided, as far as possible, to make it difficult for students who do not come from privileged, noble and wealthy families to enter our universities. Professors will no longer be appointed by university councils, but by the ministry, and so on and so forth in the same vein.[1]

20 January. The Russian *muzhik* is practically a perfect savage. He is crude, ignorant, and lacks any understanding of rights and law, while his religion consists of nodding his head and flailing his arms. He's a drunkard and a thief, but a far better person than the so-called educated, intelligent Russian. The *muzhik* is sincere; he doesn't try to appear to be what he is not; he will not slander himself, anyone, or anything. But our educated Russian is a liar from head to toe; he is a swindler in keeping with the belief that "a clever man can't help being a swindler." He is vain. He is liberal in word and servile in deed, ready to stoop to anything for the sake of rank or a decoration. He is like a thief in his flair for living on a grand scale. But the main thing and worst of all, is that he is a liar in everything he thinks, says and does. He catches on easily and quickly, mastering whatever he chooses. Therefore, he presents a gentle, well-bred, polished appearance. He is thoroughly European, a civilized man; but in reality he is a faint-hearted, spineless creature.

2 March. This winter will be a memorable one. The weather was remarkably stable and temperate for St. Petersburg, yet epidemics of typhus and recurring typhus raged through the city. More than 15,000 fell ill, and very many died. Naturally, as always, the lower classes were hit the hardest.

19 April. An article by Professor Wagner, which puzzled a great many people, appeared at the beginning of this month in *Messenger of Europe.* He tells strange stories about *tipping tables,* which he himself witnessed. Everyone is quoting Shakespeare's famous words from *Hamlet: "There are more things in heaven and earth, Horatio, than are dreamt of in your philosophy."* Wagner is now the second serious scholar who has attached any importance to spiritualism. The first was our academician, Butlerov, who now firmly believes in it. Both men are scientists. One would expect such people, least of all, to believe in the supernatural.

22 April. A commission was appointed to review university charters, that is, for the real purpose of stifling the universities as much as possible and destroying the freedom of university or higher education. The commission is composed of enemies of the universities.

4 May. According to Count Tolstoy's system, indigent students would be excluded from higher education, as though only the well-to-do were equipped to perform real mental labor and possessed those virtues which form the backbone of our society. What will these excluded, indigent students, deprived of the right to a higher education, do? They will become the most dangerous proletariat—an intellectual proletariat. Since it will be closer to the masses than the well-to-do and aristocrats, what kind of influence will this suffering, unhappy element, treated like outcasts, have on them?

29 May. Can one have any faith in the teachings of the Germans after the eminent German scholars Bluntschli and Gneist tried to justify Prussia's brazen attempt to attack France without the slightest provocation on France's part? France, they reason, is now busy building up her military strength. She wants revenge on Germany for the recent defeat inflicted on her, and, therefore, Germany must anticipate her and utterly destroy her in order to deprive her of her army or any means of taking revenge or defending herself. Have you ever heard of such logic? France is vainly trying to prove that, by concerning herself with internal affairs and raising her army to a level in keeping with the status of a great power, she is certainly not thinking about war. Not a single government in Europe can make any move relating to its internal affairs without first seeking Bismarck's consent. This is also his attitude toward Belgium and Italy. And German scholars and top ranking intellects have set out to prove scientifically the correctness of this cut-throat policy. War in France would be inevitable, and rivers of blood would flow once more as plundering German knights, like a savage hurricane, ravaged Europe's finest lands. And all because it suited Bismarck. Can a nation that has talked so much about the advances of science and civilization sink much lower in its political arrogance and greed? Has science uplifted or humanized them?

5 June. The government is very nervous. They say that various revolutionary leaflets addressed to the people have been found in large quantities in
the provinces. There are constant arrests of the people distributing them.
Meanwhile, general demoralization is increasing steadily in all classes. If all
this is true, we are indeed in sad straits. What should our intelligentsia do?
It should make a concerted effort to resist this destructive, demoralizing
trend. The government should understand the need for this and enlist the
cream of society as its ally. That is why, for example, the plan to deprive the
universities of their rights is so untimely.

8 July. The propaganda that our revolutionaries are circulating is certainly
disgusting. They preach the abolition of the family, private property, all the
elements on which human societies are based. Naturally, this will only lead
to one thing: opposition to them and their ideas by anyone with a grain of
common sense. If, instead, they were to talk about the abuses of our administration, its arbitrariness, thievery and similar evils, they could win over decent
people. By striving for the possible rather than the impossible, they could inspire the public to work for the possible. But now, with their communistic
and socialistic opposition they are only hurting the cause of national freedom
and national progress. The kind of administration we have now is still prefer-
able to anarchy.

18 July. A report was published on the Senate trial of those charged with
disseminating revolutionary ideas among factory workers in St. Petersburg and
the Moscow Guards. All these revolutionaries, that is, the chief instigators—
are young people, students from the university and the Academy of Medicine.
They called for a revolt against the government, for the introduction of socialism and communism. We don't know what to be more surprised at—the audacity or absurdity of their actions.

25 July. A memorandum has been composed on the results of the investigation of revolutionary propaganda. For some reason, it is not being made public. It seems that the evil was far more deeply entrenched than it was believed
to be. The ideas it has been preaching, that is, basic communistic and socialistic dogma, are absurd. But that's not the point: the point is that people are
extremely dissatisfied with the order of things and this dissatisfaction is nour-
ished by all sorts of ideas which promise to oppose this order. A circular from
the minister of education complains that these ideas are receiving support in
the community and in the home.

6 November. Mass and funeral service for Count A.K. Tolstoy. I arrived early,
before the mass had begun. Several litterateurs were present: Goncharov,
Kraevsky, Stasyulevich, Miller, and Kostomarov. A.K. Tolstoy was one of
our most talented poets and a good friend of mine.

1876

[*n.d.*] *Abroad.* A protracted, serious illness has forced me to go abroad. Doctors and laymen alike told me it would restore my energy and appetite, which I lost some two months ago. So I finally decided to go, though reluctantly.

20 June. [Switzerland.] When I pass beneath the colonnade of the casino, I often meet a man whose extremely unattractive appearance never fails to startle me. There is something insolent and arrogant about his whole bearing. When we were strolling with our dear friend M.A.S. several days ago, and met this man again, she said: "Do you know who that is? He was introduced to me yesterday, and here's how he introduced himself: 'I am Baron von Heckeren (d'Anthès), the man who killed your poet Pushkin.' And," M.A.S. added, "if you could have seen the smug expression on his face when he said it. I can't tell you how loathesome that man is!" Indeed, it is difficult to imagine anything more disgusting than this once handsome, but now, flabby face with its trace of coarse passions. He is a rabid Bonapartist, and because of this and his generally poor reputation, all the local Frenchmen—most of the visitors here are French—avoid him. He was a senator during Napoleon III's reign, but now is a nobody. People speak very badly of his domestic situation. So, the cat has been given his just desserts.

12 August. The politics of the East today are very simple: the Turks would like to wipe out the Christians bordering them or turn them into completely submissive slaves. England says: "I will most certainly help you if you care to be my vassal and grant me full control over the Dardanelles and Constantinople so that I can establish a market for the unlimited sale of my cotton, wool, and other goods." And what about Europe? Europe feels that England's policy is very cunning, profound, and not without grandeur, although it is not too happy about England's strategy. It either remains silent or writes diplomatic notes which Disraeli laughs at. Only Russia grumbles and tries to do something about it, but no one listens to us or fears us.

23 August. The sharp contrasts between poverty and wealth are very striking in Switzerland despite its democratic spirit. Palaces rise in the cities and there are wealthy settlements where abundance and prosperity are evident in almost every chalet. But the workers, who own neither land nor chalets, suffer in dire poverty. One only has to glance at their emaciated faces, at the rags which cover their bodies, and to observe their ceaseless labor under a broiling sun, to be convinced that the Swiss are far from prosperous.

10 September. St. Petersburg. After a protracted and serious illness I had gone abroad on March 30th, on the advice of my doctors, to regain my health in the clean, healthy, southern air. I spent five months abroad and returned to St. Petersburg on Wednesday, September 8th, via the Warsaw railroad.

My health? It hasn't been fully restored but has improved noticeably. Yet I am worried about the effects of the St. Petersburg climate.

17 September. The smell of war is in the air. We are making preparations for it. England has tempered, somewhat, its enthusiasm for the Turks and their brutality. But it still fears that Constantinople will fall into Russia's hands.

7 October. Something very unexpected happened at 11 o'clock last night. I had felt rather well during the day, but I was taken with chills and fever in the evening; also weakness and chest pain.

26 November. Something akin to infanticide occurred when four newspapers were banned or suspended at one blow: *New Times, Russian World,* the *Stock Exchange Bulletin,* and the *Stock Exchange News.* The reason? Supposedly, some chatter about vodka and Russia's financial state.[1]

3 December. Still another bank has gone under. There were, we hear, some 3,000 innocent victims; rather, I should say, guilty victims, for they put their trust in credit which is simply nonexistent in Russia. They say there are an incredible number of bankruptcies in Moscow. Luckily, an excuse has been found—the war.

6 December. A scuffle took place at Kazan Cathedral. Some unidentified revolutionaries decided to organize a demonstration. Naturally, the police stopped them and, they say, the public sided with the police. We don't know yet what it's all about. Rumors are circulating and it is impossible, naturally, to make any sense out of them. We shall have to wait for the details.[1]

11 December. Details appeared in the press, first in the *Government Messenger* and then in the *Voice,* about the demonstration on the square in front of Kazan Cathedral. It began with various indecent outbursts inside the church during the mass. Then the following words rang out on the square outside the church: "And we devote today, December 6, to the memory of our unfortunate political prisoners." A banner was raised with the inscription "Land and Freedom" and was followed by a speech that was interrupted by the police. They had planned to march to the Winter Palace and make certain demands. The police began to arrest the culprits and the people helped the police. They arrested more than thirty people, including eleven women. Huge crowds had gathered. In brief, it was a reckless revolutionary attempt. This sort of activity is so utterly foolish; now, in particular, with our preparation for war, it can prove very damaging.

[1] The demonstration was organized by the Populist's "Land and Freedom" movement.

27 December. They say that many young women who had joined the disorders at the Cathedral—some of them purely out of curiosity—were nearly beaten to death by the crowd. This is seen as a reflection of the patriotic mood of the masses! The demonstrators' banner contained the inscription: "Land and Freedom," and the crowd interpreted it to mean that the rebels wanted to take away the land and freedom already given to the people by the tsar.

1877

1 January. I am forever sick, sick, sick. One minute I try to brace myself with the thought that whatever will be will be, but that I must not, in any case, lose courage; the next I become very discouraged and depressed. And so it goes, day after day.

Be that as it may, I begin each day by summoning up my courage, although I must say that the results of this summons don't always last the day.

8 January. War or peace? That is the question on everyone's lips, and no one seems to understand anything. The transactions at Constantinople were a complete fiasco. One thing is evident: Europe is rotting away with its materialistic philosophy of life and is unconcerned with problems common to all mankind. Another thing, too, is evident: it hates Russia, wants to drag it into an unwanted and terrible war and place the responsibility for its disastrous consequences on Russia's shoulders. What course we shall take is shrouded in mystery.

16 January. Our Slavophiles are more Slav than the Slavs themselves. The Slavs in Turkey have really had an intolerable situation, and, that they finally revolted, was very understandable. But the Austrian Slavs have fairly good conditions: they receive civil protection and certainly would have nothing to gain, but much to lose, by shifting their allegiance to another power. As far as national unity is concerned, the Slavs will never have it—they are eternally battling with each other. If not for the Magyars, they could not want a better situation than they have with the Hapsburgs. The Magyars are the thorn in the side of the Austrian Slavs. Naturally, it is necessary to oppose them, but not with the idea of expelling them from Austria.

2 February. I felt so poorly all day today, that I almost began to welcome the idea of death.

3 February. And what is so unusual or frightening about death? Especially when you get used to the idea; and getting used to it is not as difficult as it seems at first.

There are two things which it is difficult to become reconciled to—Russian administration and medicine.

19 June. Our forces crossed the Danube several days ago.[m]

19 July. My health is downright vile; the summer is downright vile; and

[m] Nikitenko made no entries between 3 February and 19 June. Meanwhile, the Russo-Turkish war had broken out in April.

humanity is downright vile, because it permits the Turks to slaughter and burn people while Europe is busy with diplomacy, and England with its own interests. It is difficult not to have deep contempt for everything that lives and thinks. But one must at least protect one's self from suffering as much as one's firm and courageous spirit will permit.

Outside the wind is howling like a wild beast. It is raining and gloomy.[n]

[n] Nikitenko died on 21 July 1877.

NOTES

1826

1. Nikitenko is probably referring to General V. V. Levashev, who was conducting the investigation into the Decembrist affair. The granting of permission to move indicated that the commission did not suspect Nikitenko of belonging to the secret society.

2. Fyodor Nikolaevich Glinka (1786–1880), poet and cousin of the composer, Mikhail Glinka, and member of secret Decembrist societies involved in the conspiracy to overthrow the regime and establish a constitutional form of government. He was arrested on 30 December 1825 but immediately freed on imperial orders. He was arrested again on 11 March 1826 and spent three months in the fortress.

3. "Rostovtsev in his report to Nicholas mentioned no names . . . though Nicholas cunningly tried to learn who were the members." A. Mazour, *The First Russian Revolution, 1825* (Stanford: Stanford University Press, 1937), p. 163.

1828

1. War between Russia and Persia broke out in June 1826 when Persian troops crossed the Russian border. In 1827 hostilities shifted to Persian soil. Capitulation by the Persians was followed by the Treaty of Turkmanchay. Russia acquired the provinces of Nakhichevan and Erivan, and obtained the right to maintain a navy in the Caspian Sea.

2. "Inheriting from Alexander I the complex issue of the Greek War of Independence, Nicholas 1 took a firmer stand against Turkey . . . eventually culminating in a war between Russia and the Ottoman state, fought from April 1828 to September 1829. Yet, in the opinion of Nicholas 1, hostilities against Turkey had nothing to do with any support of the Greeks: they resulted rather from long range tensions between the two neighboring empires." The Treaty of Adrianople gave the victorious Russians the mouth of the Danube and considerable territory in the Caucasus. "But in spite of these and certain other Russian gains embodied in the treaty . . . the Russian emperor did not try to destroy its opponent, regarding Turkey as an important and desireable element in the European balance of power." Nicholas Riasanovsky, *Nicholas 1 and Official Nationality in Russia: 1825–1855* (Berkeley and Los Angeles: University of California Press, 1969), pp. 238–39.

3. "The rigid censorship law of June 10, 1826 was replaced by the more liberal code of April 22, 1828, which directed the censors merely to prevent the appearance of 'harmful publications' and relieved them of the duty of directing public opinion and correcting 'mistakes' of fact or even the style of the authors. The law of 1828 remained in force throughout the reign of Nicholas 1, but it was amended and interpreted in a manner which for all practical purposes was a return to the principles of the act of 1826." Michael T. Florinsky, *Russia: A History and an Interpretation* (New York: Macmillan Co., 1969), 2: 812.

1832

1. The *European,* a political journal published by I. V. Kireevsky, was banned on 7 February 1832 after the appearance of the first two installments. Two articles by Kireevsky in the first issue, one, "The Nineteenth Century," and the other on the Moscow production of *Woe from Wit,* were cited as the reason for the ban. Soviet notes for the *Diary* claim that the basic reason for the ban was Kireevsky's attempt, though moderate and cautious, to propagandize for constitutional ideas.

1834

1. The immediate cause of the banning of the journal *Moscow Telegraph* was Polevoy's article on Kukolnik's obsequious, pseudopatriotic play, *The Hand of the Almighty Saved the Fatherland* (1834). Since one of the enthusiastic spectators was Nicholas I, the article was seen as a political attack. But the real reasons lay much deeper and were revealed in the government's decision to get rid of the *Moscow Telegraph*'s political radicalism. Uvarov said in his report to the emperor of 21 March 1834: "A revolutionary tone . . . is evident in the journal, of which thousands of copies are circulated in Russia. . . ." M. I. Sukhomlinov, *Issledovaniia i stat 'i po russkoi literature i prosveshcheniiu* [Studies and articles on Russian literature and education], vol. 2 (St. Petersburg, 1889), p. 412.

2. Gogol's story, "The Tale of How Ivan Ivanovich Quarrelled With Ivan Nikiforovich," was published in the almanac *Novosel'e* [The housewarming], vol. 2 (St. Petersburg, 1834), pp. 479–569. For the most part the deleted passages have not been reconstructed owing to the loss of Gogol's manuscript. Prior to censoring this tale, Nikitenko had prohibited publication of "The Bloody Bandore Player," a chapter from Gogol's unfinished novel *The Hetman.* This was done at the instigation of Grech. *Literaturnoye nasledstvo* [Literary legacy], no. 58 (Moscow, 1952), pp. 545–46.

1841

1. Nikitenko's review of Lermontov's *Poems* appeared in *Son of the Fatherland,* no. 1 (1841), pp. 3–13.

2. The rumors about a manifesto were related to the activities of a special secret committee organized in 1829. The only practical result of its activities was the issuing of a decree on the "obligations of the peasants" on 2 April 1842.

1846

1. The journal *Contemporary* was founded by Pushkin. In 1840 it was purchased by Nekrasov as the voice of the liberal-radical camp.

2. Nikitenko's meeting with Alexander Herzen was related to Nikitenko's appointment to the editorial staff of the *Contemporary,* to which Herzen was a contributor. In a letter written to his wife on 5 October 1846, Herzen mentions his forthcoming meeting with Nikitenko, and in a letter dated 8 October, describes the meeting to her. Thus the 10 October date noted by Nikitenko appears to be incorrect. Herzen was impressed with Nikitenko and described him in the letter as "an amazingly kind and noble person, who welcomed me with open arms." This letter appears in Herzen's collected works: A. I. Herzen, *Polnoe sobranie sochinenii i pisem pod redaktsiei M. K. Lemke* [Collected works and letters edited by M. K. Lemke], vol. 4 of 21 vols. (Leningrad, 1919–35).

1848

1. "With the appointment on April 2, 1848, immediately after the outbreak of the revolution in France, of a secret committee on censorship under Count D. P. Buturlin, there began what is usually known as the 'era of censorship terror,' which lasted until the dissolution of the committee on December 6, 1855. The censors, spurred by threat of penalties for laxity and lack of zeal, used the red pencil with utmost freedom. . . ." Florinsky, 2: 813.

1849

1. This is the first reference Nikitenko makes to his resignations from his censorship and editorial positions. He resigned as editor of the *Contemporary* in April of 1848. Both resignations were undoubtedly inspired by the nature of the times. The revolutionary thunder in Europe frightened Russia's leadership into a veritable reign of terror, throwing liberals like Nikitenko into near panic. On 6 April 1848, Nikitenko was summoned by Count Orlov, Chief of the Gendarmes, and warned about the seditious nature of the articles appearing in the *Contemporary* under his editorship. P. A. Bugaenko, *Esteticheskie vzglyady A. V. Nikitenko* [Nikitenko's aesthetic views] (Ezhegodnik Saratovskogo universiteta, filogogicheskii fakul'tet [Yearbook of the Philology Department of Saratov University], 1958), p. 20.

1856

1. The Crimean War (1853–56) between Russia on the one hand and Britain, France, Turkey and Austria on the other, ended on 16 January 1856 with acceptance by Alexander II of the peace terms proposed in the Austrian ultimatum. The four points to which Nikitenko referred in his diary were: 1) freedom of navigation on the Danube; 2) Russia would abandon her claim to protect Orthodox Christians in Turkey and permit, instead, collective protection of Christians, regardless of denomination, by the five great powers; 3) substitution of a European guarantee for the Russian protectorate over Moldavia, Wallachia and Serbia; 4) neutralization of the Black Sea.

1857

1. On 20 November 1857, Alexander II issued a rescript in the name of V. I. Nazimov, governor-general of Vilnius, Grodno, and Kovno. It ordered the formation in these provinces of committees, composed of elected representatives from the nobility, which would work out plans for emancipation of the serfs. These plans were to be based on proposals already formulated in a note drafted by Minister of Internal Affairs Lanskoy. The publication of the rescript in the press on 17 December 1857 was the first official announcement by the government of preparations for the emancipation of the serfs.

1858

1. "The student riots in the autumn of 1858 were the first in the history of St. Petersburg University. They began with a clash between the progressive student body and the police. As far as can be judged from the incomplete facts at hand, the cause of the riots was an insult inflicted by the police on a student, Rashevsky. The latter had taken his complaint to Chief of the Gendarmes Shuvalov, who cursed him and drove him from his

office. The students took this as an insult to the entire student body. A student delegation proceeded to the office of Delyanov, Superintendent of the school district." B. L. Modzalevskii, "K istorii Peterburgskogo universiteta 1857-1859. Iz bumag L. N. Modzalevsky—'Golos minuvshogo' " [On the history of St. Petersburg University, 1857–1859. From the papers of L. N. Modzalevsky—"The voice of the past"], no. 1 (1917), p. 165.

2. An anonymous article was printed in *Illustration,* no. 35 (1858), "refuting" the demands of progressive Russian circles which called for the extension of civil rights for Jews in Russia. It was full of coarse anti-Semitic attacks. The article drew replies from the *Russian Messenger,* no. 18 (1858), and from *Athenaeus,* no. 9 (1858). *Illustration,* in its reply to them (no. 43, 1858), indulged in even cruder insinuations, which provoked a protest from a group of St. Petersburg litterateurs (*St. Petersburg Bulletin,* no. 258, 1858). Several dozen writers joined the protest; among those to sign were Nekrasov, Turgenev, Chernyshevsky, and Shevchenko.

1860

1. During the summer of 1860, while abroad, Goncharov worked on his novel, *The Precipice,* and upon his return to Russia published two chapters from it, "Grandmother" and "Portrait." The character of Vera which elicited Nikitenko's comments in his diary was basically very different from that which emerged in the novel's final version.

2. Nikitenko stated the following in his written opinion: "Nekrasov's poems flow from an elegaic mood which is very common among our own and foreign writers and, understandably, they do arouse discomforting thoughts when they fix their gaze on various aspects of people's lives and the daily life of society. The banning of such literary works would mean the elimination of one of literature's inescapable features and, by interfering, so to say, in the psychological processes of a person's inner life, the appearance of any outstanding talent in literature will be rendered impossible." V. E. Evgen'ev-Maksimov, *Nekrasov, kak chelovek, zhurnalist i poet* [Nekrasov, the man, the journalist, the poet] (Government Publishing House, 1928), pp. 229–37.

3. The Sunday schools were organized by circles of progressive intellectuals to teach adults the rudiments of reading and writing. This popular movement began in Kiev and St. Petersburg in 1859, and by 1862 there were over 300 such schools in 178 towns, with an attendance of some 20,000.

1861

1. Kostomarov's speech was cancelled because the university administration feared it would inspire student demonstrations in favor of one of their popular professors. Sergei Gessen, *Studencheskoe dvizhenie v nachale shestidesyatykh godov* [The student movement at the beginning of the sixties] (Moscow, 1932), pp. 45–46.

2. On 19 February 1861 Alexander II signed the Emancipation Proclamation and the manifesto on reforms. However, neither document was published until 6 March 1861, since the government feared disturbances. These fears inspired Governor-General Ignatiev to release the statement which Nikitenko mentions in his diary.

3. "In the summer and autumn of 1861 appeared the first revolutionary proclamations printed in Russia, forerunners of a long line of underground publications. . . . Many of the appeals issued by Herzen and other radical leaders were addressed to university youth. That they were not without effect was indicated by the outbreak in the autumn of 1861 of student disturbances. The movement had a political character and spread from St. Petersburg to Moscow and other university cities." Florinsky, 2: 1074.

4. Mikhail Illarionovich Mikhailov (1826–65), poet, novelist, publicist, revolutionary democrat, was arrested in September for his role in the drafting and distribution of the leaflet "To the Younger Generation." He was sentenced to penal servitude in Siberia. This was the first political trial during the reign of Alexander II.

5. According to the Soviet editors of the *Diary*, Nikitenko's proposal for a lighter penalty in no way reflected his sympathy for the journal. Nikitenko's report ended with the following words: "There is no doubt that the journals *Contemporary* and *Russian Word* have a significant influence on the mass of our reading public, particularly our young people. These journals should be pressured to change their tone."

1862

1. An official report of the events appeared in the *Northern Post,* no. 12., (1862). "In 1862 the gentry of Tver sent a formal petition to Alexander II asking for political rights to be given to the entire people (they were willing to renounce their own privileged position), and thirteen of them, who later put their names to a more outspoken document on the same lines, were imprisoned for a time. These were actions in favor of liberal reform, by members of the gentry acting corporately." Ronald Hingley, *Russian Writers and Society 1825–1904* (New York: McGraw-Hill, 1967), p. 234.

2. On 2 March 1862 a literary benefit was held in St. Petersburg, officially organized for needy students, in reality for exiled Mikhailov (see 1861, note 4) and Obruchev. Among the participants were Chernyshevsky, Kurochkin, and Professor of History Pavlov, who was very popular with the students. Pavlov delivered a speech which was misheard and misinterpreted by its biased listeners. The meeting ended in a fracas and Pavlov's subsequent arrest on 5 March 1862. L. F. Panteleev, "Academia," *Is vospominanii proshlogo* [from reminiscences of the past] (1934), pp. 160–61.

3. The Chief Censorship Administration in the Ministry of Education was abolished by a decree issued on 10 March 1862. The censorship apparatus itself remained in the Ministry of Education, which would continue to exercise preliminary censorship powers. However, the Ministry of Internal Affairs was given the power to check the press for violations of censorship rules. A. M. Skabichevsky, *Ocherki istorii russkoi tsenzury, 1700–1863* [Studies in the history of Russian censorship, 1700–1863] (St. Petersburg, 1892), p. 474.

4. The decree of 10 March 1862 which abolished the Chief Censorship Administration and gave supervisory and surveillance powers to the Ministry of Internal Affairs caused a great deal of confusion in the censorship department. Now it was responsible to two ministries, each of which operated independently in censorship matters, without developing any kind of coordinated plan. The Ministry of Education, almost from the very first day of the new decree, saw itself under the constant domination of the Ministry of Internal Affairs, which began to shower it with an endless stream of reports on various censorship violations, many of them very petty. Ibid., p. 477.

5. The fires that swept St. Petersburg in the spring of 1862 were ascribed to subversive elements.

6. Nikitenko is referring to the "Basic Principles," or statutes, for the reform of the judiciary, which were made public on 29 September 1862. They formed the foundation for the judicial reforms of 1864.

7. Obolensky's commission was critical of the present censorship system which divided responsibilities between the Ministry of Education and the Ministry of Internal Affairs. Its recommendation for the transfer of the entire censorship apparatus to the Ministry of Internal Affairs was implemented by 1 March 1863. *Skabichevsky,* pp. 494–95.

1863

1. The insurgent movement was directed by the Central National Committee, an agency of the Reds. . . . The rival organization of the Whites was at odds with the National Committee on practically every issue except the demand for the restoration of Poland within the frontiers of 1772. . . . On 22 January 1863 the National Committee declared "a state of insurrection" and issued a manifesto proclaiming the equality of "all sons of Poland irrespective of religion, origin, and social status." The manifesto, which was read from the pulpit of every church in Poland, promised the peasants the ownership of the land they farmed; the large landowners were to be indemnified by the state. After some hesitation the Whites endorsed this program. The unsuccessful insurrection lasted eighteen months. Florinsky, 2: 913-14.

2. From the very beginning the Polish insurrection elicited widespread sympathy in Europe. Under the pressure of public opinion, the governments of France, England and Austria sent notes to the Russian government in defense of Poland. Russia categorically rejected the interference of these powers in Russian-Polish relations. As a result of this "diplomatic duel" international relations took a serious turn, thereby arousing fears of war in Russia and the western European powers.

3. In the middle of June 1863 the English, French and Austrian ambassadors in St. Petersburg handed Minister of Foreign Affairs Gorchakov notes with a number of demands on the Polish question. The *six points* included demands for full amnesty for the Poles, a national government in keeping with the 1815 constitution, the restoration of Polish administration, freedom of religion, the introduction of Polish in the schools and official institutions. In his reply, Gorchakov categorically rejected the interference of the three powers in Russia's affairs and their attempts to act as mediator between the insurgents and the Russian government.

1864

1. Turgenev's presence was required in relation to the "trial of the 32" charged with having dealings with London-based Russian propagandists. Over a period of several months prior to the inquiry, he had corresponded with the Russian government, even writing personally to Alexander II trying to prove that he was not affiliated with any political organization. In March 1863 Turgenev was sent six questions which he answered in great detail, not only describing his relationship with Herzen, Ogarev, Bakunin and many other political émigrés, but even enclosing several letters he had received from Herzen and Bakunin. Mikhail Lemke, *Ocherki osvoboditelnogo dvizheniya shestidesyatykh godov* [Studies in the freedom movement of the sixties] (St. Petersburg, 1908), pp. 160-74. The Russian government, however, was not satisfied with this evidence and again demanded his presence in St. Petersburg. Finally, in January 1864, Turgenev appeared before the Senate, gave testimony and received permission to return abroad on condition that he return to Russia if summoned. Ibid., pp. 206-8.

2. "The statutes of the judiciary of 20 November 1864 embodied with a varying degree of thoroughness the accepted principles of western European jurisprudence: equality of all before the law; access to an impartial tribunal and the right to be heard; . . . a fair trial; uniformity of judicial procedure; separation of the judicial from the legislative and the executive power; irremovability of the judges except for misconduct in office; publicity of proceedings; representation of the parties in civil cases and of defendants in criminal cases by qualified members of the bar; trial by jury; election of judges of the lower

courts; preliminary investigation of criminal offenses by examining magistrates instead of the police." Florinsky, 2: 903-4.

1865

1. In its petition presented to Alexander II on 11 January 1865, the Moscow nobility asked for the convocation "of a general assembly composed of delegates from our Russian land to discuss the common needs of the entire nation." Alexander II and his advisors considered this petition an inexcusable, impertinent act. For publishing this petition, the editor of the *News* was prosecuted. The Moscow Nobles' Assembly was shut down. E. M. Feoktistov, *Za kulisami politiki i literatury* [Behind the scenes in politics and literature] (Leningrad, 1929), pp. 101–2. Also see Nikitenko's entries of 15 and 19 January 1865. ". . . Unlike the nobility of other provinces, they stressed the part of the landed aristocracy as the mainstay of the throne. This proposal, interpreted as an attempt at establishing oligarchical rule, was not well received. The tsar refused to accept the address, and announced in a rescript to Valuev that initiative in constitutional matters was a prerogative of the Crown and that no social group had the right to speak for the nation." Florinsky, 2: 1066–67.

2. "The censorship law introduced as a 'temporary experiment' on 1 April 1865 continued to exist without considerable changes for forty years. Preliminary censorship was abolished for books of a certain volume; for periodicals the question of exemption from preliminary censorship was left to the discretion of the Minister of Internal Affairs, and for the first time it was decided to introduce that freedom only in St. Petersburg and Moscow. The permit for publication of new periodicals was also left to the discretion of the Minister of Internal Affairs. Among the punitive measures, those introduced by the temporary rules of 1862 were retained." A. Kornilov, *A Classic History of Nineteenth Century Russia,* edited and abridged by Robert Bass (New York: Capricorn Books, 1966), p. 292.

1866

1. Count Dimitry Tolstoy, the new minister of education, from his very first days in office, began the preparation of educational reforms which were directed against the penetration of materialistic and socialistic ideas in the schools. One of the basic measures proposed was the replacement of *real* education (in which principally useful subjects such as mathematics, physics and others were a basic part of the curriculum) by classical education, with emphasis on classical languages.

2. Secretary of the Navy G. V. Fox headed an American delegation with a congratulatory message from Congress on the tsar's escape from the attempt on his life. At the same time, Fox's mission was supposed to express American gratitude for Russia's position during the Civil War.

1869

1. The closing of the Academy of Medicine and Surgery was related to the growth of an antigovernment mood among its students. At the beginning of March several clashes occurred between the students and the administration over the ban on meetings and the arrest of student leaders and delegates. When the government learned of the students' intentions to hold a large demonstration, they closed the Academy, prohibited students from loitering in its vicinity and fired its president, P. A. Naranovich. This led to wide-

spread disorders involving a number of St. Petersburg's institutions of higher education.

1870

1. A. N. Englehardt, professor of agricultural chemistry at the St. Petersburg Agricultural Institute, was arrested on 1 December 1870, together with a group of students. On 5 December he was relieved of his professorship, and on 10 January 1871 he was forbidden to engage in educational activity and was expelled from St. Petersburg for "participation in gatherings at the institute" and "for instilling immorality and democratic ideas in his students." E. M. Feoktistov, *Dnevnik, 1870* (rukopis') [Diary, 1870 (manuscript)] Pushinskii dom (the Institute of Russian Literature of the Academy of Sciences of the U.S.S.R. in Leningrad).

1871

1. Actually, eleven defendants figured in the Nechaev trial, which began 1 July 1871. Nechaev himself had taken refuge abroad and was not present at the trial on that date. In August 1871 he was arrested in Switzerland and extradited to Russia. See diary entry dated 13 January 1873.

1872

1. The *Voice* was suspended for its sharp criticism of the government's position on classical education.

1874

1. "Under the new law army service became the personal obligation of every able-bodied male on reaching the age of twenty, irrespective of his social status. . . . Not all men of twenty were actually drafted. They were classified into several categories according to their family status. Breadwinners and only sons, for instance, formed Category I, which could be called upon only by special imperial order. . . . Special privileges were granted to holders of academic diplomas. . . ." Florinsky, 2: 908.

1875

1. The Valuev Commission attributed disturbances at the universities to whatever remnants of faculty and student autonomy they retained. The Commission's proposal to limit such autonomy, as well as its proposal to limit the admission of students from the lower classes, was approved by Alexander II.

1876

1. The government wanted to halt all discussion of Russia's difficult financial situation in view of the impending war with Turkey. A manifesto declaring war on Turkey was signed by Alexander II on 24 April 1877.

INDEX

Baltic provinces, 122, 286-87, 325
Censorship
appointment of Goncharov as censor
    (1855), 151
appointment of Nikitenko as censor
    (1833), 42
arrest of Nikitenko for passing works
    (1835), 54-58; (1842), 87-90
arrests of writers, editors and pub-
    lishers: Dal (1832), 39; Kraevsky
    (1866), 319; Kulish (1847), 111-
    12; Nadezhdin (see Chaadaev) (1832),
    39; Ogryzko (1859), 190, 191-92;
    Samarin (1849), 122; Sorokin (1843),
    94; Turgenev (1852), 128-30
ban on articles relating to academic
    institutions and all government insti-
    tutions (1849), 137
ban on articles relating to Communica-
    tions Department (1845), 102
bans and suspensions at discretion of
    administration (1873), 359
bans and suspensions: Deception in the
    Caucases (1844), 100-101; works of
    A. Dumas (1836), 64; all French
    novels and stories (1836), 64; V.
    Hugo's Notre Dame de Paris (1834),
    47; Moscow (1869), 334; Moscow
    Telegraph (1834), 47; Moskvich
    (1868), 328; National Chronicle
    (1865), 297; News (1865), 293-94;
    Pisemsky's drama (1859), 202;
    Pogodin article (1855), 149-50;
    Sail (1859), 184-85; Telescope
    (1836), 65-66; theatre articles in
    Russian Veteran (1843), 94; Time
    (1863), 264, 265, 267; Voice (1872),
    350, 351, 382
Buturlin Committee (Committee of April
    2, Secret Censorship Committee)
    (1848), 116, 117-18, 121, 124,
    125-26, 140, 147-48, 186-87, 377
censorship abuses, debates, discussions
    in relation to approval of works sub-
    mitted, 32, 64-65, 109-10, 125, 127,
    134, 143, 159, 194, 206, 208, 216,
    217-18, 270-71, 272, 277-78, 279-80,
    284, 285, 286-87, 288, 290, 337
censorship committees enumerated, 126
censorship of Nikitenko's article (1827),
    20-21

Chaadaev's Philosophical Letters (1836),
    64, 65
Chief Censorship Administration, 126,
    137, 177, 195, 200, 201-2, 205,
    206, 208, 215, 216, 217, 221-22, 223,
    225, 230, 241, 246; abolished, 247-48,
    379
complaints against Censorship depart-
    ment and censors, 61, 96-97, 97-98,
    99, 101-2, 107-8, 114
Council on Press Affairs (1863), 265,
    266-67 (includes Nikitenko, Goncharov),
    268 69, 270-71, 272, 273; (1864), 277,
    277-78, 279-81, 282 (Tyutchev joins),
    284, 285, 286-87, 288, 290; (1865),
    292, 295, 301-2, 306, 312
double censorship of journal articles
    (1837), 72-73
ecclesiastical (1839), 76
Gogol: "The Bloody Bandore Player"
    from Hetman censored by Nikitenko,
    376; censorship committee bans re-
    lease of new edition of Gogol, 91;
    Dead Souls "saved" by Nikitenko,
    xix; "The Tale of How Ivan
    Ivanovich Quarrelled with Ivan Niki-
    forovich" censored by Nikitenko,
    48, 376
greater vigilance ordered, 98, 112, 166-
    67, 169-70, 246
harassment of Notes of the Fatherland
    (1844), 101
harassment of Polevoy (1834), 47-48
history of censorship, xvi-xvii
instructions for censors (1854), 142,
    148; (1855), 145-46, 147-48; (1861),
    221, 222-23
Nikitenko threatens to resign as censor
    (1843), 93
Obolensky Commission (1862), 254-
    55; (1863), 257-58
periodicals: Nikitenko assigned to
    compose new law (1841), 82
Pletnyov, chairman of Censorship Com-
    mittee (1845), 103-4
preliminary (preventive) censorship,
    xvi, 292, 297-98, 304, 381
proposals for reorganization and
    amendments to code composed by
    Nikitenko (1846), 107; (1857), 161;
    (1858), 167-68, 169-70, 174, 177-78,

179; (1865), 292, 294, 295, 296, 297-98, 381

Publishing (Press) Committee for "guidance" of literature (1858), 179, 182, 183; (1859), 186-87, 188-90, 190 (Nikitenko joins), 190-91, 192, 193-94 (emperor discusses committee with Nikitenko), 194-96, 197, 198-99, 200, 201-2 (merges with Chief Censorship Administration)

punishment of censors, 33, 85, 96, 121, 130-31, 141-42, 167

punishment of writers, editors, publishers, officials, 96, 140, 171, 215, 221-22, 225, 264, 269, 308, 309-10

Pushkin: *Angelo* (1834), 47, 48, 63; *Boris Godunov* (1837), 71; *Bronze Horseman* (1836), 63; censorship of tribute to Pushkin (1837), 70; emperor eases censorship (1837), 72; emperor issues orders (1837), 71; Filaret complains about *Onegin* (1834), 46-47; Grech reprimanded for tribute to Pushkin (1837), 70; severely harassed by censorship (1836), 64; Nikitenko opposes censorship of Pushkin (1837), 72; posthumous works assigned to censor Nikitenko (1837), 72 (1840), 77; reprimand for lampoon *Lucullus's Recovery* (1836), 63-64; special censorship orders (1837), 69; *Tales of Belkin* assigned to censor Nikitenko (1834), 48

Reader's Library assigned to censor Nikitenko (1834), 44-45

repressive measures against Delvig, 29-30, 31; against literature and press, 105, 304, 306, 318, 336, 341-42, 352, 353-54. *See also* Russian literature

revised code (1828), 25-26, 27

steps toward transfer of censorship to ministry of internal affairs (1859), 202, 203, 203-4; (1862), 248-49, 254-55, 379

translations, 98, 113-14

types of censors, 131

warnings, 29-30, 241, 304-5, 307, 308, 311, 314, 324, 325, 331, 338, 350, 355, 360

Cholera and other epidemics, 29, 33-35, 38, 114, 117, 123-24, 288, 295, 301, 314-15, 339, 345, 353

Corporal Punishment, abolition of (1863), 261

Crimean War, 136, 149 (fall of Sevastopol), 153 (peace treaty), 377

Decembrists, xiii, xv, 1, 2, 3, 4, 6, 10-11, 23, 52, 169, 375

Education
classical schools vs. *realschulen*, 315 326, 339, 346-47, 350-51, 381, 382
harassment of faculty, 118
philosophy courses, 125, 159, 188; faculty for, 216, 217, 220
reforms, 14-15
repressive measures, 12
state of universities, 222
student disorders, 176-77, 178, 180-82, 184, 218, 220, 223-24, 225, 230-40, 241, 242-43, 244-45, 247, 249, 250, 271, 279, 312-13, 333, 334, 365-66, 377-78, 381-82

Emancipation
discussion and steps toward, 81, 86, 157, 159-60, 163, 166, 170-71, 181, 201, 202, 206, 219-20, 220-21, 222 (manifesto), 376, 377, 378
peasant attitudes toward, 228, 228-29
peasant disorders, 178-79, 223, 225

Famine, 328, 352, 363

Fires in St. Petersburg, 250-51, 289, 289-90, 301, 303, 331-32, 379

France
July revolution, 29
Franco-Prussian War, 340, 341, 342, 344
Paris Commune, 345

Jews, 181, 378; pogrom, 345-46, 355

Judiciary, reforms, 254, 290; undermining of courts, 317, 323-24, 325, 379, 380-81

Ostsee Germans. *See* Baltic provinces

Persia, war with Russia, 24

Poland, 221, 256-57, 258, 259, 260, 262, 263-64, 266, 323, 380

Raskolniks (raskolniki), 52, 120, 159, 270-71, 309

Religion and clergy, 46, 95, 101-2, 119, 175, 178, 208, 279; Nikitenko on God, 285, 286

Russian literature, 32, 41, 61, 84, 105, 125, 164, 212-13, 297-98

Russians, character traits of, 5, 106, 287, 288-89, 289-90, 300, 305, 348-49; freedom of thought and intellectual life of, 38, 39, 49-50, 61, 84, 118-19, 121-22; and Germans, 340-41; in high society, 4, 7-8, 11-12, 23-24; hostility of, toward Russian-Germans, 37-38, 146-47, 154-55, 367

Russo-Turkish War, 24-25, 372-73, 375, 382

Slavophiles, 83, 111-12, 112-13, 122, 123, 165-66, 331, 372

Solovets Monastery, 51-52

Sunday (literacy) Schools, 218, 219, 378

The Third Section. *See* Benkendorf; Censorship; A.F. Orlov

Travel, restrictions on, 99-100

Zemstvos, 253, 307, 308, 320-21, 357, 362

Index of Names

Adlerberg, Count A.V. (son of V.F.)
(Publishing Committee, Chief Censor-
ship Administration, close to Alex-
ander II), 182, 183, 186, 188, 189,
191, 192, 193-94, 198-99, 200, 201,
202, 203, 204, 217, 220, 223
Adlerberg, Count V.F. (Min. Imperial
Court 1852-72), 161, 162, 168, 175
Afanasy (Sokolov) Bishop (rector St.
Petersburg Seminary, Ecclesiastic Cen-
sorship Committee), 101
Akhmatova, E.N. (writer, translator,
publisher), 272
Akhmatov, N.S. (censor), 134, 146
Aksakov, I.S. (poet, publicist, editor of
Slavophile journals), 122-23, 184,
185, 272, 290, 303, 334, 359, 360
Aksakov, K.S. (Slavophile, publicist,
historian, philologist, poet), 130, 166,
220, 226
Albedinsky, General P. P. (gov. gen. of
Ostsee, gov. gen. N. W. territory), 342
Aldridge, I. (Black actor), 180
Aleksandr Aleksandrovich (son of
Alexander II), 311-12, 328, 351
Alexander I (1777-1825), xiv, 162-63,
326-27, 329
Alexander II (1818-81, ruled 1855-81),
xvii, 153-54, 157, 161, 238, 256, 261,
282, 302, 350
  assassination attempts, 311, 312, 322,
  323
  banning of Moskvich, 328
  censorship matters, 147-48, 169, 170,
  174, 204, 205, 214
  Crimean War peace terms, 377
  demonstration of popular support for,
  262
  disorders at universities, 223-24
  displeasure with courts, 348
  emancipation manifesto issued, 222,
  378
  emancipation steps, 159, 160, 181
  heir's death, 297
  Nikitenko's audiences with, 191, 192,
  193-94, 197-98, 342-43, 365
  petitions to, 202, 379, 381
  reforms in judiciary, 254
  resignation of Kleinmichel, 150
  resignation of Kovalevsky, 226
  Sunday Schools, 219
  war declared on Turkey, 382

Andreevsky, I. E. (lawyer, prof.), 249
Annenkov, General I. V. (publisher of
Pushkin's works), 128, 166
Annenkov, General N. N. (member of
censorship Committee of April 2),
125, 247
Annenkov, P. V. (literary critic, literary
historian), 184, 207, 223
Antonovich, M. A. (publicist, literary
critic), 280, 297
Aprelev, A. F. (official), 64
Arakcheev, A. A. (high offices under
Alexander I), 336
Arendt, Dr. N. F. (Court physician),
69
Arnim, Count H. (Prussian diplomat),
365
Arseniev (chairman of Moscow District
Court), 325
Arseniev, I. A. (journalist), 246, 252
Arseniev, K. K. (lawyer, publicist, literary
critic), 208
Assandri (prima donna of the Italian opera
in St. Petersburg), 95-96
Astafiev, V. I. (helped Nikitenko win
freedom), 7
Athenaeus (Atenei, journal), 378
Babst, I. K. (prof. political economy,
journalist), 171, 244
Baer, K. M. (zoologist, academician), 288,
319
Bakunin, M. A. (anarchist), 253, 380
Balzac, H. (French writer), 47
Baranovsky, S. I. (prof., inventor), 174
Barclay de Tolly, Prince M. B. (field
marshal, commander-in-chief at
beginning of war of 1812), 326-27
Bashutsky, A. P. (journalist, writer, pub-
lisher), 85
Batyushkov, K. N. (poet), xiii, 53, 77, 105
Bazhanov, V. B. (prof., Court priest), 175
Behr (German merchant, left notes on
journey to Moscow at turn of 16th
century), 119
Beist, Count. F-F. (Saxon and Austrian
official), 344
Beketov, V. N. (censor), 165
Belinsky, V. G. (literary critic, philosopher,
political thinker), 94
Bell, The (Kolokol, Herzen's journal),
242, 253, 303
Bell, The (a student publication in imitation

of Herzen's *Bell*), 163

Belyaev, A. N. (director No. 5 Gymnasium), 352-53

Benish, Dr. (Bible expert), 212

Benkendorf, Count A. Kh. (chief of gendarmerie, director of the Third Section of His Majesty's Own Chancery under Nicholas I), 30, 46-47, 58, 63, 87, 90-91, 159
  accused of causing Delvig's premature death, 31
  arrest of Nikitenko, 88-89
  eases conditions for exiled Nadezhdin, 66
  censorship matters, 33, 46-47, 70, 85

Berezovsky, A. (Polish revolutionary, would-be assassin of Alexander II in Paris), 323

Berte, A. A. (censor, director Chancery of Min. of Education, Chief Censorship Administration), 138, 177, 208, 215, 216, 221, 223, 230

Besser, Dr. V. V. (physician, prof.), 357

Betling, O. N. (academician), 288

Bezobrazov, V. P. (statistician, economist, publicist), 317, 358

Bibikov, D. G. (gov. gen. Kiev, Min. Internal Affairs), 99, 132, 332

Biron, Count E. (favorite of Empress Anne of Russia), 106

Blagosvetlov, G. E. (publicist, literary critic, editor, publisher), 313

Blagoveshchensky (prof. St. Petersburg Univ., later rector Warsaw Univ.), 247, 322, 334, 353

Bludova, Countess A. D. (wife of Count B.), 358

Bludov, Count D. N. (high official, chairman State Council, president Academy of Sciences), 105, 125, 136, 137, 150, 151, 158-59, 161-63, 165, 166, 167, 168, 169, 170-71, 172, 178, 179, 181, 182, 195, 223, 248, 254, 272, 273, 278-79

Blumenfeld (friend of Nikitenko), 358

Bluntschli, J-K. (Swiss lawyer, prof.), 368

Bodyanksy, O. M. (prof., Historical and Antiquities Society), 118

Bogdanova, E. K. (pupil of Nikitenko at Smolny), 358

Bogolyubov, V. (student at St. Petersburg University), 177

Boldyrev, A. V. (rector of Moscow University, non-salaried censor), 65, 66

Boldyrev, Major, 56

Bolotnikov, I. I. (leader peasant uprising at beginning of 17th century), 121

Booth, John Wilkes (Lincoln's assassin), 297

Borovsky, Bishop (Catholic bishop), 119

Borozdin, K. M. (sup't. St. Petersburg school district, historian, archeologist), xv, 13, 19, 22, 27, 42, 71

Botkin, V. P. (litterateur), 184, 328

Bov. *See* Dobrolyubov

Bradke. *See* Von Bradke

Brok, P. F. (Min. of Finance, State Council), 161, 162, 167

Bryullov, K. P. (artist), 78, 81-82

Budberg, Baron A. F. (diplomat), 177

Bulgarin, F. B. (writer, journalist, publisher, informer and spy for the Third Section), 9, 21, 28, 33, 35, 36, 59, 85, 87, 96-97, 98, 107, 110, 114, 115, 116, 129, 130, 158

Bulich, N. N. (prof., historian), 217

Bunyakovsky, V. Ya. (v.p. Academy of Sciences, mathematician), 146-47, 364

Butkov, V. P. (State Council, Committee of Ministers), 181, 272, 273

Butlerov, A. M. (chemist, academician), 368

Buturlin, Count D. P. (chairman "Committee of April 2 for top-level surveillance of spirit and orientation of printed works in Russia"), 116, 117, 121, 124, 125, 377

Butyrsky, N. I. (prof., translator, censor), 5, 8, 28, 31

Bychkov, A. F. (academician, director Public Library, State Council), 317

Catherine II, Empress, 329-30

Chaadaev, P. Ya. (philosopher, writer), 65

Charukovsky, P. A. (Academy of Medicine and Surgery), 34

Cherkesev A. A. (bookshop owner, arrested in conjunction with Nechaev affair), 337

Chernyshev, Prince A. I. (Min. of War, State Council), 329

Chernyshevsky, N. G. (political thinker, writer, critic), 174, 216, 230, 243, 252, 284, 285, 297, 354, 379

Chevkin, K. V. (chief of Communications Bureau, State Council), 165, 167, 182, 219, 346, 350, 351

Chivilev, A. I. (prof., preceptor for children of Alexander II), 61, 218, 257

Chizhov, F. V. (publicist, Slavophile), 66, 83, 112

Citizen, The (*Grazhdanin,* newspaper), 353

Constant, Benjamin (French writer), 32

Contemporary Annals (*Sovremennaya*

Letopis, newspaper), 271, 317

Contemporary, The (Sovremennik, journal), xviii, xx, 64, 77, 103, 108, 109, 110–11, 115, 116, 121, 124, 141, 171, 184, 223, 230, 250, 265, 277, 278, 280, 285, 304–5, 314, 376, 377, 379

Court Messenger (Sudebnyi Vestnik, newspaper), 338

Dal, V. I. (pseudonym Kazak Lugansky; ethnographer, lexicographer, writer, physician), 39, 70, 71, 91, 111, 117, 164, 273, 358

Danichich, D. (Serbian linguist, historian, prof.), 273

d'Anthès, G. (Baron von Heckeren; Pushkin's antagonist in fatal duel), 68–69, 370

Danzas, K. K. (Pushkin's second in duel), 69

Dashkov, D. V. (literary critic, Min. of Justice), 105, 159

Davydov, I. I. (prof., academician), 113, 124, 136, 138, 143, 146–47, 155, 162, 170

Day, (Den, newspaper), 267, 303

Degai, P. I. (lawyer, senator, secret Censorship Committee of April 2), 116, 121

de Kock, P. (French writer), 47

Del, A. (university friend of Nikitenko), 56

Delavigne, C. (French poet, playwright), 31

Delyanov, I. D. (sup't. St. Petersburg school district, Deputy Min. of Education, later Min. of Education), 190, 191, 205, 216, 217, 221, 240, 241–42, 250, 258–59, 271, 279, 286, 312, 349, 352–53, 364, 377–78

Delvig, Baron A. A. (poet, publisher), 31, 32

Derzhavin, G. R. (poet), 260

Dobrolyubov, N. A. (pseudonym laibov; critic, writer), 216, 243

Dolgoruky, Prince V. A. (Min. of War, chief of gendarmerie and Third Section), 160, 161, 171, 178, 190, 192, 218, 219, 224, 285

Dondukov-Korsakov, Prince M. A. (sup't. St. Petersburg school district, chairman St. Petersburg Censorship Committee), 42, 51, 54, 56, 65, 72, 124

Dostoevsky, F. M. (writer), 287

Dostoevsky, M. M. (writer, translator, journalist, publisher), 265, 287

Drashusov, A. N. (prof., censor), 140

Druzhinin, A. V. (literary critic, writer, translator), 151, 184, 193, 207, 277, 278

Druzhinin, G. V. (brother of A. V.), 278

Dubbelt, L. V. (manager of Third Section under Benkendorf, later under Orlov), 66, 87–88, 100, 108, 112, 116, 120

Dudyshkin, S. S. (journalist, literary critic), 176, 207

Dumas, A. (French writer), 64

Dyachenko (teacher), 359

Economic Index (Ekonomicheskii Ykazatel, journal), 221-22

Economist (Ekonom, journal), 82

Efebovsky, P. V. (writer), 88

Elagin, N. V. (censor), 131, 134, 146, 149

Elena Pavlovna, Grand Duchess (patron of science and art, wife of Mikhail Pavlovich), 123, 357

Eliseev, G. Z. (publicist, journalist), 297

Elizaveta Alekseevna, Tsarina (wife of Alexander I), 7

Englehardt, A. N. (chemist, prof.), 343, 382

Epoch (Epokha, journal), 285

Eshevsky, S. V. (historian, prof.), 157

European, The (Evropeets, journal), 37, 376

Fet, A. A. (poet), 156

Filaret, Metropolitan, 46-47, 127, 241

Fischer, A. A. (prof. philosophy), 71, 143

Fletcher, Giles (English poet, ambassador to Russia, 1588), 118

Fox, G. V. (secretary U.S. navy), 381

Franklin, Benjamin, 333

Freigang, A. I. (censor), 99, 131, 146

Fuchs, V. Ya. (censor, Council on Press Affairs), 298, 302, 304

Fuss, P. N. (mathematician, academician), 146

Fyodorov, B. M. (writer, academician, informer and secret agent of Third Section), 108, 115, 116

Gaevsky, P. I. (censor), 64, 65, 82, 137, 177

Gaevsky, V. P. (lawyer, writer), 272, 363

Gagarin, P. P. (chairman State Council, Emancipation Committee), 161

Galakhov, G. P. (Ukrainian industrial magnate, various committees for peasant reforms), 222

Galich, A. I. (prof., philosopher, Nikitenko's teacher), 25, 46, 140, 296, 315

Galkin (gov. of Revel), 342

Garcia, 94, 96. *See also* Viardot

Garibaldi, G. (Italian patriot), 210, 253, 264

Gebhardt, I. K. (teacher, friend of Nikitenko), 66, 111

Gendre, N. P. (writer), 271

Gen, K. A. (law student), 232

Georgievsky, A. I. (editor *Journal of*

Min. of Education, Council of Min. of Education), 354

Gilyarov-Platonov, N. P. (censor, prof., journalist), 259, 266

Gintze, R. (journalist), 66

Glebov, I. T. (v.p. Academy of Medicine and Surgery), 235

Glinka, F. N. (poet, Decembrist), 1, 4, 9, 375

Glinka, M. I. (composer), 77

Glinka, S. N. (censor), 28

Gneist, R-G-F. (German lawyer, publicist, deputy German Reich), 368

Gogel, G. F. (adjutant general), 296

Gogol, N. V., xvii, 38, 50, 91, 129, 132, 133, 214, 215
death of, 127-28
Inspector General, 64
letter to Uvarov, 105
Nikitenko as censor of, xix, 48, 376
university teaching fiasco, 59-60

Golitsyn, Prince A. N. (Min. of Religious Affairs and Education under Alexander I), xiv, 22, 329

Golovinsky, I. P. (rector Roman Catholic Academy, metropolitan of Catholic Church in Russia), 119

Golovnin, A. V. (Min. of Education, State Council), 246, 248, 259, 267, 273, 282, 303, 325-26
appointed Minister of Education, 245
choice of Litke as president of Academy of Sciences, 279
creates Obolensky Commission for reorganization of censorship department and code, 254-55
opposed to classical schools, 346, 351
refuses to oppose arson accusation against students, 251
relieved as Minister of Education, 312-13
reopens university, 247

Goncharov, I. A., xvii, 174, 184, 190, 197, 209, 210, 211, 214, 218, 225, 236, 243, 248, 305, 316, 328, 369
as censor and in censorship administration, xviii, 151, 166-67, 278, 279-81, 282, 284, 302, 306, 307, 309
as editor of *Northern Post,* 252
letter from Nikitenko, 287
Oblomov, 176
Precipice, 211-12, 347, 378
Quarrel with Turgenev, 206-7
Skladchina, 363, 364

Gorchakov, Prince, A. M. (Min. of Foreign Affairs), 178, 182, 264, 273, 282, 337, 380

Gorchakov, Prince M. D. (adjutant general, viceroy of Poland), 190

Gorlov, I. Ya. (prof. political economy and statistics), 185, 234

Gorozhansky, A. S. (Decembrist), 52

Government Messenger (Pravitelstvennyi Vestnik, official gov't. newspaper), 371

Grech, N. I. (writer, journalist, author texts on Russian grammar and history of Russian literature), 9, 28, 35, 36, 46, 48, 62, 64, 66, 70, 76, 82, 85, 107, 158, 320, 376

Greig, S. A. (Deputy Min. of Finance, state controller), 346, 351

Griboedov, A. S. (playwright of early 19th century), 32, 305

Grimm, A-T. (teacher, preceptor for children of Nicholas I and Alexander II), 218

Grot, K. K. (high official Min. of Finance, State Council), 302, 346, 351

Grot, Ya. K. (philologist, academician), 210, 269, 272, 316, 317

Gulak, N. I. (member of secret Kirill-Methodius Society in Kiev), 112

Heir, the. *See* Nikolai Aleksandrovich (before 1865); Aleksandr Aleksandrovich (after 1865)

Herald of Free Opinion (student publication), 163

Herman, K. F. (prof., class inspector at Smolny and Catherine Institutes, academician), 31, 40

Herzen, A. (leading Russian philosopher and revolutionary thinker), 108
appeal "To the Younger Generation," 229
The Bell, 179
death of, 338
V. Gaevsky, 272
on Korf's history of decembrist uprising, 169
on legal reforms, 254
letter to emperor on heir's death, 303
on Mazzini and Garibaldi, 253
meeting with Nikitenko, 108, 376
rumor about death of, 276
smuggling of Herzen's books into Russia, 252
on student disorders, 242
Turgenev, 380
on Prince Vyazemsky, 168
on writers, 214-15

Housewarming (Novoselie, almanac), 376

Hugo, V. (French writer), xvi, 33, 47, 54, 258

Ignatiev, Count P. N. (gov. gen. St. Petersburg, chairman Committee of Ministers), 173, 221, 232, 233-34, 378

Illustration (Illyustratsiya, magazine),

225, 378
Isakov, N. V. (sup't. Moscow school district, chairman Moscow Censorship Committee), 224
Ishimova, A. I. (children's writer, publisher children's magazines), 111
Ivanov, A. A. (artist), 174
Ivanovsky, I. I. (prof. international law, censor), 111
Johnson, President Andrew, 333
Journal of Ministry of Education (Zhurnal Ministerstva Narodnogo Prosveshcheniya), 137, 141, 153
Kaidanov, Dr. Ya. K., 33
Kalashnikov, I. T. (writer, gov't. official), 115, 116
Kalmykov, P. D. (lawyer, prof.), 50
Kankrin, Count E. F. (Min. of Finance), 64
Kapustin, M. N. (prof. international law), 157
Karakozov, D. V. (would-be assassin of Alexander II), 312, 315, 316
Karamzin, A. N. (son of writer-historian N. M.), 129, 132
Karamzin, N. M. (writer-historian), 105, 163
Karamzin, V. N. (senator, son of N. M.), 310
Karatygin, V. A. (actor), 32, 36
Karniolin-Pinsky, M. M. (senator), 276
Katkov, M. N. (editor, publisher, prof. philos.), 140, 264, 266, 269, 271, 272, 273, 276, 292, 311, 346-47, 348, 350, 354
Kavelin, K. D. (historian, publicist, prof.), 157, 166, 171, 220
Kazembek, A. K. (prof. Arabic and Persian literature), 149
Kelsiev, V. I. (publicist), 212, 334-35
Kern, Anna Petrovna (close friend of Nikitenko and Pushkin), 15, 16, 17, 18, 19
Khomyakov, A. S. (poet, Slavophile publicist), 37, 127, 130
Kiprensky, O. A. (artist), 20
Kireevsky, I. V. (publisher), 130, 376
Kiselev, Count P. D. (gov't. official and diplomat), 95
Kislovsky, A. E. (vice-director of dep't. of education), 155, 156, 177, 244
Kleinmichel, Count P. A. (high ranking official), 67, 83, 87, 88, 90, 91, 95, 99, 114, 150, 151, 219
Klevanov (journalist), 257
Klimov, Governor (gov. of province of Samara), 363
Knyazhevich, A. M. (writer, translator, Min. of Finance, State Council), 50,

83, 171, 178, 295-96, 334, 350
Kologrivov, N. N. (friend of Nikitenko), 263
Koltsov, A. V. (poet), 78
Komarovsky, E. E. (official in Min. of Education), 141
Komissarov, O. I. (foiled attempt on Alexander II's life), 311, 312, 321-22
Komovsky, V. D. (historian, translator, director of chancery in Min. of Education), 105, 113
Konstantin Nikolaevich, Grand Duke (son of Nicholas I, gov. gen. Poland 1862-63, chairman State Council), 147, 151-52, 166, 173, 219, 241, 248, 262, 294, 297, 336, 351
Kopasov (teacher), 51
Korf, Baron M. A. (historian, high gov't. official, censorship Committee of April 2) 116, 121, 125, 140, 151, 169, 203, 204, 239-40, 279, 292, 294, 328
Korkunov, M. A. (archeologist, academician), 166
Kornilov, I. P. (historian, archeologist, sup't. Vilnius school district), 336, 348
Korsakov, P. A. (censor, writer, translator, editor), 64, 96, 99
Koshelev, A. I. (publicist, Slavophile), 253
Kossikovsky, V. A. (aide-de-camp of Rostovtsev), 155
Kostomarov, N. I. (Russian-Ukrainian historian, writer, prof., member secret Kirill-Methodius Society) 112, 220, 247, 276-77, 284, 285, 290, 322, 328, 369, 378
Kotsebu, P. E. (State Council, gov. gen. Novorossisk and Bessarabia), 345-46
Kovalevsky, Egor P. (mining engineer, writer, public figure), 166, 189, 195, 223
Kovalevsky, Evgraf P. (geologist, ethnographer, sup't. Moscow school district, chairman Moscow Censorship Committee, Min. of Education), 165, 166, 169-70, 174, 177, 178, 179, 181, 183, 186, 188, 189, 192, 194, 196, 202, 203, 204, 205, 219, 220, 223-24, 225, 226, 241
Kozlov, Dr. N. I. (prof., pathologist, anatomist), 333
Kraevsky, A. A. (journalist, writer, publisher), 70, 94, 96, 100, 108, 113, 176, 225, 243, 269, 308-10, 351, 353, 363, 364, 369
Krasovsky, A. I. (censor, chairman foreign censorship committee), 162
Kreutzer, G-F. (German philosopher, prof.), 50
Krusenstern (son of Admiral K.), 55

Krylov, A. L. (prof., St. Petersburg censor), 55, 64, 65, 82, 114

Krylov, I. A. (fabulist), 48, 59, 102

Krylov, N. I. (prof., Moscow censor), 100-101

Kudryavtsev, P. N. (prof., writer), 140

Kukolnik, N. V. (dramatist, writer), 45, 46, 59, 63, 70, 77, 111, 129, 376

Kulish, P. A. (Ukrainian nationalist, poet, writer, translator, historian), 111-12

Kunik, A. A. (historian, academician), 293, 316

Kurochkin, V. S. (poet, translator), editor-publisher), 379

Kushelev-Bezborodko, Count G. A. (publisher, writer), 215

Kutorga, M. S. (prof. of history), 61, 249

Kutorga, S. S. (zoologist, censor), 72, 87-90, 97, 104, 111, 280

Ladyzhenskaya, V. D. (friend of Nikitenko), 302, 303

Lamansky, V. I. (Slavicist, prof.), 296

Lanskoy, S. S. (Min. of Internal Affairs), 163, 377

Lavrov, P. L. (political thinker and critic, publicist, philologist, sociologist), 216, 217, 220, 297, 313

Lebedev, N. E. (censor), 268

Lelewel, J. (Polish historian and political figure, prof.), 44, 190

Leontieva, M. P. (director Smolny Convent), 95

Leontiev, P. M. (historian, publicist, journalist, prof.), 140, 346-47

Lermontov, M. (poet), xxi, 80, 133, 376

Leskov, N. S. (writer), 364

Leuchtenberg, Duke of (nephew of Nicholas I), 333

Levashev, General V. V. (conducted investigation of Decembrist affair), 1, 2, 375

Levshin, General D. S. (director of schools under military jurisdiction, sup't. of Kharkov, Moscow school districts), 184

Lieven, Prince K. A. (Min. of Education), 33

Lighthouse (Mayak, journal), 82

Likhachev, V. (writer, poet), 141

Lincoln, President Abraham, 297, 333

Liszt, F. (composer), 86

Literary Gazette (Literaturnaya Gazeta, newspaper), 29, 32, 105

Litke, Admiral F. P. (geographer,

voyager, president Academy of Sciences), 55, 279, 296, 351

Little Star (Zvyozdochka, children's magazine), 111

Lkhovsky, I. I. (civil servant, writer), 225

Lobanov, M. E. (dramatist, critic, academician), 45

Lobanov-Rostovsky, Prince A. B. (Deputy Min. of Internal Affairs), 341-42

Lomonosov, M. V. (scholar, poet, scientist), 293, 294-96, 298

Longinov, M. N. (literary historian, bibliographer, chairman Council on Press Affairs), 349, 355

Lorentz, O. (German historian), 84

Lvov, Prince V. V. (writer, censor), 131

Lyubimov, A. S. (lawyer, official, senator, chairman at Nechaev trial), 347-48

Lyuboshchinsky, M. N. (uncle of Nikitenko's wife, lawyer, senator, chief prosecutor of senate, State Council), 148, 173-74, 190, 206, 285, 292, 294

Magnitsky, M. L. (sup't. Kazan school district), 102, 326-27

Maikov, A. N. (poet, censor), 328
   anti-German poem, 296
   "Choice of Death," 127
   "Dreams," 151
   "Lucius's Death," 262
   review of "Two Worlds," 358, 362
   "Simeon Bolgarsky," 339
   "The Spanish Inquisition," 218
   translation of "Cassandra," 364

Maikov, V. N. (journalist, translator, publisher), 176

Maksheev, D. M. (landowner), 52

Mariya Nikolaevna, Grand Duchess (daughter of Nicholas I, president Academy of Arts), 153

Markevich, B. M. (writer, official), 310, 322, 332

Markevich, N. A. (poet, ethnographer, author of "History of Little Russia" [Ukraine]), 99

Markov, M. A. (lt. general, poet, writer, dramatist), 58

Martynov, A. E. (actor), 193

Martynov, General P. P. (commandant of guardhouse), 55, 56, 57

Martynov, S. M. (friend of Nikitenko), 102

Masalsky, K. P. (historical writer, translator, journalist, editor-publisher), 46

Mazzini, G. (leader in Italian national liberation movement), 253

Medem, Baron N. V. (chairman military censorship committee, chairman St. Petersburg Censorship Committee,

Chief Censorship Administration), 221, 223

Mekhelin, A. I. (censor), 121

Menshikov, Prince A. S. (Min. of Navy, chairman censorship Committee of April 2), 116

Meshchersky, Prince V. P. (writer, publicist, publisher), 333, 353

Messenger of Europe (*Vestnik Evropy*, journal), 360, 368

Middendorf, A. F. (zoologist, academician), 146-47, 288

Mikhaelis, E. P. (student), 232-33

Mikhaelis, M. P. (expelled from St. Petersburg for participating in demonstration during public sentencing of Chernyshevsky), 284

Mikhailov, M. I. (poet, writer, publicist), 236, 379

Mikhail Pavlovich, Grand Duke (brother of Nicholas I), 55, 67

Miklashevich, V. S. (writer, translator), 85

Miller, I. P. (uncle of Orest M.), 335

Miller, O. (literary historian, Slavophile, prof.), 218, 355, 369

Milyutin, General D. A. (State Council, Min. of War), 157, 275, 318, 346, 351

Milyutin, N. A. (sec'y. of state for Polish Affairs), 313

Minaev, D. D. (poet, translator, playwright), 365

Mitrofaniya, Mother Superior (Baroness P. G. Rosen), 365

Mordvinov, Count N. S. (State Council, Committee of Ministers), 171

Moscow (*Moskva*, newspaper), 324, 328, 331, 334

Moscow Bulletin (*Moskovskie Vedomosti*, newspaper), 266, 269, 271, 292, 311, 312, 314, 319, 336, 337, 338, 339, 348, 364

Moscow Observer (*Moskovskii Nablyudatel*, journal), 63

Moscow Telegraph (*Moskovskii Telegraf*, journal), 47, 65, 376

Moskvich (newspaper), 328

Mukhanov, N. A. (senator, State Council, Deputy Min. of Education, Publishing Committee, Deputy Min. of Foreign Affairs), 182-83, 186, 188, 190, 194-95, 198, 200, 201, 208

Muraviev, A. N. (writer), 58

Muraviev, Count M. N. (State Council, Min. of State Property), 181, 313

Muscovite (*Moskvityanin*, journal), 82, 141

Musin-Pushkin, M. N. (sup't. St. Peters-

burg school district, chairman St. Petersburg Censorship Committee), 105, 107, 113, 122, 130, 146, 150, 156-57

Nadezhdin, N. I. (prof., literary critic, journalist, editor), 83
 Chaadaev affair, 65
 exile, 66

Naranovich, Dr. P. A. (head of Academy of Medicine and Surgery), 333

National Chronicle (*Narodnaya Letopis*, newspaper), 297

Nazimov, Governor General V. I. (gov. gen. of Vilnius, Grodno, Kovro), 163, 271, 377

Nebolsin, G. P. (economist, statistician, State Council, senator), 358

Nechaev, S. G. (revolutionary, political terrorist)
 arrest of, 382
 conviction of, 357
 murder of student, 337
 trial of, 347-48

Nekrasov, N. A. (poet, publisher), xviii, 111, 174, 197, 363
 "Cemetery," 184
 censorship problems, 215, 223, 277, 278, 284
 poem in honor of Martynov, 193
 protest against anti-Semitism, 378
 purchase of *Contemporary*, 376
 Skladchina committee, 364

Neverov, Ya. M. (teacher, memoirist, sup't. Trans-Caucasia school district), 356

News (*Vest*, newspaper), 293-94, 308, 309, 334

New Times (*Novoe Vremya*, newspaper), 371

Nicholas I (1796-1855, ruled 1825-55), 12, 41-42, 138, 376
 attitude of Nikitenko toward, xv
 attitude toward literature, 298
 censorship, 140, 143
 death of, 144
 literary productivity under, xvii
 opposition to freedom of thought, 190
 relations with Europe, 153
 release of imprisoned Nikitenko, 122
 religion, 119
 steps toward emancipation, 171
 war with Turkey, 24-25, 375

Niebuhr, B. G. (German historian), 136

Nikitenko, A. V.
 Academy of Sciences: appointed corresponding member, 137; appointed full Academician, 146
 Actual State Councillor, 139
 addresses and articles, 8, 41, 71, 86, 164, 277, 357, 358
 appointed censor, xv-xvi, 42

appointed to editorial posts: *Contemporary*, xviii, 108; *Journal of Ministry of Education*, 137, 153; *Northern Post*, 240; *Son of the Fatherland*, 76
appointed to teaching posts, 28, 29, 30, 36, 45, 87, 125
appointed to Theatre Committee, 162
on the approaching crisis, 305
arrest of, xvi, 54-58, 87-90
and Decembrists, xiii, xiv-xv, 1, 2, 3-4, 6, 10-11, 23, 169, 375
early life and schooling, xi-xiv
employed by Ministry of Finance, 120-21
on Fet, 156
on freedom of thought, 318
on Goncharov: *Oblomov*, 176; *Precipice*, 211-12, 347, 378
instructions for censors, 148
introduction to government service, xv, 12-13
on Kukolnik, 63
on Lermontov, 376
on Maikov, 218, 355, 364
marriage of, 43
on the masses, 275-76, 335
member of Press (publishing) Committee (joins the "Triumverate"), 188-90, 191, 192, 194-97, 198-99, 200, 201-2, 202-3
Minister of Education Norov requests assistance of, 134
Minister of Education Norov requests N. to prepare memo on censorship, 136, 137
on Ostrovsky, 154
on Pisemsky, 268, 310, 353
on Poles, 279
on power, 208
on Pushkin, 20, 67
on Pushkin's *Onegin*, 21
on Russia, 241-42
on Russian literature, 61-62, 84, 132-33, 212-13, 358
Skladchina, 363, 364
on social activists, 216-17, 229-30
statements of N.'s philosophy, 167, 185, 214-15
threatens to resign as censor (1843), 93
on Aleksei Tolstoy, 316, 317
on Turgenev's *Smoke*, 322
on women, 269, 272, 281-82, 283-84, 286, 330-31, 332
Nikolai Aleksandrovich (son of Alexander II), 171-72, 173, 257, 292, 296, 297, 298-99, 300, 303
Nikolai, Baron A. P. (sup't. Kiev school district, Deputy Min. of Education), 255
Nodier, C. (French writer), 47
Norov, A. S. (Deputy Min. of Education, Min. of Education), 125, 134, 135, 136, 137, 139, 140, 141, 142, 143, 144, 145, 147-48, 149, 151, 152, 153, 155, 156, 169, 177, 292, 294, 300-301, 317, 329, 331, 332, 333
Northern Bee (*Severnaya Pchela*, newspaper), 33, 70, 96, 109-10, 114, 115, 129, 216
Northern Post (*Severnaya Pochta*, newspaper), 240, 241, 246, 248, 252, 257, 264, 277, 299, 304-5, 307, 314, 324, 325, 379
Notes of the Fatherland (*Otechestvennye Zapiski*, journal), xx, 77, 78, 82, 84, 87, 97, 100, 101, 103-4, 107, 113, 115, 116, 132, 141, 184, 220, 266, 268
Novikova, O. A. (publicist), 339
Obodovsky, P. G. (teacher, writer), 70
Obolensky, Prince D. A. (State Council, chairman of Commission for Reorganization of Censorship and Code), 132, 133, 254-55, 257-58, 310, 351, 379
Obolensky, Prince E. P. (Decembrist), xiv, xv, 2, 4, 6, 11
Obrezkov, A. M. (senator, diplomat), 24
Obruchev, V. A. (publicist, journalist), 251, 379
Obukhov, B. P. (Deputy Min. of Internal Affairs), 349
Ochkin, A. N. (censor, editor), 47, 55, 96
Odoevsky, Prince V. F. (writer, literary critic, philosopher, cousin of Decembrist A. I. Odoevsky), 46, 101, 151, 219, 310-11
Ogarev, governor of Nizhegorod, 317-18
Ogarev, I. I. (civil governor of Archangel), 51
Ogarev, N. P. (journalist), 380
Ogryzko, I. P. (publisher of Polish newspaper in St. Petersburg), 190, 191, 192
Oldekop, E. I. (censor), 280
Olga Nikolaevna, Grand Duchess (daughter of Nicholas I), 90
Olin, V. N. (poet, writer, translator, journalist), 44
Orlov, Count A. F. (chief of gendarmerie, chairman State Council), xviii, 110, 111, 112, 157, 161, 171, 183, 201, 377
Orlov, Count G. G. (a favorite of Catherine II), 329-30
Orlov-Davydov, Count V. P. (public figure,

Marshall of the Nobility), 293
Ostrikov, I. A., 308
Ostrogradsky, M. V. (academician, mathematician), 147
Ostrovsky, A. N. (playwright), 154, 262, 269, 273, 324-25, 353
Palauzov, S. N. (censor, historian), 202
Palen, K. I. (Min. of Justice), 323
Panaev, I. I. (writer, editor), xviii, 108, 111, 127, 156, 165, 174, 184, 197, 247
Panin, Count V. N. (Min. of Justice, State Council), 165, 167, 171, 182, 206, 219, 224, 346, 351
Pantheon (Panteon, theatre journal), 82, 141
Parrot, G-F. (academician, mathematician), 326-27
Paskevich, General I. S. (commanded army in wars with Persia and Turkey), 24
Pavlova, Karolina K. (poet, translator), 142
Pavlov (civil servant), 64
Pavlov, P. V. (prof. of Russian history and Russian art), 247, 270, 379
Pecherin, V. S. (friend of Nikitenko, 20 years in Catholic monastery, later political activist), 40, 61-62, 66, 83, 303-4, 326
Peiker, N. I. (censor), 134
Pekarsky, P. P. (historian, academician), 306, 316
Perovsky, Count L. A. (Min. of Internal Affairs), 93, 99, 117, 122
Philipson, General G. I. (sup't. St. Petersburg school district), 231, 232, 233, 244
Pietri, P-M. (French political figure, under Napoleon III prefect of Paris police and organizer of broad network of spies and provocateurs), 343
Pinsky. *See* Karniolin-Pinsky
Pisarev, D. I. (critic), 252, 307
Pisemsky, A. F. (writer, editor), 151, 202, 268, 310, 353, 355, 365
Pletnyov, P. A. (prof. and rector St. Petersburg University, academician, literary critic, publisher), 32, 35, 36, 37, 46, 48, 50, 56, 63, 67, 68, 70, 71, 103-4, 111, 132, 142, 146-47, 151, 153, 154, 155, 158, 182, 185-86, 189, 220, 240, 241, 306
Pluchart, A. A. (bookseller and publisher), 46
Pogodin, M. P. (historian, journalist, publisher), 36, 61, 129, 130, 141, 149-50, 171-72, 224, 264
Pokhvisnev, M. N. (censor, chairman

Council on Press Affairs), 141, 266, 341
Polenov, D. V. (diplomat, archeologist), 66
Polevoy, N. A. (dramatist, novelist, historian, journalist), 47, 48, 62, 76, 77, 84, 85, 107, 376
Polonsky, Ya. P. (poet, editor, sec'y. of committee foreign censorship, Council on Press Affairs), 184, 339
Popov, A. V. (prof. of Mongolian), 149
Posen, M. P. (high official, Emancipation Committee), 159-60, 161, 201
Postels, A. F. (prof., round the world voyage with Litke), 55
Poyarkov, S. F. (Pecherin's nephew), 326
Prokopovich, N. Ya. (poet), 59
Przhetslavsky, O. A. (journalist, censor, Council on Press Affairs, Publishing Committee), 206, 208, 215, 223, 225, 265, 266, 272, 277-78, 282, 285
Pushkin, A. S., xvii, 17, 20, 35, 36, 37, 46, 49, 50, 128, 166, 339
Angelo, 47, 48
and censorship, xix, 47, 48, 64, 71, 72, 77
Contemporary, 63-64, 376
death of, 68-71
Gavriliada, 300-301
Kern, Anna Petrovna, 16
Lucullus's Recovery, 63
Nikitenko on *Onegin,* 21
Nikitenko on significance of P. in Russian literature, 133, 213
Putyatin, Count E. V. (Min. of Education), 225, 229, 230, 231, 240, 241, 242, 243, 351
Pypin, A. N. (literary historian, journalist, editor, prof.), 360
Raevskaya, A. M. (great-granddaughter of Lomonosov), 295-96
Raikovsky, Archpriest A. I., 101
Ranke, L. (German historian), 101
Reader's Library (Biblioteka dlya Chteniya, journal), 44, 45, 48, 55, 58, 59, 70, 98, 99, 104, 141, 184
Rebinder, N. R. (official in Siberia, 1851-55, sup't. Kiev and Odessa school districts, director of department in Min. of Education, senator), 111, 171, 197, 217, 218, 222, 223
Redkin, P. G. (law prof.), 177, 266
Reitern, Count M. Kh. (Min. of Finance), 272, 273
Repertoir (Repertuar, theatre journal), 82
Rosen, Baron E. F. (poet, dramatist), 36, 70
Rosenheim, M. P. (poet), 328

Rostopchina, Countess E. P. (poet), 109-10, 125, 151

Rostovtsev, Ya. I. (informed on Decembrists, high posts, State Council, Emancipation Committee), 1, 2, 3, 4, 10, 11, 23, 67, 135, 136, 140, 148, 155, 156, 161, 169, 192, 205-6, 375

Rubini, G. (Italian singer), 94

Rudnitsky, K. I. (friend of Nikitenko), 287

Russian Messenger (*Russkii Vestnik,* journal), 82, 84, 184, 207, 266, 268, 288, 378

Russian Veteran (*Russkii Invalid,* newspaper), 69, 94, 299, 301, 312

Russian Word (*Russkoe Slovo*), 214, 215, 241, 250, 265, 280, 304, 307, 309, 314, 379

Russian World (*Russkii Mir,* newspaper), 371

Russkaya Starina (*Russian Antiquity,* journal), xxi, xxii, 361

Ryleev, K. F. (poet, Decembrist), xiii-xiv, xv, 2, 11

Rzhevsky, D. S. (journalist, censor), 141, 246, 249, 258

St. Petersburg Bulletin (*St. Peterburgskie Vedomosti,* Academy of Sciences daily newspaper), 115, 129, 153, 164, 184, 235, 243, 244, 249, 266, 308, 314, 315-16, 336, 338, 339, 346, 352, 353-54, 378

St. Petersburg Police Bulletin (*Vedomosti St. Peterburgskoi Gorodskoi Politsii,* newspaper), 284

Samarin, Yu. F. (publicist, Slavophile), 122

Saratov Provincial Bulletin (*Saratovskie Gubernskie Vedomosti,* official newspaper), 140, 141

Schelling, F-V. (German philosopher), 2, 13

Schneider, V. V. (Nikitenko's former teacher), 329

Scott, Sir Walter (Scottish novelist and poet), 47

Semevsky, M. I. (historian, founded *Russkaya Starina*), 361

Semyonov, V. N. (censor), 33, 36, 58

Senkovsky, O. I. (pseudonym, Baron Brambeus; prof. of Arabian and Turkish literature, journalist, editor of *Reader's Library*), 15, 44, 45, 49, 58-59, 62, 78-79, 83, 113

Serafim, Metropolitan, 54, 58

Serbinovich, K. S. (censor), 28

Serno-Solovievich, N. A. (associated with the *Bell*), 252

Shchebalsky, P. K. (historian, journalist), 184, 225

Shcherbatov, Prince G. A. (ass't. sup't. Moscow school district, ass't. sup't. St. Petersburg school district, Marshall of Nobility), 163, 165, 171, 173, 178-79, 277

Shcherbinin, M. P. (Moscow Censorship Committee, Council on Press Affairs), 302

Shenin, A. F. (writer), 64, 67

Sheremetov, Count (wealthy landowner and owner of the Nikitenko family), xi, xiv, 12, 80, 81

Shevchenko, T. G. (Ukrainian poet), 112, 193

Shevyrev, S. P. (prof., academician), 119

Shidlovsky, General M. R. (Council on Press Affairs), 341, 349

Shirinsky-Shikhmatov, Prince P. A. (poet, translator, Deputy Minister, then Minister of Education), 125, 132, 134-35, 140, 146

Shishkov, Admiral A. S. (Minister of Education), 10, 21

Shulgin, I. P. (professor), 67

Shuvalov, P. A. (1866-74 chief of gendarmerie and Third Section), 316-17, 320, 321, 337, 339, 343, 377-78

Shtatnikova (inspector at Catherine Institute), 31-32

Shterich, S. I. (friend of Nikitenko), 3, 4, 5, 7, 8, 9

Sidonsky, Father F. F., 46

Sinelnikov, N. P. (gov. gen. of eastern Siberia, senator), 359

Skaryatin, V. D. (journalist, publisher of *News*), 293-94

Smaragdov, S. N. (teacher, author history texts), 143

Smirdin, A. F. (publisher, bookseller), 44, 45, 48, 50, 58, 59, 66, 76, 78, 80

Snowdrop (*Podsnezhnik,* children's magazine), 176

Sollogub, Count B. A. (writer, dramatist), 108, 153

Soloviev, S. M. (prof., historian, author *History of Russia*), 121, 140, 244

Somov, O. M. (writer, editor), 36

Son of the Fatherland (*Syn Otechestva,* journal), 8, 58, 76, 77, 78-79, 80, 83, 88, 165, 176

Sorokin, M. P. (journalist), 94

Spark (*Iskra,* satirical journal), 194

Spasovich, V. D. (lawyer, publicist, literary critic), 347-48

Spencer, Herbert (English philosopher,

social scientist), 338

Speransky, M. I. (statesman under Alexander I), 12, 162-63, 326-27, 329

Sreznevsky, I. I. (philologist, censor), 147, 155, 238, 269, 272, 290-91, 310, 316, 317

Starynkevich, A. S. (wife of Senator S.), 305-6

Starynkevich, S. A. (senator), 214

Stasov, D. V. (lawyer, public figure), 272

Stasov, V. V. (art critic, art historian), 272

Stasyulevich, M. M. (historian, journalist, editor, publisher), 328, 369

Stefanovich, P. K. (student), 232

Steinman, I. B. (philologist), 243

Stock Exchange Bulletin (Birzhevye Vedomosti, newspaper), 346, 371

Stock Exchange News (Birzhevaya Gazeta, newspaper), 371

Strakhov, N. N. (pseudonym N. Kositsa; Time; Epoch), 252, 265, 267, 284, 285

Strauss, Johann (composer), 335

Stroev, V. M. (journalist), 78

Stroganov, Count A. G. (Committee of April 2 [Secret Censorship Committee]), 116

Stroganov, Count A. S. (high posts under Catherine II, Paul, and Alexander I), 329-30

Stroganov, Count S. G. (sup't. Moscow school district, member State Council, in charge of education of Grand Duke Nikolai Aleksandrovich), 116, 117-18, 204, 219, 224, 279, 296, 297, 351

Strugovshchikov, A. N. (poet, translator), 77, 196, 225

Sukhomlinov, M. I. (prof., academician), 243, 279

Suvorin, A. S. (journalist, writer, publisher), 353-55

Suvorov, Prince A. A. (gov. gen. Baltic provinces, later of St. Petersburg), 122, 275, 350

Taneev, A. S. (diplomat, Deputy Min. of Education), 225

Teacher (Uchitel, journal), 266

Telescope (Teleskop, journal), 65, 66

Tikhomandritsky, A. N. (teacher, mathematician), 266

Tikhonravov, N. S. (prof., academician), 273

Timaev, M. M. (ass't. inspector at Catherine Institute), 31

Timashev, A. E. (chief of gendarmerie

and Third Section, member of Publishing Committee [censorship], Min. of Internal Affairs), 178, 182, 184, 185, 186, 188, 194, 195, 197, 198, 200, 201, 203, 208, 222, 264, 329, 336, 337, 339, 341-42, 351, 352, 355, 361-62

Time (Vremya, journal), 264, 265, 267

Times (English newspaper), 320

Timkovsky, E. F. (poet), 225

Titov, V. P. (State Council, writer, critic), 171, 334, 351

Tolstoy, Count Aleksandr Petrovich (Chief Procurator Holy Synod), 139

Tolstoy, Count Aleksei Konstantin (poet, playwright)

"Death of Ivan the Terrible," 305, 310, 316, 317

death of, 369

elected Academy of Sciences, 362

"Tsar Fydor Ivanovich," 322

Tolstoy, Count Dmitry Andreevich (Chief Procurator Holy Synod, Min. of Education), 127, 241-42, 312, 325-26, 341-42, 362

Academy of Sciences, 318

banning of Dialog, 354

classical vs. Real education, 346-47, 349, 351, 353

philosophy of education, 381

proposal to exclude indigent students from higher education, 368

Tolstoy, Count Fyodor Petrovich (artist, sculptor, v.p. Academy of Arts), 45

Tolstoy, Count Lev [Leo] Nikolaevich, xvii, 151, 362

"Snowstorm," 154

War and Peace, 332

Totleben, E. I. (director engineering dep't. of Min. of War), 321

Troinitsky, A. G. (Chief Censorship Administration, Council on Press Affairs, Deputy Min. of Internal Affairs), 216, 217, 221, 242, 243, 248, 251, 252, 265, 266, 268, 271, 292, 309, 326-27, 328

Trubetskaya, Princess (wife of Voronezh governor), 358

Tsee, V. A. (St. Petersburg Censorship Committee, later senator), 264, 309

Tsion, I. F. (physiologist, prof., publicist), 365-66

Tumansky, V. I. (poet), 300-01

Turchaninov, A. P. (teacher), 41

Turgenev, I. S., xvii, 127, 151, 154, 174, 182, 183, 184, 187, 197, 277

accused of plagiarism by Goncharov, 206-7

relations with foreign writers, 278

Smoke, 357
summoned for testimony in "Trial of the 32," 276, 380
Turunov, M. N. (St. Petersburg Censorship Committee, Council on Press Affairs), 264, 265, 266, 278, 285, 301-2
Tyutchev, F. I. (poet, chairman of Committee for Foreign Censorship), 151, 162, 182, 189, 190, 223, 263, 271 284, 297, 303, 312, 322, 324, 328, 353
   appointed to Council of Press Affairs, 282
   censorship matters, 177-78, 258
   discussion with Valuev on repression, 306
   "Huss," 339
   illness and death of, 357, 358, 359, 360, 361
Urusov, Prince A. I. (lawyer, literary critic), 325
Urusov, Prince S. N. (State Council, chairman of commission to compose new press laws, 1869), 310, 336, 351
Ustryalov, N. G. (prof., academician), 46, 147, 316
Uvarov, Count S. S. (Min. of Education, president Academy of Sciences), 38, 86, 116
   bans *Moscow Telegraph,* 47, 376
   censorship matters, 97, 98, 101, 112, 127
   displeasure over tribute to Pushkin, 69
   letter from Gogol, 105
   political philosophy of, 62
   removal of Count Stroganov, 117-18
Valuev, P. A. (Min. of Internal Affairs), 240, 241, 248, 252, 285, 301, 303, 326, 367, 381, 382
   bans *Moskvich,* 328
   bans *Time,* 264
   censorship of press, 304, 318, 319
   commission on conditions among peasants, 361
   compulsory subscription to *Northern Post,* 246-47
   conflict with Nikitenko over newspaper, 250
   control of courts, 316-17
   dissolution of St. Petersburg *zemstvo,* 320
   emancipation reforms, 360
   favors classical schools, 351
   influence on *Northern Post,* 257
   new press laws, 294, 296, 297, 298
   requests Nikitenko's resignation from Council on Press Affairs, 302
   retires from ministry, 329

warning to *Moscow Bulletin,* 311, 313, 314, 318
warning to *Voice,* 325
Varadinov, N. V. (journalist, member of higher censorship offices), 249, 265, 266
Velikopolsky, I. E. (poet, dilettante playwright), 280
Verderevsky, E. A. (poet), 36
Vernadsky, I. V. (economist, teacher, journalist), 221-22
Veselovsky, K. S. (academician), 170, 272, 288, 292, 316, 319
Vessel, N. Kh. (teacher, journalist), 266
Viardot, Polina (singer), 94, 96
Villamov, G. I. (in charge of Mariya Fyodorovna's institutes for women), 31-32
Vladislavlev, V. A. (Benkendorf's aide-de-camp, writer, publisher), 100
Voeikov, A. F. (poet, journalist), 28
Voice (Golos, newspaper), 266, 308, 314, 316, 317, 325, 328, 334, 346, 350, 351, 355, 359, 364, 371, 382
Voitsekhovich, A. I. (senator), 101, 159
Volkonsky, Prince G. P. (sup't. St. Petersburg school district), 76, 87, 90, 93, 96-97, 98, 101, 103, 108
Volkonsky, Prince P. M. (Min. of Imperial Court), 96
Volkov, E. E. (official in Min. of Education, censor), 141
Von Bradke, E. F. (sup't. Kiev and Dorpat school districts, chairman commission to study university by-laws), 244
Von Heckeren, Baron. *See* d'Anthes
Von Oldenburg, Prince P. G., 86
Voronov, A. S. (teacher, journalist, government posts), 321, 322, 353, 359
Vronchenko, M. P. (translator), 93
Vyazemsky, Prince P. A. (poet, critic, Deputy Min. of Education, member Chief Censorship Administration), 28, 32, 149, 150, 151, 154, 159, 161, 167-68, 169, 189, 244, 302, 310, 332, 333
Wagner, N. P. (pseudonym Kot Murlika; zoologist, prof., writer), 368
Waltz, Dr. J-G., 273, 274, 320
Wielgorski, Count M. (chamberlain), 42, 85, 86
Work and Play (Delo i Otdykh, children's magazine), 284
Yanovsky, K. P. (sup't. St. Petersburg school district), 352-53
Yaroslavtsev, A. K. (censor), 215
Yazykov, D. I. (academician), 7, 9, 10, 19
Yazykov, General A. P. (director Law Institute), 283-84
Yazykov, M. A. (involved in *Notes of*

the Fatherland and *Contemporary* circles), 128, 171, 193

Yershov, P. P. (poet, author of "The Hunchback Horse"), 149

Yurkevich, P. I. (playwright, translator, chairman Theatre Committee), 316

Yusupov, Prince N. B. (philanthropist, patron of the arts), 252

Yuzefovich, M. V. (childhood friend of Nikitenko, ass't. sup't. Kiev school district), 339

Zamyatin, D. N. (Deputy Min. of Justice, Min. of Justice), 283

Zdekauer, Dr. N. F., 202, 203, 297

Zeleny, A. A. (Deputy Min. of State Property), 318

Zhdanov, A. D. (senator), 264

Zhikharev, S. P. (Theatre Committee,

memoirist), 187

Zhukovsky, V. A. (poet, translator), 77, 105
death of, 130
intercedes on behalf of Nikitenko's mother and brother, 80-81
interest in Gogol, 60
"Nala and Damayanti," 93
Nikitenko on Zhukovsky, 131, 132
opposition to censorship of Pushkin's posthumous works, 71, 72
publication of posthumous works of, 151

Zinoviev, General N. V. (mentor of Alexander II's sons), 296

Zotov, V. R. (writer, journalist, literary historian), 225, 284

Zvegintsev, M. E. (civil servant, Nikitenko's brother-in-law), 144, 186